Looking at the Sun

Also by James Fallows

The Water Lords

National Defense

*More Like Us: An American Plan
for American Recovery*

James Fallows
Looking at the Sun

James Fallows is the Washington Editor of *The Atlantic Monthly* and a weekly commentator for National Public Radio. With his wife and children, he lived in Asia for four years. His first book, *National Defense*, won the National Book Award in 1981.

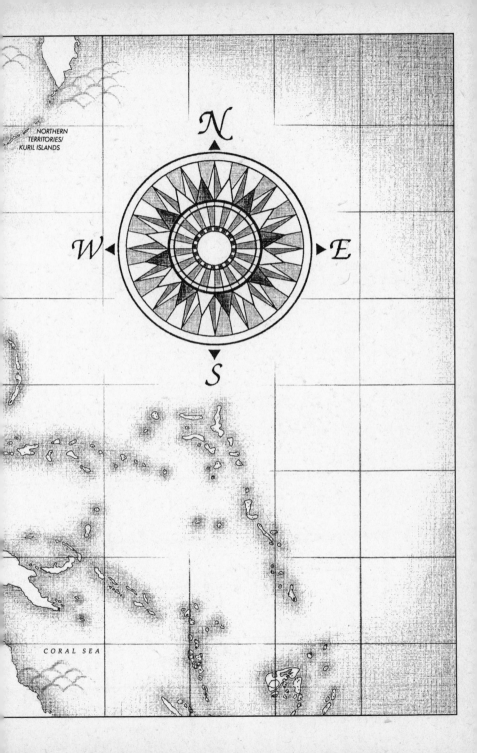

NORTHERN
TERRITORIES/
KURIL ISLANDS

N

W

E

S

CORAL SEA

Looking
at the Sun

*The Rise of
the New East Asian Economic
and Political System*

◆

James Fallows

Vintage Books

A Division of Random House, Inc.

New York

For Deb

The Library of Congress has cataloged the Pantheon
edition as follows:
Fallows, James M.
Looking at the sun: the rise of the new East Asian
economic and political system/James Fallows.
p. cm.
Includes index.
ISBN 0-679-42251-X
1. East Asia. I. Title.
DS504.5.F35 1994
950—dc20 93-38367
Vintage ISBN: 0-679-76162-4

Author photograph © Stanley Tretick

Contents

Introduction to the Vintage Edition   *xi*

Introduction   *3*

1. The Mystery of the Chips   *21*
2. The Drive to Catch Up   *72*
3. The American Years   *117*
4. The Idea of Economic Success   *177*
5. The Pan-Asian Age   *241*
6. Growth Without Development   *278*
7. On the Sidelines   *325*
8. Contenders   *375*
9. The Impact of the Asian System   *407*
10. Looking At the Sun   *437*

Acknowledgments   *454*
Notes   *457*
Index   *499*

Introduction
to the Vintage Edition

I HAD BEEN LIVING and traveling in Asia for nearly five years before I began work on this book. Through those years I had been writing frequent articles for *The Atlantic Monthly* and filing broadcasts almost every week for National Public Radio's *Morning Edition* program.

People become journalists largely because they enjoy the freedom to move from subject to subject and continually learn about new things. In deciding to spend two more years writing what became a long book about East Asia, rather than moving immediately to some other region or theme, I had four motivations in mind. The first two were straightforward. The third and fourth came to seem controversial after the publication of the hardcover edition of this book.

The first and simplest of my ambitions was to share with readers the look, the feel, the sound and smell and excitement of East Asia at this stage of its history. While living in Japan and Malaysia, while traveling through Shanghai or Bangkok or even Hanoi, I often felt distinctly privileged to be witnessing events that would be studied by historians for many years. Some of these events, particularly in China and Korea, involved political showdowns that made front-page news. But most of them were changes in business, society, technology, and culture that command less attention day by day but in the long run shift the balance of power in the world. Historians now try to describe the energy that transformed England in the days of the Industrial Revolution, or the United States as it was absorbing immigrants and becoming an economic giant at the end of the nineteenth century. I believe that East Asia of the late twentieth century will eventually be studied in the same way, and I have tried to give a journalistic account of how the transformation looked as it was going on.

My second purpose in writing the book was to try to nudge discussions of East Asia in a familiar but important direction. Everyone acknowledges the importance of history in shaping and limiting today's choices. But, especially in the United States, this recognition tends to be pro forma only. A nation built on the idea that people can reinvent their lives naturally resists reminders that what happened yesterday still matters today. There is no good place to start telling the history of a region's complications, whether that region is the Balkans or Latin America or East Asia, and I make no claim of presenting a comprehensive history of the countries I discuss. But I do attempt to explain why the colonial era still matters so much in China and Southeast Asia, and why the decade just after World War II still has such an effect on relations between Japan and the United States.

My final purposes were more directly argumentative, and they provoked more arguing back when the hardcover came out. The issues they involve will, I am convinced, be at the heart of relations between the Western world and East Asia well into the next century, so I should outline the poles of these debates.

One of these issues involved the role of economic theory. Long before I set foot in Asia, I had studied economics at universities in the United States and England. To take even an introductory economics course anywhere in the English-speaking world is to be exposed to constant claims that this discipline has sweeping, even scientific authority to explain how the world works. Economics has come to seem another branch of physics—a discipline that may not be able to predict how the stock market will move tomorrow or what the unemployment rate will be next week, but which can with great certainty lay down rules about long-term growth. The Nobel Prize in economics, which was instituted in the late 1960s, underscores the impression of scientific precision created by today's economic journals, with their articles dense with formulas and equations. Since American and British professors have won most of the Nobel economic prizes ever awarded, it is natural to think that in this field, as in many branches of science, the exploration of ultimate knowledge is being led by experts from the Anglo-American world.

After the years I spent in Asia, I became convinced that this faith was misplaced. The ideas that guided action in Tokyo, Seoul, and Taipei were not limited to the ones that were taught in Cambridge or Chicago. Western economists had consistently been wrong in their understanding of the strengths, weaknesses, and future growth prospects of Asian systems, most of all Japan's.

When the yen doubled in value against the dollar in the mid-1980s, Western authorities again took it for granted that Japanese exporters would finally be priced out of world markets. Over the next decade, industries based in Japan heavily out-invested their North America, European, and other Asian competitors, in hopes of pushing production costs down even faster than their currency was going up, and thereby to avoid being underpriced by the Taiwanese, Koreans, or anyone else. By the mid-1990s, buoyed by endless Japanese trade surpluses, the yen had moved to its highest valuation in history. Through the 1960s, one yen had been worth less than one third of a U.S. cent. (The fixed exchange rate in the postwar years was 360 yen to the dollar). Through the mid-1980s, one yen was worth less than half a U.S. cent. In 1994, shortly after the first edition of this book came out, the yen crossed the historic "parity" threshold—100 yen to one dollar, or one yen to one U.S. cent—and kept rising, to yen-per-dollar rates that were in the low eighties. Although such a highly valued currency had been barely imaginable a decade earlier, Japan's export strength remained far greater than any mainstream Western economist had foreseen. (Japan's trade surpluses fell as a percentage of Japan's total outcome through the early 1990s. Yet measured in dollar terms, they remained far higher than Western scholars had predicted, and repeatedly set records for the largest surpluses in history.)

These statistical comparisons come and go with the passing months, and their significance tends to blur. The crucial point behind them is a mismatch of theory with reality. Through the last four decades, the economies of Japan, South Korea, Taiwan, and, more recently, coastal China have grown by using techniques that, according to Western economic logic, should not have worked at all. Governments have interfered far more than Western theory says they should. Ferocious market competition has existed alongside central planning in ways that seem impossible, illogical, or certainly doomed to fail. This book lays out the argument and the evidence for the power and novelty of this Asian form of capitalism.

In theory, this description of the Asian system could fit comfortably within Western economic teachings. Many of the "Asian" aspects of today's Japanese or Korean systems are in fact based on careful study of the works of American or European analysts. Many Americans are now aware that after World War II, outside experts, including the great W. Edwards Deming, gave crucial advice to Japanese industries. Long before Deming's time, Japanese strategists had studied the work of Alexander Hamilton, the father of "industrial policy" in the United States; Friedrich List, the German writer heavily influenced by Hamilton's work in the United States; and even Adam Smith, who in the less-famous parts of *The Wealth of Nations* explained why governments might sometimes interfere with industry to expand the common wealth.

But in the politicized world of late-twentieth-century economics, analyses like mine about Asia are seen as affronts to prevailing economic theory, even as insults to the profession of modern economics as a whole. When mainstream American or English economists wrote about this book, they often said that while its travelogue and descriptions might be interesting, its fundamental outlook went counter to "known" economic principles and therefore could not be true. It may be significant that reviewers in Japan, Korea, Taiwan, and China usually made just the opposite point. "This book claims that the Asian system works on different principles from the Anglo-American model," a typical Asian review would say. "This has been obvious for years to everyone. Why should the author consider it news?"

American economists responding to this book—or to parallel analyses by increasing numbers of firsthand observers of modern Asia—generally made one of two criticisms. These criticisms contradicted each other, which itself showed the tension that Asia's rise has created for English-language economics.

The first and more common criticism was to say that Japan, Korea, and Taiwan might well be violating the "rules" of Western economics—and that therefore they were less successful than I portrayed them as being, and would certainly become less successful until they changed their ways. The long decline of the Nikkei average on the Tokyo Stock Exchange, from a high above 40,000 in the late 1980s to levels well under 20,000 in the early 1990s, was Exhibit One for this indictment. If the Japanese system was so good, why were Japan's corporate profits so bad? Exhibit Two was the case of America's semiconductor manufacturers—Intel, Motorola, and the like. This book describes their long decline through the 1980s. But in 1994 the United States again overtook Japan as the world's leading producer of computer chips. Worry about the Asian achievement must be out of date! Moreover, the signs of continued slowdown were rampant in Japan. The lifetime employment system was breaking down; the appetite for Western goods continued to rise. In these circumstances, marveling at the strength of the Asian model was, as one American economist put it, like being wowed by the Soviet productive system during Brezhnev's regime.

The impressive thing about these responses is how much evidence they had to ignore. Japan's financial system indeed went through a severe contraction in the early 1990s. Through the late 1980s, the Bank of Japan adopted a radical easy-money policy, reducing interest rates practically to zero. The country's economic leaders feared that the yen's rapid rise might choke off Japan's export business. They hoped that easy money would stimulate domestic investment and help prevent a recession. The approach worked—so well, in fact, that by 1989 Japan's central bankers were more worried about inflation than recession. Therefore, they deliberately jacked up interest rates to control the "bubble economy" of the cheap-money years. Japan's stock market fell, and the years of financial contraction began.

For all the hardship it meant for the stock market and land speculators, it is amazing how little "collateral damage" this process inflicted on the real economy of Japan. No major Japanese bank failed. Instead, at government urging, weak banks were forced to "merge" with stronger ones. Although the stock market lost two thirds of its value, no major Japanese corporation wound up in bankruptcy court. No Japanese firm announced large-scale layoffs, of the sort common in the United States and, to a smaller degree, Western Europe since the early 1980s. Precisely because of the combination of government and market forces, the Japanese system was able to absorb and deflect a shock that would have been far more devastating in other economies. Moreover, the concentration on Japan's temporary setback ignored how powerfully its model was being applied through the rest of the region.

Even the miraculous comeback of American semiconductor companies underscored, rather than contradicted, the argument of this book. After losing ground through most of the 1980s, American companies like Intel and Motorola began a comeback at the end of the decade. They did so, as the book points out, by applying a customized American version of the strategy that had proven successful in Asia.

That strategy is based on the shrewd mixture of government intervention and market competition. In the American version, the market did its part, as Intel, Motorola, Texas Instruments, and other firms reinvested in future output, paid fanatical attention to improving quality, and expanded their efforts to understand and please customers around the world. Meanwhile, the U.S. government took steps directly modeled on the Asian experience. Late in the Reagan administration, the United States slapped tariffs on selected Japanese products until the Japanese government agreed to sign a "semiconductor trade" agreement. Under this agreement, the Japanese government pledged itself to increase the sales of foreign chips in Japan, until they represented 20 percent of the Japanese market. By the time Bill Clinton took office, the target had been met. Also in the Reagan years, the U.S. government approved the formation of "Sematech," a consortium in which major American semiconductor firms would share certain research costs, to help maintain the U.S. productive base in general. By the second year of the Clinton administration, Sematech had gone far enough toward its goal that the companies that made it up said it could continue without further subsidy from the federal government.

Other economists responded to this book's argument in the opposite way. They agreed with its contention that Asian economies had been remarkably successful—but they ruled out the possibility that their success departed from American teachings in any significant degree. This view requires some convoluted interpretations of the way Asian economies actually function.

This book discusses many recent illustrations of the attempt to squeeze Japanese or Korean practices, from a toleration of cartels to widespread government-business collaboration—into Economics 101-style theories about the power of laissez faire. New examples continue to appear. Early in 1995, the Heritage Foundation, based in Washington D.C., issued a widely publicized "index of economic freedom," which showed that the economies with least regulation also grew the fastest. The two "most economically free countries" in the world, according to this list were Hong Kong and Singapore. Four other Asian economies were among the world's top fifteen freest systems.[1]

---

[1] Edward Feulner, "Land of the Free," *Far Eastern Economic Review,* January 26, 1995. The full list was:

1) Hong Kong
2) Singapore
3) Bahrain
4) United States
5) Japan
6) Taiwan
7) Britain
8) Canada
9) Germany
10) Austria
11) Bahamas
12) Czech Republic
13) South Korea
14) Malaysia
15) Australia

Therefore, the faster Asian economies grew, the more they reinforced the familiar lesson that government can help an economy best
by keeping its hands off.

But this reassuring "lesson" could be learned only by asssuming
away a number of inconvenient facts. Hong Kong and Singapore are
free economies—in some ways. Tarriffs are low. There is little discrimination against foreigners who want to sell, buy, or invest. Yet
each economy could just as easily be used as a demonstration of
the power of state planning. Singapore's people have been required
for decades to turn over as much as one third of their income
to a government-run "Central Provident Fund." This government-
enforced savings scheme created a huge government-guided capital
pool, which in turn has been used for a variety of public purposes,
such as creating a stock of low-priced housing. Hong Kong's government has historically interfered very little with trade, but used
a heavy hand to determine which borrowers would get first crack at
capital for investment.

Indeed, if these two countries, along with the others in Asia,
demonstrate any "lesson," it concerns the *combination* of markets
and planning that lies behind Asia's modern growth. Modern Asia
has clearly been a capitalist success story, but its speciality has been
"guided capitalism" of a sort considered almost a contradiction in
terms in much of Western economic discussion. This combination
is evident throughout the region, as this book tries to demonstrate.
Yet the very idea of such a mixture has seemed difficult for many
Americans, including economists, to accept. Experience has taught
them to think that "capitalism" and "free markets" must be the
same thing. After all, the modern United States has embraced both
capitalism and free markets, with exceptions—and during the Cold
War the Soviet Union rejected both of them.

The most intriguing and, for Americans, most challenging trait
of Asian economies is the way they have embraced capitalism while
limiting markets. These limits come in countless varieties, many of
them described in the pages that follow. Governments issue guidance, direct and indirect. They work thorugh networks of old-boy
relationships. They set targets that companies must meet.

Many of these approaches would fail in the different circumstances of Western governments, especially in America. But the
message of this book is not that they should be imitated. Instead,
it is that the Western world cannot possibly make sense of the
changes in the world economic landscape without a realistic understanding of how the fastest-growing societies actually work.

At the moment, the West's economic profession is hindering rather than helping the process of realistic recognition. Chalmers Johnson, author of *MITI and the Japanese Miracle* and the leading American scholar of Japanese industrialization, wrote early in 1995 that modern English-language economics "has become the Marxism-Leninism of our society—the official ideological expression of how the United States works and why it 'won' the Cold War." America's professional economists, he said,

> have the same interest in preserving their usually tenured (in violation of market forces) positions as did the masters of [Marxism-Leninism] at Moscow State University until August of 1991. The greatest single threat to their continued dominance is the prowess of the Japanese economy and the emulation of that economy by everybody else in Asia, from China to Kazakhstan. It is not the wealth of Asia that is threatening but how the Asians obtained it.[2]

Asia's wealth was intellectually "threatening," Johnson concluded, because it called into question the first principles of Western economic theory. No other branch of Western academics is having as much trouble fitting observations into established theory as economists are as they cope with Asia's growth. I am convinced now, as I was when writing the book, that developments like those it describes will play a part in changing our understanding of how the economic world works.

My ultimate motive in writing this book was to address the possible political consequences of a shift in world economic power. In their universities and business schools, Westerners often discuss economic competition as if it could be neatly separated from history and politics. In this book, I try to demonstate how deeply history, politics, and economics have been mingled in the development of East Asian systems. The very ambition for rapid economic growth has often been political. Through the centuries of European colonial dominance, and through the decades of post-World War II supremacy by the United States, societies in Asia, Africa, Latin America,

[2] Chalmers Johnson, "Intellectual Warfare," *The Atlantic Monthly*, January 1995.

and the Middle East have known how painful it is to be economically weak. Having been on the receiving end of a world order based on economic, technical, and military strength, they naturally would like to improve their bargaining position.

As Japan, China, and their neighbors continue to gain economic power, the world's political debates may change in a way that few Westerners now appreciate. This book describes efforts that began in the 1980s to challenge the Western definition of "human rights" by officials from Singapore, Malaysia, China, and even Japan. This challenge became more obvious in 1994.

The melodramatic version was the showdown between the governments of Singapore and the United States over proper punishment for Michael Fay, an American teenager who was convicted of vandalism in Singapore and then beaten with a rattan cane. A more serious long-term tension was revealed by the argument over "Most Favored Nation" trade status for China in 1994. When running for the presidency, Bill Clinton had promised to revoke China's "MFN" status, which in effect would have dried up U.S.-Chinese trade, unless China ended its prison-labor system, expanded civil liberties, and, in general, began conforming to American concepts of individual rights. But less than two years into his term, President Clinton had to back off this position. He continued China's MFN status, despite the Chinese government's flat refusal to entertain his complaints about human rights. To judge by his statements, the president changed his mind because of the way he sized up the world's power equations. Even in its moment as the world's sole superpower, the United States apparently lacked the leverage to make the Chinese government change its practices. This book argues that the Western world's leverage over China will decrease with the passing years, as China's techno-economic base grows and its connections with other Asian countries expand. The MFN showdown will not be the last confrontation with China over basic political values.

At the same time, this book suggests that Asian success should encourage the Western world, and especially America, to think about the fundamentals of its own political organization. Just as the Asian economic strategy involves a combination of government and market forces, so the political balance in much of Asia reflects a balance of individual and collective rights. Individual liberties are constrained to varying degrees in many Asian societies. Some of the constraints amount to sheer repression. But in other cases, notably Japan's, a deliberate trade-off between individual liberty and collective security seems to lie at the heart of an accepted social contract. Individual workers in Japan have for decades earned less money than their productivity would entitle them to. Individual shareholders receive lower dividends than do their counterparts in Europe or North America. Companies earn lower profits. Students are hemmed in with more requirements and restraints. Women have fewer freedoms in their career choice. Families live in smaller homes. "Salarymen" have less choice about changing jobs in mid-career.

Japanese citizens complain about every one of these constraints. Yet the complaints have always been buffered by the sense that the system, as a whole, is a success. Those who study hard are rewarded. Those who are loyal to their employers receive loyalty back. Despite widespread American reports that Japan's "lifetime employment" system had fallen apart in the 1990s, the essentials of Japan's social bargain—an understanding that companies will care more about preserving their work force than maximizing their profits—remained firmly in place. When shocks batter the system as a whole, as they did with the recession of the 1990s, the effects are more or less fairly spread.

Many parts of the Japanese-style social bargain would be impractical or unacceptable in the United States, especially the still-sharp division between "men's work" (running industry and government) and "women's work" (raising children). But the success of this system does dramatize the social problem hardest for Americans to solve. The political and economic doctrines on which American society is based emphasize individual welfare. The Declaration of Independence and the Constitution spell out liberties but not responsibilities. Free-market economic theory says that if each individual pursues his maximum economic welfare, the best possible society will result.

Many Americans sense that something is missing from this formula. Their big cities, with homeless "squeegee men" running rags across the windshields of limousines, fit no one's concept of the ideal society. Filling in the missing part of the formula, with conceptions of "the good of the nation" and "collective strength," is no problem for many Asian societies. It is much harder for Americans, whose only language for discussing collective well-being is that of national defense.

This part of the book's argument provoked the angriest response. Some reviewers said that to raise the idea of a clash of political values was to engage in "Orientalism"—that is, the idea that those Asians are quaint, colorful figures whom no Westerners will ever fully understand. Others said that the idea was condescending and even racist, since it amounted to saying that democracy was fine for white people, but not necessary for the yellow masses of the Far East.

It is obvious that some Asian arguments for "Asian political values" are self-serving exercises by political elites. Lee Kuan Yew and other spokesmen for the government of Singapore say that their country's people do not want the chaos of a free, unbridled Western-style press. Maybe so, but it would be more convincing to hear that from ordinary citizens, rather than from officials whom a free press might criticize. The ruling mandarins in China and Vietnam say that their countries cannot "afford" political liberties as they modernize. Again, this argument is too convenient to be very convincing.

Still, when all convenience and hypocrisy has been allowed for, a fact remains. The political model underlying most Asian systems differs from that of the United States. The role of the individual is more constrained. The rights of the collectivity are greater. No Asian society honors a close counterpart to Thomas Jefferson or John Locke. This difference will come out more and more in world political arguments. And it should provoke Americans especially to reflections about their own system.

In addition to the U.S.-Chinese disagreement over trade and human rights, three other developments in the year since this book's publication illustrated the main themes of the book.

One of these was the continued political turmoil in Japan. In the summer of 1993, the Liberal Democratic Party lost the hold on political power it had enjoyed since 1955. In the following eighteen months, the faces at the top of Japan's political system changed rapidly, but the underlying structure proved surprisingly robust. Morihiro Hosokawa, the reform prime minister who had led the original challenge to the LDP, took office in 1993 pledging to overturn post-war Japan's long-standing bias in favor of large companies and against consumers, urban dwellers, "salarymen," and the other foot soldiers of the country's campaigns to export and industrialize Japan. The backstage strongman who had helped engineer Hosokawa's victory, Ichiro Ozawa, published a bestselling book calling for an end to the practices that made Japan an "abnormal" nation. His recommendations ranged from allowing more regional autonomy, so that bureaucrats in Tokyo no longer micro-managed the details of educational and construction policy for the nation as a whole, to expanding Japan's military role (still in partnership with the United States).

Yet by the next year the Liberal Democratic Party was back in a coalition controlling the government, in partnership with their long-time adversaries in the Socialist party. The bureaucrats in Japan's powerful central-government ministries—the Ministry of Finance, Construction, Trade, Education—continued to make the most important decisions about the nation's future, using tactics described in many chapters of this book. As the popularity of Ozawa's book demonstrates, there is no shortage of ideas within Japan for reforming the Japanese system. Yet a central argument of my own book is that Japan's political-economic system is far stronger and more resilient than most outsiders give it credit for. The last eighteen months of Japanese politics are a reminder of that point.

Another significant development was in the United States. During its first year in office, the Clinton administration adopted a "framework" strategy for trade negotiations with Japan based on an analysis that paralleled the reasoning in this book. Rather than exerting "moral" pressure on Japan to change its "unfair" trading practices, the Clinton strategy took the strength and nature of the Japanese system for granted. While pursuing a worldwide effort to reduce trade barriers, through ratification of the North American Free Trade Agreement (NAFTA) and the latest round of the General Agreement on Tariffs and Trade (GATT), the administration took a "results-oriented" approach to Japan. U.S. negotiatiors thought that general pleas to open the Japanese market would not succeed. Instead, they concentrated on setting targets for increased sales of foreign high-tech products in Japan.

In the short run, this approach failed. Japanese government negotiators shrewdly calculated the "correlation of forces"—the balance of strengths and weaknesses—that the two sides brought to the bargaining table. They believed (according to Japanese press reports) that if President Clinton actually carried out his threat to put tariffs on certain Japanese products, the Japanese government would ultimately have to accept the demand for targets for increased imports. President Reagan had carried out exactly such a threat in 1986, and the Japanese government had accepted his demands.

But if President Clinton were merely bluffing in his demands, then the Japanese negotiators would have everything to gain by saying "no" to request for targets. They could complain publicly that this constituted a demand for "managed trade." They could point out that the Japanese economy was still stagnant, that America was on the way back, and that it would violate the spirit of NAFTA and GATT for the U.S. to impose "managed trade" on its most important economic partner.

By the Japanese government assessment, the correlation of forces lay in its favor. Its negotiatiors said "no"; most of the U.S. press criticized the administration for endorsing "managed trade"; and the Clinton administration was so beset with other problems that it essentially dropped Japan from its economic agenda until some more promising time.

The third development was the one destined to matter most for all the countries mentioned in this book. This was the trend toward increasing "Asianization" of East Asia.

Late in 1993, the first formal summit meeting of heads of state from Asian-Pacific nations took place in Seattle. A second "APEC Summit"—for "Asian-Pacific Economic Cooperation" forum— took place a year later in Bogor, Indonesia. The APEC meetings were remembered in America mainly for the photos of President Clinton at the second summit, his torso swathed in a flowing In- donesian batik shirt. Yet in Asia the APEC conferences were seen as signifying a historic change. Over the previous decade, importers, exporters, investors, and entrepreneurs in the region had worked with each other more and more closely. Although the APEC meet- ings had no immediate practical effect, they were advertised in many Asian countries as the first step toward other forms of integration, political expression, and shared regional consciousness.

The politics of most Asian countries have become increasingly attuned to relations with the rest of the region. For instance, as U.S.- Chinese relations turned bitter in 1994 and early 1995, Japanese strategy toward China boiled down to the idea of avoiding any step that might annoy the Chinese government in any way. Yet each step in this "pan-Asian" direction highlighted the great dilemma of post- war Asian politics. The region has depended, both for its prosperity and its relative peace, on the United States. From the 1950s through the 1990s American customers bought up Asia's output surplus and thereby kept capital flowing into the region. In 1993, the latest year for which final figures are available as I write, the U.S. trade deficit with East Asia as a whole exceeded $100 billion, which was nearly all of America's trade deficit and nearly all of Asia's trade surplus.

At the same time, the destroyers, frigates, and aircraft carriers of the U.S. Navy's Seventh Fleet have, as they cruised the South China Sea and through the Straits of Malacca, allowed each Asian country to worry less about its neighbors than it otherwise would. With the possible exception of North Korea, no Asian country has believed in the last two decades that the United States was about to attack it. But without the Seventh Fleet, the Taiwanese would acutely worry about the Chinese, who would in turn worry about the Japanese, who would in turn worry about the Koreans.

This is the dilemma: East Asia's welfare rested on a U.S. role that East Asia's success would eventually undermine. The more that the United States felt embattled by economic competition with East Asia, the more trouble American politicians would have explaining why, exactly, they should continue serving as the region's police force. The last two chapters of this book deal with the tangle of economic and political questions this tension will create.

Japan and China, and their neighbors, will shape our choices and stimulate our imaginations for many years. I hope that this book helps clarify their role.

James Fallows
Washington, D.C.
April 1995

Looking at the Sun

Introduction

IN LIFE THERE OFTEN IS TOO MUCH theory and not enough fact. Strangely, the opposite is true in the Western world's dealings with East Asia. The non-Asian world is awash in information about political and economic developments in Asia. But it lacks the right tools—the right theories—to give that information coherence and shape.

Each day's news brings a flood of fresh data about Japan, Korea, and China, much of it apparently contradicting the data delivered the day before. The yen is up, and Asian industries are stronger. The Korean steel industry is down, and the Asian miracle is past its peak. Japan has reorganized the rest of Asia into a co-prosperity sphere. Japan is shunned and resented by the very Asian countries that know it best. Women and students in Asian societies are rebelling against their stereotyped roles. Women and students are being forced into those roles more firmly than before. China will certainly open up to market forces and grant its citizens more liberty, since it hopes to modernize. China's leadership is determined to maintain control at any cost. American industry has been invigorated by competition from Asia. American industry is doomed. Japan is America's most important strategic partner. Japan is America's most important economic foe.

One by one many bits of data may be accurate, but together they seem chaotic, even meaningless, like a thousand conversations blurring into white noise. Most members of Western societies cope with this confusion by ignoring it, focusing on Asian matters only when a trade dispute, a coup, or a war makes its way onto the front page. Yet sometimes contradictions do have to be resolved. Should North Americans and Europeans welcome Japanese investment, or fear it? Should they assume that Asia is becoming more and more Western as it modernizes, or not? Should they criticize China and apply trade sanctions in hopes of forcing it onto a more democratic path? Or should they consider the very idea of "pressuring" China to be absurd? In such moments, when it is necessary to choose—discarding some information, putting the rest into sensible shape—observers naturally turn to the tools closest at hand, their own theories and instincts about how the world works.

Americans in particular tend to view the world as one vast potential extension of their own culture, containing billions upon billions of people who would be American if only they could. Therefore it is all but irresistible for Americans to size up foreign situations by thinking, What would we do in their place? The thought does not even have to be conscious or explicit; the instinct is still there. When Americans see Chinese students demonstrating in Tiananmen Square, they think of their own civil rights movement, if not of their Founding Fathers. They see McDonald's restaurants in Jakarta and Kyoto and think that societies must be converging on an American norm.

This universalizing instinct is the noblest thing about the American social model. But it can lead to terrible analytical mistakes. American statesmen ignored the nationalist part of Ho Chi Minh's movement against the French, seeing only its Communist component—and saw only the nation-builder in Syngman Rhee of Korea and Ferdinand Marcos of the Philippines, ignoring what was corrupt and oppressive in each of them. Many Americans later romanticized Corazon Aquino, seeing her as a Common Cause–style reformer rather than as one of the richest people in the country, taking revenge on the remnants of the Marcos regime for her husband's death. For nearly two centuries Americans have swung between romanticizing China—as a mother of civilization, a natural friend to America, a bountiful source of converts and customers—and demonizing it for its godless, despotic ways.

The American assumption that people and cultures are at their core all the same and can be understood with the same mental tools is mirrored in milder ways in other Western nations. It shows up in the instinctive belief that "progress" will inevitably make societies more and more alike. As a nation becomes scientifically advanced, commercially strong, and materially rich, it will come to resemble the Western nations that have exemplified progress for several centuries. Successful societies on every continent will grant citizens more and more individual rights. Superstition and religion will grow weaker; scientifically based rationalism will win out. Barriers among races and entire nations will eventually fall. In short, the world will become Westernized—will become fundamentally similar to Europe and North America—as it grows up.

Modern Europeans are less likely than Americans to come right out and say that the rest of the world views their society as a model. And yet, as two Australian diplomats wrote in 1989:

> The fact is that most Western opinion still assumes the contin-uing predominance of a European moral order throughout the late twentieth century global village. . . . [The] worldview [of Western leaders and academics], their political stance, and the essence of their personal confidence are still based on their assumption of a European moral order which "shows the way" to other cultures.[1]

The central argument of this book is that Western societies, espe-cially America, have been using the wrong mental tools to classify, shape, and understand the information they receive about Asia. They try to fit the facts into familiar patterns and categories—and then are hurt and frustrated when predictions derived from these patterns don't come true.

The mental habits that make Westerners leap to conclusions about the rest of the world come from three main sources:

The first is the desire to convert. The American assumption that all people want to become Americans is a variation of the broader Western missionary principle that all people should be brought to the Christian God. The common thread is the belief in mutability and elevation—that all societies can be changed, and that a change toward Western values is necessarily a step up.

The second is the assumption of superiority, no longer in the crude chauvinistic or racial sense of the colonial age but in a subtler and more important form. Western societies have led the world, materially and technically, for so many centuries that very few Amer-icans or Europeans think consciously of this as an interesting fact. The Western dominance of science, technology, and industry, es-tablished during the Renaissance and maintained for most of the time since, is instead an accepted part of the landscape, shaping other thoughts. Non-Western cultures can be "respected," "appre-ciated," welcomed politely as if they were full equals on the world stage. Western devotees can learn Zen, Tantrism, the exotica of the East. But it is very hard for Westerners truly to take another social system seriously—to imagine, that is, that it might have improved on Western rules for organizing and channeling human activity.

The third is a misplaced scientific faith. In the centuries since the Renaissance, Western scientists have refined their understanding of the natural universe. During this century many people, especially Americans, have believed that they had approached a similarly precise understanding of human behavior. The results of this effort show up under various names—operations research, management theory—but most of all in the modern "science" of economics.

The powers of "quantitative analysis," as used by modern economists and managers, are enormous but nonetheless limited. The operations-research experts of the 1960s could not imagine that a country as miserable and disorganized as North Vietnam could thwart the will and power of the United States. The economists of the 1990s cannot honestly fit the rise of Japan, Korea, and Taiwan into their models of how economies should grow. As economics has presented itself more and more like a "natural science," with mathematical formulas and an air of hard, scientific precision, it has crowded out the softer but ultimately more useful discipline of history. Economics gives us clear, logical "models" that are supposed to explain dealings among nations. History gives us different, more complicated lessons, which are more useful for understanding what is going on in Asia now.

"Stated briefly and far too boldly, the Japanese have succeeded by doing everything wrong (according to standard economic theory)." So wrote Alan Blinder of Princeton, an economist whom President Clinton appointed to the Council of Economic Advisers. "Our intellectual conceptualization of the Japanese economic system undergirds policies toward Japan. If our picture is distorted, our policies will be too."[2]

Our picture of modern Asia is distorted mainly by seeming too familiar. In this book I will suggest different pictures, which might lead to more realistic policies—and which above all might create a richer sense of how Asia's rise may change the rest of the world.

I did not expect to become interested in the ways Westerners think about Asia. When I moved with my family to Japan in 1986, I thought I was just looking for new facts.

For the previous half-dozen years, while working as a writer for *The Atlantic Monthly,* I'd concentrated mainly on issues that involved the long-term strength of American society. I wrote about federal budget policy, about immigration's impact on the United States, about morale and leadership in the U.S. military and in U.S. corporations, about the changing nature of social class in America.

In several of these areas East Asia in general, and Japan in particular, had become the standard by which the United States judged its efforts. Whatever American children learned in school, it seemed that Taiwanese or Korean children were learning much more. Whatever American industrialists did, they did partly out of fear of the Japanese. During American policy debates, I constantly heard Asian examples being used to support one side of the argument or another. But I had almost no firsthand experience in the way modern Asian business or educational systems worked. I had lived for two years in England, as a graduate student in the 1970s, and had traveled extensively in Africa and Europe, but my exposure to Asia had been limited to a brief tourist visit with my wife to Singapore and Indonesia.

To put it another way, what I "knew" about Asia, at the time I left the United States to live there, was what most educated Americans think they know about the outside world. To the extent that Japan, Korea, and Taiwan were successful, they had succeeded by besting Europeans and Americans at the Westerners' own game— or so I had read in newspapers and business magazines. The sporting world offered a seemingly perfect metaphor. Americans had invented and refined the game of baseball and considered themselves so dominant that they called their own baseball championship the World Series. But after World War II, baseball had caught on in much of East Asia. In perfectly "fair" competition, teams from Asia soon dominated world play, at least at the Little League level. From 1970 to 1993, teams from Korea, Taiwan, and Japan won the Little League World Series seventeen times; previously the championship had been an American monopoly. The Asian approach to the game differed in many ways from the American style (as the writer Robert Whiting explained in his classic books about Japanese baseball *The Chrysanthemum and the Bat* and *You Gotta Have Wa*[3]). But when American teams played against Asians for the Little League title, everyone was playing by the same rules; the only difference was, the Asian lads were playing better.

And so it seemed to be in the world of commerce. Once upon a time America had had the will to innovate its way around any obstacle. Before that, Britain had been the culture with the inspired tinkerers and entrepreneurs. Now the game was being played with extra energy by the Asians. Same game, same rules, different champions—or so I'd been told.

But what I learned while living in Asia was not what I had "known" before. I had intended to visit Japan for a few months and then travel in Southeast Asia for a few months more. As it turned out, I stayed in Japan and Malaysia, with my wife and two sons, for three and a half years. After we moved back to the United States at the end of 1989, I traveled in Asia on reporting trips for most of another two years. During this whole period I was in Korea, the Philippines, Thailand, and China for a total of several months each, and in Indonesia, Vietnam, Taiwan, and Australia for three to four weeks apiece. With my family I made frequent brief visits to Singapore and Hong Kong. Burma in those days allowed visitors to stay for no more than seven days, which is how long my wife and I spent there.

The reason we stayed so long is that we found daily life constantly surprising. Our previous beliefs, instincts, and mental pictures did not apply. We had heard for years that Japan was rich. Yet normal life, as we lived and observed it in a Tokyo suburb, would be considered needlessly grinding and difficult by most American and European standards. Homes were usually unheated. Modern plumbing was rare. In the country that produced more automobiles than any other nation, most of our neighbors had no cars. The windows of Japanese *danchi,* or huge apartment blocks, fluttered with laundry each morning because the average Japanese family did not own a drying machine.

What sort of prosperity was this, if the people who created it lived so much worse than those they were "outcompeting" overseas? It was certainly hard to explain Japan's evolution by the principles I had learned in economics courses in America and England. I had been taught that the ultimate purpose of economic growth was to make individuals rich; in Japan, individuals remained poor so that the industries could grow strong. Western economists were unanimous in saying that a country with big, chronic trade deficits—a country like Japan—was merely hurting itself. Its people were working too hard and saving too much, all for the benefit of their customers overseas. "The point of trade is to get useful things from other countries, that is, imports, which are a benefit, not a cost," an esteemed American economist said in 1993. "The unfortunate necessity of sending other countries useful things in return, that is, exports, is a cost rather than a benefit."[4] This would sound logical to most Americans who have taken an introductory economics course. Somehow the same logic did not seem so obvious in Japan—or in Korea or Taiwan.

Like most other Americans, I had heard for years that as countries became more prosperous, they would become freer and more democratic, and that prosperity would erode barriers among nations as well. As time went on, people in each corner of the world would discover more and more similarities with their fellow human beings in other corners. Within each country, rulers would finally have to respect the rights of the ruled.

In many parts of Asia I could see confirmation of these hopeful theories. Korea and Taiwan became freer as they became richer. The most repressive Asian countries—North Korea, Burma—were the most economically backward as well. As I traveled with my family, we saw signs almost daily of pop culture converging on one international norm. A toddler in the hills of northern Thailand wore a Los Angeles Raiders T-shirt. During Ramadan, the Moslem month of fasting, crowds would gather at twilight outside the Kentucky Fried Chicken outlets in Kuala Lumpur. When evening fell, they would pour into the restaurants to break their fast with chicken, biscuits, and slaw. At night, in Hanoi, we saw light spill onto the street from hundreds of small cafés in which American MTV videos were playing on Japanese or Korean VCRs.

Yet we left Asia thinking that the worldwide convergence of pop culture, the spread of blue jeans and rock music, meant less than most Westerners assume. Along with this hunger for the trinkets of the Western world, we often encountered doubts and challenges to the West's more fundamental political ideas. In many parts of Asia, the Western world is considered rich but undeserving. America is seen as an extreme case: pampered, glamorous, and enviable, yet also self-destructive, undisciplined, and perhaps terminally debauched. Western ideas more generally are being called into question in Asia, ideas as basic as the primacy of free speech or individual rights. After centuries of having to listen to Western rulers and look up to Western technology, more and more Asian leaders—the politicians, scholars, and business titans who would talk about such subjects—now say that the Western model is breaking down and that they have found a better way.

My family had the good fortune, although we did not always think of it as such at the time, to be living in East Asia when it dramatically broke through to a new plateau of economic success. In early 1986, when we arrived in Tokyo, Japan was trailing behind the United States, as the number-two economic power, in a host of different measures. Its per capita income was slightly lower than America's. Its annual investment was less. In many fields its largest manufacturers were just behind their U.S. counterparts. One U.S. dollar was worth nearly 200 Japanese yen.

Within a year, the yen had almost doubled in value against the dollar, and Japan had pulled into first place in many world economic rankings. Part of this change was purely an accounting phenomenon, reflecting how much more valuable each yen's worth of output, investment, or assets had become when counted in dollars. But the rise in the yen's value was itself a tribute to the real power of Japan's economy. And through the late 1980s, the years of Japan's *baboru keizai* or "bubble economy," raw expansive power was the most noticeable trait of the Japanese economy and the other parts of Asia that it touched.

Land prices in Japanese big cities tripled in the bubble years. (These years are usually reckoned as running from late 1985, when the yen began doubling in value against the dollar, to late 1989, when the Bank of Japan hiked up interest rates and launched a tight-money policy.) The Nikkei average on the Tokyo Stock Exchange tripled as well.[5] By 1989 the combined value of stock traded in Tokyo exceeded the value of the entire New York Stock Exchange. The Nippon Telegraph and Telephone corporation, NTT, was worth more than all the stock traded on the German stock exchange. Any Japanese family who owned land was suddenly rich, at least on paper. As of 1989, some five hundred thousand households in Greater Tokyo alone each had land worth $1 million or more. At that same moment, the land value of Japan as a whole was theoretically four times greater than that of the entire United States, even though America was twenty-five times bigger and full of the natural resources that Japan lacked.

In all corners of Asia were signs of Japan's economic preeminence. Japanese-language courses were oversubscribed in Thailand. Japanese tourists and investors filled hotels from Beijing to Sydney and every point between. The "Japanese model" was studied in government planning agencies. In Thailand, virtually every car on the road was a Toyota, Nissan, or other Japanese model. Even in Vietnam, the refrigerators and VCRs that showed up in hard-currency stores were Japanese.

As the flood of money and products out of Japan was shaping

the rest of Asia, within Japan itself its main effect was to make many people worry that the society might be losing its way. In the fall of 1988, when it seemed that the bubble years would never end, I was sitting with a Japanese diplomat in one of Tokyo's fancy French restaurants. I had learned long before this meeting that I could not enter such places unless someone else was paying. My menu had no numbers on it, but I guessed that lunch would come to about $250 a head.

Near the end of the meal, I realized that I had grossly miscalculated; the meal would certainly cost much more. My host told me that he had ordered a special dessert. After the main dishes were cleared, the waiter appeared in a tuxedo and laid down tiny dishes of chocolate mousse. Then he brought out some kind of grinder, and instead of cinnamon or flaked chocolate he began decorating my mousse with shavings of pure gold. Psychologically I found it hard to choke down the soft metallic curls. The gold had no taste and practically no texture—it was like eating Saran Wrap. At that moment I knew exactly what conspicuous consumption meant.

From within, this dramatic ride up, and then back down again, was exhilarating. During Japan's cycle of expansion, you could almost feel minute by minute that the world's balance of power was shifting. In tones that were sometimes plaintive and sometimes haughty, Japanese, Chinese, Koreans, and Thais lectured Westerners that the age of Asia had arrived.

When Japan's bubble economy began sagging in the early 1990s, some of the self-confidence went out of Japan's spokesmen. They sat more quietly at international meetings; commentators wrote fewer articles in the Japanese press about the decline of the Western industrial system. When prices on the Japanese stock market and the valuation of Japanese land plummeted in 1992 and stayed low through 1993, internal Japanese rhetoric turned bleakly pessimistic. Japan had reached the end of its productive miracle! The fundamentals of world trade had finally set limits on its growth! Japanese buyers disappeared from the markets for French Impressionist paintings and trophy buildings in Manhattan and Los Angeles. Japanese investors were ridiculed for having overpaid for their previous trophy purchases, from the Pebble Beach golf course to Rockefeller Center. In Tokyo's fanciest restaurants there were empty tables. Small-time Japanese speculators, who had believed that the value of their NTT shares or tiny square of Tokyo real estate would always go up, clogged the bankruptcy rolls.

Seeing these symptoms, the Western world drew what seemed

the obvious conclusion: that it didn't have to worry about Japan anymore. Having portrayed Japan through the 1980s as a nearly unstoppable force, much of the Western press swung to the opposite tack and minimized Japan's future prospects. In the phrase that an editor of *The Economist* magazine used as the title of a book, "the sun also sets." In the springtime of 1992, Karen Elliott House, an influential former reporter who had become a vice president of Dow Jones, wrote an essay in *The Wall Street Journal* called "Japan's Decline, America's Rise." It differed from a number of other articles and speeches of the time mainly in being clearer and more eloquent in its conclusion: that Japan had faltered, that no other Asian contender was in the wings, and that America's natural superiority had been revealed.

> TOKYO—"Shrinkies: Amazing, in four magical minutes they bake and shrink right before your eyes!" So says the box top on our five-year-old's favorite toy. . . .
>
> Something like that seems to be going on in Japan these days. . . . Americans who want to see America outperform Japan ought now to be humming the Hallelujah Chorus—not in glee at Japan's difficulties, but in confidence that America need not fear Japan. . . .
>
> An America that has won the Cold War, that has seen its political and economic values spread from Southeast Asia to South America, and that now clearly is reasserting its economic primacy over an uncertain Japan has that alternative [of being admired by others]—if only it believes in itself.[6]

Soon after President Bush's tour through Asia in early 1992, ending with the unsubtly symbolic picture of himself lying helplessly in Prime Minister Miyazawa's lap, a White House expert on Asian affairs gave a wrap-up speech. "We considered it a 'victory lap' around Asia, after the Persian Gulf war," he said. Soon afterward, in Silicon Valley, I met a lawyer who had "stuffed" Japanese clients with a number of overpriced high-tech deals. "I figure they've had a good ten years," he said of Japanese industrialists with a dismissive smirk. "Give them that. But it couldn't last."

It is possible, of course, that judgments like these will prove to be correct. Perhaps it will be clear to everyone, by the late 1990s, that Japan and Asia in general reached a peak of relative power in the late 1980s—as America did in the 1960s, as England did in the Victorian age. If that happens, I will be able to look back on the gold-covered mousse the way today's Britons might look at twenty-course banquets from the Edwardian age: it will be a specimen of a kind of confidence that is hard to imagine once it's gone. It is possible, in a more positive sense, that the political turmoil of 1993 will lead to profound and lasting reform of Japan's governing system, so that consumers, women, students, and other hard-pressed groups in Japan would have greater rights, and bureaucrats and industrialists would have less power to run the economy for the benefit of Japan's big exporters.

But it is also possible that these judgments will turn out to be wrong. More than merely "possible," this result would be consistent with a long record of systematic Western underestimation of Japan and misperception of Asia as a whole.

For at least a century, Westerners (and especially Americans) have been too quick to count profits from the vast potential market in China—and too ready to dismiss progress in Japan or elsewhere in Asia. In the decades since World War II, American observers have declared the Japanese miracle "finished" nearly half a dozen times. In the early 1970s, after OPEC seemed to bring the era of cheap energy to an end, Japan was more severely shaken than any other industrialized nation. It produced virtually no oil of its own. An island nation's worst, most elemental fears of being cut off from crucial supplies seemed to be coming true. Yet within a decade, it was clear that, far from weakening Japan, the era of oil *shokku* had made the Japanese economy relatively stronger, by jolting industries into a radical energy-efficiency campaign.

"It is almost impossible to recall now the sense of near terror that it spread through the business community and government," William Chapman, a journalist based for years in Japan, wrote in his book *Inventing Japan* in the early 1990s.[7] "It" in this case was not the oil shock, but *endaka,* which literally means "high yen" and is Japan's term for the process started by the sudden rise of the yen's value against the dollar in 1985. *Endaka,* according to Japan's big-business alliance, the Keidanren, was a crisis "unprecedented in severity" since the end of World War II.[8] Quite apart from competing with Americans, there would be no way for Japanese manufacturers to hold off ambitious but lower-priced competitors from Korea or Taiwan. As Aron Viner wrote in 1988, in a book about Japanese finance, "The strong yen seems destined to shatter forever Japan's export-based economy."[9]

"Forever" turned out to mean about two years. Within four years of the beginning of *endaka,* Japan's trade surplus was on the rise again. In 1992, with the yen worth twice as much as in 1985, the trade surplus was moving to its highest level ever. The precise reasons for this shift are not the issue for the moment. (The booming trade surpluses of 1991 through 1993 mainly reflected the slowdown in Japan's internal demand. As they tightened their belts, Japanese firms and individuals bought fewer products from overseas. Yet Japan's factories kept running, to keep its people employed, and the most active markets were overseas.) The Western world's persistent underestimation of Japan is the relevant point.

Indeed, even at the moment of its greatest apparent distress and weakness Japan retained strengths most other economies would envy. Its savings rate was at least three times higher than America's. In the short run this was a nuisance for Japan, since money relegated to savings was not available to stimulate the economy through consumer spending. It remained a formidable advantage in the long term, since it provided more money for the country's industries to invest. Japan's central government typically operates with a balanced budget, rather than the chronic deficits of the United States. In the short run this too depressed spending, but in the long run it gave the country great maneuvering room. Despite the collapse of Japan's bubble economy, unemployment rates remained lower than they had been in Europe or North America for decades.

Perhaps most important, in Japan's years of expansion its industries had, through sales and investment efforts, solidified their presence in every other corner of East Asia. Asia's overall growth was barely hampered when the Japanese bubble burst. High-rises and heavy factories sprang up in China's coastal provinces. Kuala Lumpur and Bangkok were virtually buried by new condos and office towers, and their streets were choked with cars. Through the 1980s East Asia had been the fastest-growing part of the world economy, and through the 1990s and beyond it should retain that role. Through the power of its money, its technology, its corporations, and its example of success, Japan remained at the center of this rising system. Japanese finance, even during Japan's distress, flowed through the region, drawing on the savings of Japanese citizens to create new factories and jobs. Japanese cars, construction machines, high-tech equipment, and consumer goods dominated markets throughout the Pacific littoral, from Manchuria to Singapore. Asia's other economies remained so closely linked to Japan's—as a source of capital, advanced components, and expertise—that each export success enjoyed by Taiwan, Thailand, Korea, or Malaysia was a success for Japan as well. The sun had not set.

At times, of course, outsiders have overestimated the power of the Japanese industrial system. For instance, in the mid-1980s Japanese industrialists and planners believed they could take an early lead in developing high-definition television sets, or HDTVs, by committing to an analog transmission system. (Analog is the transmission system that has been used for decades in broadcasting TV and radio signals. In an analog system signals are conveyed by variations in the frequency or amplitude of electromagnetic waves.) Western press coverage of their efforts took it for granted that whatever aproach Japanese firms chose would succeed. By the early 1990s, however, it had become clear that the Japanese developers had made the wrong choice. Firms based in the United States and Europe had shown that digital transmission systems were fundamentally superior to the analog approach, and Japan's initial approach to the HDTV industry was obsolete almost before its first products reached the market.[10]

Yet over the past century, when outsiders have misjudged the strength of the Japanese system, which during the same period has been the Asian system's productive core, they had usually guessed too low. Such consistent misjudgments, consistently in the same direction, say at least as much about the observer's biases as about the system being observed. They reveal how difficult it can be to recognize the emergence of a successful new system. How can we *see* these new ways of mobilizing and deploying human energy— and see them for themselves, not just as reflections of our own image in the glass? Finding ways to do so is my purpose in the pages that follow.

The first chapter of this book provides a detailed case study of how and why prevailing Western economic concepts fall short. Every day in the newspapers and in political speeches we hear familiar concepts about what businesses "must" do to succeed. This chapter is meant to show that none of those familiar ideas can explain, first, why the American semiconductor industry nearly vanished in the mid-1980s, or second, why it recovered in the late 1980s. Some other set of ideas and explanations is necessary.

What might those ideas concern? The second and third chapters suggest the basis for a different view of Asia's rise, one more in keeping with the way the process looks to the people who have engineered it in Tokyo, Seoul, Singapore, and Taipei. When Westerners talk about business and economics, they usually talk just about business and economics—that is, they view the rise and fall of certain industries as if this were a matter of purely commercial interest. As seen from Asia, the economic expansion of Japan and its neighbors is not primarily an economic phenomenon at all. It is better understood as a political achievement, with distinct historical motivations and roots that today's Westerners generally ignore.

Seen from the Asian side of the Pacific, Asia's modern success is the latest stage of a process that started when the European colonialists spread out through Africa, Asia, and Latin America five centuries ago. European missionaries, traders, colonialists, and warriors started showing up in Asia in large numbers in the 1600s. When they arrived, they had better weapons and machinery than the Chinese, Koreans, Malays, or Japanese possessed. Because the Europeans were stronger, they could tell the Asians what to do. The Europeans conquered many countries outright and bent the others to their will. To most Westerners, this episode is part of the distant past. In Asia its aftereffects live on today. Having seen the consequences of being weak, many of these countries resolved at all costs to become strong.

The historical background to today's economic news is especially crucial, and especially neglected in the West, in the case of Japan. From the 1960s through the early 1990s, there were two great pillars of ill will and friction between Japan and the United States. One was Japan's relentless emphasis on economic expansion; the other was the pernicious, passive/aggressive American policy toward Japan. For decades the United States has kept calling Japan "unfair" and demanding that it "change" and "open its markets." These campaigns have had virtually no effect on the underlying economic problems, yet they have built resentment in both Japan and America to ever higher levels. The Japanese feel that they are being bullied by a declining power; Americans feel that either by trickery or by hard work they are being overtaken by Japan. All in all, the relationship was much stranger and more perverse than that between any other two major "friendly" nations.

The roots of these tensions are also historic and political rather than strictly economic. They lie principally in a set of fateful decisions made in the decade after World War II, which are the subject of Chapter Three. America's Occupation of Japan was in many ways a brilliant success. During the Occupation years American and Japanese efforts put the Japanese economy back on its feet and repaired relations between countries that had been bitter enemies. Yet the aftereffects of the Occupation warped the American view of Japan by committing it to the fiction that Japan was a "baby America" that very soon would become like its American "parent" and model. More important, they warped Japan itself, especially its political system, in ways that have a major impact nearly fifty years after the end of the war.

Several decisions, all of which seemed humane and sensible at the time, had unexpected long-term consequences. One was the imposition of Japan's "Peace Constitution," drafted by the Americans, which said that Japan would renounce the right to use military force as a tool of national policy. At face value this was a sign of Japan's commitment to peace, but as the years went by it also became a reminder that Japan was an oddity among nations, the one major power that somehow could not be trusted—by its neighbors or its own citizens—to hold itself back if it possessed military force.

Yet another legacy of the Occupation was Japan's military "relationship" with the United States. Japanese and American diplomats were careful never to call this relationship an "alliance," since an alliance commits partners to come to each other's defense. The U.S.-Japanese "relationship" committed America to protect Japan but placed no reciprocal obligation on Japan, apart from that of letting the United States base its soldiers on Japanese soil. The asymmetry of this relationship may have seemed reasonable—Japan was not supposed to have a military in any case, so how could it be bound (as the British and Canadians theoretically were, through NATO) to come to America's defense? But the effect of this dependence, along with other features of the Occupation, was to keep Japan from becoming a "normal" country.

Japan's economic institutions grew stronger and stronger. Its political system atrophied. It was left with the ability to promote its industrial interests but to do very little else. This legacy of the Occupation is the fundamental source of the endless "trade frictions" between Japan and the rest of the world. The historic Japanese elections of 1993, in which the Liberal Democratic Party lost the monopoly on power it had held since 1955, could conceivably be a step toward building a system of political accountability in Japan. But at its best this process will take years, even decades—and meanwhile the economic frictions increase.

Another effect of World War II and its aftermath was to confirm the American belief in its supremacy over the world. This sense showed up not just in material ways but also in its lack of real curiosity about how other people think and how other systems work. This lack of curiosity has been especially damaging in the realm of economics. Chapter Four describes a parallel economic universe, a realm of both ideas and action whose very existence most Westerners have ignored. What the modern English-speaking world thinks of as "economics" should really be called, more narrowly, "Anglo-American economics." It represents one tradition in economic analysis—but not the only tradition, and certainly not one accepted as gospel truth in the rest of the world, least of all in Asia. The main alternative tradition is the one started by nineteenth-century German economists, for whom I use Friedrich List as a symbol. This tradition places much less emphasis on "consumer welfare," "free trade," and "global allocative efficiency"—the ideas that underlie virtually everything that is written in the United States about economic policy. Instead, this German tradition, often known as "corporatism" in Europe, views economics as essentially a tool of national strength—that is, as a *political* matter rather than as a question of dollars and cents.

It is this system—essentially, economics for political and historic purposes—whose effects the world is now beginning to recognize in Asia. The second half of this book explores the system's consequences in the rest of the region. Japan is inescapably the center of this discussion, since it is both the conceptual model and the day-by-day integrating force for most other economies in the region. From northern China to the southern reaches of the Indonesian archipelago, Japanese banks are the leading lenders in the region, Japanese trading houses are the leading exporters, Japanese cars are omnipresent, and the Japanese model is paramount in planners' minds.

Yet the Asian system is powerful precisely because it has become a broad regional system, reaching across national borders and taking on different characteristics in each place it is applied. Some nations in East Asia, especially Korea and Taiwan, have struggled to create their own counterparts to the "Japanese miracle." Others have boomed mainly because of money, factories, technology, and raw-material demand spilling over from Japan. This effect is most obvious in Thailand and Malaysia but involves Indonesia and Singapore in smaller ways. The Philippines, Burma, North Korea, and the countries that made up old French Indochina—Laos, Vietnam, and Cambodia—have for political and historic reasons been cut off from East Asia's boom. Except for the totalitarian dinosaurs Burma and North Korea, each of these excluded countries has been looking for ways in.

Meanwhile, every Asian country except China has been trying

to assess China's intentions and possibilities. All of them, including China, are aware that China is the historic titan of the region, which could rise to dominance once more if its current strategic gamble pays off. The Chinese leadership is trying to demonstrate that a country can have a powerful modern economy without allowing its people the individual freedoms that the Western world calls "human rights." The entire Asian model is based on a variant of this proposition: that it is possible to become as strong as the Western world without embracing its permissive ways.

The engine of modern Asia's power is economic, but the effects touch politics, culture, and conceptions of individual worth and collective welfare. Its economic power is based on a political model at odds with the ideals Westerners have propounded since the time of Locke and Rousseau. No one outside Asia will be forced to adopt or imitate this system, but outsiders should be sure they understand how the new system works.

It is difficult to look directly at the sun, so we turn away, view it obliquely, look at the shadows it casts. It has been difficult for Westerners, especially Americans, to think directly about the economic power that has spread to the rest of Asia from Japan. The countries are far away, the languages are hard. Most outsiders turn away, view the situation obliquely, judge it by the shadows it casts in our world.

I won't call this book a look straight into the sun, which suggests that we'd all go blind. But the Western world's reluctance to look at the Asian model directly, in all its brilliance and its heat, is the main source of friction between Japan, plus those neighbors in Asia that it increasingly dominates, and the rest of the world. There is nothing inherently dangerous in the new social and economic models being developed in Asia. There is great danger in failing to see them for what they are.

I

The Mystery of the Chips

The Age of Innocence

IN THE MIDDLE OF MARCH, the air was still hard and cold on the American East Coast. I was glad to be in California again. In peninsular California, south of San Francisco, so many things seemed soft, starting with the feel of the air on your skin. Having been inside, with chapped skin from heater-dried air on the East Coast, through the long, dark winter months, I spent a March morning sitting on a bench in Cupertino, California, just feeling the spring sun and soft air. I looked at the fresh green leaves waving on the maple trees, which in the East were still bare. This really was the place for a new start.

The blessing of California is generally the sense of newness, which at this moment, in 1980, seemed more vivid and real than in quite a long time. You could stand on sidewalks in Sunnyvale or Santa Clara and look down the straight, broad streets toward the rolling green-and-tawny foothills at their end. Up in the hills were vineyards, and in the flatlands there were still a few plum orchards, from the Santa Clara Valley's recent days as a gentle-climate agricultural center. Everyplace else, the fruits of the new economy seemed to be coming right up out of the soil.

The Santa Clara Valley had in those days just been baptized Silicon Valley, the center of the semiconductor industry for the entire world. The previous farm economy had had its own distinctive architecture. There were the redwood-clapboard warehouses that weathered to a silvery gray, the Spanish-style orange-packing houses with the picturesque workers outside, like those on the Sunkist or Real Gold labels that became collectors' art. The new economy had its own look, too, related to but subtly different from the standard American strip mall. The new buildings were sleek and low, because the San Andreas fault ran right through Silicon Valley. High, brittle buildings could be shaken down—and would seem wrong for such a flexible new business culture. The buildings looked fresh and almost flimsy without seeming cheap. They were like mushrooms that have sprung up after a rain, fragile but in their own way perfect. The walls of many of the buildings looked as if they were all window. With the sun gleaming off of them, the buildings seemed to shine.

In the downtown of Cupertino, which had been orchards barely a decade before, was a new public library with a large sculpture shaped like a conquistador's helmet. In the sun it beat out a coppery glow. Such structures were this new economy's answers to the concert halls and art museums that had gone up in Detroit and Chicago early in this century: people were making money, and they were spreading it around.

Just a few blocks from the library was one of the main sources of the money, Apple Computer, which was then growing so rapidly that its offices were scattered among half a dozen rented sites. If Cupertino had had a skyscraper, from its top you would have been able to see the other great successes of the valley arrayed along El Camino Real and Interstate 280. They included Intel, whose headquarters in Santa Clara looked slightly more composed and established than Apple's; the Xerox Palo Alto Research Center, where the "graphic interface" that led to Apple's Macintosh and Microsoft Windows was devised; upstarts such as Zilog, in Cupertino, which had been founded by exiles from Intel; and a host of others. In the late 1970s, the U.S. government published a list of the thirty-five American semiconductor companies founded since 1966. All except four were in the adjoining communities of Cupertino, Santa Clara, Sunnyvale, or Mountain View.[1]

Within a few years, it would become difficult to remember the sense of amazement and all-embracing promise that emanated from that area at that time. By the late 1980s, the newspaper-reading and computer-using public had become jaded about routine leaps forward in electronic performance, as chips the size of fingernails went from having 65,000 transistors per chip, to more than 1 million, to more than 4 million, to more than 16 million, to more than 64 million. By the 1990s, computer performance had become a numbers game; machines did the same things, only faster and faster.

But in the years before 1980, there was nothing to be jaded about. The industry was doing things that had never been done before, creating things that no one had ever seen. As Detroit had at the turn of the century, when new car companies were springing up practically overnight, Silicon Valley conveyed the sense that its own industries were actively remaking the world around them—and as with Detroit in those years, some of the people who had made the original discoveries were still on the scene and at the helm. Robert Noyce was one of several men who might reasonably be called the "father of the chip." In 1959, while in his early thirties, Noyce had proposed combining a large number of electronic circuits on a single piece of silicon. This would be the "integrated circuit," later known to the world as the chip.[2] In 1980 Noyce was still working in Silicon Valley, as part of a triumvirate that ruled Intel. (Intel's two other leaders were Gordon Moore and Andrew Grove.)

William Shockley was another creator of the industry. He had been awarded a Nobel Prize in physics in 1956 for his work a decade earlier in inventing the transistor. Before the transistor, electronic devices relied on vacuum tubes, which were clumsy, unreliable, and always burning out. Just after World War II Shockley and two other researchers at Bell Labs, John Bardeen and Walter Brattain, discovered that they could instead use the "semiconducting" properties of certain crystalline materials to do the job that vacuum tubes had done so awkwardly. By the early 1950s this discovery of "solid state" design was fostering a new electronics industry. Shockley himself moved to California in the 1950s and formed his own semiconductor company. In the late 1950s a group of young scientists broke off from Shockley's company to form Fairchild Semiconductors, which in its turn would be the incubator for the founders of Intel, AMD, and many other Silicon Valley firms. By 1980 Shockley had become embarrassing to the industry, because of his advocacy of the theory that the IQ of whites was inherently higher than the IQ of blacks. But he was still in the neighborhood, based at the University of California at Berkeley. Steven Jobs and Steve Wozniak were still together, at Apple, which was in 1980 preparing what would be a precursor of the Macintosh, a computer called the "Lisa."

Although the computer companies, especially Apple, were more glamorous and visible, the semiconductor makers—such as Intel and National Semiconductor and Advanced Micro Devices— were really the foundation of the business and of the valley. Through the late 1970s, business writers often contrasted Silicon Valley with Detroit. One was seen as symbolizing American manufacturing and innovation at the start of the century, the other at the end. One was going down, the other was going up.

The process of making computer equipment was roughly comparable to the process of making cars. Each industry started with specialized raw materials and transformed them into sophisticated products. Silicon Valley's raw materials were brick-sized loaves of pure silicon crystal; these were cut into wafer-thin slices, on whose surfaces the circuits were etched. Each industry required highly specialized machinery—precision machine tools to make car engines, lithographic etching systems to produce computer chips, their tolerances measured in millionth-of-an-inch units known as microns and their performance in billionth-of-a-second units known as nanoseconds. The semiconductor makers provided the most valuable components of the larger box that became the computer.

In Detroit, Henry Ford had brought the whole process of producing a car under one gigantic roof at the legendary Rouge plant: coal and ore came in at one end; from the other, finished cars rolled away. In between, the factory made its own glass and steel. IBM applied the same philosophy to the high-tech business, producing more semiconductors than any other company in the world and using them in its own computers. But most of Silicon Valley was based on an elaborate and precise division of labor, as separate parts of the production system were hived off into separate ventures. A division of Monsanto produced the silicon crystals. Companies such as Varian, Eaton, and Perkin-Elmer produced semiconductor-making equipment. Scores of small start-up shops specialized in designing chips. And new companies such as Advanced Micro Devices and National Semiconductor became local giants, combining the ingredients into memory chips.

The semiconductor industry was profitable for its owners and successful internationally. In 1980 American semiconductors earned about $2 billion of net foreign sales, at a time when the United States sold just about as much merchandise overseas as it bought. Semiconductor sales were part of an overall U.S. high-tech trade surplus of well over $20 billion.[3] The only American industries that provided more net exports than semiconductor makers were aircraft, led by mighty Boeing; farm products, from California and the Midwest; and entertainment, from America's movie and record companies. The sales of one semiconductor company, Intel, had risen from $283 million in 1977, to $400 million in 1978, to $661 million in 1979. In 1979 about one quarter of its revenues came from export sales.[4] In 1980 its main problem was finding enough engineers and technicians. Fourteen thousand people worked for Intel in 1980, and most of them had joined the company within the previous two years.

The Moral Success of the Semiconductor Makers

Half a dozen years later, when I was living in Japan, I wondered what it must have been like to be there during the U.S. Occupation, when Americans felt so confident of their economic strength and political insight that they unself-consciously tried to reform an ancient nation. This must have reflected a similar confidence at home. I thought I saw something similar in Silicon Valley in 1980. The industry's success could be seen as a triumph—first, of sheer technology, and second, of business skills. But those who are successful, especially in America, tend to interpret their success in moral terms, and that was so in the semiconductor industry as well.

In 1980 the United States was more than a decade past the time when its industries seemed automatically to be the best in the world. Starting in the late 1960s and continuing throughout the 1970s, one part of the industrial base or another seemed to be in trouble—automobile makers after the oil shock of the early 1970s, radio and TV makers as Japanese producers displaced them from the U.S. market, the steel industry as Brazil, Taiwan, India, and every other country moving toward industrialization promoted steel exports as a sign that it had arrived.

The shutdowns of plants were obviously inconvenient and even tragic where they happened, but they could be seen as inevitable. Historically, some industries had always been falling while new ones were rising—and the list of industries that were failing in 1980 made a certain sad sense. The industries with the biggest and most obvious problems—autos, steel, other parts of heavy manufacturing—were those that seemed oldest and least deserving.

In 1980 General Motors was getting ready to close its Vega plant, in northern Ohio. Well, it was this very plant that in the early 1970s had symbolized what was wrong with American manufacturing. Management ran the lines a little faster than the workers felt they could tolerate; union members put Coke bottles in the door panels, and kicked the cars as they passed.

Just before coming to Silicon Valley, in 1980, I had gone to Michigan to interview "workers" and "management"—it was significant that they described themselves that way—in the auto industry. At a Buick plant in Flint, I arrived wearing a suit and tie. I was outfitted with a hard hat that said "GM Visitor" on the front, and I walked along the line with a front-office keeper who also wore a suit. As we strolled at arm's length from the "workers" on the line, or viewed the whole panorama from a catwalk above, the glare of class-war hatred seemed to beat out from the factory floor. In those days it was hard to find even the semblance of the team spirit that would, by the late 1980s, be emphasized in ads like Ford's "Quality Is Job 1" campaign.

The upper management of the industry, as David Halberstam made vivid in *The Reckoning,* had less and less dirty-hands contact with the realities of building cars. More and more of them were financiers who saw factories only as entries on balance sheets and were willing to pare away any piece of productive hardware that wasn't earning its keep right now. A few days after visiting the automobile plants in 1980, I sat in an anteroom in the main GM building in Detroit, waiting for an audience with Roger Smith. Smith was then about one year away from taking over as chairman of GM. Everything about the setting called up the words "plush executive suite"—the dim lighting, the thick carpet, even a sense of unrecognized pathos, in the insulation required from the grimy downtown area that surrounded the corporate headquarters. When Smith finally came in, looking through a sheaf of papers as we talked, he confidently told me that Americans didn't really like little cars and that the Japanese cars were overrated. "Wait and see how they stand up to real road conditions. Our Midwestern winters!" When we were done he was escorted down the hall to an elevator and whisked down to the basement, where a chauffeur was waiting with a car. I'm sure the auto industry's problems must have been more complicated than this—Toyota executives have chauffeured cars, too— but if you were looking for a way to connect the ambiance with the failure, you could start with executives who didn't seem to like the hands-on experience of driving the cars they made.

Everything about the steel and auto and tire industries seemed tired and angry and old. Earlier in 1980 I had met a U.S. Steel official in Pittsburgh whose own story seemed to be a model for the life cycle of declining industries. His grandfather had come from Poland and had worked in the coal mines without ever really learning English. His father had worked in a U.S. Steel mill in the great days after World War II. The man himself had gotten a white-collar job in U.S. Steel's public relations department—and his daughter, he hoped, would get out of Pittsburgh altogether and wind up as a lawyer or consultant somewhere sunny and warm. If the old manufacturing industries were heading down, half of the people involved seemed to be thinking, Good riddance.

In the early springtime of 1980, in the sun-washed, soft-aired valleys of northern California, the spirit seemed just the opposite. The technology was new, and its freshness and profitability naturally spilled over into the way people viewed themselves. They, or their parents or grandparents, had moved from places like Pittsburgh or Youngstown to get a new start. It was too bad for the people who hadn't had the foresight to leave, but in a way it was their own fault. These new companies weren't ever going to succumb to the same, primitive us-vs.-them mentality of the old factory towns. In the proudest, richest companies—Hewlett-Packard, Apple, Intel—the millionaire bosses and owners sat right on the work floor, in little cubicles alongside everyone else, rather than holing themselves up in executive suites.

In Detroit, about a week before arriving in Cupertino, I had spent an afternoon in a recreation hall built by the United Auto Workers just after World War II. Inside, broken-down auto workers, who had grown up with the idea that a shift on the assembly line gave you as much exercise as you would ever need, padded slowly around a grimy indoor track or sat soaking their bones in galvanized metal tubs. In Silicon Valley, people wore running shoes to work and went outside at lunchtime to exercise in the sun on Parcours fitness trails. *In Search of Excellence,* by Tom Peters and Robert Waterman, was about to come out. The book was a survey of America's most successful companies, which concluded that the firms that were most flexible, least hierarchical in their internal organization, and most attentive to their employees' well-being prevailed in the marketplace, too. Silicon Valley seemed full of such companies. At Hewlett-Packard, the interior of the building had muted light and lush plants. Everyone seemed to be young.

It was not simply a matter of atmospherics. Structurally, too, the semiconductor companies seemed to be doing everything right. In the 1960s and early 1970s, the big American steelmakers had made a nearly fatal error by not modernizing as rapidly as the Japanese and Koreans did. The Japanese steel companies had nearly all converted to basic-oxygen furnaces; most of the American firms had saved money by sticking with the open-hearth process, which meant that every ton of steel cost them more to make.

The companies of the Silicon Valley believed that they would never make such a short-sighted error. The valley's high-tech industry was very proud in those days of its venture-capital system, which allowed companies to invest for the long run and which, through stock-owning plans for employees, gave everyone a stake in the company's success. Each year Intel put 10 percent of its total earnings back into research, much more than in the typical heavy-manufacturing firm. The company was a dozen years old in 1980, and with all its revenues it had not paid out a penny in dividends; its owners and venture capitalists made money as the share price went up. The previous year, Intel had put $67 million into research and $97 million into capital improvement. The employees put another $60 million, or more than $4,000 per person, into stock-buying plans. The company's three founders—Robert Noyce, the Gary Cooper–like Iowan who had helped invent the integrated circuit; Andrew Grove, a refugee from Hungary who became Intel's management specialist; and Gordon Moore, a renowned engineer who still carried pens in a pocket protector—worked in a kind of bullpen among the other employees, as their counterparts would have in Japan.

Many people were making fortunes in the semiconductor business at that time: Gordon Moore owned Intel stock worth some $60 million, and Andrew Grove and Robert Noyce had comparable stakes in the company—but almost all were close enough to the actual business to view it as something more than a mere balance sheet. There was an industrywide rather than companywide camaraderie, because people changed jobs so quickly and so many had rubbed shoulders with each other at crucial junctures in the industry's growth. The founders of most of the big companies had in the early 1960s worked for Fairchild Semiconductors, Silicon Valley's first real semiconductor-making firm. The three people who started National Semiconductor, the three who started Intel, the eight who started Advanced Micro Devices, and the three who started Precision Monolithic had all worked for Fairchild. Regis McKenna, a suave man who became the PR titan of the valley in the 1970s and 1980s, had come from Fairchild as well.

Executives from the auto and steel companies pointed out that no matter how progressive and touchy-feely they might become, they were up against certain ultimate limits. The American economy could use only so much steel—indeed, as its industries grew more sophisticated, they used less and less steel per dollar of output. (Most of the cost of an anvil is made up by the steel that goes into it. Raw materials make up very little of the cost of a camera or a computer chip.) If the overall economy grew by 4 percent, the demand for steel might go up by only 2 or 3 percent—and the number of jobs in steelmaking might continue to fall as the mills increased their productivity faster than overall demand rose. The average American family had about as many cars as it was going to buy.

The computer and semiconductor makers seemed to face no such limits. The more they made, the more they sold. People who bought the first personal computers in the late 1970s felt lucky to have a whole 8 kilobytes of memory to use. When the first IBM Personal Computer appeared in 1981, it offered a magnificent-seeming 16 kilobytes of programmable memory. A decade later, a typical desktop personal computer might have 250 times as much memory, for about the same price.

Semiconductors were used in photocopying machines and to run industrial robots. They were built into household thermostats, airplane cockpits, and programmable VCRs. By the late 1980s, the biggest single use of semiconductors was one that most customers never saw: controlling the operations and providing the displays for modern cars. In his book *Microcosm,* published in 1989, George Gilder was more rhapsodic than most observers about the industry's prospects, but he vividly captured the sky's-the-limit feeling of Silicon Valley and of the people who had created it: "As computers master new levels of the hierarchy of knowledge, human beings can rise to new pinnacles of vision and power and discover new continents of truth."[5] He was not alone in such views.

Even the physical layout of the valley seemed to promote the idea that it was the natural and good succcessor to the previous industrial order. The old industrial system had been built on big, brutish machines concentrated in hell-like factory zones. Men were roasted alive in smelters, dehumanized on auto assembly lines. In Silicon Valley, the machines were barely visible. They existed inside the low, modern production buildings, and the men and women who worked there dressed like astronauts. The semiconductor industry seemed to be human intelligence made incarnate.

One of the Apple managers of that time, Mike Markkula, said in 1980 as he sat in one of the bright offices, "My basic understanding is that if you took all the people out of the buildings, what you'd have is a bunch of buildings. The company is worth simply nothing without the people." A few years later this would sound like management-theory boilerplate, but at that moment, talent clearly seemed to be the most crucial factor of production in Silicon Valley. Engineers would leave one company on Friday night, drive across El Camino Real, and start at a new company on Monday morning. Over the hills and up the freeway lay the two ultimate sources of the region's vitality and its human talent, serving like twin suns constantly beaming out energy that sustained life. These were Stanford and the University of California at Berkeley, with their crops of technical graduates, the cadres of ambitious foreign students, and their research centers with vast experimental machines underwritten by federal contracts.

The valley served in those days as a kind of Lego-set model for an idealized economy, straight out of Econ 101 texts. Well-informed buyers and sellers made rational decisions every day, judging mainly on price and quality, without the distorting influences of emotion, monopoly, or government interference.

The manufacturers of the valley could be divided into three main categories. At the top of the industrial "food chain" were the computer makers—companies such as Apple and Hewlett-Packard, whose brand names the public knew and whose products sat on desks in offices and homes. Below the computer makers were the semiconductor makers—Intel, Motorola, Texas Instruments, Zilog, National, and countless others. As the industry grew through the 1980s the public came to know their names as well, but until very late in the decade, when computer users around the country began buying extra RAM or faster processors for their home computers, the semiconductor makers sold their products to the computer industry and other industrial consumers. At the base of this particular food chain were the semiconductor-equipment companies—Varian, Eaton, Perkin-Elmer, and the like. They were virtually invisible to the public, but without them Intel and Motorola could not have made chips, and without chips Apple and HP could not have made computers.

The varied branches of this industry were working together in California just the way American economic theory said they should. Few companies in this industry were big and integrated. Most were specialized, agile, and small. The giants of those days, IBM and Xerox, were present in the valley but served largely as brooder houses from which ambitious engineers and breakthroughs in basic research would emerge. (AT&T's Bell Labs had played the same role in the industry's early days.)[6] Every branch of the industry seemed unchallengeably strong—as makers of American cars had seemed in the 1950s, as American software houses believe themselves to be in the 1990s. Japanese manufacturers, who had already created such problems for other, less advanced-seeming American industries, were barely on the map. At the urging of the Japanese government, Japan's big firms—Toshiba, Hitachi, Fujitsu, NEC—

were building both chips and computers by the mid-1970s. But they still relied overwhelmingly on American suppliers for the chip-making equipment; they had no way to match it on their own.[7]

Because of everything that was going right in Silicon Valley, its members, and most of the American public, saw an inevitable logic to its rise. These industries were forward-looking, and they were flexible. They used advanced technology, and they created good jobs. Opinion polls in those days still showed great American confidence in the country's technical prowess. The Koreans might move from textiles to steel, the Japanese from steel to cars, but the Americans would move from cars to computer chips, and from there who could tell what would come next? The drive along El Camino Real was a bittersweet but inevitable counterpart to a trip along the old Penn Central right-of-way through New Jersey and Pennsylvania. Machine shops and gearworks in America's old industrial areas had closed, and that was poignant—but the economy of the future was growing before America's eyes!

The Industry's Collapse

Five years later, everything about this industry had changed. In some ways the look and feel of American life remained constant through those years. In the early 1990s it was possible to look at pictures of Ronald Reagan's election campaign of 1980 without the shock of thinking, Did we really dress that way? But the look and feel of the semiconductor industry had changed dramatically. The very companies that had seen themselves as demonstrating the moral superiority of the American way of doing business were making almost exactly the opposite point. What happened to the semiconductor industry, and to its constellation of customers and suppliers, is like what happened to the American automobile or steel industries—except that it happened so much more rapidly.

Through the late 1970s, American companies still dominated semiconductor production and had a virtual monopoly on the sophisticated machines necessary to make semiconductors. Of all the machines used to make semiconductors in the world, about 85 percent came from America in the mid- and late 1970s, including about 80 percent of those used in Japan.[8] A U.S. government interagency task force conducted a survey in the late 1970s of technical prowess in the semiconductor and semiconductor-making industries. Of the twenty-four areas they surveyed, American producers had a "clear" or "substantial" technical lead in eight, and a "slight" lead in six more. Japanese producers had a "clear" lead in only one area, semiconductor packaging (which means mounting the chips themselves in ceramic or plastic housings), and a "slight" lead in four others. By the late 1980s, Japanese producers had moved ahead in almost every area.[9]

By 1991, a report from the U.S. Office of Technology Assessment that covered semiconductors and other high-tech manufacturing concluded that "in sectors that contribute heavily to employment, trade, knowledge, and income, there is still a gulf between Japanese and American company performance"—a gulf that this time favored Japan. In a number of areas (such as merchant suppliers of silicon, and companies producing gas for "maskworks" used in making semiconductors) Japanese suppliers were the only suppliers; no American companies had the machinery or factories to compete. The report went on to say, using a flourish of italics unusual for government prose,

> In many cases, the gap is widening, driven by the fact that Japanese companies, flush with the profits of their market success, are investing more heavily in technological improvement and global expansion. *If there are no major changes in government policies of developed nations, we expect U.S. manufacturing competitiveness to continue to sink, compared with Japan.*[10]

By 1982 Japanese semiconductor companies were making more "dynamic random access memory" chips, or DRAMs, than American firms. These DRAM products, pronounced "dee-ram," are what most computer users think of as "memory chips." By 1985 Japanese production of semiconductor products as a whole exceeded America's. As Japanese companies increased their output of chips, they also turned more and more to Japanese suppliers for chip-making equipment. Through the late 1970s American equipment makers had dominated sales to chip-making companies in Japan, but by 1985 their share of the Japanese market had fallen to 20 percent.[11]

When the U.S. government made another survey of technology in 1987, it found that the U.S. and Japanese positions had more or less reversed. Japanese companies had clear or substantial leads in eight fields and slight leads in five others. The United States had a clear lead in only two remaining fields, microprocessors and linear-logic chips, and had lost ground in every area except one (linear logic). Another survey revealed slightly different results but the same general trend: clear Japanese lead in ten areas, U.S. lead in four, and the two countries even in three.[12]

The best-publicized American success was in the area of microprocessors—the chips that actually interpret the instructions in computer programs and control the operations of the computer as a whole. The two American powerhouses in microprocessor making were Intel and Motorola. Intel had started out as a memory-chip company—indeed, it had invented the DRAM chip in 1969, just after the company's founding—but, like many others, had been forced out of that business as the Japanese producers came in. Unlike the others, however, it had by the mid-1980s found a new and amazingly lucrative role in producing microprocessors. Motorola, which had been actively fighting trade wars in Japan and whose processor chips were used not just in the Macintosh but also in a variety of industrial applications, also prospered.

These two "victor" companies, Intel and Motorola, differed in many ways. Intel was new, specialized, the epitome of Silicon Valley culture; Motorola was older, much more diversified, with its headquarters outside Chicago rather than on the Pacific rim. But the companies shared a crucial similarity during the 1980s, the first decade of the personal-computer age: each of them made a family of microprocessing chips around which a major computer operating system had been designed. Intel's "x86" series of chips—from the 8086 used in the origial IBM personal computer to the "Pentium" chip released in 1993—was designed into Microsoft's phenomenally popular operating systems, DOS and Windows. Motorola's processors were designed into Apple computers, the most successful of which was the Macintosh. Each time Apple sold a Mac, anywhere in the world, Motorola sold a sophisticated central-processing chip. The symbiotic relationships between Intel and Motorola, on the one hand, and the Microsoft/IBM and Apple operating systems, on the other, provided a steady cash flow that buoyed these two chip makers when others around them were foundering.

There were other patches of good news, such as that from Applied Materials, a small American company whose products had been designed into a number of Japanese systems. Early in the 1990s, the U.S. semiconductor industry as a whole would regain some of the ground it had lost to the Japanese, largely because of changes in U.S. trade policy, as we will see. But by the mid-1980s the semiconductor industry as a whole had changed dramatically from the position it had held at the beginning of the decade.

In 1978 the world's two largest merchant semiconductor firms were Texas Instruments and Motorola. (IBM remained the largest producer in the world, but it used its own chips, unlike the "merchant" firms that sold them.) By 1986 the top three merchant firms were NEC, Hitachi, and Toshiba, and there were six Japanese firms among the ten leaders in the world.[13] (The non-Japanese entrants were Intel; Motorola; Texas Instruments; and Philips, based in Holland.) By 1983 the Japanese semiconductor companies were spending more on new facilities than the Americans were. By 1985 they were spending more on research and development. By 1986, in the words of one report, "most non-Japanese producers of DRAMs had been eliminated from the world market or marginalized; Japanese firms controlled 90 percent of world production of 256K DRAMs."[14]

By 1990 Japanese firms accounted for about 50 percent of total world sales.[15] By 1990 U.S.-based firms were disappearing from the semiconductor-equipment industry (steppers and so on)—and Silicon Valley was so rife with reports of Japanese-based manufacturers "holding back" their best equipment from American manufacturers that the U.S. General Accounting Office and several intelligence agencies looked into the situation. Early in 1991 I met a minister from the Korean government who had come to Washington to try to put together alliances of Korean and American technology firms. Otherwise, he said, they would both eventually be eclipsed by Japanese firms.

Newspapers reports continually referred to semiconductor chips as part of an industrial "food chain," an allusion that probably meant nothing to most readers. It had a precise meaning to those in the business. The chips were, on the one hand, raw materials for other advanced products: They went into computers, VCRs, and increasingly into cars. The top three semiconductor makers, for instance—NEC, Toshiba, and Hitachi—were best known not for their chips but for the computers, VCRs, machine tools, and similar finished goods that incorporated chips.

The classic economic theory taught in American business schools contended that a specialized approach—in which some companies made the best possible chips and others used those chips to make the best possible computers—would be the most efficient of all ways to exploit the vast potential of this new technology. Each little firm could concentrate single-mindedly on making the best possible chip, video display device, or disk drive, without carrying the overhead of supporting a big, diversified corporate structure. Yet through the 1980s the combined Japanese approach became more and more successful, by measures of world market share. The

United States has twice as many people as Japan, an economy that through the 1980s was more than twice as large as Japan's, and a computer-and-semiconductor industry that was regarded as leading the entire world. Yet by 1988 Japan's *consumption* of semiconductors—its use of them as components for cars, computers, and countless other high-value products—was greater than America's, and a Japanese industrial group projected that it would be dramatically larger by 1995.[16]

And in addition to providing the supplies for computer makers and other "downstream" industries, the chip makers were themselves major customers. They bought from the "upstream" companies that made steppers and all the other complex and expensive capital goods necessary to produce semiconductor chips. As the American semiconductor industry dwindled in the 1980s, so did the related American industries that bought from and sold to it. In theory this need not have happened—American etcher makers could in theory sell equipment to Hitachi rather than to Advanced Micro Devices, American computer makers could in theory get all the DRAM chips they needed from NEC rather than from sources nearby in Silicon Valley. But for one reason or another it did not work that way.

As the semiconductor industry itself grew in Japan, it evolved in such a way as to promote linkages with other Japanese firms—and to prevent them from developing with non-Japanese firms. In the mid-1970s Japan's Ministry of International Trade and Industry, MITI, launched its "VLSI" projects, the most visible of numerous postwar efforts to coordinate the growth of Japan's computer-related industries. The acronym stood for "Very-Large-Scale Integration," and the projects involved preferential access to capital, government-sponsored research, strategies for licensing technology from foreign (mainly American) suppliers, and other means to help Japanese producers overcome the foreign lead in high-tech production.

By the logic of American-style economic theory, such government-sponsored efforts should have been both unnecessary and self-defeating. They were unnecessary because if customers in Japan wanted chips, chip-making machines, or computers, they could always just buy them from suppliers in other countries. There was no need to go to the expense or bother of erecting new industries from scratch in Japan. And the efforts were self-defeating because government interference would raise the price that Japanese customers had to pay, handicapping the Japanese firms that used the chips.

Japanese commentators, when writing in English, often claim

that precisely this logic prevailed in Japan. "We Japanese, like people everywhere, import when other countries can provide competitively attractive goods and services," one famous Japanese spokesman asserted in 1993.[17] Yet such a nationality-blind, purely price-minded mentality cannot explain the way the Japanese semiconductor industry developed.

How Japan's Industry Grew

In the version of economic theory most American students learn in introductory courses, there is a tension between two opposing ideas. One is a concept of automatic correction. It holds that in the long run most trends will moderate or reverse themselves. The other is a concept of momentum. It suggests that once a trend happens, it will continue.

The laws of supply and demand make up the "automatic correction" part of this equation. As demand for a product goes up— whether the product is a barrel of oil, an apartment in Paris, a share of Intel stock, or a ticket to a popular play—the price of the product also rises, which in turn eventually makes demand go down. No price rises forever; market forces eventually turn most booms into busts.

But at the same time, everyone recognizes the concept of self-sustaining momentum. Once the United States develops an aircraft industry and Morocco does not, once New York becomes a financial and publishing center and Topeka does not, the gap between the leaders and followers may grow larger, rather than automatically closing itself. The industries that provide parts to aircraft makers concentrate in America, not Morocco. Even if aircraft companies eventually move some factories to Morocco (or some other lower-wage country), their most specialized and best-paying jobs will remain near the headquarters of Boeing, or Airbus, or other major manufacturers. Medical-equipment companies grow up near major hospitals and medical schools, and the more of them are in one place, the faster they move ahead. It becomes hard for regions that lack the experience and the schools and the networks to catch up.

Through the 1980s, the Japanese semiconductor industry illustrated this self-accelerating momentum. The companies that made chips were tightly connected to the companies that bought chips— and connected by something other than the prospect of business advantage that momentarily binds buyers to sellers in the American marketplace. The closest analogy from American life is the military. Just as the U.S. Air Force, with its allies in industry and the Congress, competes bitterly for budget and prestige against the Army and the Navy (and their respective allies), so do Toshiba, NEC, and Fujitsu, with their allies, compete bitterly for primacy and market share against each other. Yet competitors within each system— branches of the military in America, large corporations in Japan— recognize limits to their rivalry; fundamentally each is on the same team as its rivals, and at certain points they must pull together for the common good. According to Western economic theory there is virtually no "shared interest" among business competitors. Members of the American military system, and the Japanese business system, need no theory to articulate why they are on the same side.

By the mid-1980s, several years of bargain-basement prices from Japanese suppliers had convinced nearly all American firms to quit the DRAM (memory-chip) market. By 1986, 90 percent of all 256K chips made anywhere in the world were made by Japanese companies.

At just this point, when non-Japanese producers had virtually disappeared from the market, a strange thing happened. Before, semiconductor chips had always become cheaper as time went on. Factories became bigger and more efficient. Producers learned how to eliminate defects, which meant they had fewer flawed chips to throw away, which in turn reduced the overall cost per finished chip.

Yet starting in 1985, the 256K chips started to become "expensive" and "scarce." Prices went up and stayed up, as they never had before in the history of the semiconductor industry. In the past, high prices had always led to increased supply—the more money was coming in, the more of it the companies reinvested in factory space. But as the price of 256K chips mysteriously rose, Japanese companies did *not* invest in any more 256K production space.

This behavior would be hard to explain if you thought of the chip industry as being made of completely free agents competing ferociously against each other. It made more sense if you thought that the Japanese chip industry as a whole acted with certain common interests, a more subtle and effective version of OPEC. "The Japanese producers, probably with MITI's encouragement, had begun to act like a cartel, controlling output and prices and reaping higher profits as a result," a report from the U.S. government's Office of Technology Assessment concluded in 1991, several years after the shortage began.[18]

The exact causes of the DRAM shortage are still hotly debated in both Japan and the United States. In brief, most discussion in America assumed that the United States itself had caused this price rise, through its complaints about Japanese "dumping" of chips in the previous three years. Reports published in Japan suggest that the Japanese industry itself engineered the rise, taking advantage of the OPEC-like control over chip supplies it had finally attained. Either way, the results were unmistakable. An American high-tech industry that had fed on chips, using more and more memory to produce bigger and faster machines, suddenly was cut off from its supply. Chip prices were going up, defying the industry's collective experience—and no matter what the price, some chips seemed impossible to find.

Everyone who was in the high-tech business in those days has stories about the DRAM drought. Computer magazines began running ads for "zero cards." These were expansion boards with no memory included; the customer was on his own to find DRAM to plug into the board. Officials of MITI began regulating the flow of precious DRAM chips out of the country, much as oil ministers had regulated output during OPEC's heyday. MITI had long maintained a list of goods requiring government approval before they could be sold to customers in China. An official of Hitachi, one of Japan's major DRAM producers, said that during the shortage "it was easier to get approval from MITI to sell things [goods subject to government control] to China than it was to get approval to sell DRAMs into the United States."[19]

Japanese producers, strong in DRAMs but weak in other kinds of semiconductor production (such as "application-specific integrated circuits," or ASICs), began offering package deals to American customers on a take-it-or-leave-it basis: We'll let you have DRAM if you'll buy our ASICs. American computer makers bought expansion boards from Japanese suppliers simply so they could strip off and use the DRAM chips. The sort of panicky rumor that had swept through oil markets in the early 1970s now affected the high-tech business. Abu Dhabi, it was said, was trading crude oil for chips, since it was easier to turn the latter into cash. Billion-dollar American high-tech firms were reluctant to go to the U.S. government for help, out of fear that their Japanese chip suppliers would resent such interference and retaliate by leaving them totally cut off. As one American report pointed out:

> While U.S. producers of personal computers were hampered by
> limited DRAM availability, their Japanese rivals—who were the

world's leading DRAM producers—experienced no such difficulty. During the late 1980s they were able to export large number of PCs and work stations "crammed" with DRAMs, capturing a 16 percent share of the world PC market.[20]

The shortage lasted a little over a year. Its most lasting effect was to aggravate a division between two branches of the American high-tech industry, the chip makers and the computer makers. In Japan these industries generally saw themelves as allies—and in many cases were combined in the same firm. (One division of NEC made chips; another division used them in computers.) In America the chip and computer makers were often at odds. For the chip makers, of course, higher chip prices meant higher revenues. For the computer makers, higher chip prices meant higher costs. So while the American computer makers might theoretically agree that it was wrong for Japanese chip makers to "dump" chips, at least in the short term the dumping was good for them. More important, while the "unfairness" of dumping was objectionable in theory, the hardship caused by the chip shortage was immediate and real for the U.S. computer makers. Even after the DRAM shortage ended, most U.S. computer companies retained a "never again" mentality. They realized the dangers of exposing themselves to another DRAM shortage by antagonizing suppliers in Japan.

The disagreements between America's chip and computer companies came to a famous climax early in 1990. IBM had spent much of the previous year pushing for a new U.S. chip-making consortium. The idea behind the project was that America's biggest chip-using and chip-making companies would band together to help strengthen the domestic semiconductor industry. Computer companies such as Digital Equipment and Hewlett-Packard, which like IBM used tremendous numbers of chips, would join semiconductor companies such as Intel and LSI Logic in building a large, advanced chip-making facility to be called U.S. Memories. The computer companies would then commit themselves to buy a certain share of the plant's future output, even if in the short term they could obtain chips more cheaply from Japanese or Korean suppliers. The project's backers argued that in the long term, the computer companies and the whole domestic high-tech industry would be stronger if American-owned chip companies survived.

U.S. Memories had been proposed in 1988, during the great chip shortage. As it held its first organizational meetings, in 1989, chip prices began drifting down. By the summer of 1989, another chip glut seemed to be in the making. Japanese manufacturers had expanded their output, and U.S. computer makers could get all the chips they wanted at good prices. In September 1989, amid falling chip prices, Apple Computer announced that it wouldn't support U.S. Memories. Apple spokesmen said that there was no need for the project, now that DRAM chips were cheap and plentiful again. By November Compaq, Sun Microsystems, Unisys, and Tandy had all rejected U.S. Memories as well.

At a meeting in Dallas on January 10, 1990, Sanford Kane, president of U.S. Memories, asked the remaining partners to state explicitly how much money they would put up and how many U.S. Memories chips they would buy. IBM and Digital were the only two computer companies to make significant commitments. Hewlett-Packard, one of the original supporters of the plan, backed off. By the end of the meeting it was clear that U.S. Memories was dead.

"These guys have a tactical view of the world; they don't think strategically," Sanford Kane told Stephen Yoder of *The Wall Street Journal* shortly after the meeting in Dallas. They were able "to so quickly forget that a year ago they were screaming for this"—that is, for some alternative to Japanese suppliers. "For them, it's 'Don't worry, be happy.' Just close your eyes and blindly go on." Kenneth Flamm, a semiconductor expert who was then at the Brookings Institution (and who became a Defense Department official in the Clinton administration), said the U.S. Memories failure "goes to prove Akio Morita's contention that U.S. business has a ten-minute time horizon."[21]

With a longer perspective, the U.S. Memories backers said, computer companies would realize how deeply they were threatened by reliance on foreign suppliers. If, for instance, Compaq were selling laptop computers in competition with Toshiba, but both of them relied on Toshiba chips and screens from Sharp, then in the long run Compaq would lose.

About a year before U.S. Memories failed, Ingolf Ruge, a German technology expert, said:

> The goal of the Japanese . . . is a world monopoly on chips.
> They have even announced this publicly, and they are acting
> with this in mind. About a year ago, all Japanese manufacturers
> suddenly cut back on production, shooting prices way up. This
> monopolistic policy is currently costing companies like Nixdorf
> [a major German maker of computers] tens of millions of
> Deutschemarks.[22]

Shifts in the Balance of Dependence

Through the early 1990s, American politicians would often threaten to "deny" the American market to foreign manufacturers as a way of getting what the United States wanted. Since America was by far the world's biggest importer, this was often an effective threat. In 1992, for instance, Japan sent 30 percent of all its exports to its largest customer, the United States, versus only 6 percent to the second-largest customer, Hong Kong. But the threat was less impressive than Americans generally believed, since in so many areas Japanese companies were the only known suppliers. In 1991 one Japanese electronics maker irritated the U.S. government by selling equipment to Iran. Some federal agencies proposed punishing the company by refusing to buy its products. The main resistance came from the Pentagon: if the company were barred from selling in the United States, the American military could not develop several projects it had under way.[23] The most celebrated American weapons used during Operation Desert Storm, including the Patriot missiles that intercepted some of the Iraqi SCUDs, all relied for their operation on a kind of ceramic chip packaging that no American company could make.[24]

In the 1980s the National Security Agency, which is in charge of intercepting, processing, encoding, and decoding millions of messages per year, took the extraordinary step of building its own semiconductor-manufacturing facility. It went to this extreme to avoid having to buy foreign-manufactured semiconductors, which it believed could conceivably be "tainted" with virtually undetectable yet potentially catastrophic viruslike hostile programming. Despite its evident determination to avoid relying on foreign sources, the NSA found that such a goal was unattainable. For certain kinds of semiconductor-manufacturing equipment, it had no alternative but to buy from suppliers in Japan.

The NSA was asked what it would do when its foreign-made machines needed servicing, as they inevitably would. Would it rely on service representatives from the parent company to come to its supersecret premises and work on the machines? A government official involved in purchasing the machines smiled somewhat ruefully (according to another U.S. government official, who witnessed the exchange) and replied, "Oh, we'd never risk having a foreign citizen [i.e., a Japanese company representative] enter the facility. If we can't fix it ourselves, we'll just throw that piece of equipment out and purchase a new one, even if it means several million dollars for replacement instead of a repair for several hundred dollars."

Just before fighting began in the Gulf War, the Defense Intelligence Agency circulated a highly classified and controversial draft report about the American military's growing dependence on Japanese high-tech equipment. The report warned that the Japanese government was explicitly considering how it could exploit the military's dependency to gain additional leverage over the United States—for instance, to keep the U.S. government from proposing more aggressive trade policies toward Japan.[25]

Even more unsettling to the Pentagon were indications that it simply did not know how dependent it was on countries that did not always share America's strategic views. On June 18, 1991, ten days after a Desert Storm celebration parade rolled down Constitution Avenue in Washington, the Senate Armed Services Committee held a hearing on "America's Industrial Base as it Supports the National Security." Exhibiting candor rare for such a hearing, Admiral Donald J. Yockey, under secretary of defense for acquisition, told the committee that "we have no precise understanding of the extent of foreign sourcing."

Senator Jeff Bingaman, a Democrat of New Mexico, wanted to be sure he'd heard correctly: "We do not know the extent to which we are foreign sourcing or the extent to which we are dependent upon foreign sources?"

Admiral Yockey replied: "I will say this, we pretty much know it on a case-by-case basis on the first tier. When you get down two, three, four tiers, or down to the components, we have no idea."[26]

In 1990, Andrew Grove, one of the cofounders of Intel, gave a speech contrasting the Japanese and American semiconductor industries. One of the most striking differences, he said, was how much deeper and denser the Japanese network of suppliers was. One Japanese company had decided to get into the DRAM business and was up and operating within about a year. It could call for immediate service on suppliers of machinery and components located in Japan. "At one point," Grove said, "there were twelve hundred vendor employees"—that is, representatives of companies making the components and machinery—"swarming all over the location where this company's first facility was being built." He added: "*We couldn't do this in the United States* for love or money. There are no twelve hundred vendor employees and there are no dozens of relevant suppliers."[27]

By the early 1990s, American semiconductor and computer companies were routinely complaining to the government, but their complaints had taken on a strange, new fatalistic tone. In many cases they were not asking for a better opportunity to sell to Japanese customers, or for help in competing with Japanese firms in other markets around the world. Rather, they were complaining because they were having trouble *buying* the best equipment from Japanese suppliers. In the fall of 1991, a report from the U.S. General Accounting Office said that a third of the American companies it surveyed had had problems buying up-to-date components from Japanese suppliers, even though the components had already gone on sale within Japan. The crucial components were flat display screens for laptop computers, and the most modern version of "steppers" for producing semiconductors. One company said that the delays had cost it $1.4 billion in sales, and another said the problems in getting display screens put it "essentially out of business."[28] William J. Spencer, director of a government-sponsored consortium, Sematech (which coordinated joint research projects among major semiconductor companies), was asked early in 1992 which kind of silicon wafers U.S. manufacturers would be using in the long run. "That's easy to answer," he said. "It depends on what Japan, and to a degree Germany, will sell us. We no longer have any silicon sources of our own, so what we can make depends on what they will sell us."[29]

At about the same time, several American papers carried the news that Intel, the giant of Silicon Valley, had nearly perfected a technology called "flash memory," which could in the long run revolutionize the electronics business yet again. Because normal computer chips do not store information when the power is off, computers require bulky storage devices, especially hard disk drives. Flash memory retains its contents when the machine is turned off, so it could eventually eliminate disk drives. Perhaps more important, it could add enormous amounts of memory to small devices not normally thought of as "computers," from toys to compact disk players to "organizers" like the popular Sharp Wizard series.

This looked like a comeback for the American industry—and so it was reported in a euphoric story on the front page of *The Washington Post.* But on the same day, February 6, 1992, Jacob Schlesinger of *The Wall Street Journal* presented the same news in a very different light. Intel had come up with the technology—based, for once, on a discovery that originated in Japan. But Intel could not *make* the chips. Even Intel—*even* Intel, celebrated throughout the American press in 1992 as the classic high-tech success story—lacked the money, and it lacked the manufacturing know-how. It would rely on the Japanese company Sharp to do the actual production work. "Without Sharp, 'we would not have been able to come up with the manufacturing capacity we would need,' " an Intel senior vice president was quoted as saying. "The Intel-Sharp pact shows growing American dependence on Japan, even when the United States has the technological edge," the story in *The Wall Street Journal* concluded. "Intel, which devotes most of its resources to its bread-and-butter microprocessors, is trading its advanced flash know-how to Sharp."[30]

From Intel's point of view, the alliance with Sharp would help avoid another peril. The most valuable customers for flash-memory chips would be consumer-electronics companies—the ones that made TVs, VCRs, computer games. Those companies were mainly based in Japan. Everything in Intel's experience indicated that if it did not form a partnership with a Japanese company, it would eventually be frozen out of this market. As *The Wall Street Journal* reporters said, "The U.S. consumer electronics industry has all but disappeared, and U.S. chip companies have had difficulties selling to the dominant Japanese manufacturers." By letting Sharp produce the memories, Intel was making the best of its options, for now.[31]

In December 1990, just before the war against Iraq began, the Nomura Research Institute, connected to one of the world's largest stock-brokerage houses, Nomura Securities of Tokyo, released its survey of the world's semiconductor and computer industries.[32] Anyone who has tried to talk delicately around an unpleasant truth— "Well, I'm sure Johnny is trying his best in math"—could recognize the tone of this document. For instance, "The widely held view is that the declining market share indicates loss of American competitiveness, but we believe this is not necessarily the case."

The English version, which came out six months after the original was published in Japanese, sympathetically yet firmly expressed the conclusion that American firms simply could not compete in the future. It is impossible, the report said, for Americans to compete with Japan's "oligopolistic dominance," which came from "weeding out of weaker companies unable to keep up with heavy capital expenditure."[33] "In the technology-intensive computer and semiconductor industries, the basic trend since the start of the 1980s— market share gains by Japanese companies, market share losses by American companies—will likely continue in the 1990s."[34] Whenever American firms started to show weakness, the report said, they usually went on to collapse. "The U.S. market is hard on losers. Companies that have reached the limit of growth rarely have a chance to come back."[35] Large Japanese firms, by contrast, simply did not go bankrupt, and were able to buffer losses in one division with earnings from another.

The Nomura report—which was, again, originally intended for domestic Japanese consumption rather than for inspection by Americans themselves—included a nightmare version of a Horatio Alger story. It concerned a young, talented, and ambitious American software engineer known as Mr. A. He started with one big high-tech company, as his counterpart would in Japan. Then this company is acquired in a hostile takeover and Mr. A is laid off, a fate that, of course, would not befall his counterpart in Japan. He moves to a fast-growing company, but is laid off yet again when business slows down. He joins yet another company, but—hardened by his experience—he resolves to "keep the knowlege and skills he is acquiring to himself as a means of ensuring his job security." After five years with this firm, Mr. A considers jumping ship and starting his own firm, with the help of venture capitalists. The report concluded, in a pat-on-the-head style:

> Mr. A's experiences in the status- and class-conscious culture of the American company suggest why the United States is so imbued with an entrepreneurial spirit, yet why American industry is so sloppy when it comes to factory productivity and industrial control.[36]

When Ideas Don't Fit Reality

This is not supposed to be an ideological age, but the ideas we use to explain events are very, very powerful. The idea that Communist control of Vietnam would lead to Communist control of all of Asia required the United States to fight there. Standing up to the Viet Cong and North Vietnamese represented a chance to correct the mistake made when no one stood up to Hitler—or so it seemed, as long as the "domino" idea prevailed. In economics, the idea that there can't ever be too much competition, or that the government will gum up whatever it touches, requires us to assume that whatever happens, through the market, is for the best. During the 1992 American presidential campaign, the columnist George Will offhandedly reminded his readers that the "lesson of the late twentieth century" was government's inability to hit whatever economic target it set for itself. Therefore, it was folly for the Democrats under Bill Clinton even to talk about devising a "national economic plan." The significance of the point was that Will could make it offhandedly. He could safely assume that most educated Americans would agree:

> Aspiring planners of national economies were thick on the ground, here and especially in Europe, as recently as the 1940s and 1950s. But recent history has been chastening, at least to people paying attention. . . .Planners say, with breezy confidence: Why wait for billions of private decisions in free markets to reveal possibilities and preferences? Government in the hands of clever people like us can know what is possible and preferable.[37]

Suppose this paragraph, and the idea behind it, had been put a little differently. Suppose it had said,

> Aspiring planners of national economies were thick on the ground in America as recently as the 1950s. Even now they dominate the governments of Europe, except for England, and those of East Asia, except for Hong Kong. Perhaps it's just a coincidence, but each of these "except for" countries is the industrial sick man of its region. The European planners have failed in some ways and succeeded in others. In East Asia, government in the hands of clever people has generally achieved what it set out to do. This history might be chastening, if we could pay attention—but that's hard for us to do, because we like people to talk to us in English, and the Anglophone world tells us that what we already think is right.

This, of course, would represent a different idea, which would fit reality into different patterns, leading to different results. With a different mental map of the world, people might feel differently about the nature of economic change. The prevailing American idea requires us to view industrial rises and falls as if they were the weather. We can complain all we want, but in the long run there's nothing much we can do, except to kid ourselves with a rain dance and put on a sweater when it's cold. Or the American idea made economic change seem like an earthquake: some people were better prepared for it than others, but no one could alter or constrain the fundamental force. A different idea—that industrial decline is less like a drought than like a disease, which might be treated—would lead to different behavior.

In the early 1960s, American strategists "knew" certain things about military power. They knew that the most dangerous potential conflict was between the two superpowers. If the United States and the Soviet Union were not fighting against each other, then either of them would obviously beat whatever lesser power it faced. It was hard to make those ideas fit the later facts of Vietnam and Afghanistan. American economists "know" certain things about business competition now. It is very hard to make those ideas fit the facts of the semiconductor industry. It is the gap between prevailing ideas about industry and the history of this industry that deserves attention. Whether American or Japanese producers turn out to be stronger in the long run, America's explanatory concepts clearly need to be revised.

Attempts to Explain the Collapse

Why is the sudden change in the semiconductor industry a cause for concern? One answer is the worthy though boring response offered by the industry itself. This is not just another product, the spokesmen say. It is the fundamental building block of modern industrialism. No country could be a serious economic contender in the nineteenth century if it could not make engines, steel, and machine tools. This is what the Chinese, the Mexicans, and most other non-European societies discovered when they tried to "compete," militarily and economically, with the advanced Western world. By the same logic, no country can be a full contender in the twenty-first century if it cannot make and use semiconductor chips.

But by far the most interesting part of the semiconductor story has nothing to do with "strategic industries." It is instead a question of ideas. Whether the rapid collapse of the American semiconductor industry in the mid-1980s is good for Americans, or bad for Americans, or completely neutral in its effects, it is *mysterious*. According to the ideas by which Americans explain the workings of the world, this industry should not—indeed, could not—have failed. The industry's partial recovery in the early 1990s only compounds the mystery. By standard business theory it's hard to explain exactly why trends changed when they did.

Moments when standard explanations fail are exciting moments, although they are also uncomfortable and can be painful. According to ideals that prevailed in early-twentieth-century England, it would be unrealistic for European nations ever to fight each

other again, since their economies had become so intertwined. (In
his famous book *The Great Illusion,* published in 1910, Norman
Angell "proved" that England and Germany could never go to war.
"Even if we could annihilate Germany we should annihilate such an
important section of our debtors as to create hopeless panic in London," and so on.[38]) According to the conceptions of power that must
have prevailed in Leonid Brezhnev's Kremlin, the Soviet Army
should not have had difficulties coping with the Afghan resistance.
And according to the ideas that, even in the 1990s, dominate most
journalistic and political discussion of business matters, it should
not have been possible for American chip makers to fall so far so
fast.

"Cultural" Explanations

How can we explain what happened to the American semiconductor
industry? The familiar explanations for American industrial failure—greedy bosses, pigheaded unions, rampant short-termism,
overregulation by the meddlesome state—don't seem to apply.

The conventional Japanese explanation is simpler. During the
1980s, most Japanese high-tech industries thrived. Japanese commentators and politicians are quick to see the "unique" traits of the
Japanese people as the explanation for almost any phenomenon in
Japan. Therefore, Japanese discussions of the semiconductor industry have stressed the intrinsic traits of Japanese culture—"harmonious" working patterns, attention to detail—that supposedly
make it natural for Japanese companies to excel.

At a Hitachi semiconductor factory on the island of Kyushu,
in 1986, I walked through fabrication areas that looked very much
like their counterparts in Texas or California that I had previously
seen. The hardware and the procedures seemed so similar. Why
were Hitachi and other Japanese manufacturers doing so well?

"The starting level of production is not so different here from
in America," the manager who was escorting me told me—in English, since he had studied for a while in the United States. He
paused, and indicated thoughtfulness with the familiar Japanese
gesture of "teeth-sucking." (This involves opening the lower half of
the mouth, putting the bottom teeth against the upper lip, and
inhaling, with a sucking/slurping sound. Its body-language message
is, "Whew! I need to think about this for a minute!") When he
recovered, he said:

"The starting level is similar—but ours improves much more rapidly than in America. There is a difference of culture. It is often said that we Japanese are united as a single people, or even race. In the United States there are so many people with different backgrounds and religions and races, it is harder to work together in harmony—unless you are all Swedes in Wisconsin."

In his famous book *The Japan That Can Say No,* the Japanese politician Shintaro Ishihara told a touching story of another plant in Kyushu, where the defect rate was inexplicably worse than at other factories in Japan. A young man and woman who worked at the factory had become sweethearts. One evening, while riding bikes together, they waited for a train at a crossing—and then realized that vibrations from the passing trains must have been subtly shaking the entire factory and ruining the chips! Only the Japanese traditions of duty and purity, taught through millennia, could have led to such care, Ishihara said. A few years later, while I was living in Japan, a prominent Japanese newspaper columnist wrote that Western practices might have sufficed for the first few generations of semiconductor chips. But once the lines etched into the chip passed the "one-micron barrier"—that is, once they required resolutions finer than one millionth of an inch—only people steeped in the Shinto tradition of purity and diligence could be up to the task.

The conception that there is something inherently fine, perfectionist, and effective in Japanese production standards has taken very deep root in Japan—even more than it has taken root in other places around the world where Japanese products are popular. In the summer of 1991, my family was at the Chautauqua institution in upstate New York, sharing a house with a Japanese violinist who had worked for several years in New York. She came to the breakfast table one morning looking as if she had spent the evening crying. Her manager in Tokyo had faxed some new musical scores to her, but the transmission had been rough and she couldn't read what had come across. Something must be wrong with the machine, she said.

Wa-sei ka? asked a Japanese man, who was in fact a visiting official from MITI, in Tokyo. "Was it made in Japan?" The real meaning of the question was, Did you take the elementary precautions with this machine? Did you make sure that it had been produced by people schooled in the Japanese tradition of duty and care? These were the only words he exchanged with her in Japanese at the table, and he clearly assumed that no one else would know what they meant. (After she reassured him that the defective machine was indeed from Japan, a perplexed look came over his face.)

In the early 1980s, the consulting firm McKinsey & Company undertook a study, along with the U.S. Chamber of Commerce, to see just how many "barriers" kept foreigners from exporting to Japan. The operating assumption of the study was that it should not even consider industries in which Japanese companies were already exporters—that is, if Japanese companies could make a certain product, it was only natural that Japanese consumers would not consider buying imports. "This is an astounding statement," two American scholars observed. "If the Germans or French were to follow a similar logic, it would then mean that since both are substantial exporters of autos, there would be no place for Japanese cars in Europe."[39] It would also mean that since Americans were exporting cars in the 1950s and 1960s, they should not have considered buying any cars from Japan.

The Japanese convention of explaining events in purely cultural, and often explicitly racial, terms creates great intellectual and diplomatic difficulties. When one of my children was enrolled in a Japanese junior high school, the principal remarked, in an offhand fashion, that he was doing all right in mathematics "for a foreigner." If asked directly, he would never have said that the laws of mathematics worked differently for Japanese and non-Japanese students; but without thinking, he assumed there was such a gulf.

Americans have, in their time, fallen back on ethnic theories for success and failure. But ethnicity and race are no longer part of any respectable discussion of business trends. Instead the emphasis is on the ultimate justice of the market. In the long run, we all assume, the efficient companies will survive and the inefficient will fail. Governments can try to tamper with this law of nature by offering subsidies or shielding producers from foreign competition. But in the short run these attempts will harm the nation's consumers, by raising the prices they must pay, and in the long run they will weaken a nation's producers, by delaying the moment when old industries are cleared away so that new ones can rise.

In the late 1980s this view was summed up in a quip that was attributed to a variety of Republican officials (and was quoted by Clyde Prestowitz in his book *Trading Places*). Sometimes the words were placed in the mouth of Richard Darman, director of the Office of Management and Budget; sometimes, that of Michael Boskin, chair of the Council of Economic Advisers. Sometimes they were attributed to someone else. Each of the supposed speakers denies uttering the sentence, but the underlying argument, if not the specific words, accurately reflects a position all of them have held for years. "If our guys can't hack it," one or the other of these officials is supposed to have said in a meeting about American semiconductor makers, "then let 'em go."

Behind comments like this lie visions of the thousands of companies that have bitten the dust as the inevitable cost of economic progress. Automobile makers rise and buggy makers fall. The computer comes and the electric typewriter goes. Within any given industry, the inefficient and lazy are left behind—which is, of course, the whole point of market competition.

This vision of "creative destruction," in the famous words of Joseph Schumpeter, is indispensable as a guide to most economic activity. *But it can't quite explain the semiconductor case.* All the familiar variants of the "if they can't hack it" argument apply to certain parts of the American economy, but they don't tell us what went on in Silicon Valley in the 1980s. Consider four elements of the standard analysis:

The first and most familiar part of this analysis is that American management has simply forgotten why it is in business. Too many companies are run by financiers, not engineers or production experts. The executives have feathered their own nests, ignored and mistreated their workers, been too lazy to learn what it takes to please German or Japanese customers, and in general failed to do their best. David Halberstam presented a panorama of this failure on a large scale in his book *The Reckoning*. Two professors from Harvard Business School presented the academic version of this analysis in a famous article published in 1980 in the *Harvard Business Review* called "Managing Our Way to Economic Decline."[40]

The word "Detroit" comes to mind when Americans think of this syndrome. "Detroit" made fat, fuel-guzzling cars in the 1970s, while Toyota and Nissan quietly improved their manufacturing techniques and learned what American drivers really wanted. "Detroit" must have been dimly aware that Japanese drivers used the left side of the road, but it nonetheless kept sending cars to Japan with the steering wheel on the wrong side.[41]

A second, related cultural explanation for American business failure is that American products themselves have become shoddy and backward—and that a nation that still excels in basic science has forgotten how to put its inventions to commercial use. Many popular Japanese exports of the 1980s, from VCRs to video-game machines, were hatched in American labs. The United States, according to this hypothesis, is following the unwholesome trail blazed by the English, who were famed in the 1930s for having brilliant tinkerer-inventors but an increasingly feeble manufacturing base. Before and during World War II British scientists had come up with most of the crucial breakthroughs in radar technology. Yet the high-volume production was done in America, where the huge wartime investment in radar provided the foundation for the postwar electronics industry.[42]

The third standard belief is that American managers have been ruinously focused on the short term. Given a choice between investing $10 million in new equipment that will pay off in five years, or using the money to boost earnings next quarter, they've too often pumped up the earnings, often because their own pay is tied to results *right now*.

The fourth contention involves the government, which in various ways affects the climate for business. The most important of these ways, by far, has been the enormous, sustained federal budget deficit. According to basic economic theory, a big budget deficit does not automatically mean that business will suffer relative to foreign competitors. But, other things being equal, it makes a trade deficit more likely, which in turn means that some domestic products are losing ground to foreign rivals. The kind of school system each nation runs also affects its business. In the late 1980s, as the Soviet Union began to collapse, Americans started to debate the question of "imperial overstretch"—whether the government had taken on too many international burdens for the economy to support.

All of these failings are serious. When we examine American businesses that are floundering, one or more of them may seem to explain what's gone wrong. But they weren't true of the semiconductor industry in 1980, when it was on the verge of its precipitous decline.

Silicon Valley suffered, at worst, from minor versions of each of these ailments. In 1980, Hewlett-Packard released a study comparing the chips it bought from Japanese companies with those it bought from Silicon Valley. The defect rate for Japanese chips, it said, was lower than for the Americans'. But this was hardly a fatal objection: the quality level in both cases was better than what purchasers said they required. One of the bibles of American business studies, Michael Porter's very fat book *The Competitive Advantage of Nations,* tried to apply the first objection to the American semiconductor companies: like the car and steel companies, he said, America's chip companies had been too slow to move with changing technology. The switch to MOS (metal oxide) technology had, Porter said, "catapulted the Japanese to industry leadership."[43] Once the Japanese firms had made this switch, he said, "The world-leading group of Japanese semiconductor firms has triggered the emergence of world-leading Japanese semiconductor manufacturing equipment suppliers."[44]

But to offer this as an explanation merely raises further questions. Why hadn't the "world-leading group" of American semiconductor makers stayed that way, when there was nothing obviously flawed in their performance? Why had the emergence of Japanese equipment suppliers been "triggered" so much more powerfully, quickly, and lastingly there than in the United States?

There were almost no signs that the American chip companies suffered from fatal short-termism in 1980. Intel, despite its years of profits, paid out no dividends. Most others acted accordingly. Many of the companies were still run by the engineers who had set them up. Even the U.S. government, for all its other failings, was not handicapping the industry in any obvious way. In the five years after 1980, American makers were affected by the dramatic rise in the value of the dollar, which made their exports more costly overseas. But if that had been the crucial factor, then the collapse in the dollar's value after 1985 presumably would have promptly helped them regain whatever ground they'd lost.

To put the entire point another way: from the early 1980s, politicians, journalists, and businessmen said that various industries could have protection—if they earned it. The machine-tool industry, the auto makers, and the steel mills might have some relief from foreign competition—but only for three years, or for five, just long enough to fix the many things that were wrong with how these American firms did their work. GM would try to put its money into the Saturn plant. Lee Iacocca would say that Chrysler had learned its lesson and would build better cars. Ford would say that quality was now Job One.

However much these heavy industries might eventually improve, whatever plateau they might someday attain, the semiconductor industry of the early 1980s *was already there*. By the rules that American politicians and journalists use to explain success or failure, there was no obvious reason why it should have been eclipsed so fast—indeed, relatively much faster than any of the "bad" old industries like steel or cars. The semiconductor industry was in trouble less than two decades after its basic product was invented and barely one decade after its most rapid growth. It would be as if other industries in which the United States felt most dominant in

the early 1990s—movies and music, pharmaceuticals, university education, software—were on the skids by the end of the decade. A
Saturn plant for GM, a minimill for steel makers, a radical new
program of teaching Japanese or German in the schools—all of these
might be necessary measures for reviving the economy. But on the
evidence of what happened to Silicon Valley, perhaps such steps
would not be sufficient. On the evidence of Silicon Valley, maybe
our understanding of competition is not sufficient either.

A Difference of Systems

Why, *exactly,* would American businesses have been slower to switch
from one kind of chip to another, especially when in the preceding
decade they had seen more clearly than anyone else the importance
of moving fast? Was it simply that they were complacent and satisfied, like the barons of Detroit or Pittsburgh in their dominant
days? That doesn't seem likely—the rhetoric that poured out of
Silicon Valley in those days was full of exhortations to stay alert, to
adapt or die, to keep moving ahead. Had they forgotten that there
were competitors overseas? Did they dismiss them the way automakers had dismissed the tinny, laughable cars from Japan? Hardly.
Even in 1980 Silicon Valley rang with analyses of the "Asian
challenge."

Individual firms in America may have made strategic errors,
and individual firms in Japan may have been persistent and skillful
and shrewd. But something else was going on that did not often
show up in the speeches and the editorials about quality control and
foreign-language training and good morale on the factory floor.

That something involved factors left out of standard discussions
of "improving competitiveness" by raising morale within companies
or even improving math classes in schools. It involved a broader
shift in conceptions of how industries rose and fell, and about
whether companies based in one country and the same goals as
companies based somewhere else.

In his book *The New Realities,* published in 1989, the business
strategist Peter Drucker discussed this shift. In particular, he said,
Japan's success had changed the perceived rules of world trade:

> The emergence of new non-Western trading countries—fore-
> most, Japan—creates what I would call adversarial trade. . . .
> Competitive trade aims at creating a customer. Adversarial trade

aims at dominating an industry. . . . Adversarial trade, however,
is unlikely to be beneficial to both sides. . . . The aim in adversarial trade . . . is to drive the competitor out of the market
altogether rather than to let the competitor survive.[45]

In this changed competitive landscape, explaining economic events
such as the fall of the American semiconductor industry required
allowing for factors left out of most business texts.

One of these missing factors was government. On its way up and on
its way down, the U.S. semiconductor industry was driven not just
by private companies, although they made every crucial operating
decision and came up with every new design, but by a network of
government-business interactions.

The role of the government was often considered an embarrassing afterthought in American or British discussions of how economies should work. Yet in America as in every other country that
had spawned a semiconductor industry, government incentives and
pressures shaped the way the industry grew. All around the world,
the design and production and marketing of chips was carried out
by private firms. It was these firms—America's Intel or Japan's
Toshiba, Korea's Samsung and Thomson of France—that journalists
and politicians mainly discussed. But each of them took the shape
it did largely because of policies imposed by the respective
governments.

In fact, the crucial turning points in the modern history of the
semiconductor industry involve shifts in government-business interaction rather than purely private shifts in industrial strategy. Without
recognizing how chronic, significant, and often successful government "interference" has been, we are back in the position of not
being able to make changes in a major industry fit our main idea of
economic life.

In 1992 the Semiconductor Industry Association (SIA) published a history of the industry. It said that the industry's growth
since the 1950s could be divided into five stages.[46] The first four
were these:

1. The pioneering American efforts, from the 1940s through the
   1960s, to develop transistors and integrated circuits, and learn
   how to make them efficiently and in large quantities. In this
   stage William Shockley and his colleagues at Bell Labs played

a crucial scientific role with research on transistors, and Robert
Noyce at Fairchild and Jack Kilby at Texas Instruments developed the first semiconductors.
2. The Japanese entry into the field in the 1960s and subsequent
rapid catch-up with American producers in the 1970s and 1980s.
3. The effort of European manufacturers, principally Philips of
Holland and Siemens of Germany, to enter the business in the
late 1960s and 1970s, and to survive in the business in the 1980s
despite the American technical lead and the Japanese competitive surge.
4. The emergence of other East Asian producers, especially those
based in Korea, to challenge the Japanese in the late 1980s.

Every one of these steps, the history said (plus the fifth, to which
we'll turn later) depended *fundamentally* on government policies.
With the emphasis of italics the authors said:

> *Government policies have shaped the course of international
> competition in microelectronics virtually from the inception of
> the industry, producing outcomes completely different than would
> have occurred through the operation of the market alone.*[47]

The SIA authors were not, of course, purely detached historians;
their association has lobbied for the U.S. government to respond
more aggressively to Japan's industrial policy for semiconductors.
But the SIA, unlike its counterpart in Japan, is a distinctly private organization. (The Electronic Industry Association of Japan,
by contrast, is effectively a branch of the Japanese government. Like
many other industrial organizations in Japan, it conveys industry's
wishes to the government, relays the government's "guidance" to
the industry, and in effect administers the country's industrial policy.) And the SIA could offer evidence to substantiate its view of
events.

In emphasizing the role of government decisions, the SIA authors explained that none of these stages would have happened the
way it did without the impact of government decisions. The United
States would not have been the early world leader in semiconductor
production. The Japanese would not have caught up and moved
ahead. The Europeans would not have stayed in the business. And
the Koreans and other Asian competitors would never have had a
chance. Consider each of these four stages:

U.S. genesis. American companies led the world in semiconductor technology due to their own effort, expense, and ingenuity—but also due to U.S. government support. The government did not directly finance the crucial research that led to integrated circuits, but the companies making these investments understood that if the products were successful, the Defense Department and NASA would be standing in line as the first—and often only—customers.[48]

For instance, in 1962 NASA announced that it would use integrated circuits—the first simple chips, produced by Texas Instruments, Fairchild Semiconductors, and other suppliers—in the computer systems that would guide Apollo spacecraft to the moon, and the Air Force decided to buy ICs to guide its Minuteman missiles.[49] Every history of the semiconductor business regards these contracts as a turning point; they guaranteed a big and relatively long-term market that no private purchaser could have offered at the time.

Over the first decade of integrated-circuit production, from the mid-1950s to the mid-1960s, the U.S. government was the single largest customer for all integrated circuits and early semiconductor chips. Together, the Defense Department and the space program bought 45 percent of all U.S.-made chips in 1959, 39 percent in 1961, 33 percent by 1963. The early government purchases let manufacturers produce at higher volume. As volume went up, price went down, and commercial purchasers began buying more and more chips. This was not an "industrial policy" in the explicit sense, but it had the same effect: it gave the companies a reason to invest in new products and new factories.[50] In 1962, the average "monolithic integrated circuit"—that is, a chip as we now think of it—cost $50 apiece, and the Defense Department bought the *entire* U.S. output of this particular type of semiconductor. By 1968, volume production had driven the per-chip price down to less than $2.50, and non-Defense Department customers bought more than 60 percent of the output.[51]

The Defense Department played another crucial role. Government contracts had paid for some of the research that led to patents. When that happened, the Defense Department required companies, in effect, to share the patents with the U.S.-based industry as a whole. (Sharing with foreign producers was at this time a moot point, since there were virtually none. Moreover, since the contracts were supervised by the Defense Department, it could use national security as a justification to exclude foreign-owned companies.) This enforced cooperation spread new techniques much more quickly than they would have diffused naturally. By normal market logic, a company would have no incentive to share its discoveries with its potential rivals at almost no charge. But the government insisted that such discoveries be treated as a public good. This, of course, made it easier for the small companies that became the hallmark of Silicon Valley to find niches and go to work.

The U.S. government did not run a single semiconductor factory, but it provided conditions that *could not otherwise have existed,* especially the reliable markets in the crucial early years, and thereby got the industry as a whole off the ground.

Americans still talk about "governmental interference" and "industrial policy" as if the country faced an all-or-nothing choice between grim, Soviet-style central planning and entrepreneurs completely on their own. In reality, even this liveliest and most entrepreneurial of American industries reflected a mixture of visible and invisible hands.

Japanese ascendancy. The role of government in the rise of the Japanese industry is more familiar and obvious. "The rise of the Japanese semiconductor industry is a textbook example of how industry and government can cooperate to foster the rapid development of a high-technology industry," Kenneth Flamm has written.[52] Without heavy government involvement, Japan's semiconductor industry simply would not exist.

In the beginning, from the end of World War II until at least the early 1970s, the Japanese government forced foreign companies to sell or license their technology to Japanese firms if they wanted to do business themselves in Japan.[53] Americans who are skeptical about the importance of Japan's industrial policy often cite Sony's early difficulties in acquiring rights to the transistor. In the early 1950s, MITI bureaucrats initially turned down Sony's application to buy a license for transistor technology from Western Electric. (Western Electric was then the manufacturing arm of AT&T. AT&T's Bell Labs was where pioneering work on the transistor had been done.) To Americans this episode shows that MITI often stumbled.[54] Apparently its bureaucrats did not even realize how important the transistor would become! In fact, the episode revealed just the reverse. MITI in the 1950s had a policy of making sure that important new technologies with global export potential were assigned as far as possible to the most competent and sophisticated Japanese firms. Precisely because MITI officials recognized the transistor's tremendous commercial potential, they needed some persuading that Sony, then a tiny start-up, was the right company to handle such an important industrial policy. Moreover, in those days MITI often vetoed license requests on grounds that the royalties demanded by foreigners (usually Americans) were "too high." In effect this was a pretext for negotiating lower prices. It also kept Japanese companies from entering a destructive bidding war against each other for foreign rights.

Americans now take it for granted that the Toyota works in Kentucky will be owned by Toyota; the Japanese government, in the years after the war, took it for granted that foreign ownership of its economy should be resisted. The government had the power to review all applications for foreign investment in the Japanese electronics industry (and virtually all other industries); it routinely rejected all applications for fully-owned subsidiaries or even joint ventures in which foreigners would hold the majority share.[55] This policy prevented most U.S. manufacturers from setting up their own plants in Japan. Until 1974, semiconductor chips containing more than two hundred circuits could not be imported without special permission[56]—by that time, advanced chips contained many thousands of circuits. The only way foreign firms could get around these prohibitions was to license (i.e., teach) the technology to Japanese firms—and the Japanese government set flat royalty rates so there would be no unseemly bidding war among the Japanese firms.

Even IBM, big as it was, went along with the Japanese government's demands. Perhaps it was impressed by the statement made by a senior MITI official, in the 1950s, that "We will take every measure possible to obstruct the success of your business unless you license IBM patents to Japanese firms and charge them no more than a 5 percent royalty."[57] IBM licensed some of its leading computer technology and set up a wholly owned operation in 1960.

Texas Instruments (TI) hoped to do the same thing, but through the 1950s the Japanese government denied it permission to set up an operation. TI, for its part, refused to go in as a minority partner with a Japanese firm—and there things stood. TI knew it was in an unusually strong bargaining position, since it controlled many of the fundamental patents for making integrated circuits. It refused to license them to anyone in Japan unless the government approved its application to set up a wholly owned plant.

Finally, in 1968, TI, Sony, and the Japanese government agreed that the two companies would form a fifty-fifty joint venture, which led to several factories in Japan. As part of the deal, TI agreed to license its patents for integrated circuits to the big Japanese elec-

tronics makers—NEC, Hitachi, Mitsubishi, Toshiba—who were
nominally in bitter competition with each other and with Sony. TI
also agreed, as Michael Borrus has pointed out, "to limit its future
share of the Japanese semiconductor market to no more than 10
percent." As a further part of the deal, undisclosed in public (but,
according to Sony's chairman, Akio Morita, understood by all parties), TI would be able to buy back control from Sony when a decent
interval had passed. The deal almost fell apart when the literal-
minded Americans asked to have this buy-back understanding put
in writing.[58] A contract containing vague assurances was drawn up,
the deal went through—and in 1972 TI bought full control back
from Sony. Through the 1970s, when American chip makers dominated the world market, TI was the only American merchant firm
with a fully owned factory in Japan.[59]

There was an intriguing skew in the way that non-Japanese firms
operated in Japan, compared to their dealings elsewhere in the
world. Outside Japan, American-based manufacturing companies
made vastly more money from direct investments than they did from
licensing. For example, Du Pont would build a factory in Europe,
just as the German chemical firm BASF might build a plant in the
United States. The earnings from these factories' sales were much
larger than the mere licensing fees for technology. In the case of
American firms operating in Europe, the earnings were ten times
greater. But in Japan the pattern was reversed. There, the licensing
fees were greater than the investment earnings. Non-Japanese firms
had difficulty exporting to Japan; were forbidden to invest there;
and were forced to license their advanced technology to Japanese
producers, at fees set by the Japanese government, if they hoped to
do business in Japan at all. Laura Tyson, chair of President Clinton's
Council of Economic Advisers, and John Zysman, her former colleague at Berkeley, summed up the situation this way: "Overall in
the Japanese case American firms could only earn by *selling* their
technology, not by exploiting it as a producer."[60]

These aspects of Japanese policy had long-lasting consequences—in the 1960s and 1970s foreign suppliers could not build
up the "relationships" with customers that, they are told in the 1990s,
are essential for doing business in Japan[61]—and the rules established
by the Japanese government had nothing to do with enhancing free-
market competition as a goal in itself. Market forces were crucial
tools; Sony and Matsushita and NEC and Toshiba competed against
each other as hard as they could. But the goal, that of building an
industry in Japan, run by Japanese people, was decided on and

carried out by the government. As Laura Tyson and John Zysman put it:

> Restrictions on the ability of foreign firms to develop a permanent presence in the Japanese market have been removed only where Japanese firms have already achieved a dominant position at home and a strong, often dominant position overseas. In other words, restrictions have been removed only when they don't matter anymore.[62]

Why does this matter? Because it is so much at odds with the prevailing American *idea* about why industries rise and fall. Michael Porter, the prominent business theorist, says that Japanese semiconductor makers succeeded because of the fierce "internal competition" within Japan. This is a favorite theme in analyses of Japanese success: because their companies had to try so hard to stay alive within Japan, they were naturally better prepared for competition overseas. Yes, competition inside Japan is intense. But is that what convinced IBM and Texas Instruments to license their patents?

A leading trade economist, Gary Saxonhouse, says that an emphasis on high-value manufacturing is a "natural" part of Japan's high literacy rate and "factor endowment." With a lot of people and not much space, they naturally tend to produce sophisticated, valuable products. In isolation this may sound logical enough. But it doesn't fully explain how Japan went from having virtually no semiconductor industry in 1970, when it was already crowded and the people were already well educated, to a lead in 1990. Nor does it explain why the foreign share of the semiconductor market inside Japan remained virtually flat through most of the 1980s, no matter how the yen and dollar changed in value, no matter what shifts in technology and competitive advantage were happening around the world.[63] (Nor, for that matter, does the "natural endowment" theory explain why other crowded sites with large pools of relatively well-trained workers, such as Manila, have not "naturally" spawned semiconductor industries.)

"If our guys can't hack it"—this is a natural reflection of everything we have been taught about industrial development. But a more realistic view is the conclusion of one authoritative history of the industry, Michael Borrus's *Competing for Control*. "State policy would not have succeeded without the efforts, investments, and strategies of Japanese industry," it said. "But the industry would almost certainly have failed without the state."[64]

*   *   *

The American beginning, and the Japanese catch-up, were the first two of the phases of the industry's growth. Phases three and four, according to the historical scheme laid out by the SIA, were Europe's survival in the industry and the appearance of the New East Asian entrants. In each case, as with the U.S. and Japanese examples, government policy made a decisive difference. Several European governments promoted "national champions" in technology. For instance, the French government, in an effort to promote a domestic high-tech industry, subsidized the installation of "minitels," computer terminals for looking up phone numbers and other simple functions, in most private homes. The German government "guided" banks, brokerage houses, and manufacturers to ensure that German-owned firms had capital to invest and modernize. The results of such efforts could be considered disappointing or fruitful, depending on your perspective. The state-champion firms often lose money, as the European aircraft consortium Airbus chronically does; yet to their supporters the cost is justified by the high-tech manufacturing capacity they maintain under local ownership and control.

In Korea, successive presidents have shared a belief in state-guided industrialization. Chun Doo Hwan, who ruled through most of the 1980s, was a military strongman who took power in a coup. In the mid-1980s his advisers convinced him, in the words of a magazine report, that "the only way to crack the world semiconductor market would be to orchestrate a massive development project involving every important Korean company in the business."[65] The Korean government applied many of the steps the Japanese government had used two decades before. Government ministries "guided" Korean banks about how much to loan, and to which firms. Korea's tariff levels and import rules were set in such a way that American companies were encouraged to license their technology to Korean firms, rather than simply exporting products from the United States. The Korean government set performance standards—high investment rates, rising exports—for companies that received preferential treatment through tariffs and loans. By the end of the decade, analysts from the World Bank—which through the 1980s espoused a laissez-faire view—concluded about Korea that

> There is no doubt that the government has sought explicitly to
> encourage the development of high-tech industries like com-

puters and semiconductors by designating them "strategic industries" entitled to certain preferential treatment.[66]

Around the world, the growth and survival of semiconductor industries has not just been a matter of "hacking it," or fostering
competition, or having very good schools—although each of these
ingredients played a part. Every country that has waited for the
industry to develop "naturally," through the flux and play of market
forces, *is waiting still*. Canada is as populous as some countries that
now make semiconductors, and its people are just as well educated.
It had as much "natural advantage" for the semiconductor industry
in 1980 as Korea did—indeed, much more, since it was richer, its
people were better educated, and it was closer to major markets and
research centers in the United States. Hong Kong had as much
"natural" inclination for semiconductor making as Singapore ten
years ago—just as crowded! Just as much influenced by Confucian
culture! The governments of Korea and Singapore deliberately cultivated the industry; the governments of Canada and Hong Kong
did not. Korea and Singapore now have a semiconductor industry;
Canada and Hong Kong do not. Governments may not have been
able to "pick" winners, but they seemed to be able to "make"
winners, to create advantages for themselves.[67]

After the American genesis, the Japanese ascent, the European
survival, and the East Asian emergence, the semiconductor industry
entered a fifth stage in the early 1990s, which the SIA history called
the "U.S. revival." "Recovery" or "respite" might be more appropriate terms. Starting in the late 1980s, some parts of the U.S.-based
industry flickered back toward life. The graphs showing worldwide
market share for American-made chips dropped steadily through
the 1980s—and then, around 1988, ticked up again. Graphs for each
specific kind of chip—processors, memory chips, custom-made chips
called ASICs (application-specific integrated circuits)—all showed
the same change at about the same time. Late in 1993 U.S. semiconductor production as a whole exceeded Japan's for the first time
in eight years.

Why the sudden recovery? Was the main factor the fall in the
dollar's value, which made American chips cheaper for purchasers
around the world? Probably not—there'd been very little correlation
between currency changes and worldwide market share before. (Before 1988, when the dollar had gone up, yes, American market share
had gone down. But when the dollar had gone down, American
market share had also gone down.) Was it due to a dramatic im-

provement in American education? Hah. Was it because the companies themselves tried harder in the late 1980s than they had in the golden, early-80s age? Perhaps. The kings of the American industry, Intel and Motorola, kept racing each other with new designs and improved manufacturing processes. The industry in general, like the American auto makers it had once scorned, put new emphasis on quality and service.

But something else happened at about this time: the U.S. government intervened—"interfered," if you prefer—in the workings of the market, to protect American manufacturers. In 1986, the United States and Japan signed the Semiconductor Trade Arrangement, which was renewed and modified in 1991. The results of these negotiations differed from most trade agreements in that they did not attempt to "remove barriers" or "create a level playing field" in the Japanese market. The agreement was, in effect, a quota bill, paying less attention to the rules of competition with Japan than to the result. In 1986 the two governments expressed their "expectation" that by the end of 1991 non-Japanese companies (which in practice were mainly American) would supply 20 percent of the semiconductors purchased in Japan. At the time this agreement was signed, U.S. companies accounted for less than 9 percent of the Japanese market—and about 65 percent of the market in the rest of the world. (The deadline for reaching 20 percent was later extended to 1992.)

The Japanese government hotly denied that this "expectation" was any kind of enforceable promise. When talking to American politicians and reporters, Japanese government officials often claimed, doing their best to keep a straight face, that setting a market-share target would mean government interference with private enterprise. Surely the Americans didn't want that! Yet Japanese press reports made it clear that the government was behaving internally as if it believed it had to meet the target of 20 percent. MITI was twisting the arms of big Japanese industries, encouraging them to "design in" foreign chips when they planned new products.

In 1987 the U.S. government also decided to support a consortium called Sematech. Its purpose was to encourage American semiconductor companies to cooperate in research areas too risky or expensive for any of them to undertake independently. The government offered contracts and subsidies to defray the research expenses. The cost to the federal government was some $100 million per year, which was matched by contributions from the industry. And in the wake of this government "interference," through the semiconductor agreements and Sematech, the fortunes of the American semiconductor industry finally brightened.

After remaining flat, at about 10 percent, for years, the American share of the Japanese market neared 20 percent by the end of 1992. During the period covered by the agreement, from 1986 to 1992, the absolute volume of American chip sales in Japan more than tripled, even though the Japanese high-tech industry was in a slowdown during the early 1990s. "The existence of this agreement has made a big difference," Norman Neureiter, director of Texas Instruments Japan Ltd., told Merrill Goozner of the *Chicago Tribune* early in 1993. "Every time there has been a recession in the past, our share of the Japanese market dipped. But we expect to have gained share in 1992 at a time when the Japanese consumer electronics industry dropped 30 percent. That's pretty good." "Sematech saved the industry," Papken Der Torossian, chairman of a large semiconductor equipment company called Silicon Valley Group, said in 1992.[68]

In short: When the American industry was doing everything right, according to American economic theory, it began to collapse. When European, Japanese, and Korean producers broke all the rules of American "market rationality," they started to rise. The very existence of the American industry could not be explained by "natural" market forces—nor could its implosion, nor could its partial recovery in the late 1980s. Every one of these trends reflected not just market forces, nor just the dead hand of the state, but some interaction of the two that's usually missing from our political discussion.

You don't have to care about semiconductors, or really even about economics, to be intrigued by this tension. A well-established set of theories that undergirds our whole national policy and runs through nearly every speech and editorial about America's economic health *cannot explain* what has happened in a major industry in the real world. Academic economists have offered nuances and refinements of their theory that more closely fit the facts of the semiconductor case. For example, they emphasize that the "externalities" of a high-tech industry can make it sensible for governments to subsidize the industry's growth. Strong semiconductor or aircraft industries generate high-wage jobs and make it easier to attract other high-value industries in the future; therefore governments may be sensible in offering subsidies, even though the simplest version of economic theory says that the choice should be left strictly to the invisible hand. But very few of these refinements make their way into the public debate, where we're usually presented with the stark choice between "free markets" and "state control."

We can resolve this tension by disregarding the evidence—as most of us do when thinking of cars or TVs as the symbol of trade problems, rather than semiconductor chips. We can invent exceptions and special clauses to account for the variation—much as the Ptolemaic astronomers did as they tried to fit the motion of the planets into their theory that the sun revolved around the earth. Or we can look again at our basic ideas.

Efficiency vs. Effectiveness

What happened in Silicon Valley—on its way up, before 1980, and on its way down, through the 1980s, and upward again in the early 1990s—says something about where, *exactly,* our standard economic theories may mislead us.

Beneath all the ups and downs of high-tech competition, one difference between the Japanese and American industries matters more than anything else: the Japanese companies *had more money.* They could build bigger and newer factories because they had more money to invest. They could prevail in price wars because they had bigger war chests with which to cover losses. They could retain their work forces because in recessions they did not have to lay employees off. They could afford to invest in ten potentially promising technologies all at once (and fail at nine of them) because their R&D budgets allowed more room to spare.

This is a deceptively significant point. "Capitalism," as we all know, is finally about the use of money—capital. Its bedrock idea is that the people who own and control money will figure out the best places to put it for future development. Through countless private decisions—individuals deciding to invest, entrepreneurs deciding to borrow—the money will be collected from people who have it, and passed to the people who can most profitably put it to use. Interest rates, share prices, dividends, the hope of profits— these are the signals by which the system works. The higher the interest rate goes, the more willing the people with the money will be to lend it. The higher the rate, the more selective borrowers will be. Through the automatic magic of the market, the most promising opportunities will be the ones that get the cash.

The real drama of this American form of capitalism lies in the struggle to perfect the *rules*. According to its deepest assumptions, governments can never outguess the market about where the money should go. All that governments can—and should—do is make sure that the crucial signals flow. Signals come in the form of prices; therefore the paramount goal is to "get prices right." After that, everything should work on its own.

Governments should break up monopolies and punish manipulation of the stock market. Such abuses would distort prices and therefore keep money from flowing to its most efficient possible use. Governments should police the banking system to keep it honest, because otherwise there would be temptation for abuse. Governments should step in to correct a few, clearly recognized cases of "market failure"—for example, making sure that factories throughout the country have to obey comparable environmental standards, so that some factories don't cut costs by simply dumping their waste in the water or air. But otherwise the government should get out of the way. Its final goal should be a *frictionless* flow of signals and money.

This vision of capitalism is like the American vision of democracy. The government has no right to define what a "good" society may be. All it can do is set up the rules by which people express their views, exercise their rights, and cast their votes. According to American theory, if the system is fair, the results, by definition, must be good. So it is with the business system: if competition is on a "level playing field," if new competitors can enter the game, if customers can choose freely and fairly among the offerings, then, by definition, whatever happens will be for the best. In the long run, the right amount of money will be available for investment and the right number of new ideas will pop up for putting the money to use. It was this logic that led to the breakup of AT&T in the 1980s, the deregulation of the airlines in the 1970s, and the attack on the big industrial trusts at the turn of the century. When judges and reformers instituted these changes, they had no idea of what the "ideal" telephone or airline system might be. But they thought that if they brought in more competition, whatever system resulted would be the best. If the market was free to "get prices right," it would produce more benefits, for more people, than any other arrangement could.

By this same logic—which is, again, *the* unique and guiding logic of modern Anglo-American economics—the semiconductor industry, as of 1980, was structured about as well as any industry could be. Much of the basic scientific research had come, in the years just after World War II, from one place—AT&T's Bell Labs.[69]

Such a centralized operation was at odds with the American idea that small, agile entrepreneurs would be the greatest source of creative vigor. And so, within a few years after the war, the U.S. government had begun antitrust proceedings to make sure that Bell and AT&T did not abuse their monopoly power. Under the pressure of a government "consent order" in 1956, Bell began licensing its technology virtually to all comers, including those based outside the United States.[70] Bell held a number of crucial symposiums during the early 1950s, at which it announced its research reports, and the scientists in the business got to know each other. Later in the 1950s, Bell all but encouraged its specialized employees to branch out and form independent companies, to get the process going faster. When the industry was growing fastest, it was closest to what economists said industry should be like, with very low "barriers to entry"— especially few legal constraints or feuding over patent rights.

The chip-making merchant firms of Silicon Valley acted as much like the "economic men" of academic theory as real human beings ever will. "Economic man," as he is introduced in Ec 101 textbooks, goes through life calculating the costs and benefits of different decisions—and does not let himself be swayed by irrational or sentimental concepts, including any "buy American" (or, for that matter, "buy Japanese" or "buy French") schemes. The economic men who ran companies in Silicon Valley had every reason to sell equipment to whomever came up with money—even when they knew that many of the purchasers might, in the long run, becomes their competitors. "The independence of semiconductor equipment firms enabled them—indeed, *required* them—to sell their most advanced machines to all potential users, a practice that led routinely to the rapid diffusion of state-of-the-art production equipment throughout the world," one scholarly study said. "As long as all of the equipment firms were American, these strengths tended to hide a host of potentially serious competitive weaknesses that also derived from the U.S. industry's fragmented structure."[71] And yet this "fragmented structure" is what Anglo-American economic theory calls perfect competition.

Silicon Valley was remarkable for the high "birth rate" and high "death rate" of its firms. New products were coming out by the month, and prices were changing—usually falling—by the day. As soon as one company came up with a new product—a DRAM chip or "stepper" or hard-disk drive—other companies figured out how to do the same thing. They raced against each other to get more customers, to remove cost and waste from their own operations, to increase their production runs. Every one of these steps drove prices down, down, down. In the search for higher profits, firms were forced to scramble and innovate again and again.

Texas Instruments was one of those that scrambled—and, as in the case of its battle with MITI, the results were significant for the industry as a whole. Through the 1960s and 1970s, TI remained a master of chip technology, but the chip business became more frantic and less comfortably profitable by the day. Quaint as it now seems, the first digital watches and hand-held calculators were unveiled to the world at about the time when men first landed on the moon. These products were advanced and sexy! The manufacturers could charge premium prices, so different from their experience with price wars over chips. If Texas Instruments made the chips that, in turn, made watches and calculators possible, why shouldn't TI make the whole machines? Why not earn the profits that came from being packagers, not just parts makers?[72]

In the early 1970s, Texas Instruments and a dozen other American companies tried to win a calculator war against Japanese producers. By the late 1970s the American firms had withdrawn in defeat. They had found themselves locked in a ruinous, game-of-chicken-style price war against their Japanese rivals. Japanese firms such as Sharp seemed willing to sell calculators at a loss, for months or years, if that is what it took to dominate the market in the long run. To the non-Japanese producers this seemed irrational, even suicidal, behavior. The American companies had money for research, and for new facilities, and for generous salaries for their best scientists, and for every other element that, in the American view, should lead to competitive success. But the American companies did not have money to throw away. They saw no point in selling at a loss. If the Japanese companies were willing to do so, then they were welcome to the calculator business.[73]

It was a sign, though not widely noticed at the time, of what was to come. The American firms that had entered the calculator wars—so lean! so specialized!—were fast on their feet, and they confirmed all the American rules about how competitive life really should work. But they couldn't afford to stay in a money-losing race. They didn't see the point. The Japanese firms had a different approach, which in turn came from a different idea of how business capitalism should work.

If the American approach boiled down to "getting prices right," the Japanese approach boiled down to something different. Its essence was "getting enough money"—not worrying about theoretical efficiency, not being concerned about the best rules for competition, but focusing only on getting the nation's money into the hands of the nation's big manufacturing firms. If companies could get *more money* to work with than their competitors, then in the long run they would prevail. This is a view of capitalism that depended on *capital*. It did not concentrate on rules for ensuring frictionless markets. It focused instead on an ultimate purpose: build industry as quickly as possible. The purpose was not anything as limited or strictly financial as "maximizing profit" or "increasing shareholder value." This approach was a means, first, of catching up with others who were ahead technologically—and then of eliminating competitors. And it worked.

American semiconductor officials, when preparing a dumping complaint in 1985 against their Japanese rivals, found a copy of a Hitachi sales presentation that emphasized the "win at any cost" spirit. It said,

> *Quote 10% Below Competiton.*
> *If they requote . . .*
> *Bid 10% under again.*
> *The bidding stops when Hitachi wins. . . .*
> *Win with the 10% rule. . . .*
> *Find AMD and Intel sockets. . . .*
> *Quote 10% below their price. . . .*
> *If they requote,*
> *Go 10% again.*
> Don't quit until you *win!* . . .[74]

Three famous cases from the other end of the computer industry's food chain displayed a similar detachment from Western concepts of short-term profitability. Fujitsu and NEC, Japan's largest computer makers, were bidding against each other to supply mainframe computers to three local governments in Japan—in Hiroshima, Nagano, and Wakayama. Mainframe computers usually cost tens of thousands of dollars; indeed, in Nagano's case the local government had budgeted some 16 million yen, or about $110,000 at the time, for computer services. Fujitsu won the contracts by offering to "sell" its system for one yen, at the time about two thirds of an American cent. Clearly this was a good deal for the local governments. But what was in it for Fujitsu?[75]

What kind of system is this? What possible motives could lie behind its behavior?

The Story So Far

Late in 1991, a researcher who had specialized in East Asian development was invited to tell a group of Africans about the lessons he had learned. The East Asia success stories, he said, "are inconsistent in important ways with even a modified version of the standard economist's account" of what countries should do to grow rich.[76] "It is amazing and even scandalous," he said, that the distinguished academic theorists of economics have not even "tried to reconcile these facts about East Asian" development with their theoretical view of the world. Chalmers Johnson, of the University of California, an academic who doubles as a parlor wit, put it more tartly in a speech delivered late in 1991:

> In talking about economic issues in the Asia-Pacific region, one must begin by largely discounting or ignoring the opinions of economics professors in English-speaking countries. This is because they failed to anticipate the growth of great wealth in the area, still cannot adequately explain it, and are today concerned more with defending their arcane theories than with studying the nature and potentialities of Asian capitalism.[77]

In Japan's success, shared to some degree with its neighbors, we see a phenomenon that does not fit our prevailing models of the world. It differs from these models in means. We "know" that government messes up efficiency, but the Japanese government actively intervenes. It also differs from the model in its apparent goals. Companies lose money, citizens lead arduous lives. To understand why a system might work this way, we need to look outside our economic models, and to do that we need to understand that society's history—as seen from its own point of view.

2

The Drive to Catch Up

WHEN SIXTEENTH-CENTURY PORTUGUESE explorers found a sunny, tropical island off the southern coast of China, with a spine of steep and wooded mountains running nearly its full length, they called it Formosa, "beautiful island" in Portuguese. The island goes by a variety of terms today—Taiwan as a geographic entity, the Republic of China to its own government, Free China to its partisans, "China—Taipei" in the Olympics and similar events where it must coexist with mainland China, and "Customs Territory of Taiwan, Penghu, Kinmen, and Matsu" for the General Agreement on Tariffs and Trade, or GATT.

The island may still have its glades of loveliness, but no modern visitor has called its major cities beautiful. Taipei, the capital, is a utilitarian, get-the-job-done sprawl of factories and quickly built apartments and office blocks, all under a blanket of air pollution from decades of nonstop industrial and automotive growth.

From the jumble of buildings in Taipei, two loom up as reminders that this is not just another quickly built strip city in, say, the American Southwest. One is a gigantic structure that, from a distance, appears to be a Chinese temple, set on a hillside that overlooks the town. The apparent temple, supported by carmine-red columns ten feet thick and nearly a hundred feet tall, proves on closer inspection to be the Grand Hotel, built by Taiwanese interests in the 1960s, the most luxurious hotel in the city until the glassy Hyatts and Sheratons sprang up in the 1980s.

The other building, about a mile away, is a more understated palace-style structure surrounded by traditional Chinese gardens and lakes. This is the National Palace Museum, the greatest treasury of Chinese art in the world. It is the storehouse for the Chinese artwork taken by Chiang Kai-shek's Nationalists in 1949, when they were driven off the mainland by Chairman Mao's advancing Communist troops. The display rooms are vast, but the museum's holdings are so enormous that only about a fourth of the total can be shown at any one time. The displays change, with the seasons, through the year.

In the summer of 1991, I visited the museum and found a new historical display. Much of the ground floor was devoted to a time-line comparison of Chinese and Western civilization over the past five thousand years. In the tag end of the display, covering the years from about A.D. 1650 to the present, the Western world suddenly discovered machinery and the scientific process, and it bolted ahead of China. But the preceding 90 percent of the display showed the Westerners scrabbling their way up from a Cro-Magnon existence, while the Chinese refined their many arts. Here were the Chinese of the Hsia dynasty, with their pottery and their carvings, already having achieved a style barely improved on today. And over there were the European primitives of the same age, hammering out crude arrowheads while they huddled in caves. Here were etchings of Chinese scholars launching rockets, and there were European sorcerers of the same era, trying to cure disease with leeches or by drilling holes into some unfortunate's skull. The effect was like one of the charts depicting the whole span of geologic time, with all of mankind's activity representing a tiny blip at the end. The Western World as a whole seemed quite *arriviste*.

The weight of being a foreigner usually sat lightly on my shoulders in China and in Chinese outposts such as Hong Kong or Taiwan, compared to its effect in other societies, especially Japan. There are too many different kinds of Chinese, and too much else is going on, for them to spend much time theorizing about what makes them different from you.

But here, on the ground floor of the National Palace Museum, as the only non-Chinese among the several hundred people viewing the mural—the only heir to the Vandals and Huns!—I felt the weight of racial identity increase. How unfair the saga of recent history looked when viewed from the Chinese perspective! For century after century the Middle Kingdom and its Asian tributary states had led the world in arts and sciences. Virtually overnight, by Chinese historic standards, the upstart Europeans appeared with machines, weapons, and scientific mastery that put the rest of the world at their mercy.

America is an intentionally "ahistoric" culture. This quality has nothing to do with what its students may or may not learn in class about their nation's past. Rather it reflects the fundamental idea of America: that people should not be bound by their pasts and should be able to create new roles for themselves as they go along. Americans are routinely reminded of the effects of history on current-day events—the marks left by centuries of slavery and by the civil rights movement, by World War II and the war in Vietnam. But for most Americans, acknowledging history's effect is an exercise rather than an instinct.

The same imbalance of memory applies on a larger scale between Americans and members of most Asian societies. It is hard for many Americans to imagine that the weight of centuries of colonialism still hangs on most interactions, most days, between Asian cultures and the Western world. In their centuries of expansion, the Europeans (and eventually the Americans) changed the map of the world; uprooted supremely self-confident cultures; spread their own languages; and installed a world system based on their own ideas of logic, morality, and the rule of law. Those on the winning side of this interaction have little sense of how grating the results can seem to the losers.

The main plot line of modern history, as seen consciously or unconsciously in many Asian societies, is that Europeans and Americans *with technology* have for several centuries imposed their will on others. The crucial advantage for the Europeans was not that they were so much more cultured, nor that their political system was so much more admirable, nor that their behavior endeared them to God. They prevailed principally because their machines were better and their armies were stronger. "It was not primarily due to strategic, but rather to technical reasons that the Japanese lost the Second World War," the German historian Lily Abegg wrote shortly after the war was over, in an effort to capture the Japanese view of what had gone wrong. The Americans could rev up their mighty Arsenal of Democracy, once they were aroused by Pearl Harbor. Japan's factories were by that point already producing full-out. With their brimming output, the Americans could, Abegg said, "sweep with iron hand across the Japanese 'Go' board and fling down the complicated positions built up at such great pains. . . . [T]his was made possible only by the Americans' material superiority, for they could not have afforded to undertake these bold thrusts had the Japanese been their equals in the matter of equipment."[1]

The memory of not having been equals remains clear and important in Asia and yet is largely unrecognized in Europe and the United States. "The people of this region perceived as humiliations many features of Western colonialism that the European powers regarded merely as a matter of course," two Australian diplomats, Reg Little and Warren Reed, wrote in the late 1980s in an essay about Asia called *The Confucian Renaissance*.[2] As today's matter of course, Westerners describe their dealings with Asia almost exclusively in the language of economics—"market openings," "level playing fields," "worldwide system of free trade." Concepts derived from economics clarify some issues but can obscure questions of history and human nature that are at the heart of the Western world's current dealings with Asia.

The Start of Relevant History

In the springtime of 1592, the great Japanese warlord Hideyoshi assembled a force of 150,000 men, the greatest army in his country's history to that point. He massed them on Kyushu, southernmost of Japan's four main islands,* and prepared to sail the 110 miles across the Strait of Tsushima and the Strait of Korea to invade Korea, starting with the city of Pusan.

There is no right place to "start" the history that affects today's Asian economic developments, since every theme has a precedent that stretches back into the mists of time. Still, Hideyoshi's voyage to Korea in 1592 represents a kind of dividing line for the modern history of East Asia, as the voyage of Columbus a century before is a dividing line for the history of North America. From that point on, certain processes were under way in Japan that had not been there previously, and whose consequences affected not just Japan's development but Asian-Western relations as a whole. If the voyage

---

*The islands are Honshu, literally "main island," which is the largest island and contains most of Japan's major cities; Hokkaido (literally "northern sea road"), a frontierlike territory that nearly touches Siberia; Kyushu, which is semitropical; and the small, rural island of Shikoku. The other significant island is Okinawa, four hundred miles to the south of the main archipelago; Okinawa had been the independent Kingdom of the Ryukyus but was taken over by Japan in the nineteenth century.

had turned out differently, so might many other things about today's world.

Hideyoshi—"usually agreed [to be] the greatest man in the history of Japan," in the words of a standard history[3]—was born a commoner. Like most other plebeian Japanese of his era, he did not have a family name, and assigned himself one (Toyotomi) only after he had risen to power. He had become a hired warrior for the shoguns of his era, and he demonstrated a military genius that made him the Napoleon or MacArthur of his day. Eventually he became the ruler of all Japan.

In the few decades before Hideyoshi's excursion, the Europeans were beginning to flex their muscles around the world. In 1521, Ferdinand Magellan landed in the Philippines, where he would eventually be bludgeoned to death on the island of Cebu. In 1542, Portuguese seafarers called on Kyushu, in the first European incursion into Japan. Even now, Kyushu has a sleepier, more tropically lazy air than the rest of Japan, but centuries of direct contact with foreigners have made certain enclaves of Kyushu the most truly cosmopolitan parts of the country. Kyushu was the natural first landing site for early Europeans coming past the Malay Peninsula and up the Chinese coast through the South China Sea. It was also the natural conduit for migrants and traders going between Korea and Japan during many centuries before the European explorers set sail. After the first Europeans landed on Kyushu, successive Japanese governments decided it was an ideal long-term holding tank for them. From the sixteenth through the early twentieth century, the European merchants, diplomats, and missionaries who operated in Japan were concentrated around Nagasaki, on Kyushu's western coast.

The most important of these early foreign visitors was Francis Xavier, the Portuguese Jesuit who had more influence on Japan than any single foreigner until Matthew Perry, the American commodore who steamed into Uraga Harbor in 1853, or Douglas MacArthur, the American general who ruled occupied Japan starting in 1945. Francis Xavier's arrival, in 1549, presented the Japanese of that era with a reality that altered the fundamental conditions of Japan's strategy: foreigners were coming, and they could not be wished away or ignored.

Until that point, Japan's interactions with its neighbors in Asia had been intense at times, but had generally been on terms controlled by Japan. The straits that separate the tips of the Japanese archipelago from Korea, to the south, and the Sakhalin Island of Siberia, to the north, discouraged casual traffic. The period about a thousand years before Francis Xavier's arrival, the fourth to the sixth century A.D., was a time of great interest and interaction among China, Japan, and Korea. Japan adopted its current character-based writing system from China during this period; knowledge of the Buddhist religion reached Japan from China, through Korea; Chinese and Korean styles of architecture and ceramic design were applied in Japan. By the end of the ninth century Japan was pulling away from this involvement with the mainland, and most official trade between China and Japan did not resume until the twelfth century.

The most traumatic interaction between Japan and the outside world (which, until the Portuguese arrived, meant the Asian mainland) had occurred three hundred years before Hideyoshi's voyage, in the mid-thirteenth century. China had been in one of its periods of unity from the mid-900s until the mid-1200s, under the Sung dynasty. That period ended when the Mongols, under Genghis Khan, decided to expand their empire southward, into Asia, rather than westward, into Europe. Over the next generation Genghis Khan and his successor Kublai Khan put together their own version of the Alexandrine or Roman empires, which stretched across nearly all of modern China, the Central Asian republics of the former Soviet Union, and south toward modern-day Burma and Vietnam. Kublai Khan meant to extend this empire through the Korean Peninsula to Japan itself. He sent peremptory messages to Japan, addressed to the "king of your little country" and demanding immediate surrender. The Japanese did not comply.

In 1274 Japanese defenders barely held off a force of Mongols attempting to invade on the northern shore of Kyushu. The Japanese were aided by a windstorm, which destroyed the invaders' boats and caused thirteen thousand of them to drown. Seven years later, Kublai Khan had amassed a much larger force and was still determined to invade Japan. But this time an even larger storm, on the night of August 15, 1281, destroyed his fleet. This typhoon was to become legendary in Japan as the *kamikaze*, or "divine wind." Japan's providential protection from foreigners underscored the idea of the country's special role, at a distance from the world.

By the time the Portuguese arrived in 1542, Japan was in the late stages of what is called the *sengoku jidai,* or "warring states era." Rival *daimyo,* or feudal lords, were struggling for power within a structure that was theoretically ruled by a divine emperor but was in practice run by the shogun, or military boss, from his stronghold in Kyoto. The only taxable asset for this system was land, specifically rice land—and the emperor and shogun had no vast estates of their own to tax. They depended, therefore, on feudal tribute payments from the daimyo. They also turned their attention to trade, as a way of generating more revenue.

Despite a long lack of interest in the seafaring arts, Japanese traders had become more and more integrated into an Asian trading system by the time the Europeans arrived. The main products they had to sell were silver, from their mines, and the Japanese swords that were treasured by customers in China.

As the first Europeans reached Asia near the end of the "warring states" period, Hideyoshi's predecessor Oda Nobunaga was bringing the daimyo more and more under control. But after a decisive battle that established the primacy of central control, he was murdered in Kyoto by one of his own generals. Hideyoshi rose in his place to rule. Japan had become more unified internally just as it had a new foreign threat to confront.

Patterns of Engagement

The initial pattern of contact was revealing, because its essentials show up in Japan's relations with the outside world in the late twentieth century.

First among the constants: The rulers of Japan decided to expose the country to foreign influence only after a clear-eyed, practical decision that Japan might be imperiled if it failed to do so. Outsiders, they discovered in the 1500s and again in the 1800s, had surpassed them in certain undeniable ways. It was crucial to learn about these advances, assess Japan's weaknesses accurately, and apply the new knowledge wherever possible.

It was clear to the Japanese rulers of the 1500s that the Portuguese had mastered navigation in a way no Asian countries had. In addition to learning from their experience, Japanese could profit from trading with the Portuguese, and from using their ships to carry goods back and forth to China. The Sea of Japan was infested with a brand of Japanese pirates known as *wako,* about whom the Chinese chronically complained. Because of the predations of the pirates, the Ming dynasty had forbidden all direct trade between Japan and China in the late 1400s. The Portuguese warships, however, could dispose of the pirates without serious trouble, and soon the Portuguese had a monoply on carrying goods between China and Japan.

In weaponry as well, the Japanese learned they had fallen behind. The first Portuguese matchlock muskets had washed ashore, along with several bedraggled but still living Portuguese sailors, on the Japanese island of Tanegashima in 1542.[4] The local daimyo immediately recognized the importance of the weapons, bought them for a large sum from the sailors, and had them copied. Soon thereafter every army in Japan was equipped with guns and muskets. The systematic attempt to master foreign techniques and apply them rapidly within the country distinguished Japan from the rest of Asia in the early 1500s and again in the late 1800s, when Japan had to cope with another form of foreign threat.

The second great constant had to do with the behavior of the foreigners—in this case the Portuguese. Like Japan's leaders, the Portuguese were pursuing their own practical-minded interest, which soon became evident beneath the veneer of missionary rhetoric.[5]

In preceding decades the Portuguese had established a system of trading posts, moving around the Indian Ocean and the South China Sea—from Goa, on the Indian coast, to Malacca, on the Malay Peninsula, to Macao, on the southern curve of China, and now to Nagasaki. The reasons they gave to themselves (and the rest of the world) for the entire venture were expressed in the highest and most idealistic terms: they were bringing souls to Christ. Yet the missionary, commercial, and military aspects of the Portuguese presence were intertwined in an obvious way. The Jesuits arrived on the trading ships, guarded by the army; the profit from the trading voyages kept the missions open. Traders and missionaries alike set up their beachhead in Nagasaki, although the Jesuits were allowed to operate throughout much of the country.

The missionary component of the exercise was no doubt sincere, or at least as sincere as it was for their counterparts in Latin America at the same time. Indeed, it was precisely because the Jesuits succeeded in making converts that they eventually antagonized Hideyoshi, who had originally tolerated them because of the outside knowledge they brought. The proselytizing Catholics of that day were not believers in cultural relativism. In Japan as in other pagan lands, they insisted on all-or-nothing commitments from would-be converts, who had to turn their backs on all previous beliefs. This was a clear and uncomfortable contrast to Japan's incorporation of Buddhism (and Chinese Confucianism) many centuries before, which had been moderated and blended so as not to disrupt existing ways. Early Buddhism mixed with the native Shinto faith to include elements of the "Divine Land" principle—that Japan was the holy, heaven-blessed site among all nations of the earth. Most societies believe this about themselves, of course, but it became a formal part of Japanese Buddhism. Christianity "might have had a different history if the missionaries had been able to accept the 'Divine Land' doctrine," one Japanese scholar dryly pointed out. "Such a change, however, would have entailed a serious transformation of Christianity."[6] This pattern of behavior, in which foreigners preached idealism but also carefully pursued their self-interest, would recur in the mid-1800s, when Commodore Perry attempted to open Japan to Western trade, and in the mid-1900s, when the United States made postwar Japan its crucial Asian bastion during the Cold War.

It eventually became clear to Hideyoshi and the other temporal powers that the Jesuits constituted an important practical threat. The Jesuits' success in converting 150,000 to 200,000 Japanese to Christianity during their first three decades in the country was itself a challenge to the steady evolution of central government power, since the Jesuits announced that real Christians owed loyalty to the one true God and to no one else. Worse still, from the Japanese rulers' point of view, the converts included a number of Hideyoshi's top advisers.

In the early 1600s, the real-life episode that formed the basis for the novel *Shōgun* occurred. An English pilot of a Dutch ship came ashore in Kyushu, where the Portuguese Jesuits almost had him crucified for his Protestant heresies. The shogun of that time, Ieyasu, learned of the existence of the pilot, Will Adams, and had him brought to the court in Edo. Once there, Adams imparted information about shipbuilding and navigating, and also warned that the Catholic powers of Portugal and Spain, which were both then under the Spanish king, were preparing for a military conquest of Japan comparable to what had happened in the Americas.

The shogun's fears were intensified when refugees from a Spanish shipwreck washed ashore and revealed that there was a strong connection between the cross and the sword. Throughout the Americas, the rescued sailors said, Catholic friars had served to lull and weaken the local population before the conquering military moved in. The Jesuits in Japan had consistently professed to be shocked by any suggestion that they might be an advance wave for real conquerors. One Portuguese priest wrote in 1588 that since Hideyoshi "cannot believe that our mission is to save souls for life eternal because he does not recognize the immortality of the soul, he is ready to believe that we have no other goal but to prepare the conquest of his kingdom."[7]

Every non-Western nation that let in the Jesuits (or the Franciscans or Dominicans or other missionary orders) ended up facing a challenge to its hegemony. The Chinese approach to this challenge rested on their faith in China's most absorptive capacity. After missionaries trickled in during the 1500s, Chinese leaders tried to envelop and co-opt them, confident that they would eventually be won over by the powers of Chinese culture. In the meantime, China's rulers assumed, the Chinese system would not be deeply altered by their presence. The Jesuits, admired for their skill with languages and general mandarinlike training, became favored advisers to the emperor.

The Japanese approach was more black-and-white: after initially tolerating the Jesuits, and profiting from their presence in both economic and technological terms—learning about navigation and guns, and having Western books translated into Japanese by the scholarly Jesuits, who produced noted experts in the language—Hideyoshi took the first step against them with an expulsion order in 1587. Getting rid of all the missionaries, and even more, erasing the Christian influence, proved not to be quick or easy tasks. Over the next two decades Hideyoshi and his successor Ieyasu had to wage a long and bloody anti-Christian campaign, which at several stages involved scenes reminiscent of Romans putting Christians to death in the Colosseum. The standard means of execution for the many Japanese Christians who would not recant was crucifixion, upside down. The difference between the Roman anti-Christian campaign and the Japanese was that Japan's worked. As little as 1 percent of the Japanese population is Christian now.

Having beaten back the Christians in the West and consolidated his power through the rest of the country, Hideyoshi was more in command of Japan as a whole than any previous ruler had been. It was at this stage that he amassed his troops for the fateful drive into Korea. In so doing he underscored another of the constants in Japan's relations with outsiders: its own acute sense of vulnerability, which has affected its policies in profound ways.

Japan's Struggle to Avoid Vulnerability

Japan's fundamental predicament is that it is vulnerable to the external world in countless ways. In the late twentieth century, Japan is dependent for raw materials to keep its factories running and its people fed. For a much longer period it has been vulnerable to powerful foreigners who might overtly or subtly force their ways on Japan. Nothing like this vulnerability is part of the American historical imagination, and from the time of the Norman Conquest until the threat of a Nazi invasion it has not been part of Britain's.

In attempting to solve its problem of vulnerability, Japan has had two basic choices. One is to try to wall itself off from the outside world. The other choice is to attempt to control the surrounding environment so it will not be capable of springing surprises on the Japanese. With his attempt to conquer the Korean Peninsula in 1592, Hideyoshi tried the second alternative. The results of that attempt soon drove Japan's leader toward the opposite approach.

With the confidence that came from controlling his own territory, with the knowledge that the Europeans were prowling around and that the Korean Peninsula could someday serve as a kind of entry ramp for Chinese incursions against Japan, Hideyoshi sent a force of some two hundred thousand men in seven hundred vessels bound for Pusan in May 1592. The Japanese of Hideyoshi's era were used to warfare, with several decades of internal battling during the *sengoku jidai* behind them. Hideyoshi apparently dreamed of moving through Korea and going on to conquer China. Other forces of outsiders, from Mongolia and Manchuria, had done that in the past, but, of course, they did not have to send their armies across the sea.

In principle, the invading Japanese force could have been destroyed as it neared Pusan Harbor, because through poor planning the ships straggled in piecemeal rather than in a coordinated assault wave. But the Korean Navy was apparently still waiting for instructions from the capital, and the Japanese landed safely and stormed rapidly to the north. They seized the capital, in Seoul, and had settled down for a long occupation when a Chinese "human wave" assault came across the Yalu River in 1593 and drove most of the Japanese forces back home, thereby removing a threat to Chinese dominance of the Asian mainland. In Korea to this day, temples and palaces typically have explanatory markers laying out three relevant dates: when the structure was originally built; when it was burned, defaced, or razed by Japanese invaders (in either the sixteenth or the nineteenth century or both); and when it came back under Korean control and was restored by loving local hands.

In 1597, five years after the first invasion, Hideyoshi tried again, amassing another 150,000-man force and sending them back across the Tsushima and Korea straits. This second attack seemed an act of grandiosity or delusion. Hideyoshi was generally thinking big at this stage. For instance, he gave the Spanish notice that he didn't like their settlement in Manila and ordered them to pay tribute or suffer the consequences. One historian has compared him to the emperors of the late Roman empire—successful in battle in his early years but growing more and more decadent, cruel, and impulsive as time went on. He fared much worse on his second attempt to seize Korea. This time the Chinese and Koreans were ready. The Chinese Army was prepositioned, much closer to the attack point, and the Korean Navy, under the legendary Admiral Yi, scuttled the Japanese fleet. Today, a heroic super-life-size statue of Admiral Yi stands above the main traffic intersection in downtown Seoul. Not only did he beat the hated Japanese, but also he did so with "turtle boats," early ironclads with armor on top.

As Hideyoshi's troops were being driven back in 1598, he died and was succeeded by another of Japan's great leaders: Ieyasu Tokugawa, whose decisions, like Hideyoshi's, have consequences even now.

The next two and a half centuries of Japanese life are known as the Tokugawa era, after Ieyasu and his successors. They represented Japan's attempt to close itself off from the world. Hideyoshi thought Japan could best avoid foreign control by preemptively controlling the foreigners. The Tokugawa strategy swung to the opposite extreme: Japan could maintain control over its own fate by trying to insulate itself from outside disturbances altogether.

The result was to put Japan on a gyre leading in a different direction from almost any other country. At a time when the European powers were poised to unleash themselves full-strength upon the world, at a time when most non-European socieities were about to become the object of that outburst, Japan took a course that its geography permitted but was nonetheless quite strange. The Tokugawa leaders (unlike, say, the Yanomamo of the Amazon) knew about the existence and nature of the outside world. Ieyasu, for instance, had a globe, as an aid for studying geography. But by the 1640s his grandson Iemitsu Tokugawa had imposed a sweeping policy of isolation on the country.

Japanese citizens were in principle forbidden to have any contact with outsiders, cultural or commercial. They could trade with other Japanese but were not allowed to deal with foreigners. The emperor's subjects were forbidden to leave his domain, and if they were caught trying, the punishment was death. The few Japanese traders and sailors who were living overseas were ordered not to return; if they tried and were caught, they, too, would be killed. The systematic campaign to stamp out Christianity continued, with waves of crucifixions through the 1600s. One of the strangest parts of modern Tokyo is a slum area called Sanya. The entry to it was named long ago *namida-bashi,* the "bridge of tears," since it was the last bridge the condemned, including Christians, would cross on their way to the execution grounds.

The Tokugawa rulers left a small opening to the outside world, but this was tightly controlled. Traders from Holland would be the only foreigners allowed to deal with Japan, and they would be confined to a small settlement called Deshima, near Nagasaki. The Japanese leaders of the time were aware of the great rivalry between Holland and Portugal for commercial control of Asia. Ieyasu and the other Japanese leaders had grown deeply embittered against Portugal, and they welcomed a chance to break the powerful hold on commerce that the combination of Jesuits, warships, and merchants had given Portugal. The Japanese were also impressed by what they had heard about Dutch shipbuilding skills (mainly from Will Adams, the shipwrecked English pilot of a Dutch ship). Therefore Ieyasu chose to spite the Portuguese by favoring the Dutch, who would handle such limited business as Japan continued to transact with foreigners.

The Uses of Isolation

European historians often debate how dark the "Dark Ages" really were, and what kind of creativity preceded the Renaissance. Similarly, vast tracts of Japanology concern just what happened during the apparently static Tokugawa years, which ran from the early 1600s until the 1860s. Although the most obvious effect of this era was to let Japan be overtaken by the industrial, technological, and political developments of the outside world, some traits that now make Japan seem "efficient" and "modern" were nonetheless being formed.

For instance, a network of "village schools" spread through the country, with a strong emphasis on duty and practical skills.

"None of the assumptions concerning the functions of education provided any reason for denying it to the lower class," the British scholar Ronald Dore has written. "There was, indeed, every advantage in their getting moral instruction." This was especially important in a Confucian social model, as it would be in a Western military unit; the whole organization could not succeed unless each person understood the duties and obligations that came with his rank.[8] The breadth of Japanese education, which brings nearly everyone up to a level of basic competence, remains one of its most marveled-at features even now.

Cartel-mindedness, another of modern Japan's notable traits, was also visible during the Tokugawa days. In the 1600s and 1700s, guilds were being put on the defensive in Europe and North America, as an early capitalist economy took form. During those same years in Japan, guilds and similar arrangement to protect people from "excessive" competition were spreading in Japan. The moral and ethical rhetoric of the era placed great stress on the duties to the group, rather than the individual pursuit of happiness. Even the earliest contact with European traders had made clear that in open trading competition, Japan's small craftsmen and cottage industries, making cloth and implements, could be wiped out, and Japan could be reduced—like Java, like Luzon—to a work force that produced food and ores for the Europeans. Isolation allowed these manufacturers to survive.

The tremendous centralization and standardization of Japanese life were also visible in those years. The strangest thing about traveling in Japan now is how little it varies from place to place. Hokkaido is big and open, Kyushu is more tropically verdant than the rest of Japan; but cities, street scenes, houses, and schools look much more homogeneous than is the case even in the United States. Soon after World War II Lily Abegg wrote in *The Mind of Asia:* "Quite apart from modern industrial products, the following have been standardized in Japan since time immemorial: the size of the straw matting in houses, sliding doors, window shutters, chopsticks, towels, soup bowls, rice bowls, toilet paper and troughs for washing clothes, bed-covers, wooden patterns, brooms, feather dusters, the width of materials, the cut of the kimono, rolls of writing paper, and so on."[9]

At the beginning of the Tokugawa era, Japan, behind its closed-off veil, was putting in place the beginnings of a system of nationwide, centralized administration and taxation. Hideyoshi, the man who had dreamed of conquering China, had required oaths of loyalty from lords around the country, and reinforced them with an ingenious hostage system later institutionalized under the name of *sankin kotai* (alternative residence). Subsidiary lords, or their wives or children, were forced to live for much of each year as "guests" in Hideyoshi's castle in Osaka, reducing their enthusiasm for rebellion or surprise attack. A feudal system of tax revenue, based on shares of the rice harvest, was in place. Each regional lord, or *daimyo,* owed a certain amount of rice each year to the shogun's central government; each landowner in turn owed rice to his *daimyo.* The very center of Japan's centralized power has always been difficult to locate. The emperor, then as now, was nominally in charge of the whole governmental affair, but in effect he usually was another hostage of the shogun, like the weak popes of the ninth and tenth centuries who served as front men for German emperors. Nonetheless, from the early Tokugawa time onward, Japan could be considered a state in the full modern sense long before today's Western powers could.

That is, while it seemed to be retreating from the world, Japan took certain steps that would eventually help it cope with strangers. Then, all of a sudden, with the arrival of the Americans and Europeans in the mid-nineteenth century, Japan was shocked by the enormousness of the task it faced.

Japan, from the middle of the nineteenth century, was forced into a race against the threat of domination from overseas. The Chinese in the early 1800s had made one concession after another to the intrusive Englishmen—ceding away control of Hong Kong and the treaty ports, debauching themselves with the narcotics that British traders brought. The great kingdoms of Southeast Asia—in Java, the Malay Peninsula, Cambodia, Vietnam, and elsewhere—had been ruled by Europeans for several centuries. (The arrival of Commodore Perry did not threaten the Japanese with immediate conquest, but the Tokugawa leaders knew that interactions with a materially stronger society could turn out very badly for Japan.)

The magnitude of this shock of encounter, in which the Europeans demonstrated their complete ability to dominate other cultures, is hard for Westerners to take seriously. It was a long time ago, and it didn't happen to them. But the processes it set in motion still shape the Asia of the late twentieth century. Colonial dependence on, first, Spain and then America still affects politics and culture in the Philippines. Political parties and structures left over from the fight against colonialism still have an effect in countries as different as Singapore, Vietnam, and China.

"The intrusion of Western power into East Asia . . . shattered the Chinese idea of a world order based on the Middle Kingdom," the historian Theodore Friend has written. "In the tradition of Renaissance diplomacy, the Western imperial powers treated each other as legal equals; but in the tradition of social Darwinism they treated Asian polities as legal and moral inferiors unless counterforce proved otherwise. *Only Japanese power kept native initiative in Asia.*"[10]

Through the colonial era Japan escaped the outright control by foreigners that most other Asian societies endured. Yet the means by which it avoided external control created other, inner controls whose effects are visible in the Japan of the 1990s. To avoid foreign domination, the Japanese leadership of the late nineteenth century began a drive to learn systematically about achievements in the outside world; it imposed internal controls so that the newly acquired knowledge could be applied as quickly and efficiently as possible, without corrupting what it thought of as the cultural essence of Japan; and it began constantly looking over its shoulder to see how Japan stood, relative both to the Western powers it feared and admired and the Asian neighbors from which it was pulling ahead. Each of these habits and tendencies affects the strong, successful, fully "caught up" Japan of the late twentieth century.

The Decision to "Catch Up"

The pivotal impetus for Japan's drive to catch up was Commodore Perry's arrival with his "black ships," or *kurofune,* in 1853. But before that, other indications of trouble were making their way into Tokugawa Japan. English trading ships were snooping up from the south, and Russian missions were coming from the north. By 1825, the shogun's government, or *bakufu,* had issued sweeping orders to repel foreign intruders. The edict told loyal citizens, "All Southern Barbarians and Westerners, not only the English, worship Christianity, that wicked cult prohibited in our land. Henceforth, whenever a foreign ship is sighted approaching any point on our coast, all persons on hand should fire on it and drive it off." Japanese sentries might mistake Dutch ships for the hated British or Russians, the edict warned. "Even so, have no compunction about firing on them by mistake: when in doubt, drive the ship away without hesitation. Never be caught off-guard."[11]

But the foreigners kept coming. While in the middle of fighting Napoleon, the British sent a fleet to call at Nagasaki—as did the famous British colonialist Raffles, after the defeat of Napoleon, from his base in Singapore. Neither the British nor the Russians nor the Americans showed any inclination to abide by the arrangement Tokugawa had worked out with the Dutch, under which the Dutch would be the middlemen and filters for dealings with all foreigners.

The signs of American interest were clearly the most alarming to Japan. In one of the last acts of his administration, and by far the most consequential, President Millard Fillmore sent Matthew Perry to sea. Perry carried with him a rosewood box containing a letter ordering the Japanese to open their markets to foreign trade. Like so many subsequent American pressures on Japan, this was a combination of moral lecture and open-ended threat. The moral uplift lay in the "better life" and "higher civilization" Japan would attain through intercourse with foreigners.[12] The threat was an unspecified "or else," implicit in the big, armored steamships that Perry took fearlessly into Japanese harbors. After his first voyage, Perry told the Japanese that he would be back, next time "with a larger force." On his return he brought a telegraph; a working model of a locomotive; and, of course, many armaments.

Almost every day when living in Japan I saw a reference to these black ships, or *kurofune*—in the name of a television show, in product brands, in art exhibits of how the foreigners seemed when they arrived. Not only did the black ships bring the intruders who changed the country's history; they also represented, in themselves, the technological gap that the Japanese of the time most feared. Westerners could make warships that could traverse the wide sea; the Japanese could not. The Tokugawa leaders, after all, had explicitly forbidden Japanese craftsmen to make oceangoing vessels, as part of the plan for bottling up the country. By the time Japan's rulers glimpsed their first steamship, Great Britain had a fleet four hundred strong.[13]

Countless plays, histories, memoirs, and novels concern the minuet of the following ten years: Perry bluffed, wheedled, and demanded; the shogun's representatives stalled, dissembled, but finally gave in. The two most poignant subcharacters are undoubtedly Townsend Harris and Shoin Yoshida. Harris was the man Perry left behind to negotiate. His diaries record his cycles of hopefulness and despair. One day, he thinks the shogun's government has agreed to a new concession. Two months later, he is told that he must have "misunderstood." Like clockwork, contemporary U.S. diplomats assigned to Tokyo discover Harris's diaries as they're midway into their service. They underline passages and turn down the corners of pages, telling their colleagues: Nothing has changed. Everyone circles the poignant question Harris asked about the unrelenting American pressure. "I shall be the first agent from a civilized power to reside in Japan. . . . Query—if for the real good of Japan?"

Yoshida, Harris's Japanese counterpart in poignancy, was in his mid-twenties when Perry arrived. He seems to be a character who would have fit without trouble into an American college campus in the mid-1960s. He sopped up tales of foreign countries, dreamed of traveling overseas, and drew up plans for strengthening Japan by applying foreign techniques. He decided to smuggle his way onto Commodore Perry's ship when it made its second visit to Japan, in 1854. In the middle of the night he rowed out to the anchored American ship *Mississippi* and scrambled aboard. The Americans were impressed by his gumption but felt they had to return him to the authorities. The Tokugawa law still forbade Japanese to leave the country. Suppose this had been a test to see whether the Americans would abet a crime? Yoshida was promptly thrown into jail. Eventually he was released—but then rearrested for plotting against the shogunate and beheaded in 1859. The bill of particulars for this execution is revealing about the conflict of values then going on inside Japan:

- · Item: He tried to go to America.
- · Item: He advised the government on coastal defense while in jail.
- · Item: He opposed the hereditary succession to office and favored the selection of able men by popular vote.
- · Item: He planned to give his opinion regarding foreigners to the Bakufu [the shogun's government].
- · Item: He did such things while in domiciliary confinement, thus showing great disrespect for high officials.[14]

Perhaps Japan would have lumbered toward modernization without foreign pressure. But undoubtedly Perry's arrival brought things to a head. Within fifteen years of his first voyage, patterns that still affect Japan's response to the outside world, and in particular to America, had been put in place.

In Japan, a system emerged that was shaped for one overriding national purpose: creating modern industries and armaments as quickly as possible, to keep the foreigners at bay. To this end, Japan developed elaborate, effective, and systematic ways to learn the

details of foreign achievements. By 1868 a group of warriors, reformers, and ideologues had seized control of the country from the
toppling Tokugawa shogunate. They wanted their regime to be
known as the "Meiji Restoration," which purportedly "restored"
the imperial family to its proper role after centuries of de facto rule
by the shoguns. The emperor at that time was the fifteen-year-old
Mutsuhito, known as the Meiji emperor.* "Restoring" him to power
in effect meant giving a radically reformist regime a legitimate cover
for its acts.

Over the last third of the nineteenth century, the Meiji government shaped the political and ideological system to remove any
obstacle to modernization. Industrial growth was a *means* toward a
political and strategic *end:* making the country too strong to be
vulnerable to foreigners. This was, of course, the logic the United
States later used when it was at war with Japan: industry was the
"Arsenal of Democracy," not merely a source of consumer comfort.
For Japan, industry was the only arsenal that might preserve its
independence.

"The Japanese have ardently desired to retain their culture,
their way of life, the specific relationship between superior and inferior, and their family structure, yet simultaneously to build a modern nation endowed with power that is comparable to that of Western
countries," Michio Morishima wrote in 1982 in his book *Why Has
Japan "Succeeded"?* "This desire has persisted throughout the last
century or more—on the eve of the Meiji Revolution; when fighting
Russia in the latter part of the Meiji period; during the militaristic
period when Nazi Germany was considered the ideal; when the
country was in ruins after being defeated in the World War; and
even today when Japan has become an economic giant."[15]

The Western world reacted in many ways to this Japanese renaissance: with fascination for Japanese art and aesthetics, with a

---

*A word about the naming system for Japanese emperors. When an emperor
takes the throne, an "era name" is chosen to apply to the years of his reign.
Once the emperor dies, that era name is applied retroactively to identify
him. Thus when the fifteen-year-old Prince Mutsuhito became emperor in
1868, the Meiji era began, Meiji meaning "Enlightened Rule." Ever since
his death in 1912, he has been known as the Meiji emperor, or Emperor
Meiji. During an emperor's reign he is identified in Japan as *Tenno Heika,*
or "His Majesty the Emperor."

Dates are officially reckoned in Japan by these imperial eras. *Meiji
gan-nen,* or Year 1 of the Meiji era, was 1868; 1869, therefore, would be
Meiji 2.

missionary desire to save souls, with a mixture of respect, condescension, and nervousness about what Japan had under way. Yet Westerners, especially Americans, were predisposed not to look too closely at what Japan was doing as it modernized.

The Steps Toward Catching Up: Learning; Control; and Purity and "Proper Place"

Learning. Every culture "learns"; Japan in the Meiji era was probably unique in its *systematic* attempt to learn what the rest of the world had come up with, and apply it as quickly as possible in Japan. The result was a system that, for better and worse, works today like a valve or ratchet.

Japan is extremely well set up to take information in—books and movies in translation, scientific papers, licensed technology, and data of every form. It has never developed mechanisms for helping information flow the other way. Late in 1992 I met a Japanese official who was in charge of coordinating the "mutual" exchange of scientific information between Japan and the United States. He spent a long time describing all the projects the Japanese government and Japanese companies had launched to understand American science, to observe American research, to learn from American techniques. At the end he was asked about the other side of his job—encouraging the flow of information out of Japan. "Actually, nothing formal has been established as of yet. . . ."

The Japanese interest in foreign innovations long predated the arrival of the Europeans. Since its earliest contact with China and Korea, Japan has demonstrated (in the words of an Australian scholar) "a fascination with brilliant foreign cultures and an intense desire to import and adapt as many of their desirable features as possible."[16] Even in the late Tokugawa days, while the country was still officially closed, a cadre of specialists became *rangakusha,* or "masters of Dutch learning." As word of the European menace seeped in during the 1830s and 1840s, the *rangakusha* led a bitter debate about how Japan could best respond—by opening itself and learning what the Westerners had done, or by redoubling its policy of isolation and driving them away at all costs. The side whose motto was *sonno joi*—"revere the emperor, expel the barbarian"—lost the intellectual battle after Perry's arrival; it was no longer practical to drive the foreigners away by force. But the subsequent policy, of *kaikoku* or "opening the country," could lead to the same results—if Japan's leaders learned enough, fast enough, from the West. That is, if Japan became strong again, it could right the distorted balance of world forces and live on its own once more.

Even Shoin Yoshida, the man who was executed for trying to go to America, had recommended learning from the West in order to cope with and eventually surmount the Western powers. In 1854, while he was in prison for having tried to sneak aboard the U.S.S. *Mississippi* of Perry's fleet, Yoshida explained his reason for wanting to learn how the Westerners had built the ships and guns:

> If we dispose of sufficient naval vessels and cannon it should be possible for us to bring the [Western] barbarians under control, subdue the feudal lords, seize Kamchatka and [the Sea of] Okhotsk, to absorb the Ryukyus [Okinawa], to teach the Koreans a lesson, extract tribute from them . . . to divide up the territory of Manchuria in the north, to absorb Taiwan, and the Philippines in the south. In fact, it will be possible for Japan to establish itself as a power with a gradually expanding sphere of influence.[17]

By the 1880s there had been an explosion of Japanese research into how the outside world did what Japan could not yet do. In 1866 Yukichi Fukuzawa, who later founded Keio University and was to become one of Japan's great reformers (and whose portrait now graces the 10,000-yen bill), had published a book called *Seiyo Jijo,* or *The Situation in the Western World,* based on his discoveries during travel outside Japan. The title page showed a drawing of the globe begirdled by telegraph wires and with Western trains roaring past. The characters on the cover helpfully informed readers: "Steam Ferries People. Electricity Carries Messages."[18] Later, a man named Kenjiro Yamagawa, who was a teenager in the early Meiji era and showed great promise in mathematics, was selected by the government to go for advanced technical training in the United States, at Yale. Crossing the seas at age seventeen, in 1871, he was dumbfounded by a sight that he described in a letter home:

> In those days I had not yet overcome my ingrained contempt for foreigners. . . . But then something happened that impressed me greatly and made me realize that I needed to learn from them. In the middle of the Pacific we were informed that that evening or the next morning we would meet the boat of

the Pacific Mail Company and those who wanted to send mail to Japan should have it ready. I seriously doubted whether on this huge body of water two ships could possibly meet as planned. At three or four in the morning we in fact met up with the other ship and stopped about two hundred meters from it. A boat was let down, our letters were taken across and others received. Watching this, I was deeply impressed by the superiority of Western knowledge and decided that in the face of such massive knowledge Japan would be impotent.[19]

By the 1870s, the Naval Ministry was advised by eighty-seven Englishmen; the Army by forty-six Frenchmen; the Board of Construction by six Dutch experts; and the Medical College by eleven Germans. Americans were present as missionaries, athletic coaches, and advisers on building a university system. The public school curriculum was standardized around the country; school uniforms, still in use today, were based on those of Prussian cadets. "The culture imported by the Meiji government was not a general, unplanned import of Western culture equally from all countries," says a Japanese historian. "Its elements were selected following a careful analysis of their potential contribution to the economy and defense of the nation; these various imports were fused together to produce a Western culture unique to Japan."[20]

At the same time, Japanese society was letting out much less information than it was taking in. During the first, Perry-era contacts between outsiders and Japanese officials, the Japanese grilled the foreigners on every aspect of how their societies worked. But when the foreigners asked questions, these same officials feigned ignorance about the most basic matters—how many people lived in a city, whether there was actually an emperor of the country, what the main businesses were. "Where, we ask, did this policy of non-communication and secretiveness originate?" Masao Miyoshi, a literary critic at the University of California, has written. "A paranoiac worry over national security? A totalitarian structure depending for survival on rigid adherence to an official line? Of course. But underlying these was a philosophical attitude toward knowledge. . . . Information had to remain within the tribe."[21]

The forced-march approach toward learning from foreigners has its obvious drawbacks. It has led to extremes of emotion, like those of the young man on the boat. We're so far behind! Now we're Number One! Early in my own stay, I was at Tsukuba Science City, to the north of Tokyo, spending a day interviewing scientists in an optoelectronics lab. In this field at that time, Japanese engineers led the world, and my hosts made sure I knew it. But at the end of the day, I sat down with the scientist who directed the lab; he had once studied at the University of Pennsylvania. After we'd gone through the list of his lab's advances, he let out a big sigh and in a "my life has been wasted" tone said, "But I still get the feeling that *all* the new stuff comes from the States. We're just applying it over here."

The tradition of large-scale, systematic learning explains the Japanese business visitors who copy down everything they see and hear when touring foreign factories, and the high-volume collection of data without obvious use. Daily life in Japan is full of measurements of things that other cultures just let slide. At the barber shop, individual strands of my hair were measured, and the lengths recorded, before and after the cut. During the swimming lesson at public schools, each child's body temperature is taken before he's allowed in the water—even though the same children go to school in shorts all winter and sit in only vaguely heated rooms.

Still, when every complaint has been listed and every grievance heard, the main fact about large-scale learning is that it fostered tremendous success. It is still under way. One of the clearest examples of Japan's commitment to systematic learning is the flood of Japanese students into American business schools. Most of the students are young employees of large Japanese companies, sent to America for a year or two at corporate expense. On its face this is a strange way for Japanese corporations to spend their money. For at least a decade the Japanese press has been full of disdain not just for the skills of American workers but even more for the mentality of American managers. The presence of the Japanese students can be seen mainly as an extension of the system for learning everything that can be learned about the surrounding, possibly threatening, environment.

Control. Learning from the foreigners was but one step toward a solution. To turn the knowledge into functional factories and research labs, Japan would need money, and it would need the concerted action of everyone in the country. Nearly a century and a half later, it has come to seem natural that the Meiji leaders obtained both those things. Political speeches routinely refer to "our national tradition of savings" and "our united national spirit." It is conceivable that Japan naturally has more of each quality than some other societies do. But the Meiji leaders left very little to chance.

Money was the most straightforward problem. Petty merchants had boomed during the late Tokugawa years. But they couldn't be relied on to make the large-scale investments—in railroads, engine plants, cannon works—necessary to put Japan on a par with the outside world. They lacked any system for pooling their capital for such grand projects. If this work were to be done, the state would have to encourage it—which it did by creating, coordinating, and protecting companies large enough to achieve the country's industrial goals. "The consistent aim of successive governments from the Meiji Revolution onward was to build Japan into a strong country with a top-class military capability and a top-class industry—a country which could not be defeated by the advanced nations of Europe and America," a Japanese scholar has written.[22]

In the 1850s and 1860s, after Commodore Perry's arrival, and a century later, after the era of the American Occupation, the Japanese had two main alternatives for modernizing their industry. They could try to improve the country's abilities across the board, upgrading many industries and many regions simultaneously. Or they could choose a few industrial champions and concentrate attention on them. Each time, Japan chose the second, more focused approach. This is one reason for the strange "duality" of today's Japanese economy, in which a superproductive semiconductor plant may sit next to a steam-powered sawmill.

But even the large, favored companies would need to find money, more money than might naturally come into their hands. Again, the Meiji leaders had two choices. They could borrow the money from outside the country, or they could somehow extract it from their people. At this same moment in history, the United States was taking the first approach. It borrowed heavily from foreign investors, mainly British, to lay its railroads, build its factories, expand its farms. The Meiji officials viewed this option as amounting to colonization in another form. From the beginning of the Meiji era until the turn of the century, Japanese interests arranged only two loans from foreign banks, both of them in Britain. One loan, for nearly a million pounds sterling, was for construction of a Tokyo-to-Yokohama railway in 1870. The other, for more than two million pounds, was to fund a pension system for government employees (including a number of samurai) in 1873. Both foreign loans were quickly repaid.[23]

Viscount Inouye Masuru explained at the time that even financiers and government officials opposed such loans, "some of them crying out, 'to make a foreign loan is to sell the country.' "[24]

This was to be an enduring belief. The single most unusual trait of
the Japanese economy, then and now, is the microscopically small
share that is owned by non-Japanese interests.[25]

If the money to develop Japanese industry were not to be imported, then somehow it would have to be extracted from Japan's
own population, most of whom were peasants as the Meiji era began.
As with its success in promoting systematic learning from the outside
world, the Meiji leadership devised institutions to help solve this
problem. Essentially these were means of raising the savings rate
above what it would naturally have been and concentrating the
money in the hands of the nation's big industrial investors. These
means included taxation (which put capital in the hands of government), suppression of wages (which left more capital for industry),
and a tolerance for business cartels (which raised prices and increased business profits). The Meiji government also engaged in
extensive public-education campaigns, to convince a nation populated mainly by peasants that they must gird themselves for
modernization.

"To further its development agenda, the government intervened to a remarkable degree in shaping the thoughts and behavior
of ordinary Japanese," Sheldon Garon, a historian at Princeton,
wrote in 1993.

> In area after area the Japanese government attempted to shape
> how ordinary people thought and behaved to a degree that
> would have been unthinkable in Anglo-Saxon societies and
> would have strained the limits of continental European statism.
> During the early twentieth century, the Japanese state actively
> regulated religious organizations, mounted pervasive "diligence
> and thrift" campaigns, and mobilized local women to improve
> social mores.[26]

The Meiji system was as a result "exploitative." Workers and consumers had an artificially small share of the national wealth; industry's share was artificially large. The bias of the system was similar
to that of the American system during World War II, when civilians
were exhorted to save and work in the name of national strength.
In the twentieth century Japan's economy retains much of this bias.
Wages, measured as a share of the national product, are lower in
Japan than in other industrial countries, and working hours are much
longer. In the Meiji era one official warned the public about its
tendency to slack off on Sundays:

Even if we now cause people to run day and night, we shall not overtake the West in less than a few decades. If such is the case, how much longer will it take if they waste a day [Sunday] each week?[27]

In 1992, when Japan's Ministry of Education decided that public-school students should have one Saturday off per month, a sociologist from Nihon University said, "I almost tend to think this is some kind of plot to weaken Japan's economic prowess by attacking the final fortress—education."[28]

KOKUTAI AS AN INSTRUMENT OF CONTROL. Frugality and diligence were only part of the civic virtues the Meiji leaders wanted to promote. They also considered it crucial to create a broad sense of loyalty, if possible, or obedience at least. In the last days before Commodore Perry's arrival, a Tokugawa-era intellectual named Seishisai Aizawa had argued that a mass ethic of loyalty and duty would be the only way for Japan to preserve its place in the world.[29] He wrote a famous essay called *Shinron,* or "New Theses," advancing a concept called *kokutai.* With an emphasis on *kokutai,* the essay said, Japan would create its own state religion, which would unify and motivate people the way that Christianity had motivated Europeans during the Crusades.

With *kokutai* we encounter one of those foreign terms worth noticing, like *Volk* or *Lebensraum* in German, because its connotations have had such a significant historical effect. The first of the two characters that make up the word *kokutai* means "nation," and the second means "thing" or "body." Together they are usually translated into English as the stilted-sounding term "national polity," but from the Meiji era through World War II the term took on the mystical, blood-bond overtone of "national will," "national essence," or even "soul of the nation." A film such as Leni Riefenstahl's *Triumph of the Will,* about the Nuremberg rallies of 1934, could be thought of as celebrating German *kokutai.*

During the agonizing last months of World War II, the Japanese war cabinet insisted that preservation of *kokutai* was its main goal in arranging surrender terms; in his surrender speech, which told the Japanese people that the war had turned out "not necessarily to Japan's advantage," Hirohito emphasized that *kokutai* had indeed been preserved.

In a book called *Japan's Modern Myths: Ideology in the Late Meiji Period,* Carol Gluck, of Columbia University, described the

evolution of the *kokutai* ideology during the late nineteenth century.
The Meiji leaders undertook a dual strategy: building political institutions that would help the country develop as quickly as possible,
and meanwhile inculcating beliefs and values that would let the
institutions work.

On the surface, the political institutions looked like those in
the Western countries Japan was so attentively studying. Instead of
a shogun's court, Japan soon had a parliament, or "Diet," plus a
cabinet of ministers, a court system, and a constitution. Structurally
the Japanese government looked very much like the British parliamentary system, with French and American touches.

Functionally, however, most of the new government's powers
lay with a cadre of skillful administrators who were responsible for
guiding the country's economic and educational makeover. During
Japan's preceding centuries of isolation, when the Tokugawa shoguns
had imposed internal peace on Japan, the country's samurai warriors
had less and less real fighting to do. Many of the samurai ended up
serving as administrators of the shogun's system. By the time the
Meiji era began there was an established tradition of skillful, elite
officials applying the rules that governed the nation.

Japan's entire legal structure changed during the Meiji years,
as it later did during the U.S. Occupation. But the impact on day-
by-day administrative decisions was less dramatic than the new rules
themselves might suggest. The most powerful means of control, in
the Meiji era and in late-twentieth-century Japan as well, are usually
the informal tools and unwritten rules that don't show up anywhere
in the lawbooks or on any of the organizational charts but that in
reality make all the difference in daily life. During the 1930s, for
instance, Japan's militaristic government did not want its people
listening to anti-Japanese broadcasts coming from China or the Philippines. The Meiji constitution, which was still in effect, guaranteed
certain civil liberties, and the government did not formally abrogate
them with a radio-censorship law. It simply tightened up a system
under which each individual radio set required a license. If a family
asked for a license on a set that could receive long-distance signals,
the license was not approved.[30] I think of this whenever I hear an
American lawyer or economist say that Japan must be a real democracy, since its constitution is so admirable, or that it has no
formal barriers to trade. This is like imagining that prenuptial agreements explain how most families really work.

By American standards, the closest comparison to Meiji era
modernization is the way bureaucrats in the Department of War ran

industrial production during World War II.[31] There was an underlying warlike spirit to the Meiji effort, designed to create a climate of cooperation and compliance from the public. The Meiji leaders saw themselves confronted by powerful, seemingly united nations—the English, the Americans, the French. For self-preservation they had to build a sense of nationhood out of what had been peasants, petty bureaucrats, people from little warring fiefs.

"It was not enough," Carol Gluck wrote, "that the polity be centralized, the economy developed, social classes rearranged, international recognition striven for—the people must also be 'influenced,' their minds and hearts made one."[32] She added:

> Not unlike American nativism of the same period, late Meiji ideology insisted on social conformity as the binding principle of national loyalty. It may seem odd to compare such a homogenous society as Japan to a nation of immigrants. But in fact Japanese nativism was often invoked for very nearly the same purpose, except that its targets were those within Japan who appeared to be bearers of alien ways and thoughts. This includes those who consciously advocated such unacceptable foreign notions as individualism or socialism as well as those who unwittingly pursued . . . unhealthy Western preoccupations with materialism and personal success.[33]

Foreigners usually tick off a list of traits that make today's Japanese society unusual—the devotion to duty, the willingness to suppress individual interests for the good of the group, the passive outlook toward those with political and economic power, the sense of kinship that is believed to unite *ware-ware Nihonjin* ("we Japanese") and separate them from the rest of the world. These traits may or may not have anything to do with the long sweep of Japanese culture, but they certainly were encouraged during the Meiji years.

As an example of this personality formation: Everyone "knows" that today's Japanese are fanatically devoted to duty. While I was living in Japan, I met a young American who had come to Tokyo looking for work and found it in a Baskins-Robbins ice-cream shop. After he had been there for several weeks, he seemed completely fatalistic. No other society could compete with Japan! Why? On their own time, after the shop was closed, he'd seen his young Japanese counterparts hold "precision contests." They would take turns digging out scoops of ice cream, with a prize to the one whose scoop weighed exactly 150 grams.

Maybe this sense of devotion to work is "innate," as many Japanese spokesmen say. But the Meiji leaders apparently did not think so, since one of their first steps was to issue proclamations about the need for duty, duty, duty.

The famous Imperial Rescript on Education, which was issued by Emperor Meiji in 1890, was posted in schools in every corner of the country, read aloud by teachers and school principals, and apparently taken very seriously. It portrayed a social system in which the emperor was on top; the people were as one, and were different from outsiders; and the ultimate purpose of each person's life was to carry out his or her duty, so as to advance the *kokutai*. The burdens of duty radiated out in all directions—to emperor, to parents, to children, to spouse. Loyal subjects were advised to "bear yourselves in modesty and moderation," to pursue knowledge, and to be ready to serve the state when called.*

The good and the bad effects of this character-forming effort

---

*The full text of the rescript, which was as familiar to Japanese of the prewar era as the Hail Mary was to practicing Catholics of the pre–Vatican II era, is as follows:

> Know ye, Our Subjects:
> Our Imperial Ancestors have founded Our Empire on a basis broad and everlasting and have deeply and firmly implanted virtue; Our subjects ever united in loyalty and filial piety have from generation to generation illustrated the beauty thereof. This is the glory of the fundamental character of Our Empire, and herein also lies the source of Our education. Ye, Our subjects, be filial to your parents, affectionate to your brothers and sisters; as husbands and wives be harmonious, as friends true; bear yourselves in modesty and moderation; extend your benevolence to all; pursue learning and cultivate arts, and thereby develop intellectual faculties and perfect moral powers; furthermore, advance public good and promote common interests; always respect the Constitution and observe the laws; should emergency arise, offer yourself courageously to the State; and thus guard and maintain the prosperity of Our Imperial Throne coeval with heaven and earth. So shall ye not only be Our good and faithful subjects, but render illustrious the best traditions of our forefathers.
>
> The Way here set forth is indeed the teaching bequeathed by Our Imperial Ancestors, to be observed alike by Their Descendants and the subjects, infallible for all ages and true in all places. It is Our wish to lay it to heart in all reverence, in common with you, Our subjects, that we may thus attain to the same virtue.[34]

are visible to this day. The good effects show up in the high level of minimum education (that is, the worst-educated person in Japan knows much more than the worst-educated person in America or in most of Europe), in the air of safety, in the person-by-person attention to duty that generally distinguishes successful from unsuccessful societies.

The bad effects are connected to the weakness of Japan's political system. What the Meiji system ultimately required of its people, as Carol Gluck has pointed out, was not participation but *submission*. The Japanese people were called "citizens," but they were really subjects. "By moralizing and mystifying the nature of the state," Gluck said, "politics was depoliticized."[35] Real political disagreement was not encouraged. As in a religious group or a military unit, dissent and disloyalty were the same.

It is too big a leap to go directly from Meiji indoctrination to the Japanese politics of the 1990s, since so many dramatic events intervened—democratic stirrings in the 1920s, militaristic fascism in the 1930s, the foreign Occupation in the 1940s and 1950s, and serious debates over Japan's political future in 1960. But something like the Meiji balance has been restored. Japanese citizens are not really citizens. They are mobilized, organized, and superbly well trained by the state and its institutions, but they have not really participated in its governance. As the writer Karel van Wolferen has put it, modern Japan lacks a "civic culture" in which citizens, intellectuals, journalists, and politicians freely debate how the society should be run.

No doubt the rulers of every society would prefer submissive citizens to any other kind. But through its post-Meiji history, Japan has differed from other "industrialized democracies" in that its fundamental policies were not democratically determined. The crucial decisions that in most countries amount to "politics" were rarely part of Japan's postwar election campaigns. The balance between economic growth and other social goals, the size of the government and its proper function, the nation's diplomatic aims in the world, the emphasis in school curricula—these and countless other "political" decisions have been made not by politicians at all but by highly skilled officials in Japan's central government ministries.

Both of Japan's sustained economic miracles—the one that led up to World War II, and the one that followed the war—were overseen by one-party governments and unaccountable bureaucratic rule. "Between 1892 and 1937 the party in power was never replaced by election," Robert Wade wrote of Japan in his book on Asian development *Governing the Market.* "The legislature from the beginning to the present has had less influence in the major decisions that affect national welfare than in any other industrial democracy, while meritocratically selected technocrats have had more."[36]

At a gross level the "elite bureaucrats" who ruled Japan clearly won popular assent. In their hands the country had become powerful, and although living standards were modest, the standards kept going up. "While in most developed countries the word 'bureaucrat' carries a negative connotation, suggesting a petty official who obstructs because of a preoccupation with form over substance, the term has stirred respect among most Japanese," James Sterngold of *The New York Times* wrote in 1993. "There are just 19,000 of these mandarins, but they administer a system that influences nearly every economic decision in Japan, from the way banks operate and how much doctors can charge to how businesses grow or shrink."[37]

When the world political landscape has changed suddenly— when the United States went off the gold standard in 1971, dramatically changing currency exchange rates; when oil-producing nations raised the price of oil in the early 1970s, increasing the cost of Japan's main import—the Japanese bureaucratic system has responded quickly and deftly to protect the nation's interests. But the system has long been paralyzed when it comes to setting its own agenda or serving as a forum for discussion among Japanese citizens about the direction in which the country should go.

Until the Liberal Democratic Party (LDP) lost its monopoly on power in 1993, Japanese politicians and journalists often joked that the only "opposition party" in Japanese politics was the government of the United States. If the American government grumbled about some barrier within the Japanese system, thereby applying *gaiatsu,* or "external pressure" to the system, the Japanese government would have to respond. Otherwise its policies would roll on undisturbed.[38]

In the summer of 1993, a reform coalition led by Morihiro Hosokawa denied the LDP its parliamentary majority. In August, 1993, Hosokawa became the first non-LDP prime minister since 1955. This was the most dramatic development in Japanese politics in at least a generation. The story of Japanese politics will turn on whether any elected government can shift the balance of power and bring the bureaucratic rule that was established during the Meiji years under control.

Purity and "proper place." In 1991, Japan's Foreign Ministry conducted a poll of young foreigners who were living in Japan. They were students, and they were corporate workers. They were black, white, Hispanic, and Asian. They had come from all over the world. The government asked them whether they were glad they had had firsthand exposure to Japan. Most of them said no.

The same poll asked the foreigners what had most irritated them about their time in Japan. Anyone who has lived in the country could guess the answer without looking at the results: Non-Japanese, in Japan, felt ground down by the constant reminders of the perceived racial gap between *ware-ware Nihonjin* ("we Japanese) and everyone else.

This is "perceived" racism because it is not always prompted by what outsiders would consider racial differences. As seen from the West, the Chinese, Koreans, and many Southeast Asian people would fall within the same large racial group as the Japanese—and yet these Asians, like most other foreigners, generally say that they feel discriminated against in Japan.

In the summer of 1992, the Japan Society of New York released a research paper on relations between Japanese and African Americans. The report concluded with a backhanded compliment. "If by racism one refers to values, attitudes, actions, and structures that cause one group to denigrate another because of color, then Japanese are not racists," the report's author, Reginald Kearney, wrote. "Color is largely irrelevant to Japanese discriminatory practices. Japanese tend to treat all foreigners similarly."[39] That is, Japan displayed a kind of "racism" that applied to everyone except the Japanese.

The main "minority" group within Japanese society, the so-called *burakumin,* are a separate, reviled caste—but are not distinguishable on sight from anyone else in Japan. Just as anti-Semites must do careful research to find out who really is and is not a Jew, an elaborate family-history system in Japan allows a potential employer, or a potential spouse, to determine whether someone bears any taint of the *burakumin.* Historically, these were the people who did society's ritually unclean work, such as handling dead bodies and working with leather. Denied other employment activities, they drifted disproportionately into gangsterdom. Because of their historic connection with cattle, they have also been overrepresented in Japan's modern-day beef industry. Japanese politicians have for years dragged their feet about opening the beef market, not because beef is a "strategic industry" but because they're afraid that the gangster/packer alliance will shoot them or beat them up.

The Japanese sense of "us-ness," then, might be called racial or tribal or straightforwardly xenophobic. Its consequences are so sweeping and obvious that it seems unsporting to do more than allude to them here. Apartment-rental guides in major Japanese cities have symbols that show how much the apartment costs, how much down payment is required—and whether foreign renters are allowed. Japanese universities have made it all but impossible to hire foreign-born scholars for tenured positions.[40] Most Japanese sports leagues either strictly limit the number of foreigners who can participate, or ban their participation altogether. And on and on through a thousand other episodes anyone with experience in Japan can recount.

In the Meiji era race-consciousness became a deliberate and useful organizing tool. The concept of *tenno-sei*, or the "emperor system," was promulgated, and the Shinto religion was revived. The two were obviously connected. Shinto boils down to a worship of Japaneseness—of the country itself, which was formed by lava dripping from the early gods' great spears; of the imperial line, supposedly unbroken for more than four thousand years; of the people, all descended from the sun goddess Amaterasu, and by definition united as a tribe and separated from the rest of mankind. "As a religion, Shinto is primitive," wrote the Meiji era scholar Tetsujiro Inoue, "but it is not merely a religion; in its relation to Japan's *kokutai* it is related to Japan's fate as a nation."[41]

The rhetoric and imagery of the "emperor state" dripped with ancient references, but in fact this was a modern attempt to invent, or revive and invoke, a useful past. Mussolini in the 1930s dressed up his regime by pretending to be a Roman emperor; something similar was under way in the Meiji state. Traditions that had been ignored or lain dormant for hundreds of years were resurrected to build loyalty to the state. The Meiji emperor, a boy of fifteen when he took the Chrysanthemum Throne, went to pray shortly afterward at the Ise shrine, the holiest Shinto site. This was presented as fulfillment of an ancient custom, but he was the first emperor in centuries to do so. Seventy years later, as Japan was on its way to war, fanatical loyalty to the emperor had come to be accepted as a basic trait of Japanese life.

In his remarkably shrewd journalistic book *Inside Asia*, published just as the United States and Japan were going to war, John Gunther pointed out the political impact of the emperor system:

The emperor, as head of the nation, was also head of a vast single *family,* if Shinto doctrine is to be believed; thus—to put it crudely—Shinto could be made to serve an extremely pertinent political aim, namely, the conception of indissoluble unity of the people.[42]

A natural corollary of the emphasis on Japan's "purity" and uniqueness, from the Meiji era onward, was the country's extremely sharp sense of "proper place." If Japan really was a tribe set apart, in a world full of foreigners who could neither become Japanese nor be relied on to sympathize fully with Japan, then Japan itself would have to "catch up" to survive. And to know whether it was catching up, it would have to know which other countries were ahead and which behind. It had to keep striving to attain its "proper place," in which the European powers would not be able to boss it around, and all of its neighbors in Asia would recognize what Japan had attained.

> In recent years all the Western countries have the intention of extending their power in the Orient. Everybody has seen that France has taken Annam, England has overthrown Burma and seized the Komun islands of Korea, Germany has seized the South Sea Islands, and Russia has been trying to expand her territory southward. Japan stands high out of the Eastern Sea, and since her geographical features are favorable and her products abundant, it is obvious that the Western powers have been drooling over our country. It is not easy to maintain our independence being situated in such an imperiled place.[43]

This was from an essay called *Nihon dotoku ron,* "On Japanese Morality," by an intellectual named Shigeki Nishimura. He published the essay in 1887, after Japan had been on the catch-up trail for roughly twenty years. There was no longer an immediate peril of being conquered by the Europeans, as the Filipinos, Javanese, and tens of millions of others had been. Yet Japan faced constant reminders that Western nations were powerful and willing to use their power.

Because the Americans and British had engines, cannons, and steam-powered warships while the Tokugawa shoguns did not, Japan had to swallow a number of unequal treaties in the late 1850s. These denied Japan the sovereign right to set tariffs and control what goods

passed across its borders. The treaties were uncomfortably similar
to the notorious treaties with which the Western powers had effectively colonized mighty China, and they posed a similar threat
to Japan's economy: It "stood in danger of being stunted or
'dwarfed,' " as China's had been.[44] "It was not until 1911 . . . that
Japan fully recovered her tariff autonomy," the scholar Michio Morishima has written. "During this time the Japanese were made to
feel well aware of the *misery of being a weak country*. . . . It was
experiences such as these in Japan which formed the background
for the ideas . . . which led up to the Pacific war."[45]

As the immediate risk of being conquered receded, the Japanese sense of injustice seemed to grow. Even when Japan achieved
success on Western terms, the Americans and Europeans seemed
to treat it as just another colored nation, just another object of
contempt. Within thirty years of Perry's arrival, Japan had moved
from an Elizabethan era craft economy to the first, or nearly the
first, rank of industrial powers. Ten years after that, in 1895, the
modernized Japanese Army controlled most of the Korean Peninsula
and had so thoroughly humiliated the Chinese Navy that the Chinese
government, for millennia the masters of East Asia, had to grant
all of Japan's territorial demands.

But even this victory produced another affront to Japan's pride.
Japan's central demand was control of the Liaotung Peninsula, including the city of Port Arthur, which Japan considered indispensable for defending its Korean territory. The Russian government
objected. It feared a showdown with Japan sooner or later and
viewed a Japanese presence on the Liaotung Peninsula as too threatening to its own interests. Because the Russian military was, at the
time, still stronger than Japan's, and because neither America nor
England was interested in supporting Japan's claim, the Japanese
had no choice but to back down. The situation was, in the words of
the historian W. G. Beasley, "a savage reminder that half a century's
work had still not put Japan in a position to ignore or reject the
'advice' of one of the major powers. It is no wonder that the shock
was great and that it engendered a mood of bitterness."[46]

Within another ten years this wound would be salved as Japan's
Imperial Navy, under the famous Admiral Togo, sank the czar's
Russian fleet at the Battle of Tsushima Strait. It was described
around the world as the first war in which a nonwhite country had
beaten a European power. The Indian leader Jawaharlal Nehru was
fifteen years old at the time. He wrote in his autobiography that he
and his friends had rejoiced at the news that an Asian nation had

beaten a "European colonialist," even though the Russians were hardly leading colonialists.[47]

The powers Japan had caught up with spurned it again and again. Before World War II the United States had imposed a humiliating "gentlemen's agreement" to keep Japanese immigrants out of America; it was an early version of the "voluntary export restraints" imposed on Japanese cars in the 1980s. At the Versailles Peace Conference after World War I, the Japanese delegation proposed that the covenant of the new League of Nations include a "racial equality" clause. The clause would have had no practical effect, but the Japanese government believed it would have been a sign that Japan had at last been embraced as an "equal" by the white Western powers. The Japanese delegation was also concerned about hostility to Japanese immigrants in the United States. When the American and British delegations refused to support the clause, Japan's representatives were deeply (and understandably) insulted.

In an extraordinary document known in Japanese as the "Showa Emperor's Monologue," which Hirohito dictated to one of his assistants just after Japan's surrender in 1945 but which was not made public until his death forty-four years later, the emperor himself traced the origins of World War II to the humiliation at Versailles, which (in Japan's eyes) rubbed in Japan's status as a "have-not" nation:

> Japan's call for racial equality, advocated by our representatives at the peace conference following World War I, was not approved by the Great Powers. Everywhere in the world discrimination between yellow and white remained, as in the rejection of immigration to California and the whites-only policy in Australia. These were sufficient grounds for the indignation of the Japanese people who suffered from having a small, overpopulated territory and a lack of raw materials, yet had considerable ability to develop.[48]

Three years after the Versailles peace conference, at the Washington Naval Conference in 1922, Japan felt cornered into accepting an inferior military status. The American, British, and Japanese fleets, according to the agreement, would have a permanent ratio of 5, 5, and 3, with Japan on the short end. The Japanese Navy had to give up its cherished plans for eight new battleships. "This was taken by the Japanese as a move by America and Britain to keep them down," a Japanese historian says. "Within the Japanese people as a whole there was a shift to the right and increasing hatred" of the white, Anglo-Saxon powers.[49] From these negotiations, influential Japanese drew the conclusion that idealistic Western rhetoric counted for only so much; what mattered was being strong.[50]

Just after the Washington conference, nearly twenty years before it would go to war with the United States, the Japanese military leadership drew up an extraordinary document, which was approved by the cabinet. It said that as Japan's power expanded, America's resistance would naturally grow. War between the two countries should probably be considered inevitable; the United States "will, sooner or later, as part of its Asian policy, provoke a conflict with the empire."

> The ostracism of Japanese residents in California will gradually spread to other states and develop a more solid base. There are no grounds for optimism concerning the position of our people in Hawaii. These conflicts, growing out of years of economic problems and racial prejudice, will be difficult to solve.[51]

The inevitable conflict finally came, in the prevailing Japanese view, with the formation of the dreaded "ABCD line" in the late 1930s. This event, now barely remembered in the United States or Europe, was the collaboration of the United States, England, Holland, and China to choke off Japan's crucial shipments of raw materials and fuel. The motive behind it was to protest, and possibly to slow down, Japan's expansion into China on its northern front and Indochina to the south. (America, Britain, China, and the Dutch made up the "ABCD" bloc.) Once the ABCD line was drawn, from the Japanese perspective, war really did become inevitable. If the Japanese didn't fight, they would starve and freeze to death. And if they didn't strike first, at Pearl Harbor, they might lose their chance to fight at all, as the United States continued to rebuild its navy and as the Japanese Navy used up its scarce remaining oil. In 1943 the wartime Japanese government formed the "Greater East Asia War Inquiry Commission" to look into the causes of the war. It said of the ABCD encirclement:

> The arrogant Anglo-Saxons, ever covetous of securing world hegemony according to the principles of the white man's burden, thus dared to take recourse to measures designed to stifle Nippon to death. It is small wonder that Nippon had to rise in arms.[52]

Pan-Asian Yearnings

As they have surveyed the world, Japanese leaders from the Meiji era on have felt victimized, vulnerable, and looked down upon. One natural result was the buildup of anti-Western resentment. The other result was the encouragement of a "pan-Asian," or *Ajia ichi,* school of thought, which had sprouted in the Meiji days.

In its extreme form the pan-Asian argument held that Japan should stop seeking the recognition of the white men and instead look to Asia for its economic future, its source of morals and knowledge, and its sense of national fulfillment. If it concentrated on *Dai Toa*—"Greater East Asia"—Japan could avoid the chronic snubs it suffered from the arrogant Western world. It could apply its stewardship and its wisdom to the other nations of East Asia. It could act as their champion, since it was the only one strong enough to stand up against the colonizing West. Asia would be one big, hardworking, and harmonious family, with Japan as the stern but fair father, the role it had earned by its efforts, and each other country in its own proper place. *Hakko ichiu* was the slogan, which literally meant "eight corners of the world, one roof," or "everyone under one roof."[53] Since Westerners seemed to dead set against recognizing Japan's proper place, it could find its deserved status among its own.

A typical statement of the pan-Asian outlook came from the renowned propagandist Kita Ikki, who wrote in 1919:

> The vast wealth of Britain extends over the whole world. Russia owns vast tracts of land in the northern hemisphere. Does not Japan, which in international terms has very much the status of a have-not, have the right to fight in the name of justice to break these monopolies? . . . That Japan, a proletariat in international terms . . . has had recourse to war to correct the injustices in international territorial boundaries is something to which people ought to give their unconditional approval.[54]

A generation later, when Japan had actually gone to war to defend its "proper place,' the rhetoric naturally became far more pointed. But the essential themes remain: Japan has been denied the respect it thought it had earned from the Western world, and therefore it was all the more important to assert its proper place within Asia.

Japan's pan-Asian policy had exactly one advantage from the perspective of other Asian nations: it hastened the departure of the European colonialists. The beginning of the end for the British in

Burma, the French in Indochina, and the Dutch in Indonesia all
came with the Japanese Occupation during World War II. The Japanese presence itself was not necessarily welcomed, but it served to
evict the Europeans and was therefore convenient for many Asian
nationalists. Soon after Indonesia became independent, in 1949, an
Indonesian politician told the American novelist Richard Wright
that the Japanese had been responsible for "one of the most decisive
factors in [our] winning independence." What was the factor?
Wright asked. The Indonesian replied:

> It was how the Dutch behaved when the Japanese came. They
> caved in. The Dutch were scared; they bowed; they wept; they
> begged; they all but crawled. . . . And we Indonesians said to
> ourselves, "If the Dutch are that scared of the Japanese, then
> why ought we be scared of the Dutch?"[55]

"An entire generation remembers the Japanese with gratitude,"
another Indonesian politician told Robert Elegant, a veteran journalist, in the 1980s. "It was the end of the white man when we saw
them as prisoners of war."[56]

Built into the pan-Asian outlook was a deep internal conflict
in Japan's view toward its neighbors and cousins. One part was
embarrassment at the squalor and backwardness of the rest of Asia.
How much better for Japan to be identified with the tea-drinking
Englishmen and the Beethoven-appreciating Germans! When the
first Japanese delegation arrived in Washington, D.C., in the 1850s,
its members discovered that white Americans looked down on
blacks, and they happily embraced that attitude. As they realized
that the whites also looked down on *them*, as Asians, that "did not
bother them much," according to the scholar Masao Miyoshi, "since
the Japanese would be like the whites someday. . . . Their identification with the whites and their resultant self-hatred were soon to
take the form of wild swings between pro-Western and anti-Western
national policies. And the gradually intensifying disdain for their
fellow Asians is inseparably linked with it."[57]

The other part of the pan-Asian mix was a reembrace of Japan's
Asian heritage at moments of spurning by the West. At the beginning
of the Second World War, Emperor Hirohito issued an imperial
rescript to outline the country's war aims. A book of commentaries
on the rescript sold more than 3 million copies during the war.

It included a plea that embraced both parts of Japan's conflicted view toward Asia:

> To speak the truth, the various races of East Asia look upon the British and Americans as superior to the Nippon race. They look upon Britain and the United States as more powerful nations than Nippon. Therefore we must show our real strength before all our fellow races of East Asia. We must show them an object lesson. It is not a lesson in words. It should be a lesson in facts. In other words, before we can expel the Anglo-Saxons and make them remove all their traces from East Asia, we must annihiliate them.[58]

Pan-Asianism turned out to be fraught with conceptual and practical problems. Economically, the vision of a *Dai Toa Kyoeiken,* or "Greater East Asia Co-Prosperity Sphere," was completely unrealistic. The rest of Asia could not supply enough raw materials, or buy enough Japanese products, to make up for Japan's dealings with Europe and the United States. The scheme was strategically unrealistic, too. The Japanese government allied itself with Hitler in 1940, on the assumption that he could beat the French and English and make their Asian colonies available to Japan. But this made Japan's Asian plans dependent on the result of a European war—and only worsened Japan's problems with the United States.[59]

The idea of Japanese supremacy was plainly not as popular with the Chinese, Koreans, and other lesser peoples as it was with its proponents in Japan. Asians "who bought this liberationist rhetoric soon choked on it, for the Japanese wasted little time in demonstrating how vicious conquest and colonial control could really be," the historian John Dower has said. "What the emperor's loyal troops did instead with the time they bought was create an enduring Asian legacy of suspicion and outright hatred toward the Japanese."[60]

The Japanese leadership had blinded itself to this inevitability by imagining that the rest of Asia would fall in line with the Japanese sense of natural hierarchy. Japan had bowed to Western strength when it realized its technological inferiority (meanwhile working hard to redress the imbalance). The graceful course for its neighbors would now be to bow to Japan. The self-delusion ran quite deep. In the summer of 1940, just before Japanese troops occupied Indochina (provoking the ABCD line and all-out war), Japan's foreign minister, Matsuoka Yosuke, explained the naturalness and inevitability of Japan's expansion:

> I have always said that the mission of Japan is to proclaim and demonstrate the *kodo* [imperial way] throughout the world. Viewed from the standpoint of international relations, this amounts, I think, to enabling all nations and races to find each its proper place in the world. . . . The immediate aim of our foreign policy at present is to establish in accordance with the lofty spirit of the *kodo,* a great East Asian chain of common prosperity with the Japanese-Manchukuo-China group as one of the links. We shall thus be able to demonstrate the *kodo* in the most effective manner, and pave the way toward the establishment of an equitable world peace.[61]

Still, pan-Asianism wasn't obviously more wrongheaded than a lot of European colonial schemes. The appeal of pan-Asianism within today's Japan seems to increase whenever Japan's relations with the West in general and America in particular are bothersome.

The Asian ideal is attractive in Japan during these moments of exasperation because it holds out three promises at once. It could bring an end to the condescension of the Western powers, a condescension evident even now when the Japanese prime minister is still obviously the odd man out at annual economic summit meetings. It could bring Japan a "proper place" of prominence and respect within Asia, based this time not on military but economic strength. And it could bring an alternative to the endless quarrels about whether Japan really believes in the same concepts of "democracy," "human rights," and "free trade" as are practiced in the West. The pan-Asian romantics say that these are imposed European concepts and that Japan should be allowed to operate by different, Asian rules, which are somehow instinctively understood by the peoples who all eat rice. Some Japanese intellectuals have argued for years that the simple act of growing rice shapes culture in profound ways. People must work together to coordinate the times their fields must be flooded and drained. This supposedly builds natural cooperation, which shows up now on the shop floor. During World War II, a Japanese textbook pointed out that all the countries Japan was occupying also grew rice; therefore they would bend naturally to Japan's will.[62]

There are recent signs of Japan's recurring desire to seek refuge in Asia as an escape from Western problems. Each winter, the Swiss resort town of Davos is the site for the World Economic Forum, a masters-of-the-universe gathering of financiers and government officials. The 1992 meeting took place just after President Bush's disastrous trip to Tokyo, during which he collapsed into Prime Minister Miyazawa's lap and reinforced America's image, in Japan, as a country that could whine but couldn't produce. Former prime minister Takeshita, who had been driven from the prime ministership in Spiro Agnew-like disgrace but was still one of the most powerful political bosses in Japan, came to the Davos conference, and there engaged in a kind of public love song duet with Li Peng, the Chinese prime minister. Japan was being criticized at the conference for its chronic trade imbalances—and for doing business eagerly with China, which in turn was being criticized for its human-rights problems. Takeshita and Li, on the defensive from other members, found comfort in each other. In a matched set of speeches, they implied a "new" Asian perspective that the Westerners perhaps could not understand. Kenneth Courtis, an economist with Deutsche Bank in Tokyo, described the scene. Takeshita, he said,

> was as an Edo daimyo with his staff of twenty-three retainers, holding court for two days, supplicant visitors including the Vietnamese, Chinese, and Taiwanese delegations. What he said was essentially that Japan would change, indeed had to change, but that it would not follow the road of those countries that had adopted "excessive individualism" and which led to crime, AIDS, poor education levels, and who knows what. And Japan understood the constraints that China faced and that Chinese society shared with other Asian countries, Asian values, as supposedly does Japan. . . . Li indicated that the market reforms had entered a new phase but that did not mean that the liberalism of the West was going to be tolerated.
>
> It was this double message that spoke more clearly than ever in the past that the wave of liberalism that has risen from Vancouver to Vladivostok stops at the Great Wall.[63]

Feeling Cornered

What is the motive for Japan's industrial structure? Why should a system that accepts low returns for hard work persist after the nation has succeeded in "catching up"? Why has it taken so long for the "universal" rules of economics to kick in for Japan? The country is rich, but the people don't take vacations. Prices are high, but the system resists buying from overseas. It is the "global age," but Japanese companies and society resist foreign presence. It is the age of free societies and free markets and "getting prices right," yet the Japanese government keeps pushing companies toward new technological goals.

The current intellectual environment for dealing with questions like these is like a vast field all planted with one crop. One mode of thinking—economic theorizing about "protectionism" and "competitiveness"—has driven out the competing possibilities. There's no healthy diversity left. Perhaps economic theory has become so dominant because it is, well, politically correct. The rules seem neutral and impartial. They avoid subjective judgments about why different nations behave in different ways.

But the economic tools are not enough, and the patterns of the past 150 years do tell us things we would otherwise miss. For entirely legitimate reasons, the leaders of Japan were terrified when Westerners arrived. China could not preserve its independence in the face of superior weapons and technology. Nor could Vietnam or the Philippines. Japan could—but in so doing, it set up institutions, habits, and outlooks whose effects persist in today's Japan and whose effectiveness has served as a model in many other parts of East Asia.

In the effort to avoid control by outsiders, Japan's leaders perfected systems for acquiring foreign knowledge. They built on existing patterns to develop a political, educational, and ideological network that combined the strengths of big business and big government and that consistently put the interests of the greater society ahead of the comfort and the individual Japanese. The United States has done this in wartime; Japan has sustained it for 150 years through war and peace. Japan developed a political system that stresses loyalty to the country and the collective good but that discourages debate about larger political goals. It intensified a sense of separateness, rivalry, and victimization relative to Western powers, and of deserved supremacy relative to other nations in Asia. Every society is tempted to feel this way about foreigners; beginning with the Meiji era the Japanese system inculcated these beliefs as an organizing ethic.

When the Meiji era leaders devised these catch-up systems, they did not know what kind of society they would create. Their goal for the moment was to create a society not run by foreigners. Eighty years later, the whole experiment seemed to have been a catastrophe. After catching up with the West, Japan had gone on expanding and militarizing. By challenging the Americans militarily, Japan brought on a calamity worse than what it had hoped to forestall. It was utterly defeated, and foreign soldiers, chewing gum, roamed through the country and made the rules.

Some historians, from Japan and elsewhere, now contend that Japan's overreach was built into the Meiji system. It was an authoritarian, quasi-fascist system that eventually matured into the real thing. A year before Japanese planes flew toward Pearl Harbor, the Canadian scholar E. H. Norman's book *Japan's Emergence as a Modern State* was published. It argued that the same strong-arm institutions that guided the country into the industrialism led naturally to the war machine that flattened Asia and was about to bump up against England and the United States. In 1964, as Japan was finally recovering from the war, a historian and polemicist named Fusao Hayashi wrote an *Affirmation of the Great East Asia War (Dai Toh Ah Senso Kotei Ron),* which emphasized the seamless nature of events over the previous century. What Americans called World War II was actually the last stage in a hundred-year war against the Western presence in Asia, Hayashi said. As William Chapman, an American journalist based for years in Tokyo, wrote about Hayashi's book:

> The first shots had been fired in 1863, when the British had shelled the southern port of Kagoshima, and in 1864, when a combined foreign fleet bombarded Japanese forces at Shimonoseki. All subsequent history was in some way a repetition of those dramatic encounters on the eve of the Meiji Restoration. Japan's war with Russia, her first defeat of the Chinese, and her later interventions in Manchuria and China had to be seen in the light of a grand purpose—to expel the barbarians—according to Hayashi. . . . It was, he said, a hopeless fight, but one that had to be fought. . . . It fits quite neatly with the vision of Japan as the noble, inevitably failing victim.[64]

Other historians claim that there were many paths open for Japan after the head start of the Meiji era. In this view, a combination of bad luck, a hostile international environment, and a failure of courage by Japanese democrats pushed the country over the brink.

One way or the other, the country was pushed; it occupied the rest of Asia; it went to war against the Anglo-Saxon world it had tried to catch up with; and it was utterly crushed. Everyone knows these facts. What happened immediately afterward is not well known—indeed, American policy has been based on not really knowing it. But it shapes modern East Asia and the post–Cold War economic world in ways the United States is only dimly beginning to recognize. This is the story of what happened during the years of the U.S. Occupation.

3

The American Years

I MOVED TO JAPAN in my midthirties. For the previous decade, like many others of my generation, I had tried to get exercise every day. I didn't fully realize how I'd come to rely on running or tennis for a sense of physical well-being until I couldn't do either of them for a period of several months. In Tokyo I spent hours trudging to and from train stations and up and down subway steps, but it was not the same. I felt like hell.

There was always an obstacle. I had to take the train too early in the morning. I had to stay out too late at night drinking with business "friends." On the weekends, the streets around my family's apartment were so jammed with people that trying to run was like playing rugby. Once I rode on a bus past a group of four public tennis courts in Tokyo. About a hundred people were waiting around the courts, hitting balls against a wall.

In desperation, I discovered two places where, when the conditions were right, I could run in relative solitude. One was the campus of Gakushuin University, a lovely enclave in the Tokyo suburb of Mejiro that looked like a fancy Eastern prep school and was in fact known as Japan's Princeton, a traditional haven for the genteel class. Princess Kiko, who became the heartthrob of the nation in 1989 when she married the younger brother of the crown prince, had been a student at Gakushuin. So had the famous novelist Yukio Mishima, who set scenes from *Spring Snow* there. A mile-long loop disappeared into the trees in the back of the Gakushuin campus. Each time I ran there I realized I was not the only one who craved its solitude. I would come around a bend to find a student practicing kendo, in traditional clothing; a couple walking and holding hands; once even an aspiring saxophonist, getting as far away from the crowd as possible to practice his songs.

The other site was in downtown Tokyo, on the periphery of the Imperial Palace. Running there meant finding someplace to change my clothes in the middle of the city, not an easy thing to do, but the ambiance of the palace was so unusual that I sometimes rode the train thirty minutes, in shorts and running shoes, to the Takebashi or Sakuradamon stops so I could run around the palace grounds. I preferred these stops because of their names, which meant, respectively, "Bamboo Bridge" and "Cherry Blossom Gate."

As I trudged out of the subway stop, amid crowds of salarymen in their polyester suits, I would see the blue-green tiled roofs of the palace poking above the battlements. The palace is surrounded by steep walls and a moat, in the center of the city. During the late 1980s, news reports always pointed out that the palace grounds were worth as much as all of Canada, or all of California, depending on the yen's rate that day. This said something about land prices in Tokyo but something more about assets still under the Imperial Family's control.[1]

The palace grounds in Tokyo are virtually unchanged from the era in which photographs were first taken. As you circle around the walls, you can see the backdrops for the famous ceremonial photos from Japan's modern history, minus only the bearded Meiji era officials or stern wartime overlords who filled the foreground. After the fall of Singapore, in the beginning of 1942, Emperor Hirohito* mounted a white charger and rode from the inner palace to the *Nijubashi,* or "double bridge," in the outer grounds. He sat there motionless in the cold, for an hour, as his people came to celebrate and do homage. The picture is everywhere in history books, one of

---

*A note about the names of recent Japanese emperors. The Meiji ("Enlightened Rule") emperor, whose given name was Mutsuhito, presided over Japan's great leap into modernity. He took the throne in 1868, at age fifteen, and died in 1912. His son then became the Taisho ("Great Correctness") emperor. Within a decade of assuming the throne, the Taisho emperor became mentally unstable. His son, whose given name was Hirohito, was named regent in 1921 and became emperor in 1926, on his father's death. The "era name" for Hirohito's rule was Showa, or "Enlightened Peace." After the death of Hirohito, the Showa emperor, in January 1989, his son Akihito became emperor. Heisei, or "Achieving Harmony," was chosen as his era name.

the most famous taken in Japan during the war years. The exact scene, with carefully bent trees looking virtually the same after half a century, is there today, except for the man and the horse.

On a misty day, tired after running, I looked across at the *Nijubashi* and imagined the emperor sitting there. Then I dimly realized what building was at my back. It was an ordinary, nondescript prewar office structure, with fat columns in the front. A small metal sign said in raised, Roman letters, *Dai-ichi Seimei*, "First Life Insurance." I had heard of this building but had never known exactly where it was.

The building was completely unexceptional now, not old enough to be distinguished, like many of the other financial buildings in the Marunouchi district across from the palace, not new enough to be stylish in any way. But for a time this had been the real palace. This had been Douglas MacArthur's governing seat during his reign as coemperor of Japan; it had been the GHQ of SCAP, the general headquarters of the Supreme Command of the Allied Powers, and of the supreme commander, Douglas MacArthur.

From this building, in his big car with the five-star general's flags flying, MacArthur had driven on September 27, 1945, to the U.S. Embassy, where another of the most famous photos of the 1940s had been shot. Douglas MacArthur, in an unadorned khaki uniform, with no tie and no hat, stands with a slight slouch. His hands are on his hips, his elbows are out, his weight is on his back leg—he has a look of slight impatience as if a press photographer has called out, "Just one more, please, General!" Next to him stands Hirohito: much shorter, ramrod straight, fingers slightly curled so the tips just touch the thumb, as Japanese are taught to do in formal portraits. He is wearing perfectly pressed Western morning dress, the stripes on his trousers hang absolutely vertically, his heels are together, and his feet are angled out as if hitting marks on a stage.

Every Japanese person I have met in Japan who was born before, say, 1950 remembers this picture. It is hard for any of them to discuss it without a surge of emotion—and I can understand why. This photo is a more intense version of the scene aboard the *Missouri*, in Tokyo Bay, when a limping Japanese official in morning dress signed the instruments of surrender to the bigger, more casually dressed Americans. In his surrender speech, the emperor had told his country that it must "endure the unendurable." The phrase might well have been the caption for his photograph with MacArthur. More even than the emperor's surrender speech, the picture conveyed the helplessness yet dignity of defeated Japan. The symbol of his nation bore himself with complete rectitude, next to a man so large and confident and powerful that he could afford to slouch.

I used to wish that I'd been alive in the 1820s in America, when so many national institutions were taking shape, or been in California in the 1920s, when there was empty space and people had big plans. After being in Japan for a while, I came to wish that I'd seen it during either the Meiji or the Occupation years. The dynamism of the Meiji era, in which the effects of several centuries of Japanese isolation were reversed in just a few years, would have been breathtaking to experience. The Occupation years were more bitter and desperate, but this was another period in which everything was up for grabs.

Japanese memoirs from that time have a resigned, stoic quality. Fathers were dead, houses were burned, families sold their heirloom kimonos and Edo-era woodblock prints to buy handfuls of rice. When Americans remember those days, some sound coarse and gloating and others—more—are drippingly sentimental, in the fashion of James Michener's *Sayonara*. Nearly all of the American accounts suggest the breathtaking sense of being present at Year Zero, when everything could be remade and redone. When I have asked the American veterans of the Occupation what they remembered most, almost all have mentioned the same scene: they could stand in the heart of the Ginza, on what is now the most expensive land in the world, and see in the distance the snowy cone of Mount Fuji, fifty miles away. This was a sign not simply of how Tokyo had been flattened but also that no factories were running to sully the air. (Forty-five years later, from my family's house in Yokohama, fifteen miles closer to Fuji, the mountain was visible only three times during one year.) Those seeing this tabula rasa could have no idea of what would happen next.

No military occupation can be truly enjoyable for the loser, but this one went remarkably well. The circumstances allowed each country to show its best side. The Americans, from regally casual MacArthur to the GIs-bearing-candies who learned to take off their boots when they went inside, were at their best as winners. The Japanese were the world's best losers: uncomplaining, dignified, ready to get back to work. In July 1945, the Japanese government had been preparing its women and children to fight to the death, with knives and bamboo stakes, to keep the hated Americans from despoiling the Divine Land. In August 1945, the United States dropped atomic bombs, twice, on Japanese civilians. But by August

1950, more than two thirds of the Japanese public said, in an opinion poll conducted by the *Yomiuri* newspaper, that America was their "favorite country."[2] By the same margin, they chose the Soviet Union as the country they most disliked.

"The United States soon established itself, in the minds of many Japanese . . . as the political, economic, and cultural center of the universe," the Australian historian John Welfield wrote. "Washington became, on a grander scale, what Chang'an had been for the aristocrats of the Heian era"[3]—that is, the Middle Kingdom, the pinnacle of power and refinement, the leader whose wishes must be accommodated and whose achievements must be studied with care.

MacArthur brought in with him a cadre of starry-eyed reformers, who were ready to break up the nasty feudalism in Japan the way they and their predecessors had broken up the trusts and monopolies in the United States. Some of the reforms changed Japan permanently, and for the better. Land was redistributed from landbaron families to tenant farmers. Today you can find yesterday's aristocrats grumbling about what they lost, but even most of them concede that this was indispensable to postwar Japan's economic and social rise. In the late 1980s, as the bloom was going off Corazon Aquino's presidency largely because of her failure to break up the huge landed estates, a Filipino woman told me, "We should have been your enemies in the war! Then you might have given us land reform, too!" In the early years of the Occupation, unions got new rights; women became, in theory, the political equals of men; and everyone talked about rooting out "feudal" remnants.

Moreover, what had been most wrong with Japan in the 1930s and 1940s—that it was invading and terrorizing the rest of Asia— was decisively changed during the Occupation. Article IX of the Constituton, mandated by MacArthur, declared a Gandhi-like defense policy for Japan. In its three-sentence entirety, the article says this:

> Aspiring sincerely to an international peace based on justice and order, the Japanese people forever renounce war as a sovereign right of the nation and the threat or use of force as a means of settling international disputes.
>
> In order to accomplish the aim of the preceding paragraph, land, sea, and air forces, as well as other war potential, will never be maintained. The right of belligerency of the state will not be recognized.

Article IX acquired tremendous talismanic power in Japan, even though it is hard to square what it says—"land, sea, and air forces . . . will never be maintained"—with the 250,000 fighting men Japan now keeps under arms. Japan has resolved this apparent contradiction with a lawyerly argument, as follows: Every nation has a fundamental right to defend itself. Since that right is fundamental, it can't be abridged by a mere document, like a constitution, any more than citizens can abridge their right to liberty by selling themselves into slavery. A "self-defense force," or *Jieitai* in Japanese, could therefore coexist nicely with a constitution saying that warmaking potential would "never be maintained."

The roots of Japan's antimilitarism can be annoying to foreigners, since they rest on the Japanese perception that Japan itself was the main victim of World War II. Whenever there is a debate about rearming Japan, the opposition's case boils down to: Militarism was bad for *us*, so why should we try it again? Nonetheless, this root of self-interest has made antimilitarism very powerful in today's Japan.

For all the benefits it brought, the Occupation was also the source of the frictions between Japan and the outside world that are showing up today. The governments of the United States and Japan, for reasons that seemed wise at the time, made fateful decisions, especially about Japan's military and diplomatic role, that have become very difficult to reverse. The Occupation made Japan dependent on America in a relationship that was generally described in Japan as "big brother/little brother." The relationship depended on great American wealth—great enough so that the United States could defend Japan, great enough that it could afford to overlook economic quarrels—yet this very relationship guaranteed that the cushion of American wealth would erode. The longer the relationship went on, the more certain it became that the relationship could not continue.

America's Changed View of Japan

By the time the Occupation was over, Americans were used to thinking of Japan as an America in embryo. No one would put it just that baldly, of course, but it is impossible to explain how Americans dealt with Japan in the 1940s and 1950s and how they talked about Japan for the next thirty years without reaching that conclusion.

The explicit problem posed for the Occupation was how to keep Japan from ever "going ape" again, in the phrase George Ball used after the war to describe the country's penchant for militarism. As the war neared its end, the U.S. government had undertaken a mammoth effort to determine what had gone wrong in Japan. Ruth Benedict's famous book *The Chrysanthemum and the Sword,* written by a woman who had never been to Japan and had no knowledge of the language yet nonethless produced an insightful and influential work, was one fruit of this effort. The writings of E. H. Norman also became, for a while, tremendously influential.

Norman was a Canadian citizen who had grown up in Japan, where his parents were missionaries. He returned to North America for study before the outbreak of Japanese militarism, eventually finishing a doctorate at Harvard. In 1940, at age thirty-one, he published a *tour de force* book called *Japan's Emergence as a Modern State.*[4] Norman had become a Communist and was active in student-leftist circles in the United States and England. His book was to a degree a sorting out of two rival schools of analysis within Japanese communism. The argument between the schools involved how many stages of feudalism and bourgeois democratic reform were left before the revolution came.

Norman's book, beautifully written and free of Communist jargon, had an immediate practical lesson for American reformers. The war had started, he said, *because* of the institutions put in place during the Meiji years. The same authoritarianism, the same centralized control, the same all-obsessive attempt to catch up with the West—all these things set up a momentum that led naturally toward aggression in the rest of Asia and to war with the United States.

Naturally, Norman's argument was more elegant and subtle than this condensed version—just as Michael Harrington's argument in *The Other America* was more subtle than "America still has a lot of poor people," and Jean-Jacques Servain-Schreiber's in *Le Défi Américain* was more complicated than "Watch out for the Yanks." But books that have a political effect often have it in a one-sentence version. The boiled-down version of Norman's argument was: If you want to keep Japan from going on the warpath, make it a democracy at home. At the end of the war, the U.S. military produced indoctrination films explaining, with a tone of patronizing understanding, that the average Japanese citizen could not help behaving like a robotized brute. For the previous seventy-five years he'd been crammed with propaganda about the joy of dying for the emperor; those years of mental warping had to be undone.

As the Occupation began, in the fall of 1945, every part of the American experience suggested that, with enough time, it should be possible to remold Japan. When immigrants came to America, they could be remade, as individuals, relatively quickly. Refrigerators, nylon hose, universal suffrage, and three good square meals a day could do the same for Japan. In his book *The Reckoning,* David Halberstam quoted the reaction of Perry Miller, a renowned professor of American literature at Harvard. Miller toured Japan near the end of the Occupation and remarked that the whole undertaking "was an effort to make of Japan, a new Middle West—not, of course, the Middle West as it is, or in fact ever was, but as it perpetually dreams of being."[5] The Japanese professed their eagerness to learn from America; the Americans were enthusiastic about such willing pupils. One influential American memoir of those days was called *Remaking Japan: The Occupation as New Deal.* The introduction, by another American veteran of the era, expressed the guiding, idealistic faith of those years: "The new Japan and, especially, its economic institutions were to be rebuilt in democratic form to safeguard the peace of the world."[6]

Douglas MacArthur, whose viceregal personality affected everything about the Occupation, revealed its underlying faith in an intriguing way. MacArthur's father had been America's first military viceroy; he ruled the Philippines as military governor after the United States took over in 1898, the year young Douglas entered West Point (with his beloved mama taking up residence, to watch over him, at the West Point hotel). The younger MacArthur took to heart a speech the bloviating William McKinley had given about America's civilizing mission in the Philippines. Under American guidance, McKinley said, the Philippines would become "the gem and glories of these tropical seas, a land of plenty and increasing possibilities . . . whose children and children's children [will] for ages hence bless the American Republic, because it emancipated and redeemed their fatherland and set them in the pathway of the world's best civilization."[7]

When MacArthur, in his memoirs, quoted these words of McKinley's, he was really (as the Japanese historian Tetsuya Kataoka has emphasized) talking about his own ambitions in Japan. In 1951 he gave the U.S. Senate a famous and amazing summary of the philosophy behind his Occupation reforms:

> If the Anglo-Saxon was, say, forty-five years of age in development in the sciences, the arts, divinity, culture, the Germans were quite as mature. The Japanese, however, in spite of their antiquity measured by time, were in a very tuitionary condition.

Measured by the standards of modern civilization, they would be like a boy of twelve, as compared with our development of forty-five years. Whatever the German did in dereliction of the standards of modern morality, the international standards, he did deliberately. . . . But the Japanese were entirely different. There is no similarity.[8]

In the long term, the significance of statements like McKinley's or MacArthur's was not their condescension. It was instead their faith that "growing up," being "set . . . in the pathway of the world's best civilization" would mean *becoming like the Western world,* or at least like the United States and the Western European countries Japan thought of as its true peers. America, along with its temporarily misguided German brothers, represented social maturity, economic development. If you wanted to know what a society looked like in middle age—at "forty-five" in MacArthur's terms—you need only look at the United States.

Viewed from outside the physical and spiritual boundaries of the United States, this assumption—that to become modern is to become like America—has some obvious logical limitations. Nonetheless, the impulse to believe it is very strong in America—which has evidence each day that other nations are wearing its blue jeans and listening to its pop music—and is powerful in many other parts of the Western world. The Germans and the Dutch may realize that the world is not taking up their languages, the Italians and the Swiss may acknowledge that their pop music lacks fans anywhere else in the world. Even so, the essence of the modern Western worldview— a rational approach to science, an approach to government based on individual rights, an economic system tending more and more to laissez-faire—is catching on everywhere else. Two generations after the Occupation's end, Francis Fukuyama's essay "The End of History," in *The National Interest* magazine, presented an erudite and argued-through version of the concept that all societies must, in the long run, follow America down the road to consumer-oriented liberal democracy. Fukuyama later allowed for the possibility that Asian-style capitalism, pioneered in Japan, might be a long-term challenge to the Western liberal model. Nonetheless, without ever reading such writings or considering refinements on an "end of history" thesis, most Americans seemed to trust that the more Japan "grew up," the more familiar and American it would become.

Douglas MacArthur's own version of the ideal American society might have been different from that of his countrymen. Like

Commodore Perry, MacArthur was a quite unrepresentative American—royalist, antidemocratic in temperament, uncomfortable with the pushing and shoving of real democracy, successful largely because of his authoritarian streak. Yet he became convinced that the key to putting Japan on its feet was a series of sweeping social and economic reforms. In a conversation with George Kennan during the Occupation, MacArthur compared his supervision of Japan to Julius Caesar's rule over Britain and France, and said that his land reform was the most successful since the efforts of the Gracchus emperors of Rome.[9] The purpose of these reforms, he emphasized, was to create a society on the road to capitalism and democracy— which meant, in the only practical terms anyone could imagine, on the road to Americanism.

"SCAP officials were ordered to 'democratize' Japanese society without having any clear idea of what 'democratization,' abstractly and in a culture-free formulation, might entail, or what the end result might look like," wrote Chalmers Johnson in a history of Occupation-era labor strife. "They therefore tried to Americanize Japanese society. . . . This simplified matters a good deal—one needed to know something about America, not Japan."[10]

It all seemed to go swimmingly because of the Japanese capacity to tell the Americans what they wanted to hear—and the even greater American capacity to see what they wanted to see. This is the chronic weakness of conquerors, amplified by the American belief that, deep inside, everyone is a potential American.

In keeping with the idea that Meiji era propagandizing was the root of Japanese aggression, one of the Occupation's first efforts was to remove pernicious nationalism from Japan's schools. Throughout the country, teachers stood before their students and took them page by page through their textbooks: All right, children, everyone tear out page 23 and pass it to the front of the room. Now, on page 24, take your brushes and black out the words *Dai Toa Kyoeiken* ("Greater East Asia Co-Prosperity Sphere"). Meanwhile, American experts were announcing that the centralized Japanese education system was itself the problem. It should be more like America's, with thousands of school districts setting their own policies. And instead of all the emphasis on conformity and duty, individual self-expression should be the goal. "Citizens, not subjects" was the philosophy of the American educational system, and Japan's should work the same way.

"*Yes, yes!*" the Japanese education officials replied. "Individualism and antifascism are just what we need!" Wherever the Americans went, their plan seemed to be taking effect. "The Americans assigned young officers, one to each prefecture, to supervise the progress," Thomas Rohlen of Stanford noted in his book *Japan's High Schools:*

> [T]hese men bounced around the countryside in their jeeps supervising reform in schools and communities without in fact directing action. In Kobe, I heard stories of principals in middle schools ordering their students to begin square dancing upon the approach of an American jeep.[11]

As William Chapman observes in his book about the Occupation, *Inventing Japan,* "a gap emerged between what SCAP thought was happening and what actually was happening among the Japanese." There were sporadic efforts to close the gap. For example, Mark Gayn, a young American newspaperman, traveled through the countryside with a Lieutenant Hartley, looking for traces of backsliding among schoolteachers and average citizens. As they began to suspect that the teachers had been tipped off to their visits and had prepared Potemkin classroom scenes, they began going to schools unannounced. Still, the teachers had obviously known they were coming—when the Americans made their lodging reservations, the innkeepers had tipped off the schools. As William Chapman says,

> Dejected, Gayn and Hartley planned a stealthier school raid. The local train from Otuki passed through four small towns on its way to the city. They would board it without telling anyone their destination, then hop off at the village of Mitumine and arrive unannounced at the local school. . . . At Mitumine, they bounded onto the platform to find a greeting party which included the mayor elegantly clad in a cutaway suit. Welcome to Mitumine, the mayor said. How would they like to visit the schools? Defeated once again, the two Americans glanced over more shiny classrooms and ate more tea and rice crackers. Later they discovered why their surprise raid was not a surprise. Police had alerted mayors and school principals at each of the train's four village stops. All down the line receptions had been planned by smiling men in formal clothes and teachers with hot tea. Gayn and Hartley gave up.[12]

Leaving Prewar Institutions in Place

The American occupiers certainly did not give up on their efforts
to reform Japan's laws, nor did Americans give up on their person-
to-person contacts with the Japanese over the ensuing decades, nor
did Westerners in general give up their interest in Japan's art and
culture and religion, nor did the U.S. government give up its belief
that Japan was its linchpin in the Pacific. But from an early point in
the Occupation, perhaps from the very start, the United States gave
up any attempt to match the effort that had seemed indispensable
to Japan a century before: *really* understanding how the other culture
worked, rather than assuming it must work by the same principles
as your own.

Some of this was inevitable. MacArthur decided, early on, that
it was neither wise nor practical to have an army of occupation in
the classic sense, with Americans reaching their tentacles into every
corner of Japanese life. Americans did not control Japan's taxes;
they did not run its courts; they did not demobilize its army; they
did not take over its schools. In Germany, the Allies showed up in
a country whose government had disappeared. Japan, though thoroughly beaten, surrendered while a functioning government was still
intact. The Americans formed a thin supervisory layer[13] over a government whose operations they did not control and—for reasons of
language, manpower shortage, and disinclination—did not really
understand. This, as would become apparent after the Americans
left, had some unforeseen long-term consequences.

In his book about Japan's postwar recovery *MITI and the Japanese Miracle,* Chalmers Johnson described the way that the functions of the prewar Ministry of Munitions had been passed more or
less intact to the postwar Ministry of Commerce and Industry, which
midway into the Occupation was renamed the Ministry of International Trade and Industry, or MITI. Some two hundred thousand
Japanese bureaucrats, soldiers, and politicians were eventually
purged from the government for their activities in the war. But the
prevailing view in Japan, then and now, was that this represented
"victor's justice"—the "criminals" and purgees were being punished
for losing, rather than to atone for deep sins against the natural laws
of mankind. As soon as the purge orders expired, many of these
officials returned to politics.

Nobusuke Kishi was held in Sugamo Prison on "Class A" war-
criminal charges. He was released in 1948 and became prime min-

ister by 1957. Mamoru Shigemitsu was sentenced to seven years in prison on Class A war-crimes charges. He was paroled early, and became foreign minister in the 1950s. Okinori Kaya was sentenced to life imprisonment for "Class A" crimes, including his service in the wartime government under General Tojo. He had been paroled by 1958; by 1963, he was the country's justice minister.[14] It is hard to imagine a similar mass return of Nazi officials to the postwar West German government; the ease of so doing in Japan reflected the general sense that the country had committed no sin except losing—especially since the emperor himself, in whose name the officials served, was also absolved of guilt (as we will see).

After the Nuremberg trials were over, the West German government, prodded by its neighbors and the government of Israel, conducted several of its own Nazi-hunts and war-crimes trials. When the Tokyo trials, run by the Allies, had ended and Prime Minister Tojo and six others had been hanged, the Japanese government let the matter rest and conducted no further trials on its own. The comparison to postwar Nazi-hunts was offensive in Japan: those people may have been beasts; our problem is that we lost. Moreover, the Japanese public had not, in any broad sense, endorsed or authorized the policies that led to war. When the war was under way, Japanese citizens cheered their army's and navy's victories, as most citizens anywhere would. But the militarized government that invaded China and attacked the United States made no pretense of being a democratically chosen reflection of the popular will, as Hitler had in his early days.

While there was tremendous revulsion after the war against the militarists who had led Japan into catastrophe, not as many aspects of Japanese life were changed, or changed as deeply, as the Americans wanted to believe. "Great progress was made, and it would be foolish to underestimate SCAP's accomplishments or to belittle the genuine iconoclasm that was churned up in Japanese society by the defeat, by the release from emperor worship, and by the American presence," Chalmers Johnson wrote in his study of labor unrest:

> But it was too easy. . . . The success of the Occupation was anomalous: there was not enough arguing, backsliding, and contention to believe that anything was really happening. Japanese society did not seem to be giving off the heat that is inevitably generated by real social change.[15]

America's Need to "Reverse Course"

Everyone in Japan is familiar with two English phrases that very few people in America would recognize. They are "reverse course" (or *gyaku kosu* in Japanese) and "Dodge line." Each refers to the dramatic change in Occupation policy, driven by the Cold War, that set Japan on its current path.

During the first years of the Occupation, the fervent American reformers may have not made Japan into America, but they certainly made it more liberal than it had been before. The big prewar cartels, called *zaibatsu* (literally "financial clique"), were broken up. Fair-trade commissions went to work with a vengeance, rooting out price-fixing and the informal networks through which big companies kept in touch. Labor unions got sweeping new rights. Communists were let out of prison, and they soon were at the head of major unions. When they weren't checking dossiers to see who should be purged, the Occupation authorities were ordering factories to cease production and in some cases actually dismantling them so machinery could be shipped to the rest of Asia as reparations.

It was the full liberal package, more sweepingly imposed than it has ever been in the United States—and its results would bring grim satisfaction to any true conservative's heart. The early reform plan nearly killed Japan's economy. At least five million soldiers and civilian laborers returned from Manchuria and Southeast Asia and found no jobs to fill. Farmers and their sons and daughers were drifting from the countryside into the big cities, with little work for them. By 1946 Japan, with a total population of fewer than 80 million, had 13 million adults who were unemployed.[16] In that same year, the country's industrial output was only one third the level it had reached in 1930, and by 1948 it was barely half the 1930 level.[17] (By way of comparison, in 1948 American industrial output was nearly four times greater than it had been in 1930.) Japan's farm output was about half its prewar level. Japanese people who now reminisce about that era always begin by talking about the search for things to eat.

On May Day 1946, half a million Japanese demonstrated outside the Imperial Palace, and smaller rallies took place across the country. In 1947 radical leaders planned a nationwide general strike, which MacArthur intervened to stop at the last moment. The Communists leading many unions, especially the all-important railroads, were not simply leftist in temperament but often were instructed agents of the Soviet Union, causing disruption for its own sake. In

July 1948 there were daily incidents of train sabotage or train wrecks.[18] Early in 1949, the president of Japan National Railroads was run over and killed by a train. The case was never solved, but there were widespread suspicions that he had been murdered. Two days earlier, this same man had handed out dismissal notices to thirty-seven thousand railroad employees. Later that year, an unmanned train was sent plowing through a station in Mitaka, just outside Tokyo, where it killed six people. A group of Communists was convicted of the crime. Shortly afterward, north of Tokyo near the village of Matsukawa, a passenger train was deliberately derailed, killing two and injuring many. Another group of leftists was caught and tried.[19]

In the spring of 1986, my family lived for several months near a tiny commuter railroad station called Shiinamachi, in the northwestern suburbs of Tokyo. In 1948, a tidy-looking middle-aged Japanese man had walked into a bank in this same neighborhood and announced that he was from the Public Health Department. He asked everyone present to drink a cholera vaccine he was distributing. They complied, but the vaccine was actually cyanide poison. Twelve people died while the man robbed the bank.[20]

It was a very different Japan from the one invoked by today's rhetoric about the "harmonious rice-paddy culture" and the near-total absence of violent crime. And it was a Japan that George Kennan, who then had great influence over the shaping of the U.S. "containment" strategy toward the Soviet Union, considered potentially disastrous for American interests, when he visited Japan in 1948. Since the time when the first bright-eyed Occupation reformers had thought about leading Japan out of the feudal age, the surrounding world had changed. The United States and the Soviet Union were now locked into a full-scale Cold War. The Communists, under Mao Tse-tung, had nearly completed their takeover of mainland China. Other countries of Asia were bubbling with various degrees of anti-Western agitation. This cast the situation in Japan in a completely different light.

Even before the war had ended, conservative Japanese were warning that the real nightmare was not defeat itself but the Communist revolution that might follow. In the beginning of 1945, American troops were preparing for the invasion of Okinawa that would be the first step toward the grim task of seizing the home islands. At the same time, Vice Admiral Takijiro Onishi of the Imperial Navy, mastermind of *kamikaze* strategy of destroying the U.S. Navy with suicide-bomber planes, was calculating that it might take more

than a million *kamikaze* pilots for the final defense of Japan. At just
that moment, in February 1945, Prince Fumimaro Konoe wrote a
famous memorandum to the emperor warning him that defeat, and
something potentially worse than defeat, lay ahead. Prince Konoe
was a flamboyant nobleman who had been prime minister until just
before the attack on Pearl Harbor. He was the only wartime prime
minister not put on trial for war crimes by the Allies, a fate he
avoided by killing himself when he learned that his arrest was near.
In his memorandum, six months before the final surrender, he told
the emperor that "defeat is inevitable." Losing the war, he tactfully
pointed out, would be "a blemish on our *kokutai*." Yet there was a
worse possibility.

> More than defeat itself, what we must be concerned about from
> the standpoint of preserving the *kokutai* is the Communist rev-
> olution that may accompany defeat.[21]

After the war Japanese conservatives emphasized a similar warning
as, in their view, the Occupation reformers went wild. Shigeru Yoshida, the giant of midcentury Japanese politics who had just become
prime minister, went to MacArthur in his headquarters and asked
whether "his intention was to turn Japan Red."[22]

Kennan took this prospect more seriously than MacArthur
seemed to. Like MacArthur, Kennan was an unrepresentative American. The oddity of these men lay not just in their obvious abilities
but also in the ways their impulses veered from the American norm.
MacArthur was a royalist from a nation of small-d democrats. Kennan had devoted his life to diplomacy but was deeply skeptical of
the missionary, reformist, universalist views that pulsed through the
rhetoric of Woodrow Wilson, Franklin Roosevelt—or Douglas
MacArthur, when he talked about remaking Japan. By the time he
got to Japan, Kennan had propounded his famous "containment"
thesis for the Soviet Union. In the late 1940s, the logic of U.S.-
Soviet tensions would seem to be leading inevitably to all-out war.
"Containment," in Kennan's view, was a practical-minded way to
cordon off the most sensitive areas of potential conflict without
imagining that America was undertaking a crusade to save the Soviet
soul.

When he got to Japan in March 1948, Kennan once again saw
idealism gone amok. The Occupation's reformers had big plans and
noble ideals, but in the short run they were making life miserable
for most Japanese. The result would be to make recovery, or even

stability, impossible for Japan. In a theoretical world sweeping democratization might also help an economy get back on its feet, but in the real Japan of the immediate postwar era the two goals seemed to conflict. Kennan's most famous conclusion is too verbose to be memorable as an epigram, but its meaning comes through:

> The nature of the occupational policies pursued up to that time by General MacArthur's headquarters seemed on cursory examination to be such that if they had been devised for the specific purpose of rendering Japanese society vulnerable to Communist political pressures and paving the way for a Communist takeover, they could scarcely be other than what they were.[23]

"All we were doing," he said in much crisper form, "was tearing apart the closely woven fabric of Japanese society. Some of the young officers in GHQ SCAP were outdoing the Russians in their enthusiasm for uprooting traditional structure."[24]

From concerns like this flowed the "reverse course" and the "Dodge line" now so familiar in Japanese history. The crusade to democratize Japanese society had proven incompatible with the need to get the Japanese economy going again, at least in the short run. If the economy kept floundering, the Communist labor organizers and Communist Party propagandists would keep increasing their already considerable power. If that happened, the United States would have not just Stalin's Soviet Union to worry about, and not just the newly Communist China of Chairman Mao, but also an emerging Communist state in Japan, where America was theoretically still in control.

It was time to shift gears, forget about a Japanese New Deal, put bread (rice) on the workers' tables, and get smoke coming out of the factory chimneys again. As part of this "reverse course," the Detroit banker Joseph Dodge showed up in 1949 with a stern, eat-your-spinach package of reforms for the Japanese economy. No more overstaffed bureaucracy: he urged the government to fire one sixth of its employees. No more featherbedding at the railroads. No more deficit spending in an attempt to get the economy going; Dodge recommended higher taxes and smaller budgets. It was Republican-style economics, in the pre-1980 version.

Douglas MacArthur clearly disagreed with the program. It seemed to him bean-counting and small-minded. Yet by the middle of 1948 influence over economics was shifting from MacArthur to people who thought like Dodge.

Within another three years, after MacArthur had left Japan to command the U.N. forces in Korea, Occupation strategy had taken a more amazing lurch. As American troops were redeployed to Korea, U.S. strategists worried that they might not be able to defend a completely demobilized Japan. Soon after Kennan's trip to Japan—which is to say, less than three years after mandating the Peace Constitution—the U.S. National Security Council was discussing ways to rearm Japan by beefing up a national "police force." In July 1950, as American soliders were being drained into Korea, Douglas MacArthur ordered a seventy-five-thousand-man National Police Reserve into existence to offset the missing GIs. Three months later, the United States secretly ordered Japan to begin minesweeping operations off the Korean coast.[25] Over the next few years, under strong U.S. pressure, Japan resurrected its military—not, of course, as a real army, navy, or air force, since that was explicitly forbidden by Article IX of the Constitution, but as what eventually became known in the 1950s as a "Self-Defense Force," or *Jieitai*.

The Cold War View of Japan

Joseph Dodge arrived in Japan early in 1949. The Berlin Wall came down late in 1989. During those forty years, America's policy toward Japan—and, more important, its conception of Japan—were shaped less by Japan itself than by fears of the Soviet Union. It was indispensable that Japan itself not "go Communist" or come under the Soviet Union's political sway. The United States should do everything possible to permit its own continued use of military bases in Japan.

Japanese strategists sometimes lamented the unfairness of the country's geographic location, so close to potential enemies in Siberia, China, and Korea. From America's Cold War point of view, this location was ideal. From the far south of Japan, on the Ryukyu chain that included Okinawa, the United States could patrol the southern coast of China and Taiwan. Near the center of the country, the U.S. Navy could enjoy superb repair and maintenance facilities at Yokosuka, outside Tokyo and a natural stopping point on voyages across the Pacific. From the north, with bases on Hokkaido and the northern tip of Honshu, the U.S. Navy could menace the home port of the Soviet Pacific Fleet. That fleet's main headquarters were in Vladivostok. Any Soviet ship trying to leave that harbor for the open sea had no choice but to pass through one of four straits, all of which a Japan-based navy could bottle up. (From the north, these are Soya Strait, between Hokkaido and the southern tip of Sakhalin Island; Tsugaru Strait, between the southern tip of Hokkaido and the northern end of Honshu; and Tsushima Strait and Korea Strait, between southern Japan and Korea.) It is more or less as if the U.S. Pacific Fleet had its main base in Oakland, California—and an enemy controlled the Golden Gate.

Douglas MacArthur had felt that the United States did not need to make Japan a permanent military staging point. The United States could, instead, dot its bases through the Philippines, Midway, and even Okinawa (which the United States held until 1972), without any need to put them on the main Japanese islands. But in this as in economic policy he lost out to the Kennan view. By the late 1940s, George Kennan was arguing that bases on Japan, together with those in the Philippines, must be the "cornerstones of a Pacific security system adequate for the protection of our interests."

> If we could retain effective control over these two archipelagoes,
> in the sense of assuring that they would remain in friendly hands,
> there could be no serious threat to our security from the east
> within our time.[26]

Forty years later, in the late 1980s, whenever I interviewed American diplomats or soldiers, I would hear the same ideas in more or less the same words. Yes, it could be annoying or troublesome to maintain an overall alliance with Japan, they would tell me. But any possible alternative would be much, much worse. Did we want those impressive chip and robot makers to be selling their wares to the Soviet military rather than ours? To the Iranians or the Libyans? Did we want to find some other home for the fighter and spy planes now nestled right next to Siberia? Did we want to guarantee the Soviet Fleet free passage through the crucial straits? Did we want the Japanese government to stop picking up half the cost of keeping our forces in their country, at a time when America was having to pay Spain, Greece, the Philippines, and other countries for the right to keep our troops there?

By the end of the 1980s, the strategy that Kennan had envisioned, the historic plan for containing Soviet power, had clearly worked. The world's main Communist regime had collapsed, the Soviet empire in Europe was freed, and the two superpowers had avoided all-out war. Yet along the way to this victory the United States had been pushed to some desperate acts. It had overlooked the many things that were wrong with Anastasio Somoza in Nicaragua, Ferdinand Marcos in the Philippines, Ngo Dinh Diem in South Vietnam, and assorted other tyrants, just as it had overlooked what was wrong with Stalin during World War II. By comparison, what had to be overlooked about Japan seemed very small indeed, in light of the great reward of a secure military relationship.

But there were costs. The forty-year emphasis on the Cold War left two distinct marks on America's ability to deal with Japan: it changed the balance of power inside the American government, and it sent American academics to war.

The Pol-Mil Mind-set

Anyone who has dealt inside the U.S. government understands how its hierarchy of rank and respectability runs. The upper end of the totem pole is for people who can take the big, strategic picture— people who can go to foreign summit meetings, who can say "Sorry, that information is classified." The low end is for those who have to deal with insoluble domestic problems, who take trips to mayors' conferences in Cleveland rather than to NATO meetings or to Geneva. The U.S. secretaries of state or defense are viewed as potentates all around the world. The U.S. secretary of commerce is viewed as just another arm-twister for American business. Even within the staff of any given U.S. embassy overseas, the "pol-mil types"—those concerned with the big issues of military strategy and geopolitical alliance—have seemed, well, more serious than those dealing with mere business quarrels.

The Cold War reinforced this natural hierarchy. Within the U.S. government, the Pentagon and the State Department were almost guaranteed to win any argument about how to deal with Japan. If the special trade representative was complaining about some Japanese market barrier, if the secretary of agriculture wanted to sell more oranges or grapes, the pol-mil types could always say: Look, knock it off, because if you're not careful you could mess up The Relationship. The Relationship became an incantatory term, like The Alliance in talking about U.S.-NATO interactions. Mike Mansfield, the U.S. ambassador to Japan during nearly the entire Carter and Reagan terms, repeated the term in almost every speech or interview he gave. The U.S.-Japan relationship, Mansfield said in unvarying form, was "the most important bilateral relationship in the world, bar none."

When America's ambassadors, lower-level diplomats, and military strategists thought about The Relationship during the Cold War, they, like Mansfield, saw very little to dislike. The French, Germans, and Swedes might criticize what America was doing. Stalwart Japan almost never took a diplomatic position openly at variance with American interests. (In a number of cases it quietly charted its own course, as in its acquiescence in the Arab boycott of Israel and its extensive trade with South Africa. But it did not rub these deviations in, as the French would do.) Japan's military essentially functioned as a sub-unit of the U.S. Pacific Command. In some Japanese soldiers' eyes there was still a gleam of respect for the big, strong U.S. Army, with its big, advanced weapons—a gleam that American businessmen working in Japan had not seen for many years.

As a result, the main pol-mil goal during the Cold War was to avoid rocking the boat, to smooth over problems, to assure Americans that business difficulties with Japan were curing themselves, and that in any case bigger issues were at stake. There was a peculiar moral edge to the disagreements within the U.S. government about The Relationship, one that provided a surprising contrast to the operations of the famous military-industrial complex in the United States. When congressional investigators ask why American weapons cost so much, Pentagon officials often stand shoulder-to-shoulder as partners with U.S. defense contractors, explaining why the companies are doing their best to serve the nation's needs. Once they get to Japan, however, U.S. officers begin talking about corporate America with Ralph Nader–like scorn. The Pentagon's Japan-handlers have usually studied the Japanese language to some extent and try hard to get along with their counterparts. Their own dealings with the Japanese are pleasant and satisfactory. When they hear complaints from American businesses, their own experience tells them to classify it as whining from overpaid, shortsighted peddlers who don't appreciate Japan's strategic value to the United States and have never made enough effort to understand the Japanese market.

In 1988, when the Berlin Wall was still up and the Soviet menace was still in the air, I had lunch in Tokyo with four Japanese military officials and one uniformed officer from the U.S. Navy. "I ask my friends in America: Please, work a little harder," one of the Japanese men said, offering the conventional Japanese solution of that time to trade problems. "Yeah, the barriers are all down now," the American officer volunteered. "If American businessmen would get on the ball for once, and produce something worth buying, they'd be making those sales." I looked at him, thinking, My tax dollars are paying for this? What intrigued me was his complete disdain for the small-minded merchants who, in what he saw as special-interest pleading, were endangering The Relationship.

From the early 1950s through the late 1980s, the forces of the Cold War battled the forces of commerce inside the U.S. government, and the Cold War perspective usually won. American aircraft makers wanted to sell planes to the Japanese military, once it was revived in the mid-1950s. The Japanese government wanted its companies to learn how to build the planes themselves. The U.S. government decided not to make a point of it, and ordered the U.S. manufacturers to comply. When the U.S. government was ginning up its SDI/Star Wars projects in the mid-1980s, the pol-mil wing wanted to direct research contracts to Japanese firms. It would tie the Japanese government's prestige to the overall project and would give the U.S. military a chance to use whatever technology the Japanese companies produced. From the U.S. commercial point of view, of course, such a move seemed shortsighted: it dispersed scarce research money to the competitors that U.S. electronics companies most deeply feared. The Cold War imperatives won; in 1985, the Pentagon granted research contracts to NEC, Mitsubishi, and other firms. When American trade negotiators showed up to ask Japan to relax its quotas on imported beef or oranges, they'd send cables back to Washington, saying, We have to push harder, or the Japanese won't believe we're serious. The pol-mil section of the embassy would send its own cables saying, Be careful, don't push too hard, you don't know when they'll get mad.

"If I sat down with a cable form, I knew from the outset that if I wrote something that cast Japan in a good, cooperative light, it would just sail through the clearance process," one man who worked in the American embassy in Tokyo during the Mansfield years told me. "If I said, for instance, that Japan's market is rapidly opening to imports, no one would question my sources, the internal coherence of the argument, or where I got my evidence. It would sail into Washington. But if I sat down to write a piece critical of Japan in some way, everything would slow down. It might eventually get out, but only after a kind of inquisition."

When devising its policy toward Japan, the U.S. government could afford to look at Japan itself only part of the time. The rest of the time the United States was looking through Japan, toward Siberia and the Soviet forces that Japan helped contain.

The Cold War had comparable effects on American academia's view of Japan. The field of Japan studies, like other academic fields, has had its share of bitter feuds that matter not a bit to people outside the discipline. But one prolonged struggle, in the 1950s and early 1960s, had a major impact on American policy.

The social sciences were transforming themselves in many ways during this period. Economics was becoming a much more math-bound discipline. Adam Smith, in the 1770s, had written mainly in normal sentences, without numbers or formulas. In the 1920s and 1930s, John Maynard Keynes was vain about his polished, relatively formula-free prose style. But in the 1950 and 1960s, American economists acted more and more as if they were mathematicians or physicists—even though most of the ideas in economics could be expressed in simple words.

Economics was repositioning itself in the postwar years as a "real" science, a "hard" science. By the late 1960s economists would even have a Nobel Prize of their own. Technically it was a "Nobel Memorial Medal," separate from the long-established Nobel prizes for scientific and literary achievement, but in any form its existence underscored the connection between economics and the natural sciences. By applying theories developed by John Maynard Keynes, economists seemed to have solved the problem of great depressions, just as Pasteur, Lister, and Jenner had figured out how to cope with smallpox and other ancient scourges of mankind. Inside the United States, Keynesian economists announced that they had found ways to eliminate the ups and downs of the business cycle, which in centuries past had driven farmers off their land and thrown millions out of work. Outside America's borders, economists offered prescriptions for how other countries could earn their way to wealth.

Walt Whitman Rostow, who became best known to the general public as an adviser to Lyndon Johnson during the Vietnam War, was best known inside academia for his theory of "stages" of economic growth. Just as living beings moved in a regular progression from infancy to youth to full maturity, so economic systems would also grow—or so Rostow's theory held. It was a matter of getting developing countries up to the stage of "takeoff." The political importance of this theory, of course, is that another big, clear idea was in circulation at the same time: the Marxist idea of international class war and oppression. Marxism had great pretensions to scientific objectivity; Rostow's theory was meant to match the Communists on their own terms.

Within the world of Japan studies, Rostow's functional counterpart was Edwin Reischauer. In many ways Reischauer lived a much more charmed life than Rostow. Rostow was one of a generation of brilliant advisers—Dean Rusk, Robert McNamara, to a smaller extent McGeorge Bundy—who were torn up by America's failure in Vietnam. After Lyndon Johnson left office, Rostow went with him to Texas and continued to teach and write. But, like Rusk and unlike Johnson, he lived long enough to come to see that he would never outlive the shadows of the war. Reischauer, on the other hand, seemed to combine his academic and governmental careers in a way that enhanced both.

Reischauer was born in Japan, in 1910, while his parents were serving there as missionaries, and was always proud of feeling at home with Japanese people and the Japanese language. He became an Asian studies expert at Harvard in the pre-World War II years, trained other Americans in Japanese during the war, and was a renowned Harvard professor again after the war. In the early 1960s he was a kind of living symbol of the Kennedy era ideal of the scholar-diplomat. John Kenneth Galbraith, Kennedy's ambassador to India, may have been more famous to the general public, but when Reischauer took leave from Harvard to serve as ambassador in Tokyo in 1961, it was seen in Japan as like the coming of a second MacArthur, without the war.

At diplomatic receptions Reischauer was usually the only foreigner who could make small talk with prime ministers or even the emperor in Japanese. In March 1964 he was stabbed and seriously wounded by a crazed Japanese protester in Tokyo. His good humor after the attack deepened the veneration for him in Japan.

Reischauer's role in America's policy toward Japan was complicated and surprisingly important. "Trophy diplomats," like Galbraith (and Daniel Patrick Moynihan after him) in India had their public-relations benefits for America but did not deeply change American policy. Reischauer did—or at least symbolized the larger change America had to make because of the Cold War.

During his academic career, Reischauer had been involved in one great dispute about modern Japanese history. It concerned Japan's lurch into fascism and militarism in the 1930s and 1940s. How should this development be explained?

One school of thought, whose best-known representative was the young Canadian E. H. Norman, basically held that the attack on Pearl Harbor was ninety years in coming. Once Commodore Perry arrived, Japan set itself on a path that led naturally to war. To avoid Western domination, the Meiji leaders had fashioned a tough, organized, tight-belt, top-down society. They achieved their stated goal, that of catching up with the West. But they had created a machine that was very difficult for anyone to turn off. The authoritarianism and hierarchy of the Meiji-style state, along with the centuries of feudalism that preceded it, predisposed Japan to aggressive action. In Norman's view, a failure of democracy inside Japan led logically to warfare outside Japan. The country was run by a narrow clique that prevented real debate or democracy from emerging in Japan and imposed a quasi-military structure on the populace. When such a country became strong enough, the argument went, it would naturally seek power beyond its own borders.

This argument was not a mere matter of historical hair-splitting or score-settling: it had immediate, practical implications for how Japan should be handled. If the structure of prewar Japan, the same structure that had made the country successful, also predisposed it to war, then Japan could never be trusted—unless its structure were radically changed.

Reischauer eventually became a leading spokesman for the opposite point of view, which could be boiled down to the idea that the 1930s and 1940s were a terrible, aberrant mistake. Taken in any kind of historic perspective, this argument ran, Japan had clearly been on a liberalizing path. The Meiji leaders brought in a number of progressive reforms, and during the brief springtime of "Taisho democracy," in the late teens and early 1920s, the country was clearly becoming more liberal. In E. H. Norman's view, the prewar political parties were jokes, and debate among them made no difference to the policies the bureaucrats and soldiers actually pursued. Reischauer took the parties, the debates, and the prospects for democracy much more seriously.

The Reischauer camp had to explain why these hopeful developments had been aborted by the militarist disaster of the 1930s. Generals took control of the government; they pushed first into China and then south, toward European colonies in Asia; and eventually they led the country into suicidal war against the United States.

E. H. Norman and his intellectual allies saw Japan's aggression in those years as being a tragic inevitability. It flowed, in their view, from the all-out mobilization of the Meiji years. Reischauer argued, on the contrary, that Japan's natural course toward democratization had been disturbed by a number of outside calamities battering Japan all at once. Worldwide economic depression, racist snubs from

nstability in the rest of Asia, aggressive moves by the
n and China—none of these was inevitable, none was
sed by Japan, but all brought out the worst in Japan
1930s. The country's fledgling democratic institutions
failed during this period, but in Reischauer's view the fifteen years
of dictatorship and war should be seen as a hijacking or perversion
of Japan's drive to catch up, not as its natural fulfillment. "Democracy, however imperfectly, was becoming the dominant force in
Japanese politics," Reischauer wrote after the war. John Dower, of
MIT, concluded, in a study of Reischauer's policies: "In short, Reischauer's emphasis was on the more *successful* aspects of prewar
Japanese development, and in particular on the *democratic* tradition
in presurrender Japan."[27]

Why did this argument matter? One reason was its implications for
the Cold War. Very soon into the Occupation years, the United
States became, as we have seen, more worried about keeping Japan
both non-Communist and anti-Soviet than about any other aspect
of its development. Emphasizing the essentially positive nature of
Japan's post-Meiji development was useful from the Cold War perspective. China had been set up as the major counterexample in
Asia, under the Soviet thumb at the time and committed to communism. The Japanese example could show a better path: toward
both prosperity and democracy, in alliance with the United States.
(Indeed, one of the great mysteries of Japanology is what would
have happened if the Japanese system had been defined as a version
of communism, rather than a version of capitalism. It shares features
with each system, and several scholars have written puckish books
calling it the only Communist society that works.

For American domestic purposes, too, there was everything to
be said for the Reischauer-style view of Japan. If Japan seemed to
be an emergent democracy, it could more naturally be America's
friend. If its people seemed to have been victims of Tojo and his
militarists—just as the civilians of China and the soldiers of the
United States had been his victims—then it would be far easier to
put wartime bitterness to rest. American politics resists the idea that
the country chooses allies for reasons of shared strategic interest;
Americans want to think that there's a real friendship and idealism underneath. The Reischauer view helped them believe that this
was so.

Within academia there were active debates in the 1950s and 1960s about how to fit Japan's experience into Western development models.[28] But much more than most academic debates, this one was immediately projected onto a public screen. During the years when American Occupation officials were leaving, the purged prewar bureaucrats were returning, and the one-party governing system that held the LDP in power was being put in place, the American press was presenting Japan as a "little brother" of the United States, destined someday to grow up and share all the important family traits. The mainstream American academics, notably Reischauer, encouraged this view.

The Little-Brother View Enters Pop Culture

When I returned to America after living in Japan, I spent two weeks prowling through the stacks of a university library, reading postwar U.S. journalism about conditions in Japan. If I concealed the dates on the magazine covers and scraped away the layers of dust that hinted that some issues were older than others, I found it almost impossible to tell articles from the late 1950s or early 1960s from those published in the 1970s or early 1980s.

Through all these magazines in all these years, there was, essentially, one article written over and over again in American coverage of Japan. The people who wrote it differed, and the exact phrases and emphases changed. But the article always said this:

Despite superficial differences, Japan is becoming more and more modern and Americanized. The hard work of recovery is over now, and the Japanese are about to say good-bye to the days of belt-tightening and round-the-clock striving for market share. Today's children, raised in affluence, will not accept what their parents did. Today's women are looking for a much better deal than their mothers put up with. The mechanisms of control—one government, strong bureaucratic guidance, big industrial combines—are reaching their limits. Japan's leaders realize that their country must open itself to the world and take on international responsibilities. A new era is at hand because Japan is on the verge of rapid change.

This standard article, I came to think, represented profound delusion and self-deception. But to demonstrate that requires a contrast or comparison—showing that the magazines could have been saying something different about Japan.

Fortunately, there is an ideal subject for a compare-and-contrast exercise. It consists of two special journalistic projects launched by the *Time* magazine family. One was a special issue of *Fortune* magazine, published in September 1936, that concentrated on Japan. The other was a special issue of *Life,* published in September 1964, to coincide with the opening of the Tokyo Summer Olympics.

By the time the *Fortune* issue came out, the Japanese Army was waist-deep in China, and war between Japan and America was in some sense inevitable. (The Japanese military leaders were determined to expand their holdings in the rest of Asia; the United States was determined to draw the line at some point.) At the time, newsreel films in America were unashamed in talking about "the brutal Japs." Yet the *Fortune* articles were simultaneously sympathetic and clear-eyed—and an astonishing amount of what they said remains sensible today.

By the time of the *Life* special issue, Japan and America were fast friends. But the articles in it, nearly three decades more recent than *Fortune*'s, have aged much less well. The writers for *Fortune* demonstrated that it was possible to be sympathetic with Japan— to admire its accomplishments, to be intrigued by its culture—and still to be critical of the way it wielded political and economic power. By the time of the *Life* issue, this seemingly obvious distinction had been blurred. To be "friendly" toward Japan meant not criticizing anything about it.

The main theme of the *Fortune* special issue was the struggle for breathing room on the world stage. On one side was Japan, always on the verge of feeling cornered and underappreciated. On the other side were the old powers, Britain and America, arrogant but nervous about what Japan could do. The magazine parodied the smug, ignorant way in which Americans and Britons tried to dismiss what Japan had achieved. ("Obviously there were tricks somewhere. The Japanese by hypothesis were incapable of industrial greatness."[29]) But the same issue talked about the deep structural weaknesses of the Japanese government, which kept major questions of policy from ever reaching the Diet and kept the military beyond any civilian party's control.[30] It suggested that while the forms of Japanese capitalism resembled what was found in England or the United States, the system as a whole operated for different purposes and toward different ends. The Japanese system might include "public corporations" and "commercial banks," just as the British or American systems did, but the rules of operation were completely different. "In Japan the industrialists and the bankers are the same people," *Fortune* said: "The great industrial interests actually own the great private banks." *Fortune* said of the Japanese stock exchanges:

> In Japan there is no capital market as we know it. There is no large investing public. . . . The Tokyo and Osaka exchanges could by no stretch of the imagination be called public markets; they are markets in which a very small speculating class keeps busy and in which the capitalist interests trade in each other's securities.

More than fifty years later, when the Tokyo Stock Exchange encountered one scandal after another in the late 1980s and early 1990s, analysts inside and outside the country describe the market's problems in terms almost identical to *Fortune*'s.

Its discussion of Japan's industrial structure concluded with lines that, with minor updatings, could have been slipped into Japan's own economic newspapers more than fifty years later. "The industrial structure of Japan is a new edifice," it said. "It is so efficient that it sells beer to Germany and American flags to the American legion. . . . Nor does the Japanese system too closely resemble that of any of its competitors."[31]

Twenty-eight years later, in the late summer of 1964, *Life* magazine published its own special issue of Japan and the Japanese. *Life* was then at its zenith as the leader of the *Time-Life* empire and the embodiment of mainstream American opinion. By devoting an entire issue to Japan, in celebration of the Tokyo Summer Olympics, *Life* certified for the American public Japan's emergence as a successful, reborn nation.

Life was not obviously a political magazine, and unlike *Fortune* it did not have to write about Japan as if it were a potential enemy. But the most remarkable things about the issue now are its political biases—the unspoken Occupation and Cold War biases that portrayed Japan as tagging along with its big brother, the United States.

On *Life*'s cover was the inevitable "East Meets West" photo—a geisha, in elegant green-and-russet kimono, her hair lacquered into a huge cone, her feet in demure white *tabi* socks, rolling a garish, American-made, marbleized-red bowling ball down the alley, with a big grin on her face. Inside, Arthur Koestler, author of *Darkness at Noon,* predicted that Japan "might achieve the first real synthesis in history between the essential values of East and West—a synthesis which neither Alexander's conquering armies, nor the

Mongol invasions, nor St. Francis Xavier's missionaries were able to achieve." Koestler said that during the Meiji era, "the nation was aglow with 'European fever.' " Now, having seen what the United States had achieved, its "present hectic drive is to out-Americanize America."[32]

Life's lead editorial said that Japan had been lamentably slow to take up responsibilities in international organizations—but was just about to get much more actively involved. ("One of the least attractive aspects of postwar Japan is her reluctance to take on international commitments. . . . Standoffishness cannot last.") A picture-feature article was called "The Young in Revolt." Its message was summed up in one caption: "In growing numbers, the country's youth runs away from tradition, family, and authority." At another point the magazine announced that "The transition to a consumer economy is in full swing," and the government has been "stripping away import restrictions."[33]

A month later, and a year later, and a decade or two later, American publications would be saying exactly the same thing— that young people were goofing off, consumers were coming into their own, and import restrictions were disappearing. In the fall of 1989, exactly twenty-five years after this issue of *Life* appeared, a U.S. government official wrote an essay full of friendly advice to the Japanese government, saying that the time had finally come for Japan to open itself up, start doing its part in international organizations, stop acting as if it were different from the rest of the world. Concern about Japan, he said, is heightened by the "fairly widespread perception that Japan is not yet pulling its weight in the world, that its contributions to peace and public welfare are not commensurate with its wealth and capabilities. . . . What is eagerly awaited are *human signs* that this extraordinary country is ready and willing to pitch in voluntarily through its people with the same fervor with which it produces microchips."[34] In short, it was "now" time for Japan to do what *Life* had said was "now" necessary in 1964.

The centerpiece of the entire *Life* issue was an essay by Edwin Reischauer himself, who was still serving (after John Kennedy's death) as ambassador in Japan. He started out on a note of Japanese-style sentimentality, saying that his connection with Japan was "umbilical," since he had, after all, been born there—and that when he was away, he missed its rugged mountains and beautiful coasts. Then he presented the argument on which America's policy toward Japan was based. The countries were, he said, "inevitable partners" because they shared so many values so deeply.

> As her technological modernization progressed [during the Meiji age], Japan departed from tradition again, becoming an internationally minded trading nation and developing democratic institutions at home. . . . Thoroughly shaken by defeat in war and by the American Occupation which followed, it emerged from these experiences with an efficiently operating democratic government, supported by a populace devoted to the concepts of individual human rights, democracy, and world peace.
>
> No less important has been Japan's success with a free economy. Free enterprise accounted for the bulk of Japan's earlier economic modernization. . . . As Japan reemerged from the shadow of war, however, the free economic system was restored, and Japan became the fastest-growing economy in the world.[35]

In these few sentences lay the key to America's problems with Japan in the decades that followed. The point is not, of course, that Reischauer himself caused the problems; the potential difficulties lay with the attitude that he both symbolized and helped to shape. The vast majority of Americans would never read books or articles about Japan, or pay attention to what any scholar thought about Japan's "similarity" or "differentness." But the background noise that Americans heard, the assumptions about America's role in the world and the future prospects for its allies and competitors, were very heavily influenced by "just like us" writings such as Reischauer's. There is such a thing as a "climate of opinion," and its jet streams and cold fronts are guided by people seen to be authorities, as Reischauer was in this case.

Students of Japan's history, including Edwin Reischauer, clearly knew that the country's reconstruction involved something a little more complicated than that "the free economic system was restored." At the time Reischauer wrote those words, the Japanese government prohibited most foreign investment in the Japanese economy, authorized sweeping monopolies and cartels, directed bank policy, controlled the prices of major commodities, strictly limited the inflow and outflow of currencies, outlawed many kinds of imports—and on and on. It took all these steps precisely because of its concern that a "free economic system" would not give the country what it needed at that stage.

Most Japan scholars also had severe doubts about what Reischauer called the "efficiently operating democratic government" in Japan, which for more than a century after the Meiji restoration never transferred power through an election. Yet in his role as diplomat and public official, Edwin Reischauer—like most other American officials of the day—presented a simplified, tamed, and romanticized version of Japan.

Government officials believed that if the American public came to view Japan as an emerging version of America itself, they would like their former enemy better. If the American population had consisted of millions of Kennans or Metternichs, it might have been sufficient to say that it was in America's *interest* to be allied with Japan. But from all indications Reischauer worked from the view that the alliance would be safest if Americans were made to *love* Japan, and that Americans were most likely to do so if they thought the two countries formed a kind of natural brotherhood. This was the note on which Reischauer ended his essay:

> Most important, we [Japan and America] have come to share much the same ideals—a belief in the worth of the individual, a devotion to democratic institutions as the best way to ensure freedom and a good life for the individual, confidence in a free economy, open international trade as the best way to prosperity, and a strong belief in international law and order as the way to a lasting peace. With such shared ideals, we are inevitable partners.

In the years that followed, virtually every component in this list of claims would be shown to be untrue. Japanese spokesmen would emphasize the worth of the collective interest rather than that of the individual; would emphasize administrative institutions insulated from the ups and downs of democracy; would talk about "excessive competition" as something their economy avoided; would say that international trade should be open in only certain ways; and would claim that international order was strongest with a dominant power, rather than some abstract rule of law. American Japanologists would argue over just how "open" or "democratic" Japan had ever become. As Richard Samuels of MIT has pointed out, U.S. political scientists usually debated Japan's "potential" for democracy, making no pretense that democracy was at hand. In a book called *Asia's New Giant,* published a dozen years after Reischauer wrote his article for *Life,* Henry Rosovsky of Harvard emphasized many of the lasting differences between Japanese and Western models of "capitalism" and "democracy."[36] Yet during the Cold War, assurances like those Reischauer delivered, assurances of Japan's essential similarity to the United States, seemed necessary to make Japan a palatable ally. Because they had so much in common, the nations were bound to be friends.

Many of Japan's own intellectuals would later point out the limits to the Occupation era reforms. "The Occupation tried to import three things," a prominent literary critic named Shuichi Kato told me in 1987. "One: demilitarization and antimilitarism. Two: egalitarianism. And three: individual freedoms. The Japanese people have accepted the first two but not the third." (He explained, "Egalitarianism has developed gradually from the Tokugawa era, to Meiji, through the war. So it is an internal trend, which was encouraged during the Occupation. It is accepted now. Antimilitarism is also deeply rooted because of the war experience and the bomb. But individual freedoms are not in the Japanese tradition. The Occupation said it was a basic right but it just can't happen in fifty years. In the United States and England it was a long process.")

An Australian scholar, Ross Garnaut, pointed out in the 1980s the precise logical flaw in arguments like the one Reischauer made twenty years earlier. When Americans saw a society becoming *modern,* they thought it must necessarily be turning *American* or at least "Western," but this was not necessarily true. Garnaut wrote, "Viewed over longer historical periods, it is not 'westernisation' that we see in Northeast Asia, but [simply] 'modernisation.' "[37] When Europeans or Americans have noticed skyscrapers in Seoul and computers in Taipei, their belief that everything scientific and progressive *must be* Western has evoked the kind of rhetoric that Reischauer used in *Life.*

Garnaut said:

[C]onfusion about "westernisation" has from time to time encouraged enthusiasm for the view that Northeast Asian political models are converging rapidly toward established North American or European models. This has invariably resulted in disappointment at slow progress or . . . deviation from anticipated forms of change.[38]

Yet despite the logical objections that might be raised, the note Reischauer struck in *Life* became the dominant note in American newspaper, magazine, and television coverage of Japan for the next few decades, and in comments by American political leaders as well. In the springtime of 1992, then-Vice President Dan Quayle gave a speech about Japan that was fundamentally similar to Reischauer's essay. Late in 1991, *The Washington Post*'s Tokyo correspondent quoted a first-time visitor from America to demonstrate the essential sameness of Japan and the United States:

> "Tokyo looks just like home," said Denver public relations executive Robert Wurmstedt, who made his first trip to Japan last month. "There's so much English everywhere! Downtown on the Ginza, they have Dunkin' Donuts right next door to Dairy Queen. And I saw a motorcycle delivering Domino's Pizza . . ."
>
> As marriages get older, so the saying goes, spouses often grow to look like each other. And that's happening to the US-Japan union. . . .
>
> Americans traveling to Japan these days almost invariably comment on how much this ancient Oriental nation resembles the United States. . . .
>
> Today, the leaders of Japan's elected government happily describe their deeply pacifist nation as a "Western democracy." . . . Fifty years after their "Greater East Asia Co-Prosperity Sphere" went up in smoke, the Japanese have shown minimal interest in the idea of an "Asian bloc." . . .
>
> The engine for this 180-degree turn was the postwar American Occupation.[39]

It is not surprising that a newly arrived tourist would notice Tokyo's Dairy Queens and Dunkin' Donuts. What is significant is that nearly four decades after the Occupation ended and nearly three decades after the special *Life* issue, a major national newspaper would put this on its front page.

Japan's View of Itself—and of the "Innocent" Emperor

The Occupation, then, changed America's view of Japan. Where there had been suspicion, a sense of Japan's strangeness, and a racist hostility to Japan's ambition, there was now more condescension, tolerant indulgence, and above all the expectation of convergence in the long run.

The same years also changed Japan's view of itself. In addition to the major legal transformations—land reform, the end of militarist rule—the American years shifted the ways in which Japan discussed its own strengths and weaknesses. Some of the changes were good, but two in particular were destined to create problems in the long run.

One was the Japanese tendency to see Japan as a *victim* in the world. This had been a constant theme in Japanese political discussion since the Meiji era. In its dealings with China, Russia, England, and the United States, Japan had often felt itself at the mercy of bigger, better-armed powers, who never fully "understood" Japan but nonetheless could inflict their will on it. After the Occupation, this tendency was if anything much stronger because of the version of history the occupiers left behind. It was a version designed to protect Japan from excessive guilt and recrimination for what it had done during the war, but which ended up distorting the Japanese public's sense of politics through the assumption that no one except the evil militarists had been responsible for the war.

The second phenomenon was the lopsided development of the Japanese state. In seventy-five years after the Meiji Restoration, Japan had developed extremely strong economic and military capabilities, with barely any political institutions to control them. Under the Peace Constitution, Japan concentrated almost exclusively on economic affairs, abandoning not just the aggressive militarism that had led it to disaster in the 1930s but also most of the political traits of a modern state.

The treatment of the Showa emperor, Hirohito, was a crucial component in the first process—the reshaping of history to emphasize Japan's victimhood. In retrospect, Hirohito certainly should not have been "blamed" for World War II, as Hitler will always be blamed. But the decision, after the war, to absolve him from all *responsibility* looks in retrospect like a mistake. It encouraged his entire nation just to put "that unpleasantness" out of mind, rather than reflecting on how it happened.

Everyone outside Japan "knows" what kind of man the emperor was. Beginning in the mid-1950s, he appeared on the world stage as a meek, shyly smiling, middle-aged figure, pluckily boosting his country's spirit as it rebuilt itself and seeming to contradict, by every detail of his bearing, the worst wartime stereotypes. He toured his country during the Occupation as a "democratic" monarch, looking at coal mines and factories, invariably saying "Ah, so?" in response to whatever he was shown. Soon one of his nicknames in Japan became the "Ah, So Emperor." He was also sometimes known as *Ten-chan,* roughly "Little Empy." The emperor came to Disneyland in the early 1960s, oohed and aahed on the rides, and wore a Mickey Mouse watch. The same 1964 issue of *Life* that featured Reischauer's essay also had a long photo essay on the Japanese imperial family. It showed the kindly grandma and grandpa, the Showa emperor and empress; the stylish younger couple, who became the Heisei emperor and empress in 1989; and the toddler who on Hirohito's death became crown prince.

The photos of Hirohito showed a dowdy-looking older gent, his hat pushed down around his ears, his pudgy knees showing beneath his Bermuda shorts. The headline on the story about him was, "The Emperor: A Gentle Ruler and His Wife Go on a Search for Shellfish." The text reinforced the harmless look of the man in the photograph:

> Hirohito, now sixty-three and a small and gentle man, has had little influence on his country's course. Before Pearl Harbor, he tried ineffectually to prevent war with plaintive, questioning poems. . . . In democratic Japan, the days pass pleasantly for the gentle emperor.[40]

In the first year that my family was in Japan, we went to the Imperial Palace in Tokyo for one of the two occasions each year in which it was opened to the public. This was April 29, Hirohito's birthday, and the first in a ten-day span of holidays known in Japan as "Golden Week." After his death, April 29 was converted into a generic "Green Day" holiday so that Golden Week could still be intact. This is a mixed blessing, since everyone in Japan takes a holiday during this same period and all hotels, trains, planes, and resorts are jammed. The other occasion on which the imperial grounds are opened is for the New Year's holiday.

On the emperor's birthday, we stood with tens of thousands of citizens in the courtyard in front of the palace, waving the same *hinomaru* flags we'd been given when we arrived. (*Hinomaru* literally means "sun circle" or "round sun." The *hinomaru* flag is the familiar white background emblazoned with a red disk.) Every thirty minutes or so, the entire imperial family would step from behind curtains and present itself for viewing, separated from the crowd by thick bulletproof glass. At these ecstatic moments everyone in the crowd would wave the flags frantically, many shouting *banzai!* Everything about the stooped-but-brave little emperor seemed to fit the official version of the postwar world. He was a marine scientist and a poet, cruelly trapped and tricked by militarist madmen.

There had always been another view of the emperor, but it was, almost by definition, excluded from reasonable debate in both Japan and the United States. When Hirohito lay dying, tabloid papers in England and Australia published frothing editorials, gleefully anticipating the moment when the old emperor would begin frying in hell. After he finally expired, British war-veteran groups petitioned the royal family not to send a representative to the elaborate funeral rites. In the end Prince Philip attended, and at the crucial moment when each onlooker was supposed to bow before Hirohito's bier, the prince fractionally inclined his head, one member of royalty acknowledging another. When his turn came, George Bush executed a barely detectable nod, moving his head perhaps one quarter of an inch.

In the days before the funeral, the Japanese press had been full of comments about the anti-Hirohito bitterness in England. Bush had been the first foreign leader to announce plans to attend the funeral, which was taken as a heartening and magnanimous gesture from the kind of confident Americans the Japanese used to know. Watching the ceremonies on television in Tokyo, I half expected war to break out after Bush's minimalist bow, but the moment passed. Yet the very bitterness of protests like those in Australia and England seemed to discredit the protesters themselves, not the emperor.

Historians have produced no credible evidence to support the view that Hirohito was a Hitler-like demon, as some British and Australian diehards believed, or even the mastermind of the entire war (as the American writer David Bergamini alleged in *Japan's Imperial Conspiracy,* a one-thousand-page tract published in 1971). Rather, the emerging evidence suggested something more believable, in commonsense terms, than the stereotypes of either the "Ah, so" emperor or the scheming warlord. Hirohito had been an active sovereign who thought constantly about his country's place in the world and listened carefully to what his generals told him about its life-and-death struggles.

The full evidence of the emperor's involvement in wartime policies did not become public until after his death in January 1989. While he was alive, the mainstream Japanese press avoided discussing the emperor's wartime role at all. Especially during the grim four-month-long vigil in late 1988 during which he bled to death from abdominal cancer, a mood of "self-restraint" in Japan deterred public discussion about the "dark side" of his reign. But a few months after his death, a fascinating document appeared. This became known as the "Emperor's Monologue," and it revealed crucial truths about how the Occupation had revised history.

In the springtime of 1946, the Allied powers were preparing to conduct the Tokyo trials and hold Japan's leaders to account. At the time, it was not clear whether the emperor himself would be brought to the stand. Many of the victorious powers, with Australians and Englishmen in the lead, were urging his inclusion. In part this was sheer bloodthirstiness. But there also was a powerful logical case. The entire Japanese empire had gone to battle in the emperor's name. The emperor's subordinates had emphasized that no major step could be taken against his will. Therefore as a matter of logic it would be hard to find colonels, generals, and cabinet ministers guilty but find the emperor completely blame-free. As the American historian Richard Minear pointed out after the war, "It would take the utmost sophistry to justify, on the one hand, the conviction of the emperor's closest advisers and, on the other, the failure even to indict the emperor."[41] At the Tokyo trials, judges from Australia, France, and the Soviet Union indicated, for just this reason, that the emperor should have been tried.

The United States and its viceroy, Douglas MacArthur, finally decided that, nonetheless, it was crucial to spare the emperor. He was cooperating in every visible way with the occupiers' plans. He was setting an example of humble cooperation for his people. In renouncing the concept that he was divine, he did what he could to promote a democratic spirit. He would be far more valuable, to his nation and its new ally, the United States, remaining on the throne than as a martyr in the dock. It was one thing for the Japanese public to see the general-turned-prime minister Hideki Tojo brought to trial and put to death. Similar treatment for a man who, until very recently, had been thought to have descended from the gods would have been quite another matter.

During the war, American bombers had attacked sixty-six Japanese cities with conventional bombs before dropping the atomic bombs on Hiroshima and Nagasaki. But during this same bombing campaign the United States had deliberately refrained from attacking Kyoto. Indeed, Henry L. Stimson, as secretary of war, had specifically ordered Kyoto stricken from the list of targeted cities;

President Truman assented to this decision.[42] The American leadership calculated that they didn't *need* to destroy Kyoto, ancient cultural capital of the nation, to win. So, too, with the emperor. MacArthur decided that he did not need to prosecute him—in fact, needed not to—if he wanted maximum cooperation from the occupied nation.

"MacArthur had been ordered by the Potsdam declaration to democratize Japan," Chalmers Johnson said in 1991. "He shrewdly and accurately concluded that this was an extremely dangerous undertaking. He knew that the probable result would be for the reforms to last only so long as the conqueror was there. . . . He therefore concluded that the reforms had to have some legitimacy outside the power of the American Occupation. For his own peculiar reasons, he chose the emperor."[43]

Among those whose support MacArthur wanted was the cadre of conservative politicians who had generally opposed the war, on grounds that Japan was certain to lose. The greatest of these politicians, an Anglophile named Shigeru Yoshida, had served before the war as ambassador to the Court of St. James's. Yoshida was a traditionalist who considered the imperial tradition essential to Japan's self-respect and hopes for recovery. Therefore he believed that Japan's main goal should be to finish the Occupation with the imperial line intact. "The usefulness of the emperor as a god diminished sharply on the day of surrender," Mark Gayn wrote in his *Japan Diary,* about the Occupation years. "Now a group of shrewd old men at, and around, the Imperial Court were manufacturing a new myth—the myth of a democratic monarch keenly interested in the welfare of his people. It was a shameful conspiracy against the Japanese people and against the concept of democracy which we said we would help to establish."[44]

To put unpleasantness in the past and to help Japan look ahead, the American officials overrode the British and Australian complaints. The emperor would not stand trial.[45] When the trials of his advisers began, the lead U.S. prosecutor, Joseph Keenan, delicately and sometimes not so delicately steered witnesses toward other subjects whenever they began discussing the emperor's role. In contemporary American experience, the Tokyo trials would have been like the Watergate or Iran-contra hearings with a determined effort not to find any connection to the president. (The most famous example of selective interrogation was that of General Tojo, whose inquisitors instantly changed the subject whenever he began to talk about the emperor's role during the war.[46]) The case at the Tokyo trials, as presented by U.S. prosecutors, prefigured the version of the emperor's wartime history later presented in *Life* magazine. When the Japanese Army moved into China, when the Japanese Navy planned the attack on Pearl Harbor, the emperor was all the while "in the power of 'gangsters,' " as Keenan put it.[47]

But for several months after the end of the war, before the American intentions toward the emperor became clear, the emperor and his advisers did not know whether Hirohito himself would have to answer charges of war crimes. Between March 18 and April 8, 1946, the emperor sat down with five of his closest advisers, in five separate sessions, essentially to talk about the defense they would offer the Allied judges should that become necessary. (This account of the monologue draws heavily on Herbert Bix's 1992 article "The Showa Emperor's 'Monologue' and the Problem of War Responsibility" in the *Journal of Japanese Studies*.[48])

One aide who was present at all the meetings was Hidenari Terasaki, who had served as a diplomat in the United States and had an American wife. He took extensive notes of everything the emperor said, but neither his notes nor any other record of the meetings was ever made public. After Terasaki's death, his notes, which were, of course, in Japanese, ended up in the attic of his daughter's house in Wyoming. Terasaki's daughter, like her mother, could not read Japanese, and so (according to the official story) she was not aware of what the documents meant. After the emperor himself died in 1989, the documents came into the hands of *Bungei Shunju,* a prominent Japanese literary and political magazine. Early in 1990 *Bungei Shunju* published the transcripts of the Emperor's Monologue, touching off an enormous public debate within Japan.

The response was understandable because the monologue showed how wrong the prevailing view of the emperor had been. Hirohito had been presented as a meek and ineffectual creature who could do little during the war years except wring his hands. The Terasaki documents suggested that he had taken an active interest in how the war was being waged. There was no evidence that he had been its instigator or strategist, but the evidence made clear that he had been involved, as an active monarch, in more or less the way that King George VI had been involved in Britain's wartime plans.

The apparent purpose of the monologue was to give the emperor "deniability" if he were ever brought to trial. With his advisers he reviewed the sequence of prewar and wartime decisions, readying himself to show that he had been on the sidelines at all crucial times.

"In his monologue, the emperor (with the assistance of his aides) presents himself as a peace-minded constitutional monarch, who, when his generals and admirals resolved on war, went along because he had no choice," Herbert Bix wrote.

Yet in the very act of preparing this defense, Hirohito left abundant evidence for the opposite conclusion—that far from being a passive onlooker, he had been (as Bix put it) "obsessed with fighting and winning decisive battles." The friendly little emperor of the postwar era had been presumed to be heartsick over the attack on Pearl Harbor. But when asked about it in the monologue, the real emperor said, in effect, that war was coming sooner or later, and Japan's only chance was to strike before the Americans rearmed:

> If I had not granted permission to stand up and act in that time of crisis, when we had elite army and navy troops who had trained hard for many years, then, as time passed, our oil supplies would have been steadily depleted and the navy would have become immobilized. If we had tried to supply the navy with synthetic oil, almost all of Japanese industry would have had to be sacrificed for that one end. If that had happened, the country would have gone to ruin, and in the end, even if pressed by unreasonable demands, we would have had to surrender unconditionally.
>
> Such were the prospects for Japan's future at the time of the opening of the war. Let us assume that I had vetoed the decision to go to war. I think it would certainly have led to enormous civil strife at home. People close to me whom I trusted would have been killed, and my own life would have been endangered. I wouldn't have minded that but, ultimately a furious war would have developed anyway and would have brought about a tragedy far worse than this war [World War II]. In the end, unable to end the war, Japan would have been destroyed.[49]

Hirohito had been present at a meeting one month before the attack on Pearl Harbor, where the decision to attack was made. The document for negotiation at that meeting, which was held on November 4, 1941, said: "To break open the present crisis, to fulfill the nation's inner life and self-defense, and to establish a New Order in Greater East Asia, the Empire, on this occasion, decides to make war on the United States, England, and Holland. For this purpose the time to activate our military forces is set for early December." The emperor approved.[50]

The "passive," "uninvolved" emperor also said that he had given strategic advice to his allies in Nazi Germany:

> At the beginning, when the United States and Britain planned to conquer Africa, I warned Tojo to recommend to the Germans that rather than give priority to their war against the Soviet Union, they should give priority to Africa. . . . Next, when the United States and Britain landed in France, I asked Germany to strike the Anglo-Americans with their main force and to limit their actions against the Soviet Union to simple defense.[51]

In similar passages Hirohito speculates on the tactics used at Leyte Gulf and in the Battle of Okinawa and on other operational details. "The case for Emperor Hirohito's indictment on war crimes charges might have been harder to dismiss had his monologue been published in 1946 or before MacArthur (the representative of a nation that had not been invaded and plundered by the Japanese Army) lost interest in pursuing such charges," Herbert Bix says.[52]

Even before this document was published, there had been indications that many of those closest to Hirohito viewed him as having been involved—not evil, not particularly blameworthy, but indisputably *there*, as a loyal and dutiful sovereign, participating in the decisions that shaped his country's fate. Two of the men who served as closest advisers to the emperor before and during the war urged him, once the war was over and the survival of the Chrysanthemum Throne was ensured, to abdicate. In this way he could demonstrate his personal accountability for the devastation the nation had suffered by fighting and losing the war.

Whether or not the emperor had participated in a single decision that led to war, the greatest disaster in his country's history had happened on his watch. Hirohito's son Akihito was by then in his early teens, not much younger than the Meiji emperor had been when he took the throne at another moment of national crisis. Hirohito himself had been barely in his twenties when he began serving as regent in place of his deranged father.

One of the advisers who recommended that the emperor step down was the aristocratic Prince Fumimaro Konoe, his prime minister during the war against China. Konoe's notes and memoirs from the war years were published in May 1946. They revealed his clear feelings that the emperor was symbolically responsible for Japan's suffering, even if he had not been in any literal sense responsible for war policy, and that therefore he should abdicate.[53]

The emperor's other key adviser was Koichi Kido, "lord keeper of the privy seal." After the war Kido was tried at the Tokyo trials, convicted of war crimes, and sent to jail.[54] In 1951, from his cell, he wrote an extraordinary letter to the emperor. It asked him to abdicate as soon as Japan had concluded a peace treaty with its former enemies and seen the Occupation forces go home. Otherwise, he said, Hirohito would leave a permanent stain on the monarchy by seeming to shoulder no responsibility for his country's catastrophic defeat.

> No matter how one looks at it, the emperor bears responsibility for losing this war. Therefore, once you have fully implemented the Potsdam proclamation—in other words, when a peace treaty has been signed—I think it is most proper for you to take responsibility and abdicate for the sake of your imperial ancestors and for the nation. . . . By doing this, the families of those who died and were wounded in the war, those who were not repatriated, and the families of the war criminials will somehow feel requited. I think that should make a very important contribution to national unity centered on the Imperial House. However, if you do not do this, the end result will be that the imperial family alone will have failed to take responsibility and an unclear mood will remain which, I fear, might leave an eternal scar.[55]

This letter was not made public at the time. Indeed, until a Japanese scholar named Kentaro Awaya discovered it in the 1980s in a microfilm version of Kido's papers kept in the National Diet Library in Tokyo, it had not been published at all.

In retrospect, there might have been other ways for Occupation authorities to explore the emperor's responsibility without encouraging him to abdicate. Perhaps the list of defendants at the Tokyo trials could have been confined to war criminals in the ordinary sense, the people who ran death marches and tortured prisoners in camps, rather than including political and military leaders other than the emperor. Perhaps there should have been a political "trial" of the entire war policy, not subjecting the emperor or prime minister to personal punishment but airing the entire record of what had occurred. If, according to one historian, Douglas MacArthur "had been supremely wise and strong, he might have insisted that the roughly $9 million spent on trying Tojo and his colleagues be used instead for a nonpunitive inquiry into the mechanics of leadership which had led Japan to offend the world."[56]

Perhaps the Americans should have gone ahead and imposed a constitution, including the famous Article IX, which was meant to disarm Japan permanently. Yet such a constitution could have had a "sunset clause," saying that the Article IX and all other imposed provisions would expire in ten or fifteen years. After that, Japan, like any other country, would need to come up with a constitution of its own. Perhaps the emperor should have decided by himself to take a tour of China and Korea, to offset their profound sense that official Japan does not remember and does not care what happened during the war years.

The fact is that none of those things occurred. The emperor did not abdicate. The trials went beyond the camp commanders, but not to the emperor himself. The Peace Constitution was imposed—and remained. Japan left the Occupation years demilitarized, eager for hard work—but doing almost nothing with the wartime experience except concluding that letting the militarists run things had been a mistake. It was not until August 1993, some fifty-five years after Japanese imperial troops invaded China, that a Japanese prime minister forthrightly told Japan's Asian neighbors that the policies of the 1930s constituted "aggression" and had been "wrong." By historic accident, the prime minister who said these things, the reformer Morihiro Hosokawa, was the grandson of Prince Konoe, who had been Hirohito's prime minister and confidant during the war years.

Not "Forgive and Forget," Just "Forget"

"Forgive and forget" is often a useful policy after a war. If Abraham Lincoln had survived, this would have been his approach to the Confederacy. But the American approach to the emperor, and by extension to his whole country, was different. It was simply to attempt to forget what had gone on.

The difference was subtle but of enormous consequence. It involved a pretend version of history, one that twists Japanese-American relations to this day. In this pretend version, the emperor was always meekly standing by, in a throne room or garden someplace, while the evil militarists took the country to war.[57]

In principle, the Americans need not have invented such a myth. It should have been enough for them to say, "Hirohito was sovereign of his country, and partly responsible for its aggressive war. We cannot forget what happened, nor should he. But there is no evidence that he originated the war plans. And it is now in everyone's best interest, in Japan and America alike, that he be spared the indignity of a trial and be allowed to move his country forward, from the throne." By the same logic, it should have been possible for the United States to say, of the alliance as a whole, "Our countries are very different and share very few values. Perhaps our societies will never converge. Nonetheless, we are both better off if we can keep an alliance going. It will reduce the chances that we'll go to war again." But after the Occupation, neither of these accurate but unromantic sentiments would suffice. The emperor became cute and harmless, a kind of mascot, and Japan and America became, in Reischauer's words, "inevitable partners."

What was the harm? It lay in an infantilization of the emperor—and of Japan. Hirohito had to pose as a feckless lightweight. Japan had to pretend that ten or fifteen years of its history hadn't really occurred. The war was like a big typhoon or earthquake—unpleasant, but not anyone's responsibility. "The American Occupation under MacArthur deemed Hirohito's continued presence indispensable to its operation locally and to American priorities globally," Norma Field, of the University of Chicago, has written:

> Thus, American interests dovetailed with the emerging interests of the rehabilitated Japanese leadership to reinforce the dispensation from reflection afforded by devastating defeat. It became virtually impossible, for instance, to recall that Japan had been waging a war of aggression prior to Hiroshima and Nagasaki. . . . The difficulty of discussing war guilt in general and of imperial responsibility in particular produced a national amentia that first mobilized a labor force for stupendously hard work and then facilitated the transition to unreflective prosperity."[58]

"Dispensation from reflection" is the essential phrase. By the end of the Occupation, debate had been squelched in Japan on the very issues that should be resolved when a war is over: How did it happen? Who was in charge? What things should we feel proud of and what should we regret?

No one, in any nation, rushes to take up such questions, as Germany demonstrated after both world wars and the United States after Vietnam. The average Japanese citizen had good reason to view himself and his family as primarily victims, rather than perpetrators, of the war. Militarist Japan had no democratic institutions;

the population was controlled by the government rather than the other way around. General Tojo's government had never been voted into power, as Hitler's had, and the Japanese public had no institutional leverage over their regime, the way Germans did in the early Nazi years.

Still, there was ample ground for asking what had gone wrong with the Japanese system as a whole; this was the inquiry that the U.S.-sponsored myths of the Occupation years cut off. The idea that the emperor had been a gentle onlooker, and that the country had been inexplicably hijacked by militarists but was now safely back on track, almost guaranteed that Japan would avoid coping with its past. In the short run this made for smoother U.S.-Japanese relations, but by the 1990s such myths would account for many of Japan's difficulties in dealing with other Asians, with America, and with itself. This approach caused difficulties with the rest of Asia because of Japan's awkwardness about apologizing or atoning for the war. It made difficulties with America because it implied a permanent big brother/little brother relationship, which was hard to sustain as economic power shifted from America to Japan. And it made problems in Japan itself, as we will see, because it left a deep fear in the minds of many Japanese. The fear was that because the country's political system had not faced the failures that led it to war, it could never really be trusted to stand up to such pressures again.

"It would be ultimately better for us to have a Swedish-type army—strong, independent, and peaceable," one Japanese journalist told me in 1988. "It would be better—*if* the country itself was like Sweden, with that history, pattern of behavior, and values. But given our forgetful history, it would be dangerous for Japan and the world for us to have independent arms."

Selective Memories of the War

In the first month I was in Japan, in 1986, I met one of its most prominent intellectuals, Shuichi Kato. Kato had been trained as a medical doctor during the war and was part of the first team of physicians sent to Hiroshima to treat atomic-bomb victims. Later he became a literary critic and an influential leftist writer.

"So far as postwar antimilitarism is concerned, it is because of the war's damage to *us,* and the bomb," he told me. "*Our* suffering is the material basis for antimilitarism. Our last memory was of the Pacific war, which was a disaster. It had the effect that the First

World War had on many European nations, or World War II on the
Soviet Union. There were too many casualties." But, he said,

> There is not any sharp sense of obligation or guilt for Japanese
> destruction of other people's lives. There is lots of publicity
> about Hiroshima but not about Nanking. If the little child who
> was killed at Hiroshima should be mourned, what about the
> little Chinese child?

It may seem unchivalrous to reflect so much on the aftereffects of
a war that took place half a century ago. But the idea of chivalry
itself suggests a mutual sense of regret or guilt. If I know that you
are already punishing yourself for failing at your work or in your
family life, it is unchivalrous of me to twist the knife. But if I think
you are deliberately avoiding facing what you have done . . .

Sooner or later, the visitor to Japan starts to realize how little
guilt there seems to be about the war. I know exactly when that
feeling dawned on me. In the springtime of 1986, my wife and
children and I went to Hiroshima, along with my mother and father,
who were visiting from the United States.

My parents were slightly younger than the generation that actually fought against the Germans and Japanese. My father had been
in a training program for Navy doctors; my mother finished high
school soon after V-J Day. My wife and I had grown up when
wartime bitterness, as far as we could tell, was in the past.

Our mood as we got off the bullet train at the Hiroshima station
was like that of virtually every American who goes to the city. We
had read books like John Hersey's *Hiroshima,* with its horrifying,
understated narrative of schoolchildren burned alive and bomb victims drowning in the river in their desperate attempts to soothe their
wounds. We knew that in this place, airplanes representing our
nation had dropped an atomic bomb on civilians for the first time
in history. Like many other American visitors, we didn't exactly
want to go, but we felt obliged. I could accept, intellectually, the
argument that it was necessary to drop the first bomb, at least, and
that in ending the war this way Harry Truman saved more lives than
he took. Still, seeing the hulks of ruined buildings, riding the city
streetcar to the stop named "Atomic Bomb Dome"—these were
ways of acknowledging the lasting consequences of a nation's acts.
Although we didn't know it at the time, the phenomenon of con-
science-stricken American tourists is so well established in the area
that it has fostered various parasite industries. Hustlers who were

obviously born years after the war limp up to American-looking visitors and ask for donations for "radiation treatment."

Then we walked into the Atomic Bomb Museum and began reading the historic narrative. It informed us, in both English and Japanese, that in the springtime of 1945 American bombers "began attacking" Japan. As the culmination of this assault, the Americans dropped history's first atomic bomb on Japanese civilians. We saw the pathetic lunchboxes of students who'd been burned or crushed to death. We saw the paving stones where the shadows of mothers and children had been permanently etched by the blast, in the last milliseconds of their lives. We saw the pamphlet that said of the *Enola Gay*'s crew, "High above, they cannot hear the survivors' voices begging for help; the victors leave for home, well satisfied that their task has been completed." We did not see a single word in this museum about any act that preceded the U.S. bombing "offensive" against Japanese cities in 1945. Not the Japanese conquest of China. Not Pearl Harbor. Not the bloody struggle on Okinawa, which convinced Truman that the Japanese government would not surrender until all its citizens were dead. The atomic bomb, to judge by this shrine to its victims, was either an event of pure, unprovoked malice, the counterpart to the Nazi holocaust, or else an inexplicable catastrophe. "Our purpose is to show how citizens of Hiroshima suffered on that day," Hiroshi Harada, the director of the Hiroshima Peace Memorial, later told John Bussey of *The Wall Street Journal*. "That's why there isn't an explanation of the Pacific war as a whole."[59]

That afternoon I could see my father silently flexing his jaw muscles as we walked from one display to the next showing America's death-from-the-skies. A few years later, I met a young American who had had a similar moment of shock and discovery in Nagasaki. He wrote:

> When I visited the Peace Museum in Nagasaki, not far from Ground Zero, I found a profoundly moving exhibition of photographs and artifacts of human suffering. In a dim corner of one room, there was an open comment book. The last entry was signed by a visitor from Shanghai who had scrawled, "This place is deeply disturbing, but I know who the first murderers were."[60]

Over the next few years, I became more familiar with the "victim consciousness," or *higaisha ishiki,* that shows up so often in Japan's dealings with the outside world and readings of its own history. In addition to the Occupation's teachings, the memories of Hiroshima served to wipe the wartime slate clean. "If the Japanese ever felt remorse, it was more than compensated for by Hiroshima and Nagasaki," a career diplomat named Yukio Okamoto said near the fiftieth anniversary of the attack on Pearl Harbor.[61]

In schoolrooms around the country, children learn about the history of the 1930s and 1940s in a highly selective way. In a sixth-grade class in Yokohama, I saw an illustrated timeline of the twentieth century. There were cars at the turn of the century, and men in top hats to illustrate the Western fashions sweeping Japan at the time. For the early 1950s there was a picture of the United Nations, symbolizing Japan's emergence from the years of Occupation, and for the 1960s there was, of course, a set of Olympic rings. For the period from the mid-1930s through the mid-1940s, the years in which Japan conquered most of Asia, there was one visible reminder only: the mushroom cloud over Hiroshima.

Almost every day in Japan there are reminders of—well, of the lack of reminders. The postwar policy, as internalized in Japan, really has been forget, not forgive and forget. When the movie *The Last Emperor* opened around the world, there was a long delay before it opened in Japan. Finally it was released, but only after a two-minute segment, containing gruesome scenes from the Nanking Massacre, was cut. Nanking is a touchy point for the Japanese right wing, which argues that no "massacre" ever occurred. (Most non-Japanese historians say that Japanese troops killed at least 140,000 civilians in Nanking in December 1937 and raped at least 20,000 women. The most prominent Japanese figure to say that it was all a myth was the politician Shintaro Ishihara, coauthor of *The Japan That Can Say No*.) But unlike the "holocaust revisionists" in the United States or Europe, the Japanese right-wingers are often able to impose their views on the mainstream press in Japan. In American terms, it would be as if white supremacists intimidated any moviemakers who planned to mention that slavery existed, or that the Native American Indian population was driven out by the Europeans.

One of the campy staples of Japan's pop culture is the Takarazuka dance troupe, a group of all-female entertainers. In the fall of 1991, one of their many musicals on historic themes, this one called "Fall of the Forbidden City" *(Shikinjo no Rakujitsu)*, was changed on its second day of performance, to remove the words "Nanking Massacre." A Takarazuka spokesman was quoted as saying, "We know it happened, but it's painful."[62] The Chinese and Korean governments protest every year or two at each new iteration of textbooks from the Japanese Ministry of Education, which go over the wartime record with an extremely light touch.

The political aftereffects of the "forget" policy have been greater in Asia than in America. The Chinese and Koreans, after all, suffered much more at Japan's hands during the 1930s and 1940s than Americans did. This is why Prime Minister Hosokawa's apologies to Asia, at the very start of his term in 1993, might prove so significant in repairing Japan's relations with its neighbors. But there was another consequence of the Occupation years that had enormous significance for America: It was Japan's decision, again with American encouragement, not to become a "real" country.

The One-Function Country

Democracies all around the world complain that they're poorly governed. Politics is corrupt and turns on trivia. The big issues get ignored. Americans typically think they have the world's worst case of this disorder, but they don't. Among major countries, Japan does.

In 1992, for instance, Japan held nationwide elections for seats in the upper house of the Diet. The stock market was collapsing. The country had been deeply embarrassed a few months earlier by its inability to decide what to do about the Gulf War. In response, it had taken what was arguably the biggest foreign-policy step of the post–World War II era, authorizing Japanese soldiers to join U.N. peacekeeping forces in Cambodia. The cost of living was high and getting higher. The birthrate was low and going down. The school system was admired outside the country but bitterly criticized within Japan. George Bush had just come to Tokyo and vomited on Prime Minister Miyazawa, symbolizing the nasty tone of Japanese-American relations. The Liberal Democratic Party, which should more accurately be named the Conservative Republican Party and which had held power continually since 1955, had lost one leader after another to bribery scandals. Three years earlier, in the Diet elections of 1989, it had lost its majority in the upper house (though its control of the lower house still gave it control over the prime ministership). The domestic "malaise" was at least as acute as what Jimmy Carter faced when he was defeated in 1980. Yet in this situation the LDP won again, and once again there was virtually no discussion of any substantive issues.

A year later, in 1993, there was another election for the lower house of the Diet, and this time the result was different. A coalition of seven parties denied the LDP its lower house majority, Kiichi Miyazawa of the LDP resigned the prime ministership, and the insurgent Morihiro Hosokawa, of the Japan New Party, became the first non-LDP prime minister since 1955.

This was the biggest political news in Japan in decades, reflecting widespread disgust at personal corruption within the LDP. (A few months before the election, police had found gold bullion worth tens of millions of dollars in the home of the LDP's most visible power broker, Shin Kanemaru.) Japan's political system for the previous four decades had resembled old-fashioned "machine politics" in big American cities, like the New York of Boss Tweed or the Kansas City of the Pendergast machine. One party was in permanent control, and factions within that party struggled for control of turf and appropriations. Elections had more to do with patronage and loyalty than with "issues" in the normal sense.

Like political machines anywhere, Japan's LDP machine was undeniably effective in certain ways. Japan did perform not one but several economic "miracles" under LDP leadership—quickly rebuilding in the 1950s, doubling personal incomes in the 1960s, surmounting the oil crisis in the 1970s, rising to preeminence in many industries in the 1980s. Although Japanese living standards remained lower than those in North America and Western Europe, the country was consistently moving ahead. Yet, as with any political machine, the LDP shortchanged other interests—most notably those of consumers, women, and urban salarymen. Collectively these interest groups made up a majority of Japan's people, but the country's political system gave them almost no way of exerting control over the nation's policy. The consequential decisions were made, year in and year out, by the elite bureaucrats in the most powerful central government ministries—Finance, Education, Construction, International Trade. Election results had almost no impact on the decisions they made.

If Japan should develop a political system in which several parties compete for power, and in which election results affect national policy, then the potential of the 1993 upheaval would have been fulfilled. But there are many reasons to think that Japan's political changes will not be that dramatic.

Although Morihiro Hosokawa himself had formed his Japan New Party to challenge the LDP when it still was dominant, most other members of his coalition had been LDP loyalists until just a few months before the 1993 election. Hosokawa's two most important allies in the "reform" cabinet, Ichiro Ozawa and Tsutomu Hata, were veteran LDP power brokers who jumped ship shortly before election time. (It was Hata who, as agriculture minister in the 1980s, said that Japan could not import foreign beef because Japanese intestines were "too long" to digest foreign beef properly.)

In the short run, the "reform" coalition faced the task of changing Japan's election laws. These were heavily gerrymandered—farmers in sparsely populated rural areas had five to six times the voting power as voters in the jam-packed Greater Tokyo sprawl—and were further biased by their "multimember" nature. In the powerful lower house of the Diet, each electoral district was represented by several Diet members—two for the smallest districts, six for the largest. Yet each voter in the district could cast only one vote for a Diet representative. The system made it easier for Japan's numerous minority parties to have some representation in the Diet, since 10 or 15 percent of a district's vote was usually enough to win one of the seats. But in practice the multiseat system made campaigns even more issue-free than they would otherwise have been. In a typical four-seat district, the LDP would usually control three of the seats. But four or five LDP candidates would compete for those three seats. Since they had little or no difference of party platform to separate them, they ran mainly on name recognition and the ability to dispense patronage benefits to their supporters. One result of this system was that a majority of Diet members were sons of Diet members; this was the easiest way to solve the name-recognition problem. Another result was to remove even the pretense that the Diet was involved in basic issues of national policy.

Unless Japan's reformers could change the electoral system, which was held in place by the interest groups and politicians who had long benefited from it, they would have tremendous difficulty with the next and more important stage of democratization. This further step would be to transfer control of the country's political decisions from unelected (though highly skilled) bureaucrats to the nation's elected leadership.

If this change occurred, it could convert Japan's system into something more like the consumer-oriented democracies of North America and Western Europe. Whether or not the Japanese system changes, the question of *why* it has had a one-party structure through the postwar era remains.

One hypothesis is that this is the natural system of "capitalist democracy" in East Asia. Indeed, the Japanese model, even in its pre-1993, "unreformed" version, was admired and emulated throughout the region. Most Western societies had a hard time defending the collective interest against individual rights and entitlements. The United States tolerated tens of thousands of shooting deaths each year rather than infringe on individual rights to use guns. Western economies in general were slowed down by the "entitlement drag" as larger and larger shares of their population claimed support from the state (through pensions, medical coverage, and other benefits generally denied in Asia). Individuals had less room for maneuver in the Japanese model, but Japan as a whole productive entity grew stronger, faster than the Western economies did.

There is another, narrower explanation for the nature of Japan's postwar political system, one that is barely mentioned or examined outside Japan. The system may now seem "natural" and "inevitable" for promoting economic growth in Asia. But as a historic matter it was anything but inevitable. It grew from another fateful decision made during the Occupation: Japan's decision not to be a "real" country.

The Road Not Taken

A real country, in this sense, is one that bears responsibility for all the attributes of sovereignty. It watches out for itself in the world, perhaps in alliances with others but always with ultimate responsibility for its own defense. It makes its own policies. It is finally "sovereign" in the literal sense, answering to no political authority above its own government.

Half a century after World War II, Japan is obviously not a sovereign or independent state. In practice its foreign policy amounts to following whatever lead the United States sets, while granting itself the right to drag its feet if the policy causes economic problems. (For instance, through the 1970s and 1980s Japan observed the "Arab boycott" against trade with Israel. The rationale was that at the time Japan depended much more on OPEC's oil than other countries did, so it had to pay more attention to Arab political views.) Americans often grumble about lack of cooperation from their "allies" in Western Europe. Nonetheless, Britain, Germany, Belgium, and other European countries were formally bound together in alliance, each theoretically pledged to go to the other's defense. Japan and America have never been allies in this official sense. The postwar treaty between them was a one-sided guarantee: the United States would protect Japan. In return Japan would help protect itself, and let the United States keep soldiers on its soil.

This arrangement might seem to be all benefit for the Japanese, but in fact it has had corrosive effects. The Japanese government clearly held itself responsible for the repair and expansion of the Japanese economy. It turned to this task with utmost seriousness. But other aspects of Japanese politics remained a kind of sideshow. Japan was not really expected, by itself or by its American protectors, to say anything about international matters. Since the expert bureaucrats really were in charge of domestic policy, other politicians could remain favor-trading, log-rolling hacks.

Japan's industrial economy is probably stronger in the 1990s because Japan's politics took the form it did, starting in the 1950s. Yet the system did not have to turn out exactly this way. For at least fifteen years after the end of World War II, it was an open question whether Japan would become a "real" country, with a real political system. During the 1950s, a group of Japanese politicians and intellectuals became known as "revisionists" because they argued that the country must revise its relationship with the United States. Complete dependence on the United States was inevitable in the immediate aftermath of the war. After all, the Americans had won and could tell Japan what to do. But sooner or later, the revisionists argued, these arrangements that sprang from postwar exigency would have to be changed.

Japan's history of the 1950s, now seen in Europe and America mainly as a time of nonstop beavering toward economic improvement, in fact turned on fundamental political decisions. Shigeru Yoshida, the prewar ambassador to Britain, was the dominant politician of the era. Yoshida served as prime minister for a total of seven years between 1946 and 1954; during that period he was out of office only from the spring of 1947 to the fall of 1948, when he headed the opposition party. Yoshida was a conservative, authoritarian figure whose experience was in foreign policy and whose role as prime minister was largely to serve as "ambassador" to the occupying American forces.[63]

Within the Japanese government, Yoshida argued that the way to restore Japan's dignity, the way to bolster its strength in the long run, was to concentrate *totally* on economics and to leave everything else to the United States. In the previous century, since the arrival of Commodore Perry, Japan's goal had been to build its productive core so it could remain free of foreign control. Now, Yoshida argued, outside control was a fact of life. Galling as this might be to Japanese pride, the Americans were there. Better to be controlled by them than by, say, the Russians or Chinese. It was time to acknowledge the realities of the situation and make the most of them.

Yoshida's most famous quote from this era was a comment he made to an American official in 1952, as the Occupation was coming to an end. Japan was about to regain formal independence, but it would still have foreign troops on its soil and would lack the right or power to defend itself. Yoshida said of this arrangement, "When it is objected that Japan will become a colony of the United States, I always reply that, just as the United States was once a colony of Great Britain but now is the stronger of the two, if Japan becomes a colony of the United States, it will also eventually become the stronger!"[64]

To Americans, in the 1990s, this quote might look like a galling reminder that Japan had always had a secret plan. Actually, its significance is far more poignant (as Tetsuya Kataoka has pointed out). At just the moment when his country was nearing nominal independence and escaping the cloud of war, its greatest statesman still thought of his land as a colony.

Through the 1950s, the Yoshida strategy was under attack from the extremes. Right-wingers rolled through Tokyo with loudspeaker trucks (as they still do today), insisting that there was nothing wrong with what the emperor, the military, or the empire had done. On the other side were the leftists, including real Communists, who protested bitterly against the military arrangement that turned Japan into a base camp for the United States.

Between these two was the "revisionist" group. Its best-known politicians were the LDP leaders Ichiro Hatoyama, who succeeded Yoshida as prime minister in 1954, and Nobusuke Kishi, who became prime minister in 1957 (after his period of imprisonment and being banned from public life, because of his indictment as a Class-A war criminal, had ended). These revisionists argued that until Japan changed both its constitution and its external military relationship with America, it could not be a full-fledged state. As the historian Kataoka has pointed out, this group had four main goals: revising the "Peace Constitution" so the United States and Japan had a relationship more like allies and less like protector and ward; rearming Japan, much as Germany had done within NATO, so it could deal with other countries more as an equal; creating something like a real two-party system, rather than the one-party factionalized machine that was already beginning to evolve; and giving politicians control over entrenched bureaucrats. Even though these revisionist leaders belonged to the one party that was then in power and had the clout to remain there for decades, they argued that a real two-party system would be better for Japan. As Tetsuya Kataoka says:

> This was no mere moralizing on democracy but a matter of hardheaded calculation. These men were born to command other men. They knew that the party leader's power rested on the threat of dissolving the Diet on an issue that could be put to the judgment of the voters. But the LDP could not be thrown out of power no matter how many elections were held. Thus LDP leaders were denied the disciplinary power of dissolution— unless there was a functioning two-party system.[65]

The reform-minded politicians had a similar, realistic motive in seeking control over the bureaucrats. In the Japan of the 1990s, the Ministry of Finance has virtually inescapable control over monetary matters. In the mid-1950s, a politician named Ichiro Kono tried to get the budget power moved from these unaccountable bureaucrats to the prime minister's office—where it is in the British system and, by analogy, in the American.[66] (The U.S. Office of Management and Budget is officially part of the executive office of the president.) At the same time, reformers tried to create a "single-seat district" system for the Diet, rather than the multiseat system Japan adopted. Under a single-seat electoral system, similar to that for the U.S. Congress or the British House of Commons, candidates from two or three parties would be more likely to run against each other, head-to-head, in each district. This would in turn increase the chances that Diet races would be referendums on national issues, rather than the simple patronage and popularity contests they soon became. The Diet itself would then have more legitimacy to make national policy—at least as much legitimacy as the Congress or Parliament had.

From a similarly hardheaded perspective, the party leader Hatoyama argued that Japan *had* to rearm to develop normally as a country. "He did not question Japan's need for U.S. military protection," Kataoka says.

> But that did not mean that Japan did not owe itself an honest self-help. It was inconceivable that Japan should regard defense as a favor for America and demand a quid pro quo, as Yoshida

was doing. Hatoyama saw Japan's inner corruption down that path. For him and the other revisionists, rearmament itself was less important than political-diplomatic equality that came with it.[67]

Yet this revisionist argument, and all the other proposals for deep political reform, failed. Yoshida, suspicious by nature of disorderly, democratizing reforms, argued that Japan could not *afford* these experiments in political science or gestures toward national pride. The country's one mission was to rebuild itself; everything else must take second place. The U.S. government was exerting enormous pressure in the same direction. For the time being it saw every advantage in keeping Japan compliant and a base for its troops. And so the U.S.-Japan relationship, as we know it now, was in place by the early 1960s. The right-wingers couldn't convince Japan to go back to the old ways. The left-wingers couldn't get Japan to split from the United States. The "revisionists" couldn't get Japan onto a "real country" course like the one that Germany moved toward. Instead, Japan would depend on America for defense and foreign policy, and America would not molest Japan as it rebuilt its industries.

Month by month and year by year, the resulting division of labor was comfortable for both countries. Japan could concentrate on its own economic welfare and avoid both the furor and the expense of raising a large military force to defend itself. America could count on Japan's acquiescence to whatever foreign policy it decided on—and Japan's loyalty in the great Cold War struggle against the Soviet Union. But beneath the surface, tensions were building. The tensions were more obvious in the United States, which increasingly grumbled about the "free ride" Japan was taking on the American defense budget. The pressures within Japan were more concealed but, for that reason, probably more dangerous. They revolved around the feeling that the nation was being bullied and not given its proper due.

In the summer of 1991, *Sankei Shimbun,* a conservative newspaper chain, ran an essay showing the frustration. "Americans criticized Japan for trying to buy its way out of the Gulf War," Kenichi Matsumoto, a historian, wrote, "but few realize that Gen. Douglas MacArthur's constitution emasculated this country. . . . In renouncing the right of belligerency after World War II, Japan placed its fate in the hands of foreign mercenaries instead of homegrown patriots."[68] Thirty years earlier, the scholar Kazuo Kawai wrote, "However desirable its contents, this constitution suffers from the fatal stigma of being an alien-imposed document. As the Occupation recedes further and further into history, it is inevitable that the revival of national independence and self-respect will give increasing rise to the demand for a truly indigenous constitution."[69]

Just before troops from all the other "G-7" countries went into combat against Iraq, I was talking with a Japanese journalist who was reliably on the left of every standard political issue. He hated the war in Vietnam. He thought the war against Saddam Hussein was a mistake. But, he said, he felt strangely wistful during the Vietnam War. The Americans were on the wrong side, he said. "But they were willing to *die* for something." "Defeat in World War II not only cured Japan's militaristic delusions but also destroyed our backbone as a nation," the journalist Ryutaro Ozaki wrote in 1992. "We lost our national identity and haven't found a new one"—which was why, he said, Japan "flunked the test of leadership" by failing to protest after the Tiananmen Square crackdowns in China in 1989 or the military coup in Thailand in 1992.[70]

When the crazy-genius novelist Yukio Mishima stormed into a Self-Defense Force barracks on a November morning in 1970, a few hours after turning in the last pages of his four-part novel *The Sea of Fertility,* he berated today's Japanese for not being willing to stand up for any beliefs. Modern Japan, he shouted from the balcony, had become a society that "thinks of money, just money." From the crowd of a thousand soldiers came back cries of *baka yaroo*—approximately, "asshole!"

Immediately after this humiliation, Mishima cut his own belly, and had a young admirer finish the job by lopping off his head with a samurai sword. Mishima had failed, but fundamentally he was right. The postwar bargains made Japan into a country with only one goal.

By 1960, Japan was taking a distinctive course. It was evolving as a nation optimized for one purpose: economic expansion. Its internal political system was set up mainly for doling out pork-barrel benefits and adjudicating fights among interest groups. Its diplomatic skills consisted mainly of following the American lead. The "goals" it pursued overseas revolved almost exclusively around its economic interests—making sure the raw materials came in, making sure that foreign governments remained as friendly as possible. This is not a criticism of Japan's strategy; it was a highly successful adaptation to the postwar environment.

Economic expansion began in earnest with a boom during the Korean War, which did for Japan what the Marshall Plan did for Western Europe.[71] This reinforced Yoshida's antirevisionist message that alliance with the Americans was the only sensible course. MITI proceeded by fits and starts, much as Roosevelt's tinkerers had done during the first few years of the New Deal. By the late 1960s, when Japan's industries first posed a noticeable challenge to American or European companies, outsiders often said that there had been a great Japanese master plan, coordinated by MITI. The architects of Japan's recovery denied that claim, saying that in fact they had succeeded through brilliant improvisation. "MITI's own men were frequently astonished at their success," one American account of MITI's rise said. "Over the years a popular saying emerged to explain it all: 'We just came forward, walking one step at a time, and when we looked up we were at the top of the stairs.' "[72]

Yet in one way or another the project of rebuilding Japan's economy went forward—and the division of labor between Japan and America, which was outlined by the Peace Constitution and the security treaty, was put into practice by both sides. America did the fighting and made the big decisions; Japan concentrated on its own economic welfare.

For a while, this relationship was stable. It could last as long as two conditions were met. One is that the United States cared more about its Cold War aims in Asia than it cared about other goals, including economic competition. As long as containing the Soviet Union was America's paramount strategic aim, then the advantages of the alliance with Japan far outweighed the headaches it might cause. The other condition was the difference of scale. When America was big and Japan was little, Japan's dependent position made sense to each side. It made sense to the Americans because the economic drag was slight. It made sense to the Japanese because of another of its timeless mottoes: *Nagai mono ni wa makareyo*—"Go with the strong." Much of the country's foreign policy had been devoted to finding sources of strength—and adapting to them.

But by 1989, both of these essential conditions had been violated. When the Berlin Wall fell, soon taking with it the entire Soviet state, the United States could no longer think of the Cold War as its major problem. When the Japanese economy grew, its worldwide effects could no longer be shrugged off—as those of, say, Taiwan still were. Nor did Japan necessarily see America as "the strong."

When the conditions changed, the world began to cope with something it had not anticipated: a system that had reinvented the rules of economics.

4

The Idea of Economic Success

THE CHUO SEN, OR CENTRAL LINE, became my symbol of the bargain Japan had made with the world. The heaviest traffic on this commuter train line is between Shinjuku station, on the northwestern side of Tokyo, and the dense suburbs that reach out to the west. In the morning and evening rush hour, this is salaryman life in its fullest, most stereotyped form. "Packers," wearing neat uniforms that vary in hue with the season, and with never-varying white gloves, would line up on the platforms and shove extra passengers onto the train. If you were lucky, you could raise an arm above the sea of hair and hold a book or magazine aloft during the trip. If you were really lucky and lived two hours or more from downtown, you could get on at the beginning of a trip and sit down through the whole ride. If you were unlucky, it would be raining, and you'd be jammed into other wet bodies, giving your clothes a human steam press while water from umbrellas drooled down onto your shoes. If you were really unlucky, you'd be trapped on the late-night train with its cargo of salarymen coming back from their "business" dinners.

"Drunk, stunned, slack-jawed, slumped boneless in their seats as though flung there by a mighty hand" began a magazine story about the late train, called "White-Collar Zombies," which I read in the mid-1980s while on just such a train. "Hair like clumps of greasy lichens, arms and legs like canned asparagus, breath like death . . . these are typical Tokyo salarymen." A Japanese doctor said in the same story that the salaryman was "a machine that can get on and off the train almost indefinitely [but] is not therefore healthy—or even, in any meaningful way, alive."

At the time, my family was considering a house about an hour out of Tokyo on the Chuo Sen. I decided I couldn't face spending two hours a day this way. We wound up living on a train line that seemed even more crowded but required a shorter trip.

In the springtime of 1992, a trip on the Chuo Sen brought me unexpected good luck. I had been traveling about an hour out of town that day, to the campus of Hitotsubashi University, a school that was famous for its economics and business faculties. Like several other elite universities, Hitotsubashi was almost heartbreaking in its cuteness. The road from the station to the main campus was lined by cherry trees, and at this precise moment in April they made fluffy white clouds the entire way. My feet stirred up little puffs from the carpet of white petals as I walked. Students glided along on their bicycles, looking—realistically—as if they were enjoying the one stress-free moment of their lives. Students at Japanese universities typically are enrolled for fifteen or twenty classes each semester, each of them meeting for an hour or two each week, which might sound as if this is one more facet of the hard life in Japan. But in surveys, huge majorities of students say that they study "never" or "hardly at all" during their university careers. The ones who've made it into good universities have years of cramming behind them, in junior high and high school. Once they leave good colleges, the salaryman life lies ahead. The crucial hurdle to surmount in Japan's merit system is getting *into* a good university, not excelling once you get there. Hitotsubashi is close enough to the top of the university status system that its students can take satisfaction in their past achievements (surviving high school and cram school) and their future prospects. The right way to spend these years is to join clubs, play sports, and savor life while they can.

I had gone to Hitotsubashi to interview a professor who was, at the time, making waves. Starting in 1990, a number of Japanese businessmen and academics had begun saying publicly: Hmmmm, perhaps our business system really is different from what they have in Europe or the United States. The man at Hitotsubashi, Professor Iwao Nakatani, was one of the most prominent and respected members of this group, and I'd spent the afternoon listening to his analysis while, through the window, I watched the petals drifting down.

On the way back to the station, I saw a sign that indicated, in Japanese, that there would be Western-language books inside. I walked to the back of the narrow bookstore and for the thousandth time felt both intrigued and embarrassed at the consequences of the worldwide spread of the English language. In row upon row sat an incongruous jumble of books that had nothing in common except that they were published in English. Self-help manuals by Zig Zigler. Bodice-rippers from the Harlequin series. A Betty Crocker cookbook. The complete works of Sigmund Freud. And two books concerning Friedrich List.

Friedrich List!!! For at least five years, I'd been scanning used-book stores in Japan and America looking for just these books. I'd scoured the English-language stores in Taiwan, which until recently had specialized in pirated reprints of English-language books for about one tenth the original cost. I'd called the legendary Strand Book Store, in Manhattan, from my home in Kuala Lumpur, begging them to send me a note about the success of their search (it failed) rather than making me wait on hold. I'd looked through English-language libraries without success. In all that time, these were the first books by or about List I'd actually laid my eyes on.

One was a biography, by a professor in the North of England. Another was a translation, by the same professor, of *The Natural System of Political Economy,*[1] a short book List had originally written in German in the 1830s. Each was a slim volume, which to judge by the dust on its cover had been sitting on the shelf for years. I gasped when I opened the first book's cover and saw the price listed as 9,500 yen—about $75. For the set? I asked hopefully. No, apiece, the young woman running the store told me. Books were always expensive in Japan, but even so, this seemed steep. No doubt the books had been priced in the era when $1 was worth many more yen than it was in 1992. I opened my wallet, pulled out a 10,000-yen note, took my change and the biography, and left the store. A few feet down the sidewalk, I turned around, walked back to the store, and used the rest of my money buying the other book. I would always have regretted passing it up.

Why Friedrich List? The more I had heard about List in the preceding five years, from economists in Seoul or Osaka or Tokyo, the more I wondered why I had virtually never heard of him when studying economics in England and the United States. By the time I saw his books in the shop beneath the cherry trees, I had come to think of him as a symbol of the strange self-selectivity of Anglo-American thinking about economics.

I emphasize "Anglo-American" because, in this area, the

United States and the United Kingdom really are like each other and different from most of the rest of the world. Just how isolated they are is usually not evident to people in these Anglophone countries. Together they have dominated world politics for decades, and the dominance of the English language lets them ignore what people are saying in the vernacular overseas. The difference shows up this way: The Anglo-American system of politics and economics, like any system, rests on certain principles and beliefs. But rather than acting as if these are the "best" principles, or the ones that their societies "prefer," Britons and Americans often act as if these were the *only possible* principles and that no one else, except in error, could choose any others. That is, political economics becomes an essentially religious question—leading to the standard drawback of any religion, the failure to understand why people outside the faith might act as they do.

To make this more specific: Today's Anglo-American worldview stands on the shoulders of three men. One is Isaac Newton, father of modern physical science. A second is Jean-Jacques Rousseau, father of liberal political theory. (If we want to keep this purely Anglo-American, John Locke can serve in his place.) And the third is Adam Smith, father of laissez-faire economics. From each of these founding titans come the principles on which advanced society, in the Anglo-American view, is supposed to work. It is supposed to understand the laws of nature, as Newton indicated. It is supposed to recognize the paramount dignity of the individual, thanks to Rousseau, Locke, and their followers. And it is supposed to recognize that the most prosperous future for the greatest number of people comes from the free workings of the market. So Adam Smith taught, with axioms that were enriched by David Ricardo, Alfred Marshall, and the other giants of neoclassical economics.

The most important thing about this list is its "moral equivalence." Isaac Newton worked in the realm of fundamental science. Without saying so explicitly, today's British and American economists act as if the *economic* principles had a similar hard, provable, undebatable basis. If you don't believe in Newton's laws, with appropriate modifications by Einstein, you are by definition irrational. Modern physics books don't need to pay attention to non-Newtonian views of the universe, since they aren't worth serious attention. And so with economics. If you don't accept the views derived from Adam Smith—that free competition is ultimately best for all participants, that "protection" and "interference" are inherently wrong—then you are a flat-earther.

Outside the United States and Britain, the matter looks quite different. About science, there is no dispute. The physics of Newton and Einstein are the physics of the world. About politics, there is more debate—as we will see in later chapters. With the rise of Asian economies, some Asian political leaders, notably Lee Kuan Yew of Singapore and several more cautious figures in Japan, have been saying that Rousseau's political philosophy is not necessarily the world's philosophy. Societies may work best, Lee and others have said, if they pay less attention to the rights of the individual and more to the welfare of the group.

But the difference is largest when it comes to economics. In the non-Anglophone world, it looks as if Adam Smith was merely one of several contending theorists with ideas about organizing economies. It is not at all self-evident—in Germany, in Korea, in Japan, in Singapore—that his theories have worn well with time.*

Englishmen and Americans tend to see the last two centuries of economics as one great progression toward rationality and good sense. In 1776, Adam Smith's *Wealth of Nations* made the case against old-style mercantilism, just as the Declaration of Independence made the case against old-style feudal and royal domination. Since then, as it seems in the Anglo-American world, more and more of the world has come to the correct view. Along the way the world met such impediments as neomercantilism; guildism; radical unionism; sweeping protectionism; socialism; and, of course, communism. One by one the worst threats have given way. Except for lamentable areas of backsliding, the world has seen the wisdom of Adam Smith's ways.

Yet during this whole time, there has been an alternate school

---

*To clear up a point of national terminology: Rousseau was, of course, French, as were some of the other founders of the modern liberal worldview. The term "laissez faire" is a constant reminder of this fact. But in the late twentieth century, the system I am describing is best called "Anglo-American," because its stronghold is the governments, universities, and newspapers of Britain and the United States. *The Wall Street Journal,* the University of Chicago, *The Economist* of London, Margaret Thatcher, and Milton Friedman—these have been its pillars. Modern France, by contrast, applies a very non-laissez-faire economic policy, something like the Japanese model without the overwork. In his book *Head to Head,* the economist Lester Thurow used the term "Anglo-Saxon" to describe the laissez-faire theories of Britain and America. I prefer "Anglo-American," to avoid putting in ethnic terms what is really a matter of national policy.

of thought. The Enlightenment philosophers were not the only ones to think about how the world should be organized. During the eighteenth and nineteenth centuries, the Germans were also active—to say nothing of the theorists at work in Tokugawa Japan, late imperial China, czarist Russia, and elsewhere.

The Germans deserve emphasis because many of their philosophies endured. They did not take root in England or America, but they were carefully studied, adapted, and applied in parts of continental Europe and in Asia, notably in Japan. In place of Rousseau and Locke, the Germans offered Hegel. In place of Adam Smith, they had Friedrich List.

The German vision of economic life differed from the Anglo-American view in many ways, but the crucial differences were the following.

"Automatic" growth vs. deliberate development.   The Anglo-American approach emphasized the unpredictability and unplannability of economics. Technologies changed. Tastes changed. Political and human circumstances changed. And because life was so fluid, attempts at central planning were virtually doomed to fail. The best way to "plan," therefore, was not to plan at all, but instead to leave the adaptation to the people who were closest to the action and who had their own money at stake. These were the millions of entrepreneurs who made up any country's economy. No planning agency could have better information than they about the direction in which things were moving, and no one could have a better incentive than those who hoped to make a profit or avoid a loss. And, by the basic logic of the Anglo-American system, if each individual did what was best for him or her, the result would be what was best for the nation as a whole.

Although List and others did not use exactly this term, the German school was more concerned about what would now be called "market failures." In the language of modern economics, these are the cases in which normal market forces produce a clearly undesirable result. The standard illustration involves pollution. If the law allows factories to dump pollutants into the air or water, then every factory will have to do so. Otherwise their competitors will have lower costs and will squeeze them out. This "rational" behavior would leave everyone worse off because of pollution. The answer to such a "market failure" is for all the members of the society—that is, the government—to set standards that all factories must obey.

Friedrich List, and his best-known American counterpart Alexander Hamilton, argued that there was a more sweeping sort of "market failure" when it came to industrial development. Societies did not automatically go from farming, to small crafts, to major industries just because millions of small merchants were making decisions for themselves. If every person put his money where the return was greatest, the money might not automatically go where it would do the nation the most good. Economic development could require a plan, a push, an exercise of central power. List, as we will see, drew heavily on the history of his times—in which the British government had deliberately encouraged British manufacturing, and the fledgling American government deliberately kept out foreign competitors.

List used the term "cosmopolitan theorists" to describe Adam Smith and his ilk. Their worldview, as List characterized it, rested on the belief that if individuals were left to pursue their own interests, the national economy as a whole would automatically develop in the best possible way. By the logic of this laissez-faire view, it naturally followed that government intervention could only harm an economy, by diverting it from the optimum path it would otherwise follow.

Yet any realistic look at British economic history, List said, would raise severe doubts about laissez-faire theory. Sometimes industries did flourish in certain regions, and wither in others, for essentially laissez-faire reasons. "It may be chance that leads certain individuals to a particular place to foster the expansion of an industry that was once small and insignificant," List said, "just as seeds blown by chance by the wind may sometimes grow into big trees." But often something more than chance was involved in the evolution of industries over hundreds of years:

> In England Edward III created the manufacture of woollen cloth and Elizabeth founded the mercantile marine and foreign trade. In France Colbert was responsible for all that a great power need to develop its economy. Following these examples every responsible goverment should strive to remove those obstacles that hinder the progress of civilisation and should stimulate the growth of those economic forces that a nation carries in its bosom.[2]

Consumers vs. producers. The Anglo-American approach assumed that the ultimate good of a society is measured by its level of consumption. Competition is by definition good, because it kills off the overpriced producers. Killing them off is, in its turn, good, because more efficient suppliers will give the consumer a better deal. Foreign trade is, by the same logic, best of all, because it means that the most efficient suppliers in the whole world will be able to compete. It doesn't even matter *why* competitors in other countries are willing to sell for less. They may be genuinely more efficient; they may be determined to "dump" their goods for reasons of their own. In either case, the consumer is better off. He has the ton of steel, the cask of wine, or—in today's terms—the car or computer that he might have bought from domestic manufacturers, plus the extra money he saved by buying overseas.

In the Friedrich List view, this logic led to false conclusions. In the long run, he argued, a society's well-being and its overall wealth were determined not by what it could buy but by what it could make. This is the corollary of the familiar argument about foreign aid: Give a man a fish, and you feed him for a day. Teach him how to fish, and you feed him for his life.

List's objection to consumption was not aesthetic or moral. Instead it involved both strategic and material well-being. In strategic terms, nations ended up being dependent or independent based on their ability to make things for themselves. Why were the Latin Americans, Africans, and Asians subservient to England and France in the nineteenth century? Because they could not make the machines and weapons the Europeans could.

In material terms, a society's long-run wealth was greater if it controlled more advanced activities. If you buy the ton of steel or cask of wine at bargain rates this year, you are better off, as a consumer, right away. But over ten years, or fifty, you and your children may be stronger as both consumers and producers if you learn how to make the steel and wine yourself. If you can make steel, rather than just being able to buy it, you'll be better able to make machine tools. If you're able to make machine tools, rather than just buying them, you'll be better able to make engines, robots, airplanes. If you're able to make engines and robots and airplanes, your children and grandchildren will be more likely to make advanced products and earn high incomes in the decades ahead.

In the long run, the German school argued, emphasizing consumption would be self-defeating. It would bias the system away from wealth creation and ultimately make it impossible to consume as much. To use a homely analogy: One *effect* of getting regular exercise is being able to eat more food, just as an effect of steadily rising production is being able to consume more. But if people believe that the *reason* to get exercise is to permit themselves to eat more, rather than for longer-term benefits in itself, then they will behave in a different way. List's argument was that developing productive power was in itself a reward: "The forces of production are the tree on which wealth grows." In his best-known book, *The National System of Political Economy,* List wrote:

> The tree which bears the fruit is of greater value than the fruit itself. . . . The prosperity of a nation is not . . . greater in the proportion in which it has amassed more wealth (i.e., values of exchange), but in the proportion in which it has more *developed its powers of production.*[3]

In the German view, then, the final measure of an economic system was what it did for producers—manufacturers, inventors—rather than its immediate effect on consumers. A society was worth as much as it could make, not as much as it could buy. This emphasis on production, in the German view, was sensible both because it would permit greater consumption in the long run *and* because making things is good in its own right. A century and a half after List wrote *The Natural System of Political Economy,* Lester Thurow made a similar point in his book *Head to Head:*

> Those remembered in human history are not the great consumers. They are the conquerors, the builders, the producers—Caesar, Genghis Khan, Rockefeller, Ford. Being part of a collective effort, of a powerful group, may in fact be more important to some individuals than having a lot of personal consumption. . . .
>
> No believer in consumer economics would have built the cathedrals that play such an important part in the Kingdom of God, the buildings and roads of Rome, or the monuments of ancient Egypt. All of these projects took too long to complete and required too much up-front capital. Yet humans built them all. In Japan, the generals, the capitalists, have been willing to invest *too* much, but in doing so they are being very human, even though they're not Anglo-Saxon.[4]

Process vs. result. In economics and politics alike, the Anglo-American theory emphasized how the game was played, not who won or lost. If the rules were fair, then the best candidate would win. If you wanted better politics, or a stronger economy, you should concentrate on reforming the rules by which political and economic struggles were waged. Make sure everyone can vote; make sure everyone can bring his new products to the market. *Whatever* people choose, under those fair rules, will by definition be the best result. Abraham Lincoln or Warren Harding; *Penthouse* or Shakespeare—whatever people choose, in a fair system, will be right.

The government's role, according to this outlook, is not to tell people how they should "pursue happiness" or grow rich. Rather, its role is that of referee—making sure that no one cheats or bends the rules of "fair play," whether by voter fraud in the political realm or monopoly in the economic.

In the late twentieth century, the clearest practical illustration of this policy is the U.S. financial market. The government has been actively involved—but principally to guard the process, not to steer the results. It has run elaborate "sting" operations to try to prevent corporate officials from trading on inside information. It requires corporations to publish detailed financial reports every quarter so all investors have the same information to work from. Laws setting "fiduciary responsibility" standards oblige pension fund managers to invest their assets where the dividends are greatest; otherwise shareholders could seek damages against them in court. The government itself could take companies to court if they became too large and powerful to permit "fair" competition by other participants.

In short, when the U.S. government knowingly and happily "interferes" in American markets, it does so in the name of non-interference. It tries to correct market failures or other imperfections that stand in the way of the central goal, which is "getting prices right." Once those distortions are removed, the government's most valuable service is to get out of the way itself. If the market is free to assign every asset and input its proper price, then the money will by definition be attracted to its best possible use.

The Germanic view is more paternalistic. People might not automatically choose the best society, or the best use of their money. The state, therefore, must be concerned with both the process and the result. Identifying an Asian variant of the Germanic view, the sociologist Ronald Dore has written that the Japanese—"like all good Confucianists"—believe "that you cannot get a decent, moral society, not even an efficient society, simply out of the mechanisms of the market powered by the motivational fuel of self-interest." So, in different words, said Friedrich List.

Individuals vs. the nation. The Anglo-American view focuses on how individuals fare as consumers and how the whole world fares as a trading system. But it does not really care about the intermediate levels between one specific human being and all six billion—that is, about communities and nations.

This criticism may seem strange, considering that the title of Adam Smith's mighty work was *The Wealth of Nations*. It is true that Smith himself was more of a national-defense enthusiast than most people who now invoke his name. Smith said that the art of war was the "noblest" of the arts, and he approved various tariffs that would protect defense-related industries—which in those days largely meant sailcloth-making. He also said that since defense "is of much more importance than opulence, the act of navigation is, perhaps, the wisest of all the commercial regulations of England." This "act of navigation" was, of course, the blatantly protectionist provision that goods going to and from England must be carried by English ships.[5]

Still, the assumption behind the Anglo-American model is that if you take care of the individuals, the communities and nations will take care of themselves. Some communities will suffer, as dying industries and inefficient producers go down, but other communities will rise. And as for nations as a whole, they are not assumed to have economic interests—apart from the narrow field of national defense. There is no general "American" or "British" economic interest beyond the welfare of the individual consumers who happen to live inside its borders. One classic quotation by Winston Churchill—delivered in 1908, as his country was deciding how to deal with the "German challenge"—summed up this view:

> There came last year into our country from every land and people under the sun billions worth of merchandise so marvelously varied in its character that a whole volume could scarcely describe it. Why did it come? Was it to crush us or to conquer us or to starve us? Or was it to nourish and enrich our country? It is a sober fact that every single item, however inconsiderable, in all that vast catalog of commodities came to our shore because some citizen desired it, paid for it, and meant to turn it to his comfort or his profit.[6]

The German view was more concerned with the welfare—indeed, sovereignty—of people in groups, in communities, in nations. This is its most obvious link with the Asian economic strategy of today. Friedrich List fulminated against "cosmopolitan theorists" who assumed away the fact that people lived in nations and that their welfare depended to some degree on how their neighbors fared. If you make $100,000 and everyone around you makes $80,000, you feel well off. The community is prosperous, and you are a success. If you make $101,000 and everyone around you is a destitute beggar, you are worse off in any full reckoning of human well-being, even though your standing is higher in both absolute and relative terms. This, in a nutshell, is the case that today's Japanese make against the American economy: American managers and professionals live more opulently than their counterparts in Japan, but they have to guard themselves, physically (and morally) against the down-and-out people with whom they share the country.

For the Germans, the answer to this predicament was to pay explicit attention to the welfare of the nation. If a consumer had to pay 10 percent more for a product made by his neighbors than for one bought from overseas, it would be worse for him in the short run. But in the long run, and in the broadest definitions of well-being, he might be better off. As List wrote in *the National System,*

> Between each individual and the entire humanity, however stands the NATION, with its special language and literature, with its peculiar origin and history, with its special manners and customs, laws and institutions, with the claims of all these for existence, independence, perfection, and continuance for the future, and with its separate territory; a society which, united by a thousand ties of mind and interest, combined itself into one independent whole. . . .[7]

Economic policies, in the German view, would be good or bad depending on whether they promoted the strength of the nation as a whole.

Business as peace vs. business as war. By far the most uplifting part of the Anglo-American view was the idea that everyone could prosper at once. Before Adam Smith, the Spanish and Portuguese mercantilists had viewed world trade as a kind of battle. What I won, you lost. Adam Smith and David Ricardo demonstrated that you and I could win at the same time. If I bought your wine and you bought my wool, we would both have more of what we wanted, for the same amount of work. The result would be the economist's classic "positive sum" interaction. Your well-being plus my well-being, added together, would be greater than they were before our trade.

The Germans had a more tragic, or "zero sum"-like conception of how nations dealt with each other. Some of them won; others lost. Economic power often led to political power, which in turn let one nation tell others what to do. In the post-World War II era, American politicians have often said that their trading goal is a "level playing field" for competition around the world. This very image implies a horizontal relationship among nations in which they all good-naturedly joust as equal rivals. "These horizontal metaphors are fundamentally misleading," John Judis, an American journalist, has pointed out.

> Instead of being grouped horizontally on a flat field, nations have always been organized vertically in a hierarchical division of labor. The structure of the world economy more accurately resembles a pyramid or a cone rather than a plane. In the seventeenth century, the Dutch briefly stood atop the pyramid. Then, after a hundred-year transition during which the British and French vied for supremacy, the British emerged in 1815 as the world's leading industrial and financial power, maintaining their place through the end of the century. Then, after about a forty-year transition, the United States came out of World War II on top of the pyramid. Now we are in a similar period of transition from which it is likely, after another two decades, that Japan will emerge as the leading industrial power.[8]

The same spirit and logic ran through List's arguments. Trade was not just a game. Over the long sweep of history some nations lost independence and control of their destiny if they fell behind in trade. Therefore they had to think about it strategically, not just as a matter of where they could buy the cheapest shirt this week.

In *The Natural System of Political Economy,* List included an absorbing chapter titled "The Dominant Nation." Like many other things written about Britain in the nineteenth century, it makes bittersweet reading for twentieth-century Americans. "England's manufactures are based upon highly efficient political and social institutions, upon powerful machines, upon great capital resources, upon an output larger than that of all other countries, and upon a complete network of internal transport facilities," List said of the England of the 1830s, as many had said of the United States of the 1950s and 1960s.

> A nation which makes goods more cheaply than anyone else and possesses immeasurably more capital than anyone else is able to grant its customers more substantial and longer credits than anyone else. . . . By accepting or by excluding the import of their raw materials and other products, England—all powerful as a manufacturing and commercial country—can confer great benefits or inflict great injuries upon nations with relatively backward economies.[9]

This is what England lost when it lost "dominance," and what Japan is gaining now.

Morality vs. power. By the end of the twentieth century, the Anglo-American view had taken on a moral tone that was latent and embryonic when Adam Smith wrote his book. If a country disagreed with the Anglo-American axioms, it wasn't simply disagreeing; it was "cheating." Japan "cheats" the world trading system by protecting its rice farmers. America "cheats" with its subsidies for sugar-beet growers and with its various other restrictions on trade. Malaysia "cheated" by requiring foreign investors to take on local partners. And on and on. If the "rules" of the trading system aren't protected from such cheating, the whole system might collapse and bring back the Great Depression. At an international business conference in 1991, an American scholar reflected this view:

> We have to deal with an uneven playing field, and with the fact that rules aren't followed everywhere in the world market. There is no doubt about that. Japan did cheat, and in fact Japan continues to cheat. And there is no reason any longer for the United States or any other industrial country to accept that.[10]

In the German view, economics is not a matter of "right" or "wrong," of "cheating" or "playing fair." It is merely a matter of strong or weak. The gods of trade will help those who helped themselves. No code of "honor" will defend the weak (as today's Latin Americans and Africans can attest). If a nation decides to help itself—by protecting its own industries, by discriminating against foreign products—then that is a *decision,* not a sin.

The Triumph of the Englishmen

Why bring the Germans into it? Because they have had a lasting effect—outside the Anglo-American bloc. It was only natural for the Japanese of the Meiji era to conclude that economics was a matter of national strength, not "consumer welfare," and that it involved winners and losers. Because the Americans had machines, they could tell the Japanese what to do. The Meiji leaders were determined to get machines of their own. In theories like those advanced by Friedrich List, the nineteenth-century Japanese found a more persuasive set of prescriptions than in the laissez-faire teachings of Adam Smith.

But the most important part of the Germanic-Asian argument is its near invisibility in the English-speaking world, especially the United States. The problem is not that Americans don't accept the German analysis; in many ways it is flawed. The problem is that they *don't know it exists*. For instance, the popular *Dictionary of Economics,* edited by American and British economists and published in 1991, has a long explanation of the "Laffer curve" but no mention of List. In 1992 Robert Wade, author of an influential study of East Asian growth called *Governing the Market,* was at MIT as a visiting scholar. Wade had previously been teaching in Korea, and there he'd found translations of List's works in every campus bookstore. But in the catalogue of MIT's vast library system Wade found an entry for just a single volume by List, *The National System of Political Economy,* in an edition published in 1885. When Wade finally obtained the book he found that it had last been checked out in 1966.

Despite Robert Wade's travails at MIT, some American economists and political scientists did in effect rediscover Friedrich List in the 1980s. "Strategic trade theory," advanced by Paul Krugman of MIT, and others, has demonstrated through sophisticated economic models that in some cases protectionism can pay. According to the Ec-101 version of free-trade theory, protectionism and other forms of government interference are doomed to fail, since they raise prices for consumers and shield inefficient industries from the bracing effects of international competition. Strategic trade theory contends that under the right circumstances, tariffs and protectionist policies can give a nation more high-value industries, and therefore more overall wealth, than it would have with strict laissez-faire. This is especially true, according to the theory, when the actions of other countries, with strategic trade policies of their own, are taken into account.

Many other modern economists devote themselves to studying the "market failures," "market imperfections," and other real-world circumstances that depart from the pristine certainty of classic economic models. But very few of these caveats and refinements have trickled down to the realm where economics is usually discussed— to the realm of politicians, newspaper editorialists, TV talk shows, and the other forms of punditry that define reasonable and unreasonable ideas. When Americans talk about wealth, poverty, and their nation's place in the world, they often act as if Adam Smith's theories, in their supersimplified version, were the only theories still in play. For instance:

After the World Bank's annual meeting, which was held in Bangkok in 1991, an editorial writer for *The Wall Street Journal* proclaimed, "With a few sickly exceptions, such as the decaying Communist holdouts of China and Vietnam, it seems that the ideas of Adam Smith, of Alfred Marshall, or Milton Friedman, have triumphed. We are all capitalists now."[11]

This would be true only if we accept the most vulgar and imprecise statement of what being a "capitalist" means. The economies that have grown most rapidly over the past generation—from Germany to Thailand to Korea to Japan—all certainly believe in *competition*. Toyota and Nissan grow strong fighting against each other. Daewoo and Hyundai have competed on products from cars to computers to washing machines. But it would be very hard to find a businessman or official in these countries who would say, with a straight face, that these industries grew "automatically" or in a "natural way."

In February 1993, Sylvia Nasar of *The New York Times* wrote that industrial policy would be a bad prescription for America, since it had so little to do with Japan's success. "Two of Japan's brightest export stars, autos and consumer electronics, owe virtually nothing to government subsidies or protection."[12] Five days later the columnist Charles Krauthammer echoed this assertion, writing that "government subsidies made almost no contribution to Japan's greatest successes: autos and consumer electronics."[13]

In fact, every serious history of these two industries documents exactly the opposite conclusion. Starting in the 1950s, MITI and the Ministry of Finance coordinated plans for reconstruction of these industries (among others). Japan imposed high tariffs on foreign products. It required foreign companies to license their technology to Japanese producers if they wanted to do business in Japan at all.

(This pattern, as applied to the semiconductor industry, is discussed in Chapter One.)

In the mid-1980s, David Aikman, a journalist for *Time,* wrote a book about the "miracle" economies of Asia. The successes of Taiwan and Hong Kong, he said, "demonstrate just how faithful, consciously or not, the rulers of these two countries have been to American conceptions of free enterprise."[14] In a similar theme but with more geographic sweep, Milton and Rose Friedman wrote in *Free to Choose* that "Malaysia, Singapore, Korea, Taiwan, Hong Kong, and Japan—relying extensively on free markets—are thriving. . . . By contrast, India, Indonesia, and Communist China, all relying heavily on central planning, have experienced economic stagnation."[15]

Despite Hong Kong's relative lack of regulations, despite the small businesses that abound in Taiwan, to call either of these "American" is to drain all meaning from the term. For example, as late as 1987, most imports of steel into Taiwan had to be approved by the nation's big steelmaker, China Steel. The United States, too, protects its steel industry, but this is presumably not what Aikman meant when saying that Taiwan had been "faithful" to American conceptions of free enterprise.

"There is a great deal of misinformation about the trade regimes of [Taiwan and Korea], misinformation which is cultivated by the governments to conceal how much real protection there has been," wrote Robert Wade in a book that discussed Taiwan at length. "East Asian trade regimes are inconsistent in important ways with even a modified version of the standard economists' account of what a good trade regime looks like. . . . It is amazing and even scandalous that the distinguished academic theorists of trade policy . . . *have not tried* to reconcile these facts about East Asian trade regimes with their core prescriptions."[16]

Anyone who reads American or British newspapers or listens to political speeches in English could provide other examples. The Anglo-American theories have won the battle of ideas—wherever that battle has been carried out in English. The concepts of consumer welfare, comparative advantage, and freest possible trade no longer seem even like "concepts" but like natural laws. Yet they have three great failings.

First, they fail a test of history. They do not explain how the industrial old guard—first England, then America—rose to power. Indeed, those countries developed fastest when they paid least attention to today's Anglo-American principles of economic growth.

Second, they fail a crucial test of theory. They do not explain how one country can take a lead over others in technology or productivity, as America did in the past and as Japan is doing now.

Third, they fail a test of current evidence. In the last generation, Asian economies have grown faster than any others, for reasons that have very little to do with the celebrated Adam Smith scheme.

The Test of History

In 1991 the economic historian William Lazonick published a book called *Business Organization and the Myth of the Market Economy.* Its subject was industrial economies during the years when they became strongest—England in the eighteenth and nineteenth centuries, the United States in the nineteenth and twentieth centuries, Germany and Japan from the late nineteenth century on.

These countries varied in countless ways. The United Kingdom had a huge empire; the United States had a huge frontier; Germany and Japan had the advantage of applying technology that others had invented. Yet these success stories had one common theme, Lazonick showed. *None* of them conformed to today's model of "getting prices right" and putting the consumer's welfare first. All of the countries had to "cheat" somehow to succeed.

Friedrich List had stressed exactly this point in the 1840s, when England was the only industrial success story to be observed. The British of those days were beginning to preach free-trade theory in earnest. They abolished the famous Corn Laws in 1846, exposing their inefficient domestic farmers to competition from overseas. Yet over the previous 150 years, England had strong-armed its way to prosperity by violating every free-trade rule.[17] It would be as if Japan, in the 1990s, after finally opening its rice market to competition, then convinced itself that it had been taking a hands-off approach to its economy for the previous 100 years. When England was building its technological lead over the rest of the world, Lazonick said, its leaders did not just care about the "process" of competition. They were determined to control the result so they would have the strongest manufacturers on earth. As Friedrich List had pointed out:

> In her North American colonies England had already acted on
> those principles in disallowing the manufacture in those colonies

of even a single horseshoe nail, that no horseshoe nails made there should be imported into England.

Accordingly, England prohibited the import of goods dealt in her own factories, the Indian cotton and silk fabrics. . . . Not so much as a thread of them would England permit to be used. She would have none of the beautiful and cheap fabrics, but preferred to consume her own inferior and costly stuff. . . .

So late as the year 1750 a hat manufactory in the State of Massachusetts created so great a sensation and jealousy in Parliament, that it declared all kinds of manufactories [sic] to be "common nuisances," not excepting ironworks, notwithstanding that the country possessed in the greatest abundance all the requisite materials for the manufacture of iron. . . . The monopoly on manufacturing industry by the mother country was one of the chief causes for the American Revolution; the tea duty merely afforded an opportunity for its outbreak.[18]

British economists began talking about "getting prices right" only after they'd succeeded in promoting their own industries by "getting prices wrong." Prices were "wrong" in that cheap competition from the colonies was forbidden. They were wrong in that the Crown subsidized and encouraged investment in factories and a fleet. They were "right" in that they made British industry strong.

As Lazonick noted, by the time Adam Smith came on the scene, the British could start lecturing other countries about the folly of tariffs and protection. Why should France (America, Prussia, China . . .) punish its consumers, by denying them access to cheap, well-made English cloth? Yet the British theorists did not ask themselves why their products were so advanced, why "the world market . . . in the late eighteenth century was *so uniquely under British control*."[19] Lazonick added, "In the last half of the nineteenth century, the proponents of the unfettered operation of international markets accepted as a natural fact of life Britain's dominant position as the 'workshop of the world.' They did not bother to ask how Britain had attained that position."[20] The answers to questions of this sort would involve nothing like laissez-faire.

The full answer would, instead, include the power of the British Navy, which by routing the French and Spanish had made it easier for British ships to dominate trade routes. It would note the political measures that prevented the Portuguese and the Irish from developing textile industries that could compete with England's. It would include the Navigation Acts, which ensured a British monopoly in a number of the industries the country wanted most to develop. The answer would involve land enclosures, and a host of other measures that allowed British manufacturers to concentrate more capital than they could otherwise have obtained.

Lazonick summed up this process in a passage that exactly describes the predicament of the United States at the end of the twentieth century:

> The ultimate critique of nineteenth-century laissez-faire ideology is *not* that it ignored the role of national power in Britain's past and present. Rather it is that laissez-faire failed to comprehend Britain's economic future—a future in which, confronted by far more powerful systems of national capitalism, the British economy would enter into a long-run relative decline from which it has yet to recover.[21]

America's economic history follows the same pattern. While American industry was developing, the United States had little time for laissez-faire. *After* it had grown strong, the United States began preaching laissez-faire to the rest of the world—and began to kid itself about its own history, believing its slogans that laissez-faire had been the secret of its own past success.

The "traditional" American support for worldwide free trade is quite a recent phenomenon. It started only at the end of World War II. This period dominates the memory of most Americans now alive but does not cover the years of America's most rapid industrial expansion.[22] As Thomas McCraw of Harvard Business School has pointed out, the United States, which was born at the same moment as *The Wealth of Nations,* never practiced an out-and-out mercantilist policy, as did Spain in its colonial age. But "it did exhibit for 150 years after the Revolution a pronounced tendency toward protectionism, mostly through the device of the tariff."[23]

American schoolchildren now learn that their country had its own version of the Smith-List debate, when Thomas Jefferson and Alexander Hamilton squared off about what kind of economy the new nation should have. During George Washington's first term, Hamilton produced his famous "Report on Manufactures," arguing that the country should deliberately encourage industries, with tariffs and subsidies, to compete with the mighty British. Jefferson and others set out a more pastoral, individualistic, yeoman-farmer vision of the country's future. As everyone learns in class, Hamilton lost. He was killed in a duel with Aaron Burr; he is not honored on Mount Rushmore or in the national capital as Jefferson is; he survives mainly through his portrait on the $10 bill. Yet it was a strange sort of defeat, for during the first 150 years after Hamilton submitted his report, the United States more or less followed his advice.

In 1810 Albert Gallatin, a succesor of Hamilton's as secretary of the treasury, said British manufacturers enjoyed structural advantages that would keep Americans from ever catching up. The only truly "powerful obstacle" to American industry, he said, was "the vastly superior capital of Great Britain, which enables her merchants to give very long term credits, to sell on small profits, and to make occasional sacrifices."[24] This, of course, is exactly what American manufacturers now say about Japan's financial system. Very little has changed in debates about "free trade" and "protection" in the past two hundred years. If the antique language and references to out-of-date industries were removed from Hamilton's report of 1791, it could have been republished in 1991 and would have fit right into the industrial policy debate. "There is no purpose to which public money can be more beneficially applied, than to the acquisition of a new and useful branch of industry" was the center of Hamilton's argument—and, similarly, of most modern-day "industrial policy" plans.[25]

In the years before the American Revolution, most leaders of the colonies had supported the *concept* of British protectionist measures. They were irritated by new taxes and levies in the 1760s and 1770s—but they had seen how effective Britain's approach had been in developing industries.[26] Through the nineteenth century, the proper level of a national tariff was, along with slavery, *the* chronically divisive American issue. Northerners generally wanted a higher tariff, to protect their industries; farmers and Southerners wanted a lower tariff, so they could buy cheaper imported supplies. Many major politicians were unashamed protectionists. "I don't know much about the tariff," Abraham Lincoln said, "but I know this much: When we buy manufactured goods abroad, we get the goods and the foreigner gets the money. When we buy the manufactured goods at home, we get both the goods and the money."[27] The United States had, just before Lincoln's term, forced the Japanese to accept treaties to "open" the Japanese market. They provided that Japan could impose a tariff of no more than 5 percent on most goods. America's average tariff, at the same time, was more than 30 percent.

In the 1890s William McKinley said repeatedly that the tariff had been the crux of the nation's wealth. ("We lead all nations in agriculture; we lead all nations in mining; we lead all nations in manufacturing. These are the trophies which we bring after twenty-nine years of a protective tariff."[28]) The national tariff level had varied but stayed over 30 percent through most of the nineteenth century. The United States did not begin to preach or practice free trade until after World War II, when its dominance of the world economy seemed unchallengeable. Then the average duty paid on all imports fell from about 9 percent in 1945 to about 4 percent by the late 1970s.

In addition to the tariff, nineteenth-century America went in heavily for industrial planning—occasionally under that name but more often in the name of national defense. Government as a whole was much smaller, relative to the private economy, in nineteenth-century America than in any of today's industrialized states, and no one contends that nineteenth-century America was a rigorously "planned" economy. Nonetheless the government consistently intervened, often using the military as a means for what we would now call "rebuilding infrastructure," "picking winners," promoting research, or coordinating industrial growth. As Geoffrey Perret pointed out in his book *A Country Made by War,* many evolutions about which people now say "that was good for the country" occurred only because someone could say at the time "this will be good for the military"—giving the government an excuse to step in.

In the mid-nineteenth century, settlers moving West followed maps drawn by Army cartographers, along roads built by Army engineers and guarded by Army forts. At the end of the century, the U.S. Navy searched for ways to build bigger, stronger warships and along the way helped foster the world's most advanced steel industry. Some boosts to industry were unintended side effects. But very often in nineteenth-century America, politicians deliberately chose the military and the government as tools for jobs that would not otherwise be done. Thomas Jefferson lacked a military record and was skeptical of military virtues. But as president he thought that the private educational system was not producing enough engineers for the nation's good. Teachers and ministers, yes—these came in abundance from Harvard and Yale, but not scientists or technicians. Therefore he expanded West Point, made an engineer its superintendent, and had it set a model for technical education.[29]

Just before Jefferson took office as president, the U.S. government began an ambitious project to "pick winners." England surpassed America in virtually every category of manufacturing at the time, and so to a smaller degree did France. In 1798, Congress authorized an extraordinary purchase of muskets from a then-struggling inventor named Eli Whitney. Whitney had invented the cotton gin five years earlier, but it had not yet paid off commercially, and he was on the verge of bankruptcy. Congress offered him an unprecedented contract to provide ten thousand muskets within twenty-eight months. Getting the muskets themselves was only part of what Congress accomplished: this was also a way to induce, and to finance, a mass-production industry for the United States. Whitney worked around the clock, developed America's first mass-production equipment, and put on a show for the congressmen. He brought a set of broken-down musket locks to Washington and invited congressmen to fit the pieces together themselves—showing, of course, that the age of standardized parts had arrived.

"The nascent American arms industry led where the rest of manufacturing followed," Geoffrey Perret concluded. "Far from being left behind by the Industrial Revolution the United States, in a single decade and thanks largely to one man, had suddenly burst into the front rank."[30] It achieved this status not by waiting for it to evolve "naturally" but by deliberately promoting the desired result.

For most of the next century and a half the U.S. government was less interested in improving the *process* of competition than in achieving a specific result. It cared less about "getting prices right" and more about "getting ahead." What America actually did, while industrializing, is not what we tell ourselves about industrialization today. Consumer welfare took second place; promoting production came first. A heavy tariff on imported British rails made the expansion of the American railroads in the 1880s costlier than it would otherwise have been. But this protectionist policy coincided with, and arguably contributed to, the emergence of a productive, efficient American steel industry. The United States, trying to catch up with Britain, behaved more or less like the leaders of Meiji (and postwar) Japan, trying to catch up with the United States.

Thomas McCraw, in his history of U.S. economic policy, says that the American pattern was not some strange exception but actually the international norm. The great industrial successes of the past two centuries—America after its revolution, Germany under Bismarck, Japan after World War II—all violated the "rules" of laissez-faire. Despite the obvious cultural differences among these countries, McCraw notes, the underlying strategy was very much the same.

In all three cases the home markets remained closed to equal
competition. In the earlier period, Germany imported practically no iron and steel from her major competitors, Britain and
the United States. Similarly, postwar Japan imported very few
manufactured goods from Europe or America, irrespective of
price or quality. She freely imported only food, industrial raw
materials, and technology.

   Thus, in all three cases, the situation was one of a closed
system exploiting open ones, using the protective home markets
to service the fixed costs that helped lead to low prices for the
same items in the export market. Assuming that the open market
remained open and the closed one closed, it was a strategy that
could not possibly fail, so long as comparative productivity remained high. The outstanding recent success of Japan would
appear to underline this point, and to remind us how difficult
it is, for either Japanese free-trade advocates inside the country
or outside negotiators from the United States, to force a change
in what has been a consumately successful strategy.[31]

This is the lesson of the leading nation's histories—but not the lesson
we read about in newspapers or hear in political platforms. "One
assumes away the evidence of American, Japanese, German, South
Korean, and Taiwanese history," Walter Russell Mead wrote about
the prevailing American attitude. "Since positive economic policy
fails the test of theory, it cannot have worked in practice."[32]

The Test of Theory

In the late 1940s, near the end of his long career, Joseph Schumpeter
speculated on what he would do if he became young again. Suppose
he woke up tomorrow as a bright-eyed graduate student in economics
rather than as a wizened professor. What would he do with his new
allotment of years?

   Modern economics research follows three main branches: economic theory, statistics, and economic history. By the time Schumpeter wrote, economic theory was clearly the most glamorous of the
callings, and statistics seemed the most practical. But, Schumpeter
said, he would surely devote his life to studying economic history.[33]

   Within the modern economics profession this would be a surprising, even radical, choice. Since the end of World War II, the
glamorous work in economics has been deeply unhistorical. With

each passing year, American economics textbooks have become more and more jammed with formulas, graphs, mathematical models, and regression analyses. At the same time, they've lightened the dosage of real examples from the real word. In the mid-1980s, researchers surveyed 212 graduate students at the most prestigious American economics schools, asking them what factors were more and less essential for success as professional economists. Sixty-five percent of the graduate students said it was very important to be "smart, in the sense of being good at problem-solving" to succeed as an economist. Only 3 percent said it was very important to have "a broad knowledge of the real economy."[34]

Something much deeper lies behind this uneven emphasis. Modern economics has become exceedingly precise about one kind of problem, but less and less interested in another. Anglo-American economists focus much of their effort on "equilibrium studies" and "constrained optimization"—in essence, laboratory experiments involving economics. In a laboratory, you can control many variables—the temperature, the amount of lighting or contamination—to focus on the single factor you want to observe. The most admired of today's economists are those who can make the best "models" of the way economic processes should theoretically occur. (Early in 1993, a famous American economist gave a speech designed to rebut criticism that academic economics was out of touch with real-world problems, especially problems of international trade competition. Nothing could be further from the truth! "Take, for example, a simple two-good Ricardian model in which one country is more productive in both industries than the other . . .") In mathematical, model-making economics, you can "control" many variables by taking them for granted, and then focusing on what you want to understand. You assume, as a given, that some people are owners and others are laborers, that Korea has a semiconductor industry and Mali does not, that women earn less then men. Then you calculate, within these constraints, the best possible outcome—what trade policy Mali should pursue, what rate of inheritance tax will make an economy grow most quickly.

Within this set of laboratory conditions, the tools of economic analysis are very powerful. By "getting prices right," Mali will make the best use of the resources it has on hand. But the most interesting and important economic questions concern the assumptions and constraints themselves. Why are some countries chronically so poor? Why have others done so much to pull ahead?

To use another homely analogy: Consider the world of cooking.

If you listed every edible ingredient that was in your household, modern economic "theory" would tell you the very best way to combine and allocate them. You could figure out which ingredients would spoil when, which tastes and nutrients went best together, which members of your family required which vitamins and minerals—and you could, quite precisely, determine the best way to eat. It would just be a matter of "getting the nutrients right." Similarly in the world of sports: If you knew about every athlete who was in training in your country, the tools of economics could help you figure out how to assemble the strongest possible Olympics team. You could determine which runners to enter in the sprints, which ones should run middle distance, and which ones you could schedule for the relays without tiring them for their individual events. In this case you would be "getting the distances right." In the world of schooling, modern economic "theory" is equivalent to university admissions systems, which can help figure out the best mixture of athletes, violinists, scholarship students, and alums' children to admit. Here you would "get the transcripts right" in knowing who had what skills.

These are all "constrained maximization" decisions—making the best use of the resources at hand. They don't help you understand why you are constrained, and what you can do about it. This kind of analysis does not reveal why you had those ingredients in your kitchen—why your store stocked what it did, why you couldn't afford better food. In the Olympics, it couldn't explain why runners from another country always beat you, or why a country's overall supply of talent might deteriorate or improve. In the university, it could tell you who, among the *available* students, would make up the best class—but could not tell you why the overall talent mix was changing, or why people from certain cities or prep schools or ethnic groups or economic class backgrounds did so much better than anyone else.

And as economic-style reasoning applies to the realm of economics: it can tell you, this week, where you can get the best return on an investment. It can tell you, this year, how a change in tax rates might affect the unemployment rate. It can even tell you how, over the course of this decade, a new tariff level is likely to affect the volume of world trade. But it has a very hard time accounting for the larger rises and falls in world affairs: why it was England, and not France, that dominated the nineteenth-century economy; why it was Germany, and not Poland, that industrialized so rapidly at the end of that century; why Japan caught up in the early twentieth century and again now. Economics is a wonderful tool for analyzing

trends and changes *once nations have assumed their ran.*
ting prices right" is not so good for understanding hc
those ranks and why they change.

This would not be a serious failing except that m
believe the opposite: that "getting prices right" tells us ᴠᴏᴛɪ aᴏout
the short and the long run. Indeed, the long-run evidence suggests
just the reverse: that *getting prices wrong*—that is, violating the
"rules" of Anglo-American economics—may be indispensable for
nations trying to get ahead.

In the late 1980s, the economist Alice Amsden wrote a book
about the Korean economy called *Asia's Next Giant*. She said that
Korea's post–World War II rise shared many basic similarities with
Japan's industrial miracles and with Germany's industrialization in
the nineteenth century. In none of these cases, she said, did the
country "get prices right" by letting investors and consumers freely
decide where they would put their money. The secret was in fact
the opposite. Unless a country deliberately rigged the markets to
"get prices wrong," it had no hope of catching up in the industrial
race.

The key to capitalistic development, in this view, finally boils
down to *capital*. If you want to build factories, leapfrog your competitors in efficiency, train your people so they can outproduce others, you need *money*. If you are a poor nation, you don't have enough
money sitting around to begin with; and if you are a rich nation,
you are likely to have committed your extra money to pension and
benefit programs, as the United States has now done. Still, you need
the money—for new factories, for research, for distribution networks. How do you get it?

Historically, Amsden concluded, successful nations have gotten
extra money by rigging their markets. The goal is to get people to
save more of their paychecks, and banks to lend more money for
long-term industrial expansion, than normal market forces would
allow. To make its people save, a country needs to jack up interest
rates; to allow businesses to invest, it needs to keep the rates low.
Under Anglo-American theory the country would just let these two
forces fight it out until they reached the natural equilibrium. But
that is not how successful development has actually occurred, Amsden said:

> Industrial expansion depends on savings and investment, but in
> "backward" countries especially, savings and investment are in
> conflict over the ideal interest rate, high in one case, low in the

other. In Korea and other late-industrializing countries, this conflict has been mediated by the subsidy. . . . Thus, the government established multiple prices for loans, only one of which could possibly have been "right" according to the law of supply and demand. Moreover, the most critical price—that for long-term credit—was wildly "wrong" in a capital-scarce country, its real price, due to inflation, being negative.[35]

That is, for Korea to get enough money into the hands of its industries, it needed to bend the rules. The crucial thing about this undertaking, Amsden emphasized, is that it was not an idiosyncratic Korean quirk. Every country that has caught up with others has had to do so by rigging its rules: extracting extra money from its people, steering it into industrialists' hands.[36] Today's Americans and Britons are not obliged to follow the same rules. But to pretend that it doesn't exist, and that it hasn't worked in many cases, is like Christian missionaries assuming that Buddhism, Islam, and other "heresies" do not exist.

The Test of Current Experience

In the late 1980s and early 1990s, publications and politicians in America and Britain said that American culture was spreading and that the Anglo-American model had prevailed. The Soviet Union had collapsed; Asia was "Westernizing"; the world, as George Bush told Americans in the summer of 1992, was becoming "just like us." Yet it was during just this time that those outside the bond of the English-speaking union, and a few inside, began revealing just the opposite view. In larger and bolder numbers they announced that the Asian systems were succeeding because they had moved *beyond* Anglo-American system capitalism, not because they were still trying to "catch up" within and live by its rules.

In the summer of 1991, an economist named Narongchai Akrasanee, from the Thailand Development Research Institute in Bangkok, came to Washington to explain why Asian economies continued to grow. The key to their strength, he said, was "the difference in the forms of capitalism practiced" from those in the West. The difference in forms was greatest between Japan and America ("U.S. capitalism is based mainly on market forces. . . . Japanese capitalism is based on networks," and so on). Because this difference was usually not recognized on the American side, it led to "perpetual conflicts" between the Anglo-Americans and the Asians.[37]

A few months later, while American newspapers reported on the Russian hunger for blue jeans, Big Macs, and apparently every kind of Americana, Russian leaders were talking about their admiration for the Asian economic model. In 1987 Leonid Abalkin, the former chairman of the Economic Reform Commission, had said that someday the Soviet Union should emulate "Japanese methods of management . . . not only those of individual companies, but also national strategy as a whole." The American scholar James Clay Moltz pointed out that comments such as these got virtually no coverage in the English-language press, which emphasized the value of the Anglo-American model around the world. But the reformers in what was left of the Soviet Union were, he said, acting in accord with Abalkin's comment that "Among the capitalist countries, I would assess the Japanese highest of all."[38] In the summer of 1992, a team of Japanese bureaucrats toured the old Marxist domains, telling Russians and Ukrainians not to listen too closely to the Americans or the officials from the International Monetary Fund. The IMF's message was to concentrate on a strong currency—that is, to "get prices right"—and then wait for industries to arrive. The Japanese delegations said that it had never worked that way for them. "From our thinking, that is not enough," a MITI representative said in Russia. "Some kind of industrial policy is needed."[39]

The IMF and the World Bank themselves had become, in the 1980s, bastions of the Anglo-American orthodoxy. (One neat, reinforcing connection involved *The Economist* magazine of London. Through the 1980s and early 1990s, its editors also served as editors and ghostwriters for the World Bank's annual reports. Those reports would emphasize the need to "get prices right" in the developing world; *The Economist* would then praise the realism and clear thinking of the reports; the bank's policies would validate the argument the magazine was pushing; and the cycle went on.) But in the 1990s Asian representatives, especially the Japanese, began to rock the boat.

In 1991, for instance, an IMF team studied the economies of Southeast Asia and concluded that if they wanted to grow even faster, the key was—surprise!—"getting prices right." In particular they had to deregulate their financial systems so that investors could move money in and out as quickly and flexibly as they chose. Almost immediately, a team of advisers from the Bank of Japan appeared to warn their neighbors: Not so fast! The basic purpose of a financial system, they emphasized, was not to enrich speculators—or even investors!—but to be the "servant of the real economy."[40] Anything that helped a financial system get money into industrialists' hands was good; anything that didn't, even if it "got prices right," was bad.

"Experience in Asia has shown that although development strategies require a healthy respect for market mechanisms, the role of government cannot be forgotten," the governor of the Bank of Japan, Yasushi Mieno, told the annual meeting of the World Bank and International Monetary Fund in October 1991. This was part of an amazing and unprecedented act of heresy by Japanese officials at the World Bank–IMF meeting that fall. For years they had listened while English-speakers at the bank and the IMF had given the Anglo-American formula for economic growth—and as they listened, they knew that their own growth had not conformed to those rules. Finally, in the 1990s, they began saying so. At the 1991 meeting Japanese officials said the Western strategy was "simpleminded," out-of-date, and blind to what the Japanese, Koreans, Taiwanese, and others had actually done.[41] Shortly afterward the Japanese government sponsored a special World Bank project known as the "East Asian Miracle" study. This was an attempt to examine the Asian economies to see whether their experience matched the bank's prevailing views. When the study was published late in 1993, it acknowledged that Asian governments had played a larger role than the bank usually advocated—but then quickly stressed that the successful Asian countries had all gotten the "economic fundamentals right," through encouraging investment and discouraging inflation. Two days after the study was released, Eisuke Sakakibara, a senior official from Japan's Ministry of Finance, spoke about it with a bemused tone. "We paid for this study," he said at a breakfast in Washington. "But we didn't write it."[42]

For Japanese and other Asians to begin saying this—that their system really *was* something new, that they weren't just waiting for more and more accurate translations of *Wall Street Journal* editorials and Adam Smith—was quite a step. Since the Occupation years, Japanese leaders had tried above all to show how faithfully they were following America's lead. When the suggestion came up that the Japanese-style Asian economic system was "different" in some way, it was hurriedly knocked down by all parties involved.

But starting in the late 1980s the tone clearly changed. Iwao Nakatani, the economics professor I'd interviewed at Hitotsubashi University, said that Japan had indeed come up with a new business system. "If the entire world were to adopt the Japanese system," he said, "the world's markets would be closed and Japan's economic expansion would be stopped right there."[43] A MITI official named Koji Matsumoto published a book called *The Rise of the Japanese Corporate System*. It had been published in Japanese in the early 1980s—and in the old days would have remained exclusively in Japanese. But in 1991 it came out in English, arguing to outside readers that Japan had come up with a new kind of wheel. ("Although not widely recognized yet, a new economic system has developed and been nurtured in Japan inside a shell of capitalism. . . . The new corporate system is the source of the might of the Japanese economy.")[44] Eisuke Sakakibara, the Ministry of Finance official whom I'd heard discussing the World Bank study, published his own heretical book. It was called *Beyond Capitalism: The Japanese Model of Market Economics*, and it argued that Japan had invented something called a "noncapitalistic market economy."[45] In the future, Sakakibara said, it would be this Japanese-style system, rather than socialism or communism, that posed the main challenge to Anglo-American-style capitalism.

By the early 1990s, more and more representatives of the East Asian system felt comfortable admitting something they had seemed ashamed of in the past—that their system was not necesssarily following the Anglo-American "rules," that it was doing things a new way. Alan Blinder, of Princeton, was one of those to notice the implications. When you examined the economies of Asia and considered how they had actually grown, he said, you saw little resemblance to Anglo-American "rules." "Much has been written about Japan's formidable challenge to American industrial preeminence," Blinder said.

> But the amazing Japanese economy poses another challenge—one that has been barely noticed. I refer to Japan's challenge to received economic doctrine. Stated briefly and far too boldly, the Japanese have succeeded by doing everything wrong (according to standard economic theory). That should make economic theorists squirm.[46]

Contrasts Between the Asian and Anglo-American Systems

Every country and culture is unique, and the "Asian" system naturally means something different in Singapore from what it means in Thailand or Japan. There are obvious comparable variations among European and North American capitalist models. In their emphasis on industrial guidance and national policy, France and Germany are more "Asian" than they are American. In their approach to leisure and the good life, the Europeans are less like the new Asian model than the Americans are. Still, four main patterns distinguish the Asian system from the prevailing Western model. Some of them are descended from old clashes between the German and the Anglo-American philosophies. They involve:

- The *purpose* of economic life. In the Anglo-American model, the basic reason to have an economy is to raise the individual consumer's standard of living. In the Asian model, it is to increase the collective national strength. Ideally, the goal is to make the nation independent and self-sufficient, so it does not rely on outsiders for its survival. The Anglo-American goal is basically materialistic; the Asian-style goal is basically political, and comes from the long experience of being oppressed by people with stronger economies and technologies.
- The view of *power* in setting economic policies. The Anglo-American ideology views concentrated power as an evil ("power corrupts, and absolute power . . ."). Therefore it has developed elaborate schemes for dividing and breaking up power when it becomes concentrated. The Asian-style model views concentrated power as a fact of life. It has developed elaborate systems for improving the chances that the power will be used for the long-term national good.
- The view of *surprise* and unpredictability. The Anglo-American model views surprise as the key to economic life. It is precisely because markets are fluid and unpredictable that we believe they "work." Attempts to outwit the market by "picking winners" or defining "the good life" are bound to fail. Let the market decide. The Asian-style system deeply mistrusts markets. It sees competition as a useful *tool* for keeping companies on their toes but not as a way to resolve any of the big questions of life—how a society should be run, in what direction its economy should unfold. This is, in Western terms, a "military" view of economics. Within the American military, the Army competes with the Navy for funds, and competition within branches keeps both the Army and the Navy sharp. But the Army and the Navy don't cast votes or place bids to decide

where the nation should fight. Decisions like that are not left to a "market."

· The view of *national borders* and an us-vs.-them concept of the world. People everywhere are xenophobic and exclusive, but in the Anglo-American model this is defined as a lamentable, surmountable failing. The Asian-style model assumes it is a more natural and permanent condition. The world consists of "us" and "them," and no one will look out for "us" if we don't look out for ourselves.

The differences emerge this way:

The basic purpose of economic activity: What, finally, is an economy "for"? By the tenets of post-World War II Anglo-American economics, economic development means "more." If people have more choice, more leisure, more wealth, more opportunity to pursue happiness, society as a whole will be a success.

Of course, even the United States and Britain recognize limits to the pursuits of "more." Americans would be more comfortable if they were allowed to hire desperate people from the Third World as indentured servants or slaves. Then almost everyone in America could afford a housekeeper and a cook. Rich but ailing people would enjoy "more" life if they were allowed to buy organs from the healthy poor. Clothes would be cheaper if we got rid of child-labor laws and put idle young hands to work.

But transactions like these, forbidden even in the permissive Anglo-American system, are seen as grotesque exceptions. In theory, any deal that the market permits will, in the long run, be good for society as a whole. During the wave of corporate takeovers and buy-outs in the 1980s, it was hard to make a purely economic case that the transactions might do more harm than good. According to Anglo-American economic theory, such deals *must* have been beneficial; otherwise they would not have taken place.[47]

The same stimulus provokes a much different response from the Asian system. In the late 1980s, the American financial operator T. Boone Pickens bought 25 percent of the shares of Koito, a little Japanese firm that supplied parts to Toyota. Pickens kept lobbying for a seat on Koito's board of directors so he could learn the details of its relationship with Toyota. Koito (and, behind it, the mighty Toyota) flatly refused. Corporations in the United States and Britain often resist takeover attempts and outside directors, just as Koito did. The difference in the Japanese case is that Pickens had no recourse. There was no body of court rulings in Japan, as there is in the United States, based on the presumption that takeover bids must be good. There was no legal assumption that corporate boards should think first about maximizing shareholder value; therefore, the Koito board was under no obligation to explain why it was resisting a director who claimed that he could make the company more profitable. (Eventually Pickens sold out and went away.)

The Anglo-American system is long on theories. It is easy to pick up any English-language textbook and find theories proving that whatever gives "more" to the consumer is best for everyone in the long run. The Asian system is not so theoretically explicit. Yet the fundamental purpose of the Asian model is evident from its performance. Its goal is to develop the *productive* base of the country—the industries either within the country or under the control of the country's citizens around the world. When it comes to a choice between the consumer's welfare and the producers, it's really no choice at all. The producer matters more.

In countless other ways the most successful of today's Asian societies reveal their bias in favor of the producer rather than the consumer. A few illustrations:

Japan and Korea are famous for protecting their rice markets. Even though the small plots, high land prices, and aged rural workforce all make the price five or six times the world level, until December 1993, when each country agreed to accept limited amounts of imported rice (as part of a worldwide GATT agreement), neither country gave its customers the option of buying from overseas. In the Western world this is usually taken as a quaint affectation. After all, Japanese and Korean spokesmen usually defend their policy in quaintly emotional terms ("our precious heritage!"), and in any case even if the markets were thrown wide open there is a limit to how much foreign rice the Japanese or Koreans could eat. In short, the rice issue seems like sugar-beet protection in the United States: economically indefensible but not a major issue.

In fact, rice policy reveals a major, consequential, proproducer bias. In both Korea and Japan, it illustrates the iron alliance between farmers and politicians. The traditional ruling party in each country has guaranteed high rice prices by closing the markets. The farmers in each country, with gerrymandered electoral systems, have provided the foundation of the ruling party's support. They also recirculate part of their profits with enormous political contributions. The consumers suffer—not just in the obvious way, by spending one third of their incomes on food, but more profoundly by being squeezed out of usable land. Especially in Japan but also in Korea and Taiwan, farm protectionism is the linchpin of a sweeping anticonsumer social bargain. If there is a single ceiling on consumption in these countries, it is the extremely high price of land—and if there is a single force that keeps the price up, it is the system that sets aside so much land (half of the nonmountainous land in Japan) for the production of very expensive rice.

"High land prices have caused the Japanese to act in ways they would not have otherwise," Susan B. Hanley of the University of Washington wrote in 1992. Nearly every aspect of daily life in Japan is affected, and often distorted, by the abnormally high price of land, Hanley said. In the late 1980s, the average dwelling in Tokyo had floor space of 60.3 square meters, or 649 square feet. While rural dwellings were larger, cramped housing throughout the country limits the number of children Japanese families can have and the amount of goods they can possess. "Much of what is attributed to Japan's uniqueness in the modern world is the result of these artificially maintained high land prices," Hanley concluded.[48]

The more successful the economy in Asia, the more likely it is to have a rigged, anticonsumer, high-priced retail system. Japan's economy is the most successful, and its retail system is the most cartelized and expensive. It's not simply that imported goods are expensive; Japanese-made goods are, too. (According to a survey at the end of 1991, clothes cost twice as much in Tokyo as in New York; food about three times as much; gasoline about 2.5 times as much, and so on.)[49]

A network of laws in Japan and other countries discourages discounting and price competition. Japan's famous *dai ten ho,* or "big store law," has for decades effectively outlawed supermarkets, since it requires that little local merchants must give their approval (or be bribed into doing so) before a big store can be built. (MITI has in recent years promised to overhaul or abolish the *dai ten ho.*) "Normal" Anglo-American economic theory can explain why a retail system as cartelized as Japan's should result in high prices. It is harder for "normal" economic reasoning to accept that such a costly, anticonsumer system might last for many decades, with the tacit acceptance of a highly educated population.

The immediate reason the system endures is the political power of small merchants, who—along with farmers and the construction industries—have in Japan been traditional big donors to the LDP. The more basic reason it lasts is that it helps producers in ways to offset its penalty to consumers. When competition in Europe or America pushes down the price of VCRs, cars, and semiconductor chips there, Japanese producers can maintain high prices within Japan. In effect, they wring monopoly profits out of their own people, to build a war chest for competition overseas. When the yen doubled in value against the dollar between 1985 and 1988, retail prices in Japan should have fallen significantly—but they barely budged. Japanese corporations were basically taxing their own country's consumers, with artificially high prices, so they could maintain artificially low prices in export markets in Europe and North America. In return for this tax, Japan got strong organizations and full employment. This may not be an attractive bargain to the Western mentality, and no individual Japanese or Korean likes paying higher prices. But as a social bargain it is seen as keeping the nation's producers strong and thereby keeping the social fabric intact.

The closest counterpart in American experience is the pre-breakup AT&T. Ma Bell penalized consumers in many ways. Rates were higher than they might have been. All the equipment had to be "authorized" by AT&T. At the same time, Bell used the money to keep its research labs and all its other functions under way. This is a version of the daily practice in Japanese business: people have fewer choices than they might ideally have, and the difference is absorbed and redeployed by the corporations.

Even corporations in Japan and Korea, in their own role as "consumers," reveal the anticonsumer bias of the Asian system. Their workers have, for several decades, traded artificially low wages for the promise of full employment. The wages are "artificially low" because through much of the postwar era earnings have lagged behind the increase in corporate productivity. By "normal" Western economic logic wages should have been rising much more rapidly. Similarly, Japanese and Korean companies have traded artificially low profits for their version of "full employment," which is an ever-growing market share. In 1991, a business survey listed the thirty most profitable large companies in the world. Of them, twenty-three were American, four were British, and none was Japanese.[50]

The parts of Japanese, Korean, and Taiwanese life that encourage consumption are made difficult. The parts that encourage savings, investment, and deferred gratification are made easy and attractive—the way it was in America during World War II. The automobile market in Japan, for instance, is dominated by the *shaken* racket. The word *shaken* is pronounced "shah-ken" rather than like the English word "shaken." In effect it is a reinspection certificate that each car in Japan must have to be legally on the road. The *shaken* policy originated during the infancy of the Japanese auto industry, when the cars were such unreliable rattletraps that bureaucrats thought it would be dangerous to let them on the road without constant safety checks. The public-safety rationale for frequent reinspections is no longer compelling. Nonetheless, when a car is three years old, and every two years after that, its owner must take it in for an inspection covering more than one hundred aspects of the car's operation. Owners are expected to have the cars fully repaired before presenting them for *shaken* inspections. Japanese garages use this as an excuse for top-to-bottom overhauls that generate nearly half the garage industry's annual income. When a car becomes eleven years old, it must be presented for annual *shaken* inspections. By that point the "necessary" repairs can cost so many thousands of dollars that it is more sensible simply to buy a new car. (Nearly a third of all cars on the road in America are more than a decade old; fewer than a tenth in Japan are.[51]) The *shaken* system is a way of turning the public into captive customers for Japan's automakers and even its repair industry.

Perhaps most dramatically, the last generation has taught most Asian countries one clear lesson: they can't really go wrong by giving consumers too little, but they can easily go wrong by giving consumers too much. During the collapse of Japan's bubble economy in 1991 and 1992, government officials grumbled privately that an atmosphere of hardship was useful. Consumerism had been getting out of hand, and the bubble's collapse would have a tonic, bracing effect—without imposing real hardship on Japan or endangering Japan's long-term prospects. (Business failure rates in Japanese manufacturing and construction firms were actually lower during the "crash" years of the early 1990s than their average rate during the booming 1980s.) In Korea, the late 1980s had been very heady, proconsumer years. The 1988 Seoul Summer Olympics did for the country what the 1964 Tokyo Summer Olympics had done for Japan. Anything seemed possible. In the fashionable parts of Seoul the young women wore miniskirts and the young men hung out all night. By 1990 the trade surplus was heading for the cellar, and the government had to fight back with a massive "anticonsumption" campaign.

During the late 1980s, the Korean government had been trying to keep its electronics industries in line by threatening that it would expose them to competition. The businesses could afford not to take this threat seriously, as Alice Amsden pointed out, because of "a sobering fact about which both the Korean government and business community were keenly aware: Taiwan had liberalized its domestic market for consumer electronics prematurely, and Japanese competition had wiped out local consumer electronics producers."[52] When Koreans ask themselves why their country took so long to get going industrially, they usually say that the problem was too *weak* a government—too weak to rig the economy to get extra savings out of the public, too weak to "get prices wrong" and artificially encourage investment. They do not complain that the government was too strong.[53]

Beyond these economic calculations is a question of human nature. Anglo-American economic theory boils people down to their roles as consumers. But life experience, even in America, tells us that people have more in mind than getting the cheapest possible price and the highest possible wage. In certain circumstances, people *like* to work hard, and save, and deny themselves. Even though state lottery winners typically don't have society's most desirable jobs, many of them decide to keep working even after they have cashed in. For years, studies have shown that people who own small businesses behave in a self-exploitative, economically "irrational" way. They typically work longer hours than most employees, and earn less money than they could if they sold off their assets and invested the proceeds. Decisions like these are seen as anomalies in the Anglo-American economic world. (They are explained away with little theories about the "utility" of work.) They are recognized as central to the Asian model of individual and collective life.

The nature of power. A second deep difference concerns an attitude and approach to the interaction of political and economic power. The Western approach, most of all the American, views concentrated power as an evil; the Asian approach, most of all the Japanese, works with it as a natural phenomenon of society, like hierarchy and inequality.

The Western liberal tradition in general, and the American political tradition in exaggerated particular, have been based on a suspicion of concentrated power. In the United States the effort to break up political power and the attempt to deconcentrate economic power have been seen as two parallel steps toward liberty. The United States has a three-branch government because of fear that any one branch would become too dominant. The great reformers of the American tradition have generally risen to strike down excessive concentrations of power, from Jefferson (in his battle with

Hamilton) to Andrew Jackson to Teddy Roosevelt to Ralph Nader and Ronald Reagan, in their varying ways. The people who have argued for centralizing and exercising power have generally had the excuse of wartime: Abraham Lincoln, Woodrow Wilson, Franklin Roosevelt, Lyndon Johnson.

The deepest critique of Japanese politics, made by the Dutch writer Karel van Wolferen, is that it lacks a *center* of political accountability. In the French or American system, a president must finally make big choices, whereas in the Japanese system (in Van Wolferen's terms) the buck keeps circulating and passing and never stops anywhere.

The classic illustration of this problem was Japan's apparent paralysis during the first month after Iraq invaded Kuwait. The standard criticism by Westerners was that Japan was not "doing its fair share." This entirely missed the point (Eventually Japan came up with quite a large sum of money, when it could have made the case for not contributing money at all. The case would have been that it was foolish to go to war over this issue, and that if other countries had emulated Japan by conserving their use of oil, they could have afforded to take a longer-term view.) Rather the problem was that Japan seemed incapable of deciding what its position was.

Most other Asian societies do have a center of power. Indeed, this "center" has often been one dominant figure—the military strongman, as in Thailand, Indonesia, and often Korea; the states-man-leader, epitomized by Lee Kuan Yew of Singapore; the sheer tyrant, as in North Korea or Burma; and the standard political boss, as in Malaysia and often Taiwan.

But whether the very center of politics has been weak, as in Japan, or strong, as everywhere else, the political system as a whole has generally been authoritarian in Asia. Compared to any Western societies, and especially the Anglo-American systems, Asian states have been less embarrassed and more explicit about the government's role in shaping society. The contrast is obviously sharper with America than with, say, France, which operates a Japanese-style *dirigiste* system without the social control. The Japanese system also resembles the most successful parts of government-business inter-action in the United States, such as nuclear-weapons design and medical research.

Some scholars contend that the heavy hand of government is the living legacy of Confucius. Anglo-American ideology warns against the abuse of power and therefore tries to restrict kings, prime ministers, and presidents. The traditional Confucian "mandate of heaven" approach assumes that there will be an emperor; the real question is whether he exercises power well or poorly. Other scholars argue that such theories are cultural window-dressing, used by ruling groups to rationalize their hold on power.

Either way, the history of powerful governments in East Asia has made most governments both more competent and more "legitimate" when they work with businesses. They are more competent because the great prestige of the civil service continues to attract the best-educated people in the country. The closest American counterpart is the U.S. Supreme Court and its cadre of clerks: there are disagreements about their political stands and about the skills of any individual judge, but the Court as a whole has power because it is seen as having passed a test of merit. Something similar applies to the governmental bureaucracies of many Asian countries. For historic and social-status reasons, jobs in the government bureaucracy are still among the most desirable jobs in Korea, Japan, and other Confucian-influenced East Asian societies. Ambitious young graduates compete for positions with the Japanese Ministry of Finance or the Korean Economic Planning Board the way ambitious young Americans compete for jobs at what we drolly call "investment" banks.

Today's Asian bureaucrats always complain that the thrill is gone, that they're not paid enough, that the long hours are driving out the real talent, and so on. Still, by international standards most East Asian governments remain successful in attracting skillful members into their ministries.

In a book called *Pacific Asia,* published in the early 1990s, the Japanese writer Masahide Shibusawa called the Asian approach to government "developmentalism." This approach differed from "economic development," Shibusawa said, in that it did not necessarily lead to a liberal democratic state. Westerners took it for granted that economic development would eventually lead to political liberalization, but "developmentalism" might have quite different results. "The Western liberal-democratic state is hardly identifiable in Pacific Asia," he said. "Indeed, it is probably not even recognized as a legitimate goal."[54] The Korean scholar Jung-en Woo, writing in 1991, made the point more explicitly:

> The state as conceived by East Asians is, furthermore, a practical necessity of development. . . . The resulting protected economy may have its inefficiencies—antique rice farmers and family store owners in East Asia, as well as higher prices for

consumers to cover the costs of this "moral economy"—but who is to say, except the hegemonic power that believes in mammon and Adam Smith, that efficiency ought to reign as the only acceptable doctrine of political economy? . . .

Japan's habits of mercantilism are longstanding, of course. But from Tokyo's point of view, this has been a tried and true system that has protected its domestic society from the ravages of the world market while late-blooming Japan raced to catch up with the West. Viewed as narrow and irrational by liberal economists, this system has virtues that are rarely voiced in the United States.[55]

That is, in Anglo-American theory, the state *gets in the way* of the economy's growth and the people's happiness. In the Asian model it is an indispensable tool toward those ends.

A fundamental mistrust of the market. In 1988, the British government was negotiating with Japan to get British brokers onto the Tokyo Stock Exchange. During the negotiations, a British friend told me about his predicament:

"Our position was that, *in principle,* any company that met the financial and other standards should be allowed to enter the market. Each time we said that, the Japanese reply was, 'How many seats do you want?' We would say, 'We don't know how many, we want it to be open to any qualified applicant.' And they would say, 'Do you want two seats? Do you want three?' "

The British negotiators eventually decided that two British companies seemed qualified, so they told the Japanese, "We want two." The Japanese side went back to deliberate—and in that time another qualified British firm appeared. My friend said, "They came back to us and said that two would be all right—but by this time we were asking for three. They were incensed at us for not sticking to our word and not knowing what we wanted. I'm sure they thought it was a case of Western deception. The 'principle' of free entry never had a chance."

At about the same time, in the long wrangle over beef and citrus imports, Michael Smith, a blustery U.S. trade negotiator, got nowhere with the argument that import quotas should, in principle, be relaxed. Then his side calculated that the beef quotas caused a price increase equivalent to a 376 percent tariff—and he asked that the tariff be reduced, in stages, by 300 points. On the basis of this concrete demand, rather than an airy principle, a deal was struck.

Neither of these outcomes is neat or satisfactory by Anglo-American standards. Openness "in principle" is what the Western system craves, not quota-style, negotiated outcomes. This dynamic view of economics is connected to the main spirit of American culture. People's lives should change! The future should be full of surprise!

This is not the spirit of most Asian societies, least of all Japan. The more familiar you become with Japanese customs, in particular, the more you are impressed with the virtue of doing *the expected thing*. (Letters to friends in Japanese, for instance, are supposed always to begin with comments about the weather.) The ideal Japanese life is one from which uncertainty has been removed as early as possible—by getting into the right school, by joining the right corporation, by doing the expected thing. In 1989, pollsters asked citizens in seven countries to react to the statement "It is boring to live like other people." In America 69 percent of the respondents agreed with the statement. In Japan only 25 percent did.[56] People in every culture adjust their behavior to fit social norms, but the Asian model acknowledges and even celebrates this reality more than the American system does.

In a much broader sense the Asian systems mistrust the uncertainty the market always brings. The Asian and Anglo-American systems both rely on the market to make operational decisions—which product will succeed or fail, which companies will beat which others. The Anglo-American system trusts political and economic markets with larger decisions, as well: what is the "good" society, what is the right course for economic growth. The Asian model shrinks in horror from this possibility, much as Western parents would from the thought that "the market"—in the form of music videos, TV shows, and shopping malls—should teach their children what is right and wrong. The children *may* actually learn this way, but most parents resist. The American model says, Go with the flow. The Asian model says, Control the flow.

"The peoples of China, North Korea, South Korea, Japan, and other Confucian cultures deeply believe that the state ought to provide not only material wherewithal for its people but moral guidance" as well, Jung-en Woo wrote in 1991. "By and large, Westerners have no way to understand this point except to assert that the Asian countries suffer from a series of absences: no individual rights, no civil society, no Enlightenment, and thus a weak or absent liberalism."[57]

According to most Western political theory, the state has *no* legitimate power to say what constitutes the good life or the healthy economy. Millions of individuals make such choice for themselves every day. The choice for the society emerges naturally from these decisions. If everyone votes against taxes, taxes stay low. If people want to buy computers—or guns, or X-rated videos—those industries flourish. The trust in the market partly reflects a preference for individual liberty—people *should* be able to choose—and partly is based on the Anglo-American fear that central power will inevitably be abused.

The genius of this system is precisely that it can use individual hungers, ambitions, and jealousies as a tool. It also perfectly melds political and economic theories: political liberalism reinforces economic laissez-faire, each of which emphasizes leaving the individual alone.

Its flaw is that it suffers from "market failures." Most people would be better off if the society invested more in schools or roads, but no one wants to vote for higher taxes. Everyone feels worse off when there are extreme social divisions, but few individuals have the power to make choices that would reduce income gaps (by creating new industries or redistributing the tax base). In the American model people are left concluding that if a willing seller and a willing buyer can agree on a deal, then by presumption the result must be right.

No government in Asia believes such things. Many individuals do. But governments feel that they, not individuals, should make the big decisions of right and wrong. Edwin Reischauer himself eloquently made this point, in discussing the different connotations that words such as "markets" and "capitalism" could have in Asia and the United States:

> Take for example the term "free enterprise." For us this implies freedom from the stultifying restrictions of the bureaucratic superstate. It suggests a healthy and altogether desirable freedom for all men on their own initiative to work for their common good and not simply to serve as cogs in a ponderously inefficient machine of state in which only a handful of men at the very top can show any true initiative. Not unnaturally we emphasize the blessings of "individualism" in our war with those political systems that enslave the faceless masses to the will of a few rulers. But both "free enterprise" and "individualism" suggest entirely different concepts to most Asians. These terms raise before their eyes the picture of the ruthless monopolist, the economic gouger, the foreign or native exploiter of the economic ills of

colonial Asia. Where we take for granted that free enterprise
and individualism will find expression within the necessary limits
imposed by law and custom in behalf of the common good, the
Asian may assume that they are symbols of the disregard of all
social conscience. Obviously terms such as these cannot be used
safely in Asia, and the ideas behind them must be translated
into some other idiom.[58]

Time and again the visitor to Japan hears the phrase "confusion in
the market" or "excessive competition." These are shorthand for
the dangers of letting market forces get out of control. Each time
these phrases come up they raise intriguing translation problems.
You can almost hear the interpreters saying the phrase as if it had
quotation marks around it in English—"confusion in the market."
There is no comparable phrase in English because the concept itself
does not really exist. What the Japanese and Koreans call "excessive" competition is what Western economics texts call "perfect"
competition. What one form of capitalism avoids the other form of
capitalism seeks.

The deeper idea is the fundamental distinction between the
market as means and the market as an end in itself. Every healthy
society knows that market incentives are necessary—real price competition, failure for products that don't make the grade, reward for
innovation and enterprise. But only the Western model thinks that
nothing besides the market should theoretically be necessary.

In their early stages of economic development, especially after
World War II, it was easy for Asian governments to set targets and
plans. Above anything else, they had to overcome the Western lead.
But even now, these systems reveal their faith that the goals should
be *chosen* rather than left to the market to decide. For example:

The Korean government has for decades divided the work of
national development among its major companies. One set of companies must run the shipyards; another must collaborate with the
Americans on semiconductor projects. The law in Taiwan obliges
companies to set aside a certain share of their sales revenue for
R&D expenses. "Such measures would probably strike those South
Koreans [and Taiwanese] who have absorbed the *political* ideals of
the Anglo-Saxon model as flagrant violations of liberty," writes
Alice Amsden.

Yet this is a very Anglo-Saxon view of democracy, not a universal
one. It could just as well be argued that to leave in private hands

investment decisions that have the potential to make a major impact on the welfare of society is itself inherently undemocratic.[59]

The Korean electronics company Samsung was struggling in the early 1990s. Its profits were very low, but the company was sitting on a large tract of increasingly valuable land. "According to short-term profit-maximizing principles, [Samsung] should have sold its land and laid off its 45,170 employees," Amsden said. This, after all, is exactly what dozens of American companies were doing at the same time. "It could then have taken its profits and invested them in still more profitable ventures, possibly employing even more workers at higher wages." But the Korean government knew of other possible outcomes—that Samsung might be bought by foreigners, that the workers might never find other jobs—and it would never have permitted the sale.

The Anglo-American system tries to permit as many deals as possible. In general, if a transaction is profitable, it should be legal, unless there's a compelling argument against it. The only loyalties that are not supposed to be for sale are within a family, and to the country. You're not allowed to sell your children, and if you're caught selling military secrets to the highest bidder, you'll be executed or jailed for life. In a more general way, friendship is supposed to operate outside the market system. But especially in Japan, *business* relationships are also supposed to operate outside the market. A Japanese scholar named Michio Morishima pointed out that

> The "loyalty" market is opened only once in a lifetime to each individual, when he graduates from school or college. It is in this market that those who are able to provide loyalty meet those who are looking for it, their lords.[60]

During the Japanese stock market's long slide from 1989 to 1992, analysts in Tokyo complained that computer-program trading, introduced by the same American firms that had been given seats on the exchange, was driving the market to daily lows. This mistrust of the computer-trading programs was part of a general view that the way to save the market was to *restrict* its flexiblity—to make it more regulated again rather than to "perfect" its market forces. As a Japanese analyst's report at the time said, "Deregulation of brokers' commissions in the United States caused securities industry profits to fall and forced many firms into high-risk areas, such as aggressive mergers and acquisitions, a report by the Securities Industry Council charged." That is, letting too many decisions go to the market created instability for all.[61]

In the summer of 1991, when scandals were being revealed practically every day in the Japanese stock-market industry, there was also a strange scandal in the earth-moving industry. Many of its competitors had been paying spies to provide information about the secret strategies of Komatsu, Japan's giant of the industry. The *Nihon Keizai Shimbun* reported, in a worried tone, that with the revelations, "many thought confusion would reign in the construction industry." But, the paper said with relief, "it has been as calm as a lake in the morning—nary a ripple."

> One of the reasons for this camaraderie is the fact that the Japan Construction Equipment Manufacturers Association, the "club" of the construction machinery industry, has just been organized. Until the "club" was organized, the industry was one huge price war. And, if the war went on, no one would make a profit and all would lose. Sensing that they were cutting each others' throats, the industry finally got together. So Komatsu didn't want to ruin all that effort.[62]

Once the industry had re-formed its cartel, everyone felt secure again.

In that same summer, the president of Japan's Toray Industries, Katsunoke Maeda, showed up at a press luncheon in Tokyo to explain how his company, which makes plastic fibers and polyesters, was doing with its expansion plans in the rest of Asia. An enterprising reporter asked him why everything that Toray made cost less outside Japan than inside—and why, as it opened plants in Thailand or Indonesia, it didn't bring these cheaper products back into Japan. "If we try to sell the cheap products in our market, we think the market will be chaotic, will be confused," Mr. Maeda replied. "We are considering the balance of the economy. We cannot only think about the consumers."[63] A few months later, a spokesman from the Japanese Ministry of Agriculture told reporters that it was a "big problem" that the price of beef was going down, now that Japan had let in some foreign beef. Why was this a problem? "Naturally, consumers might be pleased," the official said. But how short-sighted! The wholesalers would be under more pressure; they would naturally squeeze their suppliers for even lower prices; and eventually the domestic beef producers would feel "confusion" too.[64]

Toyota and Nissan are bitter rivals within Japan, comparable to Coca-Cola and Pepsi. In the 1980s, both moved to the United States to build forklift trucks. When making the move, they in effect divided the market between them, to avoid confusion and destructive overlap. As Nick Garnett of *The Financial Times* of London reported, "Toyota, the biggest Japanese producer, and Nissan, the biggest exporter to the United States, shared out the market in an organized way. Toyota based operations in California to reach the Western part of the United States, while Nissan set up in Kentucky to do the same in the East." Together they drove prices down in the U.S. market, and for American competitors "retreat has been [the] chief response."[65]

The point for the moment is that one economic system operates as if it does not have to make the largest decisions about national purpose, *except* when the system is being attacked from outside in time of war. The other operates as if the state *always* has a role in continuing to guide. It is the interaction between these visions, rather than the rightness or wrongness of either of them, that creates problems at the moment. And they are connected to:

An enduring emphasis on national borders. In Western economics, it's hard to come up with a theoretical reason for concentrating on national economic well-being. In the Asian model it's not a problem at all; the importance of national economic welfare is assumed.

The crucial point here is the lack of a guiding *idea*. In daily life there is no shortage of nationalistic spirit in Western countries in general or the United States in particular. The flag waves constantly in American TV commercials. Crowds chant "USA" at international sporting events. But in the principles that guide economic policy, the Anglo-American approach has big problems with the concept of "national interest" except in strictly military terms.

Most Anglo-American concepts run, in fact, toward the opposite conclusion: that national economic interests don't and shouldn't exist. Companies move their plants overseas, because that is what business logic says they should do. Except when military security is involved, it is hard to define the concept of a "national economic interest" at all.

This "borderless" outlook seems advanced and tolerant from the Western, liberal perspective. In the summer of 1990, Roger Porter, who was then President Bush's chief domestic policy adviser, gave a speech about America's beliefs concerning world trade. Some people, he said, clung to the "old notion of nations, companies, and markets rigidly defined by national borders." But in this modern age, he concluded, such a notion was "outdated and dangerous."[66] Porter was making a partisan argument on behalf of the Bush economic program, but his assumption that nationality-consciousness was "outdated and dangerous" reflected an educated Western view that has nothing to do with party. "No one worries about trade balances between California and Texas," Kenichi Ohmae wrote in 1993, reflecting the same borderless perspective. "Why should they worry about the balance between the United States and Japan?"[67]

Ohmae himself has long advocated reforms in Japan that would make a borderless perspective more realistic—sweeping deregulation of the economy, greater openness to foreign visitors and immigrants. But his rhetorical question raises the fundamental problem with the borderless view. As a matter of principle and ideal, there *should* be no more difference between Americans and Japanese than there now is between Californians and Texans. But as a practical matter, the two situations are not at all the same. People can move freely between California and Texas to follow economic opportunities, knowing that they would enjoy the same legal rights in either place. This is not true between the United States and Japan—which is another way of saying that Texas and California are part of the same nation, and Japan and America are not. An industry that arises in Oakland, California, or Odessa, Texas, or any other place within American borders is, at least in principle, a potential source of opportunity for every American citizen. There is no legal barrier to keep any American from moving cross-country to the job site or being considered for the job. Hundreds of personal or practical barriers may emerge, of course; but they are different from the barriers that keep Americans from pursuing new opportunities that open up in Osaka or Seoul or Taipei or Hamburg. As business strategists constantly point out, money, machinery, and knowledge are mobile in this "international age." People fundamentally are not; the opportunities available within their nation's borders are, for most people, the only opportunities that count.

In the United States discussions of corporate nationality have stuck mainly in the realm of theory. According to American assumptions, it is inevitable for businesses to operate in a rootless, global fashion. Therefore when Americans discuss this issue, they usually talk as if the denationalization had already occurred. American discussion on this point has been heavily influenced by the writings of Robert Reich, who was a lecturer at Harvard's John F. Kennedy School of Government before becoming secretary of labor in the Clinton administration. Since the mid-1970s Reich had been proposing solutions for America's long-term economic problems, and his ideas about industrial policy had attracted a broad following.

During the Bush years Reich wrote a series of influential articles in the *Harvard Business Review* and a subsequent book called *The Work of Nations,* which argued that corporations had grown past the point where they could sensibly be considered American or German or Japanese. With headquarters in one country, research centers in another, factories in yet other countries, and customers all around the world, big diversified corporations could be loyal only to their own economic interests, Reich said. That Chrysler had its headquarters in Detroit and Matsushita was based in Osaka did not mean that either would necessarily care about the governments or labor forces of its home country. They would go wherever the money, the markets, and the skilled work forces drew them. Therefore, he vigorously advocated plans for improving American education and retraining American workers.

In practical terms, Reich said in 1990 in an article called "Who Is Us?," this blurring of corporate nationality meant that the U.S. government should not try to help American *companies* just because they were American-owned.[68] The government owed its loyalty to citizens and workers within its borders, and companies from Europe, Japan, Mexico, or anywhere else might offer the best chances for the American work force. When the U.S. government gave contracts to Boeing, provided bailouts to Chrysler, or negotiated on behalf of Motorola or Zenith, it might not be helping American workers in any direct way. There was no telling where the companies would manufacture the products that U.S. government money was helping subsidize. If Toyota was building plants in America and Chrysler was moving them to Mexico, then Toyota should be considered at least as "American" as Chrysler.

As a theoretical matter, this proposition is sensible and appealing. Daily life abounds with cases that seem to confirm the point. American plants do move to Mexico; Japanese and German plants open up in the United States. A large number of American commentators have embraced the "Who Is Us?" assumption, usually crediting Reich for having precisely defined the shift to a world in which corporations no longer have citizenship. Yet many of the specific illustrations on which this changed perspective is based turn out to be misleading. For instance:

In the summer of 1989, Reich published an article in *The New Republic* that provided a perfect illustration of the way a preference for home-based companies could backfire. U.S. trade negotiators, he said, had been hammering at the Japanese government to open the Japanese market to mobile phones made by Motorola. The irony, he said, was that in helping Motorola the American government was doing little or nothing for real American workers, because the phones Motorola wanted to sell were actually designed and made in Kuala Lumpur.

As a recent resident of Kuala Lumpur, I was surprised when I read this assertion, since I had known Motorola officials there and had never heard them say that they made cellular phones. As it turns out, they didn't. Motorola officials wrote immediately to *The New Republic* pointing out that the phones were made in the United States. James Caile, director of marketing for Motorola's Cellular Subscriber Group, said in his letter that whether or not Reich's general theory of stateless corporations was true, he should not use Motorola's cellular phones as evidence for it. The telephones and pagers in question were designed and made in Arlington Heights, Illinois, not Kuala Lumpur.[69]

Half a year after the exchange of letters, Reich published his seminal "Who Is Us?" article in the *Harvard Business Review*. Once again he used the Motorola paradox as a main illustration of the difference between the welfare of American companies and the welfare of American workers. Motorola, he said this time, "designs and makes many of its cellular telephones in Kuala Lumpur, while most of the Americans who make cellular telephone equipment in the United States for export to Japan happen to work for Japanese-owned companies."

After this article appeared, Richard W. Heimlich, Motorola's director of international strategy, wrote to the *Harvard Business Review* pointing out once more that the phones were made in America, not Malaysia. Heimlich's letter also questioned Reich's claim that some "Japanese-owned companies" were building mobile phones in America and exporting them to Japan. Heimlich's letter was published in the *Harvard Business Review;* Reich replied in the magazine about mobile telephones thus: "One of those [Motorola's] Southeast Asian plants, by the way, does make parts for cellular telephones, according to industry sources."[70]

Reich also sent Heimlich an angry personal letter, saying that he resented having his intellectual and academic integrity challenged. This letter referred Heimlich to a book by Edward Graham and Paul Krugman, which Reich said would substantiate his claims.

The book was called *Foreign Direct Investment in the United States.* I found when I looked at it that it says nothing at all about Motorola in Kuala Lumpur, and in a broader sense its argument is the opposite of Reich's. Its perspective is clearly internationalist, and one of its intentions is to rebut irrational American fears about the effects of foreign investment. Nevertheless, the data Graham and Krugman examined showed that corporate nationality mattered—and that it mattered most for Japanese firms. At least in the United States, foreign-owned companies behaved differently from American-owned firms in many ways. The biggest difference was that foreign-owned firms were far more likely to import their components from suppliers in the home country, rather than buying them locally. This difference was most pronounced for Japanese-owned firms.[71] In December 1991, Edward Graham published a comparison of Japanese-owned and American-owned manufacturing firms operating in the United States. He found that the Japanese-owned firms were less likely to produce goods for export from the United States, less likely to invest R&D funds in America itself—and four times as likely to import components rather than manufacturing them in the United States.[72]

In the Winter 1991 issue of *The American Prospect,* Reich once again used Motorola to illustrate the borderless nature of the new, integrated world. He wrote:

> Our trade representatives in Washington have spent considerable time and energy of late trying to force Japan to accept cellular telephones and pagers made by Motorola (mainly in Kuala Lumpur).

Heimlich of Motorola wrote another letter to the editor, saying: "Motorola does not and has not made pagers or cellular phones in Kuala Lumpur. Almost all of the pagers and cellular phones we have been able to sell in Japan as a result of prior U.S. trade negotiations are designed, developed, and manufactured in the United States."[73] Later in 1991, Reich published *The Work of Nations,* which included chapters called "The Coming Irrelevance of Corporate Nationality" and 'The Perils of Vestigial Thought." The book highlighted "one example" that summed up the folly of the U.S. government working

on behalf of U.S.-based corporations—the same one. This time
Reich presented it as follows:

> In early 1989 Carla Hills, U.S. Trade Representative in the Bush
> administration, accused Japan of excluding Motorola from the
> lucrative Tokyo market for cellular telephones and pagers. Japan
> duly loosened its restrictions. Oddly enough, primary among
> the beneficiaries of Mrs. Hill's tough talk were engineers and
> production workers in Kuala Lumpur, Malaysia—where Mo-
> torola designed and made many of its pagers and obtained sev-
> eral of its cellular phone components.[74]

The power of the Motorola example depends on the assumption
that it is one of many possible illustrations of a widespread trend.
If there really were a large number of examples to choose from, it
is hard to explain why an author would have stuck with such a
troublesome case.

In 1993, after he had become labor secretary, Reich presented
another perfect example of the "coming irrelevance of corporate
nationality." The example came in a memorandum he sent to President Clinton on March 23, concerning trade and "competitiveness"
strategies. "Our efforts should focus on opening foreign markets to
American *exports,* rather than merely to U.S. products," he said,
sensibly. American exports would employ workers in America; mere
"U.S. products," like Coca-Cola sold overseas, might do little for
America's work force. Then came the example:

> Japan's agreement to purchase 20 percent of its semiconductors
> from non-Japanese firms, for example, does not necessarily pro-
> mote high-wage production in the United States. Close to 75
> percent of the chips which Japan purchased last year from U.S.
> firms were fabricated in Japan.[75]

If true, this illustration would be even more powerful than the Motorola story in showing that corporations had transcended nationality. It would also mean that the semiconductor agreement had
completely backfired, "forcing" Japanese purchasers, Br'er Rabbit-
like, into buying more output from factories based in Japan. But
this account of the agreement's effects also turns out to be inaccurate. According to the U.S. trade representative's office, the percentage of "American" chips made in Japan was less than 30, not
"close to 75." Rather than backfiring, the semiconductor agreement

had in fact achieved its stated purpose. Most of the "American" chips sold in Japan were indeed designed and made in the United States.

In the same memorandum to President Clinton, Reich gave another illustration of the "borderless" paradox. The U.S. government was at that time deciding how, and whether, to get involved in the emerging technologies of high-definition television, or HDTV. The main decisions lay with the Federal Communications Commission, which was to decide which transmission system, among several competing proposals, should be the standard for HDTV broadcasts within the United States. At the time Reich wrote his memo, three business consortia were vying to have their standards selected.[76] One was led by the electronics makers Thomson, based in France, and Philips, based in Holland. The other two were all-American, in that their main partners were all U.S.-based institutions. One was an alliance between Zenith and AT&T. The other was led by the Massachusetts Institute of Technology and a firm called General Instruments. A fourth group, led by Japanese firms, dropped out of the competition when it became clear that its analog transmission system would lose in competition against the digital systems proposed by each of the other teams.

In his memorandum to the president, Reich said that the government should look beyond strictly technical issues to see "which standard is likely to generate the greatest amount of high-wage production in the United States." He added:

(Interestingly, the only consortium which has pledged to develop and manufacture its high-definition televisions in the United States is the Dutch-French group (Phillips-Thompson-Sarnoff) [sic]; the AT&T-Zenith group will not do so, because Zenith is moving all its television production to Mexico.)[77]

Like the Motorola and semiconductor examples, this one seemed to show the folly of helping "American" corporations. But as with the other examples, the real facts of this case undercut the "Who Is Us?" argument.

The French-Dutch consortium had indeed promised to do the final assembly of its TV sets in America if it were chosen as the winning standard. Zenith, similarly, planned to do its final assembly in Mexico. But this stage of the process boils down to what is generally called "screwdriver jobs." Final assembly is the bolting together of sophisticated, high-value components that come from somewhere else. Most of the value of a high-definition TV, which in turn means most of the sophisticated, high-wage jobs, would come from those components. The most important and valuable components would be the large number and variety of semiconductors that would control the conversion and display of incoming digital signals. The high-resolution, large-scale picture tubes would be the next most valauble components. Where these specialized products would be made, rather than where the sets would finally be put together, will determine where the highest-value jobs from HDTV would end up.

If Thomson-Philips won, the semiconductors would almost certainly come from Thomson's factories in France. If the AT&T-Zenith group won, the semiconductors would come from AT&T in the United States. In a letter to Reich, Zenith's chairman, Jerry K. Pearlman, had emphasized that the "American" consortium would produce high-skill jobs in the United States. "Let me explain why the issue is *components,*" Pearlman wrote:

> At the heart of HDTV will be state-of-the-art integrated circuits, including advanced digital signal processors, as well as application- and algorithm-specific ICs [integrated circuits]. These semiconductors are where the new high-tech jobs will be created, both in development and production. . . .
>
> We believe that the location of semiconductor jobs will vary enormously between HDTV systems proponents. For example, the video portion of the Zenith-AT&T system is based almost totally on high-performance semiconductors to be produced by AT&T Microelectronics in Allentown, Pa., and Orlando, Fl. Our system incorporates the home-grown American Dolby AC-3 audio technology based on U.S.-designed and -built chips as well. The two General Instrument–MIT systems, as we understand them, also are based on U.S. semiconductors—largely from Motorola.
>
> We believe that the European consortium's system, on the other hand, will be based on integrated circuits from Philips-Europe and Thomson-SGS Europe with minor participation by Texas Instruments. The proposed audio technology for their system is European-based.[78]

Pearlman is hardly an impartial observer, but his account of HDTV supply patterns conforms to most other accounts in the industry. It is "interesting," as Reich had said in his memorandum to the president, to speculate that the foreign-based consortium would create more high-value jobs within the United States, but it is probably not the reality.

Most other evidence, both anecdotal and analytic, confirms the antique-seeming idea that corporations do their most valuable work in the country where they are based. Early in 1991 Laura Tyson, who later became chair of Bill Clinton's Council of Economic Advisers, published a long rebuttal to Reich's "Who Is Us?" writings. Tyson's article, which appeared in *The American Prospect,* was called "They Are Not Us." It said that around the world corporations still demonstrated a clear preference for their headquarters nation. "Unlike Reich, I read the evidence as providing a strong, continuing link between American companies and the vitality of the U.S. economy," she wrote. "Who is us? American companies still are."[79]

Anglo-American *theory* instructs Westerners that economics is by nature a "positive-sum game" from which all can emerge as winners. Asian *history* instructs many Koreans, Chinese, Japanese, and others that economic competition is a form of war in which some win and others lose. To be strong is much better than to be weak; to give orders is better than to take them. By this logic, the way to be strong, to give orders, to have independence and control, is to keep in mind the difference between "us" and "them." This perspective comes naturally to Koreans (when thinking about Japan), or Canadians (when thinking about the United States), or Britons (when thinking, even today, about Germany), or to Chinese or Japanese (when thinking about what the Europeans did to their nations). It does not come naturally to Americans—especially men, especially whites, especially those who are not from the South.

But it comes naturally in the Asian system. Without belaboring the rights and wrongs of the approach, there are many indications that the Asian model, perfected in Japan, places far greater long-term stress on the difference between "us" and "them."There are more examples from Japan than from the other countries precisely because Japan got there first; Korea, for instance, would love to be just as nationalistic, but under the current balance of power it doesn't have a chance.

*   *   *

Here are a few illustrations of the way a nationalistic system operates:

"INTRA-INDUSTRY" TRADE. As a term this is confusing, and as a concept it defies intuition, but it has become a central subject in economic debates.

In theory, international trade would seem to become more specialized, by region, as time went on. Wine and cheese would come from France. Movies would come from America. Cars would come from Japan. Wool would come from New Zealand, and vodka from Russia. Each country would develop its own national skill.

In fact, the opposite occurs. Since the end of World War II, the fastest-growing type of international trade has been "intra-industry" trade. This means, essentially, that companies specialize but whole nations do not. German car companies such as Mercedes-Benz, Audi, and BMW make cars that are attractive to customers in France, Japan, and America—but some people in Germany want non-German cars. They buy Ferraris, and Toyotas, and Volvos, and Fords. Germany also has a very active auto parts industry. It sells to other automakers around the world—and its own carmakers also buy their parts from non-German makers, notably in the United States.

This pattern of two-way trade within the same industry is "intra-industry" trade. It is measured on a scale that runs from 0 to 100. An intra-industry trade rate of 0 would mean that trade in a certain industry ran only one way. A country would either only sell, or only buy, a certain product. (For instance, Saudi Arabia's index for oil sales would be 0. It only sells and does not buy.) A rate of 100 would mean that a country sells exactly as much of a certain product as it buys. Countries that have very low intra-industry trade rates are typically Third World countries or others with unbalanced economies. The classic banana republic would sell only raw materials, and import nearly all the machinery it used, giving it a low intra-industry trade rate. Among developed countries, Australia has an unusually low intra-industry rate, since so many of its exports are raw materials and it lacks the large-scale industries of Western Europe or North America. For most developed countries, the intra-industry trade rate is high and had been steadily going up. Depending on the industry, countries in Western Europe have recently had intra-industry trade rates from the low 60s through the low 80s.[80] The U.S. rate was slightly lower than the European—which is natural, since the U.S. economy is bigger and less affected by foreign trade than, say, Belgium's or Germany's.

Among industrialized countries, there is one great exception to this pattern. The exception is Japan. It has been unusual in two ways. First, its overall rate has been low. Edward Lincoln, of the Brookings Institution, in his 1990 book *Japan's Unequal Trade,* calculated that Japan's overall rate was 25, which was one third the overall rate for France and far below that of any other industrialized power. This means, in practice, that the Japanese economy buys the goods that it cannot make: fuel, food, raw materials, certain advanced products (notably airplanes) in which its industries cannot yet compete. What it could produce, it basically does not buy.[81]

The second major difference is that the Japanese rate has barely risen. For the rest of the developed world, intra-industry trade has been the main engine of trade growth during the postwar years. Countries started with different rates, but all the rates went up. Japan's rates stayed low through most of the postwar era and rose only modestly in the late 1980s, when Japanese manufacturers moved some of their plants overseas. It is not necessary to say that Japan's low rate is wise, unwise, or some mixture; its effect is to divide the world into "us" and "them" production zones and to keep as many industries as possible among "us." As Edward Lincoln put it, "The implication of this comparison is that Japan is similar in its behavior to South Korea, a small, rather protectionist nation pursuing vigorous industrial policies to develop manufacturing industries (much as Japan did thirty years ago)."[82] It sets a standard for the Asian pattern as being highly nationalistic rather than the reverse.[83]

MANAGEMENT. The people who run Western-based companies, especially American, are becoming more varied by nationality. The people who run Asian-based companies, above all Japanese, are not.

The board members of American companies are still mainly white American males, but there are exceptions. (For instance, in May 1992, *The Wall Street Journal* provided a long list of executives of major American corporations who had been born outside the United States.[84]) The computer industry is full of people who started in other countries. The magazine industry is full of Britons.

Most Asian systems are far more nationality-conscious. It would be inconceivable for a non-Korean to run one of the major Korean enterprises. As of 1992, according to Japanese press accounts, there were only three or four non-Japanese directors of all the major companies in Japan. (Japan's federation of big businesses, the Keidanren, publishes detailed studies of the way Japan is "opening up" to a foreign presence but says it has "no information" about non-Japanese directors.) Japanese firms doing business around the world had a much higher proportion of Japanese managers than American firms had of Americans, or European firms of their own nationalities. At the end of 1991, *Nihon Keizai Shimbun* surveyed Japanese-owned companies in America. It concluded, "Only about 5 percent of executives are American and delegation of authority to local companies just isn't happening."[85] The economist Lawrence Krause pointed out that when Ford or General Motors opened plants in Europe, these subsidiaries very quickly became independent of their parents, while the Japanese-owned "transplants" in the United States were much more directly run by Japanese citizens, with decisions made in Japan.[86]

INCOMING INVESTMENT. During the late 1980s, Americans debated about the higher levels of foreign investment coming into their country and whether it was "racist" to concentrate on investment from Japan rather than, say, from Holland. One answer to this question is that there was more of it from Japan. During the late 1980s, Japanese investors overtook the Dutch as the second-leading overseas holders of U.S. assets. (The leading holders were the British.) In terms of new investments, the Japanese were by far the leaders in the late 1980s.

Moreover, the British and Dutch economies were wide open for American investment. Japan's economy was not. Indeed, the tiny share of Japan's economy that is owned by foreigners is the nation's most distinctive economic trait. Systems for measuring foreign ownership vary, but in the early 1990s approximately 10 percent of the U.S. economy was now foreign-owned. For most European nations the foreign-owned share was higher, since the countries are smaller and the economics are more integrated. Yet for Japan the foreign-owned share was about 1 percent, and was virtually zero in certain crucial industries. The foreign-owned share of the North American and European economies has been steadily rising. The foreign-owned share of Japan's economy has fallen for several years—despite the collapse of prices on the Japanese stock market in the early 1990s, which should theoretically have attracted bargain hunters from overseas.

For the first few decades after World War II, Japanese laws flatly prohibited foreigners from purchasing Japanese companies.

The few foreign companies that *are* well established in Japan—Coca-Cola, IBM—are the exceptions that prove the rule. For various reasons they were able to grandfather themselves into the system. Their success is usually cited as proof that anyone who tries hard enough can make a way for himself into the Japanese system. Most other companies were forbidden to do the same thing thirty or forty years ago, when it would have been cheap—and can't afford it now.

In a book called *Rivals Beyond Trade,* which was published in 1992, Dennis Encarnation pointed out that when Japanese enterprises bought plants in Europe or North America, they almost always bought a controlling interest—100 percent if possible, 51 percent at least. When foreigners have bought shares of Japanese firms, they have almost always ended up as minority owners, and often with no seats on the board of directors. At just about the time T. Boone Pickens was giving up his fight for seats on the board of Koito, a Japanese company called Yamanouchi Pharmaceutical bought a 29 percent share of Roberts Pharmaceutical of Eatontown, New Jersey, and promptly got two seats on the board of directors.[87] The point again is not that one system is bad or good but that a sharp, enduring consciousness of "us" and "them" is built into the Asian-style political and economic regime.

TECHNOLOGY. There is a final point to emphasize about a nationally conscious business policy: it is accompanied by an aversion to relying on foreigners. This desire for autarky and self-sufficiency is understandable in historical and psychological terms, even though it is considered irrational in the realm of modern economics.

When Japan suddenly became industrialized, in the 1910s and 1920s, it lost the ability to feed its own people from its own soil. When its leaders and generals considered war against America in the 1930s, the fear that drove them to war was the knowledge that they could run out of oil. And the nightmare, among others, they faced during war was that their shipping would be cut off and they could be starved out.

Today is a very different era: suppliers' cartels can be broken, as with OPEC; people who have money, as Japan does, can find food to buy. Yet a similar mentality runs through many Japanese—and other Asian—approaches to technology. When things really matter, it is repugnant to have to buy from foreigners. In ways that no economic theory can fully explain, the goal of national policies is to bring control of the technology into Japanese (or Korean, or Chinese) hands—even if this is "irrational,"even if it means "getting prices wrong," even if it violates the spirit of the "borderless world."

The United States applies a similar policy in a few cases. Major defense contractors are, by and large, supposed to be American. When the government pays for medical research, it is mainly done at American hospitals with American equipment—though by researchers from around the world. But apart from such exceptions, American-style economic thinking says that it shouldn't matter where something is made or who controls it. What good is it to them if they won't sell it to us and earn their economic "rents"? And why should we even think about making it if someone else can do it for a lower price?

This view is sublimely rational on its own terms. But manifestly some other societies do not share this view. It clearly matters to them that their citizens, within their borders, control the technical power.

Japanese corporations practice a form of this "nationalism" on their own. Each big company typically competes with the other in every product line. This is known as the "one set" philosophy: each company makes "one set" of every product. Each beer maker produces a draft beer, a "dry" beer, a lager, and so on; each electronics company tries to produce a full range of radios, TVs, and fax machines. This is known to economists as specializing in everything, and it is supposed to be impossible. Yet big Japanese corporations freely discuss their attempts to match each other product-for-product across a huge variety of lines.

Americans may complain about the decline of their steel or semiconductor industries—that is, areas where the United States once enjoyed a lead and has had to watch factories shut their doors. But few Americans really think it is a problem if we have to buy our entire supply of CD players from overseas. The United States has no government project under way to create a domestic fax industry, and when government guidance is proposed—for semiconductors, high-definition TVs, and superconductors—it is always controversial. The Japanese assumption is again different. In 1988, after an agricultural trade conference in Montreal, a Japanese negotiator spoke to a Canadian colleague. "You know what really makes Japan unusual?" he said. "We are the only major industrial power that is not also a food exporter. If we could improve the productivity of our rice farming by 15 percent a year, in eight years we would be competitive with California." Not even Japan's least-competitive industry, agriculture, should be "conceded" to foreign competition.

Japan's policy about the aviation industry represents the most straightforward demonstration of the idea that, in principle, it should not depend on outsiders for *anything* that is important. By the logic of comparative advantage, of course, the outlook would be simple. Japan would buy airplanes from Boeing, Airbus, McDonnell Douglas, or any of the other companies that already exist and that can manifestly make planes more cheaply than the Japanese can make them themselves.

Yet for whatever the reason, this is not the way Japan views the matter. Through much of 1988 and 1989, the Japanese and American governments battled over the construction of the FSX fighter plane. In theory, this was designed as a knockoff of the American F-16 fighter. By the normal logic of the market, Japan would seem to have every imaginable reason simply to buy the plane from the United States. The most obvious reason would be cost: since the F-16 had been produced for more than a decade, it would cost much less—from one third to one half as much, according to the estimate—as a plane the Japanese would build for themselves. It would be as if the U.S. government decided that it must become self-sufficient in high-resolution radar display screens for air traffic control towers throughout the country, rather than purchasing from Sony, which has pointedly kept the advanced display-tube production in Japan.

Japan had other reasons to consider buying an American plane. Its military partnership with the United States was in principle the bedrock of its foreign policy. Using the same plane as the Americans would eliminate countless problems of "interoperability." Beyond this were the imperatives of diplomacy: here, at last, was *something* Japan could buy to reduce trade complaints from the United States. Nonetheless, the Japanese government stuck to its position that it must build its own fighter. After great pressure from the Americans, it agreed to base its model on the General Dynamics F-16 but said that next time its plane would be all-Japanese. "The struggle to be equal with and independent of the West has animated Japanese technology and security thinking for more than a century," wrote Richard Samuels of MIT, in a book about Japanese high-tech policy. The country's prevailing view, he says, "posits Japan in a hostile, Hobbesian world in which interdependence inevitably leads to dependence, and in which dependence must eventually result in domination."[88] Thus the desire to make transistors a generation ago, and to make airplanes today.

The Japanese repeatedly emphasize the country's "unique"

capacity for high-quality manufacturing as an argument for national self-sufficiency. In August 1985, the most disastrous crash in Japanese air history happened outside Tokyo. A Boeing 747 owned by Japan Air Lines took off from Haneda Airport, bound for Osaka. Shortly afterward it crashed into a mountainside, killing 520 passengers. Officials from Japan Air Lines visited the bereaved families to express the company's contrition. On investigation it proved that the principal cause of the crash was a faulty repair job carried out by Boeing engineers, which had left one of the plane's pressure bulkheads in a weakened state.

Many lessons might be drawn from the catastrophe. The high death toll was in part an indictment of bureaucratic infighting within Japan's Self-Defense Force, which squabbled for hours over which branch would do what in going to aid the victims. Autopsies showed that many people had survived the crash but died later of exposure or injuries; they could have been saved with a faster response. Nonetheless, the crash was taken in Japan as a symbol of the across-the-board shoddiness of American equipment; over the next few years I heard it mentioned in that context dozens of times.

I moved to Japan half a year after the JAL crash and less than a month after the space shuttle *Challenger* exploded. Several times in the next year, I heard quite similar comments about these aerospace disasters from people in Japan. The theme of the comments—if we had run the program, these problems wouldn't have happened. This particular field of gloating did not turn out so well for Japanese quality control experts, since their own H-2 rocket, usually described in the press as the first "pure" Japanese aerospace project, kept blowing up on the launch pad in the late 1980s and early 1990s.[89] But the general perception of shoddy American production shaped Japan's reaction to the JAL crash and the *Challenger* explosion. Early in 1992, when the speaker of the Japanese House complained about American work habits, a *Wall Street Journal* story quoted a Japanese pollster, Takayoshi Miyagawa, as saying that the comment "represents a general perception of Japanese people on the quality of American labor." The result of the JAL crash and similar U.S.-made catastrophes, he said, is that "the Japanese people think we should make ourselves whatever concerns human life."[90]

Sometimes the strategy of saving lives by restricting imports backfires. In 1988, Japan's Ministry of Health and Welfare coordinated a drive by the country's three largest vaccine-making companies to produce an alternative to an American vaccine that had not been approved for sale in Japan. The American vaccine, produced by the Merck corporation, had the trademarked name of MMR and was used to protect children against measles, mumps, and rubella (German measles) with one inoculation. Merck's vaccine was extremely safe. After it had been used on more than 100 million children, there had been no confirmed cases of serious side effects.

Merck's MMR was approved for use in much of the world but not in Japan. Despite the extensive human-safety trials conducted before its approval in the United States in 1972, the Japanese authorities would not authorize it for use in Japan unless Merck agreed to conduct a separate series of safety trials on Japanese people. Knowing that this would involve years of delay and an outlay of tens of millions of dollars, and that at the end of the process the Japanese health-care system might still prefer any domestic alternative that might have emerged, Merck did not formally apply for distribution in Japan.

To promote the growth of Japan's pharmaceutical industry and to provide a domestic alternative to Merck's MMR, the Japanese government asked three companies each to produce its best vaccine for one of the three diseases covered by MMR. When these were ready, the government combined them into a new vaccine, which despite Merck's trademark it also called MMR. Early in 1989 the Ministry of Health and Welfare began a nationwide, mandatory inoculation program for children. "Rather than use foreign products, we wanted Japanese products because they are of better quality," an official of Japan's Association of Biologicals Manufacturers told Leslie Helm, who reported the story in 1993 in the *Los Angeles Times*.[91]

In fact, Japan's combined vaccine was of worse quality than the foreign alternatives. Based on the safety record of Merck's MMR and similar foreign vaccines, the Ministry of Health and Welfare had expected that its vaccine would produce side effects in no more than one case per one hundred thousand inoculations. By the end of 1989, the incidence of side effects was at least one hundred times greater than the predicted level. The most serious side effects were meningitis and encephalitis, which killed some children and left others paralyzed or brain-damaged. By the end of 1989 the government had made inoculation with the Japanese combined vaccine optional rather than mandatory, but it left the vaccine on the market while the remaining stocks were used up and took no steps to ease the approval of the safer Merck product for sale in Japan. (Japanese doctors reverted to giving separate immunizations for the three diseases.)

The preferences of such a system cannot be explained by a desire to save lives—or primarily to protect consumers in any sense. By modern Western standards its preferences may seem illogical and self-defeating at best, brutally misguided at worst. Yet they are in keeping with the belief, widespread outside the English-speaking world, that inconvenience to consumers is less damaging in the long run than is weakness of a nation's productive base. Friedrich List would have understood.

5

The Pan-Asian Age

FOR DECADES, when I heard the word "Vietnam" I thought immediately of disputes and trauma within the United States. I first laid eyes on Vietnam as an actual country in 1988, when it was beginning to permit visits by Western travelers.

Such a journey was still "illegal" from the U.S. government's point of view. Although U.S. court rulings held that the American government could not forbid its citizens to travel where they wanted, Treasury Department regulations prohibited Americans from spending dollars in Vietnam or having any other business dealings with Vietnam. America's long-distance telephone companies were not allowed to connect calls to Vietnam from the United States. In 1989 the Lindblad travel agency in Connecticut lost more than $500,000 in fines and legal fees for daring to organize tours to Vietnam and subsequently declared bankruptcy. In practice Americans could get around these legal obstacles by going to Bangkok, obtaining a visa from the Vietnamese embassy there, and then booking a flight from Bangkok to Hanoi or Ho Chi Minh City, the former Saigon. This is what my wife and I did.

Even in 1988, to enter Vietnam was to have a strange sense of moving back in time—and moving back on several time scales at once. In the fields, teenage boys carried water from the streams in wooden buckets, as other boys might have a thousand years ago. Pillboxes along Highway One, the only north-south route, dated from the French colonial era. Rusting American jeeps were left from the 1960s, along with GI helmets used as wash buckets in the streets of Ho Chi Minh City. Decrepit Russian vehicles looked antique even when they were more or less new.

This physical sense of out-of-dateness was matched by an anachronistic mental atmosphere. Since 1975, when the North conquered the South and the last U.S. forces withdrew, Vietnam's contact with the outside world had been like Cuba's—mediated mainly through the Soviet Union and its partners in the socialist bloc. World literature was what Russian and East German writers produced. Modern technology was what could be bought from Russian auto works. A "cosmopolitan atmosphere" meant the presence of Czech or Bulgarian tourists at the beach resorts of Quang Tri. When my wife and I traveled to Vietnam in 1988, 95 percent of the children who caught sight of us ran up and shouted *Lien Xo! Lien Xo!* Pronounced "lee-en so," it means "Russian," and it did not usually have a welcoming tone. The Russians came as "socialist comrades" rather than as colonialists or combatants, like the Americans and French, but by the late 1980s they were seeming to wear out their welcome as well. One street-urchin type in Ho Chi Minh City said that the Russians were unpopular because they were so stingy—"Americans without money." In Nha Trang we ran into a group of Czech advisers helping set up a factory, who richly reciprocated the hostility between Asians and East Europeans. They showed us their steamer trunks full of Czech sausages and breads. "Pffffahhh! Who could eat the food of Vietnam? It is fit for dogs! The people are lazy and they cheat. I spit on their country!"

It was a sign of Vietnam's isolation from the mood of Asia, even more than of its frustration with its threadbare socialist friends, that when it thought of money and technology in the late 1980s, it still thought of the United States. In part this was an understandable corollary to the government's founding myth. If Vietnam had proven its determination by beating the previously unbeatable United States, then the bigger and stronger that America seemed, the greater was little Vietnam's accomplishment.

But there was also a note of sincere awe-struckness. The last time the Vietnamese had seen the outside world, the United States was made of money, and everyone else was trying to figure out how to catch up. For any foreigners in Vietnam in the late 1980s, including the Russians, the de facto currency of the country was the American dollar—literally *the* dollar, used one by one to pay drivers or to buy bottles of Saigon beer in hotel bars. When I saw Russian advisers dig out their rolls of dollars as they walked into a Hanoi restaurant, I felt the same idiotic delight that I later did when hearing a shopkeeper in Ho Chi Minh City tell a French visitor, "Speak English! No French!" In an increasingly bizarre series of conversations in 1988 both within Vietnam and with its diplomats in other countries after I left, I heard French- or English-speaking Vietnamese talk about how great it would be for Vietnam and America to bury the hatchet and get back together again. The country was poor now, they said, but when the Americans came back, everyone would have money then!

This made an impression on me, but probably not in the way the speakers intended. In a sense they were right: when the United States finally abandoned its economic embargo of Vietnam, including its opposition to loans from the World Bank and the IMF, Vietnam would be in the economic running again, along with the coastal states of China and other low-tech, hard-work societies. But the main surge of investment, technology, consumer products, and overall economic oomph was not likely to come from America (I thought but did not bother to say to my Vietnamese hosts). It would come from Japan, and the fact that they didn't realize this proved how out of touch the Vietnamese planners still were.

In 1988, when traveling by bus from Hue, near the former DMZ, to Ho Chi Minh City, 500 miles to the south, my wife and I had not seen any Japanese people in Vietnam. But when we walked into the hard-currency store in Ho Chi Minh City, where frazzled diplomats and Vietnamese who'd somehow earned dollars could buy imported goods, I saw that every motor scooter, refrigerator, videotape player, and portable air conditioner was a Japanese brand.

Within months, as the collapse of European communism was beginning and even Asian Communists were talking about the need for market incentives, Japan's human presence in Vietnam suddenly increased. The notorious Saigon hotels of the war years—the Caravelle and the Metropole, from whose rooftop beer gardens you could watch the shelling in the distance and the jammed street scenes below—were full again. Marubeni, Mitsui, and the other big Japanese trading firms had booked whole floors on a permanent basis. In 1990, when I returned for a month in Vietnam, most of the other foreigners I encountered in hotel lobbies were Japanese.

In 1988, knowing no Vietnamese, my wife and I had generally spoken French to people in the North of the country and English in the South; those two languages, plus Russian, were Vietnam's means of connection to the outside world. When I went back in 1990, French and Russian were both in steep decline, supplanted by English and—especially in the commerce-minded South—Japanese.

Signs for Japanese-language schools were displayed all over Ho Chi Minh City. When my interpreter in Ho Chi Minh City learned that I had lived in Tokyo, he was so desperate for practice that he tried to shift our conversation to Japanese for the rest of my stay.

In short, when Vietnam became prepared for full reentry into the modern commercial world, it learned that the world around it had changed. "*Lien Xo,* numbah ten! You American, numbah one!" a crowd of beggar children in Ho Chi Minh City yelled at me in 1990 shortly before several of them rammed into me to grab at my watch, pen, and wallet. They meant, "Russians are no good! We like Yanks!" They were just trying to butter me up. I took my Foreign Ministry interpreter more seriously. *Nihon wa—ichi-ban!* he helpfully informed me during our phase of communicating in rudimentary Japanese. "Japan—number one!"

The Emergence of the Asian System

An economic system in a single country, even a country as economically large and significant as Japan, is by definition a limited phenomenon. A system that organizes half the world is something else. The phenomenon the interpreter noticed was the spread and perfection of an economic system that reaches beyond any one nation's borders.

While I was living in Japan, I often grew jaded about the concept of a "pan-Asian era." It seemed like just another slogan—another of the fads or *buumu* ("booms") that sweep through the Japanese press. *Kokusaika,* or "internationalization" in the mid-1980s, *kyosei* or "symbiosis" in the early 1990s—these were the slogans of their eras; the emphasis on Asian unity, which has showed up in Japanese TV programs and in speeches since the mid-1980s, could be seen as one more fad.

I took the concept far more seriously whenever I went to the rest of the region. Near my house in Kuala Lumpur was *Bulatan Edinburgh,* or "Edinburgh Roundabout." Its name and its traffic-circle structure reflected the British influence in Malaysia, but in the late 1980s nearly every sign on its skyline represented a Japanese brand: Sony, National (Matsushita), Mitsubishi. The two exceptions were American products: Sunkist Oranges and Kentucky Fried Chicken, which was generally a far bigger hit throughout Asia than in the United States. On the Star Ferry across Hong Kong Harbor,

China is, of course, the looming presence, but the neon signs are virtually all for firms from Japan: Hitachi, Fuji, Ricoh, NEC.

"As an Asian person, I think you are a racist," a young Thai student at Thammasat University, in Bangkok, announced to me late in 1990. I didn't bother trying to argue the irony of being lectured about discrimination in a country that would make it almost impossible for me to become a citizen, on purely racial grounds. Instead I said, "What do you mean?"

"I am judging by what I read about America," he said. "Your country is declining. Your schools are too easy and you have too many lawyers. So you are blaming the Asians for trying too hard. You are a racist. The yellow Japanese are number one."

I felt older than Methuselah when the student gave his clinching proof of American discrimination:

"You were very quick to go help your white friends in Saudi Arabia," he said—this conversation occurred while troops were massing in the desert for the assault against Iraq. "But when Vietnam invaded Cambodia in 1979 and threatened our borders, you did not make any move to help a yellow Asian nation." I was too weary to explain why the United States might not have rushed its troops back to Indochina four years after the fall of Saigon.

A few months later, I met a group of Asian students at Harvard, where most of them had come to study. Higher education was one of the remaining redoubts of American excellence. The others, for the United States, were military strength, pop culture, and raw research ability (e.g., in high-tech medical care). The students had come from China, Korea, Singapore, and Taiwan, and the basic assumption they all shared was that the United States would matter less and less in their part of the world—even though they themselves were, of course, heavily influence by their stay in America. A few days later I received a letter from the students' professor, a noted expert on Japanese relations with its neighbors. The letter said:

I was particularly struck by the comments of the graduate students from Third World countries who, it seems to me, gaze over the shoulders of the Americans and see a different world, that is Japan-led, or shall we say, Japan-determined as far as life possibilities go. Its contours are far more visible to them than us, and they are quietly preparing for it. . . . When I asked the president of the number three Korean automaker, Kia Motors, who would be the world's number one car company in ten years,

he looked surprised at the question and answered Toyota without
a moment's hesitation.

In the squalid red-light districts along Mabini Boulevard in Manila,
Filipino hookers, like Vietnamese beggars, had traditionally looked
on Americans as the customers with the money. By the early 1990s
they were able to work a two-tier price system, charging $50 to $60
for a Japanese customer and $20 or $30 for an American.[1] It only
seems as if every car in Asia is produced by Japanese manufacturers.
The actual share for Japanese brands is about 80 percent throughout
Asia, with big exceptions in Korea (which makes its own cars and
virtually prohibits Japanese car imports) and Taiwan (with a surprising concentration of big American sedans). At first glance Malaysia would seem to be an exception, since so many vehicles on the
road are Proton Sagas, the Malaysian "national car." The Protons,
however, are in reality slightly altered Mitsubishi models, produced
at a factory run by Mitsubishi supervisors and stocked with Mitsubishi parts.

Kenneth Courtis, of Deutsche Bank in Tokyo, is quoted frequently in newspaper stories about the Japanese economy, since his
predications and analyses have borne up so well since the mid-1980s.
In 1993 he pointed out that the auto market in East Asia was by far
the fastest-growing in the world. Over the next decade, he said,
Asian countries other than Japan would probably account for two
thirds of the worldwide increase in unit sales of cars. To meet that
demand, East Asia will probably require sixteen new full-scale auto
plants, each producing some two hundred thousand cars per year.

"Of those sixteen new plants," Courtis said, "probably one,
or at most two, will be American, and the same for Europe. Perhaps
two will be Korean, but perhaps not. And maybe another one or
two will be built by other East Asian producers, but if so that would
be in very close collaboration with Japanese firms. At least ten, if
not twelve or even fourteen, will be Japanese. The Japanese companies are much richer than their American and European competitors, and so much less vulnerable in their home market. They
have 97 percent of the market in Japan! With the volume they will
pick up in East Asia, the world's fastest-growing market, they will
move down the cost curve more rapidly than anyone else." Their
dominance in East Asia should, by Courtis's estimate, take Japanese
producers from 38 percent of the entire world car market at the
beginning of the 1990s to 45 percent by the decade's end.[2]

Through the late 1980s, in almost every country of the region, Japan was simultaneously the largest investor; the largest exporter; the largest source of tourism; the largest foreign-aid donor; and the largest buyer of raw commodities, such as oil from Indonesia, timber from Malaysia, or coconut oil from the Philippines. Through the 1980s Japanese companies were very cautious about sinking money in long-term investments in China. Instead, while Americans and Europeans invested in China, Japanese export houses sold products aggressively and successfully there. But by 1992 Japanese companies were outinvesting American firms in China, as they were in most of the rest of the region.

Considered as a potential self-sustaining bloc, the Japan-centered Asian economic system has certain limits.

Economically, its main weakness is that it has relied crucially on customers in North America. Japan typically runs large trade surpluses with all the other countries of the region (except for big raw-material suppliers such as Indonesia, from which Japan buys oil and natural gas). These other Asian countries, in turn, typically run large surpluses with the United States—as Japan itself does as well. In all, the countries of East Asia ran trade surpluses with the United States totaling some $80 billion per year in the early 1990s. Japan has usually accounted for about 60 percent of the total, with China, Taiwan, Thailand, Singapore, and other countries in the region making up the rest. Trade within Asia has been growing more rapidly than trade across the Pacific, and in the long run Japan hopes that the rest of Asia can take up some of America's role as a consumer market. But for now, if the American market stopped being able to absorb so many Asian products, every country in the region would have to rethink its economic plans.

Japanese planners have worried for years about one particular factor that might make it harder for the United States to absorb Japanese exports: a political backlash in America based on the chronic U.S.-Japanese trade imbalance, leading to tariffs or other restrictions on Japanese products. The integration of the Asian economies may help prevent this possibility. In effect, it displaces and relocates some of Japan's politically troublesome trade surplus to other Asian countries. That is, through the new Asian system Japan is exporting less to America directly but is exporting more through the rest of Asia.

Between 1989 and 1993 Japan's trade surplus with the United States stayed almost constant, at just under $1 billion per week. But in that same period, Japan's surplus with the rest of Asia more than doubled, from $18 billion to more than $40 billion.[3] Much of this surplus consisted either of capital goods—equipment for new Japanese-owned factories through the rest of the region—or industrial components. These components were, in turn, used in Mitsubishi, Matsushita, Toyota, and similar factories in Southeast Asia to make products destined for the United States. For instance, until 1992 Sanyo VCRs sold in the United States came directly from Japan. Then (as Jacob Schlesinger pointed out in *The Wall Street Journal*) Sanyo opened a large factory outside Jakarta, Indonesia, which produced seven hundred thousand VCRs per year for the North American market. Most of the value of the VCRs consisted of parts from Japan, but now they were classified as Indonesian rather than Japanese exports.[4] Similarly, each time a Korean auto company exports a car to North America, half the value (on average) represents parts from Japan.

Compared to the situation in Western Europe, there is no political framework to hold countries together in an Asian "system," and the range from rich to poor among these countries is much more extreme. Compared to the situation in North America, the leading economic power in the Asian bloc has less ability to co-opt protest from the others. Mexican hostility toward the United States is always balanced by individual Mexicans' dreams of moving there; Chinese or Korean hostility toward Japan is not balanced by any hope of immigration.

"The British and Americans go around the world saying, 'You, too, can be like us,' " Lee Kuan Yew, the longtime prime minister of Singapore, told an American journalist in 1992. "The Japanese go around the world saying, 'We're unique. No one can be like us.' " This was a problem for Japan, he said, since a "nation can lead others only through the magnetism of its culture or the imposition of its military might."[5] Karen Elliott House, who interviewed Lee, wrote after her conversation with him,

> Nearly fifty years after the end of World War II, Asian nations from Korea to Indonesia, while tolerant of Japanese investment, remain basically bitter and hostile to the Japanese—and that ~~senti~~ment is growing. Among Americans, reaction to the Japa~~ne~~se may range from admiration to envy; among Asians they ~~ran~~ge from fear to hatred.[6]

If you were concerned strictly about pop culture, you could see traces of America everywhere in Asia, from the movies to the McDonald's outlets to the posters in record stores. (There often is a disparity between the people who are "famous Americans" overseas and those who are well known at home. On the basis of posters in Southeast Asia, no American was more famous or glamorous in the late 1980s than the youngish actress Phoebe Cates.)[7] Many Asians vote with their feet and try to immigrate to the United States; far more send their children to universities in the United States than in Japan.

Yet Westerners often place too much emphasis on the bromide that "the other Asians just hate the Japanese." This is a classic half-truth: true enough to explain some things, but not as true as outsiders, above all the nervous Americans, would like to believe. When I've asked Filipinos, Singaporeans, Thais, or their neighbors about relations with Japan, I've wished for the moment that I could present myself in a *noh* mask or otherwise conceal my national identity. It is too obvious that they know, or at least think they know, what I want to hear: "Oh, the Americans! We will always trust them so much better than anyone else. We have so much more in common with them than with those inscrutable Japanese!"[8] When talking with Japanese people in bars or restaurants in Japan, I sometimes passed myself off as a German visitor—speaking English with a Kissingerian accent, talking about my family back on the Ruhr—in an attempt to cut through the haze of what Americans "wanted" to hear.

There certainly is enough resentment in enough countries to make the tensions between Japanese and other Asians worth keeping in mind. But as a practical reality—as a political version of the phototropism that keeps growing plants directed toward the sun— most countries on the East Asian arc are redirecting their plans toward a future in which Japan is the center of technology, money, and ideas about how to succeed.

Japan's neighbors demonstrate, on the whole, a nonromantic version of "pan-Asian" practicality. They recognize that it is crucial to deal with Japan, but they do not necessarily swoon for Japan the way Japan swooned for and romanticized America in the early postwar years. "There was a period when we were just kissing Japan's feet," one adviser to Malaysia's prime minister, Mahathir bin Mohamad, told me in 1991. When Mahathir lashed out at England with his "Buy British Last" campaign in the early 1980s, he matched it with a "Look East" campaign that for a while embraced all things Japanese. "That may have gone too far," the adviser said.

> Mahathir himself spent several weeks incognito in Japan, to try to find its spirit and roots. We thought at that time that Japan would be the engine to pull us. We just had to hitch our wagons to that star. This was also a reaction against the old slavish devotion to the British. The first generation of our elites were so *veddy, veddy British*. In their schooling, their drinking habits, their dancing. Mahathir's purpose was to say, We must cease to be brown Sahibs, brown Englishmen. We must find our roots in Asia. We should look for lessons from countries with the most relevance to our needs and experience.
>
> Perhaps we went too far. Now, as we have matured in our thinking, we still pay a lot of attention to learning from the Japanese. The best-selling books in our bookstores are about Japan. The prime minister would read and underline books about Japan and make sure we had all read them, too. Business and government leaders have practically all visited Japan, and the Japanese themselves have felt they would like to teach us, too.

A similar selective practical-mindedness shows up in many other parts of the region. On a trip to Taiwan in 1991 I stumbled through my end of a conversation in Japanese with an industrialist in his sixties, who had grown up under Japanese colonial rule. For the previous few minutes we had labored along in English, a language the man had once studied to prepare himself for a sales trip to the United States. The furrows vanished from his brow and he broke into a broad grin when he believed I could speak any Japanese at all. "This is much better!" he boomed in Japanese. "You see how much more natural it is for us to work with the Japanese. We both write with characters. We're in the same time zone. Their service technicians can come over in an hour if there is a problem. It feels more natural with them."

Respect for the Power of Japan

Despite the resentment some other Asians may feel about Japan's preeminence, and their complaints about Japan's unwillingness to share its technology or its wealth, powerful forces have pulled most of East Asia into Japan's orbit. The single strongest force is the clear-minded conclusion that the Japanese have figured out the way to wealth. In every Asian country I have visited, I've heard comments along the lines of, "Those Japanese, they're the winners now."

Such comments are more grudging in Korea than anywhere else in Asia, yet even the Koreans have shown their admiration by creating the most Japanese-like economy in the region. In 1990, Prime Minister Mahathir of Malaysia showed his admiration in a different way, with a proposal for a large regional bloc centered in Japan—but excluding the non-Asians (the Americans, Canadians, Australians, and New Zealanders).

In the spring of 1992, a major Japanese newspaper published a poll of business executives and scholars in eleven Asian countries. In Indonesia, Thailand, and the Philippines, more than 90 percent of the respondents said that Japan should be the leader of Asia. (In China and Korea, a majority did not want Japan to become the region's leader.)[9] "South Koreans are often confident to the point of arrogance in believing they will eventually overtake the United States and Europe economically, but frequently appear convinced they will not catch up with the Japanese," Mark Clifford and Shim Jae Hoon of the *Far Eastern Economic Review* wrote in 1991.[10]

Late in 1991 I met two officials of the Taiwanese government who were visiting Washington, D.C. Extrapolating, it seemed, from the way things worked back home, they assumed that since I was a "reporter" I must really be a conduit to the U.S. government. They were floating a scheme: the United States should form a secret pact with Koreans and Taiwanese for technological partnership. The idea of secrecy was not to shield the idea from the People's Republic of China (to whom the U.S. government must pretend that Taiwan does not exist as a state) but to keep it secret from the Japanese. "Together, we have a chance," one of the men told me. "But we cannot say this in public because it would irritate the Japanese."

While officials from Taiwan and from the mainland Chinese government disagree on many matters, they often take the same stance about the need for teamwork against Japan. Late in 1992, officials from the People's Republic of China told American businessmen that they planned to purchase their next generation of semiconductor-making equipment, worth some $2 billion, from American rather than Japanese firms. The purchase indicated how seriously China took its own plans for entering the consumer market—but also, as Daniel Southerland of *The Washington Post* pointed out, how much they wanted to avoid relying on Japan for the machinery. "The Chinese really made it clear that they want to work with U.S. companies as opposed to other nations," Peter Younger, of the Semiconductor Equipment Division of Eaton Corporation, told Southerland. "They don't want to be dependent on Japan for equipment, particularly if they're going to be in competition with Japan in this field."[11]

"Japan is not, of course, a *potential* model for East Asia," Chalmers Johnson said in 1991.

> It is already the prototype of the capitalist developmental states—Taiwan, South Korea, and Singapore in the first tier, the ASEAN states in the second—that have transformed Pacific politics. The most important fact about the post-Cold War Asia-Pacific region is Japan's growing economic dominance and the degree to which it is integrating all the nations of the region (including mainland China) through trade, direct investment, aid, financial services, technology transfer, and Japan's continuing role as a developmental model.[12]

Year in and year out, when interviewing businessmen and bureaucrats in other Asian countries, I heard about the way the Japanese model had affected and impressed them. But one episode dramatized how the views from the Asian and American sides of the Pacific could vary.

In the fall of 1987, when the land and stock markets in Japan were still heading up and when the dollar was falling by the day, the *International Herald Tribune* held a conference in Singapore. The official theme was stultifying—"Pacific 2000: Prospects and Challenges," or something of the sort—but the conference itself was engrossing, because most of the talks focused, seemingly without plan, on the theme of the historic shift of power from America to Japan. The Thais and the Indonesians talked about how they would get their new investment capital from Tokyo, not New York. Economists from Hong Kong discussed whether it might be "too soon" to start talking about the "post-American" era. The Japanese speakers shuffled their feet and talked about what they might do with their huge piles of money. Every other phrase out of the foreign speakers' mouths seemed to be "American decline."

The most polished of these performances was by the chief of state of the host country, Lee Kuan Yew. He talked about what Britain's 150 years of technical-financial-military world leadership had in common with America's 30-odd years. Its technical advances allowed Britain to build up trade and investment surpluses around the world; the surpluses financed its military and diplomatic presence; eventually the surpluses went away and the empire had to be scaled back; and so now with America. For a while after the Second World War, the United States enjoyed a fifteen- to twenty-year lead over the rest of the world in its commercial technology, Lee said; but that lead had been lost and would never be regained. American politicians might smash Japanese radios with sledgehammers (the photograph of U.S. congressmen pulverizing a Toshiba boom box was being published and republished in every newspaper in Japan at the time), but "the skills, the knowledge, the capacity to dream up the next [product]—that cannot be broken up with a sledgehammer." Japan, at least on paper, already had a higher per capita income than America, and the Japanese "will grow richer because they are more productive, because they have concentrated all their energies, all their R&D on where it would score on the marketplace," Lee said. "America is not the surplus country, it's Japan and Germany. It is New York with the expertise but Tokyo and Bonn with the actual cash." The greatest problem for Americans, he said, was coming to terms emotionally with this shift—accepting, in our guts, that "this is a permanent change in competitive position."

This was a more polite version of a pitch that was to become very familiar to me while I was living in Japan. "It's been six years since the United States became a net debtor," the American-trained economist Haruo Shimada wrote in early 1992 in the Japanese monthly *Bungei Shunju*. "The Americans seem to think that the problem is like a simple 'temporary virus,' but it may be a case of AIDS."[13]

Of course it was possible, even at the time, to reply that Lee was overstating his case. Many non-Americans are tempted simultaneously to overestimate America's raw power and to underestimate its resilience. This is largely because so many things that can mean vitality in America—immigration, rapid political change—look like horrifying chaos from the Asian perspective. Japan's overall position, within its region and relative to America around the world, is not nearly as strong as America's was, within its region and relative to Britain, when New York overtook London as a world financial center at about the time of World War I. By that time the U.S. economy was already bigger than Britain's; the Japanese economy was only about half the size of America's when Lee spoke, on its way to 60 percent in the early 1990s. And Japan, of course, still

has little military power or overt diplomatic influence to complement
its heaps of cash.

Lee, like most of the other Asian speakers at the conference,
had obviously spent a lot of time thinking about large-scale changes
in national power, and he was trying his best to make an important,
unsettling point.

The job of defending America's regenerative powers at the
conference fell to William Safire of *The New York Times*. I had
always enjoyed Safire's columns because of their lack of pomposity,
and on the platform he embodied the best of a relaxed, confident
American style. The Asian speakers wore identical dark salaryman
suits and read word for word from prereleased scripts. Safire showed
up in a sports coat and light pants, and he ad-libbed his way through
a very funny lunchtime speech. But by the end of his talk his op-
timism didn't seem so reassuring or contagious. Like America as a
whole, in the Asians' view, he sounded confident only because he
didn't understand the facts.

Safire told the Asians they should stop paying so much attention
to America's tedious federal deficit and trade problems. Hey, those
issues would scoot right out of the headlines once there was another
good confirmation fight or primary election to cover. And all this
talk about "permanent" changes in competitive position was so much
hogwash. Did Lee Kuan Yew think America would never again have
a fifteen-year lead over the rest of the world? Just watch! All across
America, Safire said, youngsters were tinkering with computers,
preparing the way not just for new products but for whole new ways
of buying, selling, distributing, living. Meanwhile, the Soviet Union
couldn't possibly permit its people such freedom to experiment,
since that would mean instant *samizdat*. Therefore, computers would
make America's lead grow and grow.

Around the room people sat with jaws agape. The *Soviet* economy? Was this going to be America's benchmark for competitive
success? Most other people in the room knew that all across Japan,
Korea, Singapore, and other points east, youngsters were tinkering
with computers. America's looseness, creativity, diversity, and so
on may give the country a permanent edge in this field, but other
countries have other advantages, beginning with Japan's vast supply
of capital produced by its chronically huge savings rate. (A few years
later, in a column written at the end of 1992, Safire said that the
former Communist economies of Europe really had two choices.
They could be like the Americans, with ever freer markets and
political systems, or they could be like *the Chinese*, with heavy-

handed central control. Presumably there are other alternatives—
being like the Germans or the Singaporeans or the Japanese—but
these were not on the scope.)

Black Sunday

The Great Depression was the culmination of forces that had been
building for more than a generation, but in a sense it started on
October 24, 1929, the famous Black Thursday that touched off the
historic collapse of the New York Stock Exchange. The forces that
would eventually destroy European communism had been building
for two generations, but in a sense the Cold War ended and the
Communist empire collapsed on November 9, 1989, when the East
German government lifted travel restrictions and Berliners began
crossing their city's Wall. The Japanese-centered Asian economic
model depends on attitudes and policies that have been built and
refined over more than a century, but in a sense the Asian economic
era began late on Sunday afternoon, September 22, 1985.

Early that day, the finance ministers and central bank governors
from the five major industrial powers had gathered at the Plaza
Hotel, in New York. The lineup was the same as for the annual "G-
7" meetings of industrial powers, but with the Canadians and Italians
humiliatingly left out. James Baker, the American treasury secretary, and Paul Volcker, the chairman of the Federal Reserve Board,
were joined by their counterparts from Japan, Germany, England,
and France.

For the preceding five years, in the "morning in America" phase
of the Reagan presidency, U.S. officials had promoted the line that
a strong dollar meant a strong America. The dollar had plunged to
lows against the Deutsche mark and yen during the unlamented
Carter years. With Reagan in command it reached highs not seen
since America's zenith in the 1950s and 1960s. Through the early
1980s, savers in Germany, in the Middle East, and above all in Japan
poured their capital into the United States. American supply-side
theorists said this flow was the world's homage to America as a
stable investment site. It could also be seen, and was by many Democrats, as depressing proof that the country had to borrow to keep
its consumption surge going. In either case the result was to keep
the dollar's value rising, even as America's trade deficits also soared.
Under strong, steady Dwight Eisenhower, the dollar had been worth
a strong and steady 360 yen. Under Carter it sank below 200. At

midpoint in Ronald Reagan's administration, in February 1985, it reached a high of 263.65 yen.[14]

But at just this same time, with the trade deficit nearing $10 billion a month, the Reagan administration started to believe that there could be such a thing as *too* strong a currency. With the dollar worth so much, American exporters couldn't compete, and American consumers were snapping up the suddenly bargain-priced cars and computers from overseas.

The meeting at the Plaza was recognized as one kind of watershed even as it occurred. Until this point, the Reagan administration had argued that market forces would automatically take the dollar to its most desirable level. Now they were conceding that governments might have to intervene and collaborate to force currency levels up or down.

It turned out to be an even larger historic dividing point than the participants foresaw. The communiqué they issued that Sunday afternoon said that "a 10–12 percent downward adjustment of the dollar from present levels would be manageable over the near term."[15] The dollar was then worth about 240 yen. Such a reduction would have taken it to roughly 215 yen, with some participants saying that over a longer period it might fall to 200 or even 190 yen. Once the dollar was pushed down to more rational levels, Americans would stop buying so many Japanese products—and Japanese purchasers would buy more from the United States. According to one famous formulation of this view, "To achieve equilibrium in the countries' [Japan's and America's] global current accounts, the yen would have to strengthen to a range of at least 190 to 200 yen per dollar."[16]

For a few years after the Plaza agreement it looked as if things were actually unfolding according to plan. Nightly news coverage in Japan through 1987 and 1988 was full of reports about the "NIC shops," the emporiums in Tokyo that were selling cheap imports from the "newly industrializing countries," or NICs. "Taiwanese electric fans and simple pocket calculators captured dominant shares of the Japanese market," one Japanese summary pointed out—revealing the sorts of sectors in which the NICs were showing their strength. But even at the electric-fan level this was a passing phenomenon. By the end of the 1980s Japanese imports from the NICs were falling again. The share of Japan's work force and of its economy represented by manufacturing actually *rose* during the five years after *endaka*—a result completely at odds with what had been happening in the United States during its strong-dollar years and very hard to explain by normal "comparative advantage" economic theory.[17]

Eight years after the Plaza agreement, the yen had strengthened far more than any of the Plaza participants foresaw. Through most of 1993 the dollar was worth less than 110 yen. The Japanese press began carrying articles about the psychological impact of the yen's imminent rise to "parity"—the moment when one dollar was worth 100 yen. Meanwhile, Japan's overall trade surplus was more than twice as large (when measured in dollars) as it had been when negotiators met at the Plaza. In 1992 it reached a record high of $136 billion.

When measured in yen, of course, the Japanese imbalances grew by much less over this period (since the yen itself rose so much in value against the dollar). When measured as a share of the Japanese economy, which was itself growing rapidly, the imbalances actually shrank considerably in the years after *endaka*. When the dollar was strong and the yen was weak in the mid-1980s, Japan's global trade surplus had hit a peak of nearly 5 percent of its gross national product. In 1990, Japan's overall trade surplus fell to a low of 1.2 percent of the Japanese GNP, before beginning to rise once more.[18]

By some measures this change in the Japanese surplus could be seen as a success, but it was far more modest than anyone had predicted at the Plaza. The change had very little impact on the traits that made Japan most different from other modern economies: its low rates of foreign investment, of manufactured imports, and of "intra-industry" trade. In a book published five years after the onset of *endaka*, Paul Krugman of MIT wrote that "the lower dollar, while quite effective elsewhere, had virtually no effect on U.S.-Japan trade."[19]

There is no shortage of explanations about why the radical shift in currencies did not have the expected effect. The main hypotheses involve these factors:

· *Raw materials*. Japan's most crucial imports are fuel, raw materials, and food. Most of these goods are priced in U.S. dollars—oil shipments, for instance, are quoted worldwide on a dollars-per-barrel basis. Indeed, about two thirds of all Japanese imports are priced in dollars. Therefore when the dollar goes down, so do crucial input costs for industries based in Japan (or Korea or Germany). A rise in the yen's value against the dollar, meant to handicap Japanese manufacturers, helps them reduce material costs.

· *Pricing practices*. When the yen rises against the dollar, Toyotas, Sonys, and Nikons should cost more in the United States; Apple computers and Levi's jeans should cost less in Japan. Some prices did indeed behave this way, but the shift was much less—in either country—than simple economic models would have predicted.

Japanese exporters tried for as long as possible to hold down prices in the United States, absorbing the effects of the currency change in an attempt to hold on to market share. At the same time, American exporters to Japan resisted cutting prices—in part because their costs of operating in Japan were rising at the same time.

· The Japanese strategy was perfectly consistent with a decades-long preference for high market share rather than high profit—that is, to make as many sales as possible, rather than to make as much as possible on each sale. Moreover, Japanese corporations could afford to hold down their export prices by charging more to customers inside Japan. (Competition within Japan is intense, but it has usually been waged on a product's image, features, and perceived quality, rather than on price discounting. This pattern is similar to the way U.S. airlines competed in the days before deregulation: prices were high and fixed, and airlines competed with scheduling and service features.) Some German and Korean firms behaved the same way, holding down their prices in the United States even as their currencies rose. "The United States is the most competitive market in the world," the president of BMW North America said in 1992, when the D-mark was rising again. "If you base your prices here only on exchange rates, you will be out of the market immediately."[20]

The behavior of U.S.-based companies was also consistent with their emphasis on earning the highest possible financial return, and with their heavy reliance on Japanese-made components. For instance, so many components of the Apple computers sold in Japan were bought from suppliers in Japan that Apple's manufacturing prices, in dollars, went up when the yen did.[21] Other American companies simply welcomed the opportunity for windfall profits through a higher yen. In short, customers both inside and outside Japan never got the clear price message a currency shift is supposed to send.[22]

The stickiness of prices, in both Japan and America, contributed to a phenomenon called "hysteresis." This is essentially a Humpty Dumpty concept: once something's broken, you can't always put it back the way it was. In economic terms, it can mean that after an overvalued currency has driven industries out of your country, simply lowering the currency may not bring them back.

· *Investment barriers.* Some economists argued in the late 1980s that the real problem for foreign companies was not the difficulty of selling in Japan but instead the difficulty of *investing* there. All around the world, they said, corporations needed to invest in local markets if they hoped to sell there. Partly this involved commonsense steps like setting up showrooms and a sales force. In a deeper way investment demonstrated their long-term commitment to customers in a certain market. Also, overseas subsidiaries tend to buy supplies, components, and professional services from their home country. For instance, a Fujitsu factory in California tends to bring along the suppliers, banks, and insurance firms that served Fujitsu in Japan. Similarly, although to a much weaker degree, a Texas Instruments factory in Japan brings along suppliers from the United States. Almost three quarters of all Japanese exports to the United States in the early 1990s consisted of shipments from the head office of a Japanese corporation to the American subsidiary or branch plant.[23]

This connection between foreign investment and foreign trade mattered in the post-*endaka* age because, as discussed earlier, the level of foreign investment in Japan was so low. In the 1950s and 1960s, when foreign companies could have afforded to invest in Japan, the Japanese government generally wouldn't let them. In the late 1980s and early 1990s, when the Japanese government no longer objected, the cost of buying or starting businesses in Japan was prohibitive for most foreign firms. Each time the yen went up, theoretically correcting trade imbalances, the investment-cost barrier became that much worse. During the Occupation years, General Motors could have established a nationwide dealer network in Japan essentially out of petty cash—if Japanese laws had permitted it to do so. By the 1990s GM calculated that to build a dealer network in Japan rivaling Toyota's or Nissan's would cost at least as much money as the entire corporation earned in a year. When Chrysler officials priced Japanese dealerships in the late 1980s, they found that a typical urban outlet selling five hundred cars per year would cost at least $100 million for land alone.

Without their own network of dealers, the foreign automakers faced a very hard sell in Japan, since a Toyota or Nissan dealer wouldn't handle any other line. As the yen doubled in value in the late 1980s, foreign firms should have been flocking to Japan—but the skyrocketing cost drove many small operations out,[24] further blunting the corrective effects of *endaka*.

The "Third Miracle" and the Integration of Asia

There was one further factor that altered the results of *endaka* and made the Plaza agreement a watershed in a different way than its architects ever intended. Finance ministers from the world's richest nations thought that raising the value of the yen would not simply reduce Japan's trade imbalances but would also "normalize" the Japanese economy in significant ways. It would make more room for foreigners and foreign products, and would signal to Japan once and for all that it could move beyond the years of nonstop exporting to an era of consumerism and leisure.

Yet the investment strategy of Japan's big firms was designed precisely to avoid that outcome. In the long run a high yen might be good for Japan's consumers, but in the short run, it seemed threatening to Japan's industries, and they acted promptly to defend themselves. As the yen went up, they poured money into new factories and production lines that would prevent their losing ground to foreigners. In the first five years of the high-yen era, Japanese corporations invested some $600 billion, which was more than all U.S.-based corporations did during the same period. Most of this money was devoted to coping with the effects of the high yen, both by making factories inside Japan more productive and by setting up factories outside Japan for lower-value work.[25]

The strategy proved effective. Late in 1992, MITI surveyed hundreds of the nation's exporting companies and asked them how far the dollar would have to fall before they would have serious problems selling overseas. The average "break-even rate" for all companies in the survey was 126 yen to the dollar; but (as Kenneth Courtis of Deutsche Bank has emphasized) the largest companies surveyed, which accounted for most of Japan's exports, said that their break-even rate was closer to 100 yen. Indeed, Japan's success in coping with *endaka* was so great that Courtis has said that it should be considered the "third economic miracle" of Japan's post–World War II years.

The first miracle, according to this scheme, was Japan's ability to sustain its high levels of investment and rapid industrial growth through the 1960s, when the initial push for wartime recovery was over and the nation might have been expected to concentrate instead on satisfying consumer demands.

The second miracle was Japan's recovery from the repeated economic shocks of the early 1970s. In 1971 came the "Nixon *shokku*," largely unrecognized in America but politically and psychologically profound in Japan. Within a matter of weeks, the Nixon administration announced a number of steps that were not directly related to Japan but that had a huge impact on Japan.

After years of warning the Japanese (and other allies) not to deal with the Communist regime in China, Nixon suddenly revealed that Henry Kissinger had been carrying out secret negotiations with the Chinese. Japanese diplomats felt humiliated by the announcement, of which they had received no advance word. As part of a grab bag of measures to fight inflation in the United States, the Nixon administration suggested that it might make sense to cut off exports of American soybeans to customers overseas (presumably to make more of the beans available for customers at home). This was never a serious proposal, and the U.S. government specifically repudiated it a day or two after the first rumors began. Yet in Japan it had a terrorizing effect, since so much of the nation's diet was based on imported food in general and American corn, wheat, and soybeans in particular.

Also in 1971, the Nixon administration shocked the world financial system by taking the United States off the gold standard. In effect, this meant that for the first time since the end of World War II the value of the dollar would float against other currencies. This measure was aimed in part at Japan; Nixon and his treasury secretary, John Connally, had been hammering away at the "intolerable" trade imbalance with Japan, which at the time was about $3 billion per year. Letting the dollar float would presumably raise the value of the yen, which they thought should in turn even out U.S.-Japanese trade accounts. For exactly the same reason, this step was shocking to Japanese industrialists. They had based their export plans on the certainty of a 360 yen/$1 exchange rate; now nothing about the economic landscape was certain anymore.

Then, to compound all the previous blows, came the first OPEC oil shocks in 1973. Since Japan's economic growth had been based on exports, and since its industries ran almost totally on imported oil, Japan seemed more threatened by this change than any other industrial power.

Japan's second miracle, therefore, was to survive this wave of shocks with its fundamental economic strength not simply preserved but actually enhanced. Through radical energy efficiencies, Japan made itself by the 1990s consume less imported oil than the United States does. (Japan, with virtually no domestic oil reserves, used imported oil equivalent to 0.7 percent of its GNP in the 1990s. The United States, with substantial though declining domestic oil production, used imported oil worth 1 percent of its GNP at the same time.) During the buildup to Operation Desert Storm, this simple truth was mentioned frequently in the news in Japan but rarely in America. "Fragile," "vulnerable" Japan, which "depended on imported oil for its lifeblood," actually depended on it less than most other nations did. "Who will control the oil is a serious issue for the United States this time," Masamichi Hanabusa, who was the Japanese consul general in New York, said in a speech a few weeks before the fighting began. "But it is not a very serious issue for Japan. It is, of course, better that oil is in friendly hands. But experience tells us that whoever controls oil will be disposed to sell it."[26]

The third miracle was what happened in the late 1980s, after the Plaza agreement. It involved the way Japanese ministries, banks, and corporations adjusted to the sudden shift of currencies so that its results were different from what almost everyone had foreseen. The yen shocks that emanated from the Plaza were supposed to correct the largest imbalances in world trade and shift Japan's status to that of big spender and "life-style superpower." In restrospect they soon looked like yet another of the silver-lining calamities, like the oil shock or even wartime defeat, that might push the country to new levels of achievement. And they provided the impetus for Japan's expansion into the rest of Asia, which created the framework for the Asian regional economy.

The men who were in charge of Japan's industrial system understood the theory behind the Plaza agreement. They weren't about to sit around and wait for "hysteresis" or some other economic anomaly to save them from being priced out of export markets around the world. Precisely to avoid the slowdown that the high yen was supposed to inflict, Japan's financial system began the cheap-money expansion that was known, half a decade later, as the "bubble economy."

Banks lowered their interest rates, especially for industrial borrowers, until they were practically giving loans away. A variety of other financial schemes made capital virtually free for Japan's industries.[27] It was this policy that led to the shaved gold on lunchtime mousse and the tiny scraps of property worth billions of yen.

The free-money era lasted four years, from the time of the Plaza accord in the summer of 1985 until the fall of 1989, when Yasushi Mieno was appointed the new governor of the Bank of Japan. Until the time of Mieno's appointment, the free-money experiment had turned out remarkably well. Rapidly expanding a country's money supply is supposed to create inflation. But in Japan in the late 1980s, the inflation was confined to "assets"—land, stock, golf course memberships, French Impressionist art—rather than spilling over into the "real" economy.[28] Asset inflation actually proved, for a time, to be productive and useful for Japan. Companies could use their suddenly "valuable" land as "collateral" for low-interest loans with which they could modernize their factories or expand overseas.

But by late 1989, signs of real inflation were beginning to seep into the system. Over the next four years, Mieno and the Bank of Japan deliberately reversed the free-money cycle, raising interest rates and tightening the "administrative guidelines" that banks used when making loans. By 1991 the paper value of Japanese real estate had fallen by 200 trillion yen, at the time more than $1.5 trillion, or just under half of Japan's annual gross national product.[29] The Nikkei average on the Tokyo Stock Exchange had hit a peak in the 1980s of almost 40,000, roughly equivalent to 4,000 for the Dow. The Nikkei plunged below 20,000 in 1991 and was stuck in the teens in much of 1992 and 1993.

From outside Japan, it was easy to notice all the money that had been wasted during the "bubble" years, and all the harm done when the bubble burst. It was easy to see all the cases in which suckerlike Japanese purchasers had served as the "stuffees" of the world financial system, buying at top of the market and providing profits for everyone else.[30]

But there had been *so much* new money during the boom years that it was impossible to waste it all. After all the waste and all the payoffs and all the blunders, Japanese industries had enough left over to invest more money in new capacity, in absolute terms, than American companies did.

During the late 1980s, Japan was saving and reinvesting about one quarter of its rapidly growing GNP. (The United States, at the same time, was investing about 9 percent—and saving less than that, borrowing the difference from overseas.) This meant there was enough money for a mammoth investment surge within Japan, which kept the economy booming in the short term and girded Japanese industries to compete when, sometime in the future, the yen reached 100 or even 90 to the dollar. Between 1987 and 1992, Japanese companies invested some $3 trillion in new factories and equipment within Japan's borders. Most of this money was not simply to expand capacity but also to overhaul existing factories, bring in industrial robots, cut production time, and in general "set in place the economic base for long-term growth," as Kenneth Courtis said in 1992.[31] He added,

> Contrary to the popular image of Japan as a nation of compulsive copiers, the country is positioning itself to play a role in the world economy similar to that which America played in the 1950s and 1960s:
> Then new products were first developed and introduced in the U.S. market, and as the international product cycle developed, such products were released in sequence around the world. Over the 1990s, Japan will move to play increasingly the role of new product laboratory for the world.[32]

And money was still left over. There was money to build factories and buy up enterprises in Europe and North America. This, in fact, is where most of Japan's foreign investment went—through the late 1980s, Japanese firms put about five times as much money into North America as into all of Asia combined. Most of it went, of course, to the United States, in a kind of recycling process. Americans continued to receive Japanese goods; in exchange, they offered title to various assets—stocks, treasury bills, real estate.[33] But the scale of the other Asian economies was so much smaller that the Japanese presence seemed, proportionately, immense.

In 1989, Japanese firms were investing four times as much money in Taiwan as they had in 1985; five times as much in Malaysia; five times as much in South Korea; six times as much in Singapore; fifteen times as much in Hong Kong; and twenty-five times as much in Thailand.[34] "Japan has provided the focus and much of the momentum for Asia's thrust ahead," Courtis wrote in 1992:

> Its economy represents two thirds of the entire Asian economy. It has set the pattern for development and provided the model for economic management that in its many variations sets Asia in such stark opposition to the doctrines of Smith and Ricardo.
> From Japan, capital and technology flow throughout the

region. The countless decisions made by Japanese firms—where
to invest, where and what to produce, where to source, and how
and what to sell—not only powerfully amplify the broader dynamics at work in the region but also amplify the pace of regional
integration. But Japan is master of the process. [There is] talk
of the Asian car. With their complex Asian production capacity,
Toyota and Nissan already produce it.[35]

By 1990, Toshiba, Matsushita, Minebea, and similar Japanese firms
had built some 340 fully owned plants in Southeast Asia. The great
majority, including all the plants in Thailand, Malaysia, and the
Philippines, had not been there in 1985.[36] Before the age of *endaka*
began, Japanese investors had set up plants in more advanced Asian
nations, such as Taiwan and Singapore. Even there, investment doubled between 1985 and 1990. During those five years, Japanese companies put roughly $10 billion in new equipment into Southeast Asia.
U.S.-based companies invested less than one tenth as much there.
(In 1985, the U.S. investment stock in Southeast Asia was worth
about $9 billion, and Japan's about $13 billion. By 1990, Japan's had
risen to $23 billion, and America's only to $10 billion.[37]) In 1980,
Japan's cumulative investment in the rest of Asia was worth about
half as much as America's; by 1990, it was worth 30 percent more.[38]

Such comparative figures can be misleading. For instance, Malaysian government summaries of foreign investment count money
coming into the country for new factories—but not money spent to
improve or expand factories already in place. American high-tech
firms such as Texas Instruments or Advanced Micro Devices began
moving to Malaysia in the 1970s, long before Japanese firms arrived.
Thus when an American firm expands its plant, as many did in the
early 1990s, this has less impact on published figures than do the many
Japanese companies setting up shop in Malaysia for the first time.[39]
On the other hand, about half of all American corporate investment
in Southeast Asia is for the oil or natural gas businesses, mainly in
Malaysia and Indonesia; if those figures are removed, the Japanese
preeminence in manufacturing looks even more impressive.

The New Style of International Investment

The United States has seen this kind of investment outflow itself—
or thought it had. As understood in American-style political economics, a shift toward low-wage countries simply meant that fac-

tories moved from North Carolina to Mexico, much as they had moved from Massachusetts to North Carolina generations before. Those who opposed extending the North American Free Trade Agreement to Mexico worried that the movement would become even faster. Factories would go to Monterrey or Guadalajara, where the wages were lower than in Michigan, but they would make the same cars and machine parts and sell them in the same markets. The American approach was based on the idea that each corporation, with its own money on the line, would figure out where it could most efficiently make its products, and that the real beneficiaries will be the American consumers who buy goods made in Korea, Singapore, and Mexico at the lowest possible price. The barroom debater's stereotype—that American companies were "moving jobs to Mexico"—was more or less what the economists thought would happen, too.[40] The economists had a comeback argument, of course: that new jobs would open up in new industries and Americans would gain on the whole.

But the entire process of corporate globalization operated on different assumptions when Japan responded to the nightmare of *endaka*. The idea was not simply that machines once made in Osaka could be made instead in Singapore and sold, more cheaply, to the same customers back in Japan. The concept was instead that cheaper production sites beyond Japan could be incorporated, with the Japanese headquarters firms, into a production system that could export to yet other countries (in practice, mainly to the United States). It was, once again, a producer-minded rather than a consumer-minded strategy. The Third World sites would not replace or compete with factories in Japan, for the benefit of the Japanese consumer. The new plants would augment and supplement what already existed in Japan, to strengthen the Japanese productive base.

The Thai example. Thailand is the clearest example of how the process worked. In the immediate aftermath of *endaka*, Thailand was the most attractive low-wage site for Japanese investors. The country was welcoming and relatively uncrowded. Other Japanese companies were already going there, which meant that there would be a Japanese school, lots of Japanese golf courses, Japanese newspapers, Japanese-only areas in Bangkok's entertainment districts.

The Thais had less of a chip on their shoulder about foreigners in their midst, including Japanese, than did most other Southeast Asians. The conventional wisdom in Thailand held that this tolerance reflected the country's history: although Thai governments had accommodated European colonial powers as they later accommodated the wartime Japanese, the country had never officially been colonized and therefore lacked the complexes that twisted the Malaysians' dealings with Britain or the Filipinos' with the United States. Japan had long been the largest customer for Thailand's exports, mainly farm products and fish, which built gratitude among Thailand's businesses and government. At the same time, Japan had always had a trade surplus with Thailand, providing most of the refrigerators, motor scooters, cars, and later television sets and tape players sold in Thailand. Thailand's popular culture had paid more attention to fashions from Japan than had most others in the region. (Certainly more than Korea's, where much of the population would be able to understand Japanese movies and pop records but where, probably for that very reason, the government outlawed most forms of Japanese-language entertainment.) Karaoke bars are now known around the world, but they were embraced early in Thailand. "This is a golden age for Japanese in Thailand," a spokesman for the Japanese embassy in Bangkok said, superfluously, in 1990.[41]

There seemed, from the Japanese perspective, to be everything to like about the Thai-Japanese relationship. And so, after 1985, Japanese money and manufacturers poured into Thailand. Toyota had had a plant there since the early 1960s; during the boom the plant expanded dramatically. Fewer than 5,000 Japanese lived in Thailand in the early 1980s; more than 25,000 did by the end of the decade, and some 150,000 Thais worked for Japanese-owned firms.[42] And as the money poured in, Thailand became a kind of mini-Japan. Minebea manufactured ball bearings at a plant that employed 20,000 Thai workers. The big conglomerates, such as Mitsui and Mitsubishi, established dozens of factories each. The result was to put both Japan and Thailand on a stronger footing in international trade.

The ball bearings now being made in the gigantic Minebea factory outside Bangkok, the VCRs and televisions that were being assembled elsewhere in the great sprawl along the Gulf of Siam— all of these were products that factories in Japan itself could no longer efficiently make for Japanese consumption or for export to the United States. But Japanese companies were selling Thailand the recording heads that went into the VCRs, the machine tools that made the ball bearings, the construction equipment that built the factories, the computer systems that ran the production lines, the insurance policies and training programs for the people who work there. Five years of *endaka,* far from weakening Japan relative to the neighboring Asian "tigers," actually left Japan with larger trade surpluses, and greater leads in technology, than it had achieved before.

During each year of massive Japanese investment in Thailand, for instance, Japan's trade surplus with Thailand also increased, and the composition of the goods it sold there became more sophisticated and high-tech. Thailand, in its turn, sends out most of the goods made in these factories as exports to other countries (not Japan). As its trade with Japan has run larger and larger deficits, Thailand has shown increasing surpluses with the rest of the world, especially the United States. In 1985 Thailand sent a tiny trickle of electronics goods to the United States. By 1990 it was shipping more than $300 million worth. In 1989, when the yen rose to what was then an all-time high against the dollar, American imports of Japanese-made consumer electronic products fell by about one fifth. But at the same time, American imports of consumer electronic goods from Thailand rose by 2,000 percent, virtually all of them from Japanese-owned factories in Thailand.[43] By the early 1990s this pattern extended to Asia as a whole: each year, Japan had a trade surplus with the rest of Asia worth about $30 billion, and the rest of Asia had a trade surplus with the United States of about the same amount.

John P. Stern, a squarish man with the air of a younger W. C. Fields, represented the American Electronics Association in Tokyo and spoke frequently about this kind of displacement of trade deficits. He had an array of charts to show how VCR-assembly and computer-board making were shifting from Japan to Thailand, Malaysia, and Indonesia, all under the aegis of Japanese firms. In effect, low-wage labor was assembling high-value parts from Japan; the results were shipped to America as "Indonesian" or "Thai" products, rather than Japanese. "Southeast Asia is being used to shift the Japanese consumer electronics deficit with America onto the back of the NICs," Stern said.[44] The U.S. embassy in Bangkok sent a wire to the State Department in February 1990, concluding essentially the same thing. "Thailand's continued growth will allow Japanese multinational corporations to maintain or expand their global market shares in sectors where Japanese domestic production is no longer cost-competitive or in markets that are being closed to Japanese products manufactured at home." The Japanese policy toward Thailand, the embassy report said, would be

> to maintain and advance its enormous economic influence, while promoting its image as a major contributor to Thailand's and Asia's development and stability. [They] hope a strong Japanese

role here will promote similar relationships with other Asian countries.[45]

The Japanese stampede to Thailand immediately after *endaka* was more dramatic than what happened in Malaysia or Indonesia, but the essential pattern was similar. And what is significant about the pattern? Not that it is evil or tricky or malign, because it is much less of any of those than was, say, the impact of European colonialism on most Asian countries. The new factories benefit workers in Thailand and customers in the United States. The important point is how much this differs from a "normal" or "market-driven" evolution. Almost nothing about Japan's expansion into Asia makes sense if you start with the premises of Anglo-American economic analysis. Almost everything makes sense if your main concern is the history of the region—Japan's constant concern about foreign domination, the shared knowledge in the region that technology brings political power, the knowledge by weak nations that powerful ones have to be accommodated.

There are two ways to measure this "unnaturalness"—or, more precisely, the fact that this was a political expansion rather than a purely economic one. Those two means are by input and by output: by the steps that Japanese organizations took to coordinate their efforts in the rest of Asia, and by the results they achieved.

Input: The Coordinated Effort

When the U.S. government learns of trouble in Kuwait City or Mogadishu, it knows how to respond. The National Security Council brings together representatives from the State Department, the "intelligence community," and the branches of the military. Each group has its interests and its axes to grind, but they know they are all part of a team.

"When [the rise of the yen] made a hollowing-out of Japan's economy inevitable, Japan's Ministry of International Trade and Industry and Economic Planning Agency immediately upgraded the caliber of their staff in Bangkok, Thailand; Jakarta, Indonesia; and other capitals in the area," Bruce Stokes wrote in the *National Journal*. When the Japanese government learns of threats to its security it also knows how to pull separate units together into a team. "Their task was to monitor economic developments and act as marriage brokers between local governments and Japanese companies."[46] In 1990, MITI officials in the Japanese embassy in Bangkok formed a council for Japanese businesses in Thailand. MITI representatives convened the businessmen for regular meetings, to coordinate plans.[47] Similar structures soon popped up in the rest of Southeast Asia. "Officials in these countries now say Japan has better information about their economies than they do," David Arase, of the Claremont Graduate School, told Bruce Stokes.[48]

"The outsiders have better information. . . ." I have often heard just this phrase in Seoul or Manila, but there it refers to what the U.S. embassy knows. When the South Korean military wants to know about troop movements in the North, it must rely on the Americans to share their latest data; when the Philippine military dealt with its guerrillas in the 1980s, it collaborated with American assistants and advisers. The effort made by the Japanese business system in the late 1980s, involving money and private organizations and public bureaucracies and a national mobilization of talent, was very similar to the way the U.S. political/military establishment worked.

In the American model, retired military officers would come back to work for companies producing defense technology. Networks of friendships would link the intelligence services and the military staffs. The same kind of coordination pulled together the Japanese efforts in the rest of Asia, coordination on the personal as well as the overall corporate level.

A huge outcry of controversy occurred within Asia after *The Asian Wall Street Journal* reported, in 1990, the existence of a kind of war room in MITI, in which bureaucrats mapped out investment plans for the rest of Asia. Japanese firms would invest in Southeast Asia according to an agreed-on joint strategy. The companies making word processors, answering machines, athletic shoes, and faxes would set up shop in Malaysia. Those making furniture, die-cast molds, and toys would go to Thailand. Indonesia would get wood products factories, plastic works, and textile mills.[49] I went to this very office in MITI soon afterward, at which point the officials were saying they had no coordinated plans and were shocked, just shocked, at the suggestion that they did. Nonetheless, events unfolded with a logical shape.[50]

For decades the leaders of the ASEAN countries had been talking about turning themselves into a Common Market of Southeast Asia. ASEAN stands for the Association of Southeast Asian Nations; its members are Thailand, Malaysia, Indonesia, Singapore, Brunei, and the Philippines. Almost nothing happened on the

ASEAN unity front until the Japanese investors arrived, coordinating their own production across the national lines. In Bangkok in 1990 I listened while an official of the Japan External Trade Relations Organization, (JETRO), which is in effect the foreign commercial-intelligence branch of MITI, explained to me in Japanese how the work was being parceled out. For example, with televisions: Matsushita made the electron guns for TVs in its factories in Malaysia. It exported the electron guns to Singapore, where they were assembled into cathode-ray tubes ("picture tubes" to laypeople) at a Hitachi plant. Then the CRTs went back to Japanese-owned factories in Malaysia and Thailand for assembly into finished televisions, for sale in Asia and export outside the region. The Mitsubishi works outside Kuala Lumpur made car doors, which then went to a Mitsubishi factory in Thailand—and eventually, the company hoped, into cars for the North American market. It was a success where local governments had failed; it brought prosperity and jobs. Its main drawback, from the ASEAN perspective, is that virtually all of the management, design, and skilled work was done either in Japan or by Japanese officials sent by their companies to posts in the rest of Asia.

In the early summer of 1991, an official from Taiwan's Industrial Development Bureau went to Japan to propose that Taiwan be let into the regional planning business. He was proposing a scheme in which auto-related companies in Japan, Taiwan, and Thailand would form an "alliance for auto manufacturing and worldwide distribution based on the principle of mutually beneficial division of labor." Under this division, the Japanese companies would do R&D for new models and work out high-tech production schemes; Taiwan would provide components; and workers in Thailand would assemble the parts into finished cars.[51] "The combination of Japan's advanced know-how and outstanding marketing strategy, Taiwan's low-cost, quality auto parts, and Thailand's cheap labor would turn out highly competitive cars," the Taiwanese officials told the local press.[52]

The allure of investment was, of course, the most powerful tool for integrating the rest of Asia into the Japanese industrial system. Japan's foreign aid programs were an important governmental counterpart to the investment programs by Japanese corporations. U.S. foreign aid programs reflected different ideologies at different times. In many cases the United States has given money for Cold War purposes, as a means of holding back the Communists. It gives money to obtain "leverage" and to buy cooperation in certain regions, such as the Middle East. It has at times given money to promote its ideas of democratic development or human rights. Japan's programs have been far more consistent and comprehensible.They have given money, mainly in Asia, for industrial projects that mainly involve large Japanese firms.

"The philosophy and practice of Japanese foreign aid continue to be quite different from that of the United States—and may be moving farther away," Edward Lincoln of Brookings said early in 1991. "Foreign aid remains very closely tied to the interests of the [Japanese] private sector."

Lincoln was using the word "tied" in its normal, everyday sense, to indicate that the aid program and other industrial strategies worked toward the same end. "Tied aid" in its official, legalistic connotation—that is, money that can be spent only for products from the home country—is not always a feature of Japanese foreign aid, just as formal tariff barriers are not always, or even usually, what keep the Japanese market "closed." In each case a network of informal understandings and agreements has the intended effect—that of suppressing high-value imports into Japan and of steering aid purchasers back to Japanese suppliers.

Japan's aid has been concentrated in Asia, it has coordinated with Japanese business, and it has reflected a belief that Asian businesses should be run like Japanese businesses and, wherever possible, by Japanese businesses. "The effort to integrate foreign aid with private sector interests is now rather openly expressed and defended," Edward Lincoln said.[53] "Despite [Japanese] government assurances to the contrary, Japanese aid remains largely 'tied' in practice and corporate interests play an important role in carrying out assistance programs," Michael Chinworth, a defense specialist, has written. "There is no reason to suspect that [this pattern] could be altered significantly in the near future."[54] Through the late 1980s, Japanese aid represented 15 to 20 percent of the entire budget expenditures of certain countries in the region.[55]

In a book about Japanese foreign aid policies,[56] Robert Orr emphasized that foreign aid involved bureaucratic squabbling in Japan as it does anywhere else. In most Western nations, however, the dominant bureaucracies are those involved with diplomatic and military policy. In Japan, Orr said, the agency with the greatest influence over foreign aid was MITI, which constantly viewed the loans and grants as an offshoot of export policy. "The high degree of cooperation between the public and private sectors continues to suggest to some observers that Japanese ODA remains a thinly disguised export promotion program," he wrote in 1990.[57] The same judgment would be made of private-public cooperation in American overseas programs—but there the collaboration would, of course, be between the Defense Department and McDonnell Douglas, or in rarer cases between U.S. AID and construction companies like Bechtel. Both the United States and Japan concentrated their efforts on "security" but they defined the term in different ways—with an emphasis on military and strategic threats for America, and with an emphasis on economic threats for Japan.[58]

Early in 1990, the U.S. embassy in Bangkok produced an intelligence report on Japanese influence in Thailand. It noted the overwhelming role of Japanese aid donors and said, "In sum, Japan's influence as a donor in Thailand is used to support near- and long-term commercial and economic objectives."[59]

More important than the surge of Japanese aid was, of course, its concentration and shape. In Thailand and Malaysia it was "infrastructure" investment of a certain sort, preparing a nation for commercial projects. This kind of investment is good or bad according to your taste; the point is, there was a *plan*. In the embassies in Kuala Lumpur and in Bangkok were diagrams; first there would be roads and bridges, built with Japanese loans and with Japanese engineering companies, and at the end of the new road would be a Minebea or Toyota plant. In the early 1990s much of the Japanese push in Thailand has been for a huge development along the seaboard, comparable in its ideal form to the Tokyo Bay sprawl or the Los Angeles basin. Like any other form of urban growth the Bangkok plan would create both benefits and problems. Unlike the growth of either Tokyo or Los Angeles, Bangkok's planned expansion would be driven mainly by money from outside the country.[60] "It would be unusual if such a coordination of interests between the Japanese government and private sector did not result in a de facto preference for Japanese firms," Edward Lincoln concluded. "This is the essence of what I would term 'soft regionalism': The Japanese will benefit preferentially but can deny that any formal (or even informal) preference really exists."[61]

Output: A New Export Surge

In short, the effect of this enormous shift of funds was no happened when American firms went to Europe, nor happened when European or U.S.-based firms went to Africa, Latin America, or Asia itself. In all those cases something like a borderless economy emerged; in the Asian example it was more like a large-scale division of labor run from Japan on nationality-conscious lines. It would seem small-minded to call this a colonial relationship, since there is no physical force, nor even the threat of force, to back it up. But it is "colonial" in that government and business in Japan combine to devise relationships that leave them with far more power than their partners have.

The main result that demonstrates this pattern is the evolution of trade between Japan and the rest of Asia—an evolution, again, that simply cannot be explained by the pure forces of market logic.

We return here to our old friend "intra-industry" trade. This is probably the single strongest indicator of equal versus unequal economic relationships in the modern world. When the intra-industry trade index is high, it means essentially that countries are dealing as equals, buying and selling without fretting too much about where the products were actually made. This is also what people mean when they refer to a "horizonal" division of labor. When the intra-industry rate is low, it means the reverse. There are distinct national concentrations of production, which create a "vertical" relationship and raise doubts about the "borderless" era.

Throughout Asia, the pattern of trade to and from Japan is remarkably consistent. The relationshps are "vertical"; the intra-industry rate is low. The countries that have often had trade surpluses with Japan—the Philippines, Indonesia—are not those with the strongest overall economies but those with the crucial raw materials. The more advanced industrial powers—Korea, Taiwan—have enormous trade deficits with Japan. (In 1991, Korea had an overall trade deficit of about $9.5 billion, of which $8.8 billion, or about 93 percent, was its deficit with Japan. Taiwan's trade deficit with Japan was almost as large.) This pattern would not make sense by the conventional wisdom of American speeches and editorials—"let's save more, work harder, and spend more days in school." The Koreans and Taiwanese do all those things. It does fit a pattern in which the Japanese economy leans toward importing raw materials, avoiding manufactured imports, and making other countries reliant on its crucial components. For instance, Taiwanese computer makers and Korean VCR makers must get their most advanced chips and video heads from suppliers in Japan. They have not had the technical wherewithal to develop these facilities on their own, and Japanese firms have been far more careful about licensing the technology than

American firms were when dealing with Japan a generation ago.

Figures produced by Japan's Ministry of Finance showed one shift toward a more "horizontal" relationship after *endaka*, in the 1980s. "Miscellaneous manufactured products"—low- and medium-tech goods not sophisticated enough to make it into the "machinery and equipment" category—were produced more evenly around the region after the onset of *endaka*.[62] But higher-value production barely budged from its center in Japan. Even after the yen doubled in value, Japanese companies in Japan produced sophisticated goods while importing raw materials and low-tech equipment from the rest of the region. In the late 1980s, after several years of heavy Japanese manufacturing investment in Thailand, each country's leading exports to the other were as follows, listed in order of value:

Japanese Exports to Thailand	Thai Exports to Japan
1. Nonelectric machinery	Rubber
2. Vehicles and parts	Gems and pearls
3. Iron and steel	Shrimp
4. Electrical machinery	Chicken
5. Chemicals	Garments
6. Scientific/optical equipment	Sugar
7. Electrical appliances	Squid (fresh/frozen)
8. Household goods	Ball bearings
9. Tubes and pipes	Furniture and parts
10. Other capital goods	Fish
11. Motorcycles	Squid (dried)[63]

America's imports from both Thailand and Indonesia were mainly relatively simple manufactured goods; Japan's imports from Indonesia were mainly petroleum or wood.[64] Most of America's imports from Taiwan were manufactured products. Most of Japan's imports from Taiwan were food, raw materials, textiles, and other light products. Most of Japan's imports from Korea were food, fish, cloth, and shoes.[65] "What the Japanese call a horizontal division of labor"—specializing but not dominating, most countries having high rates of "intra-industry" trade—"is generally nothing of the sort when examined in greater detail," one academic study concluded.[66] The reality of the division of labor remains vertical, but, as Edward Lincoln wrote, the use of a deceptive terminology ["horizontal division of labor"] is somewhat disturbing and rather typical of the attempts of the Japanese government to provide a facade of equality and openness to its dealings with the rest of Asia.[67]

In addition to this pattern of interaction in the rest of Asia was also a difference of scale. Japanese producers were *so* strong in so many markets in Asia, and the Asian consumer markets were growing so fast, that even during the doldrums of the early 1990s its industries enjoyed a kind of base and volume that American industries approximated mainly in the movie and record business.

What American companies gained in the first half of the twentieth century by dominating the rich and fast-growing U.S. market, Japanese firms now expect to gain, on a much larger scale, from their dominance in Asia. "In this expansion of trade, Japan and North America have played opposite, but complementary roles," Kenneth Courtis wrote in 1992, in a summary of the years of *endaka*. "Through direct investment, and its own finely targeted trade expansion, Japan has supplied the region with capital and intermediate goods. Japan's activity has been instrumental in the supply-side development of Asia." And yet, he said, the process of "development" in Asia had made other countries increasingly dependent on America for customers, and on Japan for crucial supplies:

> By the end of this year, Japan's trade surplus with the principal market economies of East Asia will [be] $35 billion, equal to its surplus with the entire Common Market.
>
> In contrast, the United States has played the role of market for Asia. . . . Given the role that it has played on the input side of Asia's economic growth, Japan has also gained immensely from the expansion of Asia's exports to America. . . .[68]
>
> On aggregate, North American–based firms are in retreat from this region. European firms, preoccupied with the new challenges they face at home, are not increasing investment in the region at the same pace at which economies are expanding. In contrast, throughout East Asia, the investment of Japanese firms continues to gallop ahead.
>
> As a result, by both design and default, Japanese-based firms are moving into strategic control of the world's greatest and fastest-growing markets. That will give to these firms huge volume increases, allowing them to continue sliding down the cost curve faster than their North American and European com-

petitors. Not only will East Asian growth fuel expansion of Japan's economy, but [it] also will prove to be the trump card that corporate Japan plays in the global competitive game through the end of the decade.[69]

Other countries in Asia have, of course, their own ideas about how this game will unfold. Their strengths and weaknesses vary dramatically, which will affect their own prospects and their impact on the rest of the world.

6

Growth
Without Development

THE FIRST FEW TIMES I visited Thailand I was nagged by a sense
of familiarity that I could not attach a name to or quite pin down.
It did not have to do with Thailand's sights and sounds—the muddy
klongs or canals of Bangkok, the gold-roofed temples throughout
the country, the monks in orange robes who walked from house to
house each morning carrying their begging bowls. These were all
"exotic" to me but also quickly recognizable from books and movies
I had seen over the years.

The sense of déjà vu in Thailand seemed to come instead from
the speed with which the whole society was being turned upside
down by nonstop economic growth. Even more than in Japan during
its boom years, in Thailand in the late 1980s and early 1990s you
could see the way money was altering life. Reconstruction in Japan
tends to be as quick and unobtrusive as possible; it reminded me of
a cat bathing itself. During Japan's bubble years, we'd notice one
day that a house on our street would be covered with bamboo scaffolding, from which blue plastic sheeting would be hung. The next
day the house would be gone, and in a week a new one would have
sprung up in its place. Roads were repaired at night, as if by fairies.

There was nothing subtle or hidden about the changes being
worked on Thailand—above all in Bangkok, where most of the
country's industry was concentrated. On nights when the moon was
down or was covered by fog, it seemed possible to read by the light
of the welding torches that flickered all over town. In 1990 I was
staying with my family for a month in Bangkok, based in a twelfth-
floor apartment not far from downtown. We had to close the curtains

at night against the electric blue light that flickered around the clock from the condo that was rising, one floor per week, across the street. When dawn came and it was harder to see the welding torches, the night crews would climb down from the bamboo scaffolding. The workers were barefoot, with broad, splayed feet and with rags draped over their face, to keep out the dust. Their eyes were visible as moist spots. I had seen this procession for several weeks before I noticed a worker remove the head rags. She was a woman—and so, I eventually discovered, were about half the other laborers on the highrise. Along with the men, they had poured into Bangkok from Thailand's impoverished hinterland, known as the Northeast. At construction sites in the city they could earn as much as 100 *bhat* per day, almost $4.

Bangkok seemed at the time like a machine running so fast that gears and rods fly out in all directions and the lubricating oil smokes away. It was natural to think of smoke when you tried to breathe in Bangkok. The air in Los Angeles does not seem opaque until you view it from a distance, looking toward an invisible mountain or out from an airplane sinking into the smog. After one of Bangkok's big, smoke-belching buses roars by on Rama IV or Sukhumvit roads, it can be hard to see even to the other side of the street. Only a generation ago, canals snaked quaintly through the entire city, and the broad and mighty Chao Phraya River was Bangkok's heart. Now most of the canals have been paved and the Chao Phraya bobs with sewage and the pink plastic shopping bags that are the ubiquitous debris of the Third World.

The sidewalks along Bangkok's jammed streets were also jammed—with Thai students, Western tourists and hippies, Japanese businessmen, peasants newly arrived from the provinces, and beggars and vendors. Outside the city's major Buddhist shrines sat women in front of cages jam-packed with sparrowlike live birds. For 30 bhat, about $1, the vendors would open a box and let a bird go. This act of charity "makes merit" for the bird's benefactor, according to Buddhist teachings. Therefore the vendors were doing passersby a favor in offering this merit-making opportunity, much as Thai monks did by asking for their morning alms. (Someone else must constantly have been giving up merit by capturing new birds, since the cages remained miraculously full.[1])

Beggar gangs presented similar opportunities to make merit. The beggars in Bangkok were not as overwhelmingly numerous as those in Manila or New Delhi. Yet even as Thailand's economy was surging, on its streets visitors would find disabled children, pathetic mothers with grimy infants hanging at their breasts, blind flower-sellers, and others with their hands out in supplication. In 1990 the Thai government became sufficiently concerned about the beggars' effect on tourism that it began issuing notices in the English-language newspapers. Don't pay attention to the beggars, the stories said. Don't feel sorry for them or believe their hard-luck tales! Tourists should be aware that begging was a business. The saddest-looking children with this most pitiable disabilities were actually part of vast beggar gangs, the official warnings said. The gangs were run by evil beggar-bosses, the "Fagins of Bangkok," according to one newspaper account.

Of course! With the word "Fagin," my nagging uncertainty was resolved. The Thailand of the early 1990s did not resemble anything I had seen, but it did resemble something I had read about. The combination of rapid economic growth and chaotic social disorganization, the streets jammed with displaced country folk in search of jobs, the new factories obscured by smoke and dust, the material progress and consequent human suffering—all these conditions summed up the England of the mid-nineteenth century as portrayed by Charles Dickens. If the beggars were Thailand's Oliver Twists and the bosses were its Fagins, then perhaps Bangkok itself in the 1990s was London in the 1850s, a metropolis going through the painful and messy birth of industrial life.

Once I had made the connection to Dickens's London, I realized why it mattered to me: It raised the central question about what the future holds for countries like Thailand. What is happening in Thailand now is ugly but not unprecedented. Today's richest countries, when they were growing fastest, were at least as raw and ruthless as Thailand seems now. In England, in North America, in Germany, and elsewhere, modernization drove people from their farms and villages and put them into tenements and factories. England lost its forests to the industrial revolution. America overcut its much larger forests, plowed up its prairie, and drained its western aquifers. Each country used up people on its way toward industrialism, as Dickens showed about England and Upton Sinclair about the United States. But today's rich countries can look back on these costly eras at times of transition. When the dirty work was finished, the countries had become so prosperous that they could afford to outlaw child labor, impose safety laws, and clean up their water and air.

There is no question that Thailand and its neighbors in Southeast Asia are in a messy period. Almost by the hour you can see the forests being mowed down, the air turning dark with smoke. In 1992 Prime Minister Mahathir bin Mohamad of Malaysia made explicit the comparison between Asia's growth and that of the West. "When the rich chopped down their own forests, built their poison-belching factories, and scoured the world for cheap resources, the poor said nothing," he stated at the 1992 U.N. environment conference in Rio de Janeiro. But now hypocritical Western countries, in complaining about Asian environmental excesses, "claim a right to regulate the development of the poor countries."[2]

Today's East Asian social turmoil is so fast it is easy to feel old in a hurry. I was gone from the United States for most of four years; when I came back at the end of that time, very few things made me think, "I don't recognize this place." When I visited Jakarta or Bangkok or Taipei after an interval of only six months I found myself vainly looking for landmarks that had been razed, remodeled, or transformed while I was gone. This was economic growth, in all its glory and ugliness. The United States was where you went to see it a hundred years ago, and East Asia is today.

The question for Thailand and its neighbors, however, is where today's disorder will lead. Japan suffered terrible industrial pollution during its catch-up years. Now it is rich enough to begin coping with pollution, while enjoying the benefits of industrial strength. But other countries, from Romania to Kenya, have depleted their resources and disrupted their people with little to show for it. Today's disruption in Southeast Asia will mean one thing if it proves to be a transition toward real development, and something different and darker if it does not. Judging these prospects, in turn, means asking whether economic growth will mean for the rest of Asia what it has meant for Japan: greater control over its own destiny. For many parts of Asia, growth may mean no such thing.

National Roles in the New Asian System

Several traits apply throughout East Asia and make it sensible to talk about these diverse countries as one economic region.

· First, there is tremendous collective dynamism. Some of the countries are poor now, and many of those will probably remain poor for a very long time. Burma might "take off" someday, especially since it has such great oil and mineral reserves, but that day is not in sight. Rural areas of China have not changed dramatically in hundreds of years, and that is where most of the Chinese population lives. The Philippines is, as a whole, worse off than it was a generation ago. Other countries have their own particular problems.

Still, throughout the region there is the sense that must have prevailed in much of Europe in the 1800s and in the United States through most of the past century. This is the sense that economic activity is changing life even as you watch, making it better in many ways, worse in others, but conveying the unmistakable sense of at-the-center-ness that Asia certainly lacked during the long years of colonial control and has captured now. South Korea has grown so quickly in the past decade that it has surpassed France and Italy and a number of other established powers in total output—and yet it still is only the fifth-richest country in East Asia, in per capita terms.[3] (The top four, in order, are Japan, Taiwan, Singapore, and Hong Kong.)

· Second, the countries in this region must all look economically to Japan. Their situations obviously vary. The Philippines, as a onetime American colony, has a longer tradition of American investment than its neighbors do. Indonesia and Malaysia, as big raw-material sellers, can in principle sell their goods to any buyer looking for timber, natural gas, or oil. The United States is still a crucial market for manufacturers through Asia. Still, all the countries in East Asia know that the big buyer (especially of oil, timber, and fish), the big seller (especially of cars, consumer goods, and capital equipment), the big investor, and the big donor in the region is Japan. Its only potential challenger is China, whose long-term prospects are too uncertain for anyone to predict with confidence.

· Third, these countries share historic experience and intellectual precepts different from those that prevail in the Western world. Most were colonized by Western countries, and even the ones that weren't have been fully conscious of the West's dominance in machinery, technology, and the flow of ideas. Although many of these Asian societies have been washed in Western concepts for decades or centuries, the concepts largely remain imported rather than intrinsic. The ideal model toward which the Asian system is evolving differs from the Western ideal. It is more hierarchical, more divided in function by gender and ethnicity, more statusbound, and more authoritarian than is advocated in most of the West. The economic success of such a system in Asia is what makes its modern interactions with the West so significant and interesting. "Ultimately we shall have to realize that this challenge encompasses not only Japan but China as well, and indeed the whole of East Asia," Ivan Hall, an American scholar who has lived for decades in Japan and other parts of Asia, wrote in 1992. "With poetic justice, we are now getting a tiny inkling of the intellectual and psychological anguish thrust upon those countries by the pressures from our more dynamic civilizations."[4]

At the same time, the countries of East Asia can be divided into a variety of categories, depending on what point you want to make.

One important and familiar axis separates "Confucian" from non-Confucian countries. The countries with the strongest economies in the region also share the imprint of Confucian values. They are Korea, Japan, and the Chinese cultures of Taiwan, Hong Kong, Singapore, and coastal China. In several other countries, most notably Malaysia and Indonesia but also including Thailand, Vietnam, and the Philippines, the Chinese (and therefore Confucian-influenced) minority dominates business activity. An emphasis on Confucianism in classifying Asian countries seems commonsensical, since many of the classic Confucian traits—study, self-discipline, and filial obedience—have proven to be economic advantages. The problem with this way of explaining success is that it leaves out political factors. Fifty years ago North Korea was as influenced by Confucianism as the South, but for political reasons the two states have taken very different economic paths. The biggest Confucian country of all, China itself, has not fully attained the status of economic "success" for both political and demographic reasons.

Another way to classify East Asian countries is by the Communist-vs.-non-Communist split. Apart from Cuba, the remaining pockets of Communist orthodoxy in the world are all in Asia. North Korea leads the list, but it is accompanied by China, Vietnam, Cambodia, and Laos. All of them have been toying with reforms, North Korea more slowly than the rest, yet all are far more stalwart than the lost Communists of Europe, and far more backward than most of their neighbors in Asia. The main lesson from this classification system is to reemphasize how profoundly Communist totalitarianism has failed.

And there is another way of classifying East Asian countries, which may be the most useful way for understanding the modern Asian system. The scheme of classification is based on each country's role in the economic system that Japan has pioneered. It separates the countries of the region into three groups.

The first group consists of the "acted upon" countries—those whose economies are principally objects of the commercial dynamism emanating from Japan.

"What has happened in Southeast Asia is the emergence of ersatz capitalism," Kunio Yoshihara of Japan wrote in the late 1980s (in his book *The Rise of Ersatz Capitalism in Southeast Asia*).[5] When Yoshihara called the systems of Thailand, Indonesia, Malaysia, and other nations ersatz, he meant that they were being propelled, shaped, inflated, and in many ways changed by forces far beyond their control. As a result, he said, they were growing but not developing. Their cities were spreading; factories were sprouting up; their GNP figures were the envy of the world. Yet these economies did not seem clearly to be "developing," in the sense of gaining new leverage and strength in the world. Modernization might not do for them what it had done for Japan—increase their ability to control or steer the economic activity going on around them. Such control is what colonialism took away from most people in Asia, and it is what Japan has spent a century and a half fighting to attain for itself.

The second group of countries consists of the stragglers—the countries that for reasons of politics, geography, or sheer bad luck have been left out of the region's growth. Burma and North Korea are at the bottom of this unfortunate list, saddled with two of the very worst governments in the world. For different reasons the Philippines, Vietnam, Cambodia, and Laos have also been excluded, as has much of China. All of these countries could potentially prosper, and a generation from now several of them probably will have. But for the past generation they have been left behind as their neighbors have rapidly grown.

The last and smallest groups consists of countries whose systems fundamentally resemble Japan's and that therefore theoretically have some chance of catching up with Japan. Two countries are in this group: the Republic of Korea (South Korea) and the Republic of China (Taiwan). Neither of them could ever catch up with Japan, if "catching up" meant that they would become richer, more productive, or generally more powerful than Japan. Japan's population is three times as large as South Korea's and six times as large as Taiwan's. Its gross national product is twelve times larger than South Korea's; the difference in technology, while harder to measure, is at least as great. Yet conceivably these smaller countries could "catch up" with a satisfied, slowed-down Japan that is larger than they are, much as Japan caught up with a satisfied, slowed-down, larger United States. This kind of catching up would mean developing independent sources of technology, improving the country's relative skills and earnings, and generally gaining the political and economic leverage that comes with commerical strength.

Countries in the first and third groups—those that are "acted upon" and those that are contenders—may well gain power relative to the non-Asian world in the next generation. The struggling countries in the second category may become less miserable when their governmental policies change. Together they make for an Asian system far more powerful and consequential than Japan's economy could be by itself; yet their own struggles with Japan underscore the strength of the Japanese system. The rest of this chapter, and the following two, consider these groups of countries in order.

Thailand

Thailand is the purest illustration of growth without development in Asia, but the category also includes Malaysia, Indonesia, and—for the foreseeable future—the coastal regions of China. Singapore and Hong Kong are much richer than the other countries in this group, but they are still "acted upon" in a political and strategic sense. Hong Kong, scheduled to pass from British to Chinese control in 1997, depends on trade with China for its economic health and on the goodwill of China for its future political freedom. Singapore is a mainly Chinese city-state positioned between two much larger mainly Malay countries, Indonesia and Malaysia. Relations between Singapore and its neighbors are correct, but Singapore remains fundamentally vulnerable; for instance, nearly its entire water supply comes through a pipeline from Malaysia.

Of these countries, Thailand deserves consideration first, as the most extensive illustration of the economic and political impact of the Japan-centered system on the rest of East Asia.

One could argue, and many Thai officials do, that the ultimate explanation for the country's rapid growth lies in its own distinctive traits, not in decisions made outside its borders. Thailand, in this view, has succeeded because Thailand itself is pleasant and attractive, making foreigners, especially Japanese businessmen, eager to work there.

The crucial fact about Thailand, according to this hypothesis, is that it is the sweet-dispositioned "land of smiles," the independent-spirited and playful-minded kingdom where nothing is taken too seriously and where every interaction is greased with kindness, care, and, above all, permissiveness.

Thailand's major industries have been "guided" and controlled by the government, like most others in Asia, and through most of the twentieth century the military has been the dominant force in its government. Yet in many social mores Thailand applies a brand of laissez-faire unimaginable in many other parts of Asia.

When my family was living in Japan or Malaysia or traveling in other Asian countries, we were in various ways shielded from the rough-and-tumble of a really free market system. In Japan, everything cost more than it was really worth—so like others in the country, we were encouraged to save. In Malaysia, things that were considered bad for us, from pornographic films to books critical of the country's government, could not legally be imported or offered for sale. But whenever we went to Bangkok, we found that everything was for sale, with results both good and bad.

I stepped into drugstores on Sukhumvit or Rama IV roads and bought all of the antibiotics, hormone pills for my wife, sleeping tablets, and other products that my family thought it might need. Why bring a nosy doctor into it? In Thailand we could write prescriptions for ourselves. I could step outside the drugstore and buy a lifetime supply of Lacoste-style tennis shirts for 90 baht apiece, or a little less than $4. Or it could have been Gucci shirts or fake Rolex watches or a million other products. Sidewalk vendors carried pirated tapes, for $1, of whatever recordings were then popular in Europe or America. People could do what they wanted; it was the libertarian dream.

Prostitution was theoretically against the law in Thailand, a fact that would come as a surprise to nearly any visitor and to every resident. In any Thai village large enough to have a store or a gas station, there will be a brothel as well. Those in the big cities are on three tiers: the expensive ones for foreigners, a middle range for prosperous Thais, and the workingman's brothel. The Thai Ministry of Tourism periodically released, without comment, statistics showing that visitors to the kingdom were overwhelmingly male, usually traveling on their own. To go once to the shows in Patpong—and see the women who ingest bananas, shoot out darts and Ping-Pong balls, or blow out candles, all with their vaginas—is perhaps instructive. To do it more than once—well, since I went only once, I would think it perverse. Driving through the Thai countryside, far to the north or east of Bangkok, you will pass hundreds of bamboo or wooden huts—and then all of a sudden you will see a substantial concrete or brick structure, with a real roof and perhaps a paved walkway. The parents who live in these houses almost always have a daughter who is "working" in Bangkok, Phuket, or Pattaya and sending money back home.

By the early 1990s, the sex industry of Thailand had to drop its pretense that all was happiness and nonexploitation, since AIDS was becoming such a scourge and Bangkok, inevitably, an entrepôt for its spread.[6] (In 1987 I interviewed an official of the Thai Ministry of Health, who claimed that Asians would prove uniquely "resistant" to AIDS, despite Bangkok's enormous prostitution industry and surveys showing that minimum-wage male workers in Thailand went to brothels on an average of three times a week. By 1990 the Ministry of Health was reporting that one third of the Bangkok construction workers it tested were postive for HIV.) Nonetheless, the prevailing Thai idea was that everything was okay, everyone can please himself. *Mai pen rai.*

Mai pen rai is Thailand's version of the cliché "insight" into the national character that becomes annoying in any country. What *mañana* is supposed to be for the culture of Latin America, what *gambatte!* (never quit!) is for Japan or "I gotta be me" is for America, *mai pen rai* is supposed to be for Thailand. The phrase variously means "don't worry about it," "no problem," "never mind," or "oh, calm down." More broadly it is meant to convey tolerance and detachment from the minor frets and concerns of Western life. Don't get upset about anything, because it's all more or less a joke.

The border between Malaysia and Thailand runs across the narrow isthmus at the top of the Malay Peninsula. There is a tremendous amount of traffic back and forth, as at border towns everywhere else in the world. Malaysians go north, from their Islamic-dominated society, for the gambling and commercial sex of Thailand. (Once I got in a taxicab on the Malaysian side and said I was heading to Thailand. The driver, a Chinese Malaysian who did not speak English, understood my attempts to write the Chinese characters for Thailand. His face lit up, and he started running the finger of one hand in and out of the circled fingers of the others, in a universal gesture. "Thailand! Okay, boss!!") When the buses full of Thais, headed for who knows what reason into Malaysia, stop in gas stations on the Malay side, they nearly always leave behind them a ring of plastic bags, cigarette wrappers, soft-drink containers, and other debris, expelled from windows on all sides of the bus as its refuels.

The Malaysians more restrained and fastidious, generally seethe, and are not calmed by the refrains of *mai pen rai* that come from the passengers as the bus rolls off.

Mai pen rai I would hear from taxi drivers or Thai friends when sitting for hours in the traffic jams on Sukhumvit. *Mai pen rai,* in the sense of "there's nothing to do about it," dominates the discussion of Thailand's severe environmental problems, or the curtain of exhaust that hangs over the skies in Bangkok.

Like most clichés and stereotypes, the Thai emphasis on its open culture and the *mai pen rai* spirit obviously has something to it, yet like most clichés it omits certain crucial facts.[7] The truth in Thailand's sense that its culture accounts for its success lies in three areas: Thailand's freedom from the psychological aftereffects of colonialism, its relative success in racial integration, and its adaptation of the monarchy to modern needs. What the cultural explanation omits are the economic fundamentals that have left this country, like most of its neighbors in Southeast Asia, dependent on decisions and events made by outsiders, mainly in Japan.

"Land of the free." Just as Japanese theories of Japanese success always seem to begin with the phrase "because we are all Japanese," Thai explanations of how their country works all seem to begin, "because we were never colonized." The very word Thai, visitors are quickly told, means "free." In its dealings with the outside world, therefore, Thailand need not display either the resentment or the leftover deference of a onetime colony, since it has never had to salute a foreign flag.

As a matter of strict historical fact, Thailand's emphasis on its unbroken liberty is not completely accurate. Thailand avoided being conquered largely because its leaders shrewdly and preemptively cooperated whenever superior force came in view. In the late 1800s, Thailand (then known as Siam) could look to the east and see the French colonies of Indochina. To the west lay the British occupiers in Burma, then part of the Indian raj. Thailand's rulers ingratiated themselves to each colonial power and thereby survived as an independent buffer state.

A century later, during the Vietnam War years, Thailand's military rulers similarly ingratiated themselves to the United States. Vietnam and Thailand are old and bitter rivals in Southeast Asia, and Thailand had reasons of its own for wanting to contain Vietnam's expansion. So through the 1960s it made itself, voluntarily, into a kind of American colony, with U.S. air bases in its eastern regions and GIs recreating in Bangkok.

Between these two episodes came Thailand's most dramatic preservation of its "independence": its lightning conversion to the Japanese side just as the Imperial Japanese Army was about to move it. Throughout the 1930s and 1940s, Thai politics revolved around the rivalry of two men, Pibul and Pridi, who had two different theories about how the country could best position itself. (Thai people are often referred to only by their first name, as in the case of Pibul and Pridi.) Pibul was the country's prime minister late in 1941. On the eve of Japan's attack on Pearl Harbor, the Japanese ambassador tried to track Pibul down in Bangkok. He wanted to present a formal request that Japanese troops be allowed free passage through Thailand as they moved against British positions to the west, in Burma, and to the south, in Malaya and Singapore. Pibul avoided him by hiding in his office building. His rival Pridi, then foreign minister, received the ambassador instead—and turned down his request.

As dawn broke the next day, with the Japanese Army preparing to move across Thailand anyway, the previously missing Pibul reappeared and gave his okay to the Japanese. Through the following three years, until the Allied forces began to roll the Japanese Army back toward its home islands, Pibul served a Quisling-like role as the Japanese puppet. His rival Pridi left the government, organized a resistance movement, and when the Allies came back was installed as prime minister. (He served until he was overthrown in a military coup—led, of course, by Pibul.)

The "alliance" with Japan during World War II, like the later accommodation to America during the Vietnam War years, required certain modifications in the *mai pen rai* approach. The Japanese theory of "pan-Asian brotherhood" resembled a real family mainly in that members were not equals. Some were older and stronger, some were small and weak and not responsible for themselves. The theory held that Japan had a "responsibility" for its little brothers throughout the region, but part of that burden was to make them shape up and modernize themselves, the way Japan had previously done.[8]

In Korea, Taiwan, China, and other places where the Japanese had taken over by main force, the immediate task was to keep people under control. In Thailand, under the guise of alliance, the Japanese officials could act as if they were providing etiquette tips. As Alec Waugh wrote,

[The Japanese] pressed for Westernization. They found Pibul
most cooperative. Orders were issued that women should wear
gloves, hats, and stockings. The Japanese disliked the black teeth
that the women acquired through chewing betel nut. Pibul ordered the habit to be discontinued, and to ensure that it was,
he had all the betel nut trees cut down. . . . The Japanese did
not consider that the Thais showed sufficient respect to their
wives, and it was decreed that when a man left his house in the
morning and returned to it at night, he should bestow a kiss
upon her cheek.[9]

Thailand's cooperation in the new Asian order was apparently not
sincere. "The Japanese had a bad time in Thailand during the war
because, as an authoritarian people, they simply could not cope with
the deviousness of the Thai," one foreign author wrote in the 1960s.
"They had a naive belief that a minimum of trust could be placed
with an ally."[10]

In its role as Japan's only Asian ally, Thailand naturally was
expected to declare war on the United States. Thailand never quite
got around to this formality. Pibul's collaborationist government
relayed instructions to its ambassador in Washington, D.C., telling
him to present a formal declaration to the American authorities.
The ambassador, ten thousand miles away from the Japanese Army,
refused. By wartime's end he had become a major resistance
leader—as had Pridi, the rival of Prime Minister Pibul.

The result of this maneuvering was to give Thailand two horses
in World War II: it could be for whomever was winning at the time.
Because of Japan's "alliance" with Thailand, the Japanese Army
did not have to fight its way through the country in 1941, as it did
so destructively in the Philippines and China. Because of the resistance movement, the Allies did not have to invade, either. When
they came, they could be embraced as liberators.

Starting in the late 1980s, when nearly all the new money coming into Thailand seemed to be coming from Japan, there were signs
that the "cover all bases" strategy was being applied again. On his
visits to the United States, Prime Minister Chatichai of Thailand
gave speeches urging a larger American presence in the region so
that his grandchildren didn't have to grow up "speaking Japanese."
At the same time, inside Thailand, officials were increasingly solic-
itous of the visiting Japanese. When I interviewed politicians in
Bangkok in 1989 and 1990 I would hear, as a refrain about Japan,
"After all, we were allies in the war." As an American who lived

in Thailand wrote, "The Thai always plant respected men in active cooperation with the publicly labeled enemy so that, no matter which side is victor in big power politics, a competent Thai is always in position to take over."[11]

Still, for all the self-consoling and face-saving fictions that may be involved, Thailand has managed to avoid direct external control through its modern history. Its belief in its heritage of independence is strong enough to remove the nasty postcolonial undertone that affects dealings between so many other Asian countries and the West.

Racial assimilation. Thailand has freed itself from another form of nastiness that prevails elsewhere in Southeast Asia: racial friction between the expatriate Chinese minorities and the Malay, Javanese, Vietnamese, or other majority populations among whom the Chinese live.

The emigrants who have fanned out from southern China since the 1500s now constitute a diaspora more numerous than the Jewish diaspora of the Western world or the Indian and Pakistani diaspora in Africa. The Chinese also constitute the commercial backbone of Southeast Asia. The forebears of today's Chinese businessmen mainly arrived in Southeast Asia as coolies, to work in the great plantations of Java and Sumatra, or as clerks and traders whose entry was encouraged by the British, French, and Dutch colonialists. Like most emigrants through history they were not from the elite class of their homeland, and they had the familiar immigrant drive to become established as quickly as possible.

Established they now are: in virtually every great city of Southeast Asia, ethnic Chinese dominate the business and finance. With bonds of language and family relations, Chinese merchants form a network that connects mainland Chinese, the mainly Chinese nations such as Singapore and Taiwan, and the large Chinese enclaves in Manila, Kuala Lumpur, Jakarta, Penang, Bangkok, and even Ho Chi Minh City. In Ho Chi Minh City, in the fall of 1990, I went to a trade show where manufacturers were showing off rice-baggers, brick makers, and other mid-technology wares. Most of the exhibitors were from Taiwan, not simply because small businesses thrive on the island but also because they could do business, in Chinese, with so many of the merchants left in what had been South Vietnam.

In most parts of Southeast Asia, the conspicuous success of the Chinese is a significant political problem. The "Chinese problem" is mild in the Philippines, where most Chinese have taken

names that don't look Chinese. (For instance, the maiden name of
Corazon Aquino was Cojuangco, which looks Spanish but which
was derived from the name of her immigrant grandfather, Ko Hwan
Ko.) Anti-Chinese feelings have reached explosive proportions in
Indonesia, where the Chinese make up perhaps 3 or 4 percent of
the population but account for perhaps 80 percent of all business
activity. In 1965, huge numbers of ethnic Chinese were hacked to
death by their fellow Indonesians in a months-long pogrom touched
off by accusations that the Chinese were working as agents for the
Communist Chinese government. No one knows exactly how many
people died during this slaughter; estimates run between 500,000
and 3 million. Twenty-five years later, I was interviewing a gentle,
harmless-seeming clerk in Jakarta, who mentioned in passing that
he had been a student, in Surabaya, in eastern Java, in 1965. Delicately, or so I thought, I steered the conversation around to the
violence. Had people been killed there? "Yes. I killed many with
my *keris*," he said with nonchalance. The *keris*, pronounced more
or less like the English name Chris, is the wavy, ceremonial dagger
that is an accompaniment to manhood in the Malay areas and is
thought to have a soul and a "taste for blood" all its own.

Similar though less lurid cases of anti-Chinese activity have
occurred in Burma and Vietnam. The first waves of Vietnamese
refugees entering the United States were disproportionately
Chinese, as they were driven from the Cholon "Chinatown" district
of Saigon. Since the end of World War II, Burma's xenophobic rulers
have tried to "cleanse" the country of Chinese (along with Indians,
members of the hill tribes, and others except ethnic Burmese).

Malaysia's politics, though rarely violent, turn on almost nothing except Chinese-Malay friction. Mahathir bin Mohamad, a medical doctor who became prime minister in 1981, had first come to
political prominence in the early 1970s with *The Malay Dilemma*,
a quasi-scientific tract arguing that Chinese were inherently more
talented than ethnic Malays. ("Whatever the Malays could do, the
Chinese could do better and more cheaply," and so on.) Mahathir
was at the time fighting for control of the Malay political party; in
stressing the innate superiority of the Chinese he was making a case
for long-term government programs to help the Malays.

Compared to the situation in these neighboring countries, racial
frictions in Thailand are mild. Thailand has solved its "Chinese
problem" by acting as if the Chinese are actually Thai. Ethnic
Chinese families were required to take Thai names, from a govern-
ment-approved list. These assigned names are easily identifiable,

but the Chinese Thai and the ethnic Thai alike seem to have agreed to act as if they share a common nationality. The Chinese Thai speak the Thai language (unlike many Chinese Malaysians, who speak only a halting version of the Malay language) and present themselves as fitting in. In exchange for these efforts they are viewed as "real" Thai participants, a mental stretch that does not seem possible in most of the rest of the region.

The good king. In deciding to view its history as one of freedom and its Chinese minority as an integral part of the Thai whole, Thailand has spared itself problems that plague neighboring countries. Thinking about itself this way has been more useful to Thailand than if it dwelled on the international humiliations it has suffered or the remaining differences between the Chinese and everyone else. Another act of self-definition has been even more important than these two: the modern Thai concept that the royal family is the embodiment of the whole nation's identity.

On May 21, 1992, after Thailand had undergone another of its frequent military coups, newspapers around the world published an extraordinary photo. It showed the king of Thailand. Bhumibol Adulyadej, dressed in a light, natty Western business suit and seated on a French-style sofa. The king, who was then in his middle sixties, wore aviator-style glasses, had his receding hair neatly combed back, and generally looked as if he might be a still-sprightly professor of mathematics or perhaps gastroenterology, nearing retirement age.

The other people in the picture were the two men who had been bitterly struggling for political control of the country: Prime Minister Suchinda Kraprayoon, a longtime soldier who had taken power in the coup, and Chamlong Srimuang, who had made his reputation as a Jerry Brown–style "shake up the system" candidate and had been jailed for his opposition to the coup.*

The two politicians in the photo, Suchinda and Chamlong, were

---

*Thai people are usually referred to solely by their first names, which will be the practice here. The king's name, Bhumibol, has been varyingly rendered into English over the years in such forms as "Phumipon." This illustrates one basic fact of Thai phonology: that "l" sounds at the end of a word are actually pronounced "n." Thus Thais who speak English will refer to the famous "Orientannnn" hotel, which English speakers know as the "Oriental," or the major department store "Centrannn," spelled in English "Central." The normal Thai reference to the king would be Nai Luang, "the greatest."

on the floor, sitting on the sides of their hips with their feet pointing away from the king and their heads leaning reverently toward him. This pose allowed them to avoid the two cardinal sins of etiquette in dealing with the king: pointing your feet toward him, and allowing your own head to be higher than his. These two leaders, each contending for control of the country's government, had entered the room shuffling along the floor on their knees. Such was the status of Thailand's king. Two years earlier, in rural Thailand, I saw a photo of the prime minister who preceded Suchinda, the one who had been ousted in the coup. He had come for an audience with the king's eldest son, the crown prince. The prime minister, who was large and bulky for a Thai, resembled nothing so much as a man-sized serpent as he slid along the floor on the side of his hip toward the prince.

The reverence for the royal family in Thailand, both spontaneous and enforced, is impossible not to notice. Pictures of the king are everywhere. In every shop and office, in every restaurant and bathhouse, a photo of the king hangs in a position of pride. Sometimes he is with his wife, sometimes with the children, but most often he is on his own, in one of a hundred varied poses. The most common shot is of the king in standard, military-looking, ribbon-bedecked regalia. But often he is shown is an open-necked shirt and khaki trousers, tromping through city slums or in the forests as he visits his people. There are pictures of the king playing his clarinet with jazz orchestras; pictures of the king at the wheel of a sports car; pictures of the king behind an easel, painting dramatic landscapes. The most evocative picture is from the king's period of service as an orange-robed Buddhist monk. This photo shows him sitting cross-legged, one shoulder draped by orange robes and the other one bare. The king's head is clean-shaven, and his eyes are hidden behind dark glasses with round wire frames. He looks like an icon of cool.

In the land of *mai pen rai* few things are forbidden. Exporting Buddha images is one, and making negative comments about the royal family, in any form and with whatever justification, is another. Few people are even tempted to make negative comments about the current king. The country apparently agrees that he comes as close to meriting adulation as a mortal can. The one controversial event in his reign occurred at its very beginning. In 1946 the king's older brother, who was himself then king, was shot to death under still mysterious circumstances in the Royal Palace.[12] Today's King Bhumibol, then a slight, weak-eyed boy of eighteen, took the throne.

Ever since that time, he has been a performer of seemingly endless good works—opening dams, but opposing dams when they would destroy too much of the forest; visiting the homeless and downtrodden but still lecturing on self-reliance; serving as patron of universities and of high-tech research. He has had exhibitions of his paintings and nature photographs; he ran a jazz radio station from the palace grounds and wrote some numbers produced by Mike Todd in the Broadway play *Peepshow*. The king has won regional yachting competitions.

For more than four decades the king has generally acted as the soul and conscience of his nation, a sentence I write with no irony at all. It was in this function that he summoned the quarreling politicians to his feet in 1992, telling them to calm down and spare the country the effects of their unseemly disputes. Nearly 20 years earlier, in 1973, when students rioted at universities and the military government cracked down hard, the king appointed a university regent as prime minister, a clear signal that he was tipping in favor of the democratic, antimilitary forces.

The benefit of Thailand's emphasis on royalty, and in particular this king, is that he has provided a living manifestation of such concepts as "the public interest" and "the welfare of the nation." But this strategy creates one obvious problem. If a good king has steered the country off the shoals so often, then a bad king could presumably do comparable harm—much more so in Thailand than in, say, Britain. The great problem for the Thai monarchy is that King Bhumibol, despite his other virtues, will die someday.

"This king has been very instrumental in creating this system and legitimizing such steps toward democracy as we have," Kraisak Choonhaven told me in 1990. Kraisak, who was in his late thirties, was the son of the man who was then Thailand's prime minister, Chatichai Choonhavan. Kraisak had been a leftist professor but had become a business consultant when his father rose to power. To judge by appearances he was doing very well: he was wearing a dark suit without a single wrinkle or bit of lint or hint of sweat—this in a swamp climate where most men never wore neckties. If this were the movies he might have been played by Omar Sharif. A year after I spoke with Kraisak, his father was driven from office in a military coup, mainly because of complaints about widespread corruption. As I spoke with Kraisak I thought, This is what it must have been like to see the young Saudi princes or the children of Brezhnev in the 1970s—or the children of the Chinese leadership in the 1980s and 1990s. But nonetheless he had a sensible political scientist's point to make about the role of the king.

"The king has been a guiding figure in developing the legitimacy of state. But because he *is* a king, because every year we have ceremonies to uplift him into heaven on earth, it is a contradictory ideology. This modern king has been very effective, but the idea that any king can build democracy is contradictory."

"If the democratic system had become strong enough, with its own ideological basis and legitimacy, then if we had a king who was not as outstanding, it wouldn't matter," he concluded. But the very virtues of this king had made the country more vulnerable to the liabilities of some future king.

Reporters who are based in Bangkok, or who hope ever to return to Thailand, find it almost impossible to speculate in print about what may happen after the current king dies. In most of Asia the press is more thoroughly controlled, through formal laws and informal self-censorship, than in North America or Western Europe. The exception that proves the rule is the Philippines. There, dozens of Manila dailies print "Aliens Ate My Baby" style stories about politics, confirming the rest of the region's judgment that the press works best when most thoroughly controlled.

In Japan, the taboo subjects for the press mainly concern the imperial family and the "untouchable" class of people known as *burakumin*. In Indonesia, the most important taboo covers the business dealings of President Suharto's family. Suharto's wife, named Tien, is informally known through the country as "Madame Tien Percent," because of her standard share of public-works projects, imports, exports, and other money flows. When Steven Erlanger mentioned this fact in *The New York Times* in 1989, he was expelled from the country.

In Thailand, there is a *lèse-majesté* clause in the country's criminal code, Section 112, which says that anyone who criticizes the king, heir apparent, or regent faces between three and fifteen years in jail.[13] In 1987 a Thai politician was hauled up on Section 112 charges; his offense was to have said, in a campaign speech, that, given the choice, he'd rather have been born in the Royal Palace than have grown up tilling the soil. Foreigners in Bangkok live with the knowledge that the one unforgivable sin, the one offense that will get them kicked out of the country for good, is to comment critically about the royal family.

Therefore the principal problem facing Thailand's royal system, the personal character of the heir apparent, is almost never discussed in print. The rumors surrounding the crown prince involve his emotional volatility and physical brutality.

When I asked most politicians or journalists in Thailand about what came next, they would give me the shifty eye, as if scanning the room for those who might overhear. It was the only time in my life in which I felt as if I'd entered a spy novel. "He likes to fly fighter planes and drive fast cars," one politician told me in 1990. "This is a dangerous life." He stared at me for about fifteen seconds to be sure I had gotten the not-too-subtle point. A few months later another politician told me, "We hope the F-16 will take care of it." The F-16 is a fast, maneuverable fighter plane that the crown prince has piloted. In the mid-1980s the Thai law of succession was changed so as to permit, in principle, a princess as well as a prince to inherit the throne. The king's daughter, Princess Maha Chakri Sirindhorn, who was born in 1955, rivals her father in belovedness.

Like any society, Thailand cares first and most about its own internal developments. Therefore it is natural that, in discussing its prospects, its leaders would be proud of its political successes—avoiding the psychological aftereffects of the colonial era, defusing racial tensions, finding a powerful symbol of national unity in the form of the current king—and be apprehensive about potential obstacles, including those involving the throne.

Yet, to outsiders, the country's recent history is significant mainly for what it shows about the growth of an East Asian system, rather than for what it shows about Thailand's innate traits. Thailand had been proud-spirited and fond of its king for many years; yet it was only when Japanese manufacturers had to look overseas, in the era of *endaka,* that the Thai economy suddenly boomed. Because its growth was prompted by sources beyond its control, the growth itself may not mean for Thailand what comparable growth has meant for other countries. At least in economic terms, Thailand has remained fundamentally an object of other countries' energies and intentions.

In England, Germany, the United States, and Japan, the development of a capitalist business system has, over two centuries, increased each country's control over its surrounding world. Development gave these societies tools not simply for manipulating nature and generating material wealth but also for projecting their values onto other cultures (in the case of Western powers) or defending their values against outsiders (in the case of Japan).

As modern East Asia has become larger, more economically integrated, and more influenced by Japan, a transfer of values has also begun. Economic power sooner or later has political consequences, and in the East Asia of the 1990s the consequences of a strong, growing, Japan-centered system are visible in three ways.

The first and least surprising is "influence" in the most mundane sense—that is, payoffs to public officials. Every political system suffers from influence-buying to some degree. While Singapore's political system is clean by world standards, in most other Asian countries bribery is more widespread than in, say, Germany or Canada. Because most of the money now flowing in the region flows to, from, or because of Japan, Japanese interests are naturally the most important influence buyers in Asia.

A second political consequence is the increased attention to and interest in collective "Asian" concerns rather than country-by-country or subregional themes. The fissures that separate countries in East Asia are obvious and deep. Yet more and more politicians, businessmen, and journalists talk in "Asian" terms. A generation ago it would have been hard to imagine the prime minister of Malaysia—a raw-material-producing, English-speaking, mainly Islamic country that was invaded by the emperor's troops during World War II—finding any common ground with the Japanese. In the 1990s Malaysia's Prime Minister Mahathir has pushed for the formation of an Asian-Pacific economic grouping that would pointedly exclude the Americans, Canadians, Australians, and New Zealanders.

Third, the success of Asian economies has begun to legitimize the idea of "Asian politics." Feeling more confident on the world stage, believing that they have more interests in common, leaders from many Asian countries have begun arguing with their Western counterparts about whether universal definitions of "democracy" and "human rights" exist. The arguments come in varied forms. Japanese officials say Americans are wrong to scold China about its political repression, since the balance between individual rights and collective well-being is a matter for each nation to decide. (In the springtime of 1993, Japan's MITI encouraged Japanese automakers to invest in China, saying that "Chinese political risk is zero."[14]) After the Thai military ousted Prime Minister Chatichai in 1991, most Western governments suspended their foreign aid programs and denounced this reversion to military rule. Japan's government announced that it recognized the new regime as a "legitimate, constitutional government" and would continue its foreign aid (which amounted to three times as much as aid from all other donor countries combined).[15] Before the LDP's defeat in the Japanese elections of 1993, politicians in Korea, Taiwan, China, and elsewhere were studying Japan as a model "for how a country can have democracy and one-party rule at the same time," in the words of Gerald Curtis of Columbia University.[16] Even after the LDP lost its majority, the Japanese model remained a more plausible one in the region than two-party democracies in the British or American style. The government of Singapore has repeatedly banned or restricted foreign publications—and has done so not apologetically but forthrightly, saying that the chaos of Western countries illustrates the harm a free press can do. "The West approves the freedom of the press in India, frowns on the lack of it in China," Kishore Mahbubani, a senior official in Singapore's Foreign Ministry, wrote in 1993. "Yet which society is developing faster today and which society is likely to modernize first?"[17]

The further Asian economic development proceeds, the more important such political ramifications will become.

Malaysia

Malaysia shares a border with Thailand but little else. Thailand is libertine; most of Malaysia's population is Muslim, and since the late 1970s the prevailing version of Islam has become more conservative and doctrinaire. Although Thailand's economy is growing fast, it is still far behind Malaysia's. Malaysia's per-capita income is about 60 percent higher than that of Thailand. Thailand contains nearly 60 million people, many of whom are very poor. Malaysia has fewer than 20 million people, virtually none of whom are destitute. Thailand's growth is an extremely recent phenomenon; Malaysia has been prosperous since early in this century because of its rich tin mines and vast rubber plantations. When the pollution and congestion of Bangkok became intolerable in the early 1990s, Japanese investors diverted some of their funds to Malaysia instead. Malaysia's capital, Kuala Lumpur, is as a result more clogged and congested than it was a decade earlier; but while Bangkok seems like a Third World metropolis suddenly choked with new money, Kuala Lumpur seem like a modern, well-built city suddenly growing too fast for comfort.

In addition, the two countries differ dramatically in their political climate. Structurally Malaysia is a stable parliamentary democracy, yet it has had terrible difficulties in exactly the areas in which Thailand has succeeded—especially resolving its racial tensions and making practical use of its traditional royal leadership. Yet in the East Asian system they share one great similarity: in both countries the political and economic systems are responding to, and sometimes being shaped by, the torrent of economic energy coming from Japan.

On paper Malaysia looks like paradise, and in reality it can come close. The country is composed of the bottom half of the Malay Peninsula—known in colonial times and in the first few years of independence as Malaya—and the top quarter of the island of Borneo, whose incorporation in 1963 turned the country into Malaysia. (At about the same time, Lee Kuan Yew's Singapore split off from Malaya and became a tiny independent state.) If you can live with perpetually hot, dripping-sticky, equatorial-jungle weather, you can think of it as Eden. "It is a place where there are no seasons to speak of, neither winter nor summer; no wet or dry season, and the sun rises and sets at practically the same time all year round," a young pre–First World War Colonel Blimp type named Carveth Wells wrote in *Six Years in the Malay Jungle*.

> The mean shade temperature at sea level (about 80 degrees)
> has not varied by more than about three degrees for a hundred
> years. . . . Rain falls about two hundred and seventy days in
> the year but there is scarcely ever a wet day. The weather may
> be perfectly fine all the morning, then rain nine inches between
> noon and three o'clock, and be fine again for the evening.[18]

"Nine inches" may be stretching it—the annual rainfall is about a hundred inches—but the impression of timeless, placid lushness is correct.

Like Indonesia and the Philippines, Malaysia is packed with natural resources. Papayas, bananas, and mangosteens dropped from trees in our backyard in Kuala Lumpur faster than we could eat them. But unlike Indonesia's central island—Java—or the Philippines, Malaysia is lightly populated by East Asian terms. The schools are well funded, the roads are modern and smooth. The eastern coast of peninsular Malaysia has some of the world's most beautiful white-sand beaches, and there are still large unlogged rainforest stands. It's a nice country. During the two years my family lived there, our only discontents of daily life came from the humidity and the inside-the-house wildlife. Our colonial-era whitewashed house, with unscreened, unglassed windows, teemed with bugs and mosquitoes preying on people, lizards eating the bugs, rats eating whatever they could find, and snakes eating the lizards and rats. My children found it easy to visualize the concept of the food chain.

There is a tender, off-the-track feeling about Malaysia—particularly for Americans, who unlike Europeans and especially Australians, rarely go there. In 1988 my wife and I were at a resort, along with about six hundred other vacationers, on the Malaysian eastern coast. Before the evening variety-show entertainment, the emcee worked up the crowd with a standard routine: Let's hear it for the people from . . . AUSTRALIA!!! (Huge cheer.) Is anyone here from . . . JAPAN!!! (Louder still.) He got through Hong Kong, Luxembourg, and New Zealand and didn't even mention the United States.

Yet despite these objective advantages, and despite the gentle tone of daily life, Malaysia's politics has been troubled and sour through most of years since its independence in 1957. In contrast to Thailand's self-definition as the "land of smiles," Malaysia's political life has often made the country the "land of snarls."

The politics of race and royalty in Malaysia. The fundamental source of Malaysia's political problems is its failure in the same area where Thailand has succeeded: assimilating a racial minority group.

In the middle of the nineteenth century, when tin mining had yet to begin in earnest, the Malay Peninsula was even more lightly populated than it is today. Aboriginal tribes lived in the jungle interior; groups of Malays lived in coastal settlements by the mouths of rivers; and traders from China, Portugal, and elsewhere operated out of the few famous seaports, such as Malacca and Penang. Then, within a few decades, British colonialism, the tin boom, and rubber planting created a totally different ethnic lineup. People poured in from all over—Malays from nearby Sumatra and Java, Chinese from Guangdong and Fujian and elsewhere in southern China, and blue-black-skinned Indians from the southern Tamil regions.

Traditional Malay culture is celebrated for its stateliness and refusal to be hurried. This trait can seem either enormously dignified or tremendously exasperating, depending on whether you are attending a Malay ceremony or trying to get a check cashed in a Malaysian bank. The British colonialists were mainly exasperated and felt they needed to look beyond the Malays for the manpower to work the tin mines and staff the colonial subbureaucracy—thus the officially sponsored importation of Indians and Chinese. ("Work is about the last thing a Malay wants," the irrepressible Carveth Wells announced, reflecting the British view at the time.) By the beginning of the twentieth century, British administrators were using the percentage of Chinese settlers as an index of overall economic progress.[19]

The interpretation of past migrations has become an extremely sensitive and politically weighted subject in Malaysia, but the low precolonial population seems to indicate that most of today's Malaysians are descended from people who came from someplace else during the past century or so. Kuala Lumpur itself arose in the late 1800s much the way cities in California had arisen during the Gold Rush half a century earlier. Laborers and fortune-seekers flocked into Kuala Lumpur to try to take part in the tin boom. (The city's name means "muddy river mouth," and it refers to the confluence of two small brown rivers flowing in from the jungle.) From the city's start, many of the gangs and labor bosses who dominated there were Chinese. Nonetheless, as the Malay politicians and theorists see it, Malays are the only original inhabitants, since Malay kingdoms had historically held sway over the peninsula. Malays call themselves *bumiputra,* literally "sons of the soil." Everyone else is *pendatang*—"newcomer" or "immigrant."

The mixture of races is potentially the most charming and admirable thing about Malaysia. Officially the country believes in racial coexistence, and in many small ways the amalgamation looks successful. A typical row of shops will have signs in Malay, Chinese, English, and, less frequently, Tamil. We had both a mosque and a small Chinese temple within view of our house; our Indian landlord kept talking about erecting a Hindu shrine in our yard. Each race's religious festivals are public holidays, which gives a constant festival feeling to local life. Heavy-handed "unity" campaigns are constantly under way on TV, in which every commercial and public-service announcement is supposed to have the right mixture of Indian, Chinese, and Malay faces in smiling harmony.

Unofficially, and in large ways, things don't work out so well. No Asian society is truly enthusiastic about the melting-pot ideal, and many Malaysians, especially Malays, feel sorry for themselves because fate, plus the British, have placed other races in their midst. Through the 1980s Malaysian government officials were very active in condemning the white South African government for its apartheid policies. At a dinner party in Kuala Lumpur in the late 1980s, I asked the wife of a prominent official whether it might be more graceful for Malaysia to let some other country lead the "nonaligned" bloc's moral war against apartheid. After all, a large number of Malaysian laws granted people different legal privileges on purely racial grounds. Malaysian discrimination is not remotely as vicious or unfair as South Africa's, but still, why give the South Africans this debating-point edge? The woman erupted: As a non-Malaysian I could not possibly understand how difficult the country's problems were, I had no idea what a challenge it was to have people from different cultures living in the same society.

There are other groups in the Malaysian mix besides the main antagonists, the *bumiputra* Malays and the Chinese. In the states of Sabah and Sarawak, which constitute "East Malaysia" and form a strip on the northern coast of Borneo, indigenous non-Malay groups like Dayak and Kadazan are a significant force. The politics of those states revolves around resistance to control by the national government, which is run from Kuala Lumpur by Malays. Indian Malaysians, who make up about 10 percent of the country's population, are on the sidelines of the main political struggles between Malays, who make up about half the population, and Chinese, who constitute about a third.[20]

Shortly after Malaysia received its independence, the Chinese and Malays worked out a grand compromise, similar to the grand division of labor between Japan and the United States after the Occupation years. The Malays would dominate the government (with the official help of an Uncle Tom–like Chinese party), while the Chinese would be allowed to run the businesses.

This deal came under strain after riots in 1969, provoked mainly by the enormous economic gap between Malays and Chinese. Some two hundred people, mainly Chinese, were killed in the fighting.

Mahathir bin Mohamad, then a medical doctor in his thirties, had become extremely controversial for writing *The Malay Dilemma,* with its famous argument that Malays were inherently inferior to Chinese and so needed permanent protection, provided by the government. Deploying crackpot scientific theories, he demonstrated that the harsh climate and Malthusian pressures of life in China had already thinned the weaklings out of China's racial stock—while the lush life of the Malayan jungle had had the opposite effect on the local Malays.[21] By the time Mahathir became prime minister, in 1981, his rhetoric was milder but the insistence on preferential policies, based on race, remained.

The most important preferential provisions are grouped together as the New Economic Policy (NEP), now more than a quarter century old. Soon after the riots of 1969 the government had devised a sweeping program of quotas and affirmative-action plans designed to increase *bumiputra* control of the economy. For instance, through the 1980s some twenty thousand Malaysians per year were studying at colleges in the United States, usually making up the second-largest block of foreign students, after Taiwanese. The Malaysian government subsidized tuition and living expenses for *bumiputras* but generally not for other Malaysian students. Government-subsidized mortgages offer one rate for *bumiputras* and a higher rate for non-*bumis*.

The New Economic Policy has had most of the failures, and some of the successes, of affirmative-action plans elsewhere in the world. In 1970, as the plan got under way, the average Chinese income was 129 percent higher than the average for Malays. By the late 1980s, the gap was only 65 percent.[22] In 1970, *bumiputras* owned only 2 percent of the capital stock of Malaysian corporations. The goal was to raise this figure to 30 percent by 1990, and toward that end foreign companies investing in Malaysia had to meet elaborate quotas for taking in Malays as partners. By 1990 it had risen to 14 percent for Malay individuals, and another 6 percent for investment trusts that represented *bumiputras* only. (The main one of these was the *Tabung Haji,* a fund through which people could save up for the *haj,* or pilgrimage to Mecca.) Yet during this same period, the Chinese share of businesses rose much more dramatically, from 34 percent in 1970 to 56 percent in 1990. The difference came out of the share held by foreigners, which fell from about 60 percent in 1970 to about 25 percent in 1990. As a means of improving the *bumiputras'* absolute standing, the NEP succeeded. As a means of closing the gap with the Chinese, it completely failed.

Affirmative-action programs in the United States also have their share of problems, but Americans could at least think of quotas as a transition toward the goal of a color-blind economic system. In Malaysia few seem to believe the speeches about an eventual pure Malaysian identity. The political parties in Malaysia are all organized on explicitly racial grounds. (The principal ones are the United Malays National Organization, the Malaysian Chinese Association, and the Malaysian Indian Congress.) The leaders of the Malay bloc, in particular, know that at election time they can reliably rally support by playing on Malay fears of Chinese economic control. The

New Economic Policy has made virtually all of politics a struggle for state revenue.

Mahathir had actually foreseen something like this when he wrote *The Malay Dilemma*. "We can expect that the new environment will not be good for the Malays," he wrote just as the racial preferences were going into effect.

> They will become softer and less able to overcome difficulties on their own. Because of this, political power might ultimately prove their complete downfall.
>
> But the alternative is equally without promise. . . . Malaysia has far too many non-Malay citizens who can swamp the Malays the moment protection is removed. The frequent suggestion that the only way to help the Malays is to let them fight their own battles cannot therefore be seriously considered.[23]

In 1989 an American writer spoke with Musa Hitam, a politician who had long been a rival to Mahathir. Musa Hitam was asked whether Malaysia would eventually become a multiracial society. "No," he replied. "Like the world becoming one, or Europe achieving unity in 1992, it will never happen."[24]

Malaysia's racial difficulties constitute the fundamental barrier to a sense of national unity. The nation is further fragmented because it cannot use the tool applied so effectively in Thailand: royalty as a symbol of collective interests. As much good as Thailand's current king has done for his country, the far more numerous members of Malaysia's royal families have done the reverse.

Malaysia consists of thirteen states, many of which had their own royal families and sultans before the British arrived. Nine states retain their sultans, and under an agreement struck at the time of independence these nine participate in a rotating kingship. From their own ranks the sultans elect one member to serve a five-year term as *agong*, or national king. In practice each of the nine states takes a turn at the national throne.

Through the late 1980s, the sultan from the state of Johor had his turn as *agong*. This man, whose full name was Mahmood Iskandar ibni al-Marhum Sultan Ismail, was a full-blooded carouser then in his late fifties. Through the preceding decade he had been convicted of an assortment of felonies—including a manslaughter count in 1977, after he shot at civilians from his royal helicopter and killed one man in a boat. (The future king's side of the story was that the victim was probably a smuggler.) He was tried, convicted, and sentenced to six months in jail, but his father, then the reigning sultan of Johor, pardoned him and kept him from serving time.

In 1981, when Mahmood's father died, Mahmood took the throne in Johor, and in 1984 his turn as *agong* began. As *agong*, he used an official house in Kuala Lumpur about a hundred yards from where my family lived. He was an avid motorman, and we would hear his motorcycles and motorcades roaring around day and night. He was also an avid golfer, and shortly before the end of his reign he apparently had a frustrating day at the golf course. According to reports that were whispered throughout Kuala Lumpur in the late 1980s and finally made their way into print in 1992, the king vented his frustration by beating a caddy to death with golf clubs. The subject was, of course, taboo in the local press while the king was still in office. When I would discuss it with foreign diplomats in their offices, they would instinctively draw the shades or start talking in hushed tones. The few Malaysians who mentioned the matter glanced around nervously as they talked. The only significant allusions to the case in the local press occurred in 1989, when a new sultan was about to be sworn in for his five-year turn as *agong*. This man, the sultan of the state of Perak, had been a distinguished judge and had served as lord president, or chief justice, of the Malaysian judicial system. When he was chosen, the local press rhapsodized about how nice it would be to have such a distinguished, sober-minded, well-educated man as king.

The full story about the golfing king did eventually leak out in the Malaysian press, but it did so in a way that actually underscored how divisive rather than unifying the royalty had become. Late in 1992 this same man, the former *agong* Mahmood, beat up the coach of a field hockey team in his home state of Johor. This time he was explicitly criticized by politicians and in the press. One parliamentarian said that the hereditary sultans were a group of "robbers, adulterers, drunkards, and thugs." The *Far Eastern Economic Review*, which circulates widely in Malaysia, carried an explicit report about the caddy-killing episode. Newspapers carried reports about other affronts: The former king had had the members of a soccer team tied to trees as punishment after a defeat. He had invited a group of Muslim activists to lunch during the month of Ramadan, when observant Muslims are supposed to fast from sunup to sundown. The former king and his own eldest son, who in the normal rotation would become king someday, had reportedly been involved in twenty-three criminal incidents, including rape and assorted assaults.[25]

The reason for this flurry of attention, however, was not some new belief in press freedom but an old exercise of political power. The ruling party, which is to say the United Malays National Organization under Prime Minister Mahathir, had grown aggravated with the nation's royalty. In many states the royal family enjoyed economic privileges at odds with the central government's ability to control the nation's economy—for instance, the right to nearly unrestricted timber cutting in the country's tropical forests. Sultans of each state enjoyed immunity from national laws, and their approval was still required for major national legislation—including any laws affecting their own rights. By the end of 1992 it was clear that Mahathir's party was ready to challenge the royal families directly, and so the signals changed to permit the press to discuss the caddy episode and similar derelictions.

In the long run this episode could prove to have been a step toward political modernization for Malaysia. Mahathir was, after all, an elected leader of his country, and he was challenging traditional rulers who were clearly abusing their privileges. But at least in the short term the effect was to weaken another of the symbols of national unity.

Surplus resentment. In the early 1990s the Malaysian economy was becoming more integrated into the East Asian system. Incoming investment was predominantly from Japan, Korea, or Taiwan; cars, radios, and other consumer goods were overwhelmingly from Japan. Yet in daily life the country also seemed comfortably connected to the Western world. Because most educated Malaysians can read English, British and American books, magazines, movies, and songs are popular throughout the country. (Of course, not everyone can speak English. When American movies play in theaters in Kuala Lumpur, subtitles in three languages—Malay, Chinese, and Tamil—crawl across half the screen. I always looked for movies that were short on dialogue.) When Malaysian students go abroad to study, virtually all go to the United States, England, Australia, or Canada. Malaysia sells 70 percent of its manufactured exports to the United States, versus only 10 percent to Japan. The country's Malay political leaders are clearly aware of the advantages of English—they speak it themselves, if possible with a British accent, and they send their children to English-language schools. Prime

Minister Mahathir is sometimes ribbed for being more at ease in English than in Bahasa Malaysia, the "language of Malaysia" that since independence has been the official national tongue.

Yet in its political tone Malaysian life has become more and more aggressively anti-Western since the early 1980s. In part this is a religious phenomenon, related to the worldwide rise of fundamentalist Islam.

Compared to Indonesia, where Muslims are much more numerous, those in Malaysia are much more intense. Indonesia's population is nearly 200 million, and of them some 90 percent are officially Muslim, making it the most populous Muslim nation in the world. Malaysia's Muslims number fewer than 10 million. (A note on math: *bumiputras* officially make up half the population, or about 9 million. By legal definition, an ethnic Malay must also be a Muslim to be considered a *bumiputra*. A Malay who converts from Islam loses his *bumiputra* status.) Christian missionaries who operate in the country are allowed to proselytize Chinese or Indian Malaysians, but if they approach a *bumiputra* they can be expelled from the country. It is not always easy to tell Chinese from Malays on sight, so the missionaries have to proceed carefully.

Precisely because Islam's presence is so overwhelming in Indonesia, it can afford not to be doctrinaire. The obvious parallel is to Catholicism in France or Italy; everyone pledges fealty, but other things are going on in their lives. The most famous archaeological site in Indonesia, for instance, is the ten-tiered stone monument known as Borobudur, in cental Java. When its construction began a millennium ago, it was intended to be a Hindu shrine; by the time it was completed two hundred years later, it had become a Buddhist temple. Now Indonesia's Muslims consider it a national treasure, and the hundreds of Buddha figures that decorate it are said by the tolerant Muslims to stand not only for Buddha but also for the Hindu god Shiva, and for the Holy Spirit in general.

In Malaysia, by contrast, the Muslim population is more embattled—and therefore less tolerant. Through the late 1980s and early 1990s Malaysia was the main Asian outpost of pan-Islamic foreign policy. When the main newspapers (which were owned by the ruling party) were not praising the country's leadership, they were warning against the latest Zionist plot against world peace. A Steinberg-style map of the world, based on news coverage inside Malaysia, would consist of three main sites: Kuala Lumpur, where the government operated; the Middle East, den of Zionism; and

South Africa, center of the Third World's struggle against the white West.

With each passing year through the 1980s, Muslim women in Malaysia were more and more likely to be seen in floor-length dresses and with long scarves over their heads. Only occasionally, and mainly in Islamic strongholds such as the state of Terengganu, on the northeastern coast, would you see women entirely covered except for their eyes. In Kuala Lumpur, the workaday population was more diverse but visibly more Islamic as time wore on. The usual Kuala Lumpur street scene included a handful of resident foreigners, mainly from Europe or Japan; a trickle of hippie tourists from Germany or Sweden, often in hiking shorts that jarred the eye, since Malay men almost never wear short pants; the Chinese business class and the Malay businessmen, dressed like businesspeople in London or Los Angeles or Hong Kong; and the Malay women, with their long, hot dresses and the little squares of their faces barely visible beneath their scarves.

For much of the urban, educated Muslim population, the rules of Islamic life seemed to be just that—external rules, which they obeyed in public to avoid making a scandal but had not internalized as deep taboos. Middle-class Muslim families in Kuala Lumpur would have a little sink built into their dining rooms, for the ritual hand-washings before meals, but in many of these same houses people would drink beer. (Alcohol is in principle forbidden under Islam.) I once visited a Malaysian military unit, most of whose members were Muslim. They had clearly modeled themselves after a crack British regiment: they had the same swagger, the same preponderance of mustaches, the same sherry-drinking hour before dinner. Still, Islam is important on a large scale because it maintains a sharp line between the Malays and the Chinese. Each night in Chinese restaurants waiters bring out dishes heaped with many forms of pork. Pork is a great abomination in the world of Islam.

Even beyond the impetus provided by Islamic politics, modern Malaysia has become rhetorically anti-Western to a mystifying degree. Castro of Cuba, Qadhafi of Libya, Saddam Hussein of Iraq—these are people with real reasons to detest the Western world, since the U.S. government has tried to kill each of them. Malaysia's Mahathir often matched their rhetoric, even though he presided over a prosperous society with active business relations with the West.

Part of Malaysia's resentful tone seemed to reflect peculiarities of its own relations with England, its former colonial master, and peculiarities of Mahathir himself. He is an ambitious, serious man who, mainly because he comes from a small country, has not been viewed as a heavyweight on the world stage. One incident seemed by itself to account for much of Mahathir's bilious view of the United States. Early in the Bush administration, Mahathir and James Baker, the U.S. secretary of state, both attended a diplomatic reception in Tokyo. Baker was dressed in a business suit; Mahathir, in the traditional Malay-Islamic cap and shirt. Baker reportedly asked a Japanese diplomat, "Who's the guy in the native costume?," which infuriated Mahathir when word got back to him. Mahathir openly gloated at Bill Clinton's victory in the election of 1992—or, as he saw it, James Baker's humiliating defeat. In that same year Mahathir refused to accept a telephone call from George Bush while Bush was visiting nearby Singapore, because, in Mahathir's view, Bush had snubbed him by not also visiting Malaysia.[26] By contrast, Margaret Thatcher shrewdly backed Mahathir away from an anti-British crusade with a demonstration of personal respect. In the early 1980s Mahathir's trade slogan had been "Buy British Last!," in apparent retribution for the arrogance of the colonial Brits. This campaign tapered off after Mrs. Thatcher invited Mahathir for a long personal dinner—that is, showed that she took him seriously.

The indignities Mahathir has resented personally he has also resented on behalf of his nation as a whole. In 1985, Malaysia was excoriated by Western human rights groups, especially in England and Australia, when two young men, one from England and one from Australia, were hanged for violating the country's draconian drug-possession laws. Australia's prime minister, Robert Hawke, described the Malaysian justice system as "barbaric," and Western human-rights activists generally struck a "those Oriental barbarians!" tone. For years afterward the Malaysian press rang with resentment about the episode—and with good reason.[27] In the preceding few years they'd heard no protests about "barbarism" when they'd executed their own citizens for violating the same law. Warnings about Malaysia's drug laws were stamped, with lurid red ink, on each card tourists filled out as they applied to enter the country. Airlines landing in Kuala Lumpur were required to announce as their final words to passengers about to leave the plane: "And remember, Malaysia imposes the death penalty for drug infractions!"

Mahathir led the Third World's scolding of Western industrialists at the world environment conference in Rio de Janeiro in 1992. In 1988, while we were living in Malaysia, Mahathir received a letter from a ten-year-old schoolboy in Britain. The letter was a standard bit of youthful bleeding-heartism, about how nice it would be if Malaysia could stop cutting down its rain forests so its birds and monkeys would have homes. Most politicians would have ignored the letter, or sent back a bit of boilerplate about the country's deep commitment to the environment. Because it came from Britain—because Mahathir thought he was being condescended to, because he wanted to show the Brits who was boss now—he couldn't just ignore it. He fired off a long, personal harangue to the schoolboy, written in the "You ignorant twit!" style and asking why the lad hadn't been so concerned when his British forefathers were cutting down the rain forests to plant their beloved rubber trees.[28]

Through the late 1980s, Mahatir's personal *bête noire* was not anyone from England but a young German Swiss named Bruno Manser, an environmental activist who had been trooping through the jungles of Sarawak, in the northwestern part of the island of Borneo, trying to organize the Penan tribes to resist rampant logging there. Manser had first visited Sarawak as a tourist in 1984, when he was in his twenties, and lived there for six years with the Penan. In the springtime of 1992, Mahathir vented his grievances in an extraordinary but somehow typical letter, the most personal and vivid bit of writing by a head of state since Harry Truman's note to the critic who panned his daughter's musical performance. "As a Swiss living in the lap of luxury with the world's highest standard of living, it is the height of arrogance for you to advocate that Penans live on maggots and monkeys in their miserable huts, subjected to all kinds of diseases," the prime minister wrote. "Your Swiss ancestors were hunters also. But you are now one of the most 'advanced' people living in beautiful Alpine villages, with plenty of leisure and very high income. But you want to deny even a slight rise in the standard of living for the Penans and other Malaysians."[29]

Behind those gestures over religion and language and ethnicity, a political view was taking form. The Malaysian version of this outlook was not as polished and nuanced as what Lee Kuan Yew had advanced in Singapore, but it got more attention outside Asia than did parallel developments in Thailand or Korea or even Japan. The reason was that Mahathir, like Lee Kuan Yew, made many of his arguments in English, where they could be noticed by the very Western powers they were directed against.

The essence of the argument was a challenge to Western-style liberal democracy as the ultimate form of human social organization. Since well before the time of Woodrow Wilson, Americans, English, French, and others had been promoting the idea that their model of human freedom and individual rights was the pinnacle to which the rest of the world should ultimately rise. The Malaysia of Dr. Mahathir became one link in an Asian archipelago that, through the late 1980s and early 1990s, was suggesting an alternate vision of how the good society should work.

The practical starting point for the antiliberal view in Malaysia was its heavy-handed control of the press. In much more sweeping ways the press in Malaysia, like that in most other parts of Asia, reflected the belief that too much freedom to criticize could be a bad thing. After I left Malaysia, I looked back wistfully on it as paradise—until I remembered how often, when living there, I would grumble and grit my teeth when I walked out to get my morning copy of the *New Straits Times* and read a headline saying, "Stop the Complaining!" or "Dr. M.'s Courage Praised!" When I wasn't complaining about the papers I would often feel lobotomized. The *Star*, a mildly critical paper that had been run by the main Chinese political party, was closed for six months in 1987 when Dr. M. thought there had been too much complaining. Foreign papers such as *The Asian Wall Street Journal* and the *International Herald Tribune* were routinely detained by better-safe-than-sorry government censors whenever they contained any story at all about Malaysia. After the first few weeks of being sheltered from news and controversy, I hesitated to open a box of magazines and books that arrived, by sea mail, from home. All those opinions! All that heat and passion about trends I didn't know were under way. With the magazines stacked right on top of one another, I was surprised the box didn't melt down.

It is subtly unfair to concentrate on Malaysia as an illustration of a controlled Asian-style press. It is unfair because Thailand, Vietnam, Korea, and other countries would no doubt provide more vivid examples—but I, like the majority of Westerners, can't easily plow through newspapers in those countries to find examples, as I can in Malaysia, Singapore, and the Philippines. But the English-language countries are also important precisely because they are connected with the political world outside Asia—connected by the residues of colonialism; connected by a language that lets Malaysians read *Time* and *The Economist* and foreigners read the *New Straits Times*; connected by constitutions, parliaments, and congresses modeled after those in Britain or the United States. Because of these connections, Dr. Mahathir in Malaysia, Lee Kuan Yew in Singapore, and Ferdinand Marcos, Corazon Aquino, and others in the Philippines have felt a burden that many other Asian politicians have not—that of justifying their political views and actions to the outside world.

In Malaysia, Mahathir has generally presented the tough-guy version of the anti-Western case. In Singapore, Lee Kuan Yew dressed up his argument with allusions to age-old Confucian values. In Japan, politicians argued until the late 1980s that they simply needed time to "catch up" with the institutions and practices of the West. Mahathir, by contrast, has basically argued that the West was squalid and had lost all moral right to tell anyone else what to do.

When Western environmentalists talked about Malaysia's record with its rain forest, Mahathir let loose as he had against the English boy who wrote him a letter. When U.S. labor unions recommended tariffs against Malaysia because of the wages and working conditions in some of its factories, the political heir apparent to Mahathir, a former student leader named Anwar Ibrahim, gave a speech saying that the Western model of human rights and individual liberties was not necessarily appropriate for a nation like Malaysia. Individual rights were the basis for the Western system, he said, but they wouldn't work in an Asian-Islamic setting ("Islam rejects the notion of individuality enshrined as the most coveted principle of human rights," etc.).[30] When U.S. jets led the attack against Saddam Hussein, a brother Muslim, the Malay-language newspaper *Utusan Malaysia* published an on-the-scene report from the United States about the "vain arrogance" of the United States. "It is no surprise to see Americans, especially the whites, with a big smile gloating about their victory."

> White people's arrogance is getting out of hand. But let them be. Why? Because the white race is facing destruction from within. This race is facing all kinds of problems. Their social ills are getting worse. And their number is dwindling.[31]

A case can be made, and is being made more and more forcefully in both Malaysia and Singapore, that "American-style" human rights are inappropriate in any case for this part of the world. Malaysia and Singapore are in the middle of this argument because they are the two English-speaking states of Asia with the economic confidence to start arguing back to the West. (The third country prepared to do so linguistically, the Philippines, has other things on its mind.) At the United Nations in 1991, Mahathir explained why it was wrong and hypocritical for the United States to tell anyone else about democracy and "human rights" when it was so debauched itself:

> If democracy means to carry guns, to flaunt homosexuality, to disregard the institution of marriage, to disrupt and damage the well-being of the community in the name of individual rights, to destroy a particular faith, to have privileged institutions [i.e., the Western press] which are sacrosanct even if they indulge in lies and instigations which undermine society, the economy, and international relations; to permit foreigners to break national laws; if these are the essential details, cannot the new converts opt to reject them? . . . Hegemony by democratic powers is no less oppressive than hegemony by totalitarian states.

The point is not that Mahathir's observations about American "democracy" are so outrageous; many Americans have voiced similar concerns. Rather the significance of such speeches is their assumption of an underlying power shift. While Mahathir's resentment at a legacy of Western power must lie behind his snarling tone, the content of his statements reflects his judgment that the West is now weak. It presumes to tell others how to behave even though it lacks the moral authority that comes from making its own society strong. Each time Asian spokesmen argue that there is an "Asian" version of human rights and that Westerners should not promote their parochial concepts of individual liberty and free speech, the Asians reveal their judgment that the Asian model is stronger for the first time in many centuries.

Being acted upon. Malaysia is a rich and comfortable country. Its per capita income is only one tenth as high as Japan's, but the real living standards for most people are comparable in the two countries. Yet Malaysia is structurally an advanced version of the Thai economic model. Like Thailand, it is a country whose economy continues to be shaped by outsiders. Two generations ago it was shaped by the British; now, by the Japanese.

Malaysia's economy is driven by two external factors. One is raw material prices, for the rubber, oil, natural gas, palm oil, and tin the country produces in abundance. With its wide variety of resources, Malaysia is better off than, say, Chile, with its reliance on copper, or New Zealand, with its wool. When the price of Malaysia's tin is down, the price of its palm oil or rubber is probably up. But in the long run commodity producers are on the losing end of modern economics. (And, during the mid-1980s, the prices of all of Malaysia's commodities were down at the same time, creating a four-year-long recession.)

The other external factor is money from overseas—from Britain early in this century, from the United States in the 1970s and early 1980s, from Japan starting in the age of *endaka*. The major American investors were oil companies (mainly Esso, still operating under that quaint-seeming name after it became Exxon in the United States) and semiconductor makers, mainly Texas Instruments and Motorola. Inside modern-looking buildings on the outskirts of Penang and Kuala Lumpur, hundreds of workers assemble semiconductor chips and power supplies for computers. The workers are mainly young women, generally brought in from the rural villages. Modern as Malaysia might seem compared to China or Thailand, for most Malaysian electronics workers the factory routine is a jarring change from the way they used to live. From time to time the factories in Malaysia suffer hysteria attacks, when one young lady starts screaming and running through the factory, and then dozens of others do. These occur when a factory has been cursed in some way. The answer is to hire a *bomoh*, or traditional Malay medicine man. In the early 1980s the manager of one American semiconductor firm stood stolidly on the front step of his factory as a *bomoh* sacrificed a goat and thereby allowed production to proceed.

In other factories dotted across Malaysia, Matsushita produces air conditioners, for shipment to the United States and back to Japan. The "national car," the Proton Saga, is produced in a factory designed and supplied by Mitsubishi. The Proton Saga looks like a Mitsubishi Lancer, but with the national seal (an Islamic-style crescent moon, plus a star) built into the grille. Through the late 1980s and early 1990s the country's output rose at boom levels—8 to 10 percent per year—and Kuala Lumpur took on the traffic jams, the high-rise condos, and the fancy hotels that go with an economic boom.

So did all this mean that Malaysia was over the hump and beginning its own path to development? Not necessarily. The growth was still mainly the object of decisions and innovations elsewhere—

"technologyless industrialization," as Kunio Yoshihara called it in his book *Ersatz Development in Southeast Asia*. Factories in Malaysia, Thailand, and some parts of Indonesia might look impeccably modern, he said. "Their activities appear quite technologically sophisticated, and they are sometimes hailed as industrial pioneers; but the fact is that they are Japanese compradors. . . . If there is any technological sophistication in the operation of such plants, it is in the making of machines. But the machines are imported, so there is nothing sophisticated in what these industrial capitalists are doing."[32]

"The Malaysian industrial structure still looks like plantation agriculture," an official at the Japanese embassy in Kuala Lumpur told me in 1991. "When the British came here and established their plantations, they would be very advanced within their special zones. Right next to them would be a traditional way of farming. The plantations had no relationship to the rest of the economy. The industrial situation now is quite the same. The foreign manufacturers come, but the local companies have the old system right next door. We look for high quality from local suppliers, but. . . ." He politely declined to go on.

That is, these factories largely represent the *effects* of innovation and investment somewhere else in the world, rather than the result of either savings or innovation within the country itself. The significance of this, in turn, is that the benefits of the industrialization don't stick. When the country no longer is attractive as a site—if it becomes too polluted or too crowded or too expensive, all of which happened to Thailand in the late 1980s—then investors can just move someplace else. Malaysia was the beneficiary of this process in the early 1990s, as Japanese firms moved out of the congestion they had created in Thailand. But already, in 1991, Japanese officials were talking about "impending constraints" in Malaysia and looking at Indonesia or perhaps Vietnam.

Prime Minister Mahathir and other Southeast Asian leaders "do not realize that true industrialization is based on an economic system that encourages people to strive for innovation and creativity," Yoshihara wrote in *Ersatz Development*.

> These features are invisible and difficult to understand, while new, large factories can be quickly built with petrodollars or money from foreign lending agencies, and they can be shown to people as a concrete sign of development. . . . Technologically, however, they are almost 100 percent dependent on their

Japanese licensers, and under the present setup it would be impossible for them to become technologically independent. . . .
Their technological dependency is not temporary but, being
structural, semipermanent.[33]

In principle, this spillover of investment will bring all countries up
at the same time. If Malaysia or Thailand had to choose between
accepting and rejecting the foreign factories, clearly they would—
and have—preferred to keep them. But when Japan (and later
Korea) were trying to develop, they took a different approach—
remember Japan's bitter resistance to foreign investment after World
War II. Southeast Asia will continue to grow, but for the time being
it should be seen as part of the Japanese expansion, not a major
alternative to it.

Contrasts with Indonesia and Singapore

Thailand and Malaysia illustrate the model for Southeast Asia's
participation in the new East Asian system. After allowing for all
the factors that make Indonesia and Singapore so different from one
another and from Malaysia, in basic ways the countries share similar
economic and political traits. They have been growing with phe-
nomenal speed, which has mainly been a boon to their people but
which has brought certain problems of its own. Compared to most
countries in Latin America and Africa, they have solved the problems of prosperity and of national independence. But compared
both to much of the Western world and to Japan in particular, they
feel as if they have not solved those problems at all.

The differences among these societies are both obvious and
subtle. Politically and socially, Malaysia and Indonesia are more
alike than either of them is like Singapore; economically, Singapore
and Malaysia are closer to each other than either is to Indonesia.

Indonesia is to Malaysia as Mexico City is to East Los Angeles,
or as the Minsk of the 1890s was to the Lower East Side of New
York City. It is the cultural base and heartland from which another
culture sprang, "old-fashioned" in both the good and the bad sense
of the term.

The official language of Indonesia is *Bahasa Indonesia*, or
"Language of Indonesia." The official language of Malaysia is *Bahasa Malaysia*, or "Language of Malaysia." The languages are similar, with variations in accent and vocabulary comparable to those

between American and British English. The most obvious difference is that in Indonesia r's are deeply rolled, as in Spanish. The capital of Indonesia, as pronounced by Indonesians, is Jakarrrrrrrrta; Malaysia's is merely "Kuala Lumpur." Both languages form plurals by doubling a word. *Anak* is one child; *anak-anak* is two or more children. In written Indonesian the plural is often written with a superscript 2, as if it were "*anak* squared," or *anak*². Yet the recent linguistic histories of the two countries suggest the political and cultural gulf between them.[34]

Both *bahasas* are derived from the Malay trading language that established itself on the Indonesian archipelago, much as Swahili did in East Africa. In Indonesia, the principal rival to Malay had been Javanese, which was spoken by a larger number of people through the Indonesian archipelago. But Javanese has elaborate politeness gradations, comparable to those in Japanese, and these got in the way of its usefulness as a lingua franca. The central appeal of Malay, by contrast, is its elegant simplicity—symbolized, for English-speakers, by its streamlined spelling of English words. (When students finish high school they go to *kolej*. A big undertaking is a *projek*. When you want to go from the lobby to the fifth floor, you use the *lif*. Catsup is a thick tomato *sos*. Catsup is also a word that came to English from Malay.)

In both Malaysia and Indonesia, postindependence political leaders pushed *Bahasa* on their people, but with very different results. In Malaysia the Malay language was another symptom of racial division. For most Malays it was their first language; most Chinese spoke one or more Chinese dialects, along with English as a business language. Imposing Malay as the national language was another sign of Malay political preeminence. In Indonesia, by contrast, *Bahasa* was a genuine unifying force. The colonial language, Dutch, had not been widely enough taught to serve as a de facto national language, which English had become in much of Malaysia. The politically most powerful group in Indonesia, the Javanese, had to learn *Bahasa Indonesia* as a second language just like everybody else. Although Indonesia suffers from far more centrifugal forces than Malaysia, Indonesia has a huge, spread-out archipelago containing scores of ethnic groups—it is not troubled by one central ethnic cleavage, as Malaysia is.

For all these reasons, the campaign for *Bahasa Indonesia* was a success, in linguistic and political terms, while the Malaysian campaign called *Cintailah Bahasa Kita!*—"Let's love our language!"— on the whole failed. It didn't make the country more unified, and it squandered the English competence that had been a kind of natural resource for Malaysia. By 1990 the government shrewdly declared victory in its campaign to establish *Bahasa* and said it was time to think about English again.[35]

Arriving in Malaysia from Japan or the United States is a sensual as much as an intellectual experience. The instant you step out of the door of the airplane or come ashore from a boat, you are surrounded by the hot, wet air of the equatorial jungle and the spice-sweet smell common throughout Southeast Asia. Yet it is at least as big a change to go to Indonesia from Malaysia.

Jakarta has had a modern airport, built (like so many other public-works projects in the country) by members of President Suharto's family. This replaced the ramshackle structures that served as the main national airport through the mid-1980s and that instantly plunged visitors into a *Year of Living Dangerously* mood. Even now the air is hotter and wetter than in Malaysia or Singapore, and the smell of *kretek,* the clove-flavored cigarette that seems to provide the aroma for the entire country, is pervasive. The unearthly music of the Indonesian *gamelan*, produced from chimes of bamboo and bronze, is the audio version of this palpably exotic atmosphere.

I used to love reading business strategy books of the "borderless world" genre when I was flying into Indonesia. The island of Java, I thought, was the simplest and most satisfying rebuttal to the conventional shrinking-world view. When I heard Americans complain that mystery and diversity were gone from modern life, I hoped they'd have a chance to see Java soon.

In the center of Java, near the old cultural capital of Jogjakarta, sits the *kraton*, or palace, of the sultan of Jogjakarta, an emblem of shabby, otherwordly gentility. Although most of the sultans who had ruled in Java were deposed when Indonesia became independent, the sultan of Jogjakarta retained his title and his (at least symbolic) power because he cooperated with the anticolonial underground. According to Indonesian lore, Suharto (like many of his subjects, he has only one name) posed during the war as a barefoot peddler outside the *kraton* gates so he could relay information between anti-Dutch guerrillas and the sultan. His *kraton*, built about 250 years ago, consists of a large pounded-dirt courtyard enclosed by palace walls and dotted with open pavilions in which the sultan's family used to eat, watch musical performances, receive petitions, and generally preside. Around the courtyard laze the sultan's "guards," elderly gents in traditional Javanese dress, complete with their sacred wavy-shaped daggers, or *kerises,* jammed into the waistbands of their sarongs. Through the courtyard wafts the music of the *gamelan,* based on its seven liquid-seeming tones.

Geographically and ethnically Indonesia is far more fragmented than Malaysia. Its predicament is in this sense like those of other big, messy countries—China, the United States, the old Soviet Union. Since Indonesia's independence from Holland in 1949, its leaders have emphasized national unity above everything else. As with China in its conquest of Tibet, and the United States in its conquest of the western frontier, this has involved considerable brutality. The government's overwhelming emphasis on national unity lies behind Indonesia's main foreign policy problem: the condemnation its government receives for suppressing separatist movements in the northern portion of Sumatra and on the island of Timor. (Its other foreign policy problem is the long-term, atavistic fear by lightly populated Australia that the Indonesian masses will someday spill out of the archipelago toward Australia, in search of living space.)

Despite the various obstacles to integration it has faced, Indonesia has generated a much more impressive sense of nationalism than Malaysia has. Indonesia's Chinese minority is much smaller than Malaysia's, which is worse for the Chinese but more convenient for the nation as a whole, since the Chinese have no choice but to assimilate. Like Thailand (and unlike Malaysia), Indonesia has coped successfully with the psychopolitical issues of colonialism, race, and royalty. Like the United States and Vietnam, it won a genuine war for independence against its foreign colonizers. This struggle generated a sense of national unity and now makes it easier for Indonesia to deal with the outside world.[36] Most of the traditional Javanese sultanate is gone, but the political system in general retains a spooky, supernatural air that vests the leader with more than merely an electoral mandate. Indonesia was ruled from the mid-1960s through the mid-1990s by one Big Man, Suharto, more than by a party; Malaysia's politics are more ideological and partisan. Indonesia is vast, poor, but self-confident; Malaysia is small, comfortable, and thin-skinned.

By any objective measure, Indonesia's economic obstacles are still enormous. Apart from China, it has the largest population in the region, roughly 195 million in 1993. The island of Java, where about half of Indonesia's people live, is so densely populated that the government has for the past generation undertaken relocation schemes to entice or compel Javanese to move to other islands. Indonesia's per capita income is one twentieth as large as Singapore's (in 1993 roughly $600, versus over $12,000), and of its income Indonesia spends only one third as large a share on education as Singapore does. Farming and fisheries account for nearly half of the Indonesian economy; until the late 1980s its exports were mainly oil and natural gas. Since then it has developed a substantial textile and shoe industry.

Politically Indonesia is farther away from Western versions of democracy than nearly any of its neighbors. Its political life since independence has been dominated by the two *bapaks*—"fathers" or Big Men—Sukarno and Suharto. The military is the most powerful single force in the government; it overthrew Sukarno and brought Suharto to power in 1965 and since then has been the only potential threat to his rule. Like Japan, Korea, and Singapore, which it resembles in few other ways, Indonesia has had a skilled, technocratic bureaucracy—often known as the "Berkeley Mafia," because so many were trained there—that has been heavily involved in shaping the country's economic plans. Starting in the late 1980s these technocrats began an aggressive campaign of welcoming foreign investment. This coincided with the *endaka* investment boom in Japan and led to a tenfold increase in foreign investment coming into Indonesia between 1986 and 1991.[37] Members of this group have launched grandiose and successful plans for a satellite-communications network to unite the far-flung nation, for a national airplane, and for other high-tech schemes. Yet their efforts coexist with corrupt state monopolies, generally run by the ruling Suharto family, that drain off national wealth.

Indonesia's poverty and backwardness, relative to the rest of Asia, mean that it has no alternative to "acted upon" status for the foreseeable future. Yet its absolute scale—in terms of geography, population, and a sense of cultural pride and self-sufficiency—gives it a certain distance from the rest of the Asian system.

Singapore

Singapore, the island-state between Malaysia and Indonesia, represents the other extreme of countries in this group. It is far richer than any other Southeast Asian nation, but it is also far smaller, and it is not a "natural" country in a historic or geographical sense. (It consists of an island roughly fifteen miles square, at the southern tip of the Malay Peninsula.) Singapore has nearly universal literacy and an economy based on high-skill work. Everything about it bespeaks "good planning," which is in fact the best and the worst of what Singapore represents.

The way to mock Singapore, and to infuriate its government, is to complain about the pettifogging degree of overcontrol. Public offices have signs saying "Long-Haired Men Will Be Served Last!" complete with charts indicating exactly what constitutes "long" hair (one inch below the collarline). Flight attendants on the Malaysian air system must make an announcement about the heavy penalties for drug importation before planes touch down in Kuala Lumpur; on planes coming into Singapore, the announcement concerns penalties for importing chewing gum. Possession of a few sticks is in practice overlooked, since they are considered to be for personal use; a pack or more constitutes trafficking.

Taxis in Singapore are mandatorily equipped with little chimes that start ringing when the taxi exceeds the speed limit. The higher the speed, the faster and more annoying the chimes become. Motorists can drive from Singapore to Malaysia by crossing a causeway over the Strait of Johor. In the late 1980s Singapore passed an ordinance saying that cars could not make the trip unless their gas tanks were at least half full—who knows what might happen to them on the Malaysian side? (In fact, what might well happen is that they would buy gasoline, which was much cheaper than in Singapore.) By the early 1990s it was a three-quarters requirement. "When the Singapore government introduced the half-tank rule, my friends in Johor thought they were half-cracked," an anonymous Malaysian wrote in a letter to the editor of the *Far Eastern Economic Review*. "With the three-quarter-tank rule, they think they are now *tiga suku* (the Malay term meaning 'three quarters' and 'not quite there')."[38]

Yet in the view of Singapore espoused by its leaders and at least acquiesced to by its citizens, these small-scale regulations are part of a seamless web of social and economic guidance. When Lee Kuan Yew, as a thirty-six-year-old Cambridge-trained barrister, became the first prime minister of Singapore in 1959, the new city-state was another tropical port town. Lee ruled without interruption for the next thirty years, beating down challenges to his People's Action Party with a controlled press, a gerrymandered electoral system that virtually guaranteed him a majority—and with a record of being able to provide steady economic growth.

Every biography of Lee points out that he took a "double first," or *summa cum laude*, in his studies at Cambridge. In office Lee made no effort to conceal his belief that a meritocracy of society's brainiest creatures should be given responsibility to guide the rest.

"We are born unequal and we've got to make the best of it," he said in a speech while he was prime minister. "Whether it is fruit trees, whether it is racehorses, whatever it is, this is the way nature works. . . . Don't we want to use some common sense and say to ourselves, 'The more we have of people who can run this economy better, the better it is for everyone'?"[39]

As applied in Singapore during Lee's three decades of power, this philosophy has led to extensive social control, clear limits on freedom of speech and debate (one by one, Lee's political opponents ended up in trouble with the law) and indisputable social tranquillity and economic success. Is this so bad a bargain? Singapore's officials ask critical Westerners. "I have visited the offices of four great American newspapers, *The New York Times, The Washington Post,* the *Los Angeles Times,* and *The Wall Street Journal,*" the Singaporean diplomat Kishore Mahbubani wrote in 1993:

> In any one of the four, if you ventured out of their offices at night and strayed a few hundred yards off course, you would be putting your life in jeopardy. . . . In Singapore, you can wander out at night in any direction from the *Straits Times* and not put your life in jeopardy. One reason for this is that habitual criminals and drug addicts are locked up, often for long spells, until they have clearly reformed. The interests in the majority in having safe city streets is put ahead of considerations of rigorous due process. . . . Let me add that a city that bans the sale of chewing gum has as much a moral right to do so as a city that effectively allows the sale of crack on its streets.[40]

Because Singapore has had low tariffs and has embraced foreign firms that comes to invest, its system is often naively referred to in American as a "free trade" or "free enterprise" approach. In basic ways Singapore's "free enterprise" system has resembled the Japanese model more deeply than it has that of the United States. Singapore has relied on the state to make the big economic choices, and allowed private firms to work within the guidelines that skilled bureacrats set.[41]

In Singapore the heaviest hand of state guidance affects savings rates. Every wage earner in the country has been required to set aside one quarter to one third of his or her entire paycheck (depending on income) into the Central Provident Fund, and this money has been used for various socially uplifting projects. The most important of these has been the Housing Development Board, or

HDB, which has in effect built state-subsidized housing for every family in the country. Singapore is very densely crowded but seems less so than, say, Tokyo, precisely because it has all been so meticulously planned. As if in a game of SimCity, high-rise apartments have popped up at all the appropriate distances from offices and factories, each served by its own recreation areas, schools, bus stops, and roads.

When American theorists have looked at this model long enough to realize that it is not exactly laissez-faire, they have often scolded Singapore for its errors. For instance, early in 1992 an economist from Harvard said that Singapore's forced-saving strategy had been inefficient. It had produced so much savings and investment that each unit of investment had been less profitable than it might otherwise have been. "A fair conclusion," he said, "is that Singapore's forced savings and industrial targeting have been mistakes. These policies have led unnecessarily to reduced productivity and welfare."[42] This is the sort of analysis for which most of today's Asians have contempt. Thirty years ago, they say, their countries were poor and dependent. Now they are prosperous and confident. Americans can consider this a mistake all they want. As with the U.S. military during World War II, the approach may have been "inefficient," but it worked.

Yet like its less-well-skilled, less shrewdly run neighbors—Thailand, Malaysia, Indonesia—Singapore is now being affected by changes in the region's financial geography. All these countries are coming to rely for loans, investment, technology, and foreign aid on Japan. They rely on the United States as a military counterweight, for higher education, and as a consumer market. They are not necessarily happy—or unhappy—about this arrangement, but they are adapting to it as the new reality.

7

On the Sidelines

O-MATASE ITASHIMASHITA, "Sorry to have kept you waiting," is the unofficial motto of Japan. These words were the formula of apology that seemed to precede half my interactions in the country, coming not from me, who actually did keep people waiting when I got lost in the subway or could not find an address, but from whatever member of the Japanese service sector I was encountering at the time. If a hotel clerk turned away for moment, if a salesman had to run to the other counter to get a receipt, on return each was sure to say *O-matase* before saying anything else. Literally the words meant, "I have made you wait," which was the version I would sometimes get, in English, from people who had studied the language from not-quite-natural-sounding school phrasebooks. Reduced to this simple assertion, it always tempted me to make a denial: No, in fact, you haven't. *O-matase,* conductors would routinely say as trains neared their destination, even though the trains were almost always right on time.

I did not know whether there was a Tagalog equivalent of *O-matase itashimashita,* but in the Philippines, where Tagalog is spoken, the phrase would have come in handy—along with counterparts meaning, "I have made you suffer" and "I have cheated you." In the summer of 1990, on Mindanao, the southernmost of the main Philippine islands, I once waited with hundreds of Filipino passengers from 4:30 A.M. until 8:00 P.M. that same day for a Philippine Airlines (PAL) flight from Manila that would take us back to the capital. The airport manager appeared every few hours to say that the plane was "coming onto the radar" or "just about to land." In reality, as we learned when the manager locked up the airport for the evening, the plane never left Manila. The fuel companies that supplied Philippine Airlines were demanding cash payment before they would tank up the planes. PAL had not been able to come up with cash that day, so the flight was scrubbed. *O-matase* indeed.

The rigors endured by individual Japanese—or Koreans, or Singaporeans—are at least part of a strategy designed to build collective strength. This wasted day for several hundred Filipinos, a small inconvenience compared to others in their lives, reflected nothing more than the carelessly contemptuous attitude of those in positions of power. Two years earlier, knowing little about public transportation in the Philippines, my family had climbed onto a huge but rickety ferry for the twenty-four-hour voyage from Manila to the island of Cebu. The boat had been built after the war, in Japan, to hold a thousand passengers. Two thousand tickets were sold at the dock; three thousand people came aboard, the extras bribing their way on for a few pesos each. When the boat was full, the crew closed the doors leading from each deck to the exit stairways, and locked all the doors shut with chains. It was more convenient, after all, to keep people where they belonged until the ship reached port. People on the outer decks could not get to the ship's toilets. Several babies were sick, and by the next day the decks ran with diarrhea and vomit. We shared our part of the ship with a number of coffins being sent home to Cebu for burial. One week later, the sister ship to this ferry sank on the same route. Three thousand passengers drowned behind the chained doors.

Not every East Asian society is on the way up. Three major countries, containing a total of nearly 200 million people, have been left out of the boom going on around them. These countries are Burma, Vietnam, and the Philippines. Each of the countries is afflicted by its own peculiar pathologies. Burma's reaction to European colonialism was so extreme that, after World War II, the country tried to wall itself off from modernity altogether. The Philippines has been tormented about its relationship with the United States and about the rapacity with which its elite has mistreated the country's masses. Vietnam has for the past generation suffered the consequences both of its own Communist policies and of having humiliated the United States. All three are on the sidelines now; Vietnam will almost certainly be the first to reenter the modern Asian economic system.

Burma*

After virtually disappearing from the world's notice for about twenty years, Burma returned to the headlines in 1988 and seemed destined to remain in the news for a number of years. That is too bad, since the reports out of Rangoon are as likely to be downbeat as those from Sarajevo or Teheran.

Intuitively it seems wrong for Burma to be in such straits, since in principle it should not be poor. When Burma became independent in 1947, "it was nearly everyone's choice to blaze the Third World trail to modernity," Marvin Ott, of the U.S. National War College, has written.

> Blessed with ample resources, a trained civil service and functioning democratic institutions, Burma was Britain's prize example of how decolonization should be done.[1]

A country immediately to Burma's west is Bangladesh, which, unlike Burma, has every possible excuse for destitution. In Bangladesh more than 100 million people live on a virtually resourceless delta that has an average elevation only slightly higher than sea level and is subject to catastrophic floods. Burma has fewer than half as many people as Bangladesh (about 40 million in 1993) but almost five times as much territory and vastly more abundant resources. Although Burma, having expelled foreign oil companies in the 1960s, now barely produces enough fuel for its own fleet of antiquated cars and trucks, its petroleum deposits are thought to be among the largest in Asia, rivaling Indonesia's. Its remote northeastern regions are full of gem mines, producing rubies and sapphires that are now mainly smuggled across the hills to Thailand and China. If the gold-encrusted stupas all around the country are any indication, there is, or was, a tremendous amount of gold in Burma's soil. Many teak forests have been ravaged, but there is probably more teak left in Burma than anywhere else on earth. Burma's fertile agricultural heartland, along the wide, brown Irrawaddy River, contains ideal rice-growing territory, as was demonstrated after World War II when Burma supplied half of all the rice sold in world trade.

---

*In 1989, a military group seized control of the Burmese government and officially changed the country's name to Myanmar. In this book I have used the more familiar name Burma. As this chapter discusses, the military regime has made the use of Myanmar a politicized symbol of the regime's legitimacy.

Natural resources don't tell the whole story about a nation's prosperity, as the Japanese, Koreans, and Singaporeans so frequently point out. Still, on the basis of its endowments, Burma's fundamental situation would seem much closer to Malaysia's than to that of Bangladesh. Burma and Malaysia are both exceptions to the general Asian predicament of dense population and scarce resources. Both flourished as British colonies on the strength of raw-material industries for which there is still demand today—rubber and tin in Malaysia's case, rice and teak in Burma's. Each country's politics turns on ethnic frictions that were intensified during British rule. Burma's chronic tensions are between the ethnic Burmese who live in the heartland and the Chinese and Indian minorities in the cities, but at the moment the most acute and violent divide is between the Burmese and the hill tribesmen (such as the Shan, Karen, and Kachin tribes) who live on the rugged northeastern frontier of the country and who have waged an insurgency for more than thirty years.

The list of Burma's similarities to Malaysia, and contrasts with Bangladesh, could go on at quite some length. The point of the comparison is that while on paper Burma would seem to be a lucky country, like Malaysia, in practice Burma is almost as desperate as Bangladesh. On the United Nations' list of "least developed countries," Burma stands with Bangladesh near the bottom, with a per capita income of about $200 per year. The only truly vibrant part of Burma's economy is the drug trade, run from the frontier region by a number of warlords. The most notorious of these, Khun Sa, is a holdover from Chiang Kai-shek's Kuomintang Army, which retreated into the Burmese hills when the battle turned against it. Through the 1980s Khun Sa commanded an army of his own in the Shan states and for all practical purposes was a head of state. By most estimates Burma produces half the opium in the world.

At the root of Burma's misery is the deliberately mystical and uninformed totalitarianism known as the "Burmese Way to Socialism," which was devised and imposed by the tyrant Ne Win more than thirty years ago. Ne Win, then an army general, ousted the civilian government of Prime Minister U Nu and seized power in 1962. He then put in place the policy that led his country to destitution.

The crucial emotional fuel for Ne Win's vision was antiforeign autarky pushed to an Albania-like extreme. Burma had graduated from the colonial era with more bitterness against Britain and the

West in general than many other British colonies seemed to feel. Before the outbreak of fighting between Japan and the Allies during World War II, Burmese nationalists had secretely collaborated with the Japanese, in hopes that the war would bring deliverance from British rule. A group of Burmese nationalist leaders known as the "Thirty Comrades" had been trained in guerrilla tactics by the Japanese Army, and they joined the invading Japanese armies in December 1941. Ne Win, the future general and dictator, was one of these comrades. So was Aung San, a heroic young nationalist now revered as the father of Burmese independence.

Near the end of the war Aung San swung his support to the Allies. By 1947, as England prepared to grant Burma its independence, Aung San, then in his early thirties, was the obvious choice to become the first prime minister of independent Burma. But in the summer of 1947, Aung San and several associates were assassinated by political rivals. When Burma became independent at the beginning of 1948, the more lackluster U Nu was its first prime minister. He served for most of the period until the coup of 1962. Aung San lived on in a godlike martyr's status; his photograph hangs in buildings all over the country, and July 19, the anniversary of his death, is the national holiday Martyrs' Day.

Even though Burma's ultimate separation from Britain was peaceful (except for Aung San's death), that did not erase the memory of previous slights. After conquering Burma in the 1880s, the British further insulted it by classifying it merely as part of Greater India, a society on which most Burmese looked down. The British clearly managed to offend Burma's numerous and devout Buddhists—for instance, by garrisoning troops in temples and pagodas. At least once a day during my visit to Burma in 1988 I heard a reference to the sacrilege of thick-booted English soldiers having clomped through temple grounds where signs now say in English, "No Footwearing Allowed." In many of the Southeast Asian countries that the Japanese Army once occupied, wartime memories are still a source of suspicion and resentment toward Japan. But in Burma, the Thirty Comrades' original view of the Japanese as liberators seems to survive. Since the early 1980s Japan has been the leading foreign-aid donor to Burma, and it is usually the only foreign government to which the Burmese leadership even pretends to listen.

When Ne Win took control in 1962, he applied a sweeping policy of purification, intended to remove all non-Burmese presence and influence from the country. Many businesses in Rangoon were at that time owned by ethnic Indians. Ne Win confiscated the businesses and deprived Indians of their citizenship. Foreign businesses, products, investments, and even advertisements were restricted or outlawed. In 1988 my wife and I spent five days riding in the back of a pickup truck, going from Rangoon to Pagan, on to Mandalay, and back to Rangoon. In that time, the only message we received from the world of international commerce was a slogan on a beat-up sign for Fuji Film that had been turned into a tabletop at a tea stand on Mandalay Hill.

Until the late 1970s, most foreigners were allowed into the country for only twenty-four hours at a stretch. Given the extreme inconvenience of getting into and out of the city of Rangoon, this meant that outsiders could see nothing of Burma except the airport and, with luck, the decrepit Strand Hotel in downtown Rangoon. Early in the 1980s that requirement was liberalized to allow visits of one week at a time; by the end of the decade, when Burma was hungrier than ever for foreign currency, the visas were extended for up to two weeks. Still, into the 1990s Burma remained the Albania of Southeast Asia long after the real Albania had abandoned its attempt to keep out the world.

As part of his rejection of Western ways, Ne Win relied very heavily on numerology and astrology in determining his policies. Major decisions are scheduled for lucky days. When Ne Win's government issued new Burmese currency in 1987, it did so in denominations of 45 and 90 *kyat* (pronounced "chat")—rather than 5, 10, 100, or any other conventional amounts. The only apparent explanation is that Ne Win viewed the number 9 as an extremely auspicious figure and linked his actions to it whenever possible. (The practical significance of a shift to 45- and 90-kyat bills may not be apparent until you try counting out large sums in multiples of 45.) Throughout East Asia, official life bows to supernatural influences. Architects in Chinese cultures carefully consider the *feng shui,* or "wind and water," aspects of a building's design—for instance, whether the door and vault of a bank are so oriented that money will naturally "flow" toward the vault. The leader of Indonesia, Suharto, has disappeared from public life for weeks at a time to consult the spirits. Yet even by regional standards Ne Win represents an extreme.

From the 1960s through the 1980s the Burmese economy had languished while most of the rest of East Asia developed. Yet the tensions created by the "Burmese Way to Socialism" came to a head only with Ne Win's decision to issue new currency, which had tremendous economic and political effect.

The background to the decision was the enormous growth of black-market activities in Burma. Through the 1980s, the Burmese government tried to maintain a preposterously high exchange rate of the *kyat* against the dollar. When tourists entered the country, they were required to exchange as much as $100 at a rate of 6 *kyat* per dollar; on the black market, the rate was closer to 50 *kyat* per dollar. Burmese citizens therefore did everything possible to exchange their *kyat* for gems, assets, or hard currency obtained from visitors. Most of the cash in circulation in the country had been earned illegally, through smuggling of gems or drugs. Most manufactured products in the country had also been smuggled in, generally across the border with China in the north of Burma to marketplaces in Mandalay. The country had no functioning banking system, so each family had to hoard cash and assets representing its entire lifetime holdings.

The *kyat* notes themselves were typically tattered and grimy—physical representations of the country's decrepit economy. At Narita International Airport in Japan, I had often seen Japanese tourists at the currency exchange desk subtly recoil in disgust when they exchanged their crisp, new-looking yen notes for dirty or wrinkled American greenbacks. I could just see them thinking: Here's the key to the whole thing! A nation without pride in its money will never make good machine tools! I became more sympathetic to that Japanese outlook when I got to Burma and could hardly bring myself to touch the money.

In an attempt to regain some control of the country's mainly illicit economy, Ne Win's government announced late in 1985 that "large" bills, notably the 100-*kyat* note, would no longer be valid. This was meant to be an orderly transfer; people who held 100-*kyat* notes could exchange them for new money in authorized, smaller denominations.

Two years later, with the economy at least as chaotic as before, Ne Win announced an apparent step toward economic modernity. He said that henceforth farmers could grow rice and other crops and sell the harvest on an open market, with uncontrolled prices. But two days after this announcement, in September 1987, Ne Win declared a second "no more Mr. Nice Guy" demonetization. This time the largest remaining bills in circulation—the 25-, 35-, and 75-*kyat* notes—were all declared valueless. In their place came the auspicious 45- and 90-*kyat* notes. But this time there was no exchange program for the old bills. Their value evaporated overnight.

This second demonetization was a profound shock to the country. The value of the nation's money supply immediately fell by more than half. Some families and small businesses saw all their savings and assets disappear, irretrievably. Students in Rangoon had no money to live on. Nine months after the decree, in June 1988, the shopkeepers and students I met in Rangoon and Mandalay still spoke about the government's decision with frank hatred. A stern-looking hotel clerk in Rangoon said that he had lost the 45,000 *kyat* he had saved over the past twenty years in hopes of getting his children out of the country. A man driving a horsecart in Mandalay told me, "If we had armies from England and America, the government could not last. We need rifles, machine guns, pistols—armies we can use to kill these men."

By the time of these monetary shocks, decades of economic stagnation had made Burma reek with signs of ruin and decline. Throughout Asia, the most appealing cities were those that had preserved the illusion of time standing still. In Malacca and Penang on the Malaysian cost, in Jogjakarta in central Java, in Hanoi, even in gigantic Shanghai until the Chinese building boom of the late 1980s, the palaces, shophouses, banks, and ministries remain—and have been more or less kept up. Rangoon's buildings were old and utterly unmaintained, crumbling beneath moss and mold. As I walked past a government ministry in Rangoon, a flow of brownish water oozed out of the very bricks, onto my feet, just after I heard a toilet being flushed inside. The "Burmese Way to Socialism" may have preserved the country's purity, a prominent dissident politician named Aung Gyi wrote in a manifesto circulated in 1988. But it has "plunged [Burma] to the bottom politically, economically, and socially."

The irrationality of government dictates forced most of Burma's economic activity outside the law. In most poor countries, people are desperate to sell to visiting foreigners. In Burma, people were desperate to buy. With so few goods produced inside the country, what was for sale was either smuggled across the hills from China or brought in on visitors' backs. The items my wife and I had brought along with us without noticing were treasures to some Burmese. Ballpoint pens, sewing kits that hotels give away, matchbooks—such minor artifacts of industrial abundance were otherwise unobtainable in Burma, so people were intent on bidding for them with the only thing they had, namely *kyat*. At the Rangoon airport on our way out of the country, dirty and sick, my wife and I were approached by a sprightly Indian man in his sixties. "You have books for me, sir?" he asked in a cheery undertone. "Toilet paper? Batteries? Ball pens, lead pencils, mosquito coils, pharmaceuticals of any description? Towel? Deodorant? Toothpaste, shampoo?" He offered to buy my shirt, but that I needed, and we had by that point given away or sold everything except our clothes. As we kept moving he fell away, and then called from ten yards back. "Anything? You have anything for me, sir?"

Because of economic desperation, widespread student protests had begun in Burma in the spring of 1988. In Rangoon, police crammed more than forty-one protesting students into a small van and let them suffocate to death. In retaliation students locked two policemen into a van and set it on fire. In July, as the protests expanded, Ne Win made the shocking announcement that he would resign his formal role as the nation's leader. By September a militarists regime known as the State Law and Order Resoration Committee, or SLORC, had taken command. It brutally put down protests, killing at least four thousand people by shooting directly into crowds. It remains in control in 1993.

"Charm." After the crackdown it became very hard to remember or believe how Burma was portrayed in the press for many preceding years. Mostly it showed up as a "charming" society, quaint and picturesque. A writer for *Time* published a book just before the 1988 riots that praised Burma as "one of the only countries I had ever seen that was not goosestepping (to the sound of the Bee Gees) toward a brave new world of videos and burgers, but content to mind its own business and go its own way."[2] The bible for visitors to Burma, the Burma Travel Survival Kit, in an edition published a few months before the riots, said, "Many overseas observers feel the Burmese approach to life isn't so bad at all—Burma may have missed out on a lot of twentieth-century progress, but it has also managed to avoid a good collection of twentieth-century problems."

Such a tone may have been the result of Burma's flat prohibition of visits by journalists, which discouraged most coverage except travel writing. (The SLORC regime allowed journalists in to cover the elections in 1989 and 1990. Almost every journalist who had entered Burma in the preceding decade had gone in, like me, as a "teacher" or "sales representative.")

Moreover, there is an undeniably charming side to Burmese life, difficult as it is to appreciate because of the country's political and economic misery. Virtually every male in Burma wears a saronglike garment called a *longyi*, usually in bright if incongruous Scottish-tartan patterns. The *longyi* is comfortable and unconstraining—"We wear nothing underneath!" a man in Pagan told me and my wife, willing to prove it until we said we believed him—but in the eons of its use no one has figured out how to tie the *longyi* securely. So to walk down a street in Burma is to see an endless, graceful fluttering of arms as men retie their longyis without breaking stride. Women paint big circles on their cheeks with a thick beige "beauty" paste.

In the Strand Hotel in Rangoon, a crumbling relic of the Victorian days, waiters greeted every male visitor during our stay with a courtly, "Good evening, Gentleman"— and greeted every female in similar fashion. In the Mandalay Hotel, a harried-seeming waiter dashed to our table and, before we had ordered, threw down a plate covered with a brown material. "Tonight we serve: Food!" Then he rushed back to the far corner of the cavernous dining hall to watch, with his friends, the evening's TV feature from Burma Broadcasting: thirty minutes of *Heckle and Jeckle* cartoons. Outside the airport in Rangoon, children in *longyis* swarmed around us and ran off with our bags, in the guise of "helping" us with them. When we retrieved them they called out "Present! Present!," which struck me even in my travel-surly state as a charming euphemism for "tip."

The "charm" of Burma also involves its brand of Buddhism. Burma seems more deeply affected by religion than most Western societies have been since the Middle Ages. Stupas are everywhere, so are monks, and much of the nation's wealth appears to go into adorning religious structures. Burmese Buddhism is of the Theravada sect, which in turn is part of Hinayana or "lesser vehicle" Buddhism. (Hinayana Buddhism is the national religion of Sri Lanka, Burma, and Thailand, and is found in Laos and Cambodia. It is more ritualized and narrowly defined than Mahayana, or "greater vehicle" Buddhism, the kind found in Nepal, Tibet, China, Korea, and Japan. "Greater vehicle" Buddhism is more universalistic and embracing; "lesser vehicle" Buddhism focuses more on rituals that lead to attainment of nirvana, or salvation.)

Different religions have different effects on their adherents' daily behavior—Mormons have large families, Seventh-Day Adventists avoid meat. To my layman's eye the most obvious practical effect of Burmese Buddhism's teaching came from its constant reminders that everyone was about to die. Near the summit of Mandalay Hill, a historic and holy site covered with Buddha images and pagodas, we saw a life-size papier-mâché tableau. It showed a *longyi*-clad corpse in an advanced state of decomposition. A vulture sat on the chest and pulled out entrails with its beak. Fluid oozed from the eye sockets, and maggots crawled around the loins. There was an inscription to inform the visitor, "You will die." In Rangoon we saw a similar statue of a man, still alive, standing up. He was feeble and bent, he was ugly, his teeth were gone. The inscription said in English, "You will be old." Every religion talks about these subjects, but usually with more of a payoff. (You will die—and then you will live!) This Buddhism says, You will die—and then you will rot. It is not hard to see it as part of the general despair of the society. (You will live under General Ne Win's policies—and then you will die.) The contents of these teachings make it all the more impressive that Burmese students and religious leaders finally rebelled as they did.

Repression. Two years before the Burmese protests, a popular movement in the Philippines eventually brought down the Marcos government. One year earlier, riots and demonstrations in Korea had led to the first truly open national elections. At the time of the Burmese protests, Gorbachev and the Soviet Union were well into the changes that would bring the Soviet empire itself to an end. News of such changes moved more slowly into Burma than into most other parts of the world, but it moved nonetheless. It was easy for people to imagine that their protests would be part of some worldwide liberalizing wave.

In fact, the spiral in Burma over the next five years was steadily down, more consistently and depressingly so than in China after the 1989 protests in Tiananmen Square. China had to worry about maintaining face and commercial contacts with the outside world. Burma's years of isolation and immiseration had brought it to a rockbottom level that made its regime more or less immune to disapproval from outside.

In 1988, after Ne Win resigned as chairman of the Burma Socialist Program Party, the party passed over a few would-be reformers and selected as its new chairman perhaps the only man in the country less popular than Ne Win. This was Sein Lwin, a sixtyfour-year-old general who directed the feared and hated riot police. He had been in charge of suppressing domestic dissent ever since the 1962 coup that brought Ne Win to power and had personally directed the crackdown on student protests earlier in the year. By the end of the year the SLORC military regime was firmly in place.

Early in 1989, SLORC announced that in 1990 it would hold elections to choose a civilian government. It clearly expected to win without strain, but all calculations were overturned when the forty-three-year-old Aung San Suu Kyi made her dramatic entrance into politics. She was at that moment Burma's counterpart to Indira Gandhi or Corazon Aquino, a woman picking up the mantle of family leadership. She was the daughter of Aung San, martyred hero of Burmese independence. She had been living in England with her English husband, but had returned to Burma as the protests began in the spring of 1988.

Aung San Suu Kyi's popularity posed such an obvious threat to SLORC that she was placed under house arrest in the summer of 1989. The following spring, her opposition party nonetheless swept the national elections, but the ruling generals simply ignored the results, remained in control, and kept Aung San Suu Kyi confined. She remained under arrest as she won the Nobel Peace Prize in 1991 and as the country further estranged itself from the rest of the world. Had Aung San Suu Kyi not attracted so much attention outside the country, she would almost certainly have been killed. Lesser members of the opposition turned up dead, along with troublemakers from SLORC itself.

The name SLORC came to have, in Burma, connotations like those of "Gestapo" in Germany. SLORC rechristened the country "Myanmar," rather than Burma, and changed the capital city's name from Rangoon to "Yangon." For a while the world press obligingly went along with these changes, imagining them to be another step in the long process of postcolonial rectification of names, like the switch from Rhodesia to Zimbabwe. The usage began to swing back when people figured out that "Myanmar" was a SLORC-initiated name designed to show that history had been restarted during its regime.

Buddhists monks played an increasing role in focusing and legitimizing opposition in Burma. When police slaughtered protesters in 1988, several dozen monks were thought to have been among those killed. "The result was that nearly every sector of Burmese society rallied behind [the] opposition," Bertil Lintner has written. Lintner, originally from Sweden, is a reporter who has sneaked in and out of Burma since the early 1980s and has been the main source of outside news about repression inside the country.[3] The main streets of Rangoon, the same ones where protests had begun, were lined with a kind of chest-high metal barrier on each side of the main roadway. They served as pens, to keep protesters who had taken to the road from fleeing when the police opened fire. Within the country SLORC began relocation projects reminiscent of the Khmer Rouge, though without the accompanying slaughter. Near the end of 1990, five thousand people living in and around the temple city of Pagan were suddenly forced to move to a camp a few miles away. Refugees streamed across the border to Thailand (not many fled to Bangladesh); sixty thousand were waiting in Thailand by 1992.

Under SLORC the country's economic fundamentals were no better than before. Having divorced itself not only from its former Western colonial masters but also from the growing economies of East Asia, Burma was left with nothing to sell but its remaining raw materials. In the late 1980s, after rains in Thailand caused devastating landslides in areas where rain forests had recently been clearcut, the Thai government suddenly banned all logging in its forests. The Thai government had quietly negotiated rights for its companies to cut timber in Burma, as well as to fish in Burmese waters. The result was for Thai timber companies, usually in partnership with the Thai Army, to move huge quantities of logs across the border from Burma and off to market. "The Thais have already raped their own environment," a Western diplomat in Rangoon told the American journalists Stan Sesser. "There's not a fish left in the Gulf of Siam. Now you're going to get that here. And you're not going to have a stand of timber in Burma within ten years."[4]

Vietnam

In the early fall of 1990, just before making a trip to Vietnam, I stopped into the Bangkok office of the Japanese trade-promotion agency JETRO. I spoke with the director for an hour about Japan's relations with Thailand, and then asked him as I was leaving how he felt about Vietnam. For the previous hour he had been furrowing his brow and sucking his teeth while discussing the things that were going sour in Thailand—too much pollution, too much sin and AIDS, too little investment in education or technology. At the mention of Vietnam his face suddenly turned to smiles.

"Ah, the Vietnamese!" he said. "Even fifteen years ago they were better workers than the Thais! This was before the Communist time. They would tell the Thais, 'If you work as hard as us you can be rich.' They are good people."

It is, of course, risky to draw moral conclusions from economic performance, and whether the Vietnamese are a "good" people is not my concern. But in the 1990s they certainly give every sign of making up a purposeful and disciplined society, in much the way

Japan and Korea do. While Burma's exclusion from the Asian boom could last indefinitely, and while North Korea's seemed certain to end only when the reign of its "beloved leader," the dictator Kim Il Sung, did, Vietnam's two decades of exclusion were visibly near their end by the early 1990s.

This fact could be admitted everywhere but in America, where Vietnam was less a real country than an uncomfortable topic from the past. Thailand had been buzzing since the mid-1980s with speculation about the new trade and industrial axis that would link Bangkok with Ho Chi Minh City. Salesmen from Japan, Korea, Singapore, and Taiwan—to say nothing of France, Italy, and Australia—jostled against each other for space at the few hotels in Ho Chi Minh City and Hanoi. The longer the United States persisted with its policy of reading Vietnam out of the ranks of normal nations (meanwhile keeping up diplomatic ties with Iraq, Zaire, and Syria), the more America called attention to its own enduring mental problems about Vietnam. In its dealings with Japan since the end of World War II, the United States had been misled time and again by its tendency to see what it wanted to see, what it thought it should see, rather than perceiving what was really going on. By pretending that if it closed its eyes, Vietnam would go away, the United States revealed a similar refusal to look and see.

America's intentions. The United States had imposed an embargo on North Vietnam, under the Trading with the Enemy Act, back in 1964, when North Vietnam was a country and the United States was its military enemy. The embargo was applied to the country as a whole on April 30, 1975, when northern forces conquered the South. This date is referred to in Vietnam as "The Liberation," as in "Back before The Liberation, there was a little café on this corner. . . ." (Similarly, the former South Vietnamese regime is always referred to as "the puppets." "The puppets tried to resist, but . . .") After 1975 the embargo remained in place for years, even as the rationale for keeping it shifted and evolved.

In the early 1980s, the stated reason for excluding Vietnam was to punish it for invading Cambodia. Vietnamese troops had stormed across the Cambodian border in 1979 to drive out the Khmer Rouge forces under Pol Pot that had terrorized Cambodia, and more important from the Vietnamese point of view, threatened their own territory.

Later in the 1980s, as the Vietnamese gradually backed out of Cambodia, the American complaint shifted to the general oppressiveness of Vietnam's Communist government, and to suspicions that it was still holding American prisoners and foot-dragging about MIAs. Although the American strategy was to make a pariah of Vietnam, the longer the boycott endured, the more it isolated the United States. By the middle of the 1980s Canada, Australia, France, Italy, and most other U.S. allies were restoring relations with Vietnam. Japan was the last major domino to fall. For seventeen years after "the Liberation," Japan lined up behind this U.S. policy, as it had so many other American initiatives in the postwar era. Japan's support enabled American governments to keep the World Bank and the International Monetary Fund from making loans to Vietnam—and this, in turn, kept Vietnam's physical infrastructure in a strange, time-warp configuration. The roads were full of craters blasted out by French and American bombs; there were virtually no telephones.

As early as May 1992, the Japanese Ministry of Finance was ready to give the go-ahead for Japanese banks to start doing business in Vietnam.[5] But knowing how emotional the whole subject of Vietnam was for Americans, the Japanese government tactfully delayed this decision, along with other departures from the American orthodoxy, until three days after the U.S. presidential election in 1992. Then it announced that it, too, was breaking ranks and beginning normal dealings with Vietnam. A big loan was the first step: virtually all the money would be recirculated in purchases of Japanese earth-movers, digital phone-switching equipment, automobiles, and machine tools.

Even before the Japanese arrived, placards on the way in from the airport in Ho Chi Minh City—familiar to Americans as Tan San Nhut Airport of Saigon—advertised VCRs and refrigerators from Korean firms such as Daewoo and Samsung. While Japan was still officially observing the sanctions against Vietnam, the American journalist Richard Read encountered a bright Japanese businessman working for a tiny firm in Vietnam. Read learned that the man was a graduate of Tokyo University, and he naturally asked: So what's a Todai man like you doing working for an obscure little company? Pride forced the man to reveal that, in fact, he was working for one of Japan's biggest companies, but he had to operate under cover until Japan's policy changed.

The Vietnamese government remained both Communist and repressive during these years, but its failings could not in themselves explain the stony resolve of the American policy. By nearly any measure of what makes a country bad, the China of the early 1990s was a match for Vietnam, and yet the United States maintained China's "most favored nation" trading status after the Tiananmen Square crackdown of 1989. The real reason for America's attempt to deny Vietnam's existence was, of course, precisely that most Americans wished they had never heard of the place, and no American politician had an incentive to remind them that they once knew it all too well.

Strangely, this desire to wipe away the whole bitter U.S.-Vietnamese interaction did not seem to be reciprocated in Vietnam. Or maybe this difference was not so strange. The government of Ho Chi Minh and his successors, after all, defined itself by having beaten first the haughty French and then the mighty Americans. They do not have to bear a collective grudge, although, of course, many individuals are bitter, and especially in the North all public places carry reminders of the heroic victory over the foreigners. But it all seems a long time ago, as the Korean War does in the United States. By the fall of 1992, when George Bush was lambasting Bill Clinton about his failure to serve in Vietnam, Vietnam's median age was under twenty, so that most of its people had no personal memory of Americans on their soil. I got the feeling, when traveling through Vietnam in 1988 and again in 1990, that what Americans called "the Vietnam War" remained more important in America than in Vietnam—and that its main historical effect would be the internal damage it did to the United States. When I was in Ho Chi Minh City with a bedraggled tour group in 1988, the requisite government guide/chaperon had planned an all-day outing to a rugmaking cooperative in the Mekong Delta. We suggested instead a visit to Cu Chi, where the Viet Cong had operated an elaborate tunnel civilization beneath a U.S. Army base. The guide finally acquiesced but shook his head in puzzlement. These wacky foreigners! More interested in crumbly old tunnels than in nice new rugs!

Vietnam's intentions. The changes that began to legitimize Vietnam in the eyes of the world were well under way by the late 1980s, at the same time as those in Eastern Europe. The Vietnamese naturally wanted to encourage the analogy to Eastern Europe. When I visited a diplomat in the Vietnamese embassy in Bangkok, a few months after the Chinese repression in Tiananmen Square, he was prepared with a whole pitch explaining why Vietnam's liberalization was going to be more lasting and comprehensive than China's. "China is a big country," he said, expansively waving his arms to illustrate his point. "Vietnam is small. We will be more like Hungary. Our problems are not so confusing as China's. We will have to come down decisively for reform, even against a lot of odds like the ones we are facing now." Near the end of 1990, when I spent a month interviewing officials and fledgling "businessmen" in Vietnam, I was told time and again that the reform road was the right road, that there was no turning back, that Vietnam recognized the error of China's ways and wanted to be like the other prospering countries of Southeast Asia.[6]

In the long run it could be true. In the short run the Vietnamese officials seemed to protest too much about the differences between their approach and China's. In each case a Communist regime seemed to have reached a purely practical conclusion: that the highly centralized, state-run economic system inherited from the Soviets just wasn't going to work. If they hoped ever to catch up with the likes of Thailand or Taiwan, if they wanted ever to acquire better machinery or attract more money than what the socialist bloc could come up with—if they wanted, in short, to become modern—then the Vietnamese and Chinese alike needed to join the world market system and use some of the tools of the market inside their countries. This was not a philosophical so much as a managerial decision. By the late 1980s it was clear to any realistic person that centralized, socialist-style economics was not going to pan out. And so Vietnam and China took market-minded steps—welcoming foreign investors, eliminating price controls for food, even tolerating the emergence of such long-denounced capitalist evils as inflation and the rise of the rich.

What made China and Vietnam similar to each other, and different from most countries of Eastern Europe, is that this loosening went only so far. A more flexible market: yes. Real political openness: no. Americans believed that the two things inevitably came as a package, but many Asian regimes acted as if this were not necessarily so. In Beijing, in Hanoi, even in Jakarta and Singapore, governments were in various ways trying to use the tricks and tools of modern capitalism without giving up their accustomed political controls.

Through the early 1990s, Vietnam was clearly less committed to political reforms than most of Eastern Europe was. There were elections, but no real challenge to Communist Party control. Yet in one fundamental way Vietnam was like Poland, Hungary, and the former East Germany. Starting in the late 1980s, the details of daily life were changing almost visibly, as the country was suddenly re-connected to the outside, industrialized world, especially the system developing around it in the rest of Asia.

I first went to Vietnam shortly before the economic reforms kicked in. At that point, in 1988, every atmospheric detail announced, "This is a Soviet-style police state." The vehicles rumbling down the road were either ill-made Soviet vans and buses or ancient, rehabilitated Fords and jeeps. Motorized vehicles of all sorts were vastly outnumbered by bicycles. Street corners in Kuala Lumpur were deafening, with unmuffled motorcycles roaring past. Those in Bangkok were black with smoke. But corners in Hanoi were almost silent at rush hour, as thousands of Vietnamese swept past on their bicycles, disrupted only occasionally by a truck, bus, or diplomat's car. For nine days my wife and I rode in a Russian bus from Hué, near the old DMZ between the former North and South Vietnams, to Ho Chi Minh City, the former Saigon. For ten hours each day the bus rolled past rice fields. One time in these days we saw a functioning tractor. The rest of the time we passed plows pulled by water buffaloes or by toiling men. The road down which we rolled, Highway 1, is the main and usually the only north-south artery in the country. But for most of its length rice grains were laid out in foot-wide swaths at the edge of the road, to dry in the sun.

In those days the main market in Hanoi had little to offer except local vegetables, a few plastic tools, and the incongruously colonial-looking green pith helmets that most northern men wear. Hanoi's market also featured several tubs full of live bullfrogs. Two market ladies chatted with each other while lopping the frogs' legs off with strokes of their cleavers. Saigon's marketplace was more active, since it had once been a thriving entrepôt, but it had a deserted, after-the-bomb feel. At just this time Vietnamese officials were beginning to talk about "price reform"; their markets gave daily lessons in what was wrong with unreformed prices. The official exchange rate in Hanoi at the time was a wildly unrealistic 368 *dong* to the dollar; at a government-run store in Ho Chi Minh City $1 was worth 2,800 *dong,* and in back alleys it was worth 3,500 to 4,000 dong. At three different post offices—in Hanoi, Da Nang, and Ho Chi Minh City—I was quoted three different postage rates for letters to Western countries. "How can the price of stamps vary from city to city?" I asked the guide in Da Nang. "Oh, many things cannot be explained!" he said cheerfully. "Especially about prices!"

At "the Cuban hotel" in Hanoi, built shortly after The Liberation by Cuban engineers, imported Heineken beer was on sale for 70 American cents. This was, at least, the theoretical price. In reality, only American $1 bills were accepted for payment, and there was no change. Alongside was locally brewed Saigon Beer for 2,800 dong per bottle—or, at the exchange rate offered at that same hotel, more than $8.

Two and a half years later, near the end of 1990, quite a few things seemed similar. The ethic of a real market economy had not exactly sunk in. In the Vietnamese embassy in Bangkok, where Americans must go for visas, a sign on one side of the room announced that Visit Vietnam Year was under way. A sign on the other side laid out the nightmarish requirements for getting a visa.

In Hanoi I stayed for a week in the "government guesthouse," where I pondered each morning whether it would be more pleasant to go yet another day without bathing or to lie, on my back, in the bottom of the little tub so that I could let rusty water from the tap dribble onto my face and hair. The room next to my own was filled with a huge Soviet-bloc telephone switching system; each time I passed it I found it easier to believe that the first computers ever made had filled whole warehouses. Either because the system was so primitive, or because of a simple desire to profiteer, the hotel charged $30 per minute for calls to the United States or Europe, with a minimum of three minutes per call. (The rates were set on a sliding political scale: lowest for calling the Soviet motherland, next cheapest for Cuba, Czechoslovakia, and so on; more for the rest of Asia; most for the Yankee foe.) When I was leaving the guesthouse, I grumbled that the phone rates seemed a little pricey. Wouldn't the government bring in more money if it lowered the cost? "Yes," the receptionist said cheerily, as if we were discussing some frustrating but unalterable quirk of the landscape or weather. "All the foreigners say so!"

A few blocks from the hotel was the central post office for the capital city. Envelopes and stamps were on sale inside, but apparently the country lacked the machinery to put any kind of adhesive on them. On an addressing table sat what looked like a huge ball of phlegm, which patrons dug into with their fingers and then smeared on the stamps and envelope flaps. I followed their example, then tried to pound my envelope, with its lumpy glue, flat with my fist so it would fit through the mailing slot. That evening, when watching a Soviet-made documentary on tractor production in my "guesthouse" room, I suddenly understood why artistic celebration of heavy capital equipment had been so popular in Stalinist regimes. I considered writing an ode to a stamp-making machine. The next feature on the news was about a new automatic cigarette maker installed at the state tobacco monopoly. I watched rapt.

Yet in the midst of this torpor were unmistakable signs of a society coming alive. Hanoi's streets were much noisier than they used to be. Cars were still rare, but the streets were crawling with Japanese-made motor scooters. I had remembered Hanoi as being virtually devoid of lighting. When dusk came, the colonial bungalows would fall into utter blackness, except for little lights flickering from the windows. Now it seemed that every other building had neon lights in front announcing, "Café." An economist named Le Dang Doanh told me that some 600,000 cafés, restaurants, and other small businesses had opened up in the preceding two years. It was very hard to figure out who might patronize so many cafés; they seemed to be mainly an excuse for their owners to watch prized VCRs, most with American music videos running nonstop. In the guesthouse, when the tractor documentary was over, each night there was a showing of . . . *Love Story,* with Ali MacGraw and Ryan O'Neal.

The currency market had been liberalized. As far as I could tell, the same rate was being offered in banks and at hotel desks as in the back alley. Mammoth trade expositions were held on the outskirts of both Hanoi and Ho Chi Minh City, one sponsored by Taiwanese firms (generally in partnership with Vietnamese Chinese) and another by Koreans. I spent a day with a Taiwanese general contracting firm, which showed me the site they hoped to clear for a luxury-style "International Quarter" housing project complete with tennis courts, golf course, and school for the foreign children who would soon arrive.

The formerly depleted marketplace in Hanoi was suddenly bulging with consumer goods: blue jeans, imitation-leather bomber jackets, Japanese-style fashions with nonsense English on the back. The hotels where journalists had stayed in wartime Saigon—Rex, Majestic, Continental, Caravelle—revamped themselves, with French-style restaurants and tawdry "discos" jammed with young Vietnamese women in short skirts. Even Hanoi had an "International Club," whose clientele seemed to be 90 percent dressed-up young ladies and 10 percent tired-looking male diplomats and merchants from the outside world. Sidewalk vendors sold English-, French-, and Vietnamese-language versions of the country's new rules for foreign investment. The foreign community contained its share of old-style aid and humanitarian workers. The Swedes had a vast foreign-aid effort, the United Nations had health and agriculture projects under way. But most of the embassies seemed to be busily converting themselves into commercial attaché operations, waiting for the boom that would someday come.

The big questions for Vietnam. As Vietnam attempted to rebuild itself, the answers to several questions would determine how far it might go.

Would Vietnam find a solution to the "Chinese question," that of balancing political and economic reforms? The East Asian countries that were at least formally democratic, from Singapore to Japan, had come up with their own solution to this problem, mixing political controls and liberty in much the same way that they had mixed markets and government guidance in their economic policy. The two states that were trying to devise a form of "capitalistic communism," China and Vietnam, faced a harder challenge, since they had no established model to apply.

What would be Vietnam's competitive advantages when it entered the world marketplace? Would it do any better than Thailand had in protecting its environment, or any better than Indonesia in keeping its population growth in check? Would it be able to deal with the regional tensions that still, twenty years after the fall of Saigon, made the southern part of Vietnam seem like a different, more market-minded country than the North?

These and similar questions would occupy the Vietnamese in the future. But the answer to a more immediate question would influence the answers to all the rest. Exactly how long, and with what firmness, would the United States continue its embargo of Vietnam?

By the beginning of the 1990s the U.S. policy toward Vietnam had become a classic lose-lose situation. The policy hurt Vietnam, but not enough to make a major difference in its behavior. At the same time it hurt the United States, but not in a way that advanced any larger goal.

The official rationale for American policy had changed so often as to create substantial doubt that America was being honest, even with itself, about what it hoped to achieve by excluding Vietnam. As the Vietnamese government met, one by one through the 1980s, the stated American conditions for normalized relations, new complaints and conditions emerged.[7]

By the beginning of the Clinton administration, the main resistance to normalizing relations came from the groups of Americans who had suffered most during the war, especially the lobby for families of POWs and MIAs. This, of course, made it harder for

Bill Clinton, noncombatant, to normalize relations than it would
have been for a Vietnam veteran of his generation, such as John
Kerry or Robert Kerrey. In Japan in 1990, just before I went to
Vietnam, I met a U.S. senator of the baby boom generation who
had not served during the war. He agreed that the embargo no
longer made sense but said it might continue through inertia for
years. "I have a simple test," he said. "When the war heroes say
it's okay, then it's okay. Until then, it's not."

It would, for that matter, have been easy for George Bush to
cut the knot before he left office. As a combat pilot, he had nothing
to prove personally; as a China hand he understood the need to deal
with unpleasant governments and make the best of it. Indeed, Clinton and Bush could have done a favor for each other, and for the
country, by agreeing on a grand strategic swap during the transition
period after the 1992 election. Bush could have normalized relations
with Vietnam before he left office, a step whose time had come but
that would inevitably be awkward for Clinton. Clinton, in return,
could have agreed to pardon Caspar Weinberger and the other Iran-
contra defendants after he took office. This would have removed an
old, festering issue from the political agenda without involving Bush
in what would inevitably seem to be a self-protective move. In the
real world, of course, this deal was not struck.

The American policy was enough to make Vietnam miserable
but not enough to make the regime grovel or change course. (How
big a surprise can this be after the war years?) Nor was it enough
to stop the countless under-the-table deals by which many other
people managed to do business with the Vietnamese. Singapore,
stoutly anti-Communist in rhetoric, was the middleman for shipment
of Western consumer goods into Vietnam. By 1990 Australia enjoyed a trade surplus with Vietnam, importing fish and grains and
selling, among other things, three large satellite dishes to handle
international phone calls. ("Now I can call Paris and Bangkok," a
bureaucrat from the Ministry of Commerce told me in Hanoi. "The
problem is calling Haiphong.") The manager of a Vietnamese shipping line in Ho Chi Minh City guilelessly explained to me how
Vietnamese handicrafts reached customers in America: first the ship
goes to Vancouver, then all the documents are changed, then it goes
on to the United States.

"If the embargo's purpose is to punish us until we relent, then
it hasn't worked," a Vietnamese diplomat told me in Hanoi in 1990.
"It will have less and less power to work from now on. Its impact

is felt mainly by the poor people. And if the goal is to persuade us to continue our reforms, it has just the opposite effect. The reforms will continue on their own, not because of outside pressure."

The government of Vietnam has proven strangely inept in presenting its case to the American public. Time and again through the 1980s, especially with its foot-dragging on the POW issue, the Vietnamese government suggested that it really had no idea what America's motives and emotions were. "During the war, they kept making a distinction between the bad American government and the good American people, and it took," one Western diplomat told me in Bangkok in 1990. "But they managed to convince themselves that the American public was not just antiwar, it was pro-Vietnamese revolution. That was why they dreamed they could ask for reparations after the fall of Saigon." "They don't *really* understand America, and never did," a Vietnamese exile who now works as a translator in Bangkok told me. "It was almost by accident that they seemed to 'understand' America in the 1960s."

Nonetheless, sometime in the late 1980s, the Vietnamese government began to have a glimmer of understanding of how it could appeal to American sentiment. It started to realize that its grudging stand on the search for POWs and MIAs was its major liability. (Over the past decade the Vietnamese government had "found" one or two sets of remains every year or so and had parceled them out in a cynical way to the Americans.) By August 1987, when retired general John Vessey, former chairman of the Joint Chiefs of Staff, came to Vietnam to begin work on the POW question, his Vietnamese counterparts realized they had nothing to gain by prolonging this dispute—and, according to Vessey's reports, they were more or less cooperative.

Simultaneously, the Vietnamese government realized that it could use the old "don't abandon the moderates" argument to sway opinion in the United States. In their dealings with Iran, with Lebanon, with the old Soviet Union, and with the new Russia, American officials had always worried that if they cracked down on an unpleasant regime they would penalize and discourage the potential "moderates" in the regime working for conciliation and reform. Vietnam's moderates, who were indeed working for economic reforms in the early 1990s, made this case as well: the longer the United States withheld recognition, the harder it was for reformers to argue that the Vietnamese government would be rewarded if it loosened up. Starting in the late 1980s, Vietnamese government

officials paid enough attention to American political debate to realize that they could appeal to American age-of-decline insecurity
as an argument against the embargo.

Shortly before The Liberation, Mobil had discovered a sizable
oil field in Vietnamese waters in the South China Sea. In 1989
Vietnam assigned rights to develop this White Tiger field to companies from Canada, France, Kuwait, and elsewhere, but not to
U.S. firms. Mobil and Texaco, along with Citibank, sent exploratory
missions to Vietnam so as not to miss out on the next such
opportunity.

The leftist argument that the United States had fought in Vietnam to guard access to oil fields and rubber plantations always
seemed preposterous to me—it would have been so much simpler
and cheaper to buy oil and rubber from whoever controlled them.
But big-business pressure clearly led the way for America's return
to Vietnam. From the mid-1980s on, American businessmen based
in Bangkok and Hong Kong had been complaining about the U.S.
embargo. They generally kept the complaints to themselves; if they
publicly questioned the policy, many feared, they might be labeled
conscienceless war profiteers, more interested in the chance to sell
cola or toothpaste than in the fate of American POWs. By 1989,
however, the American chambers of commerce in Bangkok and
Hong Kong formally recommended that the embargo be lifted, to
offset "the continuing loss of U.S. business opportunities in Vietnam
to global competitors." Raymond Eaton, an Australian businessman
based in Bangkok, gave speeches throughout Southeast Asia urging
that companies from every country except America should seize the
"golden opportunity" that the embargo created and "do your very
utmost to capitalize on the total inability of American companies
to compete against you."

In 1990 the manager of a high-rise building project in Hanoi
told me, "We hoped very much to use American elevator equipment
in our building, but, you know . . ." At about the same time Vo Dai
Luoc, of the Institute for World Economy in Hanoi, told me, "In
the past the United States spent billions of dollars to establish its
influence in this part of the world. It was not possible that way, but
simply by permitting business relations the United States may succeed in obtaining a role in this region."

On the top floor of a hospital in Ho Chi Minh City, I heard a
similar argument from Nguyen Xuan "Jack" Oanh, perhaps the most
influential of Vietnam's reform economists. Oanh had once taught
economics at Harvard; he still spoke an uncanny native-speaker

American English that stunned me, after a month of trying to communicate in a haze of pidgin versions of English, French, Italian, and Japanese. Oanh, a portly, bald man in his sixties, sat in pajamas on his hospital bed, working over the text of speeches he hoped to give in Paris and Washington, D.C., on Vietnamese economic reforms.

"Let me argue purely from American self-interest in coming back here," he said. "At the end of the war years, the United States was putting something like $1 billion a year into South Vietnam. Much of it went right back as contracts to American suppliers. There are many American manufacturers who would do well again if we could expand. For example, we used to import $7 million to $10 million worth of water-pumping equipment from the Kohler company, of Illinois. The market for cars is now completely in the hands of the Japanese. Most durable goods are now of Japanese origin. I wish that instead of a Toyota plant, we could build a Ford or GM plant in Vietnam. By punishing Vietnam the United States is punishing itself. There is such a lot of *experience* between America and Vietnam. People keep asking when the Americans are coming back again."

The case for a different American policy. From the U.S. point of view there are three strategic payoffs to repairing relations with Vietnam—and all these are apart from the general benefits of being in on a growing economy and, even more important, resolving a festering problem in America's own history.

The first, most specific, and most outlandish-sounding potential benefit is for Vietnam to serve as an alternative for the naval bases the United States had to evacuate in the Philippines. Except for North Korea, almost every government in East Asia feels more comfortable with the U.S. Seventh Fleet in the vicinity than any of them would feel without it. With the Americans nearby, the Chinese, Japanese, Koreans, and Russians generally assume that none of them will attack any of the others. Without the American buffer, each of them would have reason to fear most or all of the rest.

The buffer will, of course, ultimately disappear if the U.S. economy erodes, but the main short-term threat to the American presence has been the snarling nature of U.S.-Philippine relations. When the hand of God, in the form of the eruption of Mount Pinatubo, drove U.S. Air Force out of Clark Air Force Base, north of Manila, and the Philippine Senate drove the U.S. Navy out of Subic Bay, other countries in the region quietly offered temporary accommodations. "There are certain things that certain countries cannot say," one Malaysian diplomat told me in 1990. "George Bush cannot say, 'I don't care if the spotted owl becomes extinct.' We cannot say, 'We will let the U.S. Navy have a permanent base on our territory.' But we can offer repair facilities, docking facilities. We can sign an agreement allowing U.S. troops to visit here. We just can't talk about it."

The one country in Southeast Asia with the mental confidence to talk openly about letting in the U.S. Navy may be Vietnam. It has nothing to prove about its independence or ability to stand up to Uncle Sam. Since the Soviet Union withdrew first its soldiers and then its financial subsidies from 1988 on, Vietnamese officials have "joked" repeatedly about rewelcoming the U.S. Navy to Cam Ranh Bay.

A second advantage is the potential to help solve the region's main political problem since the fall of Saigon. That is the stream of refugees out of Vietnam, Cambodia, and Laos to neighboring countries in hopes of making it to Europe, Australia, or the United States.

Between 1975 and at least 1990, the flow of refugees out of Indochina was the most important chronic political problem in Southeast Asia. It began to abate only in 1992, and it did so because of two changes. One was a "Comprehensive Action Plan," or CAP, agreed to by the "first asylum" countries of Southeast Asia, which had been temporarily receiving refugees, and the "resettlement" countries in which the refugees ultimately ended up. Under the CAP, refugees who could prove that they were suffering outright political persecution were granted asylum and resettled, but those who could not prove the case were sent back to Vietnam. Forced repatriations, which began in 1989, were designed to discourage other Vietnamese from trying to leave, and they seemed to have that effect.

The other significant change was the beginning of Vietnam's conversion into a "normal" country, with economic opportunities for its own people. The end of the U.S. embargo would hasten the conversion to normality that is already under way, and in turn further damp the flow of refugees.

Third, smoother relations between Vietnam and the outside world would in a strange way bring America's wartime goals full circle. The United States initially moved into Vietnam because it was terrified of Chinese expansion through the rest of Asia. Two generations have passed, regimes have risen and fallen in China and every other part of Asia, and the fear of Chinese expansion is once more on people's minds.

In the short run, the serious military problems of East Asia boil down to one problem, that of North Korea. It has all the classic elements of a military trouble spot: a big army, an unpredictable leadership, an impending change in command.

In the somewhat longer run, the military problems are hazier and more open-ended. The Indian Navy might assert control over shipping lanes leading toward Singapore. Islamic separatist groups might go to work in southern Thailand or the southern Philippines. The Koreas might reunite, exciting fear in Japan. Japan might decide that it has had enough of the strange relationship with the United States and strike out on its own militarily. The "independence" parties based in Taiwan might end the "one China" pretense and announce that Taiwan really is a separate country from the mainland, which might in turn goad the mainland Chinese into demonstrating their sovereignty with military force. Britain and China might somehow get into a showdown over control of Hong Kong.

This is the stuff of an endless round of "Asian Security in the Twenty-first Century" conferences. What most of the scenarios have in common is the gradual disappearance of the U.S. Seventh Fleet from its Pacific patrols. Just as the retreat of the Soviet Army uncorked all sorts of problems in Eastern Europe, so an American withdrawal could clear the way for a lot of Asian fights. Every scenario of "Japan on the march" requires a U.S. withdrawal as a precondition. As long as American warships are parked at Yokosuka Naval Base, outside Tokyo, and Japan is bound by the U.S.-Japan Security Treaty, it would be hard for the Japanese military really to stretch its wings.

There is only one serious long-term threat that does not rest on the idea of a full-scale U.S. withdrawal. That threat is the emergence of China as a stronger and stronger military force. China's absence from this role is an oddity of the past two centuries, in which it was cowed by European colonialists and by Japan. While Japan's historical imagery emphasizes its struggle to catch up with bigger rivals, and while Korea's is full of resentment about being pushed around by the big powers on its borders, China's sense of self (like America's) emphasizes its natural supremacy and centrality. The postwar governments of Japan, Korea, and the Philippines have grumbled constantly about the need to bow to the American government's wishes. China also grumbled but does not feel obliged to comply with what the United States, or anyone else, may want.

"In the long run, there is no doubt about the greatest threat to us," a Malaysian diplomat told me in 1990, just after I'd left Vietnam. "The countries strong enough to pose a problem are Japan and China. Some people worry about India, but I don't. Japan has more political influence over us—and over you Americans—through its investments. But those investments are also hostages. The United States can still control Japan in many ways.

"Not even the United States feels it can control China. It could be an immediate threat in the South China Sea"—he meant mainly in disputes over the Spratly Islands, a tiny archipelago over which China, Vietnam, and the Philippines all claim sovereign rights. "And its power will be immense eventually.

"Therefore, it is important to build a ring of states around China that are stable and independent. They would not be a military buffer against China, but they could be a political buffer. Vietnam should be part of that frontier." To any Americans old enough to remember America's warfare in Vietnam, few developments could seem more perverse than making friends with the Vietnamese Communists in order to "contain China." But that may be the way it works out.

Vietnam and the Asian economic system. Sooner or later it seems certain that Vietnam will be a success story of Southeast Asia, overtaking Indonesia and Thailand, conceivably rivaling Singapore and Malaysia. The question is how soon or how late that might be. Even now, Vietnam's population is well educated. Through the centuries it has had a tradition of scholarship and discipline much like that of Korea or Japan. Vietnam's labor costs are so low that, at least for the time being, it can underprice any other countries in the region.[8] Its coastline is perhaps the most beautiful in Southeast Asia. "If you look at the problems of Vietnam, you want to give up," Nguyen Quang Dy, a Vietnamese diplomat, told me in 1990. "But if you look at the potential, then there is no way the changes will be reversed. The Japanese must have long-term confidence in us, since they are investing in manufacturing and tourism. Thai businesses want to invest also."

"Our wages are very low compared to the rest of the region," I was told in 1990 in Hanoi by Vo Dai Luoc, director of the Institute of the World Economy. "In the North the average worker in textile mills gets $20 to $30 per month. Of course, people do as they are paid. If they are paid $30, they do little work. But if they are paid $100 per month, our workers will work excellently!"

"In terms of drive and self-discipline, the Vietnamese are very hard to beat in Southeast Asia," an Indian diplomat told me in Hanoi. "They are gifted people—gifted with languages, mechanically very adept. They lack exposure to everything modern—management ideas, commercial laws, the idea of organizing the economy. But they will make this a very dynamic society."

The following day I met an American diplomat who had fought against the Vietnamese during the war. He made a similar point with a different edge. "If you did all the macro number crunching, you would think they are going to have a very hard time for a very long time," he said. "But I don't believe that. Too many people for too many years have used computers on Vietnam to defeat Vietnam, and they've always been wrong."

In the comments I heard from them in 1990, some Vietnamese officials showed that they had drawn the same political conclusions about Japan's role as their counterparts had in Bangkok, Singapore, and Kuala Lumpur.

"My personal idea is that Japan will be among the very few countries to play an important role in Vietnam," Vo Dai Luoc of the Institute of the World Economy told me in 1990. "No, this is not only my personal idea. This is not only my personal idea but the view of many economists in Vietnam. According to the Japanese assessment and evaluation, Vietnamese workers are among the very few who are suited to Japanese technology. That is because of our education and other factors. They tell us that they value us, compared to Thais, Malaysians, Indonesians, Filipinos.

"Japan has a lot of capital. And Japan has excellent technology in processing and exporting. Japan thinks that in the near future the Europeans will close in on Europe, and the Americans will close in on America. So it may be isolated in Asia! Because of that we Asians, including Vietnam, will play a more important role with Japan. That is why so many Japanese people are here! There are ten times as many from Japan as from any other country.

"Some people are worrying in our government because they say Japan's foreign policy will be just the same as in the past. But for me, I think day by day Japan will become more independent. Before, if Japan wanted to reach the top in the world, they had to cooperate with the United States. Now, with the end of the Cold War, they should act for themselves."

The Philippines

The least successful-seeming society in East Asia is the Philippines. No one can take comfort in that fact—least of all Americans, since this is the society most heavily shaped in the American image. When Stanley Karnow called his mammoth history of the Philippines *In Our Image,* he was not exaggerating.

This is the largest country the United States ever attempted to colonize. It is the one part of East Asia to embrace most fully the "American Way" of two-party elections and an uncontrolled press. It is the one overwhelmingly Christian country in the region, a fact that U.S. president William McKinley overlooked when saying at the turn of the century that it was necessary to colonize the Philippines to "Christianize" its people. In fact, Spanish friars had been Christianizing with great success for the previous three hundred years. (Today the leading proselytizers in the Philippines are the Mormons and Iglesia ni Kristo, a nationalist/fundamentalist sect that has built futuristic-looking churches all over the country.)

At the end of World War II Manila prided itself as having been on the winning side, while Tokyo and Seoul tried to size up the conquering Americans. Today Manila is sad in the same way Rangoon is, and for a similar reason. Each has become a melancholy monument to unnecessary, self-induced decline. The desolation of Saigon at least has a traceable historic origin. This old apartment building was destroyed in the fighting; that former department store was closed down when the Communists took over. What has gone wrong in the Philippines is harder to pin down, but it is clear that something has.

It can seem bullying and gratuitous for an American to dwell on the miseries of the Philippines. Seen from Manila, the United States is so strong and rich. Seen from anywhere, the Philippines is so troubled and poor. Why pick on people who need help and sympathy? If Americans think things are wrong in the Philippines, why didn't they fix them when they were running the place, or in the years when they had leverage over the Marcos family? The Philippines ethic of *delicadeza,* the local equivalent to "saving face," encourages people to raise unpleasant topics indirectly, or, better still, not raise them at all.

Out of respect for *delicadeza,* or from a vague sense of guilt that the former colony is still floundering, or because of a genuine fondness for many Filipino people, the United States has tolerated polite fictions about the Philippines that it would have ruthlessly punctured if they concerned France, Russia, or Mexico. These fictions took one form during the Marcos years, when it was in America's strategic interest to view him as the most important friend in the region—and another form in the early days of the Corazon Aquino regime, when she was "Woman of the Year" for *Time* magazine and was generally portrayed as a vessel of redemption, hope, and reform.

By the time Aquino left office six years later, she had reached one goal that at many points in her tenure had seemed unattainable: She had made it through the full duration of her term, despite nonstop rumors of impending coups and half a dozen actual attempts. In 1992 she handed her successor, former general Fidel Ramos, a democracy that was functioning at least in formal terms. Ramos had won just over one quarter of the votes in a seven-person presidential field. Nonetheless, that was a more democratic mandate than many other East Asian leaders, including many Philippine predecessors, had relied on to rule.

Ramos's initials were "FDR," and he soon began what he advertised as a New Deal–style crusade to raise the nation's spirits and bring it new work. In principle the country has tremendous resources. It has for decades been a large agricultural exporter and often enjoys a trade surplus with Japan. Its hundreds of islands are full of spectacular beaches that could, in theory, be among the world's sought-after resorts. When its people fan out around the world, as some 2 million emigrants and itinerant workers had by 1992, they are generally successful and well regarded.[9] Philippine immigrants in the United States, for instance, have a higher average income than do native-born American whites. "These are the same people who shine under Japanese managers," a veteran politician named Blas Ople told me in 1987. "But when they work for Filipino contractors, the schedule lags."

Except for Burma, the Philippines is the only country in the region where life seems to be moving backward. In the early 1990s Malaysia's per capita annual income was nearly $2,500, Singapore's more than $10,000, Thailand's more than $1,500, and all, of course, were going up. The per capita annual income in the Philippines has been stagnant at about $700 for several years. By government estimates roughly two thirds of the people in the country live below the poverty line, as opposed to about half in the pre-Marcos era. There are technical arguments about where the "poverty line" should be drawn, but it is obvious that most Filipinos lack decent houses, can't afford education, in some areas are short of food, and in general are very poor. The official unemployment rate is about 15 percent, but if all the cigarette vendors, surplus bar girls, and other underemployed people are taken into account, something like half the human talent in the country must be unused.

In 1987, roughly one year into Corazon Aquino's term, I sat and talked with two foreign employees of the Asian Development Bank, which is the main international organization to keep its head-quarters in Manila. We met in a café off Roxas Boulevard, the once-elegant main drag that runs along the potentially beautiful Manila Bay. The bloom was just starting to go off the Aquino administration, and the men explained why they thought things were going to get worse and worse. They went down the checklist of the nation's possibilities, and why so few of them had turned out well—in terms that stood up remarkably well through the Aquino regime and the beginning of Ramos's term:

Manufacturing? "Well, there were not many viable sectors to begin with, and most of them were taken over by Marcos's cronies. The industrial sector is used to monopoly and high tariff protection. It's inward-looking, believes it cannot compete. People are used to paying a lot for goods that are okay-to-shoddy in quality. Labor costs are actually quite high for a country at this stage of development. They should be like Sri Lanka's but they're like Korea's. It's a poor country—but an expensive place to produce."

Agriculture? "It's been heavily skewed for fifty years to plantation crops. All those traditional exports are down." Agriculture was also nearly paralyzed by arguments over land ownership. Since the Spanish days land has been concentrated in a few giant haciendas, including the seventeen-thousand-acre Hacienda Luisita, owned by the Cojuangco family, of which Corazon Aquino was part, and no government had done much to change the pattern. Indeed, the moment of truth, when it became clear that Corazon Aquino would not save the Philippines, was when she decided very early in her term not to insist on land reform. She was regarded as a saint at the time—taxicabs in Manila had little Cory dolls next to their statues of Jesus or the Blessed Virgin—and could have rammed through anything she chose. But the landowners were her friends and relatives, and she declined to trouble them.

Services and other industries? "They're very much influenced by the political climate. I think this has tremendous potential as a tourist country—it's so beautiful. But they don't have many other ways to sell their labor, except the obvious one." The obvious one is the sex business, visible in every part of the country—and throughout Asia, where itinerant Filipino "entertainers" are a familiar and humiliating phenomenon. In Davao City, on the southern island of Mindanao, I watched TV one night and saw an ad repeated over and over. Women wanted for opportunities overseas. Qualifications: taller than five feet two inches, younger than twenty-one. When I took cabs in Manila, the drivers routinely inquired if I wanted a woman. When my wife returned our children's rented inner tubes to a beach vendor at Argao, the vendor, a toothless old woman, asked if she was lonely in her room and needed a hired companion. In 1990, when Iraq invaded Kuwait, the two other countries that suffered most severe damage were Bangladesh and the Philippines. Each had relied heavily on the remittances of hundreds of thousands of expatriate workers in the oil countries, many of whom lost their jobs in the tumult.

Resources? "Exploiting natural resources has always been the base here," one of my economist friends said. "But they've taken every tree they can easily get. It's not like Brazil or Borneo, with another fifty years to rip out the heart of the earth." The Philippines has more naturally spectacular mountains and vistas than Malaysia or Indonesia, but you can travel for miles in the countryside and mainly see eroding hillsides stripped bare of trees.

One of the bankers went on: "Geographically, the country is fractured beyond belief. The most controllable area is right around Manila, but beyond that the government's writ has never run very far." For instance, the newspapers that blanket Manila have virtually no circulation in the rest of the country: among a population of some 60 million, the combined readership of all twenty-plus daily papers is about 5 million. "The education system has run down terribly." The Philippines spends about one eighth as much money per student as Malaysia does. "The $15 billion to $20 billion that Marcos creamed off has had a big effect. There's a kind of corruption that just recycles the money, but all this was taken out.

"And then you have population growth, which is closer to 3 percent than 2.5, even though the government says 2.2. The population could go over 100 million in fifteen years. Since the economy doesn't grow that fast, the per capita income keeps falling." Most people I met in the Philippines asked me how many children I had. When I told them, the normal response was, "Only two!" By the end of my stay I was experimenting, raising the number to test the response. "Only six!" a priest told me on my last day. There are parts of the world in which the more-the-merrier view of population, advanced by the economist Julian Simon, makes good sense. (In his book *The Ultimate Resource,* Simon, of the University of Maryland, argued that population growth ultimately solves environmental problems, rather than aggravating them, because people keep coming up with the innovations that remove resource constraints.) The United States, for instance, probably grows richer per capita when it lets in ambitious immigrants. But I suspect that even Simon's faith might be strained by a trip to the Philippines. In urban squatter areas parents would tell me that they'd been able to send the first five or six children to school but had had to stop educating numbers seven through twelve. Many of these children drift around Manila, begging or shooting baskets at makeshift backboards.

One of my economists concluded, "All in all, you'd have to say it's a worrisome situation."

The war of each against all. You'd have to say something more than that. Most of the time I spent in the Philippines, I walked around feeling angry—angry at myself when I brushed off the latest platoon of child beggars, angry at the beggars when I did give in, angry at the rich Filipinos for living behind high walls and guardhouses in the fortified Makati compounds euphemistically called "villages," angry as I picked my way among piles of human feces left by homeless families living near the Philippine Navy headquarters on Roxas Boulevard, angry at the society that had degenerated into a war of each against all.

Smoky Mountain is, I will confess, a clichéd illustration of the miseries of the modern Philippines, but when I first saw it in 1987 I thought it reinforced an important and less-clichéd point. The "mountain" was an enormous heap of garbage, forty acres in size and perhaps eighty feet high, in the port district north of Manila, and it had been home for years to some fifteen thousand Filipinos. (Six years later, the Philippine government closed Smoky Mountain as a dump site and drove off the squatters. "I have no doubt that you will rise from this pile of garbage to become better Filipinos," President Fidel Ramos said at a ceremony formally closing the mountain on May 1, 1993.) Living there was obviously miserable: the smell of a vast city's rotting garbage was so rank and powerful that I could not breathe through my nose without gagging. I did finally retch when I felt my foot sink into something soft and saw that I'd stepped on a discarded, half-full blood-transfusion bag from a hospital, which was now emitting a dark, clotted ooze. "I have been going to the dump site for over ten years now and I still have not gotten used to the smell," Father Benigno Beltran, a young *Mod*

Squad-type Dominican priest who worked in Smoky Mountain, wrote in an article. "The place becomes infested with millions of flies that often get into the chalice when I say Mass. The smell makes you deaf as it hits you like a blow to the solar plexus."

The significance of Smoky Mountain, however, was not how bad it was but how good. People lived and worked in the garbage heap, and they said they felt lucky to do so. Smoky Mountain was the center of an elaborate scavenging-and-recycling industry that had many tiers and many specialized functional groups. As night fell in Manila, hundreds of scavengers, nearly all men, started walking out from Smoky Mountain pushing big wooden carts, about eight feet long and shaped like children's wagons, in front of them. They spent all night crisscrossing the town, picking through the curbside garbage dumps and looking for the most valuable items: glass bottles and metal cans. At dawn they pushed their carts back to Smoky Mountain, where they would sell what they'd found to middlemen, who owned fleets of carts and bailed out their suppliers when they were picked up by the police.

Other scavengers worked the garbage over once city trucks had collected it and brought it in. Some looked for old plastic bags, some for rubber, some for bones that could be ground up for animal feed. In the late afternoon at Smoky Mountain I could easily imagine I'd had my preview of hell. I stood on the summit, looking into the lowlands where trucks kept bringing new garbage and several bulldozers were at work, plowing through heaps of old, black garbage. I'd heard of spontaneous combustion but had never believed in it until I saw the old garbage steam and smoke as it was exposed to the air. Inches behind the bulldozers, sometimes riding in the scoops, were about twenty little children carrying baskets, as if at the beach. They darted among the machines and picked out valuables that had been newly revealed. "It's hard to get them to go to school," a man in his mid-twenties who lived there told me. "They can make 20 to 30 pesos a day this way"—$1 to $1.50. "Here the money is so good."

The residents of Smoky Mountain were mainly Visayans, who had come from the islands of Leyte, Negros, and Cebu in the Visayas region of the Philippines. From time to time the government, in its embarrassment, had attempted to move them off the mountain, but until the final closure of the mountain in 1993, they kept coming back. A real community had grown up in the garbage dump, with the tight family bonds that hold together other Filipino *barangays*, or neighborhoods.

The people of Smoky Mountain complained about land-tenure problems—they wanted the city to give them title to the land on which they've built their shacks—but the dozen or two I spoke with seemed very cheerful about their community and their lives. As I trudged down from the summit of the mountain, having watched little boys dart among the bulldozers, I passed the community center. It was full of little girls sitting in a circle and singing nursery-school songs with glee. If I hadn't come at the last minute, I would have suspected Father Beltran, the young priest who was organizing the community, of putting on a Potemkin Village show.

The bizarre good cheer of Smoky Mountain undoubtedly said a lot about the Filipinos' spiritual resilience. But like the sex industry, which is also fairly cheerful, it said something depressing about the other choices people have. When I was in one of the countless squatter villages in Manila, talking with people who'd built houses out of plywood and scavenged sheet metal, and who lived eight to a room, I assumed it must be better to be poor out in the countryside, where at least you had some space and clean air to breathe. Obviously I was being romantic. Back home there was no way to earn money, and even in Smoky Mountain people were only a four-cent jeepney ride away from the amusements of the big city.

In Smoky Mountain and the other squatter districts I couldn't help myself. I kept dwelling on the other cliché of Philippine life: the contrast with the opposite extreme of the nation's life. The contrast is relatively hard to see in Manila itself, since so much of the town's wealth is walled up in the fortified "villages." But one day in the warm Philippine winter, just hours after I'd listened to scavengers explain why some grades of animal bone were worth more on the resale market than others, I tagged along with a friend and visited one of Manila's rich young families in the mountains outside town.

To enter the house we had to talk our way past a rifle-carrying security guard—a standard fixture not only of upper-class areas in Manila but also of banks, office buildings, McDonald's—and then follow a long, twisting driveway to a mountaintop palace. The family was, of course, from old money; they were also well educated, public-spirited, sincere. But I spent my day with them in an ill-concealed sulk, wandering from room to room and estimating how many zillions of dollars had been sunk into the artwork, furniture, and fixtures. We ate lunch on the patio, four maids in white dresses standing at attention a few paces off, each bearing a platter of food and ready to respond instantly when we wanted more. Another maid stood behind my chair, leaning over the table and waving a fan back and forth to drive off any flies. As we ate I noticed a strange rat-a-tat sound from inside the house, as if several reporters had set up a city room and were pounding away on old Underwoods. When we finished our dessert and went inside, I saw the explanation: another two or three uniformed servants were stationed inside the cathedral-like living room, incessantly twitching their fly swatters against the walls.

Am I shooting fish in a barrel? Of course. You could easily work up a more depressing contrast between life on the Upper East Side of Manhattan and life in the South Bronx. If you were Tom Wolfe you might even make this contrast into a book. But that would mean only that America and the Philippines share a terrible problem, not that extremes of wealth and poverty are no problem at all. While the South Bronx is an American problem, few people would think of it as being truly typical of America. In the Philippines, the contrasting extremes have been and remain the norm.

Why? What went wrong? It is harder fully to account for the sadness of the Philippines than for the rise of Korea or Japan. This is partly because fewer people are attracted to a failure or feel they have a stake in deducing what its "lessons" might be. Nonetheless, the explanations for the Philippines' long slide generally fall into three categories. The blame lies, respectively, with (a) the Marcos family, (b) the United States and international bankers, or (c) God Himself. Each of these hypotheses turns out to have shortcomings, which brings another set of explanations into view.

Blaming the Marcoses. The case for blaming the Marcoses is obvious. In their nearly two decades in power they removed many billions of dollars, with few dollars to spare. Whenever you come across a crumbling, white-elephant, once-luxurious hotel or convention center in some inappropriate corner of the Philippines, you can bet it was put up by the Marcoses to suit Imelda's vision of national grandeur and to enrich the Marcoses and their cronies.

In the fall of 1990 I went on a long driving trip with F. Sionil José, one of the country's premier men of letters, and a young Russian scholar named Victor Sumsky, to the Ilocos region, whence Marcos had sprung. "The Ilocos," as it is usually called, constitutes the band of habitable land along the northwestern shore of the island of Luzon. On one side is the sea; on the other side are the steep, blue-green Cordillera Mountains; and in between are the neat gardens and intensively farmed plots of the Ilokano people.

A severe earthquake had just struck Luzon, and in each village the devastation seemed to be worse than the next. Thick-walled church towers, built by Augustinian friars centuries before (actually, built by Ilokano work gangs under the friars' control), had toppled from the shock. But as we turned inland, across Marcos Highway, we came across a huge concrete bust of Marcos's head, looming like a surreal Mount Rushmore out of the jungle hillside. A few miles farther north, near the northern tip of Luzon, we came over a rise—and before us sat "Fort Ilocandia," a vast, lavish resort set in the middle of nowhere. The sight was as incongruous as coming across London Bridge at Lake Havasu in Arizona (which is where it now stands). The closest settlement to the resort was a little hamlet that Marcos considered his hometown. It was completely refurbished for his daughter's wedding, which is when the doomed resort was also built. Through the hundreds of rooms of the hotel the wind whistled and a few nicely uniformed bellhops wandered around. We had breakfast there, along with two Mormon missionaries. Otherwise the resort was deserted—its golf course, its swimming pools, the casinos to which it had hoped to attract the Taiwanese rich.

Still, for all the damage the Marcoses did, it is hard to contend that they caused the country's problems, as opposed to intensifying them. The strongest evidence lies, perversely, in the record of their successor Corazon Aquino. She had a record for scrupulous personal honesty, but in a sense it didn't matter. While she was not corrupt, many around her were, and the downward spiral continued at a somewhat slower rate.

Aquino's triumph over Marcos in the "snap election" of February 1986 was more heroic and inspiring than it came to look in retrospect, when so many of the country's problems remained unsolved. Through the late 1980s the sight of an oppressed population pouring onto city streets, demanding rights, became a staple of the international TV news. From Seoul, from Berlin, from Moscow and Beijing came shots of people standing up for their rights. They stood up first in Manila. The moment was known in the Philippines as the "EDSA Revolution," for Epifano de los Santos Avenue, where hundreds of thousands of ordinary citizens gathered to bear witness against Marcos—and, not incidentally, to make it more difficult for tanks to roll through town. "It was perhaps the only time in this nation's history when there was democracy as it is understood in the West," F. Sionil José, a novelist known throughout the Philippines as "Frankie," wrote six years after the event. "The poor, the middle class, and the elite were there as equals. In a sense it was a truly democratic 'revolution' but Cory made it into a restoration of the oligarchy."[10]

Indeed she did. Politically the removal of Marcos was a revolution, but in sociological terms the coming of Aquino amounted to the restoration of an old order. To the Philippine aristocracy Marcos had been a usurper. His rise represented the triumph of the *nouveaux riches*. Many of the cronies he enriched were also outsiders to the old-money, old-family elite who had long dominated the country's politics. The elite groups were often referred to in shorthand by the name of a business district, "Makati," much as the Washington liberal elite is referred to as "Georgetown." Their attitude toward Marcos had much in common with Georgetown's view of Richard Nixon: clever and ambitious, but so uncouth!

When Corazon Aquino replaced Marcos, it was therefore as if Katharine Graham, having driven Richard Nixon from office through her newspaper, had succeeded him as president—or Jackie Kennedy, or Mrs. C. Douglas Dillon III. The traditional upper class was back in its traditional place.

Bad as the Marcoses had become by the end of the day, they had not been unalloyed demons throughout their regime. Again much like Richard Nixon, Ferdinand Marcos was always considered shrewd and serious, interested in land reform and economic progress for his first few years. Moreover, if his family's personal corruption were the main source of the country's woes, why weren't all the neighboring countries going downhill, too? The Suharto family in Indonesia probably rivaled the Marcoses in the scale of their personal fortune, although to be fair Suharto had three times as populous a country to work with. Except perhaps for Lee Kuan Yew's Singapore, every East Asian country supports some form of kleptocratic regime. It was in Japan, after all, that the main boss of the Liberal Democratic Party was discovered with gold bullion worth at least $40 million in his house. Simply on grounds of logic, some other factor must distinguish the Philippines.

Blaming the United States and international bankers. This line of analysis is popular in the Philippines but is more easily disposed of. Through the late years of the Marcos regime the Philippines found itself in the same bind as countless countries in Latin America and Africa. As fast as it could sell its pineapples, bananas, sugarcane, and copra, it fell farther and farther behind on debt payments to international banks. Soon after Corazon Aquino took office, the director of the Philippine economic development office, Solita Monsod, pointed out that the country was scheduled to pay $18 billion more in interest on Marcos-era loans over the next six years than it expected to receive in foreign aid.

Most of the banks receiving the interest—or, as it's often described in the Philippine press, sucking the blood—have been American. It is a short step to the conclusion that the United States in general has been deliberately manipulating Philippine politics for its own convenience.

This line of reasoning has history on its side. When Philippine nationalist forces under Emilio Aguinaldo were fighting for independence against Spain in 1898, the U.S. military lured him into a bogus alliance. Once the Spanish were out of the way, the United States turned on Aguinaldo and conquered the country. The United States belatedly agreed to Philippine independence after World War II, yet the U.S. ambassador, working from his huge office on Roxas Boulevard, has been a kind of copresident for many years.

The weakness of this second explanation is like that of the first. Nearly every country in East Asia has relied on World Bank funding. Japan was still using it in the 1960s to complete the bullet train. Everyone has incurred interest obligations; somehow in the Philippines the money was put to worse use. Similarly, the United States played a heavy role in the politics of many of these countries, perhaps nowhere more than in Japan itself during the Occupation years. Something else must be involved.

Blaming God. The most puzzling question about the Philippine failure was whether it proved the existence of God—a nasty, vengeful God whom the Filipinos, along with Bangladeshis and Somalis, had somehow wronged and whom the Japanese had pleased, so that He kept postponing the devastating earthquake for which Tokyo is overdue. Through the late 1980s the Philippines suffered typhoons. In the summer of 1990 the main island, Luzon, was rocked by a catastrophic earthquake. Massive-walled churches that had stood for centuries, since the time of the Augustinian friars, cracked and collapsed. A modern five-story hotel in the resort town of Baguio caved in, producing a heap that looked like a collapsed house of cards. Baguio itself, which the country had thought of as its sophisticated hillside resort, became a shantytown, with families making tents out of plastic bags and living along hillsides in the constant drizzling mist. A few months later, Mount Pinatubo erupted, bring-ing the nasty, ongoing debate about the future of the U.S. military bases to an unexpected end. One week, American officials had been saying that it would be impossible to replace the Crow Valley Weap-ons Range at Clark Air Force Base, where pilots could practice bombing and missile-attack runs on the best facilities outside the United States. The following week, buildings at Clark were so heav-ily laden with Pinatubo's ashes that walls buckled and ceilings caved in. The U.S. Air Force declared the base irreparably damaged and decided to go home. It was as if, in the middle of bitter American debates about abortion, all women were suddenly rendered infertile by a plague from God. There was nothing left to argue about, yet no one really felt happy about the results.

The spiritual and supernatural element is closer to the surface of Philippine politics than in many other nations. Nancy Reagan consulted an astrologer but did not publicize this fact; routinely people in the Philippines talk about "omens" and "miracles." Yet somehow this explanation, too, seems incomplete.

Blaming Rousseau. There is a fourth possibility, which takes us closer to the central arguments about the modern Asian system. In the eyes of many of its neighboring countries, the struggles of the Philippines reinforce the case against "excessive," "uncon-trolled," "Western-style" democracy.

What Americans have liked best about the Philippines has been its structural resemblance to the United States. It has a president and a congress. It has a supreme court building that would fit nicely into the architecture of Washington, D.C. Its school system was designed by Americans. Its favorite sport is basketball. The news, talk, and soap-opera programs on Philippine TV are closely copied from American models. The Philippine constitution guarantees free expression and individual rights.

These very traits, in the opinion of many Asian neighbors, are precisely the problem. The Philippines, as Lee Kuan Yew and others contend, has taken on the "luxury" of a rights-based political system that its economic base cannot yet support.

Americans have asssumed, and have told Filipinos for decades, that economic progress and political liberties are closely intertwined. For people to progress materially, they must be free politically. It is almost impossible, according to American-style political theory, to give one form of progress precedence over the other. Societies should emphasize both at once.

The issue seems less complicated from the East Asian perspective. In almost every country in East Asia except the Philippines, the choice has been clear: economic progress, and the resulting national strength, come first. Full political liberties may or may not ever come, at least not in the individually oriented Western style. If they do come, it is only after the main economic problems have been solved.

"How does a backward country like Korea make an economic miracle?" Robert Elegant asked in his book *Pacific Destiny*. "The one-word answer is *authoritarianism*." The two-or-more-word answer would, of course, involve a broader and subtler range of influences, as Elegant pointed out: "Other factors have been essential: the Confucian heritage, the technocrats, entrepreneurship, resentment of poverty and inferiority, and the compulsion to self-improvement." But every successful East Asian economy has clearly decided to put political liberty second to economic development, and sometimes even farther down the priority list. "Despite some liberalization, no Asian country is moving toward Western-style liberal democracy," Elegant concluded.

It would be too simple, and incorrect, to say that strongman governments by themselves produce economic progress. If so, Leonid Brezhnev and Mao Tse-tung would have presided over economic miracles of their own. It is, similarly, too simple, and incorrect, to say that state intervention has caused the East Asian economic boom. The genius of the Japanese-style approach, which most other nations in the region have tried to emulate, is its intermingling of state and market, its balance of authoritarian controls and laissez-faire.

In making economic policy, successful East Asian governments have intervened (as Chapters Two and Five showed) to resolve the big questions. What industries should we emphasize? How much money must our people save? Then the government has turned things over to the market—struggles between Toyota and Nissan, competition against producers in North America and Europe—to carry out the plans. A version of this balance has applied in politics. Successful Asian governments have placed certain large issues off-bounds for democratic decision. There is no functioning two-party system in any of these countries; the school systems are unashamed vehicles of teaching "productive virtues" rather than "individual fulfillment"; day-by-day policies are set either by bureaucrats or military officials who are insulated from public control. Political leaders tend to stay in office for decades—except in Japan, where the nominal head of the government, the prime minister, has so little influence that quick turnover does no harm. Yet none of these systems is totalitarian. As long as the state's power is unchallenged for the big decisions, individuals can more or less go their way in peace.

The exception to this mixed political formula is the Philippines. There the guiding theory, imported from America, has been: Rights and liberties first. Whatever follows, second. In practice, of course, the Philippines has had an abundant share of authoritarianism, yet the ideal has been that of rights and liberties. The chaos and decay of Manila, combined with the daily news stories about chaos and decay in the United States, increasingly fortify Asian governments in the view that a "rights-based" society represents a failed approach. The government of Singapore has led the rhetorical charge for this view. Late in 1992, Lee Kuan Yew traveled to Manila and told his hosts that an overemphasis on "rights" had made them poor.[11]

What is it, specifically, that "authoritarianism" has given to many East Asian countries but that rights-based, "American-style" democracy has denied to the Philippines? It can best be thought of as a useful kind of "nationalism." East Asia's economic catch-up over the past century has fundamentally had a political, rather than a purely economic, root. First Japan, then the other countries in succession, have struggled for ways to apply technology and develop industries so as to avoid weakness relative to other *nations*—not "markets," not "companies"—in the world. The function of authoritarian rule has been to see that certain national interests are served, interests that might not automatically emerge from the play of market forces or the individual pursuit of happiness.

In its report on the "East Asian miracle" economies, issued in 1993, the World Bank generally emphasized their fidelity to the free-market principles that bank representatives had been recommending for years. But it also pointed out that certain "institutional traits" had been crucial to the success of Japan, Korea, Taiwan, and Singapore. "Foremost among [these traits] is technocratic insulation—the ability of economic technocrats to formulate and implement policies . . . with a minimum of lobbying for special favors from politicians and interest groups."[12] That is, the bureaucracies needed to be protected from excessively democratic rule. Sweeping land-reform programs had also been indispensable in the growth of Japan, Korea, and Taiwan, the report said. "In each of these instances, land reform was backed and in some cases actively guided by U.S. officials who had little interest in protecting the landed elites."[13]

Because the United States had not interfered so directly in Philippine self-government, the Bank's report added, the normal lobbying of the landed interests kept the Philippines from ever enacting land reform.

The idea of a national economic interest has provided a way to limit feuds within bureacracies or among regions of a country before they threaten the collective welfare. The most obvious exception illustrates the rule: Items one through ten on Malaysia's list of economic obstacles all involve the racial divide that usually keeps its component groups from having a sense of "national" interest. Korea has come close to the same problem since loosening its political regime. The showdowns between labor and management, and the longstanding jealousies among the regions of the country, have posed serious obstacles to its plans to modernize, export, and invest. The authoritarian/nationalist regimes have offered the bargain of rapid economic progress for reduced political liberties. This bargain has been manifestly acceptable to most people in the region.

Blaming . . . ourselves? Why has this bargain not applied in the Philippines? Why, instead of authoritarianism, did it get despotism near the end of the Marcos regime? I think that the phenomenon is principally cultural and involves a failure of nationalism. If the economic story of modern East Asia is basically a story of national ambitions, fears, and resentments, then it would make sense that the distortion or lack of those ambitions could put one country on a different path from all the rest.

Nationalism, as distinct from "factionalism" or "sectarianism," can imply a unifying rather than a divisive impulse. Nationalism is divisive when it pits French against Germans or Koreans against Japanese, but it can be unifying if it helps transcend loyalties that are even narrower and more fragmented. When a country with extreme geographic, tribal, and social-class differences, like the Philippines, has only a weak sense of national unity, its public life does become the war of each against all.

As a working definition, "nationalism" gives people a guideline for distinguishing "us" from "them." In an ideal world, all of humanity, plus the earth's flora and fauna, would always be seen as "us." In the real world, individuals and societies must decide where to draw the line each day. Japan is divided into countless "us" groups, from the family to the classroom units known as *kumi* to the work group to the firm. Yet ultimately the society insists on the difference between "we Japanese" and everyone else, which provides a rationale for pulling together when "we Japanese" are challenged from outside.

Individual Filipinos are at least as brave, kind, and noble-spirited as individual Japanese, but their culture draws the boundaries of decent treatment much more narrowly. Because these boundaries are limited to the family or tribe, they exclude at any given moment 99 percent of the other people in the country. Because of this fragmentation, this lack of useful nationalism, people treat each other worse in the Philippines than in any other Asian country I have seen.

This judgment would, of course, be bitterly disputed by many Filipinos—and was when I expressed a version of it in a magazine article in 1988. But for more than a hundred years certain traits have turned up in domestic descriptions and foreign observations of Philippine society. The tradition of political corruption and cronyism, the extremes of wealth and poverty, the tribal fragmentation, the local elite's willingness to make a separate profitable peace with colonial powers—all reflect a feeble sense of national interest. Practically everything that is public in the Philippines seems neglected or abused. On many street corners in downtown Manila, an unwary step can mean a broken leg. Holes two feet square and five feet deep lurk just beyond the curb; they are supposed to be covered by metal grates, but scavengers have taken the grates to sell for scrap.

The four hundred years that the Philippines spent under Spain's thumb obviously left a lasting imprint: at first glance, the country seems to have much more in common with Mexico or Guatemala than with any other place in Asia. The Spanish hammered home the idea of Filipino racial inferiority, discouraging the native Indios from learning the Spanish language and refusing to consecrate them as priests. The Spanish rulers also took a step that set the stage for the country's economic problems in the twentieth century, giving out huge haciendas to royal favorites and consigning others to work as serfs. As in Latin America, the Spanish thereby implanted the idea that "success" meant landed, idle (that is, nonentrepreneurial or commercial) wealth.

On top of the Spanish legacy came the distorting effects of the Philippines' encounter with the United States. The United States officially ruled the Philippines for forty-eight years, from 1898 to 1946. As a colonial ruler the United States undeniably brought many benefits to the Philippines: schools, hospitals, laws, and courts. Many older Filipinos still speak with fondness about the orderly old colonial days. But American rule seemed to intensify the Philippine sense of dependence. The United States quickly earned or bought the loyalty of the *ilustrados,* the educated upper class, making them into what we would call collaborationists if the Germans or Japanese had received their favors during World War II. It rammed through a number of laws insisting on free "competition" between American and Philippine industries, at a time when Philippine industries were in no position to compete with anyone.

During World War II, Filipinos fought heroically against the Japanese. After the war the United States "gave" the Philippines its independence and was in most measurable ways its benefactor, offering aid, investing in businesses, providing the second-largest payroll in the country at its military bases. But in unmeasurable, intangible ways it seems to have eroded confidence even further, leaving Filipinos to believe that they aren't really responsible for their country's fate. Whether I was talking with Marcos-loving right-wingers or with Communists who hated the United States, whether the discussion was about economics or the U.S. bases or the course of the guerrilla war, most of my conversations in the Philippines ended on the same discouraging note. "Of course, it's not really up to us," a soldier or politician or Communist would tell me. "We have to wait and see what the Americans have in mind." In the mid-1980s the central bank proudly issued a new 100-peso bill. It depicted the dramatic moment on the nation's independence day, July 4, 1946, when the Philippine flag went up and the American flag went down. Anyone glancing at the bill would suppose it to be American, since its most prominent features, in red, white, and blue, are the Stars and Stripes.

"This is a country where the national ambition is to change your nationality," an American who volunteers in Smoky Mountain told me in 1987. The U.S. Navy accepted about 400 Filipino recruits per year at that time; in the year of the EDSA Revolution, 100,000 people applied. "You are dealing here with a damaged culture," four people told me, in more or less the same words, in different interviews. The nationalistic excesses of some other East Asian countries seem more understandable, when you see what an absence of nationalism can do.

Bases of discontent. The Philippines cannot undo its history, but in a peculiar way it may have been delivered from it. From the moment I set foot in the country in 1986, I seemed to hear about "the bases" whenever I asked anyone about anything. "The bases" were the U.S. Navy's vast installation at Subic Bay, a beautiful natural harbor to the west of Manila, and Clark Air Force Base, near Angeles City north of the capital. The American military operated a handful of other, smaller facilities, but Clark and Subic were the focuses of the debate.

The disagreement over Clark and Subic was a perfect illustration of left-brain vs. right-brain thinking, the objective versus the subjective realm. Every bit of "hard," analytical evidence weighed in favor of keeping the bases where they were. From every measurable, material perspective it was a "win-win" situation, beneficial for both sides. As long as the U.S. Navy wanted to operate in the Pacific, it would prefer Subic Bay to almost any other port site. The harbor was a perfectly shaped natural lagoon, sheltered from the strongest storms and deep enough for the biggest ships. In the nine decades since it had taken the bay from the Spanish, the Navy had invested tens of millions of dollars in equipment and improvements. The work force was large, competent, and loyal—and its rates of pay were a tiny fraction of what the Navy was charged at its nearest overseas base, in Yokosuka, Japan. From Subic, ships could easily sail southwest to the Strait of Malacca and go on to the Indian Ocean—or north, along the sea lanes to Japan. The community of Olongopo, surrounding the base, had shaped its whole economy to provide the things a navy wants when in port.

Clark, where the U.S. Army Air Force had been caught on the ground on December 8, 1941, was a less impressive natural wonder than Subic Bay. But it had one enormous and seemingly irreplaceable attraction to a modern air force: its sixty-four-thousand-square hectares included the Crow Valley Weapons Range, one of the few places outside Nevada in which aviators could train with live ordnance, shooting any kind of missile or bomb at targets and having their results judged by advanced instrumentation.[14]

From the Philippines' point of view, the advantages of the bases seemed equally obvious. First, they meant work. Clark and Subic directly employed about sixty-five thousand people, at wages that were very high by local standards. Indirectly the bases created at least a hundred thousand more jobs. In the early 1980s the RAND Corporation calculated that the payrolls from the bases made up 4 percent of the Philippine national product. The overall economy shrank after that, so the proportion went up. Second, the United States paid for the bases. Although American policy forbade the payment of "rent" to military allies, the U.S. government contributed roughly $250 million per year in "Economic Support Fund" payments to the Philippines. Perhaps more important, the presence of the bases spared the Philippines the cost of a military establishment comparable to those of its neighbors. Singapore, Malaysia, and other countries in the region spent 3 to 4 percent of their GNP on the military. The Philippines, facing a more serious insurgency threat than any of these countries, spent only about 1 percent. U.S. military aid, which was separate from Economic Support Fund payments, covered more than half the operating cost of the Philippine military.

All that was on the left side of the brain, the side that is supposed to be rational. Through the 1980s such arguments were enough to keep the United States interested in renewing the base agreement, and the Philippine public agreeable, by margins of 60 to 40 percent in most opinion polls. But you did not have to be in the Philippines very long to understand the appeal of concepts from the right side of the brain. The closest comparison was to prostitution: it was in the rational interest of each party, but it did not make them feel proud.

Logical or not, the mere existence of the bases both symbolized and aggravated the crippling Philippine sense of dependence on the United States. Nationalists in Greece, Spain, or Scotland might agitate against "neocolonialism" in the form of U.S. bases. The difference is that the Philippines actually had been an American colony, and many people seemed unable to move past that fact as long as the bases were there. More than forty years after they theoretically gained independence, Filipinos still talked as if they were helpless to control their own fate. It was hard to see how the country could ever stop deteriorating until it changed this mood.

"In 1966 I wrote an article paraphrasing Max Lerner, who said that America needed to cut the British down to brotherly size in order to use the British heritage in its drive to greatness," Raul Manglapus told me in Manila late in 1986, just before Corazon Aquino appointed him foreign minister. "We have to cut the American father down to brotherly size if we are to mature. The bases agreement is part of what we must change. It has had a profound effect on the psychology of our people."

The Philippine attitude toward America during this period was normally described as a "love-hate relationship," but the "love" seemed closely intertwined, often in the same person, with envy, suspicion, and resentment of America, precisely because the two countries cannot deal as equals.

Because Filipinos spent so much more time thinking about the United States than the other way around, and because so many Filipinos had convinced themselves that the United States would do whatever it took to retain control over the "irreplaceable" bases, the bases came to seem a symbol of fatalism and helplessness in the face of America's devious plans.

"It would have been easier if the Americans were just sons of bitches," F. Sionil José had told me the first time I met him, early in 1987, a year after the fall of Marcos. "Then we could have just kicked them out with no regrets, like the Indonesians did to the Dutch. Now the Indonesians can talk with the Dutch very directly. 'We kicked you in the ass. It's over.' It's still all very complicated and jealous here."

José reminisced, at that point, about the time more than three decades earlier when he had met Robert Frost. It was 1955. José was barely thirty and had already published a novel called *The Pretenders,* which remains one of the most admired books in the country's literature. He was visiting the United States and had talked for thirty minutes with Frost at his New England farm. The two men went walking in the woods, and were still talking three hours later.

Frost told José that he'd always admired Emilio Aguinaldo, the Philippine soldier who with American encouragement led an uprising against the Spanish in 1898, only to be turned on and beaten by the Americans once the Spanish were gone. "Robert Frost wanted to know how his country had ruled in the Philippines," José told me. "What was the most important thing it had done?"

"I said, 'Without a doubt, Mr. Frost, it was the schools. If it hadn't been for the schools the Americans built, I would be on top of a water buffalo in my village today. We have that to be grateful for.' "

José, a short, jolly man whose face was flushed from whiskey, smiled to himself for a moment. "You think of the experience of Whitman, Emerson, Melville. They were responsible for the flowering of New England—but only after they rejected European romanticism. That is what we must do! We must reject the terrific cultural domination of this country by the United States and start working with what we have, no matter how little it might be, no matter how ignominious it might seem, no matter how insignificant it might be.

"At least in our minds, we have to kill the American father." At that time, with the bloom still on Mrs. Aquino, José was sure that his country could earn its maturity only by kicking out the Americans who had educated him.

Three years later, when I traveled with José through his native Ilocos region, he had become more fatalistic. "We should get rid of the bases—but where will the people work? Thousands of our people are working there, with families to support. How will we give them jobs?"

Through the early 1990s, the Philippine government was moving in the opposite direction. The Senate rang with more and more nationalistic declarations about the need to remove the American incubus. The U.S. government, in frustration, was also moving to the conclusion that the nearly century-long Fil-Am relationship must end. The Americans were tired of the bickering, tired of the dependence—and ready to consider other options, now that the Soviet Navy had gone away.

And then Mount Pinatubo erupted. All the arguments were moot. On November 26, 1991, Clark Air Force Base was returned to the Philippines. On September 30, 1992, the American flag was taken down at Subic Bay, and the U.S. naval base was closed. Day One of true Philippine independence had come. Perhaps it would be for the best.

Even in the ways they faltered, these three left-behind countries underscored the traits that the successful East Asian economies shared. Burma let its reaction against Western power go to self-destructive and paralyzing extremes, rather than converting the impulse into a tool for modernization, as many other Asian societies had done. The Vietnamese leaders eventually realized that all-out state control of the economy would lead to failure in Asia as surely as it had in the European Communist bloc. Like the leaders of China, they began experimenting to see how much market flexibility they could allow while still retaining political control. These Communist experiments were variations on the operating hypothesis of the East Asian system as a whole: that a mixture of liberties and controls could prove more successful than either a centrally run system or pure laissez-faire. The heartbreak of the Philippines, which is on paper Asia's closest approximation to a Western-style democracy, conformed to this hypothesis.

Two other countries attempted to apply the Asian formula without the difficulties that affect Burma, Vietnam, or the Philippines. The experiences of these countries, South Korea and Taiwan, reinforced both the power of the Asian model and Japan's preeminence in putting it into effect.

8

Contenders

Korea

IN 1987 I MADE MY FIRST VISIT to South Korea, after months of traveling and interviewing in Japan. Soon after my arrival an American friend who was working at the embassy in Seoul arranged a dinner at his house so I could meet several Korean men he knew and respected. One was a businessman, three were academics, and two were members of the national government's highly skilled bureaucracy.

As we sat down for drinks before dinner, the businessman began telling me about a new kind of personal computer his company was about to market. One of the government officials, who worked in the economic-planning agency, used this as a lead-in to the larger question of government-business interaction in Korea. When I heard him introduce this theme, I volunteered, "It sounds just like Japan." Before I could take another breath to elaborate on this thought, I saw faces turn stony around the room. Through the rest of the evening I felt the chill. I had broken the number one rule of etiquette for foreigners in Korea: I had reflexively measured it against Japan.

I thought of that offense five years later, when I had returned to the United States and saw the movie *A League of Their Own*. In the film a farming couple in the American Northwest introduce their two daughters to a visiting baseball scout. This, they say, pointing to the tall, beautiful young woman they obviously prefer, is our daughter Dottie. "And this is our other daughter. Dottie's sister."

In a fair world Korea would not be stuck in the role of Dottie's

sister, tagging along and trying to steal some of the spotlight from
the more glamourous older sibling, Japan. Korea's historic vanities
about its refinement, culture, and merit are at least as great as
Japan's. Its national museums display the elegant celadon bowls and
vases that were the models for cruder copies in Japan. Its temple
architecture obviously inspired some of the most celebrated Late
Heian era structures in Kyoto. During the Yi dynasty in Korea,
which lasted from before the time of Christoper Columbus to after
that of Queen Victoria, the intellectuals of the Korean court evolved
a Confucian doctrine purer and stricter than that applied in China.
One century before Copernicus made a dent in European mysticism,
Korea's revered King Sejong had commissioned the creation of *hangul,* the most systematic and logical writing system in the world.
The maddeningly arbitrary nature of written Japanese and Chinese
makes literacy a serious challenge even for native speakers. Without
knowing a word of spoken Korean, anyone can learn to sound out
the *hangul* in a day.

Yet Korea's history, like its present predicament, turns on the
fact that the world is not fair. In the days of the agreed-on Confucian
order in East Asia, in the era before the Europeans arrived and
shattered the old regimes, Korea was an appendage to the great
Chinese Middle Kingdom. Its leaders paid tribute to the Chinese
emperor's court, since otherwise China could crush and overwhelm
them at any time. The coming of modern warships and the industrial
age shortened the distance across the Tsushima and Korea straits,
which separate the southern tip of Korea from the northern coast
of Kyushu and which had for centuries discouraged invasions from
Japan. As Russia and America rose to world power, they exerted
their influence in and around Korea.

And as the world has focused more and more on postwar Asia's
economic boom, Korea has been unable to escape the "Dottie's
sister" role. Its best and worst luck boil down to the fact that it so
nearly resembles Japan. This is a blessing for Korea, in that the
ingredients of Japan's success can be more closely approximated in
Korea than anywhere else. It is a curse in that Korea can never be
as good a "Japan" as Japan itself is. It can never be as big as Japan
and can never enjoy the two decades of postwar sheltering Japan
received from the United States. It can never escape Japan's shadow
by applying the Japanese formula—but it probably cannot progress
by doing anything else.

Accounts of Korean history typically emphasize the role of *han,* a deep and a long-nursed resentment at the injustice of life's circumstances. Foreign businessmen, journalists, and economists must constantly compare the Korean economy to the Japanese, since they are so interconnected and structurally similar. In each country, highly skilled bureaucrats have worked with large industrial combines to coordinate development of promising technologies. In each country, the level of consumption has been held down, so more money would be available for industry. In each country, expanding the industrial base has been a political as much as a strictly economic goal. The comparisons are easy to tick off, yet each time I have made the mistake of doing so in conversing with Koreans, I believe I have seen a flash of *han* in the eyes.

In the economic story of modern Asia, therefore, Korea's experience mainly illustrates how powerful Japan and the Japanese model are. Yet there is more to East Asian ferment than industrialization alone, and this is where Korea's opportunity to step out of Japan's shadow may lie. In the realm of politics Korea has been not an imitator but a creator. If there is a challenge to the idea that Asian-style "democracy" will be lastingly more repressive than the Western model, it is to be found in Korea.

Korea is not Japan. There are differences between Korea's approach to life and Japan's, and they are not hard to find. From the emphasis on doing "the expected thing" to the propagation of national myths about "harmony" and "consensus," the Japanese system tries to apply a gloss of predictability and nonoffensiveness to its day-by-day operations. Korea operates more on what Americans of the 1990s would call the "in your face" principle. In Japan, Thailand, or Malaysia I would shrink in horror when I accidentally bumped into someone aboard a bus or in a crowd. I knew I was reinforcing the impression of being another boorish and ill-disciplined Westerner, unable to control even his own gangly frame. In Korea, on the other hand, I felt as if people were deliberately altering their course along the sidewalk so they could slam their shoulders into mine when our paths crossed. When I wasn't quick enough to avoid a collision, the person who'd made contact would often glare back as if to say, "I'm tough. How about you?"

In a broader sense today's Korea seems to encourage the head-to-head confrontations, the public displays of emotion, that are shunned in Japan, Malaysia, or Indonesia. In the mid-1980s a professor from Seoul National University made up a list of traits that, in his view, constituted the "Korean national character." This list suffered from the overgeneralization that affects any such exercise, but in a gross sense it rang true. The essential "national" traits, according to the professor, Kim Kyong-Dong, included some that would apply in much of East Asia—for instance, "authoritarianism, placing strong emphasis on hierarchical relationships and order in terms of parent-child, elder-youth," or "emphasis on saving one's own or other's face and on moral pretext rather than the deep sense of ethical rightness." But many other elements emphasized how different Korea feels from Japan, since Koreans, according to Professor Kim, are:

- "extremely emotional";
- "weak in the spirit of obeying laws";
- [given to] "unusual hospitality, excessive, often irritating kindness even causing encroachment of privacy";
- "related to the above tendency is a lack of refinement in interpersonal behavior, rather crude and even offensive despite good intentions";
- "extravagant life-style, spendthrift and lazy behavior";
- "heavy eating and drinking, voracity";
- "everybody eligible wanting to become somebody by taking a position of authority."[1]

Professor Kim also stressed Koreans' intense interest in educational achievement, which may again sound like Japan but is different in a significant way. Japan has a broad and successful basic-education system but an unimpressive university establishment. Japan's most famous universities largely serve a credentialing purpose. By passing the tests necessary to get into a prestigious university, above all the University of Tokyo, Japanese students demonstrate that they are determined and hard-working. How the students do in college courses is, for most lines of work, less important than whether they are admitted to the right school. (This is one reason why so few Japanese students take undergraduate degrees overseas, including in the United States. Everyone in Japan knows what it means to be a "*Todai* man," that is, a graduate of the University of Tokyo, or a "Keio O.B.," an "old boy" from a prestigious private university like Keio. It is harder to fit foreign universities, even highly respected ones, into the Japanese status map.) The most prominent business and government officials in Japan do not have Ph.D.s.

In Korea, by contrast, to earn a Ph.D. is to guarantee that your parents will feel fulfilled. Korea has one third as many people as Japan but routinely produces more Ph.D.s. In 1987 I met an American friend in Seoul who had just received his Ph.D. and was rushing to the print shop to order a new set of business cards with the letters "Ph.D." after his name. I started to rib him about this ostentation, but in his view it was no joking matter at all. "Don't you know anything about this country?" he asked, peeved. "Leaving out a Ph.D. would be like leaving your general's stars off your uniform."

Japanese students have had no detectable role in their country's politics since the protests against the U.S.-Japan security treaty in 1960. Korean university students seem to be chronically on the warpath. Their protests set off the nationwide wave of demonstrations that eventually brought an end to military government in 1987, and on any given day the campuses of Yonsei or Seoul National universities ring with protest chants on a variety of subjects. During the 1987 convulsions, the students endlessly chanted a strong four-beat refrain, *TOK! JAE! TAH! DO!* This meant in effect "Throw the bums out"—or, in the more elaborate translation one student helpfully gave me, with a straight face, "Oppose President Chun Doo Hwan's dictatorship and his decision on April 13 to postpone constitutional reform until after the Olympic Games next year."

Since most Korean students, especially those at the elite universities who led the protests, end up being bureaucrats and businessmen like their parents, it would be tempting to write them off as spoiled brats. But they are apparently not seen that way by their countrymen, who take seriously the idea that "scholars," even baby ones, are the conscience of the nation and should stand up to right wrongs. Through the summer of 1987, Seoul was filled with tear gas night after night as crowds of students threw bricks and Molotov cocktails at squadrons of police. A sociologist would have sized up the scene as class war: the most privileged young people in the nation, university students, were taunting the blue-collar policemen and the draftees in the military's special riot police. (Because military service is mandatory for Korean young men, some of the riot policemen were recent university graduates themselves.) But most Koreans I interviewed seemed totally uncynical about the students' advantages and praised the righteousness of their stand.

Behind this attitude lay not only a history of student-led protest in the twentieth century—against the Japanese occupiers before independence and against various authoritarian rulers afterward—but also Korea's extreme version of the general Confucian reverence for scholarship. Near the end of the nineteenth century, when Japan

was already modernizing and Korea was in the terminal stage of the
Yi dynasty, the Confucian emphasis on scholarship had reached a
stagnant dead end. The practical-minded men of Meiji Japan set
about learning how to make steel and build engines; Korea's scholars
hoped the Western barbarians would go back to their caves.

But Korea is like Japan. Countless atmospheric details mean
that even as you are being reminded how different Korea is from
Japan, you can't help thinking that the two systems are pretty much
the same. Indeed, the resemblances between the Japanese and Korean approaches to modernization are so deep and vast that Koreans
who have not been to Japan often fail to recognize them. Most are
marks left on Korea during the Japanese colonial era, which ran
from 1910, when Japan formally annexed Korea as a colony, until
1945, when the Imperial Japanese Army was driven home in defeat.
Japan had taken colonial control of Taiwan in 1895, after scoring its
first military victory in the region with a defeat of the Chinese fleet.
Ten years later, after routing the czar's Russian fleet, Japan asserted
control over the southern half of Sakhalin Island and made Korea
a "protectorate."

Japan's rule was brutal and resented in many ways. Its Korean
subjects were not merely taught Japanese, as Burmese and Filipinos
were taught English during their colonial years; Koreans were forbidden to speak the Korean language in public and were given new
Japanese names. In 1986 I met one of Korea's leading novelists and
asked her, at dinner, about relations between the two countries. She
sat silent for a minute and then spat out, in Japanese, "Watashi no
namae wa Matsuda Yoshiko desu"—"My name is Yoshiko Matsuda," the name she had been assigned as a schoolgirl near the end
of the Japanese rule. I asked her how long it had taken to switch
schools, businesses, and family life back to Korean-language operation, once the Japanese left. "About five minutes," she said.

Yet beneath the obvious resentment are more ambiguous feelings. Many people in Korea, at least, know that they and the Japanese are more alike than either group usually wants to admit. Many
of the traits that make today's Korea successful look very familiar
to anyone who has been in Japan. The schoolchildren wear similar
uniforms and are trained in school systems much like Japan's. The
big Korean industrial combines are structured remarkably like those
in Japan. The office buildings in Korea are laid out in a fashion
unlike that of a typical Western office but practically identical to
that of offices in Japan. Each floor of an office building is a big,

open bullpen, with desks arranged in a series of T-formations. The long stem of each T consists of the desks of the underlings; the top of the T is the desk of that group's boss, who can look out over the others as they work. Bruce Cumings, an American historian, has written that in Korea "one encounters the curious pattern of surface rejection in toto of everything that the Japanese did, combined with de facto adoption of many Japanese practices. . . . The Japanese set up a love-hate conflict that has gnawed at the Korean national identity ever since."[2]

Moreover, as a means of preparing a society for modernization, Japanese colonial rule had undeniably useful aftereffects. The Japanese built railroads, and they built factories. They built schools in the colonies, they built telegraph systems and roads, they built modern ports to handle the colonies' exports back to Japan. The British, French, and Americans spent more time than did the Japanese arguing about what "rights" they should grant their colonial subjects, but in the hard-nosed sense of preparing people for economic progress the Japanese may have done more good. The Japanese nationalist politician Shintaro Ishihara has proposed a cause-and-effect relationship: If a country had been a Japanese colony, then it would prosper in the postcolonial age. If it hadn't, it would not do as well. Since there are only two major test cases for this hypothesis, Korea and Taiwan, it lacks rigor as a scientific theory. Yet in some way that must have come through the sternness of their colonial administration, the Japanese left a message with their colonialism that most other powers did not: if Korea or Taiwan hoped eventually to get ahead, they would have to learn to fend for themselves.

South Korea was freed from Japanese control after World War II, and was essentially a U.S. protectorate for a decade after the Korean War. But the philosophy and instruments behind its economic recovery bore close similarities to those in Japan.

The industrial combines that in Japan have been known at different times as *zaibatsu* and *keiretsu* are called *chaebol* in Korea. The largest and the best-known outside Korea are Hyundai, Samsung, and Daewoo. The *chaebol* served to unite industries with banks, rather than relying on the magic of an independent financial system to get money into industrialists' hands. As in early postwar Japan the industrial groups were shielded from foreign competition with sky-high tariffs and absolute prohibitions on many imports. "For twenty-five years no foreign cars were to be seen on Korean roads, and no Korean cars were to be seen on foreign roads," Alice H. Amsden has written about the period after the Korean War.[3]

In exchange for protection, the Korean government, like Japanese governments from the Meiji era on, imposed a tough set of standards that businesses must meet to move the nation closer to the goal of overall economic strength. Industries were instructed to keep the prices of "luxury" goods artificially high and to keep the prices of products that other industries needed artificially low. Firms had to meet export goals; keep investing their profits in new technology; take over money-losing enterprises, such as troubled shipyards or steelworks, that the government hoped to save; and otherwise act as if they were quasi-public operations. The carrot offered by the government was protection from foreign competition; the major stick was the government's power to steer capital away from companies that misbehaved. The closest counterparts from peacetime American experience would be private hospitals and defense contractors, which earn profits but which are also expected to meet public goals—and can be disciplined, by denial of government funds, if they don't cooperate.

The most acclaimed recent study of Korea's industrialization strategy is *Asia's Next Giant,* by Alice Amsden of the New School for Social Research, published in 1990. Amsden said that Korea (and, with some differences, Taiwan) faced a later, more extreme version of the problem Japan had coped with during the Meiji era.

The challenge in each country's case was not to come up with completely new products and technologies, as Britain had had to do during the original industrial revolution. Instead the task for these "late industrializing" countries was to catch up and learn as rapidly as possible—to apply in their own factories, with their own engineers and workers, the industrial technologies that were already being used in Manchester or in Detroit. This sounds simpler than blazing a trail of completely new technology, but Amsden argued that it involves working against the natural pressures of economics. Left to their own devices, after all, customers in backward countries would prefer simply to buy advanced products from efficient suppliers overseas, rather than waiting for a domestic industry to arise.

Governments in these "late industrializing" countries believed that they would have to rig the rules of business if they were to have a chance to catch up. They had to extract unnaturally large amounts of savings from their people, so there would be money to invest in new factories; they had to deny consumers access to less-expensive foreign goods; they had to make sure that industries put the money to work within their own country, rather than letting it flow to some overseas market that might offer a higher short-term return. Simply relying on cheap labor would not suffice to move the country into the industrial major leagues. The mills and machine tools in the advanced countries were so much more productive that even dirt-cheap labor could not overcome their lead. As Amsden wrote:

> Even in a labor-intensive sector like textiles, and even with aid-financed, modern infrastructure, the governments of South Korea and Taiwan *had* to intervene to offset Japan's higher productivity with a wide range of subsidies, far wider than those warranted to support infant *innovators* in the second industrial revolution. . . . Subsidies were used deliberately to get prices "wrong" in order to stimulate investment and trade.[4]

All the countries that went through this process shared certain catch-up traits, Amsden said—and it is this family resemblance, in addition to the cultural links and the historic print left by Japanese coloni-alism, that make so many parts of Korea's business operation seem so similar to Japan's.*

Korean politics has been authoritarian and nationalistically minded like Japan's, although in Korea the military has obviously played a larger role, as have individual political leaders. Certain districts in today's Seoul look the way that parts of Tokyo or Osaka did twenty years ago. One shop is full of gears, the next is full of flywheels, people are sitting on sidewalks taking engines apart and rewinding electric motors. You walk down the street and think, this is the workshop of the world! Like Japan and Taiwan as well, about one third of everything Korea exported in the early 1990s went to the United States.[5] Korea's rice policy was structurally similar to Japan's, with small farmers, high production prices, and a market closed to foreign products. More than half of Korea's farming land was used for rice, which (like rice in Japan) cost several times more than the world price for rice.

In short, with allowances made for Korea's smaller size and its

---

*Amsden's list of common traits of "late industrializers" included these fac-tors: (1) extensive government intervention, to make sure there were enough savings and investment, and not too many imports; (2) large-scale, diversified industrial groups, like the Japanese *zaibatsu* or Korean *chaebol,* which could spread the risk of a failure in any one product; (3) a concentration by both public and private authorities on "the shop floor"—that is, a close focus on the operating details of factory life; and (4) government surveillance over and discipline of industries to make sure they are pursuing national goals.

lower degree of technical sophistication, the logic and structure of Korea's development plans are more like Japan's than they are like anything else.

And for a while, in particular from 1986 through 1988, it seemed as if this formula might allow Korea to catch up with Japan, much as Japan had caught up with the United States. Starting in late 1985, when the yen soared against the dollar, the Korean central bank held down the value of the Korean *won*. Korean clothes and machinery were, at least in principle, newly competitive against Japan's. Korea had no trade surplus in 1985, an overall surplus of $4 billion in 1986, and a surplus of $8 billion in 1987. Every indicator was pointing up, and the Olympics lay ahead the following year. Korea's drive toward the 1988 Summer Olympics was very much like the herculean Japanese efforts before the 1964 Summer Olympics. In each case the country viewed this international event as a showcase of economic recovery and a demonstration of national competence. The first time I went to Korea, on a Korean Air Lines plane, the in-flight "entertainment" consisted not of movies or safety announcements but of a newsreel showing one company after another that had racked up export gains.

Very soon afterward, the trend turned around. The country was preoccupied through most of 1987 with serious political decisions. In face of nonstop demonstrations by students, factory workers, and eventually the urban middle class that occupied the first half of the year, the military government agreed to hold elections. The subsequent parliamentary and presidential campaigns occupied the second half of the year. In Korea all other events in 1988 were overshadowed by the frantic effort to prepare for and conduct the Olympic Games. By the time normality, of a sort, had returned in 1989, something surprising and abnormal had apparently happened to the export economy. The trade surplus started shrinking as rapidly as it had grown earlier in the decade. By 1990 the surplus had disappeared altogether, and the government launched a variety of austerity and anti-import campaigns to try to get things back on the previous track.

Everyone had an explanation for what had happened to Korea's export edge. When the military had released its hold on politics, the lid came off many other controls at the same time. For decades the Korean government had discouraged foreign travel, granting passports only to those with a legitimate business reason to burn up precious foreign exchange. Now it allowed pleasure travel—and people left. Its systems for encouraging thrift and holding down consumption seemed less robust than those in Japan. Especially in Seoul, prosperous-feeling consumers snapped up the imported cars, perfumes, and jewelry now allowed into the market. What the U.S. Occupation forces had deliberately staved off in Japan in the 1950s— agonizing nationwide strikes, embattled labor unions—popped up in the Korea of the late 1980s. The biggest *chaebol* companies were paralyzed by shipyard and steelworks strikes of the kind by now unimaginable in Japan. To buy peace (and put a good face on the country for its Olympics showcase), employers gave in to wage demands, so that by 1990, Korean paychecks were rising much faster than underlying industrial productivity.

Although the rapid rise of the yen was supposed to give a big edge to Korean and Taiwanese factories, it didn't help as much as Korean economists had hoped. Japanese manufacturers were surprisingly quick and effective in driving down their own prices—and leapfrogging Korea itself to invest in truly low-wage sites in countries such as Indonesia or Thailand. When *endaka* was beginning in earnest in 1986, Japanese economists fearfully predicted that it would give Korea, along with Taiwan, the surge they needed to become big-league industrial competitors. Instead it was in this very period that Korea lost ground.

The barrier Korea could not overcome. From the varied explanations for the problems of the late 1980s rose a bigger and more brutal truth for the Korean government: as long as it played Japan's game, it was destined to fall short of what Japan had achieved. On any factor-by-factor match-up with Japan, Korea's handicaps were greater and its advantages less.

Japan was big enough to incubate industries domestically before exposing them to the outside world. Korea was not. With one third as many people and a per capita income about one sixth as great, Korea's total economy was barely 6 percent as large as Japan's. Japan was forbidden, by its constitution and continuing American pressure, to sink precious capital into a large military budget. Korea was required, by the presence of Kim Il Sung to the north, to impose a universal draft of young men and to devote as much of its GNP to defense as the United States did.

Japan's crucial years of postwar expansion occurred in the most supportive political environment imaginable. Its patron, the United States, was for several decades pleased to see Japan's exporters prosper, since this capitalist success bound Japan more closely to America's side in the Cold War. By the time Korea got going, the international mood had completely reversed. In 1987 I spoke with a young bureaucrat in Seoul named Koo Bohn Young, Ph.D. "Japan has had trade surpluses for twenty years, and only now is America complaining," he told me with slight hyperbole. "This is our first year of surplus with America—and, boom! Everyone is on our back to open up." "If we were located in Europe, everybody would be talking about giving foreign aid to poor little Korea," Park Sung Kyou, Ph.D., the director of the Daewoo division that makes Leading Edge computers, told me a few weeks later. "It's only because we're in Asia that people are impressed by our 'riches' and 'success' and think we may be a 'trade problem' in the future."

The deepest difference between the Japanese and Korean prospects, however, lay in the field of technology. Japan had been modernizing long enough, well enough, to control more and more of the technology its industries needed for their most valuable products. (The biggest exception was, of course, the aerospace business, and even there the Japanese government had directed an effort to ensure that components for Boeing, Lockheed, and McDonnell Douglas planes were actually made in Japan.)

Japan's advantage in technology acquisition, apart from having started in the nineteenth century rather than the mid-twentieth, was that it was mainly trying to acquire technology from the United States, whose companies were usually willing to sell for the right price. The technology on which Korean firms relied was often controlled by companies in Japan, which were much more reluctant to take short-term profits by licensing patents and techniques.

"The major question confronting South Korea's economy is whether it will be able to upgrade its technological capabilities," an American scholar wrote in the spring of 1993.[6] Two writers for the *Far Eastern Economic Review* made a similar point:

> South Koreans are often confident to the point of arrogance in believing they will eventually overtake the United States and Europe economically. But they frequently appear convinced they will not catch up with the Japanese. . . . One of the most persistent complaints is that the Japanese are niggardly about sharing their technology."[7]

In their face-to-face talks in 1990 and again the following year, Roh Tae Woo, then the president of Korea, complained directly about technology-sharing to Toshiki Kaifu, then the prime minister of Japan. ("If one is a true Korean . . . one should start by complain-

ing," a senior Korean government official said about this approach.[8])
In the summer of 1990, Roh's government announced a seven-year
master plan for technological development that, in effect, threatened
to boycott Japanese high-tech products wherever there was an alternative. When the Korean government went shopping for big-ticket
items—airplanes, nuclear power plants, high-speed rail systems, telecommunications products—"priority will be given to foreign firms
or countries that offer to hand over sensitive core technology," according to an official news release.[9] That is, the Korean government
threatened to avoid buying from Japan unless Japanese companies
changed their ways.

These complaints and threats had little effect. Japanese-based
corporations had one distinctively Japanese-sounding explanation
for not wanting to shift advanced manufacturing processes to
Korea—that the Koreans were too sloppy and inattentive to detail—
and another reason shared by American and European firms. Korea's laws and customs protecting intellectual property were lax at
best. The streets of Seoul, like those of Bangkok, are full of vendors
selling pirate-copy versions of Reebok shoes, Adidas track suits, and
American-made movies and tape recordings. When I met an official
from the Korean Ministry of Defense in 1986, he bowed low and
presented a leatherbound edition of a book I had written about
military policy five years earlier. The ministry had translated it into
Korean, printed it, and distributed it by the thousands to the military
staff—without being slowed down by any red tape concerning copy-
right or royalties. In products more consequential than sports shoes,
watches, or even books, Korean industries had established a reputation for appropriating whatever "intellectual property" came their
way.

The result of these factors—Korea's late start, its underdevel-
oped local technology base, the chary attitude of the Japanese—
was the predicament of the late 1980s. By 1990, more than a quarter
of the country's total exports consisted of textiles and shoes.[10] The
longer Korea stayed with these products, the more vulnerable it
would be to low-wage pressure from the likes of China, Indonesia,
or Bangladesh. But the harder Korea tried to move to higher-value
exports, the greater its dependence on, and trade deficit with, Japan
would become, since more sophisticated products required more
expensive Japanese components. In the early 1990s, when Korea's
overall trade balance varied between small surpluses and small deficits, its balance with Japan was a chronic large deficit—$9 billion
in 1991, a cumulative total of more than $65 billion from the mid-

1960s through the early 1990s. Each time a Korean company exported a car, half the value added was made up of parts purchased from Japan.

"We're hooked on Japan, I'm afraid," Lee Sang Yul, director general of the international trade bureau at the South Korean Ministry of Trade and Industry, said in 1993 to James Sterngold of *The New York Times*. "When the Korean economy was just beginning to develop, we had to rely on Japan for technology and parts. Once we had their systems, we kept buying them. So as our exports to the rest of the world increased, our imports from Japan had to grow."[11]

Korea's one major attempt to develop a technology of its own was in the semiconductor industry. As described in Chapter One, the Korean government heavily subsidized its own producers in the early and mid-1980s, so that by the end of the decade they had underpriced Japanese producers in several categories of memory chips.[12] But this was too expensive an effort to be undertaken across the board. In most other advanced industries the passing years had increased the gap between Korea and Japan. Korean manufacturers had thought they would have an edge when *endaka* pushed the dollar down to 125 yen in 1987. Yet by the early 1990s, big Japanese firms were prepared to compete with the dollar at 100 yen, or below.

"Japanese companies appear to have stymied their competitors in the newly industrializing economies at both ends of the product spectrum," Urban Lehner of *The Wall Street Journal* wrote in the summer of 1991. "For sophisticated products, many Japanese companies say privately they are actually widening their technological lead. For cheaper, low-value-added products, Japanese companies have gone around Taiwan and Korea and built factories in Southeast Asia to make the same goods using cheaper labor."[13]

Korea becomes more closed . . . One other factor compounded Korea's economic difficulties and made it different from every other country in the region. This involved the peculiar combination of xenophobia and true openness in modern Korean politics.

In keeping with the elbows-out style of daily life in Korea, there is no subtlety or concealment about the antiforeign streak in Korean culture. Because the United States occupies so much of Korea's mental space—with a huge military compound located until the early 1990s in the center of Seoul, with American network TV broadcasts direct over Korean airwaves for the convenience of overseas GIs—free-form xenophobia usually expresses itself as anti-Americanism. During the 1988 Olympics, well-educated Koreans seemed sincerely to believe that NBC, which was broadcasting the games in America, had one motive, and one motive only, in its coverage: that of heaping shame on the Korean hosts. This belief was based on NBC's coverage of a brawl at an Olympics boxing match at which a Korean crowd misbehaved. This moment came and went quickly for most viewers around the world; I heard it mentioned, in interviews with Koreans, over the next four years. The Korean press seemed similarly certain in its view that unscrupulous American farmers had been dumping Alar-tainted grapefruit on trusting Korean housewives. It does no good to argue (as the U.S. embassy did in vain) that Alar is used on apples, including apples grown in Korea, but never on citrus fruit.

Korea's truculent sensitivity to fancied slights is understandable considering its position as a small country amid leviathans. When Commodore Perry's black ships steamed into Edo Bay, Japanese diplomats of the shogun's day noticed the cannons. After a number of contentious incidents, reformers in Japan got the upper hand and decided it was shrewd to compromise and modernize. When the American merchant ship *General Sherman* steamed up the Taedong River to Pyongyang almost fifteen years later, the Koreans burned it to the water line, and their shore batteries bombarded the warships sent up five years afterward on a delayed retaliatory missions. Through the late nineteenth century, Korea tried to seal itself off from Western influence at the very time when Japan was trying to catch up with the West.

When the country's trade surplus began to dwindle in the late 1980s, the Korean government responded as its forebears had to the *General Sherman*. In 1989 the press and government together launched an "antiluxury campaign" that was in effect an attempt to harass and intimidate those who dared buy foreign "luxury" goods. The Mercury Sable became the incongruous symbol of this campaign. In 1990, in Seoul, to say that a Korean neighbor had "bought a Sable" was like saying in other times or places that someone was "driving a Rolls-Royce." Even though Korea had at the time a substantial ($4 billion) trade surplus with the United States and a very large ($8 billion) trade deficit with Japan, the campaign was directed almost exclusively at American products such as the Sable, Hollywood movies, and American cigarettes. This slant was motivated not by antismoking sentiment—the government was happy to have people smoke but preferred that they buy domestic brands.

Instead, it exemplified the structure of today's Asian trade. Ninety percent of what Korea bought from Japan was capital goods or industrial components, products that were both invisible to the average citizen and indispensable for Korea's own plans. There was no quick or simple way to cut back on imported Japanese products without hurting Korean exports. The austerity campaign also reflected the Korean government's concern that everything the country had achieved could slip away if people stopped leaving their money in banks, where industries could use it, and instead started spending freely on themselves.

Late in 1989, with economic growth slipping, the national tax office announced that "extravagance beyond one's reported means" would invite tax scrutiny.[14] In effect this meant that anyone who bought a Sable, Lincoln Continental, Mercedes, or BMW could be expect to put through the tax wringer—a more serious threat in Korea than in some other countries because so much business is off the books. Tariffs and other barriers had already raised the price of these cars to more than twice as much as they would cost in the United States. That hadn't choked off sales, but the tax threat did: sales of the Sable virtually stopped after the tax men stepped in. A young journalist named Don Jacobson, writing for the American Chamber of Commerce magazine in Seoul, published dozens of articles in 1989 and 1990 chronicling the further steps of the "anti-luxury" crackdown.

Comic books were distributed in schools, urging each child to keep careful watch on Mother's purchasing habits—and inform on her if she bought foreign goods. The same books reminded children that Alar was found in American grapefruit and that "if we eat imported foods our farmers cannot have a good life." In another comic book, a teacher instructs her students on the realities of international economics. "From many years ago foreign companies pressured Japan to buy their products," the teacher says. "However, Japanese people all together did not buy imported goods! In Japan, the price of a bunch of [imported] bananas equals one [domestic] apple, but Japanese bought the apple, which is their domestic product."[15] This, the teacher concludes, is the way to national wealth.

Large-size White-Westinghouse refrigerators, which cost $1,600 to $1,800 in the United States, were priced at $4,200 in Korea—and when Korea's new-rich class still kept buying them, the largest department stores decided not to sell them anymore. The owner of a store handling Gucci products was quoted in a foreign newspaper criticizing the antiluxury campaign. Immediately afterward, tax agents began questioning her, and she was ordered to remove from her shelves any item priced at more than 1 million *won* (about $1,400).[16] New financial regulations meant, in effect, that importers had to pay cash, in advance, for all shipments of foreign luxury goods. In the spring of 1990, the Ministry of Finance applied a similar restraint to consumers by instructing banks and department stores not to accept credit cards for purchases of "expensive imported articles." At the same time, it "discouraged" the advertising business, retailers, and TV and radio networks from carrying ads for imported articles that are "liable to lead to excessive spending." The minister of trade, Park Pil Soo, announced in aggrieved tones that a wine merchant in Seoul had been found offering a bottle of rare Cognac priced at $1,909. The minister shared his thoughts on this matter with readers of the *Far Eastern Economic Review*:

> This I don't like. And there are more than 100 wines imported, even though many Koreans are not wine drinkers. Is it acceptable? No.[17]

Many diplomats, journalists, and other foreign observers in Seoul agreed that the government's fears of economic slowdown, which had led to the antiluxury campaign, had some foundation. The trade surplus was rapidly vanishing; more important, by flaunting its wealth, Korea's new-rich class was creating deep political tensions with the long-suppressed working class, whose earnings had been held down for years as another way of amassing capital for industrial expansion. Regional tensions lay just beneath the surface of Korean politics. What is now South Korea had been three separate kingdoms in the sixth and seventh centuries A.D.. Modern voting patterns and emotional loyalties largely follow those old lines. It was understandable, therefore, that Roh Tae Woo's administration would try to pull the reins in somehow, but the U.S. government grew exasperated at having American sedans and grapefruit converted into scapegoats. By the end of 1990 the United States was threatening to hit Korea with trade sanctions under the "Super 301" bill, and U.S. spokesmen were showing up in the press saying things like this: "The intent [of the antiluxury campaign] is not to stop luxury goods, it is to stop imports" and that Korea was asking for trouble if it tried to "turn back the clock" of its long-promised liberalization campaign.[18]

. . . And yet is strangely open. No other industrialized Asian country of the 1990s would have played the anti-import game quite as crudely or as visibly as Korea did. Yet no other country was as deeply open to outside influence as Korea, in some ways, proved to be.

Religion is a proxy for other kinds of cultural permeability. It is natural that the Philippines and the countries of Indochina would be the most predominantly Christian parts of Asia, after the centuries they had spent under Catholic rule. Korea, however, is Christianity's only recent success story in this part of the world. Of the Koreans who classify themselves as religious, about half say they are Christian, compared to 1 percent of the total population in Japan. The origins of this pattern are largely political. Whereas missionaries came in the conqueror's wake in much of the colonized world, in Korea the churches were, along with the universities, the centers of nationalist agitation against Japanese colonial rule. American and European missionaries came to Korea in the nineteenth and early twentieth centuries to establish churches and universities. These institutions in turn became the organizing base for many of the Korean nationalists working to subvert Japanese rule.

Like Islam and distinctly unlike Shinto, Christianity is a universal faith that reminds people every week that they have fundamental similarities to those outside their tribe. This message goes only so far, in Korea or anywhere else; Korean families are generally appalled if a son or daughter marries a non-Korean. Still, its effect is at least slightly different from the repeated Japanese emphasis on Japan's disconnection from the world. Christianity in Korea is clearly strong enough to constitute a source of moral authority independent of the state, something that barely exists in Japan. During the upheaval of 1987, for instance, Catholic priests, cardinals, and bishops were in the news every day, telling their parishioners they had a moral right to defy the state.

Language is another example of the cracks of openness in Korea's wall of particularism. The grammatical structures of Korean and Japanese are very different from those of Western languages but very similar to each other. This point is frequently mentioned in Korea but almost never in Japan; there, people are more likely to say that their language is "unique." Part of Korea's self-myth is that Koreans are a "peninsular" people, affected by and affecting the cultures that surround them. Japan, which in reality has been heavily affected by Korean and Chinese culture, emphasizes the myth of itself as an island culture, misunderstood and alone.

"You just don't find the Japanese notions that nobody can understand us, nobody can speak our language, our snow is unique, we're different from everybody else," an American businessman who has lived in Korea for twenty years told me in 1987. "Koreans seem to have a high degree of racial consciousness and the usual Asian distaste for the half-blood, but somehow it's not such a big deal as in Japan. People can easily say, 'Well, this influence came from China, and this one went to Japan, and this started out some-place else.' There is not the weird obsession with figuring out how everything is ancestrally and uniquely their own." Another longtime foreign resident, who like the first was a fluent Korean-speaker, told me, "No one has ever complained that it's hard to make true friends with Koreans."

Korea's relative openness simultaneously reinforces and challenges the idea of a new, more restrictive East Asian version of capitalism and democracy.

Korea's experience reinforces the idea because even its small degree of openness has clearly been an economic handicap, at least in the short term. If the country had been less raucous and democratic since 1987, it would not have frittered away so much time on election campaigns—or let its wages rise so much faster than its productivity rate, as Korea's major corporations did in the wake of widespread labor unrest in the late 1980s. If you care about Western-style democracy, the period between 1987 and 1993 represented an enormous step forward for Korea. If you care about the national productive base—as most governments in the region obviously do—it was a step back.

The expert bureaucracy that has guided Korea's growth is in one way fundamentally more "open" than its counterparts in Japan. For more than a century, the Japanese government has sent students around the world, so as better to understand foreign techniques. Yet these techniques have been applied in Japan in a highly selective, usually Japanized way. This is particularly true in the case of economics: Bureaucrats at MITI and the Ministry of Finance are familiar with the concepts of Western neo-classical economics, but they plainly don't believe them. These ideas—that consumer welfare should be paramount, that the state will certainly err if it interferes with trade—are at fundamental odds with the past century of Japan's policy and experience. Very few officials of Japan's powerful ministries of Finance or International Trade and Industries hold Ph.D.s in economics from American or British universities.

The Korean bureaucrats, on the other hand, have virtually all been trained in American or British universities. In the late 1980s there were thirty-six professionals at the Korea Development Institute, by far the most influential think tank for the government. At least thirty of them had earned Ph.D.s in the United States.

The most important thing about these "American-trained Korean economists" (or A-TKEs, as Alice Amsden called them in her study of the phenomenon) who dominate the Korean bureaucracy is that their training seems to have stuck. The first time I heard a bureaucrat tell me, in 1987, that Korea would have "failed" if it just built up large trade surpluses and did not offer its people an abundant life, I was highly skeptical. I had heard this too often in Japan, from people who did not themselves believe it but knew it was what Americans wanted to hear. Five years later, when I had heard the same thing from a dozen other Korean bureaucrats, I realized what I was dealing with: these were people who really had been converted by their training in Western economics, almost in a religious sense. They seemed sincerely embarrassed by the "antiluxury campaign," which was enforced by politicians and which broke the rules of economic efficiency they'd learned at Harvard and MIT. The traditional Korean emphasis on education, the vast-seeming power of the United States, the genuine intelligence of those who taught them in graduate school—these and possibly other factors had made them think in ways at odds with the mercantilist model applied in much of the rest of Asia.

And that, of course, is the problem from Korea's perspective. The title of Alice Amsden's study of "American-Trained Korean Economists," or A-TKEs, sums up the predicament: "The Specter of Anglo-Saxonization Is Haunting South Korea." The A-TKEs had embraced an ideology at just the moment when their great rival across the Tsushima and Korea straits was revealing the blind spots in Anglo-American economic theory.

Viewed in another way, however, the A-TKEs are representative of Korea's greatest modern achievement. If they have come to believe the economic part of modern Western ideology, they may believe the political part as well. They may genuinely accept, as many others in the region do not, the value of free expression, real political competition, individual rights. Since 1987 their country has moved farther in that direction than any other in East Asia. It is the first to challenge the idea that "Asian-style" democracy might be enduringly different from that of the West. Korea is a small country, still used to depending on military protection from the United States. Yet it is becoming a "real" country, responsible for itself, more rapidly than Japan has since the American Occupation years. This political development, and not cars or semiconductors, may be what lets Korea step out of its sibling's shadow and win recognition on its own.

Taiwan, Singapore, Hong Kong: "Greater China"

Since the 1970s news reports have referred to the "four tigers" or "four little dragons," the other Asian countries that were straining to catch up with Japan. The four on the standard list were the Republic of Korea, the Republic of China (Taiwan), Singapore, and Hong Kong. Until the mid-1980s, this group was often referred to as the "NICs," for "Newly Industrializing Countries." Now the politically acceptable term is "NIEs," for "Newly Industrializing Economies." (China has insisted on this circumlocution because of its view that neither Hong Kong, which is a British colony, nor the Republic of China on Taiwan, which in China's view is part of China itself, should be dignified with the term "country.")

By whatever title, the lumping together of these four countries is intriguing, since they vary so much among themselves. Korea's economy is by far the largest of the four, with a gross domestic product of just under $300 billion in 1993; Singapore's economy, the smallest, is less than one-sixth as large, less than $50 billion. (Taiwan has the second largest economy, at about $215 billion. Hong Kong's is worth $85 billion.) On a per capita basis, Hong Kong is the richest of these economies, with output equivalent to about $14,000 per person. Singapore is second, at about $13,000; Taiwan, third, at around $9,000; and Korea, fourth, at less than $7,000.

Politically each of these states faces problems, but the problems differ substantially from case to case. Hong Kong, a British colony since the nineteenth century, is scheduled for absorption by the People's Republic of China in 1997. The Republic of China's government, on Taiwan, has no formal ties with most other nations and sustains the fiction that it is the real government of all China. South Korea views itself as being artifically separated from the northern half of its country, and until the end of the Cold War was not recognized by much of the Communist bloc. Singapore alone enjoys normal diplomatic standing in the world; its political problems involve arranging the succession to Lee Kuan Yew, who ruled the country as prime minister for three decades and, in retirement in the early 1990s, still exercised great power behind the scenes.

Even the term "four tigers" now has a quaintly anachronistic feel. The implication behind it was that these countries, lean and ambitious, would challenge Japan much as Japan in its leanest days had challenged the United States. Since the late 1980s it has become clear that Japan is better prepared than the United States was to hold off this kind of rivalry. In terms of capital, technology, and commercial presence Japanese firms are farther ahead of their "four tiger" challengers than they were a decade before.

In its fundamental economic situation, Taiwan faces the same predicament as Korea. Its best economic hopes lie in applying some version of the Japanese model, but at least for the short term it simply cannot do so as well as the Japanese themselves.

Like the Republic of Korea, the Republic of China shows a mixture of heavy American influence on the educational and political systems, and heavy Japanese influence on everything else. "You cannot *find* another country that has been so influenced by the United States," Shaw Yu-ming, who was at the time director of Taiwan's Government Information Office, told me in 1991. Shaw himself had gone to the United States to study, had become a political science professor at Notre Dame, and had come back to Taiwan in the 1980s when political reforms began. "Counting our cabinet members and even the president, 70 percent were educated in America. More than one third have their Ph.D.s from the United States." Through most of the 1980s, students from Taiwan made up the largest bloc of foreigners in American colleges and graduate schools.[19] Taipei, the capital, is virtually the only big city in Asia in which American-brand cars abound. They are a relic of distribution networks set up between the early 1950s and the late 1970s, when the U.S. government recognized Chiang Kai-shek's government as the "true government of China and the Republic of China was a sort of U.S. protectorate.

But anyone familiar with Japanese pop culture can instantly see resemblances in Taiwan. The TV commercials take the same extremely indirect approach as in Japan. (While we were living in Tokyo, my children and I would amuse ourselves by placing bets as TV commercials came on. This depiction of a couple walking on the beach—would it turn out to be an ad for whiskey, electric air conditioners, life insurance, or "instant energy" drinks?) American TV styles spill over into Europe and Latin America; Japanese-style game shows and documentaries dominate the airwaves in Taiwan. Five decades of Japanese colonialism built at least a familiarity in Taiwan with Japanese working styles.

At a deeper level of economic structure Taiwan is clearly within the Japanese sphere. "When people go off to Japan, they come back talking about it as a model," a Canadian official living in Taiwan told me in 1991. "The element of high price in Japan, which is so important in the Western reaction, is not a factor. They don't come back and complain, 'We had to pay so much for a cup of coffee in Tokyo!' They say, 'How did they *do* it?' "

"People sometimes do complain about the overpresence of Japanese products," the Canadian said. "But the goods are here because people like them. They often say, 'This is the right size!' 'It's suited to Asian taste.' 'The suppliers are right in our backyard, rather than being twelve time zones away.' A preference for Japanese goods is built into the system because they produce so many things for which there is no alternative." Taiwan's numerous computer companies, for instance, depend even more heavily on Japanese suppliers of disk drives, display screens, and memory chips than American computer companies do.

Taiwan is, and seems, surprisingly richer than Korea from the consumer's point of view. In Seoul it is still easy to imagine you are in a place like eighteenth-century London, with a population streaming in from the hinterland to work in some of the rough early stages of industrial growth. Taiwan's population is more educated and urbanized; it is already housed and clothed in a way Korea would be happy to be a decade from now. Yet the Taiwanese economy has the same two fundamental links to the Japanese economy as Korea's does. As a *model* of government-business interaction, Japan has given Taiwan something to emulate; yet as a trade partner and *supplier,* Japan has made Taiwan's success more and dependent on Japan's.

In his book *Governing the Market*, published in 1990, Robert Wade provided the most nuanced description of how the Taiwanese government has tried to apply lessons learned from Japan. The Taiwanese government's crucial insight, Wade emphasized, was that any support for industry must carry conditions. That is, in Taiwan as in Japan, the government tried to shelter and nurture industries it considered particularly valuable for the country's economic future. In the early 1990s, for instance, Taiwan's government has been trying to arrange joint-production efforts between McDonnell Douglas, the American aircraft maker, and Taiwanese firms, in hopes of fostering an aircraft industry on the island. The model for this project is clearly Japan's decades-long effort to have Boeing, McDonnell Douglas, and other aircraft makers collaborate with big industries in Japan. In Taiwan as in Japan, the government has kept careful tabs on how the industries were using the breathing space the government had provided. The companies had to meet export targets, reinvest a certain proportion of their income, keep peace with labor, and in general serve the nation's long-term interests as well as their immediate corporate ends.

This concept—aid, with conditions—is the essential East Asian industrial strategy, and it has built Taiwan's success as it has that of Korea and Japan. Nonetheless, the faster Taiwan has run in this direction, the more dependent it has become on machinery and expertise from Japan. Uniquely among East Asian countries other than Japan, Taiwan needs very little foreign investment to finance its projects. Taiwan's savings rate has usually been the highest in the world. During the 1970s, for example, its net savings represented 30 percent of its national product. In that same period, Japan's savings rate was 26.3 percent, Korea's 17.5, and America's 7.6.[20] The Taiwanese government chronically runs a large budget surplus, which adds to the national savings. The reasons behind Taiwan's high savings rate are hotly debated. Some people say the most important factor is that the government offers almost no retirement benefits, so people must save on their own; others emphasize a refugee mentality left over from the days when Taiwan's leaders fled from Mao's hordes. The result is to leave Taiwan with the largest foreign-currency reserves in the world—and with increasing Taiwanese investments in other countries.

The problem for Taiwan lies in the transition to high-tech manufacturing. As is the case for Korea, the most valuable products it makes and sells, from machine tools to personal computers, are based on components imported from Japan or made on machinery purchased in Japan. Roughly half of the U.S. trade deficit with Japan is accounted for by one highly visible consumer product: cars. Millions of purchasers decide each year what kind of car to buy. At least in theory, they could freely switch their purchases if they grew uncomfortable with cars from one manufacturer or even an entire nation. Indeed, many American consumers switched back to American-made cars in the 1990s, as the cost of Japanese models and the quality of American models both went up. But like purchasers in Korea, those in Taiwan have much less maneuvering room for affecting how much their nation imports from abroad, and from where. As Urban Lehner of *The Wall Street Journal* has pointed out, only 10 percent of Taiwan's imports from Japan are consumer goods. The other 90 percent are components, machinery, and parts for the products Taiwanese factories make.[21] In 1993 Taiwan spent more than $2.5 billion importing semiconductors from Japan, which was more than Taiwan spent on crude oil.[22]

"It is, therefore, Taiwanese industry rather than consumers that is hooked on Japanese products," Lehner wrote. "The result is that when Taiwan increases its exports to Japan or the United States or anywhere else, it almost by necessity increases its imports from Japan." "Right now we don't have our own factories" for many crucial electronics parts, an official from Taiwan's Institute for Information Industry told Michael Stroud of *Investor's Business Daily* in 1992. "That means we have no bargaining position with the Japanese if they decide to raise prices."[23] Through 1992 Taiwan's trade deficit with Japan was about $1 billion per month, more than twice as much as the previous year and proportionately greater than either the American or the Korean deficits with Japan.[24]

Starting in the 1980s the Taiwanese government has tried to cope with this technological dependence with a variety of ambitious research-promotion plans. The problem it faces is the reverse side of a trait many Westerners find comforting and appealing about Taiwan: the abundance of small and medium-sized businesses that typify its manufacturing base.

Japanese industry has its small businesses, too, many of which are crucially important suppliers to big manufacturers such as Toyota, and all of which serve as shock absorbers when economic activity rises and falls. (Big Japanese companies still mainly observe the "no layoffs" policy, despite very minor reductions in the early 1990s. Small Japanese companies have no such policy and freely take on and lay off labor as business circumstances dictate.) But the Japanese trademark business organization is, of course, the large firm—rather, many large companies combined in the structure known as a *keiretsu,* with a bank at its center and links of cross-ownership. Korea's version of the same structure is, again, the *chaebol.*

Business in Taiwan has no term comparable to *keiretsu* or *chaebol* because it has no comparable economic structure. Taiwan does have a few large firms with international scope. The Evergreen shipping line company, and Formosa Plastics, which now operates factories in the United States, are two main examples. The computer-making company Acer is perhaps the Taiwanese brand name best known to Western consumers. But these are unrepresentative features on the country's economic landscape, comparable to Ayers Rock rising out of the surrounding plain of the Australian outback.

The archetypical Taiwanese firm is still a small manufacturing business run by an individual entrepreneur with his extended-family members, which concentrates on a few niche products and scrambles to survive. In a newly developed area of Taipei stands a huge, modern international trade-fair center. One week it will host a convention of leather-goods makers; the next week it will show printing equipment, or food-packaging machines, or computer parts. Week in and week out the hall contains thousands of booths, each representing a company that makes a certain kind of copper pipe, or computer keyboard, and nothing else. In her book *Cities and the Wealth of Nations,* Jane Jacobs argued that city economies were healthiest when businesses were small, numerous, specialized, and agile. Taiwan is the closest thing that Asia offers to her dream come true. Tiny firms are constantly appearing, disappearing, adjusting, thriving, and specializing in the most arcane and bizarre ways. The great divide in the business cultures of East Asia is between Japanese-style and Chinese-style management. The Japanese-style system, most closely approximated in Korea, involves large organizations with skilled, bureaucratized management. The Chinese-style system features small family-run enterprises. Taiwan represents the Chinese model on a national scale.

This difference has made Taiwan stronger in many ways. Its little firms can adapt very quickly and strike up deals around the world, and the business environment as a whole seems less monolithic and forbidding to outsiders than Japan's or Korea's has. Its great weakness is the one reflected in Taiwan's technological dependence. In Japan and to a much smaller extent Korea, the large-scale enterprises, with their ties both to the government and to banks, have been the institutions for amassing huge amounts of capital and investing it for long-term productivity increases. During the late 1980s, when Japanese firms were out-investing American companies in absolute terms, it was big Japanese enterprises—Matsushita, NEC, Toyota, Mitsubishi—that led the way. Big Korean firms, such as Samsung, led the country's efforts to make semiconductors. In Europe and even America, where tiny firms such as those of Silicon Valley pioneered many innovations of the high-tech age, it is in fact the large firms that have been able to sink money into long-term efforts to commercialize technology. Taiwan has a lot of money, but it does not have the big firms. Family entrepreneurs have not been able to invest in the same way.

The advantages of family business. In its application of the small-business model Taiwan is exceptional among the four "newly industrializing" countries. Singapore's economy, in its three decades under Lee Kuan Yew, was shaped by a much more paternalistic government policy. Its symbol was the Central Provident Fund (CPF), a nationwide enforced-savings scheme that provided capital for housing projects and other long-term investments. Hong Kong, after 150 years of British rule, abounds in tiny enterprises but also is a base for many large foreign-owned firms.

Yet in a sense the long-term prospects for Taiwan, Singapore, and Hong Kong depend on one common factor that is not a matter of economic "model" and that is almost impossible to predict. These societies are all predominantly Chinese, and the factor that matters most for their long-term development is what happens to mainland China itself.

China's future role is the great wild-card variable in Asia's future, and to an extent the future of the world. It is conceivable that a century from now, or even within fifty years, China will dominate the region far more completely than Japan does at the moment, and will be the first or second power in the world. What that would mainly require is "smart" economic management by the government. Smart management, in turn, would mean continuing to give business—and technological development—primacy over everything else.

It is also conceivable that China will stagnate for many decades to come, because of what the "everything else" entails. What it would most obviously mean is a reduction in control—political and ideological control by the Communist Party, and control of the vast regions of the country by the central government in Beijing. The more rapidly the areas of China's seacoast facing Taiwan and Hong Kong developed in the 1980s, the more troublesome they became for the central government in the North. If it wants them to entice new industries, it needs to give them liberties about making deals, letting in foreign influence, permitting wage differences, and generally escaping central government control. This was of course part of the underlying tension that led to the Tiananmen Square shootings.

For more than a thousand years, a great drama of China's history has been the balance between centrifugal and centripetal forces. Whatever government has controlled the northern capital (which is what *Beijing* and *Peking,* which are different English spellings for the same Chinese name, both mean; *Nanking* means southern capital) has ended up thinking that its fundamental responsibility is to keep China from being dismembered. What has happened to the Soviet Union since 1989 is the greatest nightmare for the people who rule China—and for those who might plausibly follow them. At the same time, whoever has ruled in the provinces, especially in the South, has always struggled against central rule and wanted more autonomy. This pressure can only grow sharper as the economic differences between North and South increase. The coastal zones in the South are becoming more and more connected to Hong Kong, Taiwan, Singapore, and even to the Chinese enclaves in Vietnam and Thailand. They are becoming richer and more modern than the North—and dramatically more than the highly populated mainly peasant interior.

A "rational" Chinese government would let this process continue, recognizing that the country's best hope and its greatest potential for attaining wealth lie in integration with the surrounding market economies. But a "rational" Chinese government, in Western terms, would never have squashed the Tiananmen Square protesters quite so thoroughly or visibly as the real Chinese government did in 1989. Other countries, through history, have put other values ahead of pure economic efficiency, and Chinese regimes have consistently valued matters of national pride and political control over what the outside world might say is "rational."

The answers to these questions of political balance within China will have more impact on more people than almost anything else that occurs in Asia; and yet they are almost impossible to predict with any confidence. What can be said is that the Chinese members of the "four tigers" list have prepared themselves to act as go-betweens as much as conditions in China permit.

In the long run, the economic weight of Japan in Asia could be offset or exceeded by that of "greater China." Since the beginning of China's fitful opening to outside investment in the late 1970s, this term has been used more and more frequently in Asia. The concept behind it is the economic linkage between China itself, with its billion-person population and huge scale, and the surrounding highly skilled, market-oriented Chinese cultures in Hong King, Singapore, and Taiwan. (The ethnic Chinese populations in other Asian countries, especially Malaysia, Indonesia, and Vietnam, would probably be part of this vision. But the idea of pan-Chinese unity transcending national borders is alarming to the governments of those other countries, so this theme is often played down.)

All of these economies are growing rapidly, although China is still on average very poor. The scale of China's economy is in a sense unmeasurable. If its national product is valued at the international exchange rate for its currency, the Renminbi Yuan, China's per-capita income is worth about $300 and its entire economy is only one-tenth the size of Japan's. Under some less conventional valuation schemes, which ignore exchange rates and measure physical output alone, China's economy can be classified as already larger than Japan's. In 1993 the World Bank estimated that within a decade the output of the "Chinese Economic Area"—China plus Hong Kong and Taiwan—could exceed Japan's and approach that of the United States.[25]

Whatever the ultimate scale of "greater China," and whatever balance of liberalization and control the Chinese government decides upon, Hong Kong and Taiwan have for now decided to embrace the idea that their economic futures are linked to China's. This is largely a bow to the inevitable, especially in Hong Kong's case, since it will almost certainly become a "Special Administrative Region" of China in 1997. Taiwan faces a more ambiguous but still perilous political relationship with mainland China. Each government, that of the Republic of China on Taiwan and the People's Republic of China, claims to be the legitimate ruler of all China, mainland and Taiwan alike. In reality, Taiwan functions as a separate independent state. Yet the government in Taiwan cannot admit that there are now two Chinas. The problem is not resistance from its own superannuated die-hards, who dream of reconquering the mainland; it lies instead with the government on the mainland, which would view a formal assertion of Taiwanese separation as an affront to its claim of sovereignty.

Yet rather than being dragged into their relationship with China, Hong Kong and Taiwan alike are in the early 1990s actively promoting links with the Chinese economy. Hong Kong has since the 1980s been the leading investor in southern China. Since 1979 Hong Kong investors have accounted for about half the capital brought into all of China.[26] By most estimates four-fifths of foreign investment in China's booming coastal zones comes from the diaspora of "greater China"—that is, from investors in Hong Kong, Taiwan, and to a smaller degree Singapore. In 1993, the chairman of Hong Kong's General Chamber of Commerce, Paul M. F. Cheng, said that some twenty-five thousand enterprises in southern China had been established by investors from Hong Kong. Together they

employed 3 million Chinese.[27] This interaction had made the Hong
Kong dollar the de facto currency of the Guangdong region, immediately north of Hong Kong.

By the logic and standards of the economic model that Japan
has created and that Korea and Taiwan, in different ways, have
applied, Hong Kong might seem to have made strategic errors. It
obviously has been unable to launch the campaigns for national
technological autonomy that have been so important to Japan. With
a population of 6 million people, its home market has been too small
for such enterprises. Moreover, as a colony it has lacked both the
motivation and the political means to carry out such schemes. There
have been fewer industrial-development schemes in Hong Kong than
elsewhere in East Asia, and at the moment fewer high-tech industries than in Korea or even Taiwan.

Instead Hong Kong has positioned itself as the financial and
trading center for the southern region of "greater China." The risk
of this strategy is that it will succeed or fail depending on trends in
Chinese politics that Hong Kong itself cannot control. If future
governments of China decide that maintaining internal political control is more important than continuing trade and investment from
overseas, then Hong Kong's role as conduit would be much less
valuable than it seems now. The advantage of this strategy is that it
acknowledges reality: one way or another the government of China
will soon control Hong Kong, and the colony's businesses are preparing to make the best of this circumstance.

Through most of the 1980s, when reversion to Chinese control
was inevitable but not imminent, Hong Kong's strategy seemed to
be paying off. The Chinese government was allowing its southern
provinces—those closest to Hong Kong—more economic latitude
than other parts of the country. Those provinces found it expedient
to use Hong Kong as a middleman for trade and investment transactions with the outside world. It was still politically awkward at that
time for Chinese businesses or officials to deal directly with other
parts of "greater China," either on Taiwan or in Southeast Asia.
(The rapprochement between the "two Chinas"—on the mainland
and on Taiwan—speeded up in the early 1990s, when each recognized commercial advantages to dealing with the other.) Many Hong
Kong businesses had family and cultural ties to neighboring Guangdong Province, which was the fastest-growing region of China in
much of the 1980s.

After the crackdown in Tiananmen Square in 1989, Hong
Kong's prospects suddenly looked much dicier. Even before this

episode there had been a distinctly transient feel to Hong Kong. Most families who lived in the colony had emigrated from southern China within the previous one or two generations. The pop culture in Hong Kong was full of reminders that people might have to emigrate again. Early each morning long lines formed outside the visa-application offices for the major "recipient" countries—Britain, Canada, Australia, and the United States. (Emigration to countries of the British Commonwealth was much easier for Hong Kong residents than being admitted to the United States, both because Hong Kong citizens held British passports and because U.S. immigration law gives first preference to those with relatives already in America.) Hong Kong's newspapers were full of ads from real estate firms in Vancouver, international moving companies, and immigration attorneys. Everyone seemed to have a story about a son enrolling in a university in Canberra or a niece getting a green card in New York. The prevailing mood was not one of a panicky, immediate desire to flee. Instead people were trying to expand their options. By purchasing property and businesses overseas, by dispersing family members in other countries, people could feel more comfortable about their ability to go to Queensland or California if the need arose.

Something more like panic was evident immediately after Tiananmen Square. Political demonstrations had been almost unknown in Hong Kong, which was essentially one big marketplace, but demonstrations in favor of human rights and against the Chinese regime occurred after Tiananmen Square. Lines of visa seekers snaked all around the embassies. Hong Kong's property market collapsed.

Through the next three years it appeared that a showdown between Western and Asian political values might occur, with Hong Kong as the battleground. An energetic British Tory politician named Chris Patten was appointed governor of Hong Kong in 1992. Practically as soon as he arrived, he began criticizing the Chinese government for its human-rights derelictions. Through the previous decade, the British government had seemed uninterested in what Hong Kong's political fate might be after the Chinese took control. For that matter, Britain had never bothered to offer democratic rule within the colony. Hong Kong's governing body, the Legislative Council, or "Legco," had sixty members, of whom only eighteen were directly chosen by the Hong Kong electorate. Patten proposed an immediate set of reforms to make the colony's government more representative and democratic, and he said that Britain had a long-term interest in human rights in Hong Kong.

The Chinese government responded with direct denunciations of Patten's meddling and with vague threats about what the future might hold for Hong Kong. And yet somehow, by 1993, the pall had lifted and the problems seem to have been resolved. Patten had tempered his demands somewhat, and the Chinese and British governments had sat down for negotiations on Hong Kong's political structure.

The more important change, however, seemed to be in the temper of Hong Kong. Soon after the shock of Tiananmen Square, Hong Kong's Chinese looked to Britain as their protector. If they were left alone, at China's mercy, they would have no rights at all! But by 1993 the air of emergency had passed. Interests from mainland China had invested heavily in Hong Kong, buying 20 percent of Hong Kong's real estate (and in the process reviving the real estate market). How radical could their intentions be?

In the spring of 1993 I met a group of Hong Kong business families. All of them had property and emigration rights in other countries, but all of them were staying for the time being in Hong Kong. "So much talk!" one of the women said, with a dismissive laugh, when I asked her about Patten's campaign. "There is money to be made!"

9

The Impact
of the Asian System

IN 1978 WILLIAM MANCHESTER, biographer of Douglas MacArthur and author of *The Death of a President,* returned to the Pacific atolls where he had fought and nearly been killed as a Marine during World War II. Everywhere he traveled he saw signs of restored Japanese economic strength. "In peace," he concluded, "Hirohito's subjects have achieved what eluded them in war: dominance of a Greater East Asia Co-Prosperity Sphere. . . . The victors of V-E and V-J days . . . have been outmaneuvered, outsold, and outsmarted by the vanquished."[1]

I was born four years after V-J day and so have no direct memory of America as victor or Japan as vanquished. I only hazily remember the days from the 1950s when "Made in Japan" meant shoddy goods. Yet when I read the memoirs of those who, like Manchester, had seen American power at its zenith and Japan in utter defeat, I have been impressed by how soon after the war most of them seized on the idea that there had been a turnabout and that Japan had in some sense "won."

In 1955, twenty-three years before Manchester made his journey and just ten years after Japanese officials signed the instruments of surrender aboard the *Missouri,* Richard Wright, author of *Black Boy* and *Native Son,* attended a conference of nonaligned nations in Bandung, Indonesia. Japan at the time had barely regained its formal independence. It was only beginning to rebuild its industrial base, largely on the strength of resupply orders coming from U.S. troops fighting in the Korean War. Its per capita income was still well below that of the Philippines. The nonaligned movement, led by Sukarno of Indonesia and Nehru of India, was being advertised as the next big force in world affairs. Nonetheless, when Wright reported on the Bandung conference in his book *The Color Curtain,* he marveled at how skillfully Japan was rebuilding its relations in Asia and the rest of the nonwhite world. Japan, Wright said, was walking a tightrope,

> bowing and smiling to all sides among people over whom she once so brutally ruled, trying to place herself at the disposal of other Asian and African nations, offering her aid as a technical expert, hoping thereby to stimulate trade and retrieve her position as the real leader of Asia. . . . One Australian journalist commented bitterly, "Bandung means that Japan really won the war in the Pacific. . . ."[2]

To say, as many Americans have, that Japan really "won" the war appeals to a sense of irony but blurs the truth. The emergence of a Japan-centered Asian economic system resembles the wartime *kyoeiken,* or "co-prosperity sphere," in certain limited ways. Now as then, Japan is the strongest member of the system. A rhetoric of pan-Asian values is again on the rise. Japan has used its relationships in Asia to help solve its worst strategic problems, which are to ensure that food and fuel keep flowing into the country and that exports keep flowing out, both of which are necessary for people to remain employed. In each case there is a dramatic gap between power and accountability: the rest of the region in shaped by forces, originating in Japan, over which it has little control. In the 1930s and 1940s that was because of a sheer imbalance of military power. Now it is because the Japanese political and business systems have lacked feedback loops to let them respond to complaints and pressures from outside Japan (except, of course, when the U.S. government issues its periodic trade demands).

But the differences between the *kyoeiken* and today's Asian system are much more obvious. Japanese troops are not stationed throughout the region. At least in formal terms, democracy applies in Japan and several neighboring countries. The spread of the system has enriched the rest of Asia far more than either European colonialism or Japanese military "co-prosperity" ever did.

It is enough to take the modern Asian system on its own terms without hauling in comparisons to a war. The region's dynamism, centered in Japan but rapidly spreading, will change life throughout

East Asia and will change the circumstances in which the rest of the world operates.

The Impact on Asia

Environment.   One tangible effect of pan-Asian growth on Asian life is environmental. Cities are polluted; oceans are over-fished; forest reserves disappear. This is also the effect about which Asian officials least like to hear lectures from the Western world. The Chinese reply that they have as much right to industrialize as the British did in the days of the dark, satanic mills. Europeans and North Americans in Greenpeace lambaste the Koreans and Tai-wanese for running factory-fishing boats; the Koreans and Taiwanese reply that, by eating fish rather than so much red meat, they are living lower on the food chain than most Westerners do. In 1990 I asked a Vietnamese official in Hanoi how the government planned to cope with the surge in logging of the hillsides. He looked at me with a "you asked for it!" expression and said, "For one thing, I can tell you that we will not spray Agent Orange on the trees."

Nonetheless, the fact remains that in some parts of East Asia—most obviously Thailand but also parts of the Philippines and China—the immediate limit on growth is environmental. After pouring investment into Greater Bangkok in the late 1980s, Japanese firms shifted elsewhere in the 1990s because air and water pollution around Bangkok had become so extreme. Throughout East Asia, environmental pressures reflect the growth of an integrated regional economy. The first real sign of renewed commerce between Cambodia and the outside world was the stream of lumber trucks rumbling from the Cambodian hinterland, through the Vietnamese hills, to Vietnam's ports in the early 1990s.

The result is a new version of the trade patterns of the colonial days. A century ago, Burma sent teak to England, Indochina sent rubber to France, and the islands of the East Indies sent spices and tea to Holland. Now oil, logs, fish, and squid flow principally to Japan and Korea from Thailand, Malaysia, Indonesia, and the countries of Indochina. Four fifths of the logs cut in Sarawak,[3] in northwestern Borneo, go to sawmills in Japan, where they are mainly used for plywood, construction, furniture, and the disposable chopsticks Japanese diners use by the tens of millions every day.[4]

In short, the growth of East Asia is chewing up the environment in ways similar in character to what happened in Europe and North America but more dramatic in speed and effect. (The pioneers who fanned out across the American prairie did not have machines to help them clear and fell.) Today, dynamite-fishing, superfreighters for log shipment, and big log-cutting rigs put the process on a completely different scale.

Migration. Rapid economic growth creates strains on any society. Large economic differences among societies create strains of a special sort: the pressure to migrate, shown most vividly in North America along the U.S.-Mexican border.

These strains exist in Asia, too. If the world ran on purely economic principles, the pressures created by the flow of money and investment within Asia would have been offset by a flow of people, like air or water moving from higher-pressure to lower-pressure zones. Peasants from the hinterlands of Thailand would not simply move into Bangkok, where they could make a few dollars a day on the construction scaffolds or the brothels. They would go all the way to Tokyo and Osaka, which even during Japan's "recession" of the early 1990s were chronically short of low-skill laborers.

To a modest degree this flow now occurs. Some foreigners do leak into Japan. At the top of the ladder among Japan's resident-alien population are First World professionals—English teachers, models, copywriters for advertising agencies, stars on Japanese baseball teams, all-purpose *gaijin*, or "foreigners," to add an international gloss to the staff of Japanese politicians or executives. At the bottom of the ladder are Asian and Middle Eastern immigrants who do strong-back work and mainly exist outside the law.

Yet both groups together amount to mere handfuls compared to the number of foreigners other industrialized countries contain. According to a government survey conducted in 1991, there were about 100,000 foreigners residing legally inside Japan, a tiny fraction of the number of foreigners living legally in Los Angeles or London.[5] The Japanese public school system as a whole contained 5,463 foreign students in 1991, or fewer than the number of Japanese students in the New York metropolitan area public schools. The principal language among these foreigners was not Chinese or Korean or Thai—but Portuguese. This was because the largest group of foreign children legally in the schools were ethnically Japanese Brazilians who flocked back to the motherland in the late 1980s in search of work.[6]

The flow of people creates for Japan, and for the Asian system more generally, a dilemma in the classic sense. To let in many more immigrants would be to challenge many of the fundamentals of the Japanese social organization. Yet to keep foreigners out is to invite resentment from the rest of the region. Lives everywhere in East Asia are affected by Japan, but most other people in the region lack the reciprocal ability to participate in Japanese life. The ability to absorb and coopt outsiders who might otherwise be rebels remains a great strategic advantage of America, as it was in its time for the Roman empire. Japan's inability to do so is its great strategic weakness.

Sentimentality and ideology. Westerners have in this century worried about the "Yellow Peril," a term used by Kaiser Wilhelm II at the turn of the century to warn about the economic challenge posed by coolie labor. For several centuries the "White Peril" has hung over Asia, posed by missionaries and colonizers. A sense of White Peril crops up particularly in Japanese politics, evoked by the feeling of being victimized and unloved by the Western world.

Since at least the Meiji era, Japanese leaders have been trying strenuously to get a little respect from the Western world—and when they have been unfairly spurned, they have often responded with an intense embrace of Asia. Where else, the pan-Asian theorists of various ages have asked, can Japan really feel at home? This emotional cycle lay behind Japan's "Light of Asia" rhetoric before and during World War II; signs of a similar resentful mood burbled up in the early 1990s.

In the late 1980s Shintaro Ishihara was the biggest vote-getter in Japanese politics and clearly spoke for something real in the Japanese psyche, much as George Wallace, Ross Perot, and Jesse Jackson have in their times revealed truths about American opinion. In 1990 I heard Ishihara talking at a dinner about the eternal conflict between the "rice paddy people" and the "forest people" that, in his view, lay at the root of trade disputes. The "rice paddy people"— Japanese and other Asians—were inherently cooperative and team-spirited because of their centuries of depending on one another. By contrast, the "forest people"—Westerners—had spent eons running through the Teutonic woods and had absorbed an "every man for himself" code. It was only natural that these two "races" would produce different economic models. "As for the question of whether the Japanese are a superior race or not, I think only our achievements will tell," Ishihara said in an interview with *Time* magazine late in 1989.[7]

"Japan is now qualified to revive a global idea called the Greater East Asia Coprosperity Sphere, which had no chance before the war," Ishihara said in 1991 in a Japanese magazine called *Sansarra*. In 1992 in Tokyo, a crowd of twenty-eight hundred people paid $220 apiece to hear Ishihara speak on the theme that the United States could not have beaten Saddam Hussein without equipment and inventions from Japan.[8] In 1993, after the newly elected reform prime minister Morihiro Hosokawa had apologized to the rest of Asia for Japan's "aggression" during World War II, Ishihara said that Hosokawa "deserved death" for this slur on Japan's past.[9]

Ishihara represents an extreme, but a more tempered and serious "pan-Asian" view has evolved in the Japan of the 1990s. This line of analysis emerged as an increasingly direct challenge to Western political theories. In particular it was a challenge to the West's conviction that, in the long run, societies should be based more on individual rights than on collective welfare.

Some parts of modern Asian experience conform well to the fundamental Western concept. South Korea is the best example: it worked hard, it grew rich, and once its assembly lines were running, its people switched from outright militarist government to something closer to electoral democracy.

Yet other Asian countries have evolved in different ways. Even as they have modernized and prospered in material terms, they have tried to steer their political systems away from the excesses of what they call "Western-style democracy." The most successful Asian societies are, in different ways, fundamentally more repressive than America and most of Europe are, and their repression has so far been a key to their economic success. Japan, Taiwan, and Singapore allow citizens much less latitude than most Western societies do. (Despite its recent liberalizations the same is still true of Korea.) And through their determination to control individuals they have up to this point made the whole society, including its business sector, function more effectively than most in the West.

The Asian model is not "superior" in any sweeping sense. It is more confining for individuals. It has so far proven inferior in generating new scientific knowledge and fostering lone creative talents. It is hard on the weak, any kind of minorities, and outsiders. It could not be applied in most Western countries, especially the United States. Like any other system, it will encounter shocks, slowdowns, and setbacks. Yet where it has been applied in Asia, its impact is undeniable. The lesson of the Soviet economic collapse would seem to be that a completely controlled economy cannot survive. The lesson of the rising Asian system is that economies with some degree of control not only can survive but also grow strong.

Yu Shan Wu, of National Taiwan University, has suggested a way to think about the combination of control and freedom expressed in the Asian economic system. The former Communist states, he says, were based on the principle of thoroughgoing control. Property was owned by the state, and investment decisions were made by the state. The Anglo-American system strives toward the ideal of thoroughgoing lack of control. In principle, private owners should control all property, and private groups should make most business decisions. Japan, Wu concludes, has pioneered what is being applied elsewhere in Asia as a new approach: private ownership of property, public "guidance" and control of large-scale economic decisions. Big industrial combines compete bitterly against each other for prominence and market share, yet the largest decisions, including the choice of goals toward which they will strive, are influenced by the state, not left to the invisible hand. This partly controlled approach reduces the freedom of each individual and each particular company that operates within it, Wu says, yet it has certain long-term advantages over the private/private system.

The crucial conceptual innovations produced by the Asian model are "excessive" choice and "destructive" competition. Classical free-market economic theory says that these ideas are virtual impossibilities—not just in economics but also in most of social life as well. There never can be too much competition in a market, just as a person never can have too much choice. In practice everyone recognizes the limits of these theories. Children do best when raised in families, and families must be held together by something more than each member's sense of short-term gain. But as a matter of principle it is very hard for modern Westerners to say that either markets or individuals can become "too" free.

In the Western context, which reaches its extreme form in the United States, the concept of individual liberty is pure, elegant, and easy to defend. The countervailing idea of "common good" or "collective welfare" is, by comparison, vague-sounding and weak. The concept of common good fits easily into American politics only during wartime, when the struggle against an enemy defines what the "common good" for Americans is. This is why so many American leaders have used war or warlike images to drum up support for what should really just be called the "national interest."[10]

Within the Asian system, societies can approach these issues from a less complicated perspective. They were built on neither an Enlightenment concept of individual rights nor a capitalist concept of free markets as a goal, and they demonstrate in countless ways their belief that less choice for individuals can mean more freedom and success for the social whole.

The division of labor between men and women is one striking example. Despite some signs of change and with exceptions in some countries, the difference between a man's "role" and a woman's is more cut and dried in Asia than in the United States. This strict assignment of sex roles is unfair in an obvious way to women, since the vast majority of them cannot really compete for business, political, academic, or other opportunities. (Roughly 40 percent of all Japanese women are technically in the country's work force, but only about 1 percent hold positions in which they supervise some other worker.) The arrangement is unfair in a different way to men, because especially in Japan the typical salaryman is cut off from the very idea of dealing with women as equals and has what looks to the outsider like an emotionally barren family life. Japanese surveys show that the average salaryman takes more emotional satisfaction from his workplace life than the average Westerner does, but less from his relations with his children and wife. Nonetheless, this system has a tremendous practical impact: by making it difficult for women to do anything except concentrate on their families, the traditional Asian system steers more of its human talent toward child-rearing than a more "open" system of career choice would. The Asian model "overinvests" in child-rearing, much as it has overinvested in factories, engineering, and production in general. Westerners need not admire each or any part of this system; but they should not fool themselves about its overall success.

The East Asian Impact on the World

The rise of the East Asian system is potentially beneficial for the world in several ways.

- It is interesting. There is something new in the world, which provides new ideas about how life should be lived.
- It has made the world's distribution of income and opportunities somewhat more fair. Two generations ago Asia was a starving continent, in whose name children were made to clean

plates in Europe or North America. For the last generation it has been the fastest-progressing part of the world.

· It is fundamentally pacific, in the small-p sense. The prospect of growing rich clearly does not make military force irrelevant or remove the national jealousies that in the past have led to war. But it just as clearly opens other channels of ambition and makes military conquest less attractive than it would otherwise be. North Korea would be less dangerous if it were more prosperous. Vietnam has become less an armed camp as it has become more oriented toward world trade.

· Finally, the wealth created in Asia is to some extent shared. America's farmers export more to Japan than to any other country. Australia's travel industry would be in trouble without prosperous visitors from Asia. The tools needed to reduce misery in the still-poor majority of the world are money, technology, and experience in applying technology to help societies leapfrog ahead. These are precisely the tools that Korea, Taiwan, Singapore, and Japan can supply.

Yet in other ways the Asian system's success will create problems for its rivals. The most serious involve the shrinking range of independent action. A century and a half ago, Japan's rush to modernize was prompted by its fear of losing independence. The success of that drive, and its spread to the rest of the region, have shifted the balance of dependence in the world. This process has involved three types of change:

· one-way shifts of industrial dependence, which make it hard for residents of some countries to catch up with residents of other countries in the long run;
· shifts in dependence for military equipment;
· shifts in the climate of culture and ideas that confine and distort arguments.

All of these shifts principally involve Japan and the United States. Japan is the one Asian country of sufficient scale and technological achievement to begin to reverse the historic balance of dependence with the West. The United States is the one Western country whose history has accustomed it to nearly complete independence of action but whose policies have rapidly increased its dependence on Japan.

Industrial Dependence

In 1993 I heard a former IBM official describe one of the company's
production arrangements with Toshiba. IBM and Toshiba each put
up $1 billion for a new factory that would make flat-panel computer
displays. IBM provided much of the fundamental technology, from
its still-vast scientific resources; Toshiba supplied the manufacturing
know-how. The companies would own the resulting venture fifty-
fifty. This joint undertaking shouldn't be thought of as either an
"American" or a "Japanese" venture, the IBM man said. The factory and design labs "happened" to be located in Japan, he said—
but that was just chance. For the next generation of products, the
factories might be located in America.

Well, they might be, but I wouldn't bet the company on it, or
even bet $10. The pattern of most such ventures was to pool both
technology and capital from the two nations—but to put them to
work inside Japan. The result was yet another indication of the
familiar difference between a system that favors consumers and one
that favors producers. The joint ventures helped America's consumers, by making new Japanese products that they could buy. And
it helped Japan's producers, by providing jobs in the short run and
the momentum for future jobs in the longer term.

"For most Japanese electronics firms this is a no-lose proposition," Bill Powell, a *Newsweek* correspondent based in Tokyo,
wrote while the IBM-Toshiba deal was in the works. "For their
investment they get access to technologies in which they lag; then
they get to manufacture in Japan. They do so knowing that long-
term success in the market comes from improving the manufactur-
ability of a given product—that is, figuring out ways to make it more
efficiently, but also improving the product itself with changes on the
production line."[11] In addition, Powell said, the Japanese firms
hoped for exactly the result illustrated by the IBM official: that the
idea of "Japanese" and "American" companies would blur, for political purposes, and U.S. government officials would think of IBM
and Toshiba as one big, stateless, transpacific consortium, even
though the "joint" manufacturing all "happened" to be done outside
the United States.

By the logic that prevails in most U.S.-based corporations, joint
ventures with Japanese partners make eminent sense. Without a
Japanese alliance, foreign firms find it difficult to get any foothold
whatsoever in the vast Japanese market. Once they take a Japanese
partner, they have a chance to distribute their products in Japan and

to take advantage of often superb Japanese manufacturing skills. In 1992, just after Intel announced that its new "flash memory" chips would actually be manufactured by Sharp in Japan, three other U.S.-based companies announced that they, too, would try to produce flash memory chips. All three said that the manufacturing would be done by partners in Japan. John Burgess, of *The Washington Post,* pointed out that virtually all the jobs resulting from these alliances would wind up in Japan, yet the American companies felt they had no choice but to enter these "strategic alliances."[12] Their dependence on foreign partners—for money, manufacturing skill, and access to potential customers in Japan—left them with no realistic alternative of making the products in the United States. If past developments were any indication, the next generation of chips, and the next and the next, would also be easier to make in Japan, since that is where engineers and designers were getting firsthand experience.

Were the Japanese companies "dependent," too? Evidently so, since they willingly joined the alliances rather than trying to make flash memory chips on their own. Could the American companies learn from the partnership, in a way that would prepare them for future breakthroughs? In principle they could, especially by studying Japanese manufacturing techniques. In reality, however, such reciprocal learning was unlikely; the U.S. business system was arranged to send information out, and the Japanese system to take it in. In 1991 the Hitachi corporation announced that if its American employees wanted to improve themselves through further education, the company would pick up part of the cost. "The company offers you the opportunity to prepare yourself for more opportunity and higher pay," the brochure said. It listed the rules for eligibility: Employees must have worked for Hitachi for at least a year, they must have had good performance ratings, they must have used up the other scholarships and schooling benefits available to them. And oh, yes, there was one other rule: "Japanese language courses are *not* eligible under this plan."[13] American employees who spoke Japanese would have more independence of action within the company—and in dealing with other Japanese firms. It is hardly Hitachi's responsiblity to teach them all Japanese; it is intriguing that this should be the one form of self-improvement the company would not subsidize.

The general pattern of dependence shifts has been for American firms, especially in high-tech, to become more reliant on what Japanese firms could offer, and for Japanese firms to become less reliant on supplies or techniques from the United States. American firms often described this process as "globalization" or "interdependence," but the results were not as symmetrical as such terms would suggest.

In 1990, officials from the American semiconductor-making consortium Sematech visited technical trade shows in Japan. They concluded that Japanese producers were making components and machinery available to other industries in Japan before offering the same products to customers in the United States. Their report said,

> There is a six-month or longer delay before new tools are introduced into the United States. This is due to an emphasis on first filling the market needs in Japan and Asia. . . . The most key point of the SEMICON show [a Japanese technical exhibit] is that a lot of advanced equipment was shown in Japan that is not yet available in the United States.[14]

The following year the U.S. General Accounting Office released a study titled *U.S. Business Access to Certain Foreign State-of-the-Art Technology*.[15] It concluded that American firms chronically received key parts or tools six months to a year after their Japanese counterparts, and that most of the delays could not be explained as cases of "nationality-blind" corporate competition. That is, if Toshiba's semiconductor-making division had been preferentially selling chips to Toshiba's computer-making division, that would be easy to explain as a simple matter of corporate self-interest. But, according to the investigators, Japanese firms sold to *competing* firms within Japan at the very time they were withholding supplies from U.S.-based competitors: "Most of the U.S. firms that cited instances of Japanese withholding said they knew the products they were seeking from Japanese suppliers were being sold to other Japanese companies," the GAO report said. "They had seen them in use at Japanese plants."[16] It added that most of the U.S. government officials it interviewed "thought withholding by Japanese suppliers was a serious and fairly pervasive problem."[17]

In the fall of 1989, Robert Noyce, one of the venerated founders of Intel, gave a congressional committee a specific illustration of "withholding." Senator Jeff Bingaman, of New Mexico, pointed out that even if all the companies that made "steppers," "etchers," and other semiconductor-producing equipment were Japanese, these firms were still competing against each other. Therefore, if Nikon was for some reason reluctant to sell steppers to American companies, some other Japanese firm would presumably be happy to make the sale. Noyce agreed that this made sense but said that, in reality, it did not work that way. He gave this example:

> At a conference in Hawaii recently, the man responsible for exporting the Nikon steppers to America was asked directly when the [new model], the latest and greatest, would be available in America. His reponse, as recorded, was "when appropriate." We feel a little uncomfortable about that.[18]

The possiblity that companies might throw their weight around favoring some clients and punishing others, is hardly unique to the new Asian economy. In the early 1990s the American computer industry was full of similar allegations about domestic firms—that Microsoft gave some software developers an advantage over others by revealing details of its operating systems ahead of time, or that Intel made sure that some computer companies got its advanced processing chips sooner than their rivals. The difference in the Japanese case is the possiblity of a preference based on nationality rather than corporate rivalry—that is, a political rather than a purely commercial version of throwing weight around.

If the world ran on the straightforward supply-demand principles spelled out in economic texts, a company like Cray Research would not have to worry about relying on chips from Fujitsu's semiconductor division while also competing against supercomputers made by Fujitsu and other Japanese firms. As long as Cray offered top dollar, it would in theory get the chips at the same time as any competitors in Japan. In the world of real commerce, Cray and dependent companies like it have something real to fear. In 1987 the U.S. Defense Science Board issued exactly this warning about Cray. At the time, Cray relied on Japanese suppliers for all the memory chips it used in its computers. "As Japanese firms evolve from the role of merchant semiconductor manufacturers into computer/telecommunication *system* builders, *it would not be an illogical strategic business policy to delay release of the most advanced chips to competitors in the systems market,* including those residing in the United States."[19] (Emphasis as in original.)

Indeed, the German company Siemens had already felt the consequences of such a strategy. In the early 1980s, Siemens shifted its emphasis heavily into high-tech products, including telecommunications systems. "More than once, product development stalled when the Japanese refused to sell their newest chip to Siemens as both raced to develop competing telecommunications products," *Business Week* said in a corporate profile of Siemens. "We were being manipulated," the head of Siemens' semiconductor division, Jurgen Knorr, said in 1989.[20] A famous Japanese commentator, Hajime Karatsu, said at about the same time, "If Japan stopped exporting semiconductors, the United States would be turned upside down. This gives Japan an extraordinary amount of bargaining power."[21]

This pattern of dependence has naturally been most visible in the electronics industry, since its fast-changing technology makes supply delays especially critical. But similar patterns have appeared elsewhere. The MIT Commission on Industrial Productivity, for instance, investigated a shift of dependence in the machine-tool industry in the 1980s. Virtually every modern industry requires machine tools, which are classified as machines that make other machines. They range from simple lathes to exotic computer-controlled robots. Until the early 1980s the United States dominated world production of machine tools. Since then, Japanese manufacturers have done so. In the mid-1980s the director of a General Motors study on machine tools told the commission, "If you buy the very best from Japan, it has already been in Toyota Motors for two years, and if you buy from West Germany, it has already been with BMW for a year and a half." The commission concluded:

> The crucial implication here is that domestic user industries that are dependent upon foreign machine tools for manufacturing key components will chronically lag [behind] their foreign competitors, and perpetually be trying to catch up rather than to lead.[22]

The Branch-Plant Syndrome

Not being able to get first-line products is an extreme manifestation of dependence. A subtler but in the long run more important one concerns the pattern of economic activity. When one national economy becomes dependent on another for the oomph in economics— for the best technology, for investable capital, for the most exciting new products—it suffers the familiar woes of a "branch plant" economy. The big decisions are made by someone else somewhere else. At least so far, the result of Japanese branch-plant growth in America has been to move jobs out of the country even faster than U.S.-based firms were already doing.

"Japanese-owned plants have become a significant factor in the U.S. trade deficit because they increasingly buy parts and materials from parent companies and other foreign sources," the U.S. Commerce Department said in a study released early in 1992. In 1977, Japanese-owned firms in the United States imported 33 percent of all the materials and components they used. Ten years later, they were importing 43 percent of the materials."[23] According to a study conducted at the University of Michigan in 1993, the average car produced in a Japanese transplant in the United States contained more than $3,400 worth of parts imported from Japan. The average car made by Ford, Chrysler, or General Motors in the United States contained less than $100 worth of imported Japanese parts.[24] In 1993 Toyota ran an extensive ad campaign in American newspapers and magazines, pointing out how many thousands of jobs its factories had created. (The campaign was "for educational purposes, about a global company with a Japanese name," Toyota's manager of external affairs told *The New York Times*.[25]) On a net basis, the transplants had, of course, eliminated many thousands more jobs at U.S.-based auto and auto-parts firms. In 1992 Ford, General Motors, and Chrysler directly employed more than six hundred thousand people in their American plants. Toyota, Nissan, and Honda together employed fewer than thirty-five thousand Americans. In October 1993, the U.S. Department of Labor released a study comparing employment patterns in Japanese-owned and American-owned automobile plants in the United States (based on data collected in 1989). In the Japanese-owned plants, 86 percent of the labor force was in low-skill jobs; the average for all automobile plants in the United States was 61 percent. Similarly, professional workers made up only 6 percent of the work force in Japanese-owned plants, versus 22 percent for all U.S. automobile plants.[26]

Until the borderless tomorrow arrives, each person's prospects for a satisfying and rewarding job rise and fall with the welfare of companies based in his or her homeland. (Ask anyone in Britain.) If Northern Telecom, based in Canada, loses market share to Fujitsu, there will be fewer opportunities for Canadians. They will not sit on the Fujitsu board, nor supervise Fujitsu's labs, nor decide about Fujitsu's line of credit at the major banks in its corporate family, nor serve as its company doctors, nor do the architectural design and construction for its new plants. They may eventually get to work at branch plants and dealerships it sets up in Canada, but that will never be the same. In his book *Head to Head,* Lester Thurow used Canada to illustrate the branch-plant predicament. With their integration into the U.S. and increasingly the Japanese economies, Canadians will always be comfortable, Thurow said. But "they can never have the best," because they don't run the companies.

> The best jobs (CEO, CFO, head of research, etc.) are back at headquarters, and that is somewhere else. Even if Canadians were to get those jobs, and they don't, they would have to live abroad. There is something at stake! . . .
>
> What is always true is even more true in Japanese corporations. Sixty-nine per cent of the senior managers of Japanese subsidiaries in America are Japanese. In contrast, only 20 percent of senior managers of American subsidiaries in Japan are American. American managers working for Japanese firms usually find that there is a promotion ceiling beyond which they cannot go.[27]

Once a country becomes fundamentally dependent on another for technology and money, then it clearly is happier to get investment than to have it go somewhere else. Malaysia would rather attract new Japanese factories and department stores than watch them slip past to Indonesia. The United States would rather attract a Matsushita air-conditioning plant than have it go to Mexico, for shipment back to customers in Miami or New Orleans. But it is clearly better to have more control over the decision yourself—or by people subject to the constraints of your political system and social mores. Public control is weak enough in the best circumstances; the "investors" who engineered the takeover boom of the 1980s were mainly American citizens subject, at least in theory, to American mores and American laws. An economy's vulnerability is all the greater when the big decisions are completely beyond its power to affect.

In a study of Japanese international investment called *Japan, Disincorporated,* published in 1988, Leon Hollerman pointed out what this kind of dependence can mean. Japanese investment in the United States has been simultaneously high- and low-tech, he said. Biotechnology and tire-making. Computer laboratories and resorts:

> In the high-technology fields, its primary purposes have been to acquire technology, know-how, or distribution networks. In low technology, its primary purposes have been to liquidate Japan's own dual economy and to jump over existing or antic-

ipated U.S. protectionist barriers. By attracting . . . Japan's low- and middle-technology firms, the United States would be building or reinforcing its own dual economy while helping to liquidate the dual economy in Japan. . . . Japan's resources would be allocated primarily to high technology while those of the United States would be dissipated in obsolete activities supported by the welfare state."[28]

The "dual economy" Hollerman refers to is what every modern nation wants to avoid: shoeshine boys bowing and scraping to stockbrokers, minimum-wage burger-flippers alongside researchers and doctors. Because its policy has focused on reducing dependence, Japan has had more power to push its economy in the direction it wants, avoiding this social bifurcation and the other undesirable effects of economic change. The United States has increasingly been pushed in a direction it doesn't like, as economic dynamism has shifted beyond its control.

A Temporary Problem?

Perhaps these shifts in dependence have been either accidental or temporary. That is, if Japanese firms are favoring suppliers from their own country, they may be doing so unintentionally—and, even if they are doing it deliberately, they might already be evolving toward a more "borderless" approach. The evidence to date runs the other way.

In the 1990s as in the 1970s and the 1930s and the 1890s, Japanese policy abounds with statements about the importance of producing "purely" Japanese products and continuing to reduce dependence on the outside world. In 1991 MITI released a paper comparing research-and-development efforts in Japan, Europe, and the United States. For the previous few years, it noted, Japan had achieved a positive trade balance in high-tech products, after long years of importing technology from the United States. The clashes between Japan and America over semiconductors and supercomputers merely confirmed that "Japan's technology will soon be overtaking U.S. technology." In these circumstances, MITI concluded, Japan had to redouble its efforts so it could "maintain its leadership in world technology as a whole."[29] That is, it shouldn't sit back and let "interdependence" occur.

There are countless other illustrations of the principle that many Japanese firms and most parts of the Japanese government still view "self-sufficiency" as a virtue and dependence as a weakness to be corrected over time. MITI planning documents use language similar to that of military documents in the 1930s, emphasizing the need to be "free" from reliance on foreign supplies. In the springtime of 1993, Japan's Space and Technology Agency announced that henceforth it would use the "genuinely domestically manufactured" H-2 rocket, rather than the American space shuttle, to move material to an international space station.[30]

"Japanese computer companies would desperately like to be free of American microprocessors," John Stern, of the American Electronics Association, told me in 1991. "They will probably succeed if the computer world goes to open-architecture RISC chips and freely licensed UNIX"—that is, to designs that can be produced anywhere (rather than Intel's and Motorola's tightly licensed models). In 1993 Japan's National Institute for Fusion Science announced that a new supercomputer from NEC was successfully handling the institute's computational chores—thereby eliminating the "need" for supercomputers from Cray.[31]

Military Dependence

In 1952, Japanese manufacturers were finally pulling themselves out of the rubble, helped by contracts to supply the U.S. military on the Korean front. U.S. policy encouraged Japan to recover as quickly as it could. The only exception concerned the aircraft industry: the United States flatly prohibited Japanese companies from buiding airplanes. Ishikawajima–Harima Heavy Industries had been a leader in Japan's prewar aviation industry. In 1952 its president, Toshio Doko, said that someday Japan must again have an aircraft industry of its own. "If Japan does not build jet aircraft," he said, "it will be a third-tier country."[32]

Uncomfortable as Americans have been with "industrial policy" in general, they have usually accepted the need for a "military-industrial" policy. Whether they fear the strength of what Dwight Eisenhower first called the "military-industrial complex" or conversely fear that it is not strong enough, Americans have generally conceded that its size and nature are legitimate subjects of governmental attention.

Therefore it is not surprising that the kind of dependence that has received greatest attention from the U.S. government involves the military. More than at any other period in its history, the sources of America's military supplies do not now lie within its borders. Japanese chauvinists such as Shintaro Ishihara may be exaggerating when they say that Japanese suppliers could stop the U.S. military in its tracks by cutting off shipments, or by selling to an enemy. But the Pentagon and the CIA are close enough to that view to have commissioned repeated studies and policy papers since the early 1980s about ways to reduce their vulnerability.

In 1991 Mel Levine, then a Democratic congressman from southern California, made public a report, *Foreign Ownership and Control of U.S. Industry.*[33] The report had been prepared by the Defense Science Board for the under secretary of defense. It contended that while foreign investment in the United States was on the whole good economically, it reduced the military's assurance that it could get the supplies it wanted when it needed them most. The report told the story of the lowly but indispensable product known as the miniature ball bearing. Virtually every weapon in an advanced arsenal uses at least some ball bearings. Without them turrets cannot rotate and jet engines cannot run. But it is not a simple matter to begin producing them all of a sudden—especially the tiny, precision bearings required for advanced instruments.

In 1985, the Minebea company of Japan bought the largest American producer of precision ball bearings, New Hampshire Ball Bearings (NHBB). The sale was controversial inside the Reagan administration. Despite Minebea's assurances that it would invest in the New Hampshire plant to keep it running, some U.S. government officials feared that Minebea would have no reason to keep producing these military-critical parts in the United States. Prime Minister Nakasone of Japan made a personal appeal to President Reagan to permit the sale; Reagan agreed. Shortly thereafter, the fears expressed by critics were confirmed. Minebea shifted production of most of its precision ball bearings to Thailand. The company closed a factory in New Hampshire and said it was shifting the plant's production to a facility in Chatsworth, California. But after an investigation, officials from the U.S. Customs Service and the Department of Defense (DoD) accused Minebea of falsifying its production figures to conceal how much manufacturing had been moved outside the United States. This is an extreme-sounding case; nonetheless, the Customs Service contended that Minebea was making the bearings in Singapore and Thailand, shipping them to Chatsworth, and then repackaging them and stamping them "U.S.A."

"In view of the fact that 80 percent of America's ball bearings

...rom foreign sources and that NHBB may have been the largest ...cer of certain ball bearings, Minebea's substitution of foreign ...orts for all or part of the production seriously threatens the a..ured access of the U.S. military," the Defense Science Board said. "Even before losing Minebea DoD could not meet its estimated bearing surge requirements for a conventional war."[34]

With variations in detail, and usually with products more impressive-sounding than ball bearings, the same pattern has occurred in other areas of U.S. military supplies. Since 1983, the Japanese and American militaries have been linked, at least in theory, through a technology-sharing agreement. Each side agreed to transfer military technology to the other, to avoid wasted effort and to have a more efficient joint defense. Under this agreement, and the defense arrangements that preceded it, the United States transferred or licensed thousands of systems to the Japanese *jieitai,* or self-defense force; in turn, these have formed the core of Japan's effort to build its own aircraft and space programs. Back the other way have come a handful (fewer than ten) of relatively low-tech innovations. During the first few years of the agreement, for instance, the most impressive transfer to the U.S. was a new system for organizing dry-dock repairs of warships, based on Japan's own highly successful shipbuilding industry.

In 1989 the Japanese military moved toward full-scale development of the FSX fighter plane, to replace its F-1 fighter. The U.S. government claimed, ineffectively, that Japan should simply buy an American fighter plane; as a result of these complaints the Japanese government finally agreed to base the FSX's design on the existing F-16, made by General Dynamics—and to share with American companies the new technologies that Japan added to the plane. The systems that were especially attractive from the American point of view, since Japanese companies were so strong in these fields, included composite-material technology, especially for making wings; phased-array radar; and the inertial reference system. By 1992 the U.S. General Accounting Office was reporting that American producers had tremendous trouble getting information about most of these advances from their Japanese partners.[35]

As Allied troops were massing in Saudi Arabia, Pentagon officials went to Tokyo, bringing a "wish list" of ten high-tech items they hoped the Japanese military would transfer without delay. The negotiations went nowhere. The Japanese government, more and more publicly critical of America's bellicose threats against Saddam Hussein, would not comply with the request. (One of its arguments was that the technologies were controlled by private companies in

Japan, not by the government itself. This sounds plausible on its face but is at odds with a decades-long reality of government-co-ordinated technology projects, especially those involving defense.)[36]

Brief and decisive as the combat in Iraq turned out to be, it went on long enough to remind the U.S. military that its equipment depended on parts that were no longer produced inside the United States. A few months after the fighting ended, the Japanese government announced a punishment for a Japanese-based high-tech company that was half owned by Nippon Electric Company (NEC). The firm, Japan Aviation Electronics Industry (JAEI), had been caught selling parts and equipment to Iran during the Iran-Iraq war, in defiance of Japan's general ban on exports of military goods. This ban usually includes an exception for sales and transfers to the United States. The Japanese government said that, for its punishment, JAEI would be forbidden for eighteen months, to export products to anyone, *including* customers in the United States.

The result, in the U.S. military and among defense contractors, was barely concealed panic. The U.S. Justice Department had secured its own grand-jury indictment of JAEI for breaking the export ban. But the Defense Department and Honeywell, Inc., lobbied bitterly against any attempt to punish JAEI. Honeywell had received a large contract to build aircraft collision-avoidance systems, and without LCD display-screen components from JAEI it could not complete the project. JAEI offered to move assembly of the systems to the United States, to avoid the ban—but Hosiden, another Japanese company that made the LCD screens themselves, refused to agree, in protest of duties the Bush administration had recently imposed on Hosiden products. Indeed, in the summer of 1991 Hosiden suspended shipments of LCD screens to *all* customers in the United States, in particular Apple Computer, to protest the American tariffs. Hosiden said it would still supply those companies—but only at their factories outside the United States. The result was to force Apple and other makers of laptop computers to shift production to Singapore and other sites, where they could still receive the Japanese components on which they relied.[37]

The JAEI case revealed to the U.S. defense industry the dilemma of its dependence. It had faced the same dilemma in 1987, with the revelation that Toshiba Machine had sold propeller-making equipment to the Soviet Navy. For reasons of military strategy, the United States wanted to protest the sales by boycotting Toshiba products—but for reasons of technological dependence it could not afford to do so.[38]

With enough warning and investment, LCDs, ceramic packages, and almost any other component could be produced in American facilities. But "with enough warning" is a big "with" for a military establishment that will not always be able to choose the time, place, and circumstances of its combat as easily as it did in Iraq.

"I would consider it to be a rather good thing if the dependence of American advances in weaponry on Japanese technology increased," Ronald Dore, a British expert on Japan, wrote just before the final collapse of the Soviet Union. "Now that the Russians are so far behind in the new technology stakes, one could do with more dispersal of that kind of power."[39] Many countries around the world must feel the same way. But no country, including the United States, would willingly or deliberately shrink its own freedom of action, which is what a shift in dependence necessarily means.

Intellectual and Political Dependence

Semiconductors are only semiconductors, and miniature ball bearings, important as they may loom in "for want of a nail" scenarios, are finally just ball bearings. But there are times when a society's economic vigor affects its deeper values. Its political institutions, its conception of the good and desirable life, the traits that make it distinctive—all of these things rise or fall, in the long run, with its perceived success in its work.

This relationship is, of course, not linear or airtight. Italy is admired for many things even when its industries are suffering. South Africa was for years the richest country on its continent but not the best-loved. Yet in the long run a society will have a greater chance of making its values attractive, within its borders and without, if the society also works in a material sense. English is today the world's second most widely spoken language (after Mandarin Chinese) because of the military, economic, and political power of Britain in the eighteenth and nineteenth centuries and the United States in the twentieth. The artistic and literary achievements of Russian culture are celebrated now, but might be even more so if twentieth-century Russia had been a material success rather than rotting from within.

Economics textbooks can't really cope with this sense of being a "successful" or "winning" society, but I don't know how anyone could observe modern Asia and not think that it is something real.

The desire to catch up, to win, to escape inferiority and dependence is, after all, what has motivated Asian economic development for a century at least.

At the other end of the process, if a system has the sense of falling behind, economic dependence can aggravate existing problems in its politics and public discourse. This is happening in several ways in the United States.

The need to humor foreign funders.   In the old days, which is to say during the four decades after World War II, the main background factor in U.S. foreign-policy decisions was the Cold War. Marcos and Somoza were dictators, but they were *our* anti-Communist dictators. Vietnam was small and far away, but it was a place to draw the line against the Russians, or perhaps the Chinese.

With the disappearance of the Soviet Union and the introduction of huge, chronic international debts for the United States, a new background factor emerged: the need to keep foreign money flowing in. Nicholas Brady, who before his tenure as George Bush's treasury secretary investigated the five-hundred-point crash of the New York Stock Exchange in 1987, concluded that the basic cause of the crash was nervousness overseas. "People ask me, What was it that blew it off on the nineteenth of October?" he said in 1989. "Was it the twin deficits? Was it the tax legislation? . . . I don't think it was any of those things. . . . The real trigger was that the Japanese came in for their own reasons and sold an enormous amount of government bonds, and drove the thirty-year government bond rate up through 10 percent."[40]

At that point, with bond rates going up, the return on American stocks looked pallid—and from then on, through his term as treasury secretary, Brady seemed always to be glancing behind him, weighing his position in every dumping case or trade dispute against the need not to scare off the Japanese. Early in 1992, Ryutaro Hashimoto, who was then Japan's minister of finance, was caught in one of Japan's frequent scandals over "money politics." He was unloved in his own party, pilloried in the Japanese press—and publicly supported only by Nicholas Brady, constant in his desire to stay on good terms with Japanese capital. As Japan's stock market fell in 1992 and 1993, Japanese investors began pulling money out of the United States. But as long as the United States has the world's largest budget deficits and Japan has the world's largest pool of savings, the United States will need Japanese money.

Since the mid-1980s, when the United States settled into its role as a long-term, large-scale importer of the world's capital, many other officials have had to look over their shoulder at foreign investors in the same way. In the summer of 1991, U.S. trade representatives found themselves in the middle of a bizarre trade dispute with the French government. France had struck a "voluntary" agreement with Japan to limit Japanese cars to 3 percent of the French market. The U.S. government was applying pressure on France to admit cars from Honda's Marysville, Ohio, plant outside this quota, as American-made rather than "Japanese" cars.

Trade specialists could argue about whether the cars should be considered more "American" than "Japanese." According to most accounts, the "local content" of cars made at Honda's Marysville plant consisted mainly of engine blocks that were cast in Ohio plus various other parts purchased mainly from American subsidiaries of Japanese firms. The firms, in turn, were mainly assembling and repackaging components imported from Japan.

While Honda's vehicles were apparently less "Japanese" than the cars assembled in other Japanese transplants, such as Nissan's or Toyota's, none of the transplants even approached the domestic content of cars made by Chrysler, General Motors, or Ford. After a hands-on audit of Honda's Marysville operations in 1991, the U.S. Customs Service concluded that the cars made there did not even qualify for preferential treatment under the U.S.–Canada Free Trade Agreement. (That standard required merely that the value-added of the cars be more than 50 percent local. In effect, the Customs Service concluded that even the Marysville Hondas were "mainly" Japanese.) According to authoritative estimates, final assembly of a car—that is, the work Americans perform in Japanese transplant factories—accounts for less than 10 percent of the value of the finished vehicle. But because the American economy needed jobs, even lower-value ones at branch plants, the U.S. government's negotiating power was enlisted to get Honda Aerodecks into France. At just the time when its victory in the Cold War should have freed the U.S. government from one kind of distortion, its continuing economic dependence created another.

No outside power could ever censor discussion in the United States or elsewhere in the Western world. But self-censorship—tongue-biting to avoid saying the wrong thing—has become an important distorting factor in America's ability to consider its relations with Japan. It principally affects three groups:

- scholars who need future research contacts in Japan and future funding for the world's most expensive research site;
- students who have trained in the Japanese language or Japanese studies and know that Japanese-based corporations are the most likely market for their skills;
- government officials who know that someday they will leave the Commerce Department or the Treasury Department, and that when they leave their skills and contacts are likely to seem most valuable to large companies based in Japan.

For many of these people there is a powerful climate of self-control that far exceeds any limits that could be enforced on them. Anyone who has dealt in these fields since the bubble economy began in 1985 has heard comments like these: "It would be the end of my career to say that," or "I'll write about it many years from now."

In 1992, in a speech at the annual meeting of the Association for Japanese Business Studies, Robert E. Cole of the University of California at Berkeley, a specialist in Japanese business studies, described an episode of this kind. It started, he said, "with an innocent visit to a Japanese" auto transplant in the United States.

During the visit one of the Japanese managers mentioned to Cole that the plant had a hiring rule: Anyone who worked there had to live within thirty minutes of the plant. Cole asked about the reason for the rule. The Japanese manager, according to Cole, "said flat out that it was to avoid hiring blacks living in a nearby city just beyond the thirty minutes' commute." Cole said he was "stunned—partially by the fact that he was so frank." Cole noted that he could not conclude from this that the Japanese managers were necessarily more racist than American managers; they may simply not have learned what was and was not appropriate to say in public in America. Then Cole and an African-American colleague cross-referenced data about the racial makeup of American communities and the location of Japanese transplants. The real problems emerged after he published his results, showing a pattern of minority hiring well below the percentage of minority population living in the vicinity of their plants.

> I did effectively get blackballed, no pun intended, at a number of U.S. auto transplant operations. And indeed, at least one of my colleagues at Michigan was denied admission to one transplant site. He told me that this was because of my work. That really stunned me. I was prepared for losing access myself but

it never occurred to me that my colleagues might. To be sure, this was a short-term reaction by the American managers of these Japanese subsidiaries. But it made me realize that I couldn't anticipate all the possible outcomes of my decision to publish this research.[41]

When Cole traveled to Tokyo, an executive of a Japanese auto firm invited him to a meal in a private room in one of the city's priciest hotels. The executive began a heated criticism of Cole for writing the article. "I especially recall his saying that it didn't matter to him what I wrote in Japanese but I shouldn't have published it in English. This was a man whose idea of academic freedom was constrained by geographical location."

And this, according to Cole, was the heart of the problem for today's Japan scholars. To succeed in the long run they needed cooperation from sources in Japan, yet they were in chronic peril of losing that cooperation if they ever published uncomfortable truths. "It is my strong experience in collaborative research with Japanese scholars, for instance, that the American or European scholars in a joint project are far more willing to criticize the behavior of American or European managers or their country's government policy than are Japanese scholars willing to criticize Japanese managers or government. The reason, I believe, is clear: Japanese managers have orders of magnitude more difficulty accepting the idea of objective social science." He concluded:

> The bigger problem is perhaps how we Japan scholars unconsciously censor ourselves to avoid embarrassing our hosts or to avoid endangering our sources of future data. . . . We tend not to write what we think might offend our Japanese hosts.

The more scholars and business men know about Japan, the more they understand how its political system has resisted the idea of "constructive criticism" and free debate. "Especially in the ranks of the civil service, there is a distrust of opposition of all kinds," David Apter, an American scholar, wrote in 1984. "Mediation, yes; opposition, no. Nor are such views limited to the bureaucracy. Many senior officials of the LDP share them as well.[42]

The racist overhang.　America's worst problems have to do with race, and the Western world's entire history of interaction with Asia has, as Robert Elegant put it, been saturated with "racial contempt and cultural arrogance" on both sides.[43] White Americans have historically viewed Asians in general and Japanese in particular as another nonwhite race worthy of condescension, suspicion, and hostility. Meanwhile, modern Japanese often portray America with the stereotypes America has applied to its African-American minority. "Americans" as stereotyped in Japan, much like "black Americans" as stereotyped by whites, are "athletically strong and talented, dangerous when riled, sexually potent," but not as "disciplined, determined, or frugal" as the Japanese or white Americans doing the stereotyping.

The walking-on-eggs nature of any discussion involving race in America has greatly complicated its efforts to produce a sensible policy toward Asia. Japanese commentators are accustomed to making sweeping generalizations about the differences between "us" and "them." Educated Americans find this whole exercise potentially dangerous. Japan and the United States can be defined as two separate nations; two largely distinct economic systems; or two mainly different racial groups. In Japanese discussion these three levels are often run together. Statements beginning *ware-ware Nihonjin*, "we Japanese . . . ," might refer to the Japanese nation, the Japanese business system, or the Japanese "race." Educated Americans often fear that the American masses will also think in *ware-ware Nihonjin* terms—that is, they fear demagogues and bigots who say, "Japanese companies cheat, because that's how the Japs are. Remember what they did in Bataan!" The knowledge that statements about the Japanese business system might be taken as slurs on the Japanese "race" further distorts discussion in the United States. The least bigoted of Americans, those who are most worried that U.S.-Asian trade frictions might spill over into hostility toward the Asian-American minority in the United States, are most apprehensive about even opening the subject of economic tensions or political tensions.

Out of reflex, the United States of the 1980s and 1990s has classified as "racist" subjects with no necessary racial content. For example, in 1992 the Japanese family that owns the Nintendo company was considering buying the Seattle Mariners. The consensus on American sports and editorial pages was that any opposition to the deal must at some level rise from "racism."

Japan's professional baseball league does not have, and explicitly forbids, foreign ownership of its teams. Under its rules teams can use no more than two non-Japanese players at a time. This policy has an obvious "racial" effect. It confines ownership to members of the Japanese "race," and it limits the number of white, black, and Hispanic players from North America, who would dominate the lineups if there were no limit. But Japan's outlook toward baseball is usually called, by its critics, "nationalistic," "protectionist," even "xenophobic," rather than "racist." The U.S. baseball policy might be described in similar terms. (It does allow "foreign" ownership, from Canada, but Canada is, of course, the site of major-league teams.) Once we have used "racism" to describe disagreements for which there are sufficient nonracial explanations, there's not much left with which to describe real bigotry.

Rather than being careful with the term "racist" or its functional synonym "Japan-bashing," Americans have thrown the terms around cavalierly. Early in 1992 a headline in *USA Today* read, "Despite Japan-Bashing, Toyota Sales Increase." Its use has become comparable to calling any disagreement with Israeli government policy "anti-Semitism."

In an interview with the *Nikkei Weekly* in the fall of 1993, an American professor described how—and why—he had coined the term "Japan-bashing." In 1977, Robert C. Angel was directing the Japan Economic Institute, (JEI), a think tank in Washington, D.C., that is funded by Japan's Foreign Ministry. His job was to answer criticisms of Japan's foreign and economic policies. Angel said that he recognized the power of the term "anti-Semitism" to dismiss criticism of Israeli government policies. Therefore he started using the term "anti-Japanism" to describe critics of Japan's policies.

He found that the term didn't take. The *Nikkei Weekly* described his next steps:

> His next idea came from a television program on Pakistani immigrants to Britain, in which the inflammatory term "Paki-bashing' was used. Angel then coined the term "Japan-bashing."[44]

"I looked around for a phrase to use to discredit Japan's critics, and I hoped to be able to discredit those most effective critics by lumping them together with the people who weren't informed and who as critics were an embarrassment to everybody else," Angel told John Judis, for another article about the origins of "Japan-bashing," published in the *Columbia Journalism Review* in 1992.[45]

Angel found that the strategy worked. First the term was adopted in the Japanese press, and then, within a year, American journalists began using "Japan-bashing" as a shorthand for any criticism of Japanese practices. According to the *Nikkei Weekly* account:

So far, says Angel, the term has worked in Japan's favor, as many prominent Americans—especially in the fields of business and academia—are so afraid of being tagged Japan-bashers that they have toned down their criticisms of Japan.

"I view that modest public relations success with some shame and disappointment," Angel told John Judis. "Those people who use [the term] have the distinction of being my intellectual dupes."

Angel eventually left the JEI and taught at the University of South Carolina. In the early 1990s he published a book about U.S.-Japanese economic tensions in the Nixon era. It was called *Explaining Economic Policy Failure,* and its central argument was that the Japanese political-economic system could not respond quickly to a changing international environment. The U.S. government, he said, asked time and again for Japan to "open its markets" and reduce its trade surplus. Japanese bureaucrats and industrialists failed to do so; ultimately the Nixon administration was forced to the radical step of going off the gold standard and devaluing the dollar.[46]

Angel's analysis was characterized by some of its critics as "Japan-bashing."

Interdependence

To end on a more positive tone: The United States should make itself less dependent on Japan, because otherwise it will have more and more difficulty remaining Japan's partner. Westerners have over the centuries evolved many theories about how to deal most successfully in and with Japan. To seem weak and vulnerable has never been part of the formula.

"Japan does not look on its relationship with the United States as something that inherently is desirable for its own sake, or as one that should be maintained out of a sense of philosophical comitment to shared ideals," Michael Chinworth, a defense analyst specializing in Japan, wrote in 1988. "Japan, for example, certainly does not view the current security situation as a permanent one. . . . If Japan perceives an American decline—and many policymakers already see that happening—it will be extremely difficult to secure Japanese cooperation."[47]

Fifty years earlier, the German exile Kurt Singer had come to the same conclusion in his book *Mirror, Sword, and Jewel.* The book's most renowned line said that the people of Japan "are pe-

culiarly sensitive to the smell of decay, however well screened."
Therefore, he said, Japan

> seeks the friendship and guidance of a foreign power so long as
> the nation is strong, certain of her will and mission and able to
> command the ready sacrifice of individual happiness for the
> common good.[48]

If a society would choose to be Japan's friend and partner today, if
it would choose to respond to the stimulus of the Asian economic
achievement, such strength, certainty, and mission are what it should
display.

IO

Looking at the Sun

IN THE SUMMER OF 1989 I was traveling in Shanghai. The crackdown on democracy protesters in Beijing's Tiananmen Square had begun one month before. Political control under the Communists had been looser in Shanghai and the South of China than in Beijing and the North, but even in Shanghai the controls had tightened dramatically in the aftermath of the protests. When my wife and I had visited previously, in 1987 and 1988, we had been stopped constantly on the street by young Chinese determined to practice the English they'd learned from the Voice of America or from older Chinese who had studied in missionary schools. This time I could walk through the vast crowds on Shanghai's Nanjing Road and barely make eye contact with a soul. While I was riding in a taxi to an aircraft factory outside town where I had scheduled interviews, the car rounded a curve and then slammed to a stop at a roadblock manned by Chinese soldiers. One pointed a rifle toward me through the open back window, while the others spent twenty minutes inspecting the driver's legal documents before letting us go. I could not understand what the policemen were saying, but I didn't have to understand the words to know that the driver was terrified.

On previous trips I had spent the evenings walking with my wife in People's Park or along "the Bund," the grand embankment beside the wide and sluggish Huangpu River. Now Shanghai was under curfew, and at night I sat in the deserted lobby of my hotel, reading through the stack of books I had hauled along with me.

The books concerned Shanghai's architecture, its culture, its history, but they had a deeper common theme. In one way or another they all concerned national decline. The things that made Shanghai so memorable for a visitor in the 1980s were artifacts of the collapse of national power more than a century before.

In the early 1800s European merchants and missionaries had poured into Shanghai, turning what had been a minor settlement into the nation's commercial center. China's government of the time had no power to resist or even place conditions upon the influx. The British, the French, later the Americans, and later still the Japanese carved out tracts of territory, or "concessions," that were essentially removed from Chinese control. Within these concessions, the foreigners could live under their own laws and ignore what China's authorities said. Through southern China as a whole they could sell imported opium for silver and silk. The French concession in Shanghai had a Cercle Sportif and street names like Rue du Moulin; the large ring road encircling a Chinese settlement was named Avenue des Deux Républiques. The American concession was full of churches and missionary schools. The British built a racetrack, gardens, and numerous drinking and country clubs. They named their major thoroughfare Bubbling Wells Road. The Chinese government could do little but accede to their demands.

Artistically and architecturally, the years of foreign domination left a spectacular legacy in Shanghai. Until the very end of the 1980s, when a building boom began to transform the look of the town, Shanghai was a living museum of European design. French-style apartment buildings marched block after block through the city's center. Behind the apartments were rows of semidetached English family homes. Above the Bund, overlooking the Huangpu, rose the graceful Art Deco tower of the Peace Hotel. Until the old buildings were razed so that the high-rises of the 1990s could go up, much of Shanghai looked the way Berlin, Paris, or Manhattan must have looked in the 1920s. In the Park Hotel, the epitome of chic in prewar days, the cavernous dining room was still outfitted in the 1980s with tattered hangings in Jazz Age shades of pink and blue. At the Peace Hotel, where Noël Coward is said to have finished *Private Lives* when the hotel was called the Cathay, aged Chinese jazz musicians performed in the lobby at night. Along the streets of the old French concession, residents pedaled along on their bicycles beneath leafy plane trees, brought by the French to befit their concept of Shanghai as "the Paris of the East."

All of these traits made Shanghai evocative to Western visitors. Yet from the Chinese perspective each historic European hotel, garden, or leftover sporting club was a galling reminder of how weak their country had been. "Shanghai's apogee from the 1890s to the 1930s coincided with the nadir of Chinese national pride," Larry Robinson, an official with the U.S. Consulate in Shanghai, wrote in the mid-1980s in a report called "Life in the Big City." "The idea of Shanghai is linked historically in the Chinese consciousness with corruption and foreign domination."

The most stylish structure in the town, the Cathay Hotel along the Bund, was built with money the Sassoon family of England had extracted from China through the opium trade. In the 1920s and 1930s tubercular coolies coughed their lungs out as they ran along Bubbling Wells Road, hustling huge blocks of ice toward the foreigners' mansions to cool the swimming pools. On the banks of the Huangpu River, near the center of town, was a notorious public garden. The rules posted outside its gate said that no dogs, and no Chinese, would be allowed in. Largely in response to foreign domination, the Chinese Communist Party got its start in Shanghai.

When walking through Shanghai I thought frequently of Meiji Mura, outside the industrial city of Nagoya in central Japan. Meiji Mura, whose name means "Meiji Village," is like preskyscraper Shanghai a display of transplanted Western building styles, but with a crucial difference. The buildings that gave Shanghai its grace were relics of outside domination; those in Meiji Mura were indications of Japan's own resilience and strength. At Meiji Mura, on a 250-acre outdoor display site, were arrayed scores of buildings that had gone up all over Japan in the late nineteenth and early twentieth centuries, when the country was intensely studying and learning from the outside world. Like the buildings in Shanghai, many of these looked as if they might have fit into the Amsterdam or Paris of an earlier age. Unlike those in Shanghai, few of those at Meiji Mura were foreign creations. Most had been designed, planned, built, and used by Japanese of the Meiji era. This Prussian-looking police station, that American-style bungalow—these and the other structures were signs of Japan's active attempt to change its own practices in light of what the foreigners had achieved.

Under Western pressure, neither Japan nor China fully Westernized itself or became something at radical odds with what it had historically been. But Japan was able to make crucial adjustments, within the possibilities that its history and institutions allowed; China could not do so. As a result, Japan maintained its independence of action during the age of colonialism more than almost any other non-Western nation. With its motto of *wakon yosai*—"Japanese spirit, Western knowledge"—Japan coped successfully with the Western challenge until its own institutions failed in the 1930s and 1940s.

Japan's nineteenth-century success in matching foreign attainments was the beginning of the East Asian system that is now reshaping the region. The success of the Asian system as a whole now poses a challenge to Western nations. There is no prospect of conquest now, no head-on collision of national interests like that between the European powers of the colonial age and the weakened Chinese. At the end of the twentieth century, the world faces the possibility of mutual enrichment—financial, cultural, scientific, human—of a kind unimaginable during the era of colonial expansion and through the Cold War. Yet the terms of this new interaction will vary tremendously with the strengths and knowledge of each participant. People in each society, and societies as a whole, will end up either winners or losers, depending on how well they can adapt to the world's new rules. The adaptability of Western societies will depend on whether they can bring themselves, as did the nineteenth-century Japanese, to learn everything they can about powerful new systems and change their own practices where necessary— or whether, like the Chinese of the same era, they deal with unsettling new evidence by wishing it away.

In the United States, discussion about coping with Asia's achievement often begins and ends with what America should "make" other countries do. The United States should apply sanctions to change China's human-rights policy. It should use its military presence as a lever for greater trade concessions in Southeast Asia. It should punish Vietnam until it renders a fuller accounting of wartime casualties. Above all, it should pressure, cajole, lecture, and threaten Japan until it "opens its markets" and offers a "level playing field" for trade.

Some of these ideas, at some times, make sense. Except for North Korea, every nation in East Asia values the presence of the U.S. military. As long as the U.S. Seventh Fleet remains in the vicinity, no major East Asian nation expects to be invaded by any other. (North Korea's unpredictability again makes it the exception.) Without the U.S. presence, China, the two Koreas, Japan, and Russia would each be preemptively arming against all the rest. It is difficult for America to use its military commitment as an out-and-out bargaining tool in economic negotiations. Yet its diplomats can make clear that the United States can sustain this commitment only if its industrial base is strong.

Because the Asian system as a whole will almost certainly be the main source of worldwide economic energy for the next generation, Western economies should make every effort to remain involved in it. The expansion of Western economies is likely to remain slow through the 1990s; East Asia's growth will be the main offsetting force. If the Asian market remains dominated by Japanese suppliers, or by aspiring competitors in Korea and Taiwan and "Greater China" who themselves depend on Japanese companies for their highest-value components and technologies, it will be all the harder for Western economies to modernize, employ their people, or compete even in their own territory.

Because the United States and other Western nations share a political credo in which the individual is paramount and accountable democracy is the ultimate political goal, they can continue to criticize departures from this ideal in China, in Burma, in Indonesia, in Malaysia, or wherever else they may occur. They should advance these principles both to be true to themselves and because the complaints may sometimes embarrass or inconvenience other governments enough to end specific abuses. Because the United States in particular believes in mobile societies and open competition, it should feel free to criticize the closedness of various forms, without imagining that it can thereby change conditions elsewhere.

Yet efforts to remake other cultures come second. Western societies should first concentrate on whether and how to remake themselves. Like England, Japan, Germany, and the United States in their respective eras of success, today's Western societies should take the steps they deem sufficient to protect their interests regardless of whether anyone else "changes," "slows down," or "opens up." This does not mean imitating techniques that have proved successful in Asia; in some cases it may actually mean doing the reverse. For instance, Japan since the Meiji years has promoted an ethic of national "purity." The United States should rely on the opposite ethic of inclusion, so it can continue to absorb the energies of people from other parts of the world. The Philippines adopted the *form* of successful Western societies—a democratically elected legislature, rules guaranteeing a free press—but did not become successful. The leaders of Meiji Japan looked at the *result* Western powers had achieved and devised their own route to get there. Western powers should now recognize the result the successful Asian economies have achieved.

In practical terms, the most important response to the Asian achievement will come in the United States, if it is to come at all. America's economic difficulties with Asia are much greater than Europe's difficulties; yet its scale of operation, and therefore its potential for recovery, is greater too. The daily realities of American culture, along with the deep underpinning of American ideology, are further removed from Asian practices than is the case in Europe. The United States resembles a handful of nations—principally Canada and Australia—in believing that it can absorb immigrants into a multicultural society; most European and Asian countries are suspicious of this attempt. The United States resembles only Great Britain in believing its own postwar economic theories about the inadvisability of government-business interaction. East Asian countries wage no holy wars against the French, Germans, or Italians over principles of "protectionism" or the "level playing field," since they all share a practical belief in national economic policies. These differences make the American system the clearest contrast to the Asian model and, at least in principle, give Americans more room to consider whether and how their system should change.

For America, Asia's success raises questions about four aspects of its own policies. They are education, industrial strategies, trade policies, and investment in all its forms. Each of these is a familiar subject, but the implications of Asia's success cast all of them in a new light.

Education. Most industrial nations have economic strategies. The plans are clearest and most assertive in East Asia; they are haziest and most hesitant in the English-speaking countries, which have told themselves since World War II, and increasingly since Ronald Reagan and Margaret Thatcher, that economic strategies are doomed to fail. When the Asian and Anglo-American systems interact, the natural result is for the system without a strategy to become the object of strategies made by the other side. Thus, when Japan and Korea decided in the 1980s to develop their own semiconductor industries, the American industry became an object of those strategic choices—until the United States responded at the end of the decade with a strategy of its own.

Being the object of others' strategies is harmful ultimately because it is polarizing within a nation. If the world were shaped by economic forces alone, the natural tendency of a globalized economy would be to make each nation a cross section of the income distribution of the entire world. The poorly trained workers inside each nation would compete against poorly trained workers everywhere; the best-trained would sell their services to a larger and richer world market. The two American cities that are most open to global economic forces, New York and Los Angeles, are the most polarized in this way.

Nations avoid this polarization mainly by attempting to blunt the workings of purely economic forces. Protectionist policies and industrial strategies often raise prices for consumers but keep a larger share of "good" jobs within a nation's borders than would otherwise be the case. Japan is the extreme example of this trade-off. Because of its policies, all of its consumers are burdened by high prices and limited access to the world's products. Yet in their roles as workers more of its people can find "good" jobs than their counterparts in other countries. Therefore Japan as a whole is less polarized than any other industrialized power.

Yet for such a strategy to work, in Japan or elsewhere, the nation's people must be prepared to take advantage of it. In Japan for more than a century, and in South Korea, Taiwan, and Singapore since the end of World War II, the object of educational policy has been to bring most of the nation's people up to a basic level of functioning competence, so they can take advantage of the opportunities a growing economy creates. Anyone who has compared these systems with American schools quickly sees their strengths and limits. The East Asian educational model has been extremely effective in making the *worst*-trained students competent, and extremely ineffective in fostering freethinkers and individual talents. The limitations of this educational model are rubbed into the Japanese psyche each fall, when the list of Nobel Prize winners is dominated by Americans and Europeans. Yet the strength of the model is manifest in East Asia's decades of economic expansion. Training workers is not, by itself, enough to attract industry. Ireland, India, the Philippines, and Russia have at various times had a far greater supply of trained talent than jobs for them to perform. But a trained work force plus an economic strategy has, on the evidence, been a formula for growth.

America's educational challenge is more complicated than that of Japan or Korea. It has distinctive strengths it must not sacrifice— its adaptability to local circumstances, its tremendous openness to outsiders, its success in promoting individual creativity. America's university system is, in international terms, the country's most dominant and "competitive" product. The best-trained 10 or 20 percent of America's high school students are more thoroughly and broadly prepared for life than their counterparts anywhere else.

Yet the American system's most acute failure is in the area of the Asian system's greatest success: ensuring that the *worst*-trained people are competent. The roots of America's polarized school system—so good at the top, so bad at the bottom—obviously involve factors other than the schools themselves. But because schooling plays so crucial a role in the overall economic prospects for the country, as well as largely determining what kinds of Americans can hold what jobs, in the short term it is worthwhile to concentrate on the schools themselves. In the short term America's biggest educational problem is that its worst schools and students are so bad; as long as this is true, social polarization can only become worse. One way to address this problem is through a much more equal system of school funding. At the moment the students with the most troubled family backgrounds and bleakest life prospects go to the worst-funded schools. Better-funded schools will not solve the students' other problems, but worse-funded schools naturally make the problems worse.

The United States does not need a school system as centralized and standardized as Japan's, or even as that of France. But it can learn from the successes of such systems—and one way it can see similar results in an American context is through its own military. In the years since the Vietnam War the U.S. military has come close to solving three of the great problems that bedevil civilian American society: defining a national interest that is worth some sacrifice of immediate personal comfort or gain; surmounting racial barriers; and investing money and care in bringing all members of a unit up to a level of competence. In the years immediately after Vietnam, America's military was tormented by its failures. It is time to apply some of the lessons of its recent success.

Industrial strategies. "Industrial policy" has become a thought-stopping term in American politics. People are either for it or against it on reflexive, axiomatic grounds. Yet the reality behind this unfortunate term has been part of every nation's economic development. When the U.S. Congress enacted Medicare in the 1960s, it also enacted a form of industrial policy, by expanding the flow of money into hospitals, nursing homes, pharmaceutical firms, and physicians' fees. Farm subsidies are an industrial policy. Building highways has been an American industrial policy; it encourages certain industries, from car building to suburban home construction, and discourages others, such as railroad building. America's defense budget has had a major effect on America's industrial structure for more than half a century. The mortgage-interest deduction has for decades steered additional resources toward the home-building industry. Just as MITI's strategies for automobiles and electronics have left Japan with a larger stake in those industries than it would otherwise have had, America's mortgage policy has left it better housed than any other nation.

The real question about industrial policy is not whether a nation should have one—all will—but whether its existence should be admitted. A conservative argument, prevalent in America through the 1980s, holds that industrial policy will be least damaging if mention of the subject is suppressed. The big risks of government intervention are that support for promising industries will become pork-barrel subsidy to each politician's favorite industry, and that the government will make worse and more expensive errors when picking winners than private capitalists, risking their own money, ever will. Therefore, according to this view, to discuss any kind of industrial policy is dangerous. Like discussing "safe" narcotics, it legitimizes inherently harmful activity.[1]

The world's evidence indicates the reverse: the countries that have practiced the most successful industrial polices, with the least damaging side effects, have done so with their eyes open.

Alice Amsden and Robert Wade are two of the scholars who have studied exactly how Asian systems have put industrial policies into effect. They have emphasized several elements usually left out of American discussion of this issue. One is a constant interaction of guidance and market competition: typically, the government sets a general goal, but then companies compete vigorously to meet the goal. This is one reason why Asian industrial policy has been so much more successful than the dead hand of state-run enterprises in the old Communist world. Another factor is what Alice Amsden has called "discipline of capital": if companies do not meet performance standards, the government's support rapidly dries up.[2] Although Amsden and Wade have not put it exactly in this form, from their work a three-stage model of successful industrial policy can be deduced:

· *Intervention by the government.* The government supports or encourages a certain industry by steering more money toward it than the market would otherwise provide. In the early days of Japan's electronics industry, this meant government guidance to banks to ensure that they made loans available on favorable terms, plus barriers that kept foreign competitors from making sales in Japan.

· *Execution by the market.* The government then relies on businesses, entrepreneurs, and competitive market forces to make all the fine-grained decisions about how the extra money should be used. In the Japanese case, Matsushita, NEC, and ambitious new companies like Sony competed fiercely to bring the best possible electronic products to market, at the lowest cost.

· *Conditions.* The government sets conditions, rules, incentives, and standards to increase the chances that the additional money has the intended effect. The Japanese electronics makers operated with the understanding that they would expand export sales as quickly as they could in order to improve the nation's balance of trade. When the Korean government wanted to encourage and subsidize its *chaebol,* or big business groups, it offered them protection—but also set price ceilings, export targets, investment standards, and other conditions in an attempt to have the corporations act in the national interest. If major corporations did not follow these guidelines, the Korean government could (and sometimes did) cut off their credit and drive them into bankruptcy.

For historic, political, and institutional reasons, carrying out this scheme of "protection with conditions" is easier in the East Asian system than in the United States. Bureaucracies in many Asian countries are powerful and widely respected; the custom of interaction between business and government leaders is so well established that all parties know what is expected of them. But there is nothing uniquely Asian about the concept that the state can provide incentives while also setting conditions. Indeed, America's successful "industrial policy" for home building fits exactly into the scheme:

· *Intervention by the government.* The mortgage-interest deduction encourages people to buy homes, which in turn encourages other people to build them. The result is to steer more of the country's assets toward housing than would otherwise be the case.

· *Execution by the market.* The government does not try to build, maintain, or manage most of the nation's housing stock. Instead it relies on market competition to determine how many houses will be built, and at what price. Government tax policy sends out a pro-housing signal, and then millions of individuals work out the details.

· *Conditions*. While providing incentives, the government has also applied rules and conditions to shape the growth of the housing industry. Until the early 1980s, the savings-and-loans industry, which issued most mortgages, operated under guidelines about the kinds of properties that deserved loans, the size of the down payment that purchasers must put up, and the amount of insurance that homeowners must hold. Buyers or sellers who applied for mortgages underwritten by the Veterans Administration or the Federal Housing Administration had to meet further standards, such as those prohibiting racial discrimination. That is, in supporting the home-building complex, the government also had some idea of the spillover social effect that expanded housing should have.

When Chrysler was on the verge of bankruptcy, in 1979, Congress agreed to underwrite its loans—but only if Chrysler's management and unions accepted conditions and compromises to help the company survive. When the American semiconductor industry was in its infancy, the U.S. government provided little direct financing—but said it would buy the initial output if the companies could figure out how to make reliable chips. At the end of World War I, Franklin Roosevelt, then a young assistant secretary of the Navy, offered Navy procurement contracts to a fledgling firm known as the Radio Corporation of America.[3] The Navy put up cash to support an American radio-making consortium, and said it would buy the resulting products. In exchange RCA had to agree to share the patents it developed with other American companies that would like to produce radios, rather than keeping them for itself. These requirements were very similar to the burdens that MITI imposed on Sony and other Japanese producers after World War II. In RCA's case, as in Sony's, they worked. Young companies were sheltered at a time when they were not rich or strong enough to survive on their own, and as they developed they expanded the nation's technological base.

Not all of these collaborative efforts succeed, of course. Yet the historic evidence from Asia, Europe, and North America suggests that intervention is more likely to succeed if the government admits that it *is* intervening. That way, it can think about the tools that make interventions work—relying on markets for the details, applying performance standards—rather than holding its nose and guiltily dispensing government aid to whatever industry or politician pushes hardest at the moment. As Clyde Prestowitz has pointed out, the United States has fifty state industrial policies and about a dozen city policies—but is embarrassed about having any one national policy, for fear of "distorting" trade. The result is a grotesque distortion, as Kentucky bids against Arkansas and Atlanta against Seattle, but the national government feels it would be improper for it to enter or affect the bidding war.

Trade policies. Through most of the Cold War era, America's trade policy was based on an ideal, in the best and worst sense. The ideal was that with passing years the world's economies would interact more freely, as Adam Smith and David Ricardo had prescribed. The best side of this belief was that America did keep pushing for open trade. Through successive rounds of tariff reduction coordinated by the General Agreement on Tariffs and Trade, formal trade barriers came down, and more of the world's people grew more prosperous more quickly than at any other time in history.

The problem with America's approach was its underlying moralism. When countries deviated from its view of a free and open trading system, the United States was always tempted to call them wrong, rather than merely "self-interested" or "pragmatic" or "hard-nosed." If these countries' economies were small, like those of Taiwan or South Korea or even Japan in the 1960s, the United States could pressure them into changing their evil practices—or decide to overlook their transgressions for larger reasons of foreign policy. Yet the underlying moral condemnation remained. It shows up now in aggrieved complaints about "hidden barriers" and the lack of a "level playing field," and the warnings that any interference with free trade would bring back the Smoot-Hawley tariffs and worldwide hard times. Behind such comments is the idea that there is one way, our way, to play the game fairly. While the United States talks about "fair play" and "obeying the rules," other nations sensibly observe the principal rule of defending their own interests.

In its trade policy, the United States should stop trying for what is "best" and work for what is "better." It recognizes this distinction in other forms of foreign policy. During World War II it readily allied with Stalin to fight the Nazis. In the best world it would not have had to consort with such a brutal dictator, but dealing with him was clearly better than letting Hitler's empire expand. Much of the time the United States views political and military power as questions of practicality, not outright moralism. It asks, Who is weak and who is strong? Whose interests coincide with ours? It automatically understands that in certain cases the threat or even use of force may be the best way to guarantee peace.

The same approach would help in economic policy. Often the United States can improve its own economic prospects and help make world trade better by violating the "best" ideal of untrammeled free trade. Western European nations have found that they can expand trade, among themselves and with other nations, by setting certain limits and rules. For instance, in cases when the Europeans did not set any "local content" requirements for imported products, Japanese manufacturers shipped direct from their factories at home. When the Europeans interfered with trade, by imposing local-content standards, Japanese manufacturers were far more willing to set up plants in Europe, creating a better and even more "borderless" result. Through the 1980s the United States repeatedly "broke" the rules of free trade by unilaterally imposing tariffs, under the dreaded Section 301 of its trade law, against nations whose markets it considered closed. The threat or use of these weapons was enough to convince Korea, Thailand, and other countries to open themselves more fully to imports and thereby expand world trade.

In the case of Japan, seeking the "best," through lectures about the full opening of Japanese society, has outlived its usefulness. To the Japanese it seems like bullying, from a declining power unwilling to reform itself. To Americans it reinforces the mistaken idea that Japan's economic policy somehow amounts to breaking the rules. But economic problems between Japan and the outside world have often been made better through specific, practical-minded arrangements. (For negotiating purposes, "the outside world" has meant the United States, since it has been the only country with the leverage to strike major trade deals with Japan.)

The clearest example of this approach is the "expectation" expressed in a 1986 U.S.-Japan agreement that foreign-made semiconductors would represent 20 percent of sales in Japan by the middle of 1991. This agreement differed from most trade agreements in two ways. First, it concerned a target, not a process. The goal was for Japanese companies to buy a certain number of chips, not to become "open" or "fair." Second, it eventually worked. By the end of 1992 (the revised deadline, under a renewal of the arrangement), foreign chips, mainly from American companies, represented 20.2 percent of the Japanese market. The result was not the best imaginable outcome; it was, however, better than any realistic alternative.[4]

Several decades of experience have shown that the opposite approach—cajoling, negotiating, holding hands, waving sticks, and all the whole asking for "openness" and "change"—leads nowhere economically. Worse, it pumps up moralistic fury on both sides of the Pacific, among Japanese who feel they are being bullied and Americans who think they are being tricked. Settling for what is better involves less wear and tear yet will do more good than trying for the "best."[5]

Investment. Many Americans felt prosperous in the 1980s, because in those years America consumed more than it produced. Life will be more difficult for most Americans unless this pattern is reversed. Countries on the way up economically differ in countless ways. The one trait they all share is high savings and investment rates, which in turn mean deferring today's consumption for tomorrow's greater return.

Nations can go too far in encouraging savings. John Maynard Keynes changed economic orthodoxy with his *General Theory,* by demonstrating that worldwide oversaving had caused the Great Depression. Japan's sustained high savings rate is the main force behind its huge trade surpluses. The savings rate means, in effect, that Japan's total output is greater than Japan's own people can consume; the extra output is sold to the rest of the world, producing a trade surplus. If every nation had the same internal pattern of oversaving, the result would necessarily be a worldwide slowdown like the one Keynes first diagnosed.

For the time being, the United States is in no danger of oversaving. Its economic well-being depends on its ability to invest—in education, in factories, in transportation, in public safety, in research—and for more than a decade the country has failed to save enough money to cover its own investment needs. Over the last decade, industrialized countries have, on average, saved about 8 percent of their annual economic output. Japan's savings rate has been twice as high as that average; America's has been half as high as the average, or one quarter of Japan's. In the short term America's savings shortfall has been made up by international borrowing; this is the force that transformed the United States from the world's largest net creditor to the largest net debtor within one decade. In the longer term the country must find a way to save more, or else prepare for the political and social costs of certain economic decline.

People save, as individuals and in businesses, but their actions are heavily influenced by government policy. For more than a generation the U.S. government has in practice strongly discouraged savings. Its deficit is in itself a huge source of dis-saving. Since the early 1980s, the federal government has had to borrow nearly as much money to cover its deficits as American consumers have saved. The structure of American tax law has generally encouraged consumption and penalized savings. The tax treatment of interest payments is the classic illustration: interest paid out for debt, especially for homes, is tax-deductible; interest earned, on savings, is taxable.

To expand its future possibilities and preserve its present power, the United States should change the incentives it offers for savings and debt. East Asian and European countries rely less on income taxes and more on consumption taxes than the United States does. The main consumption taxes are a heavy tax on gasoline and a much lower "value-added tax" on purchases in general. The virtue of this approach is that it applies the same logic as in successful industrial policies. The government intervenes to send a signal: in this case, that the country needs more savings and less consumption. Then normal market competition lets each customer and firm respond to this signal in the most efficient way.

The United States should follow this example, shifting more of its tax stream to a value-added tax, with a tax on gasoline rising faster than on other products. A sudden increase in the gasoline tax would of course have inflationary effects for the economy as a whole. But, adjusted for inflation, gasoline prices were lower in the early 1990s than they had been since World War II. During that war, the country put up with inconveniences far worse than expensive gasoline for a long-term national goal. The United States will probably never again face such a full-scale military challenge. But if it cannot even consider how to endure, and share, inconvenience at the moment for longer-term strength, it will have lost an economic war.

In the mid-nineteenth century, the Ottoman Empire seemed a better bet than the Japanese to cope with the commercial and military expansion of European power. The Ottomans had held their own against rivals in Europe for many years, and through steady contact they had the opportunity to develop a more realistic idea of what the competition had achieved. In the late twentieth century, it seems odd even to compare the Ottoman response to European expansion with Japan's. Something had prevented the Ottoman leaders and populace from keeping up with a deeply changed world, and something had allowed the Japanese, at the same moment in history, to adapt.

Bernard Lewis, the historian of Islam, has written that the Ottoman problem was not exactly "rot" or "loss of will," the maladies that American commentators often emphasize when explaining the rise and fall of empires. Instead, Lewis said, the fatal defect for the Ottomans was their inability to see or believe how the world had changed around them. In the eighteenth century, European companies had perfected the tools of mercantilism to gain markets for textile makers from England and vintners from France. The refinement of mercantilist trading techniques, Lewis said, "helped European trading companies, and the states that protected them, to achieve a level of commercial organization and a concentration of economic energies unknown and unparalleled in the East."

> The Western trading corporation, with the help of its business-minded government, represented an entirely new force. Thanks to this growing disparity of economic strength and purpose, Western merchants, later manufacturers, and eventually governments were able to establish an almost total control of Middle Eastern markets, and ultimately even of Middle Eastern manufacturers. Middle Eastern textiles, once highly regarded in the West, were driven first from external, and then even from domestic, markets by more efficiently produced and aggressively marketed Western goods. . . . By the late eighteenth century, when a Turk or an Arab indulged in a cup of sweetened coffee, in all probability the coffee was brought by Dutch merchants from Java, and the sugar by French or British merchants from the West Indies. Only the hot water was of local provenance. In the course of the nineteenth century, even that was doubtful as Western companies dominated the rapidly expanding utilities in the Middle Eastern cities.[6]

Bernard Lewis wrote about the Ottoman failure late in 1991, just as the Soviet Union was dismantling itself. But the closest parallel to the Ottoman predicament, he said, was not to be found in the visibly disintegrating Soviet bloc. "It is rather the consumer-oriented societies of Western Europe and, even more, North America." Like the Ottomans, today's Westerners were negligent about perceiving what their competitors had accomplished. They did not recognize that the countries of East Asia "have found new ways of mobilizing and deploying the economic power of their societies."

The Western world, especially its English-speaking countries, has described economic competition as if it were a matter of right or wrong, fair or unfair. Historically economics has involved something different: the interaction of strong and weak, actors and acted-upon, the alert and the inattentive. Now as in the past it favors those who are determined to make their own luck.

Acknowledgments

My family lived this entire project with me, during the three and a half years we spent in Asia and the three and a half subsequent years in which I was traveling by myself or home finishing the book. My wife, Debbie, and my sons, Tom and Tad, have my deepest love and thanks. We learned together everything I have described in this book, and they must feel as if we wrote the whole thing together too.

My employers at *The Atlantic Monthly*, William Whitworth and Mortimer Zuckerman, gave me tremendous latitude to take the time I needed to explore the subjects I wanted to learn about. It is very rare in journalism to respect all the people you work with, to be proud of every issue they produce, and to feel that others' suggestions and changes have always made your own work better. The operation that Bill Whitworth and Mort Zuckerman have created at *The Atlantic Monthly* has given me that privilege. Jack Beatty, Corby Kummer, and Cullen Murphy at the magazine edited articles I wrote from and about Asia. Eric Haas, Amy Meeker, Sue Parilla, Martha Spaulding, Barbara Wallraff, and Lowell Weiss made the articles clearer and more accurate than they would otherwise have been, and Judy Garlan made their presentation more attractive. I am grateful to everyone at the magazine but owe special thanks for their help to Avril Cornel, Fred Drasner, and Kim Jensen.

Linda Healey, of Pantheon Books, has been an ideal editor— patient when patience was called for, insistent at other times, insightful throughout. Every writer should be so fortunate. I feel fortunate again to have worked with Wendy Weil as my agent. William D. Drennan, Jeanne Morton, and Bitite Vinklers provided careful, thorough, yet always reasonable copy-editing advice, and Altie Karper managed the whole book-production process with great skill.

When I returned from Japan to America in 1989, Maryann Aquilino played an indispensable role in helping me establish an office life in America. At the end of this project, in 1993, Kathy Sylvester played a similarly indispensable role in helping me cope with research, citations, and the final production of the manuscript. Liz First and Steve Hendrix have my gratitude for their help and friendship between these times. Chandler Burr has been an indefatigable source of ideas about Asia and America.

Everyone interested in modern Asia owes a lasting debt to Chalmers Johnson, for the research, writing, and thinking he has done. I owe him specific gratitude for his careful comments on this manuscript. Others whose comments helped me greatly are Kenneth Courtis, Glen Fukushima, Jim Impoco, Nicholas Lemann, Clyde Prestowitz, Karel van Wolferen, and another person, who has asked that he not now be named. I hope to be able to thank him publicly in the future for his time and unselfish advice.

I owe thanks to many other people for their support, advice, and criticism while I was developing this book. They include Jodie Allen, Alice Amsden, Robert Angel, Michael Borrus, Bruce Carter, Pat Choate, Malcolm Clarke, Steve Clemons, Steven Cohen, Donald Cooke, Michael Crichton, Nicholas Dawidoff, Jason DeParle, Eamonn Fingleton, Robin Gaster, Richard Gephardt, Eric Gower, Ivan Hall, Sheila Johnson, John Judis, Kevin Kearns, Kathy Kriger, Robert Kuttner, Burgess Laird, Edward Lincoln, Michael Lind, Mike Millard, Taggart Murphy, Robert Neff, Robert Poe, Richard Samuels, David Sanger, Jeff Shear, Derek Shearer, Craig Sherman, David Spector, Alan Tonelson, Laura Tyson, Robert Wade, Steven Weisman, Mike Wessell, William Wetherall, and John Zysman.

Stephen Banker, Lincoln Caplan, David Ignatius, and Paul Jensen provided moral support of a particular kind during the long months when the book was "almost done" but not in fact finished. As an alumnus of *The Washington Monthly,* I am obliged in perpetuity to thank Charles Peters for giving me my first journalistic job and for his guidance and influence since then. I am grateful to Michael Janeway for his skillful help when I was developing ideas about Japan and America in my previous book, *More Like Us.* Charles McCarry has been a friend and an example of how to understand and describe foreign cultures. David Halberstam, among his other acts of patronage over the years, first suggested in 1985 that my family try living in Japan.

So many people helped my family during its years in Asia that I feel graceless naming a few and potentially slighting many others. But I would feel worse not to thank Mary Carlin, William and Christine Chapman, Anne Convery, Lydia and Steven Gomersall, Jon Harger, Shigeki and Gerd Hijino, Jeff Irish, Hiroshi Ishikawa, Bunkichi Itoh, F. Sionil Jose, Amy Katoh, David and Jo Pierce, Margaret and Larry Robbins, Itsuko Sakai, Nobuyuki Sassa, Lona Sato, Murray and Jenny Sayle, the Shohtoku family of Kuala Lumpur and Osaka, Wick Smith, Henry Tung, M.D., Pari Vathi, the Wada family of Yokohama, and Sumimah Yusof. Ruri Kawashima and John Wheeler of the Japan Society of New York helped make possible our initial trip to Japan. Peter Grey of CEDA in Australia made an extended trip to Southeast Asia possible.

Finally a word about technology. Four kinds of software made this a more pleasant and successful enterprise than it could otherwise have been. IBM's new computer operating system, OS/2 2.1, freed me from the headache of computer crashes and gave me a reliable way to have my research notes, my outline, and my word processor all running and available at the same time. An OS/2-based word processor called DeScribe is faster, more powerful, and more disaster proof than any other writing software I have used. I paid it the most sincere compliment I know how, by switching all my drafts and research material to it halfway through the project. Without two brilliant programs originally sold by Lotus Development Corporation, Magellan and Agenda, I would have despaired of trying to organize years' worth of research material. I sincerely thank Bill Gross for inventing Magellan; Mitch Kapor, Ed Belove, and Jerry Kaplan for creating Agenda; and the current management of Lotus for leaving the programs on sale long enough for me to buy copies, before Lotus pulled the plug on both.

Notes

INTRODUCTION

1. Reg Little and Warren Reed, *The Confucian Renaissance* (Sydney: The Federation Press, 1989), pp. 25–26.
2. *Business Week* (October 8, 1990, p. 21).
3. Robert Whiting, *The Chrysanthemum and the Bat: Baseball Samurai Style* (New York: Macmillan, 1990); *You Gotta Have Wa: When Two Cultures Collide on a Baseball Diamond* (New York: Vintage Books, Departures Series, 1990).
4. Paul Krugman of MIT, quoted in *The Washington Post* (February 24, 1993).
5. Of the many useful articles on the "bubble economy," one of the best is Clay Chandler's profile of Yasushi Mieno, governor of the Bank of Japan, *The Wall Street Journal* (June 15, 1993).
6. Karen Elliott House, "Japan's Decline, America's Rise," *The Wall Street Journal* (April 21, 1992).
7. William Chapman, *Inventing Japan: The Making of a Postwar Civilization* (New York: Prentice Hall Press, 1991), p. 171.
8. Ibid., p. 159.
9. Aron Viner, *The Emerging Power of Japanese Money* (Homewood, Ill.: Dow Jones–Irwin, 1988), p. 2. William Chapman discussed this and other overreactions to *endaka* in *Inventing Japan*.
10. In a digital system, pictures are converted into 0 or 1 binary data, like data used by a computer. The TV signal consists of streams of these data, which are then reconstituted into a picture on the receiving end. The result is much more precise and error-free than analog transmission.

CHAPTER 1. THE MYSTERY OF THE CHIPS

1. U.S. Senate, Committee on Commerce, Science, and Transportation, *Industrial Technology* (Washington, D.C.: U.S. Government Printing Office, 1978), p. 91;

cited in Michael G. Borrus, *Competing for Control: America's Stake in Microelectronics* (Cambridge, Mass.: Ballinger, 1988), pp. 80–81.

2. T. R. Reid's book *The Chip: How Two Americans Invented the Microchip and Launched a Revolution* (New York: Simon & Schuster, 1984) is a lively story of the roles of Noyce, Jack Kilby of Texas Instruments, and others who might claim patrimony of today's semiconductor industry.

3. In 1980 the United States had a trade surplus of $5.9 billion in office machines and computers, of $1.4 billion in pharmaceuticals, of $14 billion in aircraft parts and engines, and of $4 billion in scientific equipment. These categories total $25.3 billion.

4. For comparison, in 1992 Intel's net revenue had risen to $5.8 billion, and exports made up just less than half of its total revenues.

5. George Gilder, *Microcosm: The Quantum Revolution in Economics and Technology* (New York: Simon & Schuster, 1989), p. 382.

6. Xerox's Palo Alto Research Center, where Alan Kay did the work that eventually led to the graphics-oriented approach of the Macintosh computer and the Windows operating environment, was the exception that proved the rule. Xerox introduced this approach with its "Star" work stations in the early 1980s but could not popularize the approach in the marketplace.

7. In 1975 U.S. suppliers represented 80 percent of Japan's semiconductor equipment market. By 1985 they had only 20 percent. Jay S. Stowsky, "Weak Links, Strong Bonds: U.S.-Japanese Competition in Semiconductor Production Equipment," in *Politics and Productivity,* ed. Chalmers Johnson, Laura D'Andrea Tyson, and John Zysman (Cambridge, Mass.: Ballinger, 1989), p. 256.

8. These figures are reviewed in Stowsky, "Weak Links, Strong Bonds," pp. 241–74.

9. The four areas of slight Japanese lead in the late 1970s were: dynamic RAM chips, or DRAMs; static RAM chips, or SRAMs; optoelectronics; and heterostructures. The five areas of parity were: custom and semicustom logic; silicon; chemical vapor diffusion; and assembly.

By the late 1980s, in the four technologies in which Japanese companies had held a "slight" lead, they now held a "clear" or "substantial" lead. In ten areas where U.S. companies had held a lead, Japanese companies were ahead of or even with the U.S. firms. In only two areas of the two dozen surveyed (linear logic and ion-implantation technology) had U.S. firms improved their position during the 1980s. From U.S. Government InterAgency Working Group on Semiconductor Technology, cited in Stowsky, p. 267.

10. U.S. Congress, Office of Technology Assessment, *Competing Economies: America, Europe, and the Pacific Rim,* OTA-ITE-498 (Washington, D.C.: U.S. Government Printing Office, October 1991), p. 7. It went on to say:

There will be more emerging technologies in which the dominant power is Japan, not the United States, and established industries will remain behind the Japanese world leaders. This situation also faces producers in Western Europe. . . . The difference between the United States and Europe, at this point, is that European governments are taking an active role in trying to bolster their competitiveness, while the U.S. Government takes the position that the best aid to competitiveness is a free market.

11. These shifts are described in Thomas R. Howell, Brent L. Bartlett, and Warren Davis, *Creating Advantage: Semiconductors and Government Industrial Policy in the 1990s* (Washington, D.C.: Dewey Ballantine/Semiconductor Industry Association, 1992).
12. Ibid., p. 18 (figure 8).
13. The rankings for merchant firms, those who sell their product to other companies, were as follows, with sales in millions of dollars:

1978	*1990*
Texas Instruments—990	NEC—2,638
Motorola—720	Hitachi—2,305
NEC—520	Toshiba—2,261
Philips—520	Motorola—2,025
National—500	Texas Instruments—1,820
Fairchild—500	Philips—1,356
Hitachi—460	Fujitsu—1,310
Toshiba—400	Matsushita—1,233
Intel—360	Mitsubishi—1,177
Siemens—270	Intel—991

This list excludes IBM, which does not publicly report how many chips it produces and uses in its own machines. Borrus, *Competing for Control*, p. 16.
14. *Creating Advantage*, p. 34.
15. The top ten in descending order were:

NEC
Toshiba
Hitachi
Intel
Motorola
Fujitsu
Texas Instruments
Mitsubishi Electric
Matsushita Electric
Philips

Japan's world share was 49.6 percent in 1991, up from 48.7 percent in 1990. The U.S. share was 35.9 percent, down from 37 percent, and Europe's was 10.7 percent, up from 10 percent. Dataquest figures, as reported in *Asahi Shimbun* (January 13, 1992).
16. Electronics Industry Association of Japan, quoted in *The Japan Digest Weekly* (Arlington, Va.: April 1, 1992). Its prediction was that worldwide demand will grow 9.7 percent per year, to $92.8 billion by 1995, Japan's market will grow by 10.6 percent, to $32.6 billion (because of strength in computers and electronic devices that demand chips), with the United States at $30.7 billion and Western Europe at $21.8 billion. In 1989 North America was at $18.1 billion, Japan at $17.8 billion, and Western Europe at $12 billion.
17. Kenichi Ohmae, "US-Japan Trade Fictions," *The Wall Street Journal* (May 27, 1993).

18. *Competing Economies,* p. 12.
19. In comments to a U.S. government official after the shortage was over.
20. Charles Ferguson, "DRAMs, Component Supplies, and the World Electronics Industry: An International Strategic Analysis," an unpublished paper originally prepared for Digital Equipment Corporation (August 1989).
21. Stephen Kreider Yoder, *The Wall Street Journal* (January 16, 1990). Yoder's story included the comments by both Kenneth Flamm and Sanford Kane.
22. *Der Spiegel* (April 24, 1989), quoted in *Creating Advantage,* p. 34
23. The company is the Japan Aviation Electronics Industry, or JAEI, which is half owned by NEC. In July 1991 the company admitted having sold parts and weapons to Iran during its war with Iraq. The U.S. Justice Department secured a grand jury indictment against the company in September 1991. But the Pentagon and Honeywell resisted applying sanctions—Honeywell in particular because it had received the contract for making collision-avoidance systems, and JAEI is the world's only supplier of LCD components that go into the system. Without them, Honeywell claimed, it could not provide the systems. JAEI proposed making the systems inside the United States to avoid the ban, but Hosiden, the maker of the screens, said it would stop shipping them to America because of the duties imposed. This was discussed by Jacob Schlesinger and Eduardo Lachica in *The Wall Street Journal* (September 16, 1991).
24. The Patriots, Tomahawk missiles, the HARM missile, and many others all depend on ceramic-chip packaging produced by Kyoto Ceramics, or Kyocera. As Jacob Schlesinger pointed out:

> The story of Kyocera's domination of this market follows closely the script of how Japan has come to control countless mundane but crucial links along the high tech food chain. The initial designs were drafted in the mid-1960s by Fairchild Semiconductor Corp., since 1987 part of National Semiconductor Corp., but then a leading U.S. chip maker. But "we couldn't find any American companies that wanted to build it for anything other than an exorbitant price," recalls Bill Phy, a former Fairchild packaging researcher. So he took the idea to a quirky Japanese company founded in 1959 as Kyoto Ceramics, now Kyocera. It "was very anxious to get into the electronic end of the ceramics business," says Mr. Phy, and Kyocera agreed "to tool it at no cost to Fairchild."
>
> By the early 1980s Kyocera had an estimated 70 percent of the world market. . . . "American and European makers had the know-how and the capacity . . . but the [lack] of effort made the difference" [says Shunji Nosaka, managing director of Kyocera]. And, he notes, at the time Kyocera entered the business, Coors [Ceramics] was the world's leading maker of ceramic semiconductor packages. "That company gave us a dream as a target to catch up with," says Mr. Nosaka. "I'm grateful to that company." [*The Wall Street Journal* (February 5, 1991)]

25. Personal interview with government source.
26. Senate Armed Services Committee, "America's Industrial Base as It Supports the National Security," hearings (June 18, 1991).
27. Andrew S. Grove, Intel Corporation, from a speech given September 26, 1990; quoted in *Creating Advantage,* p. 19.
28. U.S. General Accounting Office, "U.S. Business Access to Certain Foreign State of the Art Technology," GAS/NSIAD-91-278 (Washington, D.C.: U.S. Gov-

ernment Printing Office, September 1991). Also *The New York Times* (September 25, 1991).

29. William J. Spencer, from a speech given at George Washington University, Washington, D.C. (February 12, 1992).

30. Jacob Schlesinger, *The Wall Street Journal* (February 6, 1992) and T. R. Reid, *The Washington Post* (February 6, 1992).

31. Ibid.

32. Kiyohisa Ota and Hunt Macnguyen, "Semiconductors and Computers: A Study of U.S. Industry and Company Competitiveness in the World" (New York: Nomura Research Institute America, Inc., June 1991). This report was published in English six months after the original came out in Japanese, as *Kyuju Nendai no Computa/Handotai Sangyo,* or "The Computer and Semiconductor Industries of the 1990s."

33. Ota and Macnguyen, "Semiconductors and Computers," p. 8.

34. Ibid., p. 7.

35. Ibid., p. 11.

36. Ibid., p. 15.

37. *Newsweek* (July 13, 1992).

38. Norman Angell, *The Great Illusion: A Study of the Relation of Military Power to National Advantage* (New York: G. P. Putnam's Sons, 1910; reprint 1913), quoted in George Friedman and Meredith Lebard, *The Coming War with Japan* (New York: St. Martin's Press, 1991), p. 201.

39. *Politics and Productivity,* p. 106, quoting McKinsey & Company, Inc., and the U.S.-Japan Trade Study Group, *Japan: Business Obstacles & Opportunities* (Tokyo: President, Inc., 1983).

40. William J. Abernathy and Robert H. Hayes, "Managing Our Way to Economic Decline," *Harvard Business Review,* Vol. 58, No. 4 (July–August 1980), pp. 67–77.

41. The "wrong side" problem must have been more complicated than most Americans assumed. The best-selling imported cars in Japan, BMWs and Mercedes from Germany, also had their steering wheels on the wrong side. Moreover, Ford and GM had long been big sellers in such "wrong side" countries as Australia and the United Kingdom. For cars sold there, "Detroit" had been perfectly capable of switching the steering wheels to the right side. Its resistance to doing so for cars sold in Japan was based on the Big Three's belief that other barriers would keep their cars off the Japanese market even if the "wrong side" problem went away.

42. Geoffrey Perret elaborates on this in *A Country Made by War: From the Revolution to Vietnam—the Story of America's Rise to Power* (New York: Random House, 1989), pp. 126, 382, 400–404, 439.

43. Porter makes this point on page 97 of his book (New York: The Free Press, 1990)—and makes it again on page 169. The version on page 169 is "American semiconductor firms, for example, were slow to abandon bipolar technology in favor of the newer metal oxide semiconductor (MOS) technology, allowing Japanese firms to gain position." This doesn't answer the question, which part of this book will attempt to answer, of why the Japanese firms were trying to get into an industry in which they were almost certain to lose money unless the Americans made large mistakes.

44. This is from page 138 of Porter's book, and it is his only mention of the subject.

45. Peter F. Drucker, *The New Realities: In Government and Politics, in Economics and Business, in Society and World View* (New York: Harper & Row, 1989). A similar note was struck by the author of the Semiconductor Industry Association report:

> International competition in microelectronics has become a competition, in significant degree, between differing national economic systems. Individual firms can pursue their own strategies within this milieu and in some cases are able to swim against the tide, bucking adverse trends through their own efforts. However, even the most competitive firms ultimately cannot escape from the environment in which they must operate. . . . There is substantial evidence that Japan's rise and America's consequent relative decline in the 1980s were in large measure attributable to fundamental differences in the Japanese and American versions of capitalism—differences in industrial structure, in what constitutes generally acceptable business behavior, and, most importantly, in the relationship between government and industry. [Quoted in *Creating Advantage*, p. 23]

46. *Creating Advantage*, p. v.

47. Ibid.

48. "While the work that led to the development of Integrated Circuits (ICs) was not directly financed by the government it was 'undertaken with the clear understanding that, if it were successful, there would be a massive government market.' In the pivotal year of 1962, NASA announced that it would use ICs in the guidance system for the Apollo spacecraft, and the Air Force decided to make maximum feasible use of ICs in the guidance system for the Minuteman ICBM. Procurement featured high prices (about $100/unit) and high volume (200,000 units for the Apollo program). Such purchases enabled U.S. firms to improve yields and efficiency through volume production, and encouraged wider application of IC technology, first in other military systems and eventually in industrial and commercial uses." From Thomas Howell and Warren Davis, *Nation-States in International Semiconductor Competition* (Washington, D.C.: Dewey Ballantine/Semiconductor Industry Association, 1991), pp. 18–19; quoting Richard R. Nelson, *High Technology Policies: A Five Nation Comparison* (Washington, D.C.: American Enterprise Institute for Public Policy, 1984).

49. *Creating Advantage*, p. 26. It also cites Nelson, *High Technology Policies*, p. 43, and National Bureau of Research Standards, *The Influence of Defense Procurement and Sponsorship of Research and Development on the Development of the Civilian Electronics Industry* (June 30, 1977).

50. Borrus, *Competing for Control*, p. 71. Borrus further cites Eli Ginzberg, Thierry Noyelle, and Thomas Starback, *Economic Impact of Large Public Programs: The NASA Experience* (Boulder, Colo.: The Westview Press, 1986), p. 58.

51. Borrus, p. 72.

52. Kenneth Flamm, "Making New Rules: High Tech Trade Friction and the Semiconductor Industry," *The Brookings Review*, Vol. 9, No. 2 (Spring 1991), pp. 22–29.

53. Mark Mason discusses this phenomenon in his book *American Multinationals and Japan: The Political Economy of Japanese Capital Controls, 1899–1980* (Cambridge, Mass.: Council on East Asian Studies, Harvard; distributed by Harvard University Press, 1992).

54. See Karl Zinsmeister's article "The Industrial Policy Hoax," *The Wall Street Journal* (March 10, 1993). For follow-up discussion of Zinsmeister's claims, see *The American Prospect*, Vol. 70 (Summer 1993), pp. 21–27.

55. See Borrus, pp. 118–22.

56. Ibid., p. 120.

57. *Politics and Productivity*, p. 101.

58. Morita says in his autobiography that TI was eager to operate in Japan, but "under the existing Japanese regulations, the only way TI could come in was through a joint venture with a Japanese firm."

> I offered TI a joint venture with Sony—we were also a maker of semiconductors—and the Ministry of International Trade and Industry seemed agreeable to the arrangement by which we would sell our 50 percent in three years. We hit a snag when the TI side said they needed a guarantee in writing from the government that the sale of our 50 percent of the company would be approved three years hence. . . . "You must trust us," I told one of the TI negotiators, but he insisted it had to be on paper. We finally created a satisfactory written document that just barely managed to satisfy the American lawyers.

Akio Morita with Edwin M. Reingold and Mitsuko Shimomura, *Made in Japan: Akio Morita and Sony* (New York: E. P. Dutton, 1986), pp. 192–93.

59. See Borrus, pp. 120–22; also *Politics and Productivity*, p. 101.

60. *Politics and Productivity*, p. 102 (emphasis added).

61. As two American scholars put it, "Past discrimination lives on in the institutions of the economy and the attitudes of the community. Arrangements of suppliers and of distribution have been established in a closed market. They are now remarkably difficult for foreigners to penetrate." *Politics and Productivity*, p. 105.

62. Ibid., p. 111.

63. Tyson and Zysman (*Politics and Productivity*, p. 104) make the point more elaborately thus:

> At the beginning of the 1970s, Japanese producers were not cutting-edge competitors on world markets. Between that time and the mid-1980s, the Japanese market for semiconductors grew to match the scale of the American market. The industry underwent three virtual product revolutions. The market positions of firms throughout the world were reshuffled. Japan's share of the American and European markets went up. Yet, the American share of the Japanese market remained constant throughout these changes, it neither rose nor fell. Literacy and savings rates cannot account for intrasectoral patterns of trade such as this one.

64. Borrus, p. 102.

65. "Korea Aims for Top in VLSI by 1991," *Electronics* (April 2, 1987); quoted in *Creating Advantage*, p. 349.

66. World Bank, *Korea: Managing the Industrial Transition*, Vol. 2 (Washington, D.C., 1987); quoted in *Creating Advantage*, p. 349.

67. *Creating Advantage* concluded on this point:

> Indeed, it can now be said that Korea has created a comparative advantage in DRAMs, the mainstay of the global semiconductor trade, and is determined to achieve world-class status in higher value-added devices [p. 350].

68. Merrill Goozner, *Chicago Tribune* (March 18, 1993). Papken Der Torossian, quoted in *Time* (November 23, 1992).

69. Borrus, pp. 55–95.

70. As Borrus says about this process:

> Bell Labs' rapid dissemination of research reports helped develop the semi-conductor industry in the United States. The policy of dissemination was part of the corporate culture of public service that AT&T as a regulated monopoly strove to cultivate. At the same time, with the Justice Department's 1949 an-titrust complaint hanging on the horizon, the company could not afford even the appearance of monopoly. . . . In the development of semiconductor tech-nology, antitrust policy had the impact of widely diffusing Bell's basic tech-nology, thereby diversifying the domestic research base and creating competitive pressures and market incentives for the technology's further refinement, de-velopment, and application [p. 59].

71. Jay S. Stowsky, "Weak Links, Strong Bonds," p. 248.

72. This is described in Borrus, pp. 80–85.

73. See Borrus, p. 8: "The chief victors in the calculator wars were, of course, Japanese producers. Their success demonstrated that merchant U.S. chip pro-ducers were vulnerable to the problem of insufficient resources in competition with vertically integrated systems producers."

74. This is from "Japanese Market Barriers in Microelectronics: Memorandum in Support of a Petition Pursuant to Section 301 of the Trade Act of 1974 as Amended, Prepared for the Semiconductor Industry Association by Dewey, Ballantine" (June 14, 1985). The statement says that when Hitachi learned that the memorandum had been leaked, it denied that it reflected the company's policy, but reporters found a number of other companies who confirmed this experience with Hitachi.

75. See Robert Neff's commentary "And Now, Another Form of Japanese Hardball: Lowball Pricing," in *Business Week* (November 20, 1989, p. 50), and David Sanger's in *The New York Times* (November 2, 1989). They provide one possible answer to the "What was in it?" question, saying that the companies each hoped to get the local governments locked into their computer system so that in the future they could monopolize sales of software, accessories, and other services. The *Business Week* article said, "Japanese companies figure that once they have bought their way into a relationship, they will enjoy a lifetime of orders. As a result they don't mind giving away short-term business and dividing up the bidding with their Japanese rivals."

76. Robert Wade, Afterword, *African Development: Lessons from Asia* (Arlington, Va.: Winrock International Institute for Agriculture Development, 1991), p. 254 (proceedings of a seminar on strategies for the future of Asia sponsored by the Africa Bureau, U.S. Agency for International Development and Winrock In-ternational, Baltimore, Md., June 5–7, 1991).

77. Chalmers Johnson, "History Restarted: Japanese-American Relations at the End of the Century," in R. Higgott, R. Leaver, and J. Rowenhill, eds., *Pacific Eco-nomic Relations in the 1990s: Cooperation or Conflict?* (Boulder, Col.: Lynne Rienner, 1993), p. 49.

CHAPTER 2. THE DRIVE TO CATCH UP

1. Lily Abegg, *The Mind of Asia* (London: Thames & Hudson, 1952), p. 275.

2. Reg Little and Warren Reed, *The Confucian Renaissance* (Sydney: The Federation Press, 1989), p. 31.

3. George Sansom, *History of Japan,* Vol. 2, *1334–1615* (Tokyo: Charles E. Tuttle, 1974), p. 369.

4. Ibid., pp. 265ff.

5. As Little and Reed write in *The Confucian Renaissance,* "The Japanese response to the Jesuits . . . is the key to understanding Japanese political and commercial strategy over the past 500 years. . . . Integral to this is a recognition that moral and spiritual values were being used by Europeans in a very pragmatic and expedient way to further political and commercial objectives" [p. 20].

6. Michio Morishima, *Why Has Japan "Succeeded"?: Western Technology and the Japanese Ethos* (Cambridge: Cambridge University Press, 1982), p. 41.

7. Derek Masarella, *A World Elsewhere: Europe's Encounter with Japan in the Sixteenth and the Seventeenth Centuries* (New Haven, Conn.: Yale University Press, 1990), p. 46.

8. Ronald Dore, "The Legacy of Tokugawa Education," in *Changing Japanese Attitudes Toward Modernization,* ed. Marius B. Jansen (Princeton, N.J.: Princeton University Press, 1965), p. 107.

9. Abegg, *Mind of Asia,* p. 182.

10. Theodore Friend, *The Blue-Eyed Enemy: Japan Against the West in Java and Luzon, 1942–1945* (Princeton, N.J.: Princeton University Press, 1988), p. 54.

11. Bob Tadashi Wakabayashi, *Anti-Foreignism and Western Learning in Early-Modern Japan: The New Theses of 1825* (Cambridge, Mass.: Council on East Asian Studies, Harvard University, and Harvard University Press, 1986), p. 60. The document he cites is *Tokugawa kinreiko,* ed. Shunsuke Kikuchi (Tokyo: Yoshikawakobunkan, 1932), pp. 609–10.

12. George B. Sansom, *The Western World and Japan: A Study in the Interaction of European and Asiatic Cultures* (Tokyo: Charles E. Tuttle, 1977), p. 277.

13. Morishima, *Why Has Japan "Succeeded"?,* p. 65.

14. Sansom, *Western World,* p. 274.

15. Morishima, pp. 52–53.

16. John Welfield, *An Empire in Eclipse: Japan in the Postwar American Alliance System* (London: The Athlone Press, 1988), p. 3.

17. Ibid., p. 7; quoting Senshi Kenkyu Shiryo, *Dai Hon'ei Rikugun Bu, Dai Toa Senso Kaisen Ni Kansuru Kosatsu,* HRO-5, Boei Kenshujo Shenshi Shitsu (1976), p. 3.

18. Described in Masao Watanabe, *The Japanese and Western Science,* trans. Otto Theodor Benfey (Philadelphia: University of Pennsylvania Press, 1990), p. 123.

19. Ibid., p. 10; quoted from Kenjiro Yamagawa, *The Writings of Baron Yamagawa* (Tokyo, 1937), pp. 48–49.

20. Morishima, p. 135.

21. Masao Miyoshi, *As We Saw Them: The First Japanese Embassy to the United States* (Berkeley: University of California Press, 1979), p. 120.

22. Morishima, p. 97.

23. E. H. Norman, *Origins of the Modern Japanese State: Selected Writings of E. H. Norman,* ed. John Dower (New York: Pantheon Books, 1975), p. 222.

24. Ibid., p. 224.
25. Extensive discussions of this pattern are found in Mason, *American Multinationals and Japan,* and Dennis Encarnation, *Rivals Beyond Trade: America Versus Japan in Global Competition* (Ithaca, N.Y.: Cornell University Press, 1992).
26. The first sentence is from Sheldon Garon, "Women's Groups and the Japanese State: Contending Approaches to Political Integration, 1890–1945," *Journal of Japanese Studies,* Vol. 19, No. 1 (Winter 1993), p. 6. The extracted quote is from Sheldon Garon, "The World's Oldest Debate? Prostitution and the State in Imperial Japan, 1900–1945," *The American Historical Review,* Vol. 98, No. 2 (June 1993), p. 711.
27. Quoted in Carol Gluck, *Japan's Modern Myths: Ideology in the Late Meiji Period* (Princeton, N.J.: Princeton University Press, 1985), p. 18.
28. Andrew Pollack, *The New York Times* (September 11, 1992). The authority he quoted was Miyuki Ohashi, professor of sociology at Nihon University.
29. His work is the main subject of Bob Tadashi Wakabayashi's book, *Anti-Foreignism and Western Learning in Early-Modern Japan.*
30. John Gunther's surprisingly fascinating and prescient *Inside Asia* (New York: Harper & Brothers, 1939), published just before America joined World War II, discusses this on page 36.
31. The journalist Eamonn Fingleton described this process nicely:

> Before the 1850s, when U.S. gunboats led a Western attempt to colonize the country, Japan's system of rule by respected and highly motivated bureaucrats had already accumulated the longest continuous history of sophisticated administration of any major country. The Japanese authorities quickly reasoned that their secluded and virtually defenseless nation had a better chance of avoiding being pushed around by the great powers if Japan put in place the formal government and legal structures that mirrored those of the "civilized" West. As a result, between 1870 and 1890 the bureaucrats gave the nation a cabinet, a full set of law courts, and finally a parliament. But it was always understood that these institutions were subordinate to the will of the bureaucrats, who were entrusted by the nation with no-questions-asked powers to regulate the economy virtually free from interference from the courts, politicians, or the press. [Eamonn Fingleton, *Institutional Investor* (October 1990, p. 72)]

32. Gluck, *Japan's Modern Myths,* p. 3.
33. Ibid., p. 38.
34. Ibid., p. 121.
35. Ibid., p. 5.
36. Robert Wade, *Governing the Market: Economic Theory and the Role of Government in East Asian Industrialization* (Princeton, N.J.: Princeton University Press, 1990), p. 327.
37. James Sterngold, *The New York Times* (September 13, 1993).
38. For instance, when the U.S. and Japanese governments were wrangling in the late 1980s in the "structural impediments initiative," many Japanese consumers favored the American side. How else were they ever going to break up the cartels and price-fixing arrangements inside the Japanese economy, unless powerful outsiders complained? When the Japanese Supreme Court finally agreed, in the mid-1980s, that citizens could take notes during court sessions, it was because

an American lawyer had persisted for years with a suit demanding this seemingly obvious right.

39. Reginald Kearney, *Reconcilable Differences: Issues in African American-Japanese Relations* (Japan Society of New York, 1992).

40. The American scholar Ivan Hall, who was taught for many years in Japanese universities, discusses this and related issues in "Samurai Legacies, American Illusions," *The National Interest*, No. 28 (Summer 1992), pp. 14–25.

41. Gluck, p. 142.

42. Gunther, *Inside Asia*, p. 9.

43. Jansen, *Changing Japanese Attitudes Toward Modernization*, p. 215; quoting *Nihon dotoku ron* (February 1887), Sosho, 1.8. Quotes in 1890s from Shigeki Nishimura of imperial advisers, on the menace from the West. Donald H. Shively, "Nishimura Shigeki: A Confucian View of Modernization," in Jansen, *Changing Japanese Attitudes Toward Modernization*, p. 215.

44. John Dower, Introduction to Norman, *Origins of the Modern Japanese State*, p. 15.

45. Morishima, p. 68 (emphasis added).

46. W. G. Beasley, *The Rise of Modern Japan* (London: Weidenfeld & Nicolson, 1990), p. 147.

47. *Aera* (July 16, 1991).

48. Herbert P. Bix, "The Showa Emperor's 'Monologue' and the Problem of War Responsibility," *Journal of Japanese Studies*, Vol. 18, No. 2 (1992), p. 334.

49. Morishima, pp. 122–23.

50. John Dower, *Empire and Aftermath: Yoshida Shigeru and the Japanese Experience, 1878–1954* (Cambridge, Mass.: Council on East Asian Studies, Harvard University, and Harvard University Press, 1988), p. 47.

51. The full passage was,

> In recent years the United States, having developed its national power, and disposing of limitless national resources, has embarked on a policy of economic aggression. In China, especially . . . the United States threatens the position that the empire has acquired as a result of many risks and sacrifices. It is not possible to bear this situation any longer. . . . The ostracism of Japanese residents in California will gradually spread to other states and develop a more solid base. There are no grounds for optimism concerning the position of our people in Hawaii. These conflicts, growing out of years of economic problems and racial prejudice, will be difficult to solve. . . . In this situation, the United States, which possesses immense armaments and has many bases throughout East Asia and the Pacific, will sooner or later, as part of its Asian policy, provoke a conflict with the Empire. [Quoted in Welfield, *Empire in Eclipse*, pp. 14–15]

52. John Dower, *War Without Mercy: Race and Power in the Pacific War* (New York: Pantheon Books, 1986), pp. 59–60.

53. Friend, *Blue-Eyed Enemy*, pp. 59–60.

54. Kita Ikki, *Kita Ikki Sho Sakushu* (Tokyo: Misuzu Shobo, 1971).

55. Richard Wright, *The Color Curtain: A Report on the Bandung Conference* (Cleveland: World Pub., 1956), p. 10.

56. Robert Elegant, *Pacific Destiny: Inside Asia Today* (New York: Crown Publishers, 1990), p. 9.

[57.] Miyoshi, *As We Saw Them,* p. 64.

[58.] This is from a commentary on the Imperial Declaration of War, selling more than 3 million copies. Cited in Tokutomi Iichiro, "Commentary on the Imperial Rescript Declaring War on the United States and the British Empire," *Sources of Japanese Tradition,* Vol. 2, ed. and trans. Wm. Theodore de Bary, Ryusaku Tsunoda, and Donald Keene (New York: Columbia University Press, 1964), p. 293.

[59.] This is the subject of the first parts of Akira Iriye's book *Power and Culture: The Japanese-American War 1941–1945* (Cambridge, Mass.: Harvard University Press, 1981).

[60.] John Dower, essay in *Deadline for the Media,* ed. Tom Engelhardt (New York: Center for War, Peace, and the News Media, New York University, Fall 1991).

[61.] *Papers Relating to the Foreign Relations of the United States, Japan: 1931–1941,* Vol. 2 (Washington, D.C.: U.S. Government Printing Office, 1945).

[62.] Ben-Ami Shillony, *Politics and Culture in Wartime Japan* (Oxford: Oxford University Press, 1981), pp. 141–42.

[63.] Kenneth Courtis, ed., "Bi-Weekly Comments" (Tokyo: Deutsche Bank Capital Markets, Asia, February 9, 1992).

[64.] Chapman, *Inventing Japan,* p. 237. The book he quotes is Fusao Hayashi, *Dai Toa Senso Kotei Ron* (Tokyo: Brancho Shobo, 1964).

CHAPTER 3. THE AMERICAN YEARS

[1.] One eighty-acre tract of suburban Osaka, its existence not acknowledged on city maps, is the burial ground of Emperor Nintoku, who reigned sixteen hundred years ago. It is surrounded by a moat and high wall and not marked in any way.

[2.] John Welfield, *An Empire in Eclipse: Japan in the Postwar American Alliance System* (London: The Athlone Press, 1988), p. 56.

[3.] Ibid.

[4.] The text of this book and the material about Norman come from John Dower's indispensable introduction to a reissue of the book under the title *Origins of the Modern Japanese State: Selected Writings of E. H. Norman.*

[5.] David Halberstam, *The Reckoning* (New York: William Morrow, 1986), p. 276.

[6.] Theodore Cohen, *Remaking Japan: The American Occupation as New Deal,* ed. Herbert Passin (New York: The Free Press, 1987), p. 2.

[7.] Quoted in Tetsuya Kataoka, *The Price of a Constitution: The Origin of Japan's Postwar Politics* (New York: Taylor & Francis, 1991), p. 30.

[8.] Ibid., p. 31, citing congressional testimony.

[9.] Ibid.

[10.] Chalmers Johnson, *Conspiracy at Matsukawa* (Berkeley: University of California Press, 1972), p. 13.

[11.] Thomas P. Rohlen, *Japan's High Schools* (Berkeley: University of California Press, 1983), p. 67.

[12.] Chapman, *Inventing Japan,* p. 18; the memoirs he quotes are in Mark Gayn, *Japan Diary* (New York: William Sloane Associates, 1948), pp. 84–92. Japanese orthography does not permit a "tu" sequence in spelling, so the names "Otuki" and "Mitumine" would normally be spelled "Otsuki" and "Mitsumine." This excerpt preserves the spelling Chapman used in his book.

13. The "supervisory layer" phrase comes from Kazuo Kawai's intriguing book *Japan's American Interlude* (Chicago: University of Chicago Press, 1960), p. 19.

14. Herbert P. Bix has a valuable summary of this process in his article "The Showa Emperor's 'Monologue,' " pp. 360–63.

15. Johnson, *Conspiracy at Matsukawa*, p. 248.

16. See John Dower, *Empire and Aftermath: Yoshida Shigeru and the Japanese Experience, 1878–1954* (Cambridge, Mass.: Council on East Asian Studies, Harvard University, and Harvard University Press, 1988), p. 293, for information on this general era.

17. Johnson, p. 1.

18. Kataoka, *Price of a Constitution*, p. 63.

19. Chalmers Johnson's riveting *Conspiracy at Matsukawa* tells all about this case.

20. See William Triplett, *Flowering of the Bamboo* (Kensington, Md.: Woodbine House, 1985), for information about this case.

21. Quoted in Dower, *Empire and Aftermath*, p. 260.

22. Ibid.; the quotes are from Dower, not Yoshida.

23. Quoted in Kataoka, *Price of a Constitution*, p. 53.

24. Ibid.

25. Ibid., p. 88. Kataoka says:

> This was done on his own initiative and without prior instruction from Washington. . . . Justin Williams, a GS official, called in the leaders of the two opposition parties, the JSP and the former Minseito, and told them that the Diet had no power to discuss the police reserve issue and that any violation of his order would be punished. A mere executive order seemed to override the constitution and founded what everyone thought was a new Japanese army. Later, in October 1950, another SCAP order—this time secret—had created minesweeper units manned by former Japanese naval personnel, and they were deployed around the Korean coast. Here was the origin of Japan's illegitimate army and the never-ending controversy over it.

26. Quoted in Welfield, *Empire in Eclipse*, p. 28.

27. Dower, Introduction to Norman, *Origins of the Modern Japanese State*, pp. 50, 51.

28. John Dower extensively discusses this in his introduction to *Origins of the Modern Japanese State*.

29. *Fortune* (September 1936, p. 51).

30. For instance, "In most constitutional countries the military branches are under the control of the civil government. In Japan there is no such control: the Diet has power to regulate the service budgets but in case of a failure to agree—which can always be arranged—the previous year's budget is continued. In Japan the army may not only act without governmental authorization but may even issue proclamations on foreign policy independently of the foreign office."

31. *Fortune* (September 1936, p. 68). It also said, "Because monopoly gives its possessor the maximum control over financing, manufacturing, and marketing—for whatever ends the possessor wishes this control. Among the private capitalisms, Japan is the nearest to this ideal structure. It is Exhibit A in private monopoly capitalism."

32. Arthur Koestler, "For Better or Worse, Her Course Is Set," *Life* (September 11, 1964, p. 63).

33. "The Unique Era, but What Now?" *Life* (September 11, 1964, p. 3; unsigned editorial).

34. Private draft prepared by U.S. Information Service official (September 1989).

35. Edwin Reischauer, "Inevitable Partners," *Life* (September 11, 1964, pp. 27–28).

36. For instance: "Few Japanese came to accept the traditional Anglo-American belief that the self-oriented, profit-maximizing behavior of firms and optimizing behavior of individuals would, through competition, automatically create the maximum output and lowest prices for the benefit of consumers." Henry Rosovsky, *Asia's New Giant: How the Japanese Economy Works,* ed. Hugh Patrick and Henry Rosovsky (Washington, D.C.: Brookings Institution, 1976), pp. 10–11. Rosovsky continued:

> Rather, many Japanese, especially in the government bureaucracy, have noted the deviations in practice from the competitive model: the existence of oligopolistic markets, the efficiency of large-scale economies, lumpiness of large investment requirements in certain industries and consequent problems of excess capacity, and situations of market failure—all of which allegedly compel government intervention. And . . . not only did the Occupation reforms directed at the concentration of business power not go very far, but rapid growth has substantially influenced further the conditions of industrial organization.

37. Ross Garnaut, *Australia and the Northeast Asian Ascendancy* (Fyshwick, A.C.T.: Canberra Publishing and Printing Company, 1989), p. 124.

38. Ibid., pp. 124–25.

39. T. R. Reid, *The Washington Post* (December 1, 1991, p. 1).

40. *Life* (September 11, 1964, p. 45).

41. Richard H. Minear, *Victors' Justice: The Tokyo War Crimes Trial* (Tokyo: Charles E. Tuttle, 1971), p. 116.

42. Chalmers Johnson, in *Conspiracy at Matsukawa,* points out that the Kyoto railroad station had been an important rail junction during the war. "When I arrived in the city in 1953, it had clearly been bombed and replaced by the only new building in the city," Johnson says.

It is widely believed in Japan that the savior of Kyoto was Langdon Warner, curator of the Oriental collection at Harvard's Fogg Art Museum before the war. When Warner arrived in Japan after the war, however, he denied that he had influenced the decision. The major discussion of this issue is in Otis Cary, *The Kodansha Encyclopedia of Japan,* Vol. 8, p. 228.

43. Johnson's full argument, as expressed in an interview with me, was this:

> What the Americans did was technically illegal in international law. There is nothing in international law that says you get to reform a conquered country. You can disarm it. You can exact reparations from it. You can execute violators of the Hague Convention. But there is nothing that says you get to do what either the Americans or the Soviet Union did to conquered nations at the end of World War II.
>
> . . . In order for the Japanese to get Article I of the Constitution, saying that the emperor shall be the symbol of the state, Article IX was the price.
>
> MacArthur realized that there had long been a history of separation of power and authority in Japan. Many Japanese were sympathetic because the

emperor had had authority but no real power. Nonetheless, the emperor had been head of state during the war. For whatever reasons, he had signed the declaration of war and done similar things. Article IX, which disarmed Japan, was the cost of Article I.

　　　You might conclude that it was unwise of the Americans to try to democratize Japan. But having chosen to do so, I believe these were all rational decisions that followed.

44. Gayn, *Japan Diary,* p. 140; quoted in Bix, "Showa Emperor," p. 299.

45. The British and Australian resentment of this episode shows up even now. In the late 1980s an Australian film company produced a film called *Prisoners of the Sun.* In it, a group of Australians is tortured in a Japanese camp in the Dutch East Indies. After the war the Americans rig the testimony to free the Japanese commander—who has become part of the postwar government in Japan and has bigger fish to fry—leaving the honorable, just-following-orders camp guards as the only ones to be punished.

46. In his history of the trials, *Victors' Justice,* Richard Minear gave extensive illustrations of the selective questioning. As chief prosecutor at the trial, Joseph Keenan was determined to avoid discussion of the emperor's involvement in wartime policy. The presiding justice, William Webb of Australia, took the opposite view. Webb remained convinced of the emperor's culpability; twenty-five years after the Tokyo trials were over, he wrote a laudatory introduction to David Bergamini, *Japan's Imperial Conspiracy* (New York: William Morrow, 1971), the book in which Bergamini said that Hirohito had been the mastermind of the war.

　　　During Tojo's testimony at the trials, Webb made a remark that indicated his views about the emperor:

> TOJO: "And I further wish to add that there is no Japanese subject who would go against the will of His Majesty; more particularly, among high officials of the Japanese government or of Japan. . . ."
> WEBB: "Well, you know the implications from that reply."
> [Minear, *Victors' Justice,* p. 115; from Proceedings, pp. 36, 521]

　　　According to notebooks kept by Seiichi Yamazaki, the private secretary to chief prosecutor Keenan during the trials, Keenan was deeply upset when he heard Webb's comments in the courtroom. That same evening, Keenan met with Yamazaki and with a Japanese witness for the prosecution. According to Yamazaki, they designed an elaborate plan to convince Tojo that it would be indecent and dishonorable to keep dragging the emperor's name into the trial. Yamazaki says that Tojo got the message and understood. One week later, with Tojo again on the stand, Keenan asked him to clarify his earlier comments about the emperor's role:

> KEENAN: "While we are discussing the subject matter of emperors, it might be an appropriate moment to ask you a few questions on the relative positions of yourself and the emperor of Japan on the matter of waging war in December of 1941. You have told us that the emperor on repeated occasions made known to you that he was a man of peace and did not want war, is that correct?"
> TOJO: "I was then speaking to you of my feeling toward the emperor as a subject,

and that is quite a different matter from the problem of responsibility, that is, the responsibility of the emperor."

KEENAN: "Well, you did make war against the United States, Great Britain, and the Netherlands, did you not?"

TOJO: "War was decided on in my cabinet."

KEENAN: "Was that the will of Emperor Hirohito, that war should be instituted?"

TOJO: "It may not have been according to his will, but it is a fact that because of my advice and because of the advice given by the High Command the emperor consented, though reluctantly, to the war."

INTERPRETER: "The first part should be corrected: 'It might have been against the emperor's will.'"

TOJO (continuing): "The emperor's love for and desire for peace remained the same right up to the very moment when hostilities commenced, and even during the war his feelings remained the same. The emperor's feelings in this regard can be clearly ascertained from the imperial rescript given on the eighth of December 1941, declaring war. That portion of the rescript was included because of the emperor's wishes on the responsibility of the government. That is to say, the imperial rescript contains words to this effect: This war is indeed unavoidable and is against my own desires."

[Minear, pp. 114–15; from Proceedings, pp. 36, 779–81]

When the trial was over and Tojo had been sentenced to death, his Japanese lawyer reported that nonetheless "Tojo's mind is eased very much by the verdict, knowing that he has given no additional trouble to the emperor." Minear, p. 115; citing *The New York Times* (November 13, 1948, p. 9).

47. Minear, p. 117; quoting *The New York Times* (January 14, 1949, p. 11). Minear says that he didn't find a record of this in the trial transcript itself.

48. Bix, "Showa Emperor," pp. 295–363.

49. Ibid., p. 350.

50. General Hajime Sugiyama, *Sugiyama Memo,* Vol. 1 (Tokyo: Hara Shobo, 1967), pp. 388–406. These are papers of Japan's wartime Army Chief of Staff.

51. Bix, pp. 352–53.

52. Ibid., p. 333.

53. Ibid., p. 313.

54. Between January 1930 and December 1945, a period that covered the whole of Japan's militarist phase, Kido had kept detailed diaries of his observations inside the government. These diaries, which were published in Japan in 1966 as *Kido Nikki* ("Kido Journals"), are a major historical source about wartime policy and intrigue.

55. Bix, pp. 315–16.

56. David Bergamini offered this speculation in his book *Japan's Imperial Conspiracy,* p. 1066. As mentioned before, Bergamini's view of Hirohito as wartime mastermind is discredited. Yet this insight about MacArthur rings true.

57. This reworking of history was easier in Japan than in Germany because of the way the war ended. When the Allies stormed into Germany, they found a country whose government had ceased to function, and they could immediately confiscate tons of documents indicating who had done what during the Nazis' years of terror. But the wartime Japanese government kept on functioning until the mo-

ment of surrender. As an American scholar pointed out, "Most of the top-secret wartime records of the leaders in Japan were either deliberately destroyed in the weeks before General MacArthur's arrival, or else falsified and hidden, leaving wartime memoirs and oral testimony as the main basis on which the Allies could prosecute war criminals." Bix, p. 295.

58. Norma Field, *In the Realm of a Dying Emperor* (New York: Pantheon Books, 1991), p. 41.

59. John Bussey wrote about this in *The Asian Wall Street Journal* (August 9, 1993). The museum, he said, "is at once a reminder of the horror of nuclear weapons— and a remarkable monument to Japan's selective memory."

60. Marck C. Medish, Kyoto Kitsch and Tokyo Cafes, *Stepping Stones,* Vol. 1, No. 2, November 1992.

61. *Newsweek* (November 25, 1991).

62. *Japan Free Press* (December 9, 1991); quoting *Asahi* (November 30, 1991).

63. John Dower emphasizes this "diplomatic" role in *Empire and Aftermath*, pp. 274–76.

64. Kataoka, *Price of a Constitution*, p. 87; citing *Foreign Relations of the United States* (1950), Vol. 6, p. 1166.

65. Kataoka, p. 150.

66. Ibid., p. 151.

67. Ibid., p. 139.

68. Kenichi Matsumoto, Asia Foundation Translation Series, TSC #1488 (July 29, 1992); originally published in *Sankei Shimbun.*

69. Kazuo Kawai, *Japan's American Interlude*, p. 57.

70. *Japan Views* (July 1992); originally published in *Sankei Shimbun* (May 24, 1992).

71. "The Korean War was in many ways the equivalent for Japan of the Marshall Plan. Between June 1950 and 1954 the United States spent close to $3 billion in Japan for war and war-related supplies. This *tokuju keiki,* or *tokuju* boom (from the name of the U.S. procurement orders, called 'special needs' or *tokubetsu juyo*), overcame the depression caused by economic stabilization and started the economy on its upward course." Johnson, *Conspiracy at Matsukawa*, p. 23.

72. Chapman, *Inventing Japan*, p. 100.

CHAPTER 4. THE IDEA OF ECONOMIC SUCCESS

1. Friedrich List, *The Natural System of Political Economy,* trans. and ed. W. O. Henderson (London: Frank Cass, 1983).

2. List, *The Natural System*, pp. 42–43.

3. Friedrich List, *The National System of Political Economy,* trans. Sampson S. Lloyd (New York: Augustus M. Kelley, 1966), p. 144.

4. Lester Thurow, *Head to Head: The Coming Economic Battle Among Japan, Europe, and America* (New York: William Morrow, 1992), pp. 119, 129–30.

5. Adam Smith, *The Wealth of Nations* (New York: Random House, 1965), p. 431.

6. Quoted by William F. Buckley, "Firing Line Debate: Resolved, That American Industry Does Not Need Protection," Oxford, Mississippi (September 3, 1992).

7. List, *The National System*, p. 174.

8. John Judis, "Trade, Investment, and the Critical Election of 1992," *In These Times* (May 27, 1992).

⁹· List, *The Natural System,* p. 47. There is this further addendum:

> What England does depends upon whether her economic policy is inspired solely by self-interest and national passions and prejudices or whether her policy is inspired by a higher morality and by nobler aims. The latter is hardly to be expected at all times and in all circumstances.

¹⁰· This is Henry Nau, of George Washington University, the author of *The Myth of America's Decline,* in "America Can Compete with Japan," keynote address, *Fortune* Magazine Corporate Communication Conference, Palm Springs, Calif. (March 11, 1991).

　　In September 1992, William Buckley's *Firing Line* program held a two-hour televised debate about trade policy and industrial protection. I was the stealth member of the group, whose other members were mostly big names. Arguing that American industry did not need any protection were Henry Kissinger, Buckley, Jack Kemp, and a right-wing congressman from Texas named Dick Armey. Arguing that protection was sometimes necessary were Richard Gephardt, Lester Thurow, Jerry Brown, and me. To my mind the most revealing colloquy was one that may have seemed totally obscure to the audience. Buckley and Kissinger repeatedly asked for "moral" and "political" judgments about different trading practices. If another country was trying to hurt our industries, or was deliberately using economic power for political effect, as in the OPEC boycotts, then it was proper to retaliate against them. But if they didn't necessarily mean to harm anyone else, if their only motive was to build their own strength, then we had no standing to complain—or resist. Beneath these questions, of course, was the half-religious, half-legal perspective that has descended from Adam Smith. It assumes that there is one "right" and "fair" way to trade—that it's a level playing field, where we'll all practicing the same sport. At the end of World War II, Yoshida and the other men who led Japan did not ask whether the outside world "meant" to keep Japan weak. They observed that its weakness was a problem, and resolved to correct it.

¹¹· Claudia Rosset, *The Wall Street Journal* (November 6, 1991).

¹²· Sylvia Nasar, *The New York Times* (February 28, 1993).

¹³· Charles Krauthammer, *The Washington Post* (March 5, 1993).

¹⁴· David Aikman, *Pacific Rim: Area of Change, Area of Opportunity* (Boston: Little, Brown, 1986).

¹⁵· Milton and Rose Friedman, *Free to Choose: A Personal Statement* (New York: Harcourt Brace Jovanovich, 1980), p. 57; quoted in Robert Wade, *Governing the Market: Economic Theory and the Role of Government in East Asian Industrialization* (Princeton, N.J.: Princeton University Press, 1990), p. 22.

¹⁶· His full comment, with names included, was:

> Taiwan has not been an unusually low-protection country, and still less has Korea. Neither has Japan. It is amazing and even scandalous that the distinguished academic theorists of trade policy like Jagdish Bhagwati, Anne Kruger, James Riedel, and many others have not tried to reconcile these facts about East Asian trade regimes with their core prescription for sensible development policy. The reason why this neglect of what is, *prima facie,* a set of contrary cases is so serious is that trade policy is not just one policy among many. It is, according to these theories, the queen of policies. Get your trade policy right, and everything else will be much easier. [Robert Wade, Afterword, *African*

Development: Lessons from Asia (Arlington, Va.: Winrock International Institute for Agricultural Development, 1991), pp. 254–55 (proceedings of a seminar on strategies for the future of Asia, sponsored by the Africa Bureau, U.S. Agency for International Development and Winrock International, Baltimore, Md., June 5–7, 1991)]

17. John Judis wrote in 1992:

> As the British discovered in 1846, when they abolished the Corn Laws, their tariff on agricultural imports, countries alone on top of the pyramids have nothing to lose and everything to gain from free trade even if other countries do not always reciprocate. Because the industries of leading nations enjoy higher productivity, they can dominate their own markets without the need of tariffs, and by eliminating tariffs on imports of food and raw materials, they can lower their own cost of production. [John Judis, "Trade, Investment, and the Critical Election of 1992"]

18. List, *The National System,* pp. 42, 43, 94–95.
19. William Lazonick, *Business Organization and the Myth of the Market Economy* (Cambridge: Cambridge University Press, 1991), p. 2 (his emphasis).
20. Ibid., p. 5.
21. Ibid.
22. "In our own time, we have become so used to thinking of the United States as a bastion of liberalism in foreign economic policy that we forget that our traditional position was not free trade but protectionism," said Thomas McCraw of Harvard Business School. Thomas McCraw, "Mercantilism and the Market: Antecedents of American Industrial Policy," in *The Politics of Industrial Policy,* ed. Claude E. Barfield and William A. Schambra (Washington, D.C.: American Enterprise Institute for Public Policy Research, 1986), pp. 33–62.
23. Ibid.
24. Ibid., pp. 5–6.
25. Quoted in McCraw, p. 6. For instance:

> HAMILTON: "There is a degree of prejudice against bounties, from an appearance of giving away the public money without an immediate consideration, and from a supposition that they serve to enrich particular classes, at the expense of the community.
>
> "But neither of these sources will bear a serious examination. There is no purpose to which public money can be more beneficially applied, than to the acquisition of a new and useful branch of industry; no consideration more valuable, than a permanent addition to the general stock of productive labor."
> TODAY: This is essentially the argument about a deliberate industrial policy at the end of the twentieth century—whether the cost to society as a whole outweighs the benefits to specific industries.
>
> HAMILTON: "The apprehension of failing in new attempts is, perhaps, a more serious impediment. There are dispositions apt to be attracted by the mere novelty of an undertaking; but these are not always the best calculated to give it success. To this it is of importance that the confidence of cautious, sagacious capitalists, both citizens and foreigners, should be excited. And to inspire this description of persons with confidence, it is essential that they should be made

to see in any project which is new—and for that reason alone, if for no other, precarious—the prospect of such a degree of countenance and support from governments, as may be capable of overcoming the obstacles inseparable from first experiments."

TODAY: In convoluted form, this is the argument made about semiconductors and other high-tech industries. If American investors know that an industry has been "targeted" by a foreign government, they will shy away from investing in it. In principle they might be able to make CD players, semiconductor-steppers, or any other machine as well as a foreign competitor, but the sheer knowledge that their opponents will be subsidized makes them look for other, safer investments.

HAMILTON: "The superiority antecedently enjoyed by nations who have preoccupied and perfected a branch of industry, constitutes a more formidable obstacle than either of those which have been mentioned, to the introduction of the same branch into a country in which it did not before exist. To maintain, between the recent establishments of another country, a competition upon equal terms, both as to quality and price, is, in most cases, impracticable. The disparity, in the one, or in the other, or in both, must necessarily be so considerable, as to forbid a successful rivalship, without the extraordinary aid and protection of government."

TODAY: Again, in an antique and convoluted form, Hamilton was making the case that Americans and Europeans now make about the Asian automobile or electronics industries. Simple market forces, no matter how "level" the playing field, will never allow nonsubsidized companies to close the gap. [Hamilton quotations from Alexander Hamilton, "Report on Manufactures," in *Powernomics: Economics and Strategy After the Cold War*, ed. Clyde V. Prestowitz, Jr., Ronald A. Morse, and Alan Tonelson (Lanham, Md.: Madison Books for the Economic Strategy Institute, 1991), pp. 134–35]

26. "We should recall, however, that for more than a century before 1775 the American colonists had supported the elaborate system of trade regulations that governed the British empire," McCraw wrote. "Our revolution in fact was directed much less against British mercantilism than against the specific new revenue acts of the 1760s and 1770s." McCraw, p. 35.

27. This is from McCraw with citation to George B. Curtiss, *The Industrial Development of Nations and a History of the Tariff Policies of the United States, and of Great Britain, Germany, France, Russia, and Other European Countries*, Vols. 2, 3 (Binghamton, N.Y.: Curtiss, 1912).

28. Ibid.

29. "This was his best chance to reform higher education: an institution that would teach modern languages, not dead ones, offering instruction in technology, not theology. . . . From the creation of Harvard in 1636 up to the Civil War, the main role of American colleges would be to produce lawyers and preachers. For more than half a century, West Point pioneered in the modernization of American education." Geoffrey Perret, *A Country Made by War: From the Revolution to Vietnam—the Story of America's Rise to Power* (New York: Random House, 1989), p. 101.

30. Ibid., p. 97.

31. McCraw, p. 56.
32. Walter Russell Mead, "The Bush Administration and the New World Order," *World Policy Journal* (Summer 1991, p. 38).
33. His argument was this, which bears up very well with the years:

> First, the subject of economics is essentially a unique process in historical time. Nobody can hope to understand the economic phenomena of any, including the present, epoch who has not an adequate command of historical facts and an adequate amount of historical sense of what may be described as historical experience.
>
> Second, the historical report cannot be purely economic but must inevitably reflect also "institutional" facts that are not purely economic: therefore it affords the best method for understanding how economic and noneconomic facts are related to one another and how the various social sciences should be related to one another.
>
> Third, it is, I believe, the fact that most of the fundamental errors currently committed in economic analysis are due to the lack of historical experience more often than to any other shortcoming of the economist's experience. [From Joseph A. Schumpeter, *History of Economic Analysis* (New York: Oxford University Press, 1954); quoted in Lazonick, *Business Organization and the Myth of the Market Economy,* p. 115]

34. David Colander and Arjo Klamer, "The Making of an Economist," *Journal of Economic Perspectives* (Fall 1987, p. 100). A publication of the Bionomics Institute in California made a similar point in 1993: "Though economic historians often share the same floor in faculty office buildings with economic theorists, they remain a breed apart. Instead of wasting time massaging highly aggregated National Income Accounts data with impenetrable mathematical models, economic historians roll up their sleeves and dig out the hard facts of daily economic life." *Solving the Productivity Paradox: A Bionomic View* (San Rafael, Calif.: The Bionomics Institute, 1993).
35. Alice H. Amsden, *Asia's Next Giant: South Korea and Late Industrialization* (New York: Oxford University Press, 1989), p. 144.
36. What List argued, using a much more primitive version of technology, was that there was a kind of contest: some nations developed technology—and with it, they could develop more and pull ahead. It was, in a sense, like the argument a century and a half later, by the new trade theorists.
37. "The difference in the capitalistic system of the two countries will always lead to conflicts. For whatever is considered normal in Japan can be considered unfair by the United States. And it is unlikely for either side to change its business practice in the foreseeable future." Narongchai Akrasanee, in a speech delivered to the Commission on U.S.-Japan Relations in the Twenty-first Century, Washington, D.C. (July 16, 1991).
38. James Clay Moltz, "Soviet Assessments of the East Asian Economic Model," *Soviet Economy,* Vol. 7, No. 3 (1991), with cites to *Der Spiegel* (July 6, 1987). "But Abalkin's statements were largely ignored by Western capitalists, absorbed at this time with Soviet revelations regarding American capitalism. . . . Most Western observers of economic perestroika have tended to argue that the Western market economies will provide the model for Soviet reforms and represent the best chance the Soviets have for becoming economically competi-

tive. . . . [But] evidence from the world's rising economic powers—especially the East Asian NICs—suggests that the Western capitalistic model may not be the most successful in dealing with the economic challenges of the modern world."

39. "The IMF first seeks macroeconomic stability. After that, they think the market will decide," says Hiroya Tanikawa, a senior research fellow at the Ministry of International Trade and Industry's Research Institute. "From our thinking that is not enough. Some kind of industrial policy is needed to supplement." *The Wall Street Journal* (July 21, 1992).

40. This phrase is Anthony Rowley's from a column in the *Far Eastern Economic Review* (September 24, 1992).

41. According to a report in *The Los Angeles Times:*

> Japan is pressing the World Bank to shift its strategy for promoting economic development in the Third World—a move that could put Tokyo at loggerheads with the United States, bank sources say.
>
> They said the Japanese approach, which stresses a bigger role for government in the economy, is a direct challenge to the Western-oriented, market-driven strategy pursued by the bank in the late 1980s and championed by the United States. . . . They call that approach "simpleminded" and say it is based on outmoded Western concepts that fail to take into account the successful strategy that Japan and some of its Asian neighbors pursued.
>
> "Experience in Asia has shown that although development strategies require a healthy respect for market mechanisms, the role of government cannot be forgotten," Bank of Japan governor Yasushi Mieno told the annual meeting of the World Bank and International Monetary Fund in October. Japanese officials said developing countries should be encouraged to target certain industries for development and should be allowed to shelter those "infant industries" from foreign competition, until they can stand on their own. [Reuters, *The Los Angeles Times* (December 11, 1991)]

42. *The East Asian Miracle: Economic Growth and Public Policy,* A World Bank Policy Research Report (New York: Oxford University Press, for the World Bank, 1993). Sakakibara made his comments at a breakfast sponsored by the Economic Strategy Institute, in Washington, on October 1, 1993.

43. Quoted in *Japan Times Weekly* (February 15, 1992).

44. Koji Matsumoto, *The Rise of the Japanese Corporate System: The Inside View of a MITI Official,* trans. by Thomas I. Elliott (London: Kegan Paul International Ltd., 1991), p. vii.

45. Eisuke Sakakibara, *Beyond Capitalism: The Japanese Model of Market Economics,* intro. Clyde V. Prestowitz, Jr. (Washington, D.C.: University Press of America for the Economic Strategy Institute, 1993).

46. Alan Blinder, *Business Week* (October 8, 1990, p. 21). "There are capitalists, then there are Japanese."

47. That is: if you believe that market forces are rational, then you believe that the price of a company's stock reflects the company's overall strength. If the stock price goes up, then whatever is happening to the company *must* be good. If in the very act of bidding for a company, a takeover specialist raises the price per share, then the takeover bid must be beneficial, since people are willingly paying

more for the stock. Yes, there may be aftereffects—a large burden of debt, the need to lay off employees or to carve up the company. But in theory all those pluses and minuses will be reflected in the stock's price today.

48. Susan B. Hanley, "Traditional Housing and Unique Lifestyles: The Unintended Outcomes of Japan's Land Policy," in *Land Issues in Japan: A Policy Failure?*, ed. John O. Haley and Kozo Yamamura (Seattle: Society for Japanese Studies, 1992), pp. 195–99.

49. The New York prices, with Japan at 100:

> Rice, 35
> Land, 44
> Rent, 64
> Shoes, 77
> Health, 132
> Education, 133
> Gasoline, 38
> Clothes, 45–50
> Sugar, 58
> [Survey in *Japan Times* (November 11–17, 1991)]

50. Thurow, *Head to Head*, p. 130.

51. Andrew Pollack, *The New York Times* (September 12, 1993).

52. Alice H. Amsden, "The Specter of Anglo-Saxonization Is Haunting South Korea," *Korea's Political Economy: The International Perspective Series* (Honolulu: East-West Population Institute, East-West Center, December 1991), p. 25.

53. "[L]ate industrialization in Korea was retarded by a state too weak to intervene and stimulate capital expenditures. . . . [W]hen industrialization began to accelerate it did so in response to government initiatives and not to the forces of the free market. . . . [T]hese processes can be thought of as general propositions applicable to similar countries." Amsden, *Asia's Next Giant,* p. 27.

54. Masahide Shibusawa, *Pacific Asia in the 1990s* (New York and London: Routledge, 1992), p. 4.

55. Jung-en Woo, "East Asia's America Problem," *World Policy Journal* (Summer 1991, p. 466).

56. Seymour Martin Lipset, "Pacific Divide: American Exceptionalism—Japanese Uniqueness," paper presented to a conference of the Research Committee on Comparative Sociology of the I.S.A., Kurashiki, Japan (July 5, 1992); quoting *Nanakakoku Hikaku: Kokusai Leisure Chosa '89* (Tokyo: Yoka Kaihatsu Center, 1989), p. 47.

57. Jung-en Woo, "East Asia's America Problem," p. 466.

58. Quoted in John Dower, *Origins of the Modern Japanese State,* p. 48.

59. Amsden, "The Specter of Anglo-Saxonization," p. 29.

60. Michio Morishima, *Why Has Japan "Succeeded"?: Western Technology and the Japanese Ethos* (Cambridge: Cambridge University Press, 1982), p. 11.

61. *Japan Digest* (February 5, 1992).

62. In *Japan Free Press* (August 12, 1991).

63. *The Wall Street Journal*'s Jacob Schlesinger pointed out, "Mr. Maeda's remarks were a rare public declaration of what many observers suspect—that Japanese companies sometimes operate by different values." *The Asian Wall Street Journal* (July 8, 1991).

64. *The Wall Street Journal* (January 24, 1992).
65. Nick Garnett, *Financial Times* (July 29, 1987).
66. "The Uruguay Round and U.S. Economic Policy," address (June 6, 1990).
67. The full quote was: "No one worries about trade balances between California and Texas, which are both fully participating members of the dollar 'trading zone.' So why should they worry about the balance between the United States and Japan, which are too?" Editorial, *The Wall Street Journal* (May 27, 1993).
68. "Who Is Them?" *Harvard Business Review* (March–April 1991), and preceding article, "Who Is Us?" *Harvard Business Review* (January–February 1990).
69. Reich had also claimed in his article that the only Americans who would benefit if Motorola sold more phones in Japan would be the handful "who provide managerial, financial, and strategic services to Motorola's worldwide operations." This was inaccurate, the Motorola letter said. "The thousands of people in Illinois who design and build Motorola cellular telephones and systems find that conclusion pretty silly." James Caile, director of marketing, Cellular Subscriber Group, Motorola, letter to the editor, *The New Republic* (July 11, 1989).
70. This exchange was in the *Harvard Business Review* (May–June 1990).
71. In one of many passages at odds with the whole thrust of Reich's "who is us?" argument, Graham and Krugman wrote:

> In most respects Japanese firms in the United States look quite normal. For example, the widespread belief that Japanese firms keep high value-added activities or R&D at home is not borne out by the data. Japanese firms in the United States do, however, import considerably more per employee even in comparable activities than do other foreign direct investors, and much more than do domestically owned firms. Japanese firms and Japanese government officials argue that this is a transitional phenomenon reflecting the newness of their direct investment here. We hope that this turns out to be the case; otherwise a rethinking of U.S. openness to direct investment will become difficult to avoid. [Edward M. Graham and Paul R. Krugman, *Foreign Direct Investment in the United States* (Washington, D.C.: Institute for International Economics, 1991), p. 130]

Like Reich, Graham and Krugman say they are in favor of continued American openness; unlike him, they say that there is still a difference between "us" and "them" when it comes to domestic vs. foreign corporate ownership.

72.

	U.S. Affiliates of Japanese Companies	U.S. Affiliates of Foreign Companies	All U.S. Firms
Exports per worker	14.73	15.6	17.8
Imports per worker	18.47	41.2	11.3
Value added per emp	48.1	49.8	46.0
Compensat per empl	35.2	36.4	33.9
R&D per worker	3.88	2.88	3.36

Graham emphasizes that the difference in performance by Japanese firms is not because of their "newness," since many of them are takeovers of existing firms. These acquisitions have increasingly been the main means for expanding foreign direct investment. Volume of foreign direct investment in the United States, comparing acquisition of existing businesses with establishment of new businesses, is as follows (in billions of dollars):

	1982	1986	1989	1990
Acquisitions	4.8	25.6	59.7	56.8
New businesses	3.2	4.9	11.5	7.7
(New businesses as % of takeovers):	66	19	19	14

[Edward M. Graham, "Foreign Direct Investment in the United States and U.S. Interests," *Science*, Vol. 254 (December 20, 1991, pp. 1740–45)]

73. Letter to the editor, *The American Prospect* (February 6, 1991).

74. Robert B. Reich, *The Work of Nations: Preparing Ourselves for Twenty-first-Century Capitalism* (New York: Alfred A. Knopf, 1991), p. 164.

75. Memorandum to President Clinton, "High Wage Production in the United States" (March 23, 1993).

76. One of the groups offered two proposals, so there were a total of four transmissions standards for the FCC to choose among.

77. Memo (March 23, 1993).

78. Letter to Robert Reich, secretary of labor (March 4, 1993), from Jerry K. Pearlman, chairman and president, Zenith Electronics Corporation.

79. Laura D'Andrea Tyson, "They Are Not Us: Why American Ownership Still Matters," *The American Prospect* (Winter 1991, p. 47).

80. In 1987, Robert Lawrence, then of the Brookings Institution, produced a chart on intra-industry trade, showing the following rankings:

INTRA-INDUSTRY TRADE LEVELS, SELECTED COUNTRIES, 1980

Country	Intra-Industry Trade Index Number*
France	82
Belgium	79
Netherlands	78
United Kingdom	78
Canada	68
Sweden	68
Germany	66
Italy	61
Switzerland	61
United States	60
Norway	51
Finland	49
South Korea	48
Japan	25
Australia	22

*Based on 94 industries. The intra-industry trade index is scaled here to vary between zero (no intra-industry trade) and 100 (complete intra-industry trade).

[From Robert Z. Lawrence, "Imports in Japan: Closed Markets or Minds?" *Brookings Papers on Economic Activity*, Vol. 2 (1987), p. 520; cited in Edward J. Lincoln, *Japan's Unequal Trade* (Washington, D.C.: The Brookings Institution, 1990), p. 40]

81. As Edward J. Lincoln put it in *Japan's Unequal Trade* (Washington, D.C.: The Brookings Institution, 1990), p. 39, "In a variety of ways Japan's behavior in intra-industry trade is startlingly different from that of other countries."

82. Lincoln, *Japan's Unequal Trade,* pp. 43–44, 55.

83. One reason why Japanese trade has been such a problem for America, in particular, is that this pattern applies against the products the United States is best at exporting. In short: in those industries in which the United States exports successfully to Japan, Japan also exports successfully to the United States. But the reverse is not true: the industry in which Japan exports most successfully, it virtually does not import. In 1985, for instance, motor vehicles were, surprisingly enough, the leading category of U.S. exports in volume, but Japan's intra-industry index was only 3.7 percent. (Germany's was 39.9 percent—that is, despite its work ethic and its craftsmanship, it imported sizable numbers of cars.) The same was true for virtually every other category of significant U.S. exports. And the only one in which Japan imported more than it exported was aircraft (Lincoln, p. 56).

84. *The Wall Street Journal* (May 21, 1992).

85. *Nihon Keizai Shimbun* (December 11, 1991); quoted in *Japan Free Press* (December 16, 1991).

86. "In the automobile industry, the long-lived Ford investment in the United Kingdom and the General Motors investment in Germany are almost completely independent of their parents, while the Japanese 'transplants' in the United States are closely linked. Of course this may be a characteristic of Japanese investment in general, but since it is Japanese investment that has been dominant in the Pacific Basin in the 1980s the degree of economic integration generated thereby may be very significant." Lawrence B. Krause, "Can the Pacific Save the U.S.-Japan Economic Relationship?," a speech delivered to the Commission on U.S.-Japan Relations in the Twenty-first Century, Washington, D.C. (July 16, 1991).

87. *Japan Digest* (January 23, 1992).

88. Richard J. Samuels, *"Rich Nation, Strong Army": National Security and the Technological Transformation of Japan* (Ithaca, N.Y.: Cornell University Press, 1994), p. 89.

89. For example, see *Japan Digest* (July 13, 1992) about the catastrophe of the Japanese rocket plans.

90. *The Wall Street Journal* (January 23, 1992).

91. Leslie Helm, *The Los Angeles Times* (May 3, 1993).

CHAPTER 5. THE PAN-ASIAN AGE

1. This was the result of my own investigations in Manila. In 1990 Karen Emmons of the *Japan Economic Journal* quoted a teenager in Manila with the same price range. "Japan in Asia," special supplement, *Japan Economic Journal* (Winter 1990, p. 13).

2. Interview (April 14, 1993). See also Mike Millard, "The Global Game of Go," *Tokyo Business Journal* (September 1993).

3. James Sterngold reported these figures in *The New York Times* (April 13, 1993).

4. Jacob Schlesinger, *The Wall Street Journal* (March 22, 1993).

5. Karen Elliott House, *The Wall Street Journal* (August 14, 1992).

6. Ibid.

7. Among the best articles on the general Japan-in-Asia phenomenon is Andrew Tanzer's "What's Wrong with This Picture," *Forbes* (November 26, 1990, pp. 154–63).

8. After writing this paragraph, I came across a study-group report from The Pacific Institute, published in 1993 under the title "What's Wrong with Japan, Anyway?" It summarized a discussion of East Asian-Japanese relations and included this passage:

> [A]nother discussant retorted that the perceptions of Americans, especially American diplomats, about how Japanese are viewed in Asia are overblown. Their wishful thinking of hatred of the Japanese because of the atrocities in World War II is fed by those, especially Filipinos and Singaporeans, who tell the Americans what they want to hear. ["What's Wrong with Japan, Anyway?," ed. Dorothy Robins-Mowry (New York: The Pacific Institute, 1993), p. 48]

9. *Nihon Keizai Shimbun;* in *The Weekly Japan Digest* (April 27, 1992).

10. In *Japan in Asia: The Economic Impact on the Region,* ed. Nigel Holloway (Hong Kong: Review Publishing Co., 1991), p. 35.

11. *The Washington Post* (November 18, 1992).

12. Chalmers Johnson, "History Restarted."

> Much more important than the European single market or the North American free trade agreement as an influence on Japanese thinking was the Plaza Accord of 1985. . . . Although this devaluation of the dollar was expected to give North American and European firms a window of opportunity to compete with Japan, they failed to capitalize on it and the opportunity has now passed. At the same time, Japan undertook a major restructuring of its industries, including massive investments domestically and overseas. Out of this experience came Japan's proposal for a new regional order, a new and much more prosperous version of the Greater East Asia Coprosperity Sphere; and it has not been distracted from that goal by Americans' harping on the failed GATT negotiations or the Persian Gulf War. If I am right it may be that just as the people of Moscow and East Berlin now joke that socialism was the shortest route from capitalism to capitalism, the people of the Pacific will soon be saying that Asian capitalism was the shortest route from the Greater East Asia Coprosperity Sphere to the Greater East Asia Coprosperity Sphere.

13. *Bungei Shunji* (February 1992). The translated phrases are Chalmers Johnson's, in his paper "Capitalism: East Asian Style," presented to the Panglaykim Foundation, Center for Strategic and International Studies, Jakarta, Indonesia (December 15, 1992).

14. For this exact exchange level, and for much of the chronology of the Plaza meeting, I am relying on Yoichi Funabashi, *Managing the Dollar: From the Plaza to the Louvre* (Washington, D.C.: Institute for International Economics, 1988).

15. Funabashi, *Managing the Dollar,* p. 17.

16. C. Fred Bergsten and William R. Cline, *The United States-Japan Economic Problem* (Washington, D.C.: Institute for International Economics, 1985), p. 6.

17. In the United States, of course, the share of the GNP represented by manufacturing has been more or less steady since the early 1950s. During that same time, the percentage of the work force employed in manufacturing has gone down, precisely because productivity has been going up. This is the "normal"

advanced-country pattern; Japan's results are intriguing in suggesting that modern nations can take a different course.

18. Kenneth Courtis, ed., "Bi-Weekly Comment" (Tokyo: Deutsche Bank Capital Markets, Asia, September 23, 1991).

19. Paul R. Krugman, *The Age of Diminished Expectations: U.S. Economic Policy in the 1990s* (Cambridge, Mass.: MIT Press, 1990), p. 122. The average number of yen to the dollar through the 1980s was as follows:

1981	209
1982	240
1983	238
1984	225
1985	258
1986	179
1987	151
1988	127

[Fuji Bank, Tokyo, 1989]

20. *The New York Times* (December 1, 1992).

21. *The Wall Street Journal* discussed this pattern on May 21, 1993.

22. "Every part of the Washington economists' reasoning for why a stronger yen will bring Japan's trade surplus down is false," John Stern, the Tokyo representative of the American Electronics Association, said early in 1993 during another wave of *endaka*. "Japanese companies don't raise their prices in lockstep with the yen. American consumers don't buy fewer Japanese products. American companies don't lower their prices in Japan in lockstep with the dollar, and Japanese don't buy American products because they're cheaper." *The Wall Street Journal* (April 21, 1993).

23. See James Impoco, "Currency Undercurrents," *U.S. News & World Report* (May 31, 1993).

24. John Stern of AEA said that during that five-year period of *endaka*, the number of U.S. electronics firms opening new offices in Japan dropped from forty-one per year to twenty-two. *The Wall Street Journal* (April 21, 1993).

25. As Kenneth Courtis wrote 1991:

> What drove this explosion of investment was not the simple accounting identity of recycling the country's current account surplus. Japan's foreign investment was half again as large as that. More fundamentally what was at work was the strategic repositioning of corporate Japan as it raced first to relocate abroad low value-added, high labor content production, and then to widen its production and distribution base in key world markets. . . . So rapid has been the adjustment that Japanese competitors are once again back on the attack in foreign markets with new, knock-out products, but now competitive at 120Y to the dollar. These dynamics have put the trade surplus well on course to exceeding $100 billion by 1993. [Courtis, "Bi-Weekly Comment" (October 21, 1991)]

26. *Business Week* (January 28, 1991).

27. The main idea behind these gimmicks was that big industrial companies would issue bonds that were convertible into shares of the company's stock, at a fixed price. Since the stock market was in what seemed to be a permanent bull market

at the time, investors typically exercised their options to buy stock rather than demanding repayment of the principal of the bond. The result, as long as it lasted, was free money for industries.

As Robert Cutts wrote, "The Finance Ministry also responded admirably: first, it conveniently yielded to foreign pressure to lower national interest rates to the lowest in the developed world; second, it pursued deregulation and domestic stimulation in ways that flooded the national economy with extra cash." Robert L. Cutts, "Power from the Ground Up: Japan's Land Bubble," *Harvard Business Review,* Vol. 68, No. 3 (May–June, 1990), p. 167.

28. At the Royal Economic Society's meeting in April 1993, Richard Werner of Oxford published a paper ("Towards a Quantity Theorem of Disaggregated Credit and International Capital Flows with Evidence from Japan") emphasizing how odd this selective inflation was, and exploring the reasons for it. His findings were discussed in *The Economist* (June 19, 1993).

29. "The total value of land in Japan declined Y202 trillion ($1.6 trillion) in 1991, the equivalent of 44 percent of the GNP, *Nihon Keizai* reported. It said the figure was extracted from a report on the national economy prepared by the Economic Planning Agency. Japan's total assets, including stocks and land, dropped by Y219 trillion ($1.78 trillion)." *Nihon Keizai Shimbun* (December 21, 1991); in *Japan Digest* (December 28, 1992).

30. At the end of 1989, when Mitsubishi Estate bought a 51 percent share of Rockefeller Center, the real symbolism of the purchase was not American national "decline," as many suggested at the time, but the Japanese role as stuffee. When it came time to submit bids for Rockefeller Center, Mitsubishi offered $846 million. The next-highest bid was for less than half as much. In Michael Lewis, *Pacific Rift* (New York: W. W. Norton, 1992), p. 113.

31. Kenneth Courtis, "Japan in the 1990s," *Business & the Contemporary World* (Winter 1992).

32. Ibid.

33. The *Far Eastern Economic Review* puts it this way: Nearly half of all of Japan's foreign investment between 1986 and 1991 went to North America, which was about three times as much as the share invested in all of Asia. This is one of many statistics from the very valuable compendium *Japan in Asia: The Economic Impact on the Region,* ed. Nigel Holloway (Hong Kong: Review Publishing Co., 1991).

34. Courtis figures.

35. Kenneth Courtis, "Asia: Movements and Contradictions, Issues for Business," a speech delivered at the Center for Strategic and International Studies International Councillors meeting, Tokyo (October 23, 1992).

36. See Bruce Stokes, *National Journal* (June 29, 1991).

37. Ibid.

38. In 1980, $16.7 billion for the United States vs. $9.8 billion for Japan. In 1990, $32.7 billion for the United States vs. $41.5 billion for Japan. Richard P. Cronin, "Japan's Expanding Role and Influence in the Asia-Pacific Region: Implications for U.S. Interests and Policy" (Washington, D.C.: Congressional Research Service, Library of Congress, 1990), p. CRS-2.

39. Laurence Zuckerman reported on this anomaly in *The Asian Wall Street Journal Weekly* (August 9, 1993).

40. For instance, "The majority of local production of electronic parts is exported

to the U.S.," says Kazumasa Iwata of the University of Tokyo in a paper prepared for the Commission on U.S.-Japan Relations for the Twenty-first Century, Washington, D.C. (July 16–17, 1991).

41. Paul Addison, *The Rising Tide: Japan in Asia,* special supplement to *Japan Economic Journal* (Winter 1990, p. 8).

42. Ibid.

43. Kent Calder discusses this pattern in *Japan's Changing Role in Asia: Emerging Co-Prosperity?* (New York: Japan Society, 1991).

44. In interview with me, but also in Stokes, *National Journal* (June 29, 1992).

45. U.S. embassy cable, Bangkok, No. 010604/01 (February 1990).

46. Stokes, p. 1623.

47. Edward J. Lincoln, "Japan's Changing Role in Asia," a paper prepared for the David MacEachron Policy Forum, Japan Society, New York (March 15, 1991, p. 15).

48. Stokes, p. 1623.

49. *The Asian Wall Street Journal* (August 20, 1990). This is also discussed in Cronin, "Japan's Expanding Role and Influence," p. CRS-24.

50. For instance, "Anxious Japanese government officials generally deny to Americans that any such trend is emerging," Edward J. Lincoln of the Brookings Institution wrote in 1991. "But the evidence that the nation as a whole is drifting in this direction"—toward coordinated regional economic plans for Asia—"is quite clear." Edward J. Lincoln, "Japan's Ambivalent World Role: Economic and Political Dimension," a paper prepared for the Washington Strategy Seminar (March 21, 1991).

51. *China News* (Taipei, May 14, 1991, p. 9).

52. Ibid.

53. Lincoln, "Japan's Ambivalent World Role."

54. Michael W. Chinworth, "Thoughts on U.S.-Japanese Security and Economic Linkages in East Asia," MIT Japan Program report MITJSTP 88-11 (1988), p. 11.

55. Robert M. Orr, Jr., "The Rising Sum: What Makes Japan Give?," *The International Economy* (September–October 1989, p. 83).

56. Robert M. Orr, Jr., *The Emergence of Japan's Foreign Aid Power* (New York: Columbia University Press, 1990).

57. Ibid., p. 5.

58. Orr makes a valuable point in *The Emergence of Japan's Foreign Aid Power*:

> One possible explanation for this practice has been a subconscious desire to re-create the "Japan model" through development. In the Meiji period, it can be argued that foreign threats helped to stimulate Japan's economic development and as a result the private and public sectors were forced to collaborate closely. Adam Smith's clear-cut separation between government and business was never present in Japan [p. 5].

59. U.S. embassy cable, Bangkok, No. 10604 (February 1990).

60. Lincoln, "Japan's Changing Role in Asia," p. 14.

61. Ibid.

62. Statistics from background papers for "Japan's Changing Role in Asia," David MacEachron Policy Forum, Japan Society, New York (March 15, 1991).

63. U.S. embassy cable, Bangkok, No. 10604 (February 1990).

64. These comparisons are again from David MacEachron Policy Forum paper.

65. *Korea Times* (May 23, 1991).

66. Lincoln, "Japan's Changing Role in Asia."

67. Ibid.

68. Courtis, "Asia: Movements and Contradictions."

69. Last two paragraphs are from Kenneth Courtis, "Japan: The Heisei Cycle," *Japan Close-Up* (September 1992, pp. 13–18).

CHAPTER 6. GROWTH WITHOUT DEVELOPMENT

1. Some of Thailand's rare, outnumbered environmentalists had recently done an exposé on the merit-making business. Along with the birds, vendors offered turtles that could be "released" into a pond in Bangkok's Lumpini Park. Most of the turtles, unfortunately for them, were land tortoises, captured in the countryside and hauled by the basketful into the city to fulfill this role. The lucky ones were recaptured, within a few seconds of their liberation in the water, by boys who returned them to the merit baskets. The others drowned. "The turtles spend a few days in the basket, a few minutes in the water, and they finally die of exhaustion," Pisit Na Patalung of the Thailand Wildlife Fund had said in his exposé of this business. "They do not eat, they do not rest. They just go into this cycle until all of them are dead. This is making merit." "Discussion Excerpts," *Culture and Environment in Thailand: A Symposium of the Siam Society* (Bangkok: The Siam Society, 1989), p. 499.

2. Mahathir Bin Mohamad, speech at U.N. Conference on Environment and Development, Rio de Janeiro (June 13, 1992).

3. Stephen B. Schlossstein emphasized this comparison in *Asia's New Little Dragons* (Chicago: Contemporary Books, 1991).

4. Ivan Hall, "Samurai Legacies, American Illusions," *The National Interest,* No. 48 (Summer 1991), p. 24.

5. Quezon City: Ateneo de Manila University Press, 1988.

6. Early in 1992, epidemiologists estimated that half a million people, or 1 percent of the entire Thai population, were infected with the HIV virus. Infection rates were increasing much faster than in North America or even Africa. In 1991, North America and Europe had three times as many AIDS cases as all of Asia. By 2000, according to the World Health Organization, Asian countries (notably India, along with Thailand) would have two and a half times as many cases as North America and Europe. (Africa had thirteen times as many HIV infections as Asia in 1991; by 2000, Asia may have half as many cases as all of Africa.) *The Far Eastern Economic Review Special Report on AIDS* (February 13, 1992).

7. It was also the title of an illuminating foreigner-among-the-natives work published just before Thailand's economy was transformed by the Vietnam War. This is *Mai Pen Rai Means Never Mind,* by Carol Hollinger (Boston: Houghton Mifflin, 1965).

8. The view toward the "little sisters" of the region was more overtly sinister. *Ianfu,* or "comfort women," were taken by the hundreds of thousands from surrounding Asian countries to work in Japanese Army bordellos. The Japanese government's reluctance to face this issue squarely or apologize for it remained a thorn in its relations with its neighbors through the 1990s. It was only in 1993, on Kiichi

Miyazawa's final day in office as prime minister, that the Japanese government finally acknowledged that the wartime Army had actually enslaved the women and operated the brothels. Until then, the government had insisted that the "comfort women" were camp followers of the sort who turn up in every war, or at worst were coerced by private enterprises operating the brothels.

On August 4, 1993, the government's statement acknowledged that "the then-Japanese military was, directly or indirectly, involved in the establishment and management of the comfort stations and the transfer of comfort women." It added that in many cases the women "were recruited against their own will through coaxing, coercion, etc." This was reported in international papers on August 5.

9. Alec Waugh, *Bangkok: Story of a City* (Bangkok: Orientations, 1970), pp. 200–202.

10. Hollinger, *Mai Pen Rai,* p. 99.

11. Ibid.

12. Today's king was born not along the banks of the mystic Chao Phraya but alongside the Charles, in Greater Boston's Mount Auburn Hospital, while his father was a student at Harvard Medical School and had brought his young family along. At the time, the ruling king was an uncle, and the family tree was so large and tangled that Bhumibol's family was nowhere near the expected line of succession.

But the reigning king was overthrown in a military-run but placid coup in 1932. (This coup is the subject of the main Thai novel that is available in English, *Si Phaendin,* or "Four Reigns," by Kukrit Pramoj, of whom there will be more to say. English version by Tulachandra, Editions Duang Kamol, Bangkok, 1981.) The king remained as a constitutional monarch, but he grew melancholy under this arrangement, sailed on a trip to Europe in 1934, and from there in 1935 sent word that he wanted to abdicate. By that time the next person left in the line of succession was the older brother of today's Thai king—that is, the oldest son of the man who had been studying at Harvard Med. This son's name was Ananda, he was a student in Switzerland, and he was at the time ten years old.

Ananda was quickly brought back from Switzerland to serve as a boy regent in the constitutional monarchy (which has, in practice, left the military and various civilian bureaucrats mainly in control). He sat in place during the war years, and just after the war got ready for what was to be a brief trip to the United States. The trip did not take place. In circumstances that have never been explained and that are to Thai politics what the John F. Kennedy assassination is to American conspiracy theorists, he was found dead, on the eve of the trip, in his room in the Royal Palace. A single bullet had gone into his brain.

The aftermath of this event played out over the next dozen years and was the occasion for the disappearance of Pridi, the man who had organized Thai resistance during the war, from the political scene. There were three main hypotheses about how the young king could have died: accident, suicide, and assassination. The first seemed completely implausible, and the idea of the second was unacceptable to Thais in general. This left the third, murder, which required a murderer. The suspicions eventually centered on a faction surrounding Pridi, who had not gotten along with the king. Eventually three underling-type chamberlains were executed for the crime—one of them because he had chronically behaved "disrespectfully" around the king. The damning detail was that he had once crossed his legs in the king's presence, thereby committing the heinous sacrilege of pointing his foot at a king.

13. Ben Barber described this in *The King of Thailand in World Perspective* (Bangkok: Foreign Correspondents Club of Thailand, 1989), reprinting an article from the *Toledo Blade*.

14. *Asahi Shimbun* (May 15, 1993).

15. See *The New York Times* (May 20, 1992).

16. Gerald L. Curtis, "Sino-Japanese Relations Through Chinese Eyes," Institute Reports, East Asian Institute, Columbia University (June 1993, p. 6).

17. Kishore Mahbubani, "Perspectives on Political Development and the Nature of the Democratic Process: Human Rights and Freedom of the Press," a paper delivered at the Conference on Asian and American Perspectives on Capitalism and Democracy, Singapore (January 28–30, 1993).

18. Carveth Wells, *Six Years in the Malay Jungle* (Singapore and New York: Oxford University Press, 1988).

19. Cited in Sue Dorson, "The Identification of Socio-Economic Status with Ethnic Group Affiliation as an Impediment to a Homogeneous Malaysian Identity," master's thesis, Manhattanville College (April 1992).

20. Malaysia's racial situation, like that of most other countries in Southeast Asia, is complicated by the role of various indigenous groups. In Borneo these are forest-dwellers such as the Penan, whose society is threatened by large-scale logging operations. On the Malay Peninsula itself the aborigines consist of a tribe of some forty thousand small, dark-skinned people who live in the jungle and are known as *orang asli,* or "original people." The condition of the *orang asli* is roughly comparable to that of Australia's aborigines or Native American tribes in the United States. Some *orang asli* have become city-dwellers or live in government-sponsored camps. Those who live in the forest are often hired by logging companies; because the *orang asli* know the hills and trees so well, they are expert at felling trees in the jungle, and they can earn a few dollars a week cutting down their homes. In the Malaysian states of Sabah and Sarawak, in the northern and northwestern parts of the island of Borneo, the Penan and other groups have more of their original societies intact, but they are more immediately threatened by the lumber companies.

21. "Hunger and starvation, a common feature in countries like China, were unknown in Malaya. Under these conditions everyone survived. Even the weakest and the least diligent were able to live in comparative comfort, to marry and procreate. . . . Whatever the Malays could do, the Chinese could do better and more cheaply. . . . Removal of all protection would subject the Malays to the primitive laws that enable only the fittest to survive. If this is done it would perhaps be possible to breed a hardy and resourceful race capable of competing against all comers. Unfortunately, we do not have four thousand years to play with." Mahathir bin Mohamad, *The Malay Dilemma* (Kuala Lumpur: Federal Publishers, 1970), pp. 25, 31.

22. Figures in this section are from Dorson, "The Identification of Socio-Economic Status," pp. 59–60, quoting Malaysian government figures.

23. Mohamad, *The Malay Dilemma,* p. 31.

24. Schlossstein, *Asia's New Little Dragons,* p. 269.

25. Michael Vatikiotis, "Bending the Rules," *Far Eastern Economic Review* (De-

cember 24–31, 1992, p. 16). Also, "Malaysia's Scandalous Sultans," *The Washington Post* (December 29, 1992).

26. James Impoco, "Malaysia: Asia's New Heavyweight," *U.S. News & World Report* (December 21, 1992, p. 71).

27. The men were held and eventually hanged in Pudu Prison, a fortress in the middle of Kuala Lumpur's commercial zone. Although outsiders could not see in, its downtown location gave all executions there a hint of the eighteenth-century public hanging. The prison was surrounded by high stucco walls, on which convicts had been encouraged to exercise their talents in a constructive way. The result was a gigantic city mural designed to remind average citizens of what they might lose if they turned to a life of crime. "*Dadah* made my life a hell!" a typical inscription said, *dadah* being the Malay term for narcotics. The accompanying picture showed an idyllic Malaysian beach scene, with a happy family resting beneath the palm trees—and next to it a gallows, the logical terminus of the *dadah* road.

28. A year or two later, Americans were beginning to occupy mental space in Malaysia, because the U.S. government had criticized Mahathir's government for imprisoning its political foes. Over the next few months the *New Straits Times,* the daily paper that is owned by the ruling party, had a charming series of editorials. How fat Americans are; how disgusting their food is; how hypocritical they are to complain about other countries, and so on.

29. Doug Tsuruoka of the *Far Eastern Economic Review* obtained the letter's full text, which was quoted in *Far Eastern Economic Review* (August 27, 1992, pp. 8–9):

> 3rd March, 1992
> Herr Manser,
>
> If any Penan or policeman gets killed or wounded in the course of restoring law and order in Sarawak, you will have to take the blame. It is you and your kind who instigated the Penan to take the law into their own hands and to use poison darts, bows, and arrows, and parangs to fight against the Government.
>
> As a Swiss living in the laps of luxury with the world's highest standard of living, it is the height of arrogance for you to advocate that Penans live on maggots and monkeys in their miserable huts, subjected to all kinds of diseases. It is fine for you to spend a short holiday tasting the Penan way of life and then returning to the heated comfort of your Swiss chalet. But do you really expect the Penans to subsist on monkeys until the year 2500 or 3000 or forever? Have they no right to a better way of life? What right have you to condemn them to a primitive life forever?
>
> Your Swiss ancestors were hunters also. But you are now one of the most "advanced" people living in beautiful Alpine villages, with plenty of leisure and very high income. But you want to deny even a slight rise in the standard of living for the Penans and other Malaysians.
>
> The Penans may tell you that their primitive life is what they like. That is because they are not given a chance to live a better life like the other tribes in Sarawak. Those of the Penans who have left the jungle are educated and are earning a better living [and] have no wish to return to their primitive ways. You are trying to deny them their chance for a better life so that you can enjoy

studying primitive peoples the way you study animals. Penans are people and they should be respected as people. If you had a chance to be educated and live a better life, they too deserve that chance.

Stop being arrogant and thinking that it is the white man's burden to decide the fate of the peoples in this world. Malaysians, the Penans included, are an independent people and are quite capable of looking after themselves. Swiss imperialism is as disgusting as other European imperialism. It is about time that you stop your arrogance and your intolerable European superiority. You are no better than the Penans. If you have a right to decide for yourself, why can't you leave the Penans to decide for themselves after they have been given a chance to improve their living standards?

30. In the *New Straits Times* (July 28, 1989) he also said, "In Islam, the interrelationship of human beings and the community is the bedrock of the principle of human rights. The status of a human being as a trustee of God casts an entirely different perspective on community relationship. It contrasts with the so-called inalienable individual rights superior to the rights of the community."

31. Zulkafly Baharuddin, column, *Utusan Malaysia* (March 2, 1991).

32. Kunio Yoshihara, *The Rise of Ersatz Capitalism in South-East Asia* (Manila: Ateneo de Manila Press, 1988), pp. 111–12.

33. Ibid.

34. A history of the languages of this region is in Asmah Haji Omar, *Language and Society in Malaysia* (Kuala Lumpur: Dewan Bahasa dan Pustaka, 1982).

35. "The premier status of Bahasa Malaysia is unquestionable," the government-mouthpiece newspaper announced in an editorial in 1990. "There is now no need to feel insecure about any possible threat to it. . . . As Prime Minister Datuk Seri [roughly, "His Highness"] Dr. Mahathir Mohamad put it, 'Some of us must shed our fanatical attitude toward Bahasa Malaysia.' " *New Straits Times* (June 29, 1990).

36. Malaysia has manufactured a myth of an independence fight, but it received its independence from Britain in a gentlemanly process that culminated in 1957. There had been a bloody guerrilla war before independence, but it pitted the British and Malayan forces, on one side, against the mainly Chinese "Communist terrorists," or CTs, on the other.

37. *The East Asian Miracle: Economic Growth and Public Policy* (New York: Oxford University Press, for the World Bank, Washington, D.C., 1993), p. 139.

38. Anonymous letter, *Far Eastern Economic Review* (February 14, 1991).

39. Schlossstein, *Asia's New Little Dragons*, p. 373.

40. Presentation at conference on "Asian and American Perspectives on Capitalism and Democracy," sponsored by the Asia Society (United States), the Institute of Policy Studies (Singapore), the Institute of Southeast Asian Studies (Singapore), and the Singapore International Foundation (January 30, 1993), Singapore.

41. "Although the Singaporean state has played an equally strong [to Taiwan] role in developing the city-state's economic development strategies, the strong character of the state frequently has been ignored. [This difference] . . . stems primarily from the fact that the Singaporean government has allowed a greater degree of international involvement in the country and relied more on free-market mechanisms. . . . The importance of international actors in Singapore's

economy is, however, second to the power of the state. The People's Action Party maintains primary control over economic policy-making." Kelly S. Nelson, *The Asian Wall Street Journal Weekly* (July 20, 1992).

[42.] The Harvard economist was Robert J. Barro, writing in *The Wall Street Journal* (April 1, 1992).

CHAPTER 7. ON THE SIDELINES

[1.] Marvin C. Ott, "Troubled Burma Casts Its Lot with China," *The Asian Wall Street Journal* (April 27, 1992).

[2.] Pico Iyer, *Video Night in Kathmandu, and Other Reports from the Not-So-Far East* (New York: Vintage Books, 1989).

[3.] His books include *Outrage: Burma's Struggle for Democracy* (London: White Lotus Press, 1990) and *Land of Jade: A Journey Through Insurgent Burma* (Edinburgh: Kiscadale Publishers, 1990).

[4.] Stan Sesser, *The Lands of Charm and Cruelty* (New York: Alfred A. Knopf, 1993), p. 201.

[5.] Report from *Nihon Keizai Shimbun,* in *Japan Digest* (May 13, 1992).

[6.] Early in 1993 the Vietnamese government announced that had dissolved twenty-five hundred to three thousand state-owned enterprises as part of its general commitment to a market economy. Of course, nine thousand to ninety-five hundred of them remained. See *Far Eastern Economic Review* (March 25, 1993).

[7.] To summarize, through the 1980s the principal American indictments against Vietnam were: its occupation of Cambodia, its maintenance of an unusually brutal regime at home, and its general lack of cooperation on refugee issues. By the end of the 1980s most of these issues had been resolved, in the view of most other Western nations. The point was not that Vietnam had attained a perfect record on all these points, but that its record was not obviously worse than China's or that of many other countries.

[8.] This is so even though the Vietnamese government, following the examples set in China and the old Soviet Union, has tried to shake down foreign travelers and investors with sky-high fees for rent, office assistants, legal fees, and so on.

[9.] The Philippine government's official count of Filipinos employed overseas was 686,461 in 1992. Most other estimates of the total are much higher.

[10.] F. Sionil José, letter to the editor, *The New York Review of Books* (September 24, 1992).

[11.] The Philippine reaction was cool, but Lee was not deterred. Back at home the government of Singapore was at the same time expressing alarm that 30 percent of the country's families were speaking English at home, rather than Mandarin or a dialect of Chinese. This complaint reflected "genuine dismay at the violence and social disorder it sees in the West," according to one Western account. "If that is where Western values lead, it argues, why should Singapore follow?" *The Economist* (November 28, 1992).

[12.] *The East Asian Miracle,* p. 167.

[13.] Ibid., p. 169.

[14.] Most of the territorial expanse of Clark, 58,625 hectares of the 64,025-hectare total, was officially returned to Philippine control in 1979. De facto both Clark and Subic operated as American bases until 1992, when the United States officially withdrew.

CHAPTER 8. CONTENDERS

[1] Kim Kyong-Dong, "Koreans: Who Are They? A Comparative Approach" (Seoul: Korean-American Business Institute, 1986).

[2] Bruce Cumings, "The Legacy of Japanese Colonialism in Korea," in *The Japanese Colonial Empire, 1895–1945,* ed. Ramon H. Myers and Mark R. Peattie (Princeton, N.J.: Princeton University Press, 1984), p. 482.

[3] Alice H. Amsden, "Diffusion of Development: The Late-Industrializing Model and Greater East Asia," *Papers and Proceedings of the American Economic Association* (May 1991, p. 285).

[4] Ibid., p. 284.

[5] In 1990 they each exported 32 to 34 percent of their exports to the U.S. market. See *Far Eastern Economic Review* (September 10, 1992, p. 74).

[6] Alice H. Amsden, "The South Korean Economy: The Mid-Tech, Middle-Country Complex," in *Korea's New Challenges and Kim Young Sam,* ed. Christopher J. Sigur (New York: Carnegie Council on Ethics and International Affairs, 1993), p. 75.

[7] *Japan in Asia: The Economic Impact on the Region,* ed. Nigel Holloway (Hong Kong: Review Publishing Co., 1991).

[8] Ibid.

[9] *Newsreview* (July 14, 1990, p. 12).

[10] Amsden, "The South Korean Economy," p. 77; quoting Bank of Korea annual statistics for 1990.

[11] *The New York Times* (April 13, 1993). The story also said, "Japanese officials 'have this model in which Japan controls everything, and they are just applying that model to a new area, Asia,' said Chuh Young Souk, vice chairman of the Korea-Japan Economic Association, an industry body."

[12] See further discussion by Damon Darlin, *The Wall Street Journal* (July 29, 1991). The dilemma is that U.S. companies have the lead in microprocessors, and Japanese companies have the money for the next generation of memory chips, and it is hard for Korea to move forward.

[13] Urban Lehner, *The Wall Street Journal* (July 8, 1991).

[14] Lho Joo-Hyoung, "Imports Spark Controversy," *Korea Business World* (November 1989, p. 33).

[15] John Maggs, *The Journal of Commerce* (November 20, 1990).

[16] Described by Mark Clifford in *Far Eastern Economic Review* (May 17, 1990).

[17] Ibid.

[18] Quotes from *The Journal of Commerce* (November 20, 1990).

[19] In the early 1990s they were in third place, behind students from China (No. 1) and Japan (No. 2).

[20] Robert Wade, *Governing the Market: Economic Theory and the Role of Government in East Asian Industrialization* (Princeton, N.J.: Princeton University Press, 1990), p. 61.

[21] *The Asian Wall Street Journal Weekly* (July 8, 1991).

22. Michael Stroud of *Investor's Business Daily* highlighted the chip/crude oil comparison in *The New York Times* (October 25, 1992).

23. Ibid.

24. *Free China Journal* (November 17, 1992).

25. Kyodo News Service (May 15, 1993).

26. *The Asian Wall Street Journal Weekly* (May 25, 1993). The next three are Taiwan, the United States, and Japan; Singapore is fifth.

27. Paul M. F. Cheng, "Here Comes Greater China," *International Herald Tribune* (May 27, 1993).

CHAPTER 9. THE IMPACT OF THE ASIAN SYSTEM

1. William Manchester, *Goodbye, Darkness: A Memoir of the Pacific War* (Boston: Little, Brown, 1980), p. 63.

2. Richard Wright, *The Color Curtain: A Report on the Bandung Conference* (Cleveland: World Pub., 1956).

3. Two states on the northern and northwestern coasts of Borneo, Sabah and Sarawak, are part of Malaysia. The tiny principality of Brunei lies between them. The rest of the island belongs to Indonesia and is known as Kalimantan. The western half of New Guinea is Indonesian and is called Irian Jaya; the eastern half is the country of Papua New Guinea.

4. This estimate is from the Japan Tropical Forest Action Network, an environmental-action group, but it is in line with other estimates in Malaysia.

In 1991 a report commissioned by the government of Papua New Guinea concluded that Japan's foreign-aid agency, the Japan International Cooperation Agency (JICA), was accelerating the deforestation. JICA loans were in theory going to the Papua New Guinea government for reforestation and similar projects. But according to the report, the loans were in reality going straight to Japanese trading houses such as Nissho Iwai and Japanese lumber firms. The firms, in turn, used the money to build logging roads into the jungle, ports at river mouths, and other ingredients of an "infrastructure" to send the logs on to Japan. *Japan Times Weekly International Edition* (October 7–13, 1991). The report was conducted by Australian judge Thomas Barnett at the request of the Papua New Guinea government. In Sarawak as well, JICA has put up the money for logging roads.

5. *Japan Times Weekly International Edition* (July 13–19, 1992).

6. *The Weekly Japan Digest* (April 17, 1992).

7. *Time* (November 6, 1989). Ishihara presumably used the word *minzoku* when making this comment in Japanese. This could be put into English in the milder form of "people" or "folk"—or more or less directly into German as *Volk*. The comparison with *Volk* only underscores the problem.

8. *Japan Digest* (July 12, 1992).

9. *Japan Digest* (October 6, 1992).

10. This is one of two central problems in American politics, the other being the aftereffects of slavery. The classic discussion of the subject is William James's essay "The Moral Equivalent of War." James observed that the American Civil War, which killed more Americans than all other wars combined, brought out

some of humanity's noblest as well as its darkest traits. People shared, persevered, dared, and loved—all while trying to pulverize the other side. The challenge of politics, he concluded, was to find less destructive ways to evoke the same collective effort.

11. *Newsweek* (August 3, 1992).
12. *The Washington Post* (September 6, 1992).
13. Hitachi internal memo. Emphasis in original.
14. "Technology Transfer: SEMICON Japan 1990 Trip Report," Austin, Tex. (January 29, 1991); quoted in *U.S. Business Access to Certain Foreign State-of-the-Art Technology,* U.S. General Accounting Office, GAO/NSIA-91-278 (September 1991), p. 21.
15. *U.S. Business Access to Certain Foreign State-of-the-Art Technology.*
16. Ibid., p. 24.
17. Ibid., pp. 20–21.
18. Hearings, Senate Armed Services Committee (November 29, 1989).
19. "Foreign Ownership and Control of U.S. Industry," Defense Science Board Report on Defense Semiconductor Dependency (Washington, D.C.: Defense Science Board, 1987).
20. *Business Week* (February 20, 1989). According to a Pentagon report released in 1991, something similar already occurred in the United States. Without giving details, the report said, "A Japanese firm is known to have withheld the sale of an advanced microelectronics package for supercomputers to a U.S. firm, because the sale would have stripped another Japanese producer of its competitive advantage." From "Foreign Ownership and Control of U.S. Industry," Defense Science Board Report.
21. *Sekai* (January 1988, p. 82). Discussed in a working paper by Steven K. Vogel, "Japanese High Technology: Politics and Power," BRIE Research Paper No. 2, Berkeley Roundtable on the International Economy (March 1989).
22. MIT Commission on Industrial Productivity, Working Papers, Vol. 2.
23. *The Wall Street Journal* (January 21, 1992).
24. Michael S. Flynn, Sean P. McLainden, Godfrey Cadogan, and Brett C. Smith, "The U.S.-Japan Bilateral Automotive Trade Deficit," University of Michigan Transportation Research Institute, TRI Study 93-30 (July 1993).
25. *The New York Times* (July 21, 1993).
26. Martin Tolchin, *The New York Times* (November 3, 1993).
27. Thurow, *Head to Head,* p. 201.
28. Leon Hollerman, *Japan, Disincorporated: The Economic Liberalization Process* (Palo Alto, Calif.: Hoover Institution, 1988), p. xvii.
29. Transcription #JPRS-JST-91-035-L, Foreign Broadcast Information Service, Washington, D.C. (1991).
30. *Yomiuri Shimbun* (March 13, 1993).
31. *The New York Times* (March 2, 1993).
32. Richard Samuels, *"Rich Nation, Strong Army": National Security and the Technological Transformation of Japan* (Ithaca, N.Y.: Cornell University Press, 1994), p. 89.
33. Prepared for the undersecretary of defense for acquisition, Department of Defense, and dated June 1990. Made public by Representative Mel Levine at a press conference (May 13, 1991).

34. *Foreign Ownership and Control of U.S. Industry,* Defense Science Board Report.
35. See *Japan Digest* (June 15, 1992). Also, *Japan Times Weekly International Edition* (June 29–July 5, 1992).
36. See, for example, Jacob Schlesinger's report in *The Wall Street Journal* (September 24, 1990).
37. See *The Wall Street Journal* (August 25, 1991).
38. Jacob Schlesinger and Eduardo Lachica discussed this in *The Wall Street Journal* (September 16 and October 28, 1991).
39. Ronald Dore, "An Outsider's View" in *Japan's Economic Structure: Should It Change?,* ed. Kozo Yamamura (Seattle: Society for Japanese Studies, 1990), p. 361.
40. Quoted in *The Los Angeles Times* (May 7, 1989).
41. All quotes from Cole are from "Between a Rock and a Hard Place: Japan Scholars in an Era of Rising U.S./Japan Trade Friction," an address prepared for the Association of Japanese Business Studies' sixth annual meeting, New York (January 8–10, 1992).
42. David E. Apter and Nagayo Sawa, *Against the State: Politics and Social Protest in Japan* (Cambridge, Mass.: Harvard University Press, 1984), pp. 226–27.
43. Robert S. Elegant, *Pacific Destiny: Inside Asia Today* (New York: Crown, 1990), p. 502.
44. *Nikkei Weekly* (September 13, 1993).
45. John Judis, *Columbia Journalism Review* (November–December 1992).
46. Robert C. Angel, *Explaining Economic Policy Failure: Japan in the 1969–1971 International Monetary Crisis* (New York: Columbia University Press, 1991).
47. Michael W. Chinworth, "Thoughts on U.S.-Japan Security and Economic Linkages in East Asia," MIT Japan Program, MITJSTP 88-11 (1988).
48. Kurt Singer, *Mirror, Sword, and Jewel: The Geometry of Japanese Life* (Tokyo: Kodansha International, 1973), pp. 39–40.

CHAPTER 10. LOOKING AT THE SUN

1. Robert Wade described this prevailing view in a paper published in 1993:

   The neoclassical mainstream believes that most such interventions are a mistake—not just one mistake among many but a mistake so big as to constitute the main reason for the slow progress of most developing countries. . . . Real world markets, in this view, may well be imperfect, but real world governments are even more imperfect.

   Wade went on to demonstrate in this paper that the axiomatic "intervention will fail!" view was not borne out in the examples he studied most closely, those of Korea and Taiwan. There "the government has managed trade in such a way as (probably) to help more than hinder the economy's growth and transformation. . . . These propositions pose a challenge to the theories and beliefs in the very heartland of mainstream economics." Robert Wade, "Managing Trade: Taiwan and South Korea as Challenges to Economic and Political Science," *Comparative Politics,* Vol. 25, No. 2 (January 1993), pp. 147–67.
2. "Late industrialization everywhere has involved a high degree of discipline of labor," Amsden concluded. "What distinguishes East Asia is not just its disci-

pline of labor but also its *discipline of capital*." Alice H. Amsden, "Diffusion of Development: The Late-Industrializing Model and Greater East Asia," *Papers and Proceedings of the American Economic Association* (May 1991, p. 284).

This "discipline of capital" prevails throughout the successful illustrations of East Asian growth. The World Bank's study *The East Asian Miracle* emphasized how carefully the Korean government monitored businesses for compliance with its guidelines—and how strictly it has punished corporations that fail to meet its goals. Industries in Thailand and Malaysia have enjoyed government benefits only so long as they have met guidelines for increasing exports and raising the proportion of high-tech components they acquire from local industries. This "discipline of capital" is the essential difference between "industrial policy" and "pork-barrel subsidies." Protection given without conditions becomes a giveaway. Protection with conditions has been used successfully in Japan, Korea, Taiwan, Singapore, and other nations of the region.

3. Robert Cohen discusses this story in "Picking Winners: The Historical Record," in *Powernomics: Economics and Strategy After the Cold War*, ed. Clyde V. Prestowitz, Jr., Ronald A. Morse, and Alan Tonelson (Lanham, Md.: Madison Books for the Economic Strategy Institute, 1991), pp. 138–46.

4. The semiconductor arrangement "is one of the worst agreements Japan has ever made and most of us are determined not to repeat this mistake," Hiroshi Hirabayashi of the Japanese embassy in Washington told Peter Behr of *The Washington Post* when foreign chips hit the 20 percent threshhold. *The Washington Post* (March 13, 1993). "We have learned a lesson—that if we set numerical targets, the U.S. side will act as if the number is a commitment, or guarantee," Tetsuya Terazawa, an official in the Americas division of MITI, told Behr and Paul Blustein. *The Washington Post* (March 23, 1993).

From exactly the same evidence—that a "target" turns into a "commitment, or guarantee"—foreign negotiators should draw exactly the opposite conclusion. "The fact that Japan is so outspoken in its unwillingness to go along demonstrates that Japan views [the chip accord] as a success for the United States and costly to them," Laura Tyson, chair of the Council of Economic Advisors, said in June 1993. "That's a pretty strong argument in its favor." Quoted in *The Wall Street Journal* (June 8, 1993).

5. Targets have the goods and the bads of the American system of "affirmative action" hiring. Indeed, the scholar T. J. Pempel has proposed that Americans think of the Japanese trade problem as comparable to the aftereffects of slavery in the United States. In each case, he said, people are still benefiting in the 1990s from discrimination practiced by their parents and grandparents. Japanese firms benefit from a legacy of closedness; white Americans get a leg up from decades of segregation and unequal opportunities for blacks. "Saying that the Japanese market [now] is more open than that of most other major industrialized economies ignores the fact that from the 1950s well into the early 1970s the Japanese market was hardly more open than Albania's," Pempel wrote late in 1991.

As a result, Japanese firms were provided with the capacity to thrive and develop market niches, distribution networks, and customer loyalties that today offer them unprecedented advantages over foreign competitors, even those who choose to enter Japan's now opened markets. . . . It is absurd for advocates of "the market," whether Japanese or American, to be so blind to the importance of past advantages that they presume that if conditions are relatively open, fair, and free, then past advantages do not play a major part. . . . [This is like] considering it a fair race if, after running twenty miles in a marathon, a runner is forced to race against another who now starts "even" with him after ridden the first twenty miles in a BMW. [*The Washington Post* (December 29, 1991)]

The strongest argument for each approach is that it can do things mere "openness" will never accomplish: give African-Americans a chance in professional schools and corporations; give U.S. semiconductor makers a chance to sell to Toyota and Nissan. The argument against each approach is that it is cumbersome and anticompetitive. But targeted trade has one big advantage over affirmative action. White American society resents the idea of numerical quotas and puts up with them mainly because they're sold as a "temporary" solution to a problem with centuries-deep historic roots. Japanese business culture, by contrast, is made for the targeted-trade approach. The idea of setting targets and meeting them is ingrained into every part of the business-governmental system. It is how business is done. MITI works with the industries to set overall targets. The banks work with the big companies to allocate capital year by year. The big companies work with the little companies to plan production. Everyone is more comfortable with the certainty of a target than with the vagueness of unbounded possibilities. When the U.S. government imposes affirmative-action targets on college and industries, it is going against the grain. When foreign negotiators set sales targets for Japan, and when Japanese ministries apply them, they are working with the grain; they are water flowing downhill.

6. *The Wall Street Journal* (December 26, 1991).

Index

Abalkin, Leonid, 205
ABCD line, 108
Abegg, Lily, 74–75, 85
Acer company, 399
Adams, Will, 80, 84
Advanced Micro Devices, 23, 24, 28, 265
adversarial trade, 54–55
Affirmation of the Great East Asia War (Hayashi), 115
Aguinaldo, Emilio, 364, 373
AIDS, 287, 487*n*6
Aikman, David, 193
aircraft industry, 237–38, 397, 424, 426
Aizawa, Seishisai, 97
Akihito, Emperor, 118*n,* 158
Akrasanee, Narongchai, 204–5, 477*n*37
Amsden, Alice H., 203–4, 213–14, 220–21, 381, 383–84, 394, 445, 496*n*2
Angel, Robert C., 434–35
Angell, Norman, 48
Anglo-American economic system, 18
  Anglo-American belief in system's triumph, 192–94
  "Anglo-American" designation, 181*n*
  and Asian economic system:
    comparison with, 207–40
    inevitable conflict with, 204–5, 477*n*37
  competition, faith in, 67
  consumption vs. production, 183–85, 208, 209–10, 214
  current experience, inconsistency with, 204–7, 214, 269
  government intervention, 182–83, 191
  historical developments, failure to explain, 194–200
  individual vs. group concerns, 187–88, 218–20
  Japan's rejection of, 205–7, 478*n*41
  Korea, influence in, 393–95
  List's criticism of, 183
  market unpredictability, 208–9, 217–23
  morality vs. power, 190, 474*n*10
  national economic interests and, 223–31
  political and economic power, interaction of, 208, 214–17
  positive sum vs. zero sum issue, 188–90
  process vs. result, 185–86
  self-selectivity of, 179–81
  semiconductor industry and, 67–69
  theoretical shortcomings, 200–204
Anglo-American worldview, 180
Anwar Ibrahim, 313
Apple Computer, 22, 23, 27, 33, 40, 427
Applied Materials, 33
Apter, David, 432

Aquino, Corazon, 4, 121, 292, 355
  results of presidency, 356, 362–63
Arase, David, 270
arms industry, 199
Asian Development Bank, 356
Asian economic system, 18–19
  and Anglo-American economic
      system:
    comparison with, 207–40
    inevitable conflict with, 204–5,
        477n37
  Asian attitudes toward U.S. and,
      245, 249, 252–55
  beginning of Asian economic era,
      255–56, 483n12
  branch-plant syndrome, 420–23
  classification of countries within,
      283–85
  collective dynamism, 281–82
  consumption vs. production, 208,
      209–14
  developmentalism and, 216–17
  environmental issues, 409–10, 494n4
  "excessive" competition concept,
      220
  full employment, 212
  gendered division of labor, 414
  German system's influence on, 191
  governmental bureaucracies and, 216
  government-developed economic
      goals, 220–21
  growth in 1980s and 1990s, 14
  historical-intellectual bonds, 282–83
  individual rights, 218–20, 367–68,
      412–14
  industrial dependence and, 416–24
  intellectual/political dependence
      and, 428–35
  intra-industry trade, 274–76
  Japanese investment in Asia, 263–65
    "colonial" relationship resulting
        from, 273–77
    coordinated approach, 269–73,
        486n50
    foreign aid programs, 271–73,
        486n58
    producer-minded strategy, 266–69
  Japan's central role, 10, 14–15, 18,
      243–47, 282

Japan's economic power, respect for,
    250–52
Japan's image within Asian nations,
    248–50, 483n8
Japan's promotion of, 205–7
market unpredictability issue, 208–
    9, 217–23
"messy" transition to industrialism,
    280–81
migration of labor, 410–11
military dependence and, 424–28
national economic interests and,
    223, 231–40, 367–68
Pan-Asian view, 411–12
peaceful relations and, 415
political and economic power, inter-
    action of, 208, 214–17, 298–
    99
prewar "co-prosperity sphere,"
    comparison with, 408
regional planning, 271
Russian interest in, 205, 477n38
semiconductor industry and, 62–63
trade between Japan and rest of
    Asia, evolution of, 274–76
U.S. export market and, 247–48
West's failure to recognize Asian
    achievements, 13–15, 451–53
worldwide impact, 414–35
yen-dollar exchange rate and, 13–
    14, 255–60, 262, 483n12
Asia's New Giant (Rosovsky), 149
Asia's Next Giant (Amsden), 203–4,
    383–84
Association of Southeast Asian Na-
    tions (ASEAN), 270–71
AT&T, 30, 67–68, 212, 229, 464n70
atomic bombings, 163–65
Aung Gyi, 332
Aung San, 329
Aung San Suu Kyi, 336
Australia, 232, 339, 346
automatic correction concept, 36
automobile industry, 51, 53
  branch-plant syndrome, 421
  decline in U.S., 25–26
  domestic-content standards, 430
  East Asian auto market, 246
  Japan's *shaken* policy, 212–13

management nationality issue, 234, 482*n*86

semiconductor industry, comparison with, 23–24

U.S. penetration of Japanese market, 259–60

"wrong side" problem of exports to Japan, 51, 461*n*41

Awaya, Kentaro, 159

Baker, James, 255, 310
Ball, George, 122–23
ball bearings, 425–26
Bangkok, Thailand, 278–80
Bangladesh, 327, 328
Bank of Japan, 206–7, 263
Bardeen, John, 23
baseball, 7, 433–34
Beasley, W. G., 106
beef quotas, 217, 222
beggars, 279–80
Bell Labs, 30, 67–68, 464*n*70
Beltran, Benigno, 358–59, 360
Benedict, Ruth, 123
Bergamini, David, 153
Beyond Capitalism (Sakakibara), 207
Bhumibol Adulyadej, King, 293–96
Bingham, Jeff, 42, 418
Bix, Herbert, 156, 157, 158
black ships (*kurofune*), 87, 88
Blinder, Alan, 6, 207
Borrus, Michael, 60, 61
Boskin, Michael, 50
Brady, Nicolas, 429
branch-plant syndrome, 420–23
Brattain, Walter, 23
Brunei, 270
Buddhism, 77, 80, 334–35
Bundy, McGeorge, 140
burakumin minority group, 103
Burgess, John, 417
Burma, 281, 284, 326, 374
    anti-Westernism in, 328–29
    black-market activities, 331, 332–33
    Buddhism in, 334–35
    charming side of, 333–35
    Chinese minority, 292
    colonial period, 329
    demonetization program, 330–32

drug trade, 328
economic situation, 330–33, 337
foreign travelers, restrictions on, 330, 331
Japan's relations with, 329
Malaysia, comparison with, 328
"Myanmar" name, 327*n*, 336
natural resources, 327, 337
potential for success, 327–28
supernatural influences in official life, 330
suppression of dissent, 333, 335–37
totalitarian governments, 328–33
in World War II, 329
Bush, George, 12, 153, 166, 204, 310, 346, 427
Business Organization and the Myth of the Market Economy (Lazonick), 194
Bussey, John, 164

Caile, James, 226
Cambodia, 283, 284, 338, 350, 409
Canada, 63, 339, 421–22, 434
capitalism:
    ersatz capitalism, 284
    money's central role, 66–67, 203–4
    see also Anglo-American economic system
Cates, Phoebe, 249
cellular phones controversy, 226–28, 480*n*69
censorship:
    press censorship, 296, 299, 312
    U.S. self-censorship regarding things Japanese, 430–32
Challenger explosion, 238
Chamlong Srimuang, 293–94
Chapman, William, 13, 115, 127
Chatichai Choonhavan, 290, 295
Cheng, Paul M. F., 403
China, 4, 18–19, 142, 261, 281–82, 284
    Communist government, 131, 283
    Confucianism and, 283
    democracy protests of 1989, 437
    economic reform, 341
    economic size and wealth, 403
    environmental issues, 409
    European colonialism, 86–87, 438–39

China (*cont.*)
  future economic prospects, 401–2
  "greater China" economic sphere, 402–4
  historical development, 73–74
  Hong Kong, takeover of, 404–6
  Japan, economic relations with, 247, 298
  Japan's domination of, 106, 165–66
  Japan's history, role in, 77
  Korea, relations with, 376
  military threat to East Asia, 350–52
  missionaries in, 81
  pan-Asianism and, 113
  regional tensions within, 401–2
  semiconductor industry, 251–52
China, Republic of: *see* Taiwan
China Steel, 193
Chinese minorities in Southeast Asia, 291–93, 301–5, 320
Chinworth, Michael, 272, 435
Christianity, 79–81, 84, 308, 354, 392
Chrysanthemum and the Bat, The (Whiting), 7
Chrysanthemum and the Sword, The (Benedict), 123
Chrysler Corporation, 259, 421, 447
Chun Doo Hwan, 62
Churchill, Winston, 187
Citibank, 348
Cities and the Wealth of Nations (Jacobs), 400
Clark Air Force Base, 365, 370–74
Clifford, Mark, 251
Clinton administration, 345–46
Cold War, 131
  containment policy, 131, 132, 135
  Japan-U.S. relationship and, 134–43, 175
  legacy of U.S. policy, 135–36
  pol-mil mindset of U.S. policy, 136–38
Cole, Robert E., 431
colonialism, 74, 75, 86–87, 109–10, 329, 380, 381, 438–39
Color Curtain, The (Wright), 408
"comfort women," 487n8
communism, 123, 130–33, 139, 283; *see also* Cold War
Compaq company, 40

Competing for Control (Borrus), 61
Competitive Advantage of Nations, The (Porter), 52–53
computer industry; *see* semiconductor headings
Confucianism, 215–16, 283
Confucian Renaissance, The (Little and Reed), 75
Connally, John, 261
"constrained maximization" decisions, 202
containment policy, 131, 132, 135
corporate nationality, 224–31
corporate takeovers, 209–10, 478n47
cosmopolitan theorists, 183
Country Made by War, A (Perret), 198
Courtis, Kenneth, 113, 246, 260, 264–65, 276–77, 484n25
Cray Research, 419, 424
cultural explanation for corporate success, 48–50
Cumings, Bruce, 381
Curtis, Gerald, 299

Daewoo company, 381
Dai-ichi Seimei building, 119
Darman, Richard, 50
Defense Department, U.S., 57, 427, 462n48
Defense Intelligence Agency, U.S., 42
Defense Science Board, U.S., 419, 425
Der Torossian, Papken, 65
"destructive" competition, 220, 413
developmentalism, 216–17
Dictionary of Economics, 191
Digital Equipment, 39, 40
discipline of capital, 445, 496n2
Dodge, Joseph, 133, 134
Doko, Toshio, 424
domestic-content standards, 430, 449
Dore, Ronald, 85, 186, 428
Dower, John, 111, 142
DRAM chips, 32, 33, 34, 37–40
Drucker, Peter, 54–55
drug trade, 328

earth-moving industry, 222
Eaton, Raymond, 348
Eaton company, 30

economics, discipline of, 6, 139, 200–
203, 477nn33, 34
economic systems: *see* Anglo-American
economic system; Asian economic system; German economic
system
Economist, The (magazine), 205
education:
East Asian model, 443
in Japan, 84–85, 93, 97, 126–27,
178
Korean attitude toward, 378–80
in United States, 443–44
Electronic Industry Association (Japan),
56
Elegant, Robert, 110, 366, 432–33
emperor system, 104–5, 155
Encarnation, Dennis, 235
endaka (high yen) crisis, 13–14, 255–60,
262, 483n12
"End of History, The" (Fukuyama), 125
environmental issues, 182, 311, 313,
409–10, 487n1, 494n4
Erlanger, Stephen, 296
ersatz capitalism, 284
Ersatz Development in Southeast Asia
(Yoshihara), 316–17
Evergreen company, 399
"excessive" competition, 220, 413
exchange rates, 13–14, 255–60, 262,
483n12
Explaining Economic Policy Failure
(Angel), 435
Exxon company, 315

Fairchild Semiconductors, 23, 28
Field, Norma, 161
Fillmore, Millard, 88
Flamm, Kenneth, 40, 58
flash memory chips, 43–44, 417
Ford Motor Company, 24, 421
foreign aid programs, 271–73, 486n58,
494n4
*Foreign Direct Investment in the United
States* (Graham and Krugman),
227, 480n71
*Foreign Ownership and Control of
U.S. Industry* (report), 425
Formosa: *see* Taiwan

Formosa Plastics, 399
Fortune special issue on Japan, 144–
45, 469nn30, 31
France, 62, 181n, 215, 233, 339, 430
Free to Choose (Friedman and Fried-
man), 193
Friedman, Milton and Rose, 193
Friend, Theodore, 87
Frost, Robert, 373
FSX fighter plane, 237, 426
Fujitsu company, 30, 70, 419
Fukuyama, Francis, 125
Fukuzawa, Yukichi, 92

Gakushuin University, 117–18
Galbraith, John Kenneth, 140
Gallatin, Albert, 197
Garnaut, Ross, 149
Garnett, Nick, 223
Garon, Sheldon, 96
Gayn, Mark, 127, 155
gendered division of labor, 414
General Accounting Office, U.S.,
418
General Agreement on Tariffs and
Trade (GATT), 72, 448
General Instruments, 229
General Motors, 25–26, 259, 421
Genghis Khan, 77
German economic system, 18, 179, 182
Anglo-American attitude toward,
191–92
Asian system, influence on, 191
consumption vs. production, 183–85
government intervention, 182–83
individual vs. group concerns, 187–88
morality vs. power, 190
positive sum vs. zero sum issue,
188–90
process vs. result, 185–86
Germany, 62, 128, 129, 158, 419–20
Gilder, George, 29
Gluck, Carol, 97–98, 99, 101
gold standard, 261
Goozner, Merrill, 65
Governing the Market (Wade), 102,
193, 397
government involvement in economy:
see industrial policy

Graham, Edward, 227, 480*nn*71, 72
Grand Hotel (Taipei), 72–73
Great Britain, 86, 87–88
  economic supremacy, rise to, 194–96, 475*n*17
  Hong Kong and, 405–6
  Tokyo Stock Exchange and, 217
  see also Anglo-American economic system
Greater East Asia Co-Prosperity Sphere, 111, 407, 408
Great Illusion, The (Angell), 48
Grove, Andrew, 23, 28, 42
Gunther, John, 104–5

Halberstam, David, 26, 51, 124
Hall, Ivan, 283
Hamilton, Alexander, 183, 196–97, 475*n*25
Hanabusa, Masamichi, 262
Hanley, Susan B., 211
Harada, Hiroshi, 164
Harris, Townsend, 88–89
Hashimoto, Ryutaro, 429
Hata, Tsutomu, 168
Hatoyama, Ichiro, 171, 172–73
Hawke, Robert, 310
Hayashi, Fusao, 115
Head to Head (Thurow), 181*n*, 185, 422
Hegel, G. W. F., 182
Heimlich, Richard W., 226–27
Helm, Leslie, 239
Hersey, John, 163
Hewlett-Packard, 27, 39, 40, 52
Hideyoshi (shogun), 78, 79
  government of, 85–86
  invasion of Korea, 75–76, 82–83
  missionaries and, 80–81
high-definition television (HDTV), 15, 229–31, 457*n*10
Hills, Carla, 228
hinomaru flag, 152
Hirabayashi, Hiroshi, 497*n*4
Hirohito, Emperor, 97, 107, 110–11, 118–19
  abdication issue, 158–59, 160
  funeral of, 153

  public image, 151–53, 161
  surrender to U.S. forces, 119–20
  war-guilt issue, 129, 151, 153–61, 470*n*43, 471*n*46
Hiroshima, Japan, 163–64
Hiroshima (Hersey), 163
Hitachi company, 30, 34, 38, 48, 60, 70, 417, 464*n*74
Hitotsubashi University, 178
Ho Chi Minh, 4
Holland, 84, 234
Hollerman, Leon, 422–23
Honda company, 421, 430
Honeywell company, 427
Hong Kong, 63, 86, 193, 244–45, 285, 401
  China's takeover of, 404–6
  Confucianism and, 283
  diplomatic standing in world, 395
  economic size and wealth, 395
  emigration from, 405
  "greater China" economic sphere, 402–4
  Japanese investment in, 264
Hosiden company, 427
Hosokawa, Morihiro, 102, 160, 166, 167, 412
House, Karen Elliott, 12, 248
H-2 rocket, 238
hysteresis, 258–59
Hyundai company, 381

IBM, 24, 30, 34, 39, 40, 59, 416
Ikki, Kita, 109
Imperial Palace (Tokyo), 118–19, 152
Imperial Rescript on Education, 100
individual rights, 180
  Anglo-American economic system and, 187–88, 218–20
  Asian economic system and, 218–20, 367–68, 412–14
  Islam and, 491*n*30
  Japan's *kokutai* ideology, 97–101, 104
  in Korea, 394–95
  in Malaysia, 312–14, 491*n*30
  in Philippines, 365–68
Indonesia, 110, 270, 282, 284
  Chinese minority in, 292

Confucianism and, 283
economic obstacles, 320–21
exotic atmosphere, 319–20
Islam in, 308
Japan, economic relations with,
274–75, 321
language of, 317–18
Malaysia, comparison with, 317–18
national unity, sense of, 320
political system, 321
press censorship, 296
industrial policy:
Asian model, 445–46
discipline of capital and, 445, 496n2
in Japan, 58–61, 95, 192–93, 445–46
in Korea, 213–14, 220–21, 446
neoclassical view of, 496n1
in United States, 55–58, 63–65, 197,
198–200, 444–48, 462n48,
475n25
Inoue, Tetsujiro, 104
In Search of Excellence (Peters and
Waterman), 27
Inside Asia (Gunther), 104–5
Intel company, 22, 23, 24–25, 27, 28,
33, 39, 53, 64, 419
flash memory chips and, 43–44
intellectual property laws, 387
International Monetary Fund (IMF),
205–6, 339, 478n39
intra-industry trade, 232–33, 274–76,
481n80, 482n83
Inventing Japan (Chapman), 13, 127
Ishihara, Shintaro, 49, 165, 381, 411–
12, 425
Ishikawajima-Harima Heavy Indus-
tries, 424
Islam, 299, 308–9, 491n30
Italy, 339

Jackson, Andrew, 215
Jacobs, Jane, 400
Jacobson, Don, 390
James, William, 494n10
Japan:
antimilitarism in, 122, 149, 162
"catch-up" drive, 87, 89–108
colonial policies, 381

Confucianism and, 283
cultural explanation for corporate
success, 48–50
defense policy, 121–22, 134, 169–70,
172–74, 469n25
education system, 84–85, 93, 97,
126–27, 178
egalitarianism in, 149
emperors, naming system for, 90n,
118n
Europeans' arrival in 1500s, 76
fascist militarism, explanations for,
140–42
flag of, 152
foreign aid programs, 271–73,
486n58, 494n4
foreign policy, 137, 146, 169–70
"four tigers" and, 396
historical experience, legacy of,
113–14
holidays, 152
immigration to, 410–11
independence from European powers, 86–87
islands of, 75n
isolation period, 83–86
kokutai (mass ethic of loyalty and
duty), 97–101, 104
Korean War, 134, 175, 473n70
living standards, 8
Meiji Restoration, 90
military resurgence, possible, 351
missionaries in, 79–81, 465n5
Mongol invasions, 77
motto, unofficial, 325
nationalism in, 174, 368–69, 392–93
oil dependency, 13, 261–62
opening to foreigners (1500s), 78–79
opening to foreigners (1800s), 87–89
pan-Asianism in, 109–13, 411–12
Persian Gulf War, 215
press censorship, 296
"proper place" concept, 105–8
racial attitudes in, 103–5
resentment toward West, 105–8
rice policy, 210–11
salarymen, 177–78
secretiveness policy, 91, 93

Japan (*cont.*)
  solitude, lack of, 117–18
  Space and Technology Agency, 424
  standardization of Japanese life, 85
  unification of, 78
  university establishment, 178, 378
  unpredictability, distaste for, 218
  "victim consciousness," 151, 161–
    62, 164–65
  vulnerability problem, 82–84
  warring states era, 77–78
  Western technology, interest in, 78–
    79, 81, 91–94
  see also Japanese economic system;
    Japanese politics; Japan-U.S.
    relationship; Ministry of Inter-
    national Trade and Industry
    (MITI); semiconductor industry
    (Japan); U.S. Occupation of
    Japan; World War II; Japan
    headings under specific countries
Japan Air Lines crash (1985), 238
Japan Aviation Electronics Industry
  (JAEI), 427, 460*n*23
Japan-bashing, 434–35
Japan Diary (Gayn), 155
Japan Disincorporated (Hollerman),
  422–23
Japan Economic Institute (JEI), 434
Japanese economic system:
  automobile market, regulation of
    (*shaken* policy), 212–13
  beef quotas, 217, 222
  bubble economy, 10–11, 213, 262–
    63, 484*n*27
  cooperation among companies, 85,
    222–23
  economic expansion as country's
    sole purpose, 170–71, 174–75
  economic shocks of 1970s, recovery
    from, 13, 261–62
  endaka (high yen) crisis, 13–14,
    255–60, 262, 483*n*12
  exploitation of workers and con-
    sumers, 96–97
  Fortune article on, 144–45, 469*nn*30, 31
  gendered division of labor, 414
  industrial development in 1800s, 90,
    94–96

  industrial policy, 58–61, 95, 192–93,
    445–46
  inflation, 263
  intra-industry trade, 233, 482*n*83
  investment in by foreign firms, 59–
    61, 234–35, 259–60
  investment overseas, 227, 234, 263–
    77, 480*nn*71, 72
  investment surge (1987–92), 263–65
  joint ventures, 416–17
  land prices, 118, 211
  loans from foreign countries, 95–96
  management nationality issue, 233–
    34, 482*n*86
  market share, preference for, 258
  nationalistic system, 231–40
  Occupation-era conditions, 130
  postwar rebuilding, 175
  pricing practices, 258–59, 484*n*22
  recession of 1990s, 11–12
  retail system, 211–12
  savings rate, 14, 398, 450
  self-sufficiency issue, 235–40, 423–24
  small businesses, 399
  trade, 14, 78, 105–6, 257
    with Asian nations, 274–76
    with United States, 64, 65, 228–
      29, 247–48, 449–50
  Western misperception of, 3–4, 13–
    15, 451–53
  see also Asian economic system;
    semiconductor industry (Japan)
Japanese politics, 13, 17
  bureaucratic system, 98–99, 101–2,
    172, 393, 466*n*31
  centralized administration and taxa-
    tion, 85–86
  citizen participation, absence of,
    101–2
  control of citizens' thoughts and be-
    havior, 96–101
  development of institutions, 98
  electoral system, 168, 172
  emperor system, 104–5, 155
  Hosokawa reform coalition, 102,
    167–68
  informal and unwritten rules, 98
  one-party structure, 166, 167, 168–
    69

Peace Constitution, 17, 121–22, 173–74

revisionist group of 1950s, 170, 171–73

two-party system, movement for, 172

weakness of institutions, 151, 215

Japan External Trade Relations Organization (JETRO), 271

Japan New Party, 167

"Japan's Decline, America's Rise" (House), 12

Japan's Emergence as a Modern State (Norman), 115, 123

Japan's High Schools (Rohlen), 127

Japan's Imperial Conspiracy (Bergamini), 153

Japan's Modern Myths (Gluck), 97–98

Japan studies, discipline of, 139–43

self-censorship by U.S. scholars, 431–32

Japan's Unequal Trade (Lincoln), 233

Japan That Can Say No, The (Ishihara), 49

Japan-U.S. relationship, 16

as "big brother/little brother" relationship, 122

branch-plant syndrome, 420–23

business-military conflict within, 137–38

Cold War and, 134–43, 175

colonial status of Japan, 170–73

"emergent democracy" view of Japan and, 139, 140–43

foreign policy leadership by U.S., 137, 169–70

immigration to U.S., 107

Japanese investment in U.S., 264

joint ventures, 416–17

"just like us" view of Japan in U.S., 143–50

military relationship, 17, 134–35

mutual resentment, 173–74

opening of Japan in 1800s, 87, 88–89

pol-mil mindset of U.S. policy, 136–38

racial concerns, 431–35

self-sufficiency issue and, 237–39, 423–24

trade, 64, 228–29, 247–48, 449–50

U.S. financial dependence, 429–30

U.S. industrial dependence, 416–23

U.S. military dependence, 41–42, 424–28, 460*nn*23, 24

U.S. pressure on Japan for internal changes, 102, 466*n*38

U.S. self-censorship regarding things Japanese, 430–32

U.S. strength as key to relationship, 435–36

see also U.S. Occupation of Japan

Jefferson, Thomas, 196–97, 198, 214–15

Jesuit missionaries, 79–81

Jobs, Steven, 23

Jogjakarta, sultan of, 319–20

Johnson, Chalmers, 71, 126, 128, 129, 155, 252, 470*nn*42, 43, 483*n*12

Johnson, Lyndon, 215

joint ventures, 416–17

José, F. Sionil, 361, 363, 373–74

Judis, John, 189, 434, 435, 475*n*17

Jung-en Woo, 216–17, 218

Kaifu, Toshiki, 386

Kane, Sanford, 40

Kanemaru, Shin, 167

Karatsu, Hajime, 420

Karnow, Stanley, 354

Kataoka, Tetsuya, 124, 171, 172–73, 469*n*25

Kato, Shuichi, 149, 162–63

Kawai, Kazuo, 174

Kaya, Okinori, 129

Kearney, Reginald, 103

Keenan, Joseph, 155, 156, 471*n*46

Kennan, George, 126, 131, 132–33, 135

Keynes, John Maynard, 139, 450

Khmer Rouge, 338

Khun Sa, 328

Kido, Koichi, 159, 472*n*54

Kiko, Princess, 117

Kilby, Jack, 56

Kim Il Sung, 338

Kim Kyong-Dong, 378

Kishi, Nobusuke, 128–29, 171

Kishore Mahbubani, 323

Kissinger, Henry, 261, 474*n*10

Knorr, Jurgen, 420

Koestler, Arthur, 145–46

Koito company, 209–10

kokutai (mass ethic of loyalty and duty), 97–101, 104
Komatsu company, 222
Kono, Ichiro, 172
Konoe, Prince Fumimaro, 132, 158, 160
Koo Bohn Young, 386
Korea, North, 283, 284, 338, 351, 440
Korea, South, 4, 77, 204, 246, 251, 282, 284–85
  Anglo-American economic theory, influence of, 393–95
  antiforeign attitude, 388–91
  antiluxury campaign, 213, 389–91
  Christianity in, 392
  Confucianism and, 283
  diplomatic standing in world, 395
  economic size and wealth, 395
  education, attitude toward, 378–80
  environmental issues, 409
  export economy, 384–85
  individual rights issue, 394–95
  industrialization strategy, 381–83
  industrial policy, 213–14, 220–21, 446
  intellectual accomplishments, 376
  intellectual property laws, 387
  national character, 377–78
  "open" aspects of culture, 392–95
  political system, 383, 384, 394–95
  rice policy, 210–11, 383
  savings rate, 398
  semiconductor industry, 62–63, 388
  student protests, 379
  technological development, 386–88
  United States, relations with, 388–92
Korea-Japan relationship:
  colonial rule by Japan, 380, 381
  differences in cultures, 377–80
  economic relations, 264, 274–75
  invasions by Japan (1590s), 75–76, 82–83
  Japan's advantages, 385–88
  resentment toward Japan, 375–77
  similarities in cultures, 380–85
Korean War, 134, 175, 473n70
Kraisak Choonhavan, 295–96
Krause, Lawrence, 234
Krauthammer, Charles, 192

Krugman, Paul, 191, 227, 257, 480n71
Kuala Lumpur, Malaysia, 302, 309
Kublai Khan, 77
Kyoto, Japan, 154–55, 470n42
Kyoto Ceramics (Kyocera), 460n23
Kyushu, Japan, 75, 76

laissez-faire economics: *see* Anglo-American economic system
land reform, 356, 367–68
Laos, 283, 284, 350
Last Emperor, The (film), 165
late-industrializing countries, 382–83
Lazonick, William, 194, 195, 196
LCD display-screen components, 427
League of Nations, 107
Le Dang Doanh, 344
Lee Kuan Yew, 181, 215, 313, 367
  governing, approach to, 322–23
  on Japan's image in East Asia, 248
  on post-American era, 252–53
Lee Sang Yul, 388
Lehner, Urban, 388, 398–99
Lerner, Max, 372
Levine, Mel, 425
Lewis, Bernard, 452–53
Liberal Democratic Party (LDP), 17, 102, 166, 167
"Life in the Big City" (Robinson), 439
Life special issue on Japan, 144, 145–47, 148, 152
Lincoln, Abraham, 197, 215
Lincoln, Edward J., 233, 272, 273, 275–76, 486n50
Lintner, Bertil, 336
Li Peng, 113
List, Friedrich, 18, 179, 182, 183, 185, 186, 188, 189–90, 194–95; *see also* German economic system
Little, Reg, 75
Locke, John, 180
longyi (Burmese garment), 333–34
LSI Logic company, 39

MacArthur, Arthur, 124
MacArthur, Douglas, 76, 121, 130, 132
  "civilizing mission" in Japan, 124–25
  and Cold War role of Japan, 135

emperor's war-guilt issue, 154, 155, 470*n*43
headquarters in Tokyo, 119
Japanese surrender, 119–20
reform accomplishments, 125–26
"reverse course" campaign, 133
McCraw, Thomas, 196, 199–200, 475*n*22, 476*n*26
McDonnell Douglas company, 397
machine-tool industry, 420
McKenna, Regis, 28
McKinley, William, 124, 198, 354
McNamara, Robert, 140
Maeda, Katsunoke, 222
Magellan, Ferdinand, 76
Maha Chakri Sirindhorn, Princess, 297
Mahathir bin Mohamad, 251, 298, 308
anti-Westernism of, 309–14, 490*nn*28, 29
individual rights issue, 312–14
Japan, attitude toward, 249–50
on "messy" transition to industrialism, 281
racial views, 292, 303, 305, 489*n*21
Mahbubani, Kishore, 299
Mahmood Iskandar ibni al-Marhum Sultan Ismail, 305–7
Malay Dilemma, The (Mahathir), 292, 303, 305, 489*n*21
Malaysia, 244, 249–50, 251, 270, 282, 284, 298
anti-Westernism in, 307–14, 490*nn*28, 29
automobiles in, 246, 315
Burma, comparison with, 328
Confucianism and, 283
drug laws, 310
economic dependence on external factors, 314–17
economic prosperity, 299
environmental issues, 311, 313
independence for, 491*n*36
individual rights issue, 312–14, 491*n*30
Indonesia, comparison with, 317–18
Islamic conservatism, 299, 308–9
Japanese investment in, 264, 273, 315
language of, 317–18, 49*n*35

military expenditures, 372
natural resources, 300–301
New Economic Policy (NEP), 304–5
per capita annual income, 355
press censorship, 312
racial tensions, 292, 301–5, 489*n*20
royal families, 305–7
Thailand, comparison with, 299–300
U.S. investment in, 265, 315
management nationality issue, 233–34, 482*n*86
Manchester, William, 407
Manglapus, Raul, 372
Manser, Bruno, 311
Mansfield, Mike, 136
Mao Tse-tung, 131
Marcos, Ferdinand, 4, 136, 355, 361–63
market failures, 182–83
market unpredictability, 208–9, 217–23
Markkula, Mike, 29
Marshall, Alfred, 180
Masuru, Inouye, 95
Matsumoto, Kenichi, 173–74
Matsumoto, Koji, 207
Matsushita company, 265, 315
Mead, Walter Russell, 200
Meiji Mura, Japan, 439
Meiji Restoration, 90
mercantilism, 452
Merck corporation, 239
merit-making business, 279–80, 487*n*1
Mexico, 266
Michener, James, 120
Microcosm (Gilder), 29
Microsoft company, 33, 419
Mieno, Yasushi, 206, 263
migration of labor, 410–11
military problems of East Asia, 350–52
Miller, Perry, 124
Mind of Asia, The (Abegg), 85
Minear, Richard, 154, 471*n*46
Minebea company, 265, 267, 425*n*26
Ministry of International Trade and Industry (MITI) (Japan), 128, 175, 192, 298, 423
investment in Asia and, 269–71, 272
semiconductor industry and, 35, 37, 38, 58–59, 64

Mirror, Sword, and Jewel (Singer), 435–36
Mishima, Yukio, 117, 174
missionaries, 5, 79–81, 308, 392, 465n5
MITI and the Japanese Miracle (Johnson), 128
Mitsubishi company, 60, 138, 246, 267
Mitsui company, 267
Miyagawa, Takayoshi, 238
Miyazawa, Kiichi, 12, 166, 167, 487n8
Miyoshi, Masao, 93, 110
Mobil company, 348
Moltz, James Clay, 205, 477n38
momentum, concept of, 36
Mongols, 77
Monsod, Solita, 364
Moore, Gordon, 23, 28
moral interpretation of success, 25–31
Morishima, Michio, 90, 106, 221
Morita, Akio, 40, 60, 463n58
Motorola company, 30, 33, 34, 64, 315
    cellular phones controversy, 226–28, 480n69
Musa Hitam, 305
Mutsuhito, Emperor, 90, 118n
Myanmar. *See* Burma

Nader, Ralph, 215
Nakasone, Yasuhiro, 425
Nakatani, Iwao, 206–7
Nanking Massacre, 165–66
NASA, 57, 462n48
Nasar, Sylvia, 192
national economic interests, 209, 223
    in Anglo-American economic system, 223–31
    in Asian economic system, 223, 231–40, 367–68
nationalism, 368–70
National Palace Museum (Taipei), 73
National Security Agency, U.S., 41–42
National Semiconductor, 23, 24, 28
National System of Political Economy, The (List), 185, 188, 191, 194–95
"natural endowment" theory, 61
Natural System of Political Economy,

The (List), 179, 185, 188, 189–90
NEC company, 30, 34, 39, 60, 70, 138, 424, 427
Nehru, Jawaharlal, 106–7, 408
Neureiter, Norman, 65
New Hampshire Ball Bearings, 425
Ne Win, 328, 329–30, 331, 333
Newly Industrializing Economies (NIEs), 395
New Realities, The (Drucker), 54
Newton, Isaac, 180
Ngo Dinh Diem, 136
Nguyen Quang Dy, 352
Nguyen Xuan "Jack" Oanh, 348–49
Nishimura, Shigeki, 105
Nissan company, 223, 421
Nixon administration, 261, 435
Nomura Research Institute, 44–45
nonaligned movement, 407–8
Norman, E. H., 115, 123, 140–41
North American Free Trade Agreement, 266
Noyce Robert, 23, 28, 56, 418–19
Nu, U, 328, 329

Oble, Blas, 355
Oda Nobunaga, 78
Ohmae, Kenichi, 224
oil shocks of 1970s, 13, 261–62
Okamoto, Yukio, 165
Okinawa, 135
"one set" philosophy, 236
Onishi, Takijiro, 131–32
"On Japanese Morality" (Nishimura), 105
Orr, Robert, 272–73
Ott, Marvin, 327
Ottoman Empire, 451–52
Ozaki, Ryutaro, 174
Ozawa, Ichiro, 168

Pacific Asia (Shibusawa), 216
Pacific Destiny (Elegant), 366
pan-Asianism, 109–13, 411–12
Papua New Guinea, 494n4
Park Pil Soo, 391
Park Sung Kyou, 386
Patten, Chris, 405–6

Pearl Harbor attack, 157
Pearlman, Jerry K., 230
Pempel, T. J., 497n5
Penan tribes, 311, 490n29
Perkin-Elmer company, 30
Perret, Geoffrey, 198, 199, 476n29
Perry, Matthew, 76, 80, 87
Persian Gulf War, 41, 166, 173, 174,
    426–27
  Japan's response, 215
Peters, Tom, 27
pharmaceutical industry, 238–39
Philip, Prince of Wales, 153
Philippines, 4, 76, 121, 135, 246, 270,
    282, 284, 326, 374
  agricultural sector, 356
  Aquino presidency, 356, 362–63
  Chinese minority in, 291–92
  Christianity in, 354
  colonial experience, 86, 124, 369–70
  Confucianism and, 283
  contemptuous attitude of those in
    power, 325–26
  debt to international banks, 363–64
  economic stagnation, 355–58
  election of 1992, 355
  environmental issues, 409
  individual rights issue, 365–68
  industrial sector, 356
  Japan's trade with, 274–75
  land reform, 356, 367–68
  Marcos regime, 361–63
  military expenditures, 372
  nationalism, failure of, 368–70
  natural resources, 355, 357
  per capita annual income, 355
  population growth, 357–58
  poverty and wealth in, 358–61
  press, freedom of, 296
  revolution of 1986, 362–63
  sex industry, 356–57
  spiritual and supernatural element,
    364–65
  United States, relations with, 124,
    354–55, 364, 369–70
  U.S. military bases in, 365, 370–74
Philips company, 56, 229
Pibul (Thai statesman), 289, 290
Pickens, T. Boone, 209–10

Plaza Accord of 1985, 255–56, 483n12
Pol Pot, 338
population growth, 357–58
Porter, Michael, 52–53, 61
Porter, Roger, 223–24
Portuguese missionaries and traders,
    76, 78–81, 84
Powell, Bill, 416
Precision Monolithic company, 28
Prestowitz, Clyde, 50, 448
pricing practices, 258–59, 484n22
Pridi (Thai statesman), 289, 290
Prisoners of the Sun (film), 471n45
Pudu Prison (Kuala Lumpur), 490n27

Quayle, Dan, 150

racial attitudes in Japan, 103–5
racial tensions:
  in Asia, 291–93, 301–5, 489n20
  in Japan-U.S. relationship, 431–35
Ramos, Fidel, 355, 358
Rangoon, Burma, 332
RCA company, 447
Read, Richard, 339
Reagan administration, 255–56, 425
Reckoning, The (Halberstam), 26, 51,
    124
Reed, Warren, 75
Reich, Robert, 225–31, 480n69
Reischauer, Edwin, 140, 141–43, 146–
    47, 148, 161, 219–20
*Remaking Japan: The Occupation as
    New Deal* (Cohen), 124
retail systems, 211–12
Rhee, Syngman, 4
Ricardo, David, 180, 188
rice-growing cultures, 112
rice policy, 210–11, 383
rights-based political systems: *see* indi-
    vidual rights
*Rise of Ersatz Capitalism in Southeast
    Asia, The* (Yoshihara), 284
*Rise of the Japanese Corporate System,
    The* (Matsumoto), 207
Rivals Beyond Trade (Encarnation),
    235
Roberts Pharmaceutical, 235
Robinson, Larry, 439

Rockefeller Center, 485n30
Rohlen, Thomas, 127
Roh Tae Woo, 386, 391
Roosevelt, Franklin, 215, 447
Roosevelt, Theodore, 215
Rosovsky, Henry, 149, 470n36
Rostow, Walt Whitman, 139, 140
Rousseau, Jean-Jacques, 180
Ruge, Ingolf, 40
Rusk, Dean, 140
Russia, 106, 205, 477n38
Russo-Japanese War, 106–7

Safire, William, 254–55
Sakakibara, Eisuke, 206, 207
salarymen, 177–78
Samsung company, 221, 381
Samuels, Richard, 148, 237
samurai warriors, 98
Sanyo company, 248
Sarawak, 311, 494n4
savings rates, 14, 398, 450–51
Saxonhouse, Gary, 61
Sayonara (Michener), 120
Schlesinger, Jacob, 43, 248, 460n24
Schumpeter, Joseph, 51, 200, 477n33
SDI/Star Wars projects, 138
Sein Lwin, 335
Sejong, King, 376
self-sufficiency issue, 235–40, 423–24
Sematech consortium, 43, 64–65, 418
semiconductor industry (Asia), 62–63
semiconductor industry (China), 251–
    52
semiconductor industry (Europe), 62
semiconductor industry (Germany),
    419–20
semiconductor industry (Japan), 30–31
    calculator war, 69, 464n73
    as cartel, 35, 36–40
    combined approach to manufactur-
        ing, 34–35
    cultural explanation for success, 48–
        50
    DRAM products, 32, 34, 37–40
    foreign investment in, 59–61
    government's role, 58–61
    joint ventures with U.S. companies,
        416–17

money availability issue, 66, 69–70
    rise vis-à-vis U.S. industry, 31–35,
        458n9
    supplier network, 42
    U.S. dependence on Japanese chips,
        41–44, 416–19, 460nn23, 24
    "win at any cost" approach, 69–70,
        464n75
    "withholding" practice, 418–20,
        495n20
semiconductor industry (Korea), 62–
    63, 388
semiconductor industry (U.S.), 15, 21–
    22
    Anglo-American economic analysis
        of, 67–69
    automobile industry, comparison
        with, 23–24
    calculator war, 69, 464n73
    companies of, 22, 33
    competitive disadvantage, 44–45
    consortium of chip producers, 43,
        64–65, 418
    consortium of chip producers and
        users, 39–40
    cooperation among companies, 57–
        58
    cultural explanation for decline, 48,
        50–54
    decline vis-à-vis Japanese industry,
        31–35, 458n9
    division of labor, 24
    flash memory chips, 43–44, 417
    government's role, 55–58, 63–65,
        447, 462n48
    hierarchy of, 30
    Japanese market, penetration of,
        59–61, 64, 65, 463nn58, 63
    Japanese suppliers, dependence on,
        42–44, 416–19
    joint ventures with Japanese compa-
        nies, 416–17
    "limitless" prospects, 28–29
    money availability issue, 66, 69–70
    moral interpretation of success, 25–
        31
    origins of, 23
    personnel for, 29–30
    physical layout in Silicon Valley, 22, 29

profitability of, 24–25
related industries, 35
revival in late 1980s, 63–65
short-term perspective of U.S. industry and, 40
specialized approach to manufacturing, 30, 34–35
standard explanation for decline, 47–48, 65–66
venture-capital system, 27–28
"withholding" practice, 419
worker-management relations, 27
Semiconductor Industry Association (SIA), 55–56
Semiconductor Trade Arrangement (U.S.-Japan), 64, 65, 228–29, 449–50, 497n4
Sesser, Stan, 337
sex industry, 286–87, 356–57
shaken policy, 212–13
Shanghai, China, 437–39
Sharp company, 44, 69
Shaw Yu-ming, 396
Shibusawa, Masahide, 216
Shigemitsu, Mamoru, 129
Shimada, Haruo, 253
Shim Jae Hoon, 251
Shinto religion, 104, 105
Shockley, William, 23, 55
"Showa Emperor's Monologue," 107
"Showa Emperor's 'Monologue' and the Problem of War Responsibility" (Bix), 156
Siemens company, 56, 419–20
Silicon Valley: *see* semiconductor industry (U.S.)
Simon, Julian, 357–58
Singapore, 270, 285, 313, 321–22
anti-Westernism in, 492n11
Confucianism and, 283
economic system, 323–24, 395, 401, 491n41
government control of daily life, 322–24, 401
"greater China" economic sphere, 402, 403
independence for, 300
Japanese investment in, 264

military expenditures, 372
per capita annual income, 355
press censorship, 299
semiconductor industry, 63
succession problem, 395
Vietnam, relations with, 346
Singer, Kurt, 435–36
Situation in the Western World, The (Fukuzawa), 92
Six Years in the Malay Jungle (Wells), 300
Smith, Adam, 139, 180, 181, 187, 188
Smith, Michael, 217
Smith, Roger, 26
Smoky Mountain community (Philippines), 358–60
Somoza, Anastasio, 136
Sony company, 58–59, 60, 237
South Africa, 302–3
Southerland, Daniel, 251–52
Soviet Union, 130, 131, 132, 254
"Specter of Anglo-Saxonization Is Haunting South Korea, The" (Amsden), 394
Spencer, William J., 43
steel industry, 25, 26, 27, 28–29, 193, 199
Stern, John P., 268, 424, 484n22
Sterngold, James, 102, 388
Stimson, Henry L., 154
stock-market crash of 1987, 429
stock-market industry, 221–22
Stokes, Bruce, 269, 270
strategic trade theory, 191
Stroud, Michael, 399
structural impediments initiative, 466n38
Subic Bay Naval Base, 370–74
Suchinda Kraprayoon, 293–94
Suharto, President, 296, 319, 320, 321, 363
Sukarno, President, 321, 408
Sumsky, Victor, 361
Sun Microsystems, 40
Supreme Court, U.S., 216

Taipei, Taiwan, 72–73
Taisho emperor, 118n

Taiwan, 72–73, 193, 211, 246, 250, 284–85
Confucianism and, 283
diplomatic standing in world, 395
economic size and wealth, 395
environmental issues, 409
"greater China" economic sphere, 402–3, 404
industrialization strategy, 397–98
Japan, economic relations with, 274–75, 396–97, 398–400
Japan's colonial rule, 380, 381
regional planning proposal, 271
savings rate, 398
small-business orientation of economy, 399–401
sovereignty issue, 403
teamwork against Japan, promotion of, 251
technological development, 398–400
United States, relations with, 396
Takarazuka dance troupe, 165–66
Takeshita, Noboru, 113
Tandy company, 40
targeted trade, 449–50, 497n5
tax policy, 451
"teeth-sucking" gesture, 48
Terasaki, Hidenari, 156
Texaco company, 348
Texas Instruments (TI), 30, 34, 59–60, 69, 265, 315, 463n58
Thailand, 10, 270, 284
assassination of king (1946), 294, 488n12
Burmese resources, exploitation of, 337
Chinese minority, 291, 292–93
Confucianism and, 283
coup of 1991, 298–99
environmental issues, 409, 487n1
exports, 268
independence, history of, 288–91
Japanese investment in, 264, 266–69, 273
laissez-faire ethos, 286–87
"land of smiles" image, 285–86
Malaysia, comparison with, 299–300
merit-making business, 279–80, 487n1

"messy" transition to industrialism, 278–80
national character (*mai pen rai* spirit), 287–88
per capita annual income, 355
royal family, reverence for, 293–97
sex industry, 286–87
World War II "alliance" with Japan, 289–90
Thatcher, Margaret, 310
"They Are Not Us" (Tyson), 231
Thomson company, 229
Thurow, Lester, 181n, 185, 422
Tojo, Hideki, 129, 154, 155, 158, 162, 471n46
Tokugawa, Iemitsu, 83
Tokugawa, Ieyasu, 80, 81, 83, 84
Tokyo Stock Exchange, 145, 217
Toray Industries, 222
Toshiba company, 30, 34, 60 265, 416, 427
Toyota company, 209, 223, 267, 421
trade:
adversarial trade, 54–55
Japan-U.S. trade, 64, 65, 228–29, 247–48, 449–50
pragmatic approach to, 448–50
strategic trade theory, 191
targeted trade, 449–50, 497n5
Trading Places (Prestowitz), 50
Truman, Harry S, 155, 163, 164
Tyson, Laura, 60, 61, 231, 463n63

Ultimate Resource, The (Simon), 358
Unisys company, 40
United States:
as "ahistoric" culture, 74
Asian achievement, proposed response to, 440–51
Asian attitudes toward (1990s), 9, 245, 249, 252–55
Asian exports and, 247–48
budget deficit, 52, 429, 450–51
business failure, cultural explanation for, 51–52
"common good" concept, 413, 494n10
concentrated power, suspicion of, 214–15

economic change, assumptions about, 45–47
education reform, 443–44
foreign aid programs, 271–72, 273
foreign ownership of companies, 227, 234, 264
gold standard, 261
government hierarchy, 136
government intervention in economy, beliefs about, 186
housing policy, 445, 446–47
imports of Japanese products from third countries, 268–69
industrial policy, 55–58, 63–65, 197, 198–200, 444–48, 462n48, 475n25
intra-industry trade, 232–33, 482n83
investment overseas, 265–66, 315
Japan studies in, 139–43, 431–32
Korea, relations with, 388–92
management practices, 51
military-industrial complex, 424
military presence in East Asia, 134–35, 349–50, 440–41
"Nixon shocks" of 1970s, 261
and Philippines:
    military bases in, 365, 370–74
    relations with, 124, 354–55, 364, 369–70
pop culture, international popularity of, 249
protectionism, history of, 196–98, 475n22, 476n26
remaking Asian cultures, efforts at, 440–41
savings and investment policy, 398, 450–51
SDI/Star Wars projects, 138
self-sufficiency issue, 236
short-term perspective of business, 40, 52
social polarization, 442–44
Taiwan, relations with, 396
tax policy, 451
Thailand, relations with, 288–89
trade policy, 448–50
Vietnam policy, 241, 338–40, 345–52, 492n7

worldview of Americans, 4, 7
World War II, 74–75, 163–64
yen-dollar exchange rate, 13–14, 255–60, 262, 483n12
see also Anglo-American economic system; Cold War; Japan-U.S. relationship; semiconductor industry (U.S.); U.S. Occupation of Japan
U.S. Business Access to Certain Foreign State-of-the-Art Technology (GAO report), 418
U.S. Memories consortium, 39–40
U.S. Occupation of Japan, 16–17, 116
    Communist takeover concerns, 130–33
    democratization campaign, 126, 133
    "Dodge line," 130, 133
    economic conditions in Japan, 130
    education reforms, 126–27
    emperor's war guilt issue, 154–56, 470n43
    gap between U.S. impressions and Japanese reality, 127
    Japanese attitude toward Americans, 120–21
    Japanese governmental institutions, maintenance of, 128–29
    Japanese surrender, 119–20
    legacy of, 122
    MacArthur's headquarters, 119
    "new beginning" attitude, 120
    Peace Constitution, 121–22
    radicalism and social disruption, 130–31
    reform accomplishments, 121, 125–27, 130, 149
    remaking of Japan in America's image, 122–27
    "reverse course" campaign, 130, 133–34
    war crimes trials, 128–29, 154–56, 159, 160, 471n46
U.S. Steel, 26

Varian company, 30
Vessey, John, 347
Vietnam, 4, 10, 284, 326, 374
    Cambodia, invasion of, 338

Vietnam (*cont.*)
China as threat to, 350–52
Chinese minority in, 291, 292
communism and, 283
Confucianism and, 283
economic conditions prior to reform, 342–44
economic reforms, 340–41, 344–45, 492n6
economic success, potential for, 352–53
environmental issues, 409
international contacts, 337–38, 346
Japan, economic relations with, 243–44, 339, 353
out-of-dateness, sense of, 241–43
political reforms, 341–42
POW/MIA issue, 347
refugees from, 350
Soviet bloc countries and, 242
U.S. embargo against, 241, 338–40, 345–52, 492n7
as U.S. military base site, 349–50
U.S. viewed as economic savior, 242–43
war era, attitude toward, 340
Vietnam War, 45, 340
Viner, Aron, 13
Vo Dai Luoc, 348, 352–53
Volcker, Paul, 255

Wade, Robert, 102, 191, 193, 397, 445, 474n16, 496n1
war crimes trials, 128–29, 154–56, 159, 160, 471n46
Warner, Langdon, 470n42
Washington Naval Conference (1922), 107–8
Waterman, Robert, 27
Waugh, Alec, 289–90
Wealth of Nations, The (Smith), 181, 187
Webb, William, 471n46
Welfield, John, 121
Wells, Carveth, 300, 302
Western perception of East Asia:
conversion issue, 5
Japan's economic decline and, 11–12
science and, 6
superiority issue, 5–6
underestimation of Japan and misperception of Asia as a whole, 3–4, 13–15, 451–53
Western model as basis of, 4–5
West Point Academy, 198, 476n29
"White-Collar Zombies" (story), 177–78
Whiting, Robert, 7
Whitney, Eli, 199
"Who Is Us?" (Reich), 225, 226
Why Has Japan "Succeeded"? (Morishima), 90
Will, George, 45–46
Wilson, Woodrow, 215
Wolferen, Karel van, 101, 215
Work of Nations, The (Reich), 225, 227
World Bank, 62–63, 192, 205–6, 339, 364, 367
World Economic Forum, 113
World War II:
atomic bombings, 163–65
in Burma, 329
"comfort women," 487n8
Hirohito's role, 129, 151, 153–61, 470n43, 471n46
"inevitable" view of, 107, 108, 114–16, 467n51
Japan as victor, 407–8
Japanese-Thai "alliance," 289–90
Japan's apologies for, 160, 162, 166
Japan's pretend version of history, 160–66, 472n57
Japan's war aims, 110–11
kamikaze strategy, 131–32
Pearl Harbor attack, 157
technological superiority of West and, 74–75
Wozniak, Steve, 23
Wright, Richard, 110, 407–8
Wurmstedt, Robert, 150

Xavier, Francis, 76
Xerox company, 22, 30, 458n6

Yamagawa, Kenjiro, 92–93
Yamanouchi Pharmaceutical, 235
Yamazaki, Seiichi, 471n46

Yi, Admiral, 83
Yockey, Donald J., 42
Yoder, Stephen, 40
Yoshida, Shigeru, 132, 155, 170–71, 173, 175
Yoshida, Shoin, 88, 89, 92
Yoshihara, Kunio, 284, 316–17
Yosuke, Matsuoka, 112

You Gotta Have Wa (Whiting), 7
Younger, Peter, 252
Yu Shan Wu, 413

Zenith company, 229, 230
Zilog company, 22, 30
Zysman, John, 60, 61, 463*n*63